LEARNING TEXT

LAW OF TORTS

John Lewthwaite would like to dedicate this book to Judy

LEARNING TEXT

LAW OF TORTS

Second Edition

John Lewthwaite LLB, LLM, ACIS
Senior Lecturer in Law, Nottingham Law School

and

John S. Hodgson MA, LLM, Solicitor
Principal Lecturer in Law, Nottingham Law School

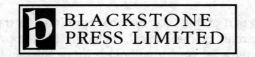

BLACKSTONE PRESS LIMITED

First published in Great Britain 1996 by Blackstone Press Limited,
Aldine Place, London W12 8AA.   Telephone 0181–740 2277

© Nottingham Law School, Nottingham Trent University, 1996

ISBN: 1 85431 816 0

First edition 1996
Reprinted 1997
Second edition 1998

British Library Cataloguing in Publication Data
A CIP catalogue record for this book is available from the British Library.

Typeset by Style Photosetting Limited, Mayfield, East Sussex
Printed by Livesey Limited, Shrewsbury, Shropshire

FOREWORD

The books in the LLB series have been written for students studying law at undergraduate level. There are two books for each subject. The first is the *Learning Text* which is designed to teach you about the particular subject in question. However, it does much more than that. By means of Activities, Self Assessment, and End of Chapter Questions, the *Learning Text* allows you to test your knowledge and understanding as you work. Each chapter starts with 'Objectives' which indicate what you should be able to do by the end of it. You should use these Objectives in your learning — check them frequently and ask yourself whether you have attained them.

The second book is a volume of *Cases and Materials*. This is cross-referenced from the *Learning Text*. It contains the primary sources of law such as statutes and cases plus subsidiary sources such as extracts from journals, law reform papers and textbooks. This is your portable library. Although each volume can stand alone, they are designed to be complementary.

The two-volume combination aims to support your learning by challenging you to demonstrate your mastery of the principles and application of the law. They are appropriate whatever your mode of study — full-time or part-time.

CONTENTS

Foreword   v

Preface   ix

Table of Cases   xi

Table of Statutes   xxv

1 Liability in Tort   1

1.1 Objectives — 1.2 Introduction — 1.3 Capacity — 1.4 Vicarious liability —
1.5 Contributions between tortfeasors — 1.6 Summary — 1.7 Further reading — 1.8 End
of chapter assessment question

2 General Defences   32

2.1 Objectives — 2.2 Introduction — 2.3 The remaining major defences — 2.4 Summary
— 2.5 Further reading — 2.6 End of chapter assessment question

3 Negligence   70

3.1 Objectives — 3.2 Introduction — 3.3 Duty — 3.4 Liability in contract and tort —
3.5 Public bodies and negligence — 3.6 Specific issues in relation to duty — 3.7 Breach
of duty — 3.8 Damage — 3.9 Summary — 3.10 Further reading — 3.11 End of chapter
assessment questions

4 Causation and Remoteness of Damage   95

4.1 Objectives — 4.2 Introduction — 4.3 Causation — 4.4 Proof of causation —
4.5 Remoteness — 4.6 Sensitive plaintiffs — 4.7 Intention/recklessness — 4.8 Summary
— 4.9 Further reading — 4.10 End of chapter assessment question

5 Negligence: 'Pure' Economic Loss/Negligent Misstatement   120

5.1 Objectives — 5.2 Introduction — 5.3 Acts: the principle — 5.4 The decision in Junior
Books v Veitchi — 5.5 Misstatements — 5.6 Summary — 5.7 Further reading — 5.8 End
of chapter assessment question

6 Negligence: Nervous Shock/Psychiatric Damage   157

6.1 Objectives — 6.2 Introduction — 6.3 The legal cause of action — 6.4 Summary —
6.5 Reform — 6.6 Further reading — 6.7 Answer to Activity 28 — 6.8 End of chapter
assessment question

7   Liability for Dangerous Premises and Land   187

7.1 Objectives — 7.2 Introduction — 7.3 Liability arising in various capacities in negligence—7.4 Liability arising under the Defective Premises Act 1972—7.5 Occupiers' liability to lawful visitors — 7.6 Occupiers' liability to entrants other than visitors coming within the terms of the 1957 Act — 7.7 Summary — 7.8 Further reading — 7.9 End of chapter assessment question

8   The Action for Breach of Statutory Duty and the Employers'
Common Law Duty of Care to their Employees   236

8.1 Objectives — 8.2 Introduction — 8.3 The action for breach of statutory duty — 8.4 The elements of the cause of action for breach of statutory duty — 8.5 Defences — 8.6 An employer's liability at common law — 8.7 Summary — 8.8 Further reading — 8.9 End of chapter assessment question

9   Trespass Torts   287

9.1 Objectives — 9.2 Introduction — 9.3 General historical background to the trespass torts — 9.4 Trespass to the person and false imprisonment — 9.5 Interference with goods — 9.6 Title conflicts — 9.7 Trespass to land — 9.8 Summary — 9.9 Further reading — 9.10 End of chapter assessment question

10   Nuisance and Harassment   325

10.1 Objectives — 10.2 Introduction — 10.3 Definitions — 10.4 Private nuisance — 10.5 Public nuisance — 10.6 Harassment — 10.7 Relationship of public and private nuisance — 10.8 Summary — 10.9 Further reading — 10.10 End of chapter assessment question

11   Hazardous Activities   352

11.1 Objectives — 11.2 Introduction — 11.3 How the 'hazardous activities' rule developed — 11.4 Fire — 11.5 Summary — 11.6 Further reading — 11.7 End of chapter assessment questions

12   Defamation   365

12.1 Objectives — 12.2 Introduction — 12.3 General considerations — 12.4 Defamation in general — 12.5 What is defamatory? — 12.6 Reference to the plaintiff — 12.7 Publication — 12.8 What must the plaintiff prove? — 12.9 Defences — 12.10 Remedies — 12.11 Summary — 12.12 Further reading — 12.13 End of chapter assessment questions

13   Product Liability   390

13.1 Objectives — 13.2 Introduction — 13.3 Contractual remedies — 13.4 Tortious remedies: common law — 13.5 Statutory liability — 13.6 Summary – 13.7 Further reading — 13.8 End of chapter assessment questions

14   Animals   410

14.1 Objectives — 14.2 Introduction — 14.3 Dangerous animals — 14.4 Livestock trespass — 14.5 Defences — 14.6 Summary — 14.7 Further reading — 14.8 End of chapter assessment question

15   Remedies   416

15.1 Objectives — 15.2 Introduction — 15.3 Self-help — 15.4 Damages — 15.5 Injunctions — 15.6 Summary — 15.7 Further reading — 15.8 End of chapter assessment questions

Index   437

PREFACE

Any text on torts is a compromise. The subject is vast. Indeed there is debate over whether it is properly tort (suggesting a unified basis of liability for all the wrongs one person can do another) or torts (suggesting that each type of wrong is unique and distinct). We tend to the latter view, while recognising that there are family groups of torts: the negligence family, the nuisance family and the trespass family to name the three which occupy most of this text. Negligence and breach of statutory duty (which often arises on the same facts, although the underlying reason for liability is different) inevitably occupy the lion's share of the text. They account for some 90 per cent of all tort-based litigation, and the judges seldom tire of improving the law in this area. The other torts should not be neglected. They protect important interests and are also important in many cases as the mechanism for litigating issues which at first glance raise problems associated with other areas of law, such as personal property and civil liberty.

The authors have taken responsibility for different sections of the text. There are no prizes for spotting where the changeover occurs. John Lewthwaite has endeavoured to put negligence into an ordered structure. This is difficult, because the definition of the tort 'breach of a duty of care causing foreseeable physical or consequential loss' is so deceptively simple, but any comprehensive explanation is bedevilled by the number of cases and the fact that the judges keep changing or modifying the rules. These chapters therefore contain detailed consideration of cases which are not always easy to reconcile. John Hodgson, in dealing with a selection of the nominate torts, where it should be easier to see the wood for the trees, has looked at the way causes of action are used for varying purposes and has tried to introduce some wider policy issues. This reflects, as this series is designed to do, the variety of approaches which a lecturer would normally incorporate in his lectures.

The authors would like to express their gratitude to Sue Webb for her assistance in preparing the manuscript.

John Lewthwaite
John Hodgson

TABLE OF CASES

A and Others v Tameside and Glossop Health Authority and Another, The Times,
   27 November 1996   179
A & W Hemphill Ltd v Williams [1996] 2 Lloyd's Rep 10   26
AB v South West Water Services Ltd [1993] QB 507   344, 429
Abbott v Strong, The Times, 9 July 1998   154
AC Billings & Sons Ltd v Riden [1958] AC 240   327
Adam v Ward [1917] AC 309   381
Adams v Ursell [1913] Ch 269   335, 338
Addie (Robert) and Sons (Collieries) Ltd v Dumbreck [1929] AC 358   202, 221, 224
Admiralty Commissioners v SS Chekiang [1926] AC 637   422
Adsett v K & L Steelfounders [1953] 1 WLR 773   256
A-G v Corke [1933] Ch 89   355
A-G v Cory Bros [1921] AC 521   355
A-G v PYA Quarries Ltd [1957] 2 QB 169   341
A-G v Staffordshire CC [1905] 1 Ch 336   433
A-G's Reference (No. 6 of 1980) [1981] 2 All ER 1057   297
Aiken and others v Stewart Wrightson Members' Agency Ltd and others
   [1995] 3 All ER 449   136
Airfix Footwear Ltd v Cope [1978] ICR 1210   8
Al Nakib (Investments) Jersey Ltd v Longcroft [1990] 3 All ER 321   138
Al Saudi Banque v Clarke Pixley [1989] 3 All ER 361   137
Alcock v Chief Constable of the South Yorkshire Police [1991] 4 All ER 907,
   [1992] 1 AC 310   72, 170, 178, 181, 184
Alcock v Wraith, The Times, 23 December 1991   6
Alexandrou v Oxford [1993] 4 All ER 328   80
Allen v Gulf Oil Refining [1981] 1 All ER 353   339
Allied Maples Group Ltd v Simmons [1995] 4 All ER 907   100
Allsop v Church of England Newspaper [1972] 2 All ER 26   375
Ambergate Rly v Midland Rly (1853) 2 E & B 793   322
American Cyanamid v Ethicon [1975] AC 396   432
AMF International Ltd v Magnet Bowling Ltd [1968] 2 All ER 789   201
Ancell v McDermott [1993] 4 All ER 355   80
Anchor Brewhouse Developments v Berkeley House (1987) 2 EGLR 187   320
Anderson v Rhodes [1967] 2 All ER 850   135
Andreae v Selfridge [1937] 3 All ER 255   335
Andrews v Hopkinson [1957] 1 QB 229   396
Anns v Merton LBC [1978] AC 728   73, 189
Arbuthnott and Others v Feltrim Underwriting Agencies Ltd and Others
   [1994] 3 All ER 506   136
Argy Trading Development Co. Ltd v Lapid Developments Ltd [1977] 3 All ER 785   130
Armory v Delamirie [1558–1774] All ER Rep 121   310
Arpad, The [1934] P 189   114
Arthur v Anker (1996) 146 NLJ 86, The Times, 1 December 1995   40, 322, 323
Ashby v White (1703) 2 Ld Raym 938   238
Ashdown v Samuel Williams and Son Ltd [1957] 1 QB 409   218
Ashton v Turner [1981] QB 137   57
Aswan Engineering Establishment Co. v Lupdine Ltd [1987] 1 All ER 135   122, 398, 405
Atkinson v Gateshead Waterworks Co. (1877) 2 ExD 441   240
Attia v British Gas [1987] 3 All ER 455   158, 182
Austin Rover v HM Inspector of Taxes, The Times, 15 August 1989   258
Auty v NCB [1985] 1 All ER 930   425

Baird v Williamson (1863) 15 CB (NS) 376   330
Baker v Hopkins and Son Ltd [1958] 3 All ER 147   54
Baker v Willoughby [1969] All ER 1528   97
Ballard v Tomlinson (1885) 29 Ch D 115   330, 332
Bamford v Turnley (1862) 3 B & S 62   333
Bank of Credit and Commerce International (Overseas) Ltd v Price Waterhouse,
    The Times, 4 March 1998 (CA)   141
Banque Keyser Ullman SA v Skandia (UK) Insurance Co. Ltd [1989] 2 All ER 952   134
Barnes v Hampshire County Council [1969] 3 All ER 746   108
Barnes v Nayer, The Times, 19 December 1986   36
Barnett v Chelsea Hospital [1969] 1 All ER 428   96
Barrett v Lounova [1982] Ltd [1989] 1 All ER 1   189
Barrett v Ministry of Defence [1995] 3 All ER 87   75
Barton v Armstrong [1969] 2 NSWR 451   299
Bartonshill Coal Co. v McGuire (1853) 3 Macq 300   5
Baseley v Clarkson (1681) 3 Lev 37   33
Bates v Parker [1953] 2 QB 231   210
Batty v Metropolitan Property Realisations [1978] QB 554   190
Beard v London General Omnibus Co. [1900] 2 QB 530   12
Bellew v Irish Cement [1948] IR 61   335
Beloff v Pressdram [1973] 1 All ER 241   9
Benning v Wong (1969) 122 CLR 249   358
Benson v Lee [1972] VR 879   160
Bernstein v Skyview and General [1977] 2 All ER 902   321
Berry v Humm & Co. [1915] 1 KB 627   428
Billings v Riden [1958] AC 240   194
Bird v Holbrook (1828) 4 Bing 628   222
Bird v Jones (1845) 7 QB 742   302
Birmingham Corporation v Sowsbery [1970] RTR 84   422
Bishopsgate Motor Finance v Transport Brakes Ltd [1949] 1 KB 322   315
Black (or Butler) v Fife Coal Co. Ltd [1912] AC 149   270
Black v Carmichael, The Times, 25 June 1992   322
Blake v Barnard (1840) 9 C & P 626   300
Bland v Stockport Borough Council, New Law Journal, 12 February 1993   280
Blennerhasset v Novelty Sales Services Ltd (1933) 175 LT Jo 393   370
Blue Town Investments v Higgs & Hill [1990] 1 WLR 696   434
Boardman v Sanderson [1964] 1 WLR 1317   160
Bolam v Friern Hospital Management Committee [1957] 1 WLR 582   83, 84
Bolitho v City and Hackney Health Authority [1997] 4 All ER 771   85
Bolton v Stone [1951] AC 850   85
Bonnington Castings v Wardlaw [1956] AC 613   258
Borag, The [1981] 1 WLR 274   115
Bottomley v Bannister [1932] 1 KB 458   188
Bourhill v Young [1943] AC 92   157, 163, 184
Boyle v Kodak Ltd [1969] 2 All ER 439   239, 264
Bradburn v GWR (1874) LR 10 Exch 1   426
Bradford v Robinson Rentals Ltd [1967] 1 All ER 267   110
Braithwaite v South Durham Steel Co. [1958] 1 WLR 986   204
Bridlington Relay v Yorkshire Electricity [1965] 1 All ER 264   337
Briggs v Gunner (1979) 129 NLJ 116   131
British Celanese Ltd v A H Hunt (Capacitors) Ltd [1969] 1 WLR 959,
    [1969] 2 All ER 1252   121, 356
British Railways Board v Herrington [1972] AC 877   222, 223
Broome v Cassell [1972] AC 1027   429
Bryanston Finance v De Vries [1975] QB 703   377, 381
BTC v Gourley [1956] AC 185   426
Buckland v Guildford Gas Light and Coke Co. [1944] 1 KB 410   194
Bull v Devon Area Health Authority [1993] 4 Med LR 117   29
Bunker v Brand [1969] QB 480   199
Burnett v British Waterways Board [1973] 1 WLR 700   51
Burris v Azadani, The Times, 8 August 1995   346
Burton v Islington Health Authority [1991] 1 All ER 825, [1992] 3 All ER 833   81, 151
Burton v Winters [1993] 3 All ER 847   322
Bux v Slough Metals [1973] 1 WLR 1358   257
Byrne v Dean [1937] 2 All ER 204   371

C R Taylor (Wholesale) Ltd v Hepworths Ltd [1977] 1 WLR 659   422
C v C (Non-molestation Order: Jurisdiction), The Times, 16 December 1997   347
Calveley v Chief Constable of Merseyside [1988] 3 All ER 385,
    [1989] 1 All ER 1025   78, 245

Cambridge Water Co. v Eastern Counties Leather (unreported, 31 July 1991),
   [1994] 1 All ER 53   113, 328, 330, 332, 349, 353, 356
Caminer v Northern and London Investment Trust [1951] AC 88   329
Campbell v Percy Bilton, The Guardian, 17 February 1988   110
Candler v Crane Christmas and Co. [1951] 1 All ER 426 (CA)   128
Candlewood Navigation Corporation Ltd v Mitsui OSK Lines Ltd [1985] 2 All ER 935   125
Canterbury v Spence (1972) 464 F 2nd 772   294
Caparo Industries plc v Dickman [1989] 2 WLR 316 (CA), [1990] 1 All ER 568 (HL)
                                      72, 74, 90, 91, 92, 136, 183, 328, 397
Capital and Counties plc v Hampshire County Council and others [1997] 2 All ER 565   80
Caporale v C W Blakeslee Inc (1961) 149 Conn. 79, 175 A 2d 561   355
Capps v Miller [1989] 2 All ER 333   61
Carlgarth, The [1927] P 93   204
Carmarthenshire County Council v Lewis [1955] AC 549 (HL)   108
Carr v Mercantile Produce Ltd [1949] 2 KB 601   263
Carstairs v Taylor (1871) LR 6 Ex 217   359
Cassidy v Daily Mirror [1929] 2 KB 331   375, 376, 386
Cassidy v Ministry of Health [1951] 2 KB 343   29
Cattle v Stockton Waterworks (1875) LR 10 QB 453   120
Cattley v St John's Ambulance Brigade (1988) QBD (unreported)   84
Cavalier v Pope [1906] AC 428   188
CBS Songs Ltd v Amstrad Consumer Electronics plc [1988] AC 1013   255
Central Newbury Car Auctions v Unity Finance [1956] 3 All ER 905   317
Century Insurance Co. Ltd v Northern Ireland Road Transport Board [1942] AC 509   12
Chadwick v British Railways Board [1967] 1 WLR 912   55, 161
Charleston v News Group Newspapers [1995] 2 All ER 904   376
Charlton v Forrest Printing Ink Co. Ltd [1980] IRLR 331   277
Chatterton v Gerson [1981] 1 All ER 257   293
Chaudhry v Prabhaker [1988] 3 All ER 718   132
Chipchase v British Titan Products Co. [1956] 1 QB 545   260
Christie v Davey [1893] 1 Ch 316   334
Clarke v Bruce Lance and Co. [1988] 1 All ER 364   143
Clarke v Taff Ely Borough Council (1983) 10 HLR 44   195
Clarke v Taylor (1836) 2 Bing NC 654   383
Clarkson v Bransford (1987) Huddersfield County Court (unreported)   411
Clay v A J Crump & Sons [1964] 1 QB 533   148, 398
Clayards v Dethick (1848) 12 QB 439   63
Clayton v Woodman [1962] 2 QB 533   148
Clifford v Charles H Challen & Son Ltd [1951] 1 KB 495   276
Clifford v Drymond [1976] RTR 134   62
Close v Steel Co. of Wales [1962] AC 367   260
Cockroft v Smith (1705) 2 Salk 642   36
Cocks v Thanet District Council [1983] 2 AC 286   79, 251
Cole v Turner (1704) 6 Mod 149   297
Collins v Renison [1754] Say 138   38
Collins v Wilcock [1984] 3 All ER 374   296
Coltman v Bibby Tankers Ltd [1987] 3 All ER 1068   272
Condon v Basi [1985] 2 All ER 453   50, 83, 297
Condon v Condon [1977] RTR 483   62
Connelly v RTZ Corporation [1997] 4 All ER 335   281
Conway v George Wimpey and Co. Ltd [1951] 2 KB 266   13
Coote v Stone [1971] 1 WLR 279   242
Cope v Sharpe (No. 2) [1912] 1 KB 496   59, 418
Cornell v Green, The Guardian, 13 February 1998   104
Corporacion Nacional Del Cobre De Chile v Sogemin Metals Ltd [1997] 2 All ER 917   61
Coupland v Eagle Bros Ltd (1969) 210 Estates Gazette 581   214
Crook v Derbyshire Stone Ltd [1956] 1 WLR 432   29
Crossley v Rawlinson [1981] 3 All ER 674   55, 111
Cunard v Antifyre [1933] 1 KB 551   194
Cunningham v Harrison [1973] QB 942   424
Cunningham v Reading Football Club Ltd [1992] PIQR 141   207
Curran v NI Co-Ownership Housing Association Ltd [1987] AC 718   74
Curtis v Betts [1990] 1 WLR 459   413
Cutler v United Dairies (London) Ltd [1933] 2 KB 297   55
Cutler v Vauxhall Motors [1974] 1 QB 418   97
Cutler v Wandsworth Stadium Ltd [1949] AC 398   239, 253

D & F Estates v Church Commissioners for England [1988] 2 All ER 992,
   [1989] AC 187   126, 191
Daly v Surrey County Council, The Times, 25 October 1997   80

Daniels v Griffiths (1997) 147 NLJ 1809   380
Daniels v R White and Sons [1938] 4 All ER 258   392, 399
Daniels v Whetstone Entertainments Ltd [1962] 2 Lloyd's Rep 1   15
Dann v Hamilton [1939] 1 KB 509   67
Darbishire v Warran [1963] 1 WLR 1067   422
Davidson v Chief Constable of North Wales [1994] 2 All ER 597   305
Davie v New Merton Board Mills [1959] AC 604   270
Davies v Swan Motor Co. (Swansea) Ltd [1949] 2 KB 291   64
Day v Brownrigg (1878) 10 Ch D 294   432
Dear v Newham LBC, The Times, 24 February 1988   246
Deeny and Others v Gooda Walker Ltd and Others [1994] 3 All ER 506   136
Denny v Supplies & Transport [1950] 2 KB 374   398
Department of the Environment v Thomas Bates and Son Ltd [1990] 2 All ER 943   193
Derbyshire CC v Times Newspapers Ltd [1993] AC 534   369
Dexter v Tenby Electrical Accessories Ltd, The Guardian, 22 February 1991   258
Dodd Properties (Kent) Ltd v Canterbury City Council [1980] 1 All ER 928,
   [1980] 1 WLR 433   115, 422
Doe d. Murray, Lord Bishop of Rochester v Bridges (1854) 1 B & AD 847   239
Dollman v Hillman [1941] 1 All ER 355   342
Donaghey v Boulton and Paul Ltd [1968] AC 1   261
Donoghue v Stevenson [1932] AC 562   26, 70, 71, 90, 182, 183, 392, 396
Dooley v Cammell Laird and Co. Ltd [1951] 1 Lloyd's Reports 271   161
Doughty v Turner Manufacturing Co. [1964] 1 All ER 98   111
DPP v Parmenter [1991] 4 All ER 698   298
Drinkwater v Kimber [1952] 1 All ER 701   64
Dulieu v White [1901] 2 KB 669   159
Duncan v British Coal Corporation   176, 183
Dunster v Abbot [1953] 2 All ER 1572   203
Dutton v Bognor Regis UDC [1972] 1 QB 373   190
Dymond v Pearce [1972] 1 QB 496   349

Earl of Oxford's Case (1615) 21 ER 485, 576   431
Eastern Distributors v Goldring [1957] 2 All ER 525   317
Eastern SA Telegraph Co. v Cape Town Tramways [1902] AC 381   360
Edwards v Railway Executive [1952] AC 737   202
Electrochrome Ltd v Welsh Plastics Ltd [1968] 2 All ER 205   121
Elguzouli-Daf v Commissioner of the Metropolis [1995] 1 All ER 833   75
Elleanor v Cavendish Woodhouse [1973] 1 Lloyd's Rep 313   14
Elwes v Brigg Gas Co. (1886) 33 Ch D 562   311
Environment Agency (formerly National Rivers Authority) v Empress Car Co.
   [1998] 2 WLR 350   359
Esso Petroleum Co. Ltd v Southport Corporation [1956] AC 218   59
Esso v Mardon [1976] QB 801   130
Esterhuizen v Allied Dunbar Assurance plc, The Times, 10 June 1998   146
Euro-Drain Ltd v Bathurst [1988] 2 All ER 23   65
Evans v Triplex Safety Glass [1936] 1 All ER 283   399
Ex parte Island Records Ltd [1978] 1 Ch 122   238

Farr v Butters Bros [1932] 2 KB 606   398
Farrell v John Mowlem & Co. [1954] 1 Lloyd's Rep 437   342, 349
Faulkner v Chief Adjudication Officer, The Times, 8 April 1994   15
Ferguson v Welsh [1987] 3 All ER 777   198, 206
Filliter v Phippard (1847) 11 QB 347   361
First Interstate Bank of California v Cohen Arnold and Co., The Times,
   11 December 1995   100
Fisher v CHT Ltd [1966] 2 QB 475   200
Fisher v Prince (1762) 3 Burr 1364   26
Fitzgerald v Lane [1987] 2 All ER 455   23, 99
Fookes v Slaytor [1979] 1 All ER 137   60
Fowler v Hollins (1878) LR 7 QB 616   307, 308
Fowler v Lanning [1959] 1 All ER 290   291
Francis Aston v Imperial Chemical Industries Group (unreported, 21 May 1992)   183
Francovich v Italian State (Cases C-6 and 9/90) [1992] IRLR 84   407
Fraser v Berkeley (1836) 7 C & P 621   36
Freeman v Home Office [1983] 3 All ER 589   64
Freeman v Home Office (No. 2) [1984] 1 All ER 1036   42, 295
Froom v Butcher [1976] 1 QB 286   62
Frost and Others v The Chief Constable of the South Yorkshire Police,
   The Times, 3 July 1995   175, 178, 183, 280
Furniss v Fitchett [1958] NZLR 396   179

Gaffney v Aviation and Shipping Co. Ltd [1966] 1 Lloyd's Rep 249 — 214
Galt v BRB (1983) 133 NLJ 870 — 162
General Cleaning Contractors v Christmas [1953] AC 180 — 275
General Engineering Services Ltd v Kingston and St Andrew Corporation
[1988] 3 All ER 867 — 15
Generale Bank Nederland NV v Export Credits Guarantee Dept., The Times,
4 August 1997 — 16
Giles v Walker (1890) 24 QBD 656 — 355
Gill v Edouin (1894) 71 LT 762, 72 LT 579 — 359
Gillingham BC v Medway (Chatham) Dock Co. [1992] 3 All ER 923 — 339
Ginty v Belmont Building Supplies [1959] 1 All ER 414 — 259, 260
Glasgow Corporation v Taylor [1922] 1 AC 44 — 209
Gold v Haringey Health Authority [1987] 2 All ER 888 — 85
Goldman v Hargrave [1967] 1 AC 645 — 331
Goldsmith v Bhoyrul [1997] 4 All ER 268 — 369
Goldsmith v Sperrings Ltd [1977] 2 All ER 55 — 378
Goodwill v British Pregnancy Advisory Servie [1996] 2 All ER 161 — 146
Gorris v Scott (1874) LR 9 Ex 125 — 260
Gough v Thorne [1966] 1 WLR 1387 — 63
Graham v Saville [1945] 2 DLR 489 — 295
Grant v Australian Knitting Mills [1935] All ER Rep 209, [1936] AC 85 — 392, 399
Grant v National Coal Board [1958] AC 649 — 261
Gray v Barr [1971] 2 QB 554 — 37
Gray v Jones [1939] 1 All ER 798 — 369
Greater Nottingham Co-operative Society Ltd v Cementation Piling and Foundations Ltd
[1989] QB 71 — 76, 125, 183
Green v Chelsea Waterworks Co. (1894) 70 LT 547 — 360
Green v Fibre Glass Co. [1958] 1 QB 245 — 84
Greenhalgh v British Railways Board [1969] 2 QB 286 — 205
Gregory v Kelly [1978] RTR 426 — 63
Groves v Lord Wimborne [1892] 2 QB 402 — 243

H v Home Office, The Independent, 6 May 1992 — 304
Hale v Jennings Bros [1938] 1 All ER 579 — 359
Hale v London Underground (1992) 11 BMLR 81 — 174
Haley v London Electricity Board [1965] AC 778 — 86, 163
Halford v Brookes [1991] 1 WLR 428 — 289
Halsey v Esso Petroleum [1961] 2 All ER 145 — 348
Hambrook v Stokes Bros [1925] 1 KB 141 — 160, 182
Hands v Rolls-Royce (1972) 69 LSG 504 — 260
Harper v Haden & Sons [1933] Ch 298 — 342
Harris v Birkenhead Corporation [1976] 1 All ER 341 — 200
Harris v Bright's Asphalt Contractors Ltd [1953] 1 All ER 395 — 268
Harris v Wyre Forest DC [1989] 2 All ER 514 — 134
Harrison v British Railways Board [1981] 3 All ER 679 — 54
Harrison v Lawrence Murphy & Co., The Chartered Secretary, 1 March 1998 — 270
Harrison v Michelin Tyre Co. Ltd [1985] 1 All ER 918 — 12
Harrison v National Coal Board [1951] AC 639 — 239
Harrison v Vincent [1982] RTR 8 — 50, 83
Hartley v Mayoh & Co. [1954] 1 QB 383 — 241
Harvey v O'Dell [1958] 1 All ER 657 — 28
Haseldine v Daw [1941] 2 KB 343 — 213
Haydon v Kent County Council [1978] QB 343 (CA) — 77
Haynes v Harwood [1935] 1 KB 146 — 53, 102
Heasmans v Clarity Cleaning Co. Ltd [1987] ICR 949 — 17
Hedley Byrne and Co. v Heller and Partners [1963] 2 All ER 575, [1964] AC 46
— 71, 76, 126, 128, 153
Hegarty v EE Caledonia Ltd [1997] 2 Lloyds Rep. 259 — 177, 183
Hegarty v Shine (1878) 4 LRIr 288 — 52
Heil v Hedges [1951] 1 TLR 512 — 404
Helby v Matthews [1895] AC 471 — 319
Hemphill Ltd v Williams [1966] 2 Lloyd's Rep 101 — 13
Henderson and Others v Merrett Syndicates Ltd and Others [1994] 3 All ER 506
— 76, 136, 152, 153, 397
Henderson v Henry E. Jenkins & Sons [1969] 3 All ER 756 — 88, 89
Herd v Weardale Steel Coal and Coke Co. [1915] AC 67 HL — 302, 303
Heron II, The [1969] 1 AC 350 — 112
Herring v Boyle (1834) 1 Cr M & R 377 — 306
Hevican v Ruane [1991] 3 All ER 65 — 171
Hewett v Alf Brown's Transport Ltd [1991] ICR 471 — 266

Hewitt v Bonvin [1940] 1 KB 188   18
Hicks v Chief Constable of South Yorkshire [1992] 2 All ER 65   428
Hicks v Wright [1992] 2 All ER 65   179
Hill v Chief Constable of West Yorkshire [1989] AC 53   78
Hill v Tomkins, The Guardian, 18 October 1997   99
Hillesdon Securities v Ryjack Ltd [1983] 2 All ER 184   312
Hills v Potter [1983] 3 All ER 716   294
Hilton v Burton (Rhodes) Ltd [1961] 1 WLR 705   13
Hinz v Berry [1970] 2 QB 40   158, 160
Hiort v Bott (1874) LR 9 Exch 86   309
Hogan v Bentinck Collieries [1949] 1 All ER 588   106
Holbeck Hall Hotel Ltd and Another v Scarborough Borough Council, The Times,
    15 October 1997   331
Hollywood Silver Fox Farm v Emmett [1936] 1 All ER 825   335
Holt v Payne Skillington, The Times, 22 December 1995   76
Home Office v Dorset Yacht Co. [1970] AC 1004   3, 72, 108
Honeywill & Stein Ltd v Larkin Bros Ltd [1934] 1 KB 1991   8
Hopp v Lepp (1980) 112 DLR (3rd) 67   294
Horrocks v Lowe [1975] AC 135   382
Horsley v MacLaren ('The Ogopogo') [1971] 2 Lloyd's Rep 410 (Canada)   55
Hotson v East Berkshire Health Authority [1987] 2 All ER 909   99
Housecroft v Burnett [1986] 1 All ER 332   424
Howard E Perry & Co. Ltd v British Rail [1979] 2 All ER 579   309
Howard Marine v Ogden [1978] QB 574   128
Hubbard v Pitt [1975] 3 All ER 1   337, 338, 349
Huckle v Money (1763) 95 ER 768   429
Hudson v Ridge Manufacturing [1957] 2 QB 348   269
Hughes v Lord Advocate [1963] 1 All ER 705   111, 210
Hulton & Co. v Jones [1910] AC 20   373, 386
Hunt v Severs [1994] 2 All ER 385   424, 425
Hunt v Wallis, The Times, 10 May 1991   413
Hunter v British Coal Corp. and Another [1998] 2 All ER 97   177, 182, 183
Hunter v Canary Wharf [1997] 2 All ER 426   327, 328, 338, 341, 345, 346, 359
Huntingdon Life Sciences Ltd v Curtin and Others, The Times, 11 December 1997   347
Hurley v Dyke [1979] RTR 265   396
Hussain v New Taplow Paper Mills [1988] AC 514   426
Huth v Huth [1915] 3 KB 32   377
Hyatt v Great Western Railway Co. [1948] 1 KB 345   56
Hyde v Tameside Area Health Authority, The Times, 16 April 1981   46, 105

Ilkiw v Samuels [1963] 2 All ER 879   25
Imperial Chemical Industries Ltd v Shatwell [1965] AC 656   5, 51, 66, 262
Ingram v Little [1961] QB 31   306
Invercargill City Council v Hamlin [1996] 1 All ER 756   193
Iqbal v London Transport Executive [1973] KIR 329   12
Irving v The Post Office [1987] IRLR 289   15

Jaensch v Coffey (1984) 54 ALR 417   165, 167, 184
James McNaughton Paper Group Ltd v Hicks Anderson and Co. [1991] 1 All ER 134   139
Janvier v Sweeney [1919] 2 KB 316 CA   345
Jauffur v Akhbar, The Times, 10 February 1984   2, 108, 199
JEB Fasteners Ltd v Marks Bloom and Co. [1983] 1 All ER 583   73, 131, 142
Jefford v Gee [1970] 2 QB 130   423
Jerome v Bentley & Co. [1952] 2 All ER 114   318
Jobling v Associated Dairies [1982] AC 794   98
John Summers v Frost [1955] AC 740   255
Johnson (AT), The Times, 22 May 1996   341, 346
Johnstone v Bloomsbury Health Authority [1991] 2 All ER 293   76, 278
Jolley v London Borough of Sutton [1998] 3 All ER 559   210
Jones and Others v Wright (Chief Constable of South Yorkshire) [1991] 1 All ER 353   168
Jones v Department of Employment [1988] QB 1   78
Jones v Lawrence [1969] 3 All ER 267   63
Jones v Livox Quarries Ltd [1952] 2 QB 608   63
Junior Books Ltd v Veitchi Co. Ltd [1982] 3 All ER 201, [1983] 1 AC 520   73, 124, 153, 397

Kandalla v BEA [1981] QB 158   428
Kay v Ayrshire and Arran Health Board [1987] 2 All ER 417   99
Kay v ITW Ltd [1967] 3 All ER 22   26
Keating v Elvan Reinforced Concrete Co. [1968] 1 WLR 722   241
Kelly v Corston [1997] 4 All ER 466   82

Kelsen v Imperial Tobacco [1957] 2 All ER 343 320
Kemsley v Foot [1952] AC 345 385
Kennaway v Thompson [1981] 3 All ER 329 432, 433
Khorasandjian v Bush [1993] 3 WLR 476, [1993] 3 All ER 669 327, 328, 345, 432
King v Liverpool City Council [1986] 3 All ER 544 105
King v Phillips [1953] 1 QB 429 160
Kirk v Gregory (1876) 1 Ex D 55 60, 313
Kirkham v Anderton (Chief Constable of Greater Manchester) [1990] 3 All ER 246 105
Kirkham v Chief Constable of Greater Manchester [1990] 3 All ER 246 45, 48, 56
Kite v Napp, The Times, 1 June 1982 413
Klein v Canadian Propane (1967) 64 DLR (2d) 220 131
Knapp v Railway Executive [1949] 2 All ER 508 241
Knightley v Johns [1982] 1 All ER 851 96, 101
Knowles v Liverpool City Council [1993] 4 All ER 321 272
Knupffer v London Express Newspapers [1944] 1 All ER 495 372
Kralj v McGrath [1986] 1 All ER 54 158
Kubach v Hollands (1937) 53 TLR 1024 396
Kuwait Asia Bank EC v National Mutual Life Nominees Ltd [1990] 3 WLR 297 139

L v Bournewood Community and Mental Health NHS Trust, The Times,
    30 June 1998 305
Lamb v Camden London Borough Council [1981] 2 All ER 408, [1981] QB 625 70, 95, 102
Lambert v Lewis [1981] 2 WLR 713 122
Lane v Holloway [1968] 1 QB 379 36
Lane v Shire Roofing Co. (Oxford) Ltd, The Times, 17 February 1995 10
Larner v British Steel plc [1993] 4 All ER 102 256
Latham v R Johnson and Nephew Ltd [1913] 1 KB 398 208
Latimer v AEC Ltd [1953] AC 643 273
Latter v Braddell (1881) 50 LJQB 448 295
Lawrence v Osborne, The Times, 8 November 1997 104
Lawton v BOC Transhield Ltd [1987] 2 All ER 608 142
LCC v Cattermoles (Garages) Ltd [1953] 2 All ER 582 13
Leakey v National Trust [1980] 1 All ER 17 331
Leigh and Sillavan Ltd v Aliakmon Shipping Co. Ltd [1986] AC 786,
    [1986] 2 All ER 145 74, 124
Leigh v Gladstone (1909) 26 TLR 139 59
Letang v Cooper [1964] 2 All ER 929 291, 345
Lewis v Averay [1973] 2 All ER 229 306
Lewis v Daily Telegraph Ltd [1963] 2 All ER 151 374
Liddle v Yorkshire (North Riding) County Council [1934] 2 KB 101 209
Liesbosch Dredger v SS Edison [1933] AC 449 115, 423
Lim Poh Choo v Camden & Islington AHA [1980] AC 174 424
Limpus v London General Omnibus Co. [1862] 1 H & C 526 12, 13
Lister v Romford Ice Co. [1957] AC 555 282
Litster v Forth Dry Dock Engineering Co. Ltd [1989] 1 All ER 1134 407
Livingston v Ministry of Defence [1984] NI 356 291
Livingstone v Rawyards Coal Co. (1880) 5 App Cas 25 417
Lloyd v DPP [1992] 1 All ER 982 322
Lloyd v Grace, Smith & Co. [1912] AC 716 16
Lochgelly Iron Co. v M'Mullan [1934] AC 1 258
Lodge Holes Colliery Co. v Wednesbury Corporation [1908] AC 323 422
Lomax v Stott (1870) 39 LJ Ch 834 360
London Congregational Union v Harriss & Harriss [1985] 1 All ER 335 422
London Passenger Transport Board v Upson [1949] AC 155 256
Lonrho Ltd v Shell Petroleum Co. Ltd (No. 2) [1981] 2 All ER 456 240
Lonrho plc v Fayed [1988] 3 All ER 464 135
Lonrho plc v Tebbitt and Another [1992] 4 All ER 280 79
Lowery v Walker [1911] AC 10 202
Luxmoore-May v Messenger May Baverstock [1990] 1 All ER 1067 (CA) 131

M v Newham LBC [1995] 3 All ER 353 78, 80
MacPherson v Buick Motor Co. (1916) 217 NY 382 395
Maes Finance Ltd v A L Phillips and Co., The Times, 25 March 1997 64
Malcolm v Broadhurst [1970] 3 All ER 608 173
Malfroot v Noxall (1935) 51 TLR 551 396
Malone v Laskey [1907] 2 KB 141 327
Marc Rich Co. AG and Others v Bishop Rock Marine Co. Ltd and Others,
    'The Nicholas H' [1994] 3 All ER 686, [1995] 3 All ER 307 75, 91, 149, 151
Margereson and Hancock v J W Roberts Ltd (two cases heard together),
    The Times, 17 April 1996 92

Mariola Marine Corp v Lloyd's Register of Shipping ('Morning Watch')
  [1990] 1 Lloyd's Rep 547   138
Marleasing Case (106/89) [1992] 1 CMLR 305   407
Marshall v Osmond [1983] QB 1034   58
Martin v Dean [1971] 3 All ER 279   243
Martindale v Duncan [1973] 1 WLR 574   115
Mason v Williams & Williams and Thomas Turton [1955] 1 All ER 808   399
Matheson v Northcote College [1975] 2 NZLR 106   355
Matrix-Securities Ltd v Theodore Goddard (a firm), The Times, 13 November 1997   83
Mattocks v Mann [1993] RTR 13   116, 423
McAuley v Bristol City Council [1992] 1 All ER 749   196
McCarthy v Chief Constable of the South Yorkshire Police and Others, The Times,
  12 December 1996   181
McConkey v Amec plc (1990) 27 Construction LR 88   11
McCord v Swansea City AFC, The Times, 11 February 1997   83
McCullagh v Lane Fox, The Times, 25 January 1994   145
McDermid v Nash Dredging and Reclamation Co. Ltd [1987] 2 All ER 878   267
McFarlane v EE Caledonia Ltd [1994] 2 All ER 1   176
McGeown v Northern Ireland Housing Executive [1994] 3 All ER 53   205
McGhee v National Coal Board [1972] 3 All ER 1008   86, 87, 98, 100
McKay v Essex Area Health Authority [1982] 2 WLR 890   81
McKew v Holland [1969] 3 All ER 1621   102
McLoughlin v O'Brian [1982] 2 All ER 298   158, 165
McNerny v Lambeth LBC (1988) 21 HLR 188   188
McWilliams v Arrol [1962] 1 All ER 623   258
Meade & Belt's Case (1823) 1 Lewin 184   298
Meah v McCreamer [1985] 1 All ER 367   103, 289
Meah v McCreamer (No. 2) [1986] 1 All ER 943   103, 289
Mears v LSWR (1862) 11 CBNS 850   313
Meering v Graham-White Aviation (1919) 122 LT 44   306
Mepstead v DPP [1996] Crim LR 111   296
Mercantile Credit v Hamblin [1964] 3 All ER 592   318
Mersey Docks and Harbour Board v Coggins and Griffiths (Liverpool) Ltd
  [1946] 2 All ER 345   10
Metropolitan Asylum District Managers v Hill (1881) 6 App Cas 193   339
Middleweek v Chief Constable of Merseyside [1990] 3 All ER 662   304
Midland Bank Trust Co. Ltd v Hett, Stubbs and Kemp [1979] Ch 384   147
Midwood v Manchester [1905] 2 KB 597   357
Miller v Jackson [1977] 3 All ER 338   334, 335, 433
Mills v Winchester Diocesan Board of Finance [1989] 2 All ER 317   140
Ministry of Housing v Sharp [1970] 1 All ER 1009, [1970] 2 QB 223   141, 255
Minories Finance Ltd v Arthur Young [1989] 2 All ER 105   140
Mint v Good [1951] 1 KB 517   338
Minter v D & H Contractors, The Times, 30 June 1983   63
Moeliker v Reyrolle & Co. Ltd [1977] 1 All ER 9   424
Monk v Warbey [1935] 1 KB 75   18, 243
Moorgate Mercantile v Twitchings [1976] 2 All ER 641   317
Morgan Crucible Co. v Hill Samuel Bank Ltd [1990] 3 All ER 330   139
Morgan v Odhams Press [1971] 1 WLR 1239   375, 376, 386
Morgans v Launchbury [1972] 2 All ER 606   18
Morris v Breaveglen Ltd [1993] IRLR 350   277
Morris v C W Martin and Sons Ltd [1965] 2 All ER 725   16
Morris v Marsden [1952] 1 All ER 925   2
Morris v Murray [1990] 3 All ER 801   43, 44, 45, 56, 66
Morris v W Hartlepool Navigation Co. [1956] AC 552   85
Motherwell v Motherwell (1977) 73 DLR (3rd) 62   327
Mughal v Reuters Ltd, The Times, 10 November 1993   279
Muirhead v Industrial Tank Specialities [1985] 3 All ER 750, [1986] QB 507   125, 398
Mulcahy v Ministry of Defence [1996] 2 All ER 758   277
Mullard v Ben Line [1970] 1 WLR 1414   263
Mullen v Barr & Co. (1929) 45 SC 245   392
Mullin v Richards [1998] 1 All ER 920   87
Multigroup Bulgaria Holdings Ltd v Oxford Analytica Ltd (1997) (unreported)   367
Murdoch v Glacier Metal Ltd, The Times, 21 January 1998   334
Murphy v Brentwood District Council [1990] 2 All ER 908, [1991] 1 AC 398
                                              78, 80, 123, 126, 144, 192, 398
Murphy v Culhane [1976] 3 All ER 533   37
Murray v Haringey Arena Ltd [1951] 2 KB 529   50
Murray v Ministry of Defence [1988] 2 All ER 521   306
Musgrove v Pandelis [1919] 2 KB 43   356, 361, 362

Mutual Life and Citizens' Assurance Co. Ltd v Evatt [1971] AC 793   130

Nahhar v Pier House (Cheyne Walk) Management (1984) 270 EG 329   29
National Coal Board v England [1954] AC 403   58
Nettleship v Weston [1971] 3 All ER 581, [1971] 2 QB 691   43, 84
Newstead v London Express Newspapers [1940] 1 KB 377   373, 386
Ng Chun Pui v Lee Chuen Tat [1988] RTR 298   88, 89
Nitrigin Eireann Teoranta v Inco Alloys Ltd [1992] 1 All ER 854   151, 193
Nor-Video v Ontario Hydro (1978) 84 DLR (3rd) 221   337
Norberg v Wynrib (1992) 92 DLR (4th) 449   295
Norris v Moss [1954] 1 WLR 346   264
Norwich City Council v Harvey [1989] 1 All ER 1180   41
Nova-Mink v Trans-Canada Airlines [1951] 2 DLR 241   72

O'Grady v Westminster Scaffolding [1962] 2 Lloyd's Rep 238   422
O'Kelly v Trusthouse Forte plc [1983] ICR 728   8
O'Loughlin v Chief Constable of Essex, The Times, 11 December 1997   296
O'Reilly v Mackman [1983] 2 AC 237   251
Ogwo v Taylor [1987] 3 All ER 961, [1988] AC 431   111, 194
Oliver v Birmingham and Midland Motor Omnibus Co. Ltd [1933] 1 KB 35   63
Olotu v Home Office and Another [1997] 1 All ER 385   75
Oppenheimer v Attenborough and Sons [1908] 1 KB 221   318
Ormrod v Crosville Motors [1953] 1 WLR 409   18
Oropesa, The [1943] P 32   103
Osman v Ferguson [1993] 4 All ER 344   80
Oxy Electric Ltd v Zainuddin [1990] 2 All ER 902   434

Pacific Motor Auctions v Motor Credits (Hire Finance) [1965] 2 All ER 105   319
Page v Smith [1994] 4 All ER 522   173
Page v Smith (No. 2) [1996] 3 All ER 272   75, 99, 165, 174, 175, 181, 183
Pannett v McGuiness and Co. Ltd [1972] 3 All ER 137   223
Pape v Cumbria County Council [1991] IRLR 493   277
Paris v Stepney Borough Council [1951] AC 367   85, 276
Parker-Tweedale v Dunbar Bank PLC (No. 2) [1990] 2 All ER 588   145
Parker v British Airways Board [1982] 1 All ER 834   311
Parnell v Duguid, The Guardian, 22 July 1997   108
Parry v Cleaver [1970] AC 1   426
Parsons v Uttley Ingham [1978] QB 791 (CA)   115
Peabody Donation Fund v Parkinson [1985] AC 210   73
Pearson v British Midland, The Times, 10 February 1998   161
Pearson v Coleman Bros [1948] 2 KB 359   204
Penn v Bristol and West BS, The Times, 19 June 1995   146
Pepper v Hart [1993] AC 593   403
Performance Cars v Abraham [1962] 1 QB 33   98
Perl v Camden LBC [1984] QB 342   105
Perrett v Collins, The Times, 23 June 1998   151
Perry v Kendricks Transport [1956] 1 WLR 85   359
Perry v Sidney Phillips [1982] 3 All ER 705 (CA)   115
Phillips v Britannia Hygienic Laundry Co. [1923] 2 KB 832   241
Phillips v Whiteley [1938] 1 All ER 566   51, 64, 84
Phipps v Rochester Corporation [1965] 1 QB 450   209
Photo Production Ltd v Securicor Transport Ltd [1980] AC 827   17
Pickford v Imperial Chemical Industries plc [1998] 3 All ER 462   279
Pickstone v Freemans [1988] 2 All ER 803   407
Pigney v Pointer's Transport Services Ltd [1957] 2 All ER 807, [1957] 1 WLR 1121   46, 105
Pitts v Hunt [1990] 3 All ER 344   41, 45, 57, 65
Pocock v North East Essex Mental Health NHS Trust, The Guardian, 3 March 1998   279
Polemis, Re [1921] 3 KB 560   109
Pollard v John Parr & Sons [1927] 1 KB 236   16
Pontardawe RDC v Moore-Gwyn [1929] 1 Ch 656   355
Powell v Bolady, The Times, 26 November 1997   179
Preist v Last [1903] 2 KB 148   392
Pride of Derby & Derbyshire Angling Association v British Celanese [1953] Ch 149   432
Prosser v Levy [1955] 1 WLR 1224   359
Pullman v Hill [1891] 1 QB 524   377

R H Willis and Son v British Car Auctions [1978] 3 All ER 392   309
R v Billinghurst [1978] Crim LR 553   297
R v Bournewood Community and Mental Health NHS Trust, ex parte L [1998] 3 All ER 289   60
R v Brown [1993] 2 All ER 75, [1993] 2 WLR 556   52, 297, 298

R v Burstow & Ireland [1997] QB 114   299, 344
R v Cheshire [1991] 3 All ER 670   107
R v Chief Constable of Devon & Cornwall, ex parte CEGB [1982] QB 458   322
R v Coney (1882) 8 QBD 534   297
R v Deputy Governor of Parkhurst Prison, ex parte Hague [1992] 1 AC 58   245, 303
R v Ireland [1997] QB 114   299, 346
R v National Insurance Commissioner, ex parte Michael [1977] 1 WLR 109   15
R v Northavon DC ex parte Palmer, The Independent, 22 February 1994   79
R v Savage [1991] 4 All ER 698   292, 298
R v Self [1992] 3 All ER 476   305
R v St George (1840) 9 C & P 483   300
R v Wilson [1955] 1 All ER 744   299
R v Wilson [1996] Crim LR 573, [1996] 3 WLR 125   298
Racz v Home Office [1994] 1 All ER 97   27
Rainham Chemical Works v Belvedere Fish Guano [1921] 2 AC 465   356
Ramwade Ltd v W J Emson & Co. Ltd [1987] RTR 72   423
Rance v Mid-Downs Health Authority [1991] 1 All ER 801   81
Rantzen v Mirror Group Newspapers [1993] 4 All ER 975   387
Ravenscroft v Rederiakiebolaget Transatlantic [1991] 3 All ER 73, [1992] 2 All ER 470   171
Read v Croydon Corp [1938] 4 All ER 631   396
Read v J Lyons [1946] 2 All ER 471, [1947] AC 15   354, 356
Ready Mixed Concrete (South East) Ltd v Minister of Pensions and National Insurance
   [1965] 2 QB 497   9
Reeves v Commissioner of Police for the Metropolis, The Times, 20 November 1997   48, 65
Reibl v Hughes (1980) 114 DLR (3rd) 1   294
Reid v Rush and Tomkins [1989] 3 All ER 228   280
Revill v Newbery [1996] 1 All ER 291   37, 223, 224, 226
Richards v Cresswell, The Times, 24 April 1987   380
Richardson v Pitt-Stanley and Others [1995] 1 All ER 460   247
Richardson v Stephenson Clarke Ltd [1969] 1 WLR 1695   268
Richardson v West Lindsay DC [1990] 1 All ER 296   193
Rickards v Lothian [1913] AC 263 PC   355
Rigby v Chief Constable of Northamptonshire [1985] 2 All ER 985,
   [1985] 1 WLR 1242   35, 59, 357
Rigby v Chief Constable of Northants [1985] 2 All ER 985   35
Rigby v Chief Constable of Northants   357
Rimmer v Liverpool City Council [1984] 1 All ER 930   188
Roberts v Ramsbottom [1980] 1 All ER 7   2
Roberts v Wyatt (1810) 2 Taunt 268   309
Robertson v Ridley [1989] 2 All ER 474   233
Robinson v Balmain New Ferry Co. Ltd [1910] AC 295   302
Robinson v Harman (1848) 1 Exch 850   417
Robinson v The Post Office [1974] 2 All ER 737   114
Robson v Hallett [1967] 2 QB 939   203
Roe v Minister of Health [1954] 2 All ER 131, [1954] 2 QB 66   85, 95, 399
Rogers v Nightriders [1983] RTR 324   26
Roles v Nathan [1963] 1 WLR 1117   210
Rondel v Worsley [1969] AC 191   82
Rookes v Barnard [1964] AC 1129   429
Rootes v Shelton [1968] ALR 33   83
Rose v Miles (1815) 4 M & S 101   343
Rose v Plenty [1976] 1 WLR 141   14
Ross v Associated Portland Cement Manufacturers Ltd [1964] 2 All ER 452   259
Ross v Caunters [1979] 3 All ER 580, [1980] Ch 297   73, 100, 141
Rowe v Herman, The Times, 9 June 1997   26
Rowling v Takaro Properties [1988] AC 175 (PC)   78, 80
Royscot Trust Ltd v Rogerson [1991] 3 All ER 294   128
Ruddiman & Co. v Smith (1889) 60 LT 708   12
Ryan v Manbre Sugar Ltd (1970) 114 SJ 492   263
Rylands v Fletcher [1861–73] All ER Rep 1, (1886) LR 3 HL 330   6, 328, 332, 353

S v Distillers Company (Biochemicals) Ltd [1969] 3 All ER 1412   161
S v Newham LBC, The Times, 5 March 1998   380
SA de Rémorguage à Hélice v Bennetts [1911] 1 KB 243   121
Sadgrove v Hole [1901] 2 KB 1   377
Saif Ali v Mitchell [1980] AC 198   82
Salmon v Seafarer Restaurants Ltd [1983] 3 All ER 729   111, 195
Salsbury v Woodland [1969] 3 All ER 863   26
Saltpetre case (1606) 12 Rep 12   59
Saunders v Edwards [1987] 2 All ER 651   58

Schneider v Eisovitch [1960] 2 QB 430 — 164
Scholfield v Chief Constable of West Yorkshire, The Times, 15 May 1998 — 175
SCM v Whittall [1971] 1 QB 337 — 121
Sedleigh-Denfield v O'Callaghan [1940] 3 All ER 349, [1940] AC 880 — 331, 333
Shanklin Pier v Detel Products [1951] 2 KB 854 — 398
Sharpe v Avery [1938] 4 All ER 85 — 148
Shiffman v Order of St John [1936] 1 All ER 557 — 103, 359
Sidaway v Bethlem Royal & Maudsley Hospital Governors [1985] 1 All ER 643 — 294
Sim v Stretch [1936] 2 All ER 1237 — 371
Simaan General Contracting Co. v Pilkington Glass (No. 2) [1988] 1 All ER 791,
 [1988] QB 758 — 134, 154, 398
Sime v Sutcliffe Catering (Scotland) Ltd [1990] IRLR 228 — 10
Simkiss v Rhondda Borough Council [1983] 81 LGR 460 — 209
Simms v Leigh Rugby Football Club [1969] 2 All ER 923 — 207
Sion v Hampstead Health Authority [1994] 5 Med LR 170 — 177
Skinner v Secretary of State for Transport, The Times, 3 January 1995 — 75
Slater v Baker (1767) 95 ER 860 — 294
Slatter v British Railways Board [1966] 2 Lloyd's Rep 395 — 113
Smith v Baker and Sons [1891] AC 325 — 51, 267
Smith v Bradford Metropolitan Council, The Times, 22 June 1982 — 195
Smith v Bush [1989] 2 All ER 514 — 134
Smith v Crossley Bros (1951) 95 SJ 655 — 269
Smith v Kenrick (1849) 7 CB 515 — 330
Smith v Leech Brain [1962] 2 QB 405 — 114
Smith v Littlewoods Organisation [1987] 1 All ER 710, [1987] AC 241 — 73, 81, 106, 126
Smith v Scott [1973] Ch 314 — 338, 355
Smith v Scott Bowyers Ltd [1986] IRLR 315 — 268
Smith v Stages [1989] 1 All ER 833 — 11, 29
Smith v Vange Scaffolding Ltd and Another [1970] 1 All ER 249 — 220
Smoker v London Fire & Civil Defence Authority [1991] 2 AC 502 — 426
Smolden v Whitworth, The Times, 23 April and 18 December 1996 — 83
Sochacki v Sas [1947] 1 All ER 344 — 361
Sole v WJ Hallt Ltd [1973] 1 QB 574 — 215
South Australia Asset Management Corporation v York Montague Ltd
 [1996] 3 All ER 365 — 141
South Staffs Water Co. v Sharman [1896] 2 QB 44 — 311
Southwark London Borough Council v Williams [1971] Ch 734 — 60
Spartan Steel & Alloys Ltd v Martin & Co. (Contractors) Ltd [1972] 3 All ER 557,
 [1973] 1 QB 27 — 95, 108, 121
Speed v Thomas Swift and Co. Ltd [1943] KB 557 — 275
Spicer v Smee [1946] 1 All ER 489 — 329
Spittle v Bunney [1988] 3 All ER 1031 — 428
Spring v Guardian Assurance plc [1993] 2 All ER 273, [1994] 3 All ER 129 — 100, 142, 143, 280
Square D Ltd v Cook [1992] IRLR 34 — 274
St Helen's Smelting Co. v Tipping (1865) 11 HL Cas 642 — 336
Stansbie v Troman [1948] 2 All ER 48 — 103
Stapley v Gypsum Mines Ltd [1953] AC 663 — 61
Stennett v Hancock & Peters [1939] 2 All ER 578 — 396
Stephens v Myers (1830) 4 C & P 349 — 300
Stevenson Jordan and Harrison Ltd v Macdonald and Evans [1952] 1 TLR 101 — 9
Stone v Taffe [1974] 3 All ER 1016 — 205
Storey v Ashton [1869] LR 4 QB 476 — 28
Stovin v Wise [1996] 3 All ER 801 — 77, 80, 81
Strand Electric v Brisford [1952] 1 All ER 796 — 312
Stubbings v Webb [1993] 1 All ER 322 — 289, 292
Sturges v Bridgman (1879) 11 Ch D 852 — 333, 336
Sutcliffe v Pressdram [1991] 1 QB 153 — 387
Sutherland Shire Council v Heyman (1985) 60 ALR 1 — 91, 138
Swain v Puri [1996] PIQR P442 — 226

T (a minor) v Surrey County Council and Others [1994] 4 All ER 577 — 148
Tai Hing Cotton Mill Ltd v Liu Chong Hing Bank [1986] AC 80 (PC) — 75
Targett v Torfaen Borough Council [1992] 3 All ER 27 — 193
Tarrant v Ramage [1998] 1 Lloyd's Rep 185 — 277
Tarry v Ashton (1876) 1 QBD 314 — 329
Tate and Lyle v GLC [1983] 1 All ER 1159 — 125, 343
Taylor v Shieldness Produce Ltd [1994] PIQR 329 — 177, 178
Taylor v Somerset Health Authority [1993] PIQR 262 — 177
Tetley v Chitty [1986] 1 All ER 663 — 337
Thomas v Bishop [1976] CL 1872 — 103

Thomas v NUM [1985] 2 All ER 1 — 300
Thomas v Winchester (1852) 6 NY 397 — 395
Thompson-Schwab v Costaki [1956] 1 All ER 652 — 338
Thompson v MPC [1997] 3 WLR 403 — 429
Thornton v Kirklees Borough Council [1979] QB 626 — 249
Tidman v Reading Borough Council — 133
Titchener v British Railways Board [1983] 3 All ER 770 — 208
Tolley v Fry [1931] AC 333 — 375
Tolstoy Miloslavsky v UK Case 1995/520, [1995] 20 EHRR 442 — 387
Topp v London Country Bus [1993] RTR 279 — 75
Toronto Power Co. v Paskwan [1915] AC 734 — 272
Tremain v Pike [1969] 3 All ER 1303 — 110
Trevett v Lee [1955] 1 All ER 406 — 342
Truckell v Stock [1957] 1 WLR 161 — 433
Tubervil v Stamp (1698) 1 Salk 13 — 362
Tuberville v Savage (1669) 1 Mod Rep 3 — 299, 418
Turner v MGM [1950] 1 All ER 449 — 36
Tutin v Mary Chipperfield Promotions (1980) 130 NLJ 807 — 412
Tutton v AD Walter [1986] QB 61 — 232
Twine v Bean's Express Ltd (1946) 175 LT 131 — 13

Vacwell Engineering v BDH Chemicals [1971] 1 QB 88 — 112
Van Oppen v Clerk to the Bedford Charity Trustees [1989] 3 All ER 889 — 135
Vaughan v Menlove (1837) 3 Bing NC 468 — 362
Vernon v Bosley (No. 1) [1997] 1 All ER 577 — 180
Vicar of Writtle v Essex County Council (1979) LQR 656 — 108
Victoria Park Racing v Taylor (1938) 58 CLR 479 — 338
Victorian Railway Commissioners v Coultas (1888) 13 App Cas 222 — 180
Videan v British Transport Commission [1963] 2 All ER 860 — 53, 224
Virgo Steamship Co. v Skaarup Shipping Corporation [1988] 1 Lloyd's Rep 352 — 122
Vizetelly v Mudie's Select Library [1900] 2 QB 170 — 378

W v Meah [1986] 1 All ER 935 — 289
Wagner v International Railway Co. (1921) 133 NE 437 — 53
Wagon Mound, The (No. 1) [1961] AC 388 — 109, 161
Wagon Mound, The (No. 2) [1966] 2 All ER 709, [1967] 1 AC 617 — 113, 332, 349, 358
Wakley v Cooke (1849) 4 Exch 511 — 383
Walker v Northumberland County Council [1995] 1 All ER 737 — 279
Wallace v Newton [1982] 2 All ER 106 — 413
Walters v W H Smith [1911–13] All ER Rep 170 — 305
Walton v British Leyland (1978) (unreported) — 399
Waple v Surrey CC [1998] 1 All ER 624 — 380
Ward v Cannock Chase DC [1985] 3 All ER 537, [1986] Ch 546 — 102, 422
Ward v Tesco Stores Ltd [1976] 1 WLR 810, [1976] 1 All ER 219 — 88, 208
Warren v Henlys Ltd [1948] 2 All ER 935 — 15
Watkins v Birmingham City Council (1976) 126 NLJ 442 — 9
Watson v Buckley, Osborne Garrett & Co. Ltd [1940] 1 All ER 174 — 396
Watt v Hertfordshire CC [1954] 1 WLR 835 (CA) — 85
Watt v Longsdon [1930] 1 KB 130 — 381
Weldon v Home Office [1992] 1 AC 58 — 303
Weller v Foot and Mouth Disease Research Institute [1966] 1 QB 569 — 121, 358
Wells (Merstham) Ltd v Buckland Sand & Silica [1965] 2 QB 170 — 398
Wells v Cooper [1958] 2 QB 265 — 84, 213
Wells v Wells, The Times, 20 July 1998 — 425
Wentworth v Wiltshire County Council [1993] QB 654 — 244
West & Son Ltd v Shephard [1964] AC 326 — 424
West Wiltshire District Council v Garland and others [1993] 4 All ER 246 — 254
Westwood v Post Office [1974] 3 All ER 184, [1974] AC 1 — 243, 263
Whatman v Pearson [1868] LR 3 CP 422 — 12
Wheat v Lacon [1966] AC 552 — 200
Wheeler v Copas [1981] 2 All ER 405 — 199
White v Blackmore [1972] 3 All ER 158 — 219
White v Holland Precision Castings [1985] IRLR 215 — 277
White v Jones [1995] 1 All ER 691 — 100, 133, 144, 145, 146, 153
White v St Albans City and District Council, The Times, 12 March 1990 — 226
Whitehouse v Jordan [1981] 1 WLR 246 [HL] — 83
Whittaker v Minister of Pensions [1967] 1 QB 156 — 9
WHPT Housing Association Ltd v Secretary of State for Social Services [1981] ICR 737 — 7
Wieland v Cyril Lord Carpets [1969] 3 All ER 1006 — 102, 114
Wigg v British Railways Board, The Times, 4 February 1986 — 55, 168

Wilkes v Wood (1763) 98 ER 489   429
Wilkinson v Downton [1897] 2 QB 57, (1897) 66 LJQB 493   158, 345, 346, 348
Wilks v Cheltenham Home Guard Motor Cycle and Light Car Club [1971] 2 All ER 369   49
Williams v British Coal Corporation, The Times, 24 January 1998   277
Williams v Humphreys, The Times, 20 February 1975   296
Williams v Natural Life Health Foods [1998] 2 All ER 577   131
Willson v Ministry of Defence [1991] 1 All ER 638   427
Wilsher v Essex Area Health Authority [1986] 3 All ER 801   29, 84, 87, 100
Wilson v Pringle [1986] 2 All ER 440   296
Wilson v Tyneside Window Cleaning Co. [1958] 2 QB 110   273
Wilson v Waddell (1876) 2 App Cas 95   330, 355
Wilsons and Clyde Coal Co. v English [1938] AC 57   182, 183, 267
Withers v Perry Chain Co. [1961] 1 WLR 1314   277
Wood v The Law Society, The Times, 30 July 1993   80
Woods v Durable Suites Ltd [1953] 1 WLR 857   276
Woodward v Mayor of Hastings [1954] KB 74   213
Wooldridge v Sumner [1963] 2 QB 43   49
Wright v Lodge and Shepherd [1993] 4 All ER 299   107
Wringe v Cohen [1939] 4 All ER 241, [1940] 1 KB 229   329, 338
Wrotham Park Estate v Parkside Homes [1974] 1 WLR 798   433
Wyatt v Hillingdon London Borough Council (1978) 76 LGR 727   248

X and Others v Bedfordshire County Council (and Other Appeals) [1995] 3 All ER 353   80, 250

Yianni v Evans [1982] QB 438   135
Young v Charles Church (Southern) Ltd, The Times, 1 May 1997 (CA)   165, 261
Young v Edward Box and Co. Ltd [1951] 1 TLR 789   14
Youssoupoff v MGM (1934) 50 TLR 581   368
Yuen Kun Yeu v A-G for Hong Kong [1988] AC 175   74, 134

TABLE OF STATUTES

Abortion Act 301
Administration of Justice Act 1982
  s.1(1)(b) 424
Animals Act 1971
  s.1-s.6 411
  s.4 354
  s.6(2) 412
  s.7 322, 418
  s.8 412
  s.9 322

Broadcasting Act 1990 367
  s.166 367

Child Care Act 1980 80, 251
Children Act 1989 80, 251
Children and Young Persons Act 1969 251
Chronically Sick and Disabled Persons Act
  1970 248
Civil Aviation Act 1982 360
  s.76 321
Civil Aviation Act 1983
  s.3 151
Civil Evidence Act 1968
  s.11 87, 267
Civil Liability (Contribution) Act 1978 1, 18,
  20, 21, 23, 60, 201, 271, 282, 400
  s.1(1)-(2) 21
  s.1(3) 22
  s.1(4) 21
  s.1(5) 22
  s.1(6) 21
  s.2(1) 22
  s.2(2) 23
  s.2(3) 22, 23
  s.3-s.4 20
  s.6(1) 22
Coal Mines Act 1911 261
Companies Act 1985 3
Congenital Disabilities (Civil Liability) Act
  1976 81
Consumer Credit Act 1974 319, 320
Consumer Protection Act 1987 193, 265, 390,
  400, 401, 402, 403, 404, 405, 406, 407
  Part I 265
  Part II 265, 272
  s.1 401
  s.1(1) 407
  s.1(2) 402
  s.1(3) 404
  s.2(1) 405
  s.3 403

Consumer Protection Act 1987 – *continued*
  s.4(1)(e) 406, 407
  s.5(1) 405
  s.6(4) 405
  s.10 391
  s.12 391
  s.41 265, 391
  s.45(1) 402
Copyright, Designs and Patents Act 1988
  253, 429
County Courts Act 1984
  s.38 431
Courts and Legal Services Act 1990 154
  s.8 387
  s.62(1)-(2) 82
Crime and Disorder Act 1998 346, 348
  s.1 348
  s.1(1) 348
  s.11 348
Criminal Justice and Public Order Act 1994
  322
  s.61 322
Criminal Law Act 1967
  s.3 65
Criminal Law Act 1977 322

Dangerous Dogs Act 1991 412, 413
  s.2(1) 413
  s.2(2) 413
  s.2(2)(b)-(c) 413
  s.3-s.4 413
  s.5(1) 413
  s.5(2)-(3) 414
  s.5(4)-(5) 413
  s.5(6) 414
  s.8(1)-(2) 413
  s.9 414
Data Protection Act 1998 127
Defamation Act 1952 373
  s.2 369
  s.5 383, 384, 385
  s.6 385
Defamation Act 1996 369, 373, 386, 387
  s.1 378
  s.1(3)(a) 378
  s.1(5)(c) 378
  s.2 373
  s.2(2)-(5) 386
  s.3 373
  s.3(2)-(6) 386
  s.4 373, 379
  s.4(2)-(3) 386

Defamation Act 1996 – *continued*
  s.8-s.9   387
  s.15   382
Defective Premises Act 1972   187, 188, 189,
    196, 232, 233
  s.1   196, 197, 233, 397
  s.2-s.3   197
  s.4   194, 195, 196, 197, 233
Dogs Act 1906   410
Dramatic and Musical Performers Protection
    Act 1958   253

Education Reform Act 1988   3
Employers' Liability (Compulsory Insurance)
    Act 1969   281
Employers' Liability (Defective Equipment)
    Act 1969   267, 271, 272, 273, 394
  s.1(1)   271
Environmental Protection Act 1990   341

Factories Act 1961   237, 243, 258, 263, 266, 281
  s.7   260
  s.14   260
  s.14(1)   255
  s.29(1)   256, 258, 259
Factors Act 1889   308, 318, 319
  s.1(1)   318
  s.2(1)   318
  s.8   319
  s.9   319, 320
Factory and Workshop Act 1891   243
Fair Trading Act 1973   80
Family Law Act 1996   345, 346, 347, 348,
    389
  s.42   347
Fatal Accidents Act(s) 1846–1976   428
Fatal Accidents Act 1976   46, 259
  s.1A   428
  s.3(3)   428
Financial Services Act 1986   127
Fires Prevention (Metropolis) Act 1774   361
  s.86   361, 362

Health and Safety at Work Act 1974   258, 265,
    266, 284
  s.2   284
  s.4(2)   258
  s.22   266
  s.47   265
Highways Act 1980   205, 244, 245
Housing Act 1985   348
  Part III   79, 249, 251
  s.62-s.63   251, 252
  s.65   251, 252
Housing Act 1988   237, 348
  s.16   188
Housing Act 1996   346, 348
Housing (Homeless Persons) Act 1977   79,
    249, 251

Land Charges Act 1972
  s.10(6)   141
Landlord and Tenant Act 1985   195
  s.11-s.13   188
Latent Damage Act 1986   193
Law Reform (Contributory Negligence) Act
    1945   23, 45, 46, 47, 61, 62, 102, 220, 226,
    228, 257, 262, 264, 281
  s.1(1)   61
  s.4   61, 64

Law Reform (Miscellaneous Provisions) Act
    1934   169
Law Reform (Personal Injuries) Act 1948   269
  s.2(4)   424
Limitation Act 1980   292, 308
  s.2   400
  s.4A   369
  s.10   22
  s.11   400
  s.11A   400, 405
  s.14A-B   400
  s.33   400
Local Government Act 1972
  s.221   339, 342
Lord Cairns' Act 1858   433

Matrimonial Homes Act 1983   321
Mental Health Act 1983   60
  s.131   60
Mines and Quarries Act 1954   266
  s.83   183
Misrepresentation Act 1967   127, 128
  s.2(1)   127

National Assistance Act 1948
  s.36   248
National Insurance (Industrial Injuries) Act
    1965
  s.5(1)   15
National Parks and Access to the Countryside
    Act 1949   200, 206, 229, 231, 234
  s.60   223
Nuclear Installations Act 1965   237, 360
Nurseries and Child-Minders Regulation Act
    1948   148, 149

Occupiers' Liability Act 1957   187, 188, 194,
    197, 198, 199, 200, 202, 203, 204, 205, 206,
    207, 208, 214, 215, 216, 218, 220, 221, 224,
    227, 230, 231, 233, 234, 237, 238, 265, 274
  s.1   220
  s.1(1)   198
  s.1(2)   198, 199, 202
  s.1(3)   199–200, 202, 220
  s.1(4)   200, 202
  s.2   215
  s.2(1)   216, 218
  s.2(2)   198, 206, 207
  s.2(3)   206, 208
  s.2(4)   206, 210–11
  s.2(4)(a)   229, 230
  s.2(4)(b)   211, 212, 213, 214, 215
  s.2(5)   219
  s.2(6)   202, 216
  s.3   215, 216
  s.3(1)   215
  s.3(2)   216
  s.3(4)   216
  s.4   195, 233
  s.5(1)   215
Occupiers' Liability Act 1984   187, 188, 194,
    201, 203, 205, 206, 209, 219, 221, 223, 224,
    225, 226, 227, 228, 229, 230, 231, 232, 233,
    234, 237
  s.1   223, 224, 226, 227, 228
  s.1(1)   224
  s.1(1)(a)   206
  s.1(3)   224, 225, 226, 227, 230
  s.1(3)(b)   226, 227
  s.1(4)   224, 225, 226, 227, 228

Occupiers' Liability Act 1984 – *continued*
   s.1(5)   229, 230
   s.1(6)   229
   s.1(7)   205
   s.1(8)-(9)   231
   s.2   217, 218
   s.2(2)   218
Offences Against the Person Act 1861   291
Offices, Shops and Railway Premises Act
   1963   243, 266
   s.7   280

Police Act 1964   9
Police and Criminal Evidence Act 1984   65
   s.24   304, 305
   s.24(4)(b)   305
Prison Act 1952   245, 304
Protection from Harassment Act 1997   346,
   347, 348
   s.1   347
   s.3(2)   158
Public Health Act 1936   190
   s.64   192
Public Order Act   299
   s.1–3   299
   s.4-s.5   299
Public Passenger Vehicles Act 1981   217
   s.29   40
Public Utilities Street Works Act 1950   241

Reservoirs Act 1975
   s.28   360
Road Traffic Act 1930   243
   s.35   243
Road Traffic Act 1960
   s.201   243
Road Traffic Act 1988   14, 57, 217, 243, 244
   s.75   391, 397
   s.149   14, 41, 57, 67

Sale of Goods Act 1893   393
Sale of Goods Act 1979   319
   s.21   314
   s.22   316
   s.23   314, 316
   s.24-s.25   314, 319
   s.26   314
Sale of Goods (Amendment) Act 1994   316
Sale and Supply of Goods Act 1994   394
Slander of Women Act 1891   369
Social Security (Recovery of Benefits) Act
   1997   426
Suicide Act 1961   184
Supply of Goods (Implied Terms) Act
   1973   394
Supply of Goods and Services Act 1982   394
Supreme Court Act 1981
   s.31   79, 251
   s.32A   427

Supreme Court Act 1981 – *continued*
   s.37(1)   431
   s.50   340, 433

Theft Act   298
Torts (Interference with Goods) Act 1977   306,
   307, 311
   s.2(2)   307
   s.3   312
   s.6   312
   s.8   311
Town Police Clauses Act 1847   4

Unfair Contract Terms Act 1977   40, 51, 135,
   198, 215, 217, 218, 219, 231, 233, 394, 396
   s.1(3)   217
   s.1(3)(b)   198
   s.2(1)   217
   s.2(2)   135
   s.2(3)   51, 219
   s.2(5)   219
   s.11   218
   s.11(3)   135
   s.14   217

Vaccine Damage Payments Act 1979   237

Water Industry Act 1991
   s.209   360
Waterworks Clauses Act 1847   240
Workmen's Compensation Acts   106

Australian legislation
Law Reform (Miscellaneous Provisions)
   Ordinance 1955 Act   166

European legislation
Directive 85/374/EEC   400, 401, 402, 404, 406
   art.1   404
   art.2   402
   art.4   404
   art.6   403
   art.7(e)   406
   art.8.2   405
   art.9   405
   art.15   402
   First recital   400
Directive 93/13/EEC (Unfair Contract Terms)
   394
Directive 95/46/EEC (Data Protection)   127
Directive (Consumer Protection)   390
EC Treaty
   art.30   400
   art.85   400
   art.100   401
   art.169   401, 406
   art.169(3)   406
European Convention on Human Rights   347
   art.8   347
   art.10   347

CHAPTER ONE

LIABILITY IN TORT

1.1 Objectives

By the end of this chapter you should be able to:

■ define 'capacity' in relation to the commission of a tort;

■ define the difference between 'primary liability' and 'vicarious liability';

■ appreciate the difference between an 'employee' (or 'servant') and an 'independent contractor';

■ understand the circumstances in which the torts of an independent contractor may lead to liability on the part of the person who engaged him (his 'employer');

■ understand the vicarious liability of an employer for the torts of his employee, committed in the course of the latter's employment;

■ understand the special vicarious liability imposed on the owners of vehicles for the negligence of persons permitted to drive those vehicles;

■ understand the differences between the various categories of tortfeasor;

■ understand the provisions of the Civil Liability (Contribution) Act 1978.

1.2 Introduction

The parties to an action in tort are *prima facie* ('of first appearance') the 'plaintiff and the defendant', but the actual position is somewhat more complex, and we have to consider the following matters:

(a) capacity to commit a tort;

(b) **vicarious** liability;

(c) contributions between **tortfeasors** (a 'tortfeasor' is 'one who commits a tort').

1.3 Capacity

A defendant, or 'tortfeasor', must be capable, legally, of being **sued** and a **plaintiff**, the aggrieved party, must have the capacity to **sue**. This is not always the straightforward issue that it might appear to be.

The Crown, unincorporated associations, trade unions, foreign sovereigns and diplomats, aliens, business partnerships, the postal authorities, bankrupts, assignees, convicted persons and the judiciary; all of these may present special technical, procedural problems in relation to 'capacity'. We cannot deal with them here; our task is limited to the consideration of:

(a) persons suffering from mental disorder;

(b) minors;

(c) corporations.

1.3.1 PERSONS SUFFERING FROM MENTAL DISORDER

There is a paucity of English authority on the point, but the general consensus of opinion is that much will depend on the state of mind required by the tort in question.

Thus, in *Morris* v *Marsden* [1952] 1 All ER 925, the defendant was sued in tort for trespass to the person, i.e. assault and battery, which is dealt with in detail in **Chapter 9**. This form of interference with the person requires only a voluntary act (perhaps also a **general** intent to cause **some** 'harm' on the part of the defendant, it does not require any specific intent to injure or cause damage). The defendant was found liable in trespass, although he had earlier been found unfit to plead in a **criminal** court for the same interference; it was enough for **this** tort that he was capable of committing a 'voluntary' act of hitting the plaintiff. The court indicated that the decision would probably have gone the other way, had the defendant's mental condition been such that he was incapable of a voluntary act.

In *Roberts* v *Ramsbottom* [1980] 1 All ER 7, the defendant was driving his car when he suffered a stroke. He carried on driving and, some 20 minutes later, injured the plaintiff. The defendant pleaded that he had been unable to drive properly because of the stroke, and the court accepted that this was indeed the case, but he was found liable in the tort of negligence on the basis that he was negligent in knowingly continuing to drive after the onset of the stroke.

It was said that the decision might have gone the other way had the defendant's condition turned him into an automaton, i.e. a person unable to control his actions. On the facts, however, he had retained **some** control over his actions and fell to be judged by the standards of the reasonably competent driver (**standard of care** in the tort of negligence is discussed in **Chapter 3**). Since his driving fell short of that standard, he was liable to pay damages for negligence to the plaintiff. In the circumstances, the 'reasonable man' would have stopped driving immediately after the onset of the stroke.

1.3.2 MINORS

Minors, in English law, are persons below the age of 18, and they are **generally** liable for their own torts. Their parents, or guardians, are **not vicariously** liable in tort (unless the minor is an employee or agent of his parent or guardian), though these persons may be liable **personally** in tort for breach of an obligation to control the activities of their charges. A good illustration of a parent's **personal** liability in this context can be found in *Jauffur* v *Akhbar*, *The Times*, 10 February 1984, which is discussed at **7.5.1**.

Winfield on Tort (14th edn.) at p. 714 says that a parent or guardian may be liable personally if he 'expressly' authorises 'or possibly' ratifies the minor's act.

Minors, like persons of unsound mind might, however, not be liable, depending in this case on their **age**, with regard to torts which require some specific state of mind or intent.

It is always necessary in such cases that the defendant should be capable of forming the relevant intent.

In the tort of negligence, it is unlikely that very young minors would be capable of reaching the required standard of care (the tort of negligence is discussed in **Chapter 3**). This, in the absence of authority on the subject, must be a matter to be determined in the light of each case.

By analogy with cases on the defence of contributory negligence, discussed in **Chapter 2**, minors who reach an age of understanding can be liable in the tort of negligence, and will be judged, no doubt, according to what would be expected from a minor of similar age, intelligence and experience.

Where a minor is immune from liability in **contract**, however, it is not possible to sue him in **tort** if to do so successfully would have the effect of enforcing that contract against him.

With respect to the prosecution of an action in tort, minors can sue and be sued through their 'next friend', a responsible adult, who may, where appropriate, be the minor's parent or guardian.

1.3.3   CORPORATIONS

Corporations are 'legal personalities', so-called 'artificial legal persons', who can sue and be sued in the corporate name. Legal persons are created by statutory procedures of incorporation, for example, limited companies registered under the Companies Act 1985; higher education corporations created under the Education Reform Act 1988, for example, The Nottingham Trent University; bodies created by Royal Charter. All local authorities, for example, Nottingham city council, are legal persons in this sense.

These 'persons' can be personally liable for wrongs committed **on behalf of the corporation**, and **vicariously** liable for their employees' actions.

A corporation can be defamed, for instance, but not falsely imprisoned, so there are obviously a number of situations in which they cannot sue, because they cannot be affected **tortiously**.

1.4   Vicarious Liability

'Vicarious liability' means liability which falls on one person as a result of an action of **another** person, i.e. it is not personal, primary, liability. In terms of the law of **tort**, it means that one person is made to account for the damage caused by **another** person's tort.

In the law of tort **generally**, liability is of a **primary** nature, i.e. tortfeasors are responsible only for damage caused by their **own** tortious behaviour. However, where there is a legal relationship between persons and a tort is committed by one party to the relationship, and that act is specifically referable to the relationship, it is possible that the law of tort will impose vicarious liability on **another** party to the relationship.

There are, as you will find later, many relationships in tort where one party is found liable for the behaviour of another party, but that liability is **personal** liability; for example, in the tort of negligence there may be a breach of a **personal** duty to control the behaviour of someone else, as in *Home Office* v *Dorset Yacht Co.* [1970] AC 1004 which is discussed in **Chapter 3**. It may also be the case that X **employs** Y to commit a tort, or

authorises him to do so: again, X's liability is of a **personal** nature. We are not dealing with **personal** liability in this chapter; it is our exclusive concern here to explore the principles of **vicarious** liability.

Often, someone may be **vicariously** liable, **as well as personally** liable. Thus, for example, a pedestrian who is injured as the result of negligent driving by a van driver may sue not only the driver personally, he may also sue the driver's employer for vicarious liability (where the conditions set out below are satisfied) **and**, where the employer has negligently chosen an incompetent driver, he can sue the employer in negligence for breach of his **own**, personal, obligation to employ competent staff. ('Duty of care' in negligence is discussed in **Chapter 3**.) Usually, however, in such a situation a pedestrian will sue an employer only for vicarious liability because it may well be difficult to prove **personal** negligence on the part of the employer in engaging incompetent employees. This example is given only for purposes of simple **illustration**; it is not intended to portray a situation that is common in legal proceedings. What **is** common are actions by **employees** against their **employers** for (i) breach of the employer's **personal** common law duty to take reasonable action for the safety of his employees which includes an obligation to his employees to engage competent fellow employees; **and** (ii) **vicarious** liability for the tort of **that** incompetent employee. This special, **personal**, duty of the employer is discussed in **Chapter 8**.

The important point to grasp at this stage is that although it might be difficult to separate **personal** liability from **vicarious** liability in many factual situations, it is imperative that they are kept distinct. **Primary**, i.e. **personal** liability is, in the law of tort, largely based on some notion of **fault** on the part of the actor; vicarious liability is **strict** liability, i.e. it does **not** rest on the proof of any fault on the part of the person who is found vicariously liable.

Liability of a vicarious nature occurs in a number of instances in tort, for example in relation to principal and agent, and partnership. We are concerned only with **two** instances of vicarious liability:

(a) the vicarious liability of an employer for his employee (by far the most common instance of this form of liability);

(b) the special vicarious liability of vehicle owners for their drivers.

It is important to clarify what we are referring to when we speak of 'vicarious liability' in the **present** context. We are concerned **only** with **vicarious** liability at **common law**, and **not** with any **special** responsibility which **statute** may impose on one person for the acts of another. Thus, for example, the Town Police Clauses Act 1847 imposes liability on the owners of taxicabs or 'hackney carriages' (**not** 'minicabs') for their drivers' torts, although the drivers are **not** employees of the owners.

1.4.1 AN EMPLOYER'S VICARIOUS LIABILITY FOR THE TORTS OF HIS EMPLOYEE

This form of liability is based on the satisfaction of the following **three** conditions:

(a) there must exist a relationship of 'employer' and 'employee' (in older, traditional, language there must be a relationship of 'master' and 'servant'); and

(b) that employee must have committed a tort (for which he is **always personally** liable); and

(c) that tort must have been committed 'in the course of the employment' of the employee.

SAQ 1

Can you think of two reasons why employers are, where appropriate, vicariously liable for their employees' torts?

It is commonly said that the reasons behind the doctrine of vicarious liability are first, that the employer is in a better position to absorb the legal costs either by purchasing insurance or increasing his prices. Secondly, that the imposition of liability should encourage the employer to ensure the highest possible safety standards in running his business. In *Bartonshill Coal Co.* v *McGuire* (1853) 3 Macq 300, Lord Chelmsford LC said: 'every act which is done by a servant in the course of his duty is regarded as done by his master's orders, and consequently is the same as if it were his master's own act.'.

Indeed, there was a theory, current many years ago, that the employer was vicariously liable for any 'act' committed by the employee in the course of his employment. It is the modern view, however, that that 'act' must be a tort.

E. McKendrick, *Tort Textbook*, 6th edn. (London: HLT Publications, 1992) points out, however, that the doctrine has, on the whole, no clear rationale. You can read an extract from his discussion on the point in *Cases and Materials* (**1.1.1**).

As Lord Pearce said in *Imperial Chemical Industries Ltd* v *Shatwell* [1965] AC 656: 'The doctrine of vicarious liability has not grown from any very clear, logical or legal principle but from social convenience and rough justice.'.

SAQ 2

Do you think that all persons 'employed' by any particular 'employer' are of one, general, homogeneous group?

They are not, and the law draws a distinction, for various purposes, between ordinary 'full-blown' employees ('servants') and 'independent contractors'. The distinction, broadly, is between employed persons who are paid a wage or salary, and self-employed persons working under a contract. Thus, it is important to know whether or not someone is an independent contractor for example, for the purposes of taxation, social security, and some statutory duties imposing safety regulations.

You will see, in **Chapter 8**, that in the law of tort employers owe a special duty of care to their employees, but **not** to their independent contractors.

1.4.1.1   Independent contractors and employees

The distinction is also important in the law of tort in the **present** context, for the reason that employers of independent contractors are **not generally** liable for their **contractors'** torts, whereas employers **are** generally vicariously liable for their **employees'** torts.

Employers **are** under a **personal** common law obligation, in the tort of negligence, to take reasonable care in the selection of contractors; the contractors must therefore be reasonably competent, but no question of **vicarious** liability arises in such circumstances. The same is true of an employer's obligation to employ an **adequate number** of people.

The case law has also generated a number of special situations in which employers might be liable where their independent contractors commit torts, although it is a moot (i.e. arguable) point whether it can be claimed that there are instances of employers being liable for their **contractors'** torts. It is more likely that **both** parties are **personally** liable, as joint tortfeasors: see *Winfield* (p. 615).

These special situations are as follows:

(a)   where the contract is to perform an illegal act like a nuisance and the employer in effect authorises or ratifies the act;

(b)   where the employer 'takes over', and directs, the work of the independent contractor.

In *Winfield's* words, however (p. 615): 'The true question in every case in which an employer is sued for damage caused by his independent contractor is whether the employer himself was in breach of some duty which he himself owed to the plaintiff.'.

This is also the explanation for the so-called 'non-delegable duty', which an employer may owe to a plaintiff injured **solely** by the wrong of an independent contractor. There is no exhaustive list of such duties; all that can be said in general terms is that where common law or statute imposes some special onerous duty to achieve a particular result or to see that all care is taken (rather than to take reasonable care) it may be classed as of a non-delegable kind, and it will be no excuse for the person upon whom it has been placed to plead simply that he took all reasonable care by entrusting its performance to a competent independent contractor. He will, in effect, be expected to ensure that the result is achieved, or that all care has been taken, without the commission of a tort by the person to whom the **performance** of the obligation has been delegated.

Where the contractor tortiously injures the plaintiff in performing the obligation, not only will the contractor be personally liable, say for negligence, but his employer will remain also personally liable.

You can read about the interesting decision in *Alcock* v *Wraith*, *The Times*, 23 December 1991 in *Cases and Materials* (**1.1.1**).

A good example of such a duty is that owed by an employer to his employees, discussed in **Chapter 8**.

Other examples of this non-delegable duty are as follows:

(a)   where the employer is under a common law obligation involving strict liability (you can read about strict liability at common law, including liability arising under the rule in *Rylands* v *Fletcher* [1868] LR 3 HL 330, at **11.3**);

(b)   where the employer is under a statutory obligation involving strict liability, for example, industrial legislation (you can read about this legislation in **Chapter 8**);

(c)   where the work entrusted to the contractor inherently contains the risk of the contractor committing a public or private **nuisance** (you can read about the law of nuisance in **Chapter 10**).

The performance of a duty of care in negligence (owed by the employer) may be delegated, i.e. it may be a defence for the employer to plead that he has taken all reasonable care in the circumstances to employ a competent contractor to do the work. (You can find an example of such a delegable duty in the occupiers' duty, arising under the Occupiers' Liability Act 1957, in **Chapter 7**.)

When we speak of 'delegable' and 'non-delegable' duties, exactly what are we saying in legal terms?

In strict legal terms, if a duty is 'non-delegable', it cannot be delegated to another person. A distinction is drawn in the law, however, between legal responsibility for the **performance** of such a duty and delegation in practical terms. It is evidently the case that some tasks require expertise not possessed by the employer, and it is therefore necessary that a contractor be called in to do the job. Indeed, unless this is done the employer will not, in such cases, be able to perform the obligation imposed on him by law.

The fact, however, that performance is delegated in these cases does not itself relieve the employer from **legal** responsibility in the event of the contractor committing a tort whilst he is undertaking the work in question.

We now have to consider how the law distinguishes between 'independent contractors' and 'employees' (or 'servants') because you will now appreciate that the employer is only **vicariously** liable for the tortious behaviour of the latter.

1.4.1.2   Who is an employee (or servant)?

It is very important to be able to identify an employee, but you may be surprised to learn that the law is rather uncertain on the definition of 'employee' (or 'servant').

An independent contractor is said to have a contract for his **services** with his employer, whilst an employee (or servant) works under a contract of **service**. Thus, a convenient starting point for our inquiry is the terms of the contract between the parties: how does the contract classify the person in question, as an employee or as an independent contractor?

The terms of the contract, however, are not conclusive where liability to third parties is concerned and, in any case, the contract may be silent or ambiguous on the matter. Nevertheless, this must be a factor which is considered by the court in a case of difficulty.

In general, however, as we will see, the court considers **all** the facts of the case before it, and does not necessarily regard any one factor as conclusive of the issue.

In *WHPT Housing Association Ltd* v *Secretary of State for Social Services* [1981] ICR 737, Webster J said:

   . . . the difference between a contract of service [servant] and one for services [independent contractor] must reside, essentially, in the terms of the principal obligation agreed to be undertaken by the employee — a word which I use without begging the question. In a contract of service, it seems to me, the principal obligation . . . is to provide himself to serve: whereas in a contract for services the principal obligation... [is to provide] his services for the use of the employer.

The cases on this point are drawn not just from the context of general vicarious liability; some of the authorities are concerned with matters of social security, taxation and employment legislation. The policy factors underlying decisions from different contexts are **not**, however, identical and you should always bear this factor in mind; but **all the** decisions can at least be used for the purpose of constructing an agrument by way of analogy.

In *Airfix Footwear Ltd* v *Cope* [1978] ICR 1210, for example, a worker who was classified as self-employed by the Inland Revenue was nevertheless found to be an employee for the purposes of employment protection legislation. Again, in *O'Kelly* v *Trusthouse Forte plc* [1983] ICR 728, bar staff, who were called 'regular' casual workers, and who worked only when called in to work as required by their employers, were held **not** to be employees for purposes of claiming unfair dismissal. The workers could refuse any work that was offered to them, and the Court of Appeal emphasised the lack of **mutuality of obligation** in the relationship.

The classification of a worker, i.e. the label that is attached to him, in cases of doubt must depend on the legal issue before the court. As McKendrick puts it in 53 *MLR* 770 ('Vicarious Liability and Independent Contractors — A Re-Examination'):

. . . the test for the existence of an employment relationship should depend upon the legal question which is being asked and on the fact that there is nothing irrational in classifying a worker as an employee for the purposes of vicarious liability but not for the purposes of employment law, social security law and taxation.

1.4.1.3   The tests

Although no single test for determining this issue is available, various tests have been formulated in the cases. The oldest of these is the 'control' test.

As Salmond and Heuston, *The Law of Torts* (21st edn.), puts it at p. 449:

The test [for determining who is an employee] is the existence of a right of control over the agent in respect of the manner in which his work is to be done. A servant is an agent who works under the supervision and direction of his employer; an independent contractor is one who is his own master. A servant is a person engaged to obey his employer's orders from time to time; an independent contractor is a person engaged to do certain work, but to exercise his own discretion as to the mode and time of doing it — he is bound by his contract, but not by his employer's orders.

In *Honeywill & Stein Ltd* v *Larkin Bros Ltd* [1934] 1 KB 1991, for example, it was held that a person is a servant where the employer retains the control of the actual performance of the work.

The weakness of this traditional approach is that in the case of modern, highly specialised tasks it is difficult for the employer to exercise control over the **method** of doing the work, for example, in the case of lawyers and surgeons. (Since 1991, National Health Service (NHS) hospital authorities have funded the defence of medical negligence cases through the system of Crown Indemnity and hospital doctors are no longer contractually bound to insure themselves against claims in negligence. Previously, when a health authority was found vicariously liable for a doctor's negligence it would seek an indemnity from him or her via this insurance.)

Apart from this difficulty, it is clear that a relationship of employer and employee does not come into existence because of the mere fact that one person exercises control over another.

Thus, for example, in *Watkins* v *Birmingham City Council* (1976) 126 NLJ 442, a schoolboy, aged ten, was given the task of taking milk round his school by his teacher. He left his cycle outside a classroom door, and a teacher fell over it and was injured. It was held by the Court of Appeal that the boy was not an employee of the education authority, because it was **part** of his **education** to do the job.

Other tests have, therefore, been suggested from time to time. In *Stevenson Jordan and Harrison Ltd* v *Macdonald and Evans* [1952] 1 TLR 101, Denning LJ suggested the 'organisation or integration test':

> under a contract of service a man is employed as part of the business, and his work is done as an integral part of the business; whereas under a contract for services, his work, although done for the business, is not integrated into it but is only accessory to it.

A chauffeur would, for example, be an employee, whereas a taxi driver would be an independent contractor on this reasoning.

This test was applied in *Whittaker* v *Minister of Pensions* [1967] 1 QB 156, in which a circus trapeze artist was held to be a servant, and in *Beloff* v *Pressdram* [1973] 1 All ER 241, a newspaper political and lobby correspondent was held to be a servant for the purposes of copyright in an internal memorandum about a cabinet minister which was published by *Private Eye*.

This test has, however, been little used as a discrete formula; it is regarded by *Street on Torts* (9th edn.) at pp. 486–7 as just another, wider, way of looking at 'control'.

The same can be said for the 'economic reality' test suggested by MacKenna J in *Ready Mixed Concrete (South East) Ltd* v *Minister of Pensions and National Insurance* [1965] 2 QB 497. This would take into account such factors as the method and frequency of payment, and the power of selection, suspension and dismissal, and the intention of the parties.

However, no test can be regarded as conclusive and the courts will have to look at **all** the elements of the relationship.

Under the Police Act 1964, Chief Constables (the Metropolitan Commissioner in London) are responsible for the torts of police officers committed in the course of their employment, with the police fund meeting the costs and damages.

SAQ 4

Can you think of three other factors that might have to be considered by a court in the present context? Write down a short list of these factors.

You might have included in your list: holiday entitlement; pension rights; whose tools, equipment and premises are to be used? It is still probably the case that 'control' is the main criterion considered by the courts. *Salmond* says (at p. 449) that the right to control is 'a **necessary**, but not a **sufficient**, mark of a contract of service'. It is not, however, as we have seen, the only criterion.

You should read about the decisions in the following cases:

(a) *Sime* v *Sutcliffe Catering (Scotland) Ltd* [1990] IRLR 228, a Scottish case, which of course is of **persuasive** authority only in this country, in which 'control' was the **determining** factor; and

(b) *Lane* v *Shire Roofing Co. (Oxford) Ltd*, *The Times*, 17 February 1995, in which 'control' was considered as only **one** of the factors to be taken into account in deciding whether the plaintiff was an employee, for purposes of health and safety at work. See *Cases and Materials* (**1.1.1.1**).

1.4.1.4 Borrowed employees

This issue raises the problem of **who** employs the loaned person.

On the authority of *Mersey Docks and Harbour Board* v *Coggins and Griffiths (Liverpool) Ltd* [1946] 2 All ER 345, where an employer lends an employee to someone else, the 'lender' will usually still be responsible for the torts of that employee. In this case the Harbour Board hired out a crane and its skilled operator to Coggins. Although the power of dismissal remained with the Board, the contract provided that the operator was to be the servant of the hirers. The operator was negligent in handling the crane while under the immediate control of Coggins in unloading a ship, although the hirers could not instruct him in the **working** of the machine, and the court had to decide who would be vicariously liable.

The House of Lords held that the Board still had ultimate control over the operator and the crane and were therefore vicariously liable. Their Lordships emphasised that there was a heavy burden of proof on the lending employer if he wished to establish that the hirer should be vicariously liable in such circumstances.

In fact, there is a rebuttable **presumption** in such a case that the employee is still in the employment of the **lender**, and the lender will only shift the presumption in exceptional circumstances.

It seems that the lender in *Mersey Docks* was still in sufficient possession and control of the machinery and operator to be vicariously liable, therefore it is going to be necessary for the lender to show that he no longer has sufficient control in this sense.

Again, each case must turn on its own facts, and the familiar questions of power of dismissal, etc, will no doubt be raised. It may be easier to show complete transfer of control where a contract, or agreement, provides for the loan of 'labour only', particularly in the case of unskilled labour. In such a case, there will be no equipment to operate, therefore the borrower may have more control over **how** the work is actually done. Even where equipment **is** involved, it may make a difference that the machinery is of a simple nature, such as an ordinary motor van: see *Winfield* at p. 599 and Jones, *Textbook on Torts* (4th edn.) at p. 274.

In *Sime* (above) a borrower of labour only was found vicariously liable on the basis of 'control'.

You may be interested to learn that many 'lenders' in these situations put a clause into the contract of loan, providing that the 'borrower' is to indemnify the 'lender', where the lender pays damages for the loaned employee's tort.

There is a further point to note; the borrower can, in any event be liable vicariously (as **principal** for his **agent's** wrongs) with regard to a tort committed by the loaned employee while carrying out a **specific** instruction issued by the borrower: see Jones at p. 274.

Of course, if the lender passes on **defective equipment** or an **incompetent operator**, he will be in breach of his **personal, primary** duty in such matters, where damage is caused thereby. You can read about the decision in *McConkey* v *Amec plc* (1990) 27 Construction LR 88 in *Cases and Materials* (**1.1.1.2**), which illustrates this point.

We have now considered the question 'who is a servant?'. Can you remember the other conditions required to establish liability on the part of an employer for his employee?

The remaining conditions are the commission of a tort by the employee; and proof that this tort was committed in the course of the employee's (i.e. servant's) employment.

Proving that an employee has committed a tort is a task which is no different from establishing proof in any other case, therefore we do not have to consider this point any further. We do, however, have to examine the issue of whether the tort was committed in the course of the employee's employment.

1.4.2 COURSE OF EMPLOYMENT

The question here is 'Was the employee acting in the course of his employment at the time of the accident, or incident?'. It is for the plaintiff to establish that this was indeed the case.

The principle is easy to state, but often difficult to resolve in practice because the issue is essentially one of **fact** in **each case**. Thus, although the decided cases are useful for purposes of analogy and illustration, they must be treated with caution, and not regarded as binding authority other than in relation to the issue(s) before the court in the particular case.

You will find the decision of the House of Lords in *Smith* v *Stages* [1989] 1 All ER 833, in *Cases and Materials* (**1.1.2**). The speeches in this case offer some **general guidance** on the issue of 'course of employment'.

Most of the cases cannot, therefore, be reconciled with each other. The decisions turn frequently on fine distinctions, and are influenced quite clearly by policy factors.

We can, however, identify a few guidelines.

1.4.2.1 Authorised acts

Although each case turns very much on its own facts, the courts have evolved a general rule that if an employee is performing an act that he is not expressly or impliedly authorised to perform, he will not be acting in the course of his employment, and the employer is not liable.

If, however, he is still doing his job, but performs it in an unauthorised **manner** this factor alone will not take him outside the course of his employment.

The **terms of the employment**, i.e. the contract of 'service' are, therefore, always an important factor to consider in these cases, but these terms cannot be binding on third parties, and are not necessarily conclusive of the issue.

In *Limpus* v *London General Omnibus Co.* [1862] 1 H & C 526, a bus driver, employed by the defendant, injured the plaintiff when he negligently drew his bus across the road, contrary to orders, in order to obstruct a rival driver. The defendant was found vicariously liable for the driver's negligence, which was committed within the course of his employment because he was doing his job at the time, albeit in an unauthorised way.

Again, in *Century Insurance Co. Ltd* v *Northern Ireland Road Transport Board* [1942] AC 509, the driver of a petrol tanker, while transferring petrol from the vehicle to the tank at the garage, struck a match to light a cigarette, causing an explosion and subsequent fire. His employers were found vicariously liable because the driver was doing what he was authorised to do, in an unauthorised way, i.e. delivering petrol while smoking.

In *Harrison* v *Michelin Tyre Co. Ltd* [1985] 1 All ER 918, employers were held liable when their employee, as a joke, deliberately steered his vehicle at the plaintiff, who was at his place of work in a factory at the time. The plaintiff was injured as a result of this tomfoolery. The truck was driven a few centimetres from an officially designated passageway in the factory in order to 'catch' the plaintiff, but the act was found to be within the prankster's course of employment, because he was still **driving** at the relevant time, although he was momentarily motivated by the 'joke'.

On the other hand, in *Beard* v *London General Omnibus Co.* [1900] 2 QB 530, the employer was not vicariously liable when the **conductor**, instead of the driver, turned the bus round at the terminus, injuring the plaintiff.

This decision was followed by the Court of Appeal in *Iqbal* v *London Transport Executive* [1973] KIR 329, in which the defendant was found not vicariously liable where a conductor, negligently and contrary to instructions, drove a bus, injuring the plaintiff. The conductor was acting outside the 'course of his employment', since he was employed to 'conduct', not to drive.

1.4.2.2 Spatial factors

The question of authorised limits of time and place have often to be considered in the present context. As a general proposition, if the employee can still be said to be substantially pursuing his employment he will be regarded as acting in the course of his employment during, or within a reasonable time outside, his normal working hours.

Thus, in *Ruddiman & Co.* v *Smith* (1889) 60 LT 708, a clerk was held to be still within the course of his employment when, shortly after finishing work, he used the company washroom and left a tap running, with the result that the plaintiff's premises were flooded.

There are several cases concerned with the situation where the drivers of vehicles have deviated from their 'official' routes. The courts have taken a 'common sense' approach to this problem, looking at the **degree** of the detour or deviation in **each** case.

Thus, for example, in *Whatman* v *Pearson* [1868] LR 3 CP 422, an employee who was in charge of a horse and cart drove a quarter of a mile out of his way, without permission, to have lunch at home. The horse, left to its own devices outside the employee's house during the lunch break, bolted and injured the plaintiff. It was held that this incident occurred during the employee's course of employment.

In *Hilton* v *Burton (Rhodes) Ltd* [1961] 1 WLR 705, four workmen, permitted by their employer, the defendant, to use the defendant's van to travel to work to a demolition site, decided to stop work and drive to a café. While on this 'frolic', one of them drove negligently, injuring another, who failed to win damages from the defendant because there was no vicarious liability on his part; the negligent employee was acting **outside** the course of his employment at the time of the accident.

This colourful expression 'frolic' ('frolic of his own') is used often in the cases. It first appeared in an early nineteenth century case, and is nothing more than a **label**, used to describe behaviour that falls outside the course of employment.

The House of Lords, in *Hemphill Ltd* v *Williams* [1966] 2 Lloyd's Rep 101, an appeal from Scotland, held that taking an unauthorised **'route'** on an **authorised journey** is **within** the employment, but an **unauthorised journey** takes the employee outside his employment. This reasoning suggests that the **journey**, rather than the route, which is merely a means to an end, must be completely independent of the job if it is to be outside the course of employment . The objective of the employee in pursuing the journey is going to be an important factor in determining whether the employee is still acting within the course of his employment.

You should consult *Smith* v *Stages* (see **1.4.2** above) on this matter.

1.4.2.3 Expressly forbidden acts

Problems have arisen where an employee does something that he has been expressly forbidden to do. Again, it is a question of fact in each case whether the prohibition relates to the scope of his employment, or the method of performance.

In *Limpus* v *London General Omnibus Co.* [1862] 1 H & C 526, a bus driver, contrary to express instructions, raced a rival bus to collect passengers at a bus stop. This was held to be within the course of his employment because he was simply doing what he was authorised to do, but in a wrongful and unauthorised manner.

Similarly, in *LCC* v *Cattermoles (Garages) Ltd* [1953] 2 All ER 582, a garage assistant was employed to move vehicles inside a garage by **pushing** them; he was forbidden to drive the vehicles. His employer was found vicariously liable when he drove a van on to the nearby road to make a space in the garage, and damaged the plaintiff's vehicle on the road.

There is a group of cases in which employees, engaged to drive vehicles, have disobeyed express orders from their employers to give lifts in their vehicles to unauthorised persons (often hitch-hikers). The question of the employer's vicarious liability has arisen where the driver's negligence, in controlling his vehicle, has injured the unauthorised passenger.

In *Twine* v *Bean's Express Ltd* (1946) 175 LT 131, the driver of a vehicle, contrary to express orders from his employer, gave the plaintiff a lift and, due to the driver's negligence in relation to his driving, the passenger was injured. Not only was the plaintiff passenger a person who fell outside the group of persons that the driver had been told he was authorised to carry, there was also a notice in the cab of the vehicle which limited the people who could travel in the vehicle. The Court of Appeal held that this prohibition limited the very scope of the employee's employment, not just the way of performing his job, therefore the defendant employer was not vicariously liable for the driver's negligence.

It was also suggested that the passenger was a 'trespasser' on the vehicle, in relation to the defendant as 'occupier' of it, therefore no liability arose on the part of the defendant also for that reason. This decision was followed by the Court of Appeal in *Conway* v *George Wimpey and Co. Ltd* [1951] 2 KB 266, on the same grounds.

The 'trespasser approach', however, is not now favoured; it was said in *Rose* v *Plenty* (below) that there was little point today in taking this approach, since an occupier's duty to his trespassers is of a **substantial** nature. (You can read about this 'occupier's duty' in **Chapter 7**.)

In any event, as Denning LJ pointed out in *Young* v *Edward Box and Co. Ltd* [1951] 1 TLR 789, a passenger's injury in such a case arises **not** because of the **state** of the **vehicle**, but because of the **driver's negligence in handling his vehicle** in the course of his employment, therefore the ordinary rules of negligence would apply. It might be otherwise if the injury was caused by a defective vehicle.

Young v *Edward Box* suggests that where the plaintiff passenger is **also** an employee of the defendant employer he may have a better chance of success when the question of authorisation for the lift falls for determination. In the event of an express order from the employer against the giving of lifts being **effective** in limiting the actual **scope** of the employee's course of employment, i.e. not merely determining the **mode** of performance, a superior servant, such as a supervisor, may have sufficient 'ostensible', i.e. **apparent**, authority to sanction the otherwise unauthorised lift, so making the employer vicariously liable for the driver's negligence.

One of the more modern leading decisions on this topic is that of the Court of Appeal in *Rose* v *Plenty* [1976] 1 WLR 141. In this case the employee was a milkroundsman employed by the defendant. Despite a prohibition against such conduct, the employee engaged the plaintiff, a boy aged thirteen, to help with the round. The plaintiff fell off the milk float whilst assisting the employee, and was injured by the employee's negligent driving. By a majority it was held that the defendant was vicariously liable, subject to a reduction of 25 per cent for the plaintiff's contributory negligence.

Lord Denning MR based his decision on the ground that the boy had **benefited** the defendant by helping with the milkround, whereas Scarman LJ, whilst assenting to the idea of 'benefit' to the employer, generally contented himself with the argument that the court should take a broad approach to the definition of course of employment.

Thus, according to the majority, the prohibition in this case limited only the **way** in which the employee did his job, it did not affect the course of his employment. Lawton LJ dissented, and you should read the extract from his judgment and the extracts from the judgments of Lord Denning and Scarman LJ, in *Cases and Materials* (**1.1.2.1**).

Under the Road Traffic Act 1988, insurance for passengers in vehicles used on the public highway is compulsory, and the question of whether an 'unauthorised' passenger can claim against the insurance policy of the owner of a vehicle, where the passenger is injured as the result of the negligent driving of an employee of that owner, will depend on the determination of the 'course of employment' issue.

This is a matter **separate** from that of the effect of s. 149 of the 1988 Act on the defence of *volenti non fit injuria*. You will find this issue discussed in **Chapter 2**.

The drivers in these cases are always **personally** liable to their passengers, and the fact that the 'lift' falls outside the course of employment does not necessarily affect any vicarious liability to other plaintiffs, for example pedestrians, i.e. the driver can still be acting **within** the course of his employment to **some** plaintiffs, though he is acting **outside** his employment regarding the **passenger**.

1.4.2.4 Connection with employer's business

Winfield (p. 608) says that an act may come within the 'course of employment if it is necessarily incidental to something which the servant is employed to do'.

Thus, in *Elleanor* v *Cavendish Woodhouse* [1973] 1 Lloyd's Rep 313, it was in the employer's interest, and ancillary, though not central, to the employee's employment, that he should give a lift home to the plaintiff, who was a fellow employee. Due to the driver's negligence the plaintiff was injured; it was held that the driver was acting in the course of his employment whilst giving the lift.

In *R* v *National Insurance Commissioner, ex parte Michael* [1977] 1 WLR 109, however, a policeman who was injured whilst playing football for his force could not claim industrial injury benefit under s. 5(1) of the National Insurance (Industrial Injuries) Act 1965, which provided that such benefit could only be claimed for injuries suffered in an 'accident arising out of and in the course of employment'. See also *Faulkner* v *Chief Adjudication Officer, The Times*, 8 April 1994, in which the Court of Appeal followed *ex parte Michael*, in *Cases and Materials* (1.1.2.2).

Much, it seems, may depend on the nature of the tort which the employee has committed. In the case of intentional, deliberate wrongs, rather than casual acts of negligence, it may be more difficult to satisfy the requirement of 'course of employment'. There are several cases in which employees have committed acts of trespass to the person, and the courts have refused to find that the employees were acting within the course of their employment at the time.

In *Warren* v *Henlys Ltd* [1948] 2 All ER 935, the employee, an attendant at a petrol filling station, thought that the plaintiff, a motorist, was trying to avoid paying for his petrol; after an argument, the attendant punched the plaintiff. It was found that the employee was acting outside the course of his employment at the time.

Again, in *Daniels* v *Whetstone Entertainments Ltd* [1962] 2 Lloyd's Rep 1, the employee, a doorman ('a bouncer') at a dance hall assaulted the plaintiff whilst evicting him from the premises. This act was found to be outside the doorman's course of employment, because it was said to be an act of **personal revenge**.

In *Irving* v *The Post Office* [1987] IRLR 289, an employee, who was authorised to write on letters for the purpose of ensuring that the mail was properly despatched, wrote racial abuse on a letter addressed to the plaintiffs, his neighbours, with whom he was not on speaking terms. The Court of Appeal held that writing the abuse was not an authorised act, therefore the employee was not acting in the course of his employment at the time he uttered the abuse, and his employer was therefore not vicariously liable for his actions.

Finally, in *General Engineering Services Ltd* v *Kingston and St Andrew Corporation* [1988] 3 All ER 867, firemen were involved in a work to rule, i.e. a 'go slow', in support of a pay claim. They took 17 minutes rather than the usual three and a half minutes to reach a fire at the plaintiff's premises which were destroyed as a result of the delay. According to the evidence, if the firemen had been 'on time' the premises might not have been destroyed completely. The Privy Council found that the employees, the firemen, were not employed to proceed to a fire as slowly as possible, thus their conduct amounted to an **unauthorised** act: it was **not** an authorised act performed in an unauthorised way. It is, of course, hardly surprising that the court should find industrial action to be outside the course of employment.

SAQ 6

Pause for a moment at this point. Do you think, from what you have read so far, that deliberate conduct could never amount to an 'authorised' act?

The answer to this question, as you might have guessed is: 'It all depends on the circumstances of the case'!

Deliberate acts, committed by the employee in the reasonable belief that they are necessary for the protection of his employer's property, may come within the course of his employment.

In *Pollard* v *John Parr & Sons* [1927] 1 KB 236, an employee of the defendant mistakenly, but on reasonable grounds, suspected that the plaintiff, a young boy, was stealing sugar from his employer's truck. He hit the plaintiff, a young boy, who fell, and was injured. The employer was found vicariously liable because the act was committed in defence of the employer's property, and was not sufficiently excessive to be outside the scope of the employee's employment.

Indeed, it is possible for **criminal** acts to come within the terms of an employee's employment.

In the leading case of *Lloyd* v *Grace, Smith & Co.* [1912] AC 716, a firm of solicitors employed a senior managing clerk to handle conveyancing transactions on his own. He dishonestly conveyed the plaintiff's property for his own benefit. The House of Lords held that the solicitors were vicariously liable, because it was the position in which they had placed the clerk which enabled him to carry out the fraud.

In effect, the clerk **represented** the firm of solicitors, so the circumstances were rather special. The clerk was regarded as the **agent** for the solicitors rather than a mere employee. As Lord Loreburn put it: 'If the agent commits the fraud purporting to act in the course of business such as he was authorised, or held out as authorised, to transact on account of his principal, then the latter may be held liable for it.'.

The Court of Appeal in *Generale Bank Nederland NV* v *Export Credits Guarantee Dept., The Times*, 4 August 1997, had to consider whether the tort of **deceit** came within an employee's course of employment. The employee had become liable to X as a **joint tortfeaser** with Y in deceit (Y and the employee having acted together, in concert). It was held that Z, the employer, could only be vicariously liable if the deceit was within the employee's actual or ostensible authority. The employee's authority ran to the underwriting of guarantees and it was this act which the court had to examine, i.e. did it fall within the course of employment? It was found that **deceit** did **not** come within the employee's course of employment.

ACTIVITY 1

Please consider the decision in *Morris* v *C W Martin and Sons Ltd* [1965] 2 All ER 725, which you can find in *Cases and Materials* (1.1.2.2), and answer the following questions:

(1)   What was the outcome of the case?

(2)   Were the reasons given by the members of the Court of Appeal for their unanimous decision on similar lines?

You should have answered as follows:

(1) The employers were found vicariously liable for their employee's theft of the plaintiff's mink stole.

(2) Their Lordships gave different reasons for their decisions:

(a) Lord Denning MR found against the employers on the ground that their non-delegable duty to take care of the stole had been broken.

(b) Diplock and Salmon LJJ regarded the employee as having committed the theft in the course of his employment, thus making his employers, the defendants, vicariously liable for his dishonesty.

It was pointed out in *Morris*, however, that it is not enough that an employee is given an **opportunity** by his job to steal or otherwise act dishonestly. The act must have been committed 'in the course of doing that class of acts which the company had put the servant in its place to do': Diplock LJ. Thus the company would not have been liable if the stole had been stolen by an employee who was not employed to clean it or have care and custody of it.

This reasoning was applied in *Heasmans* v *Clarity Cleaning Co. Ltd* [1987] ICR 949. The defendants provided cleaning services to the plaintiffs, and one of the defendants' employees, whilst on the plaintiffs' premises, made illegal use of the plaintiffs' telephones. The Court of Appeal found that before an employer could be liable vicariously for the wrongful acts of an employee there must be some 'nexus' between the employee's tortious or criminal act and the circumstances of his employment. In the present case apart from the obligation to dust and, once a week, to disinfect the telephone, nothing more existed than the provision of the **opportunity** to commit the tort or crime. As Purchas LJ said, that factor was insufficient to establish a nexus in the present case and the defendants' appeal was allowed: they were not vicariously liable for their employee's illegal act.

Do you think it possible that an employer can escape his vicarious liability by means of an appropriate exclusion clause in some cases?

In *Photo Production Ltd* v *Securicor Transport Ltd* [1980] AC 827, the defendant's employee, employed to guard the plaintiff's factory, had burnt it down in the course of his employment, but the House of Lords found that the defendant had effectively excluded its liability by a term in the contract with the plaintiff, notwithstanding the fundamental breach of the contract.

We now proceed to examine the special liability of vehicle owners, which is the second major object of our attention in the context of **vicarious** liability.

1.4.3 VEHICLE DRIVERS

The decisions here have been especially influenced by policy considerations; the courts try to see that road-accident victims may recover from the insurers. Frequently the driver of the defendant's car is described as the defendant's 'agent' rather than his 'servant' or 'employee', but 'the word "agency" in contexts such as these is merely a concept, the meaning and purpose of which is to say "is vicariously liable" . . .' in the words of Lord Wilberforce in *Morgans* v *Launchbury* (below).

Thus, it is best to regard this form of vicarious liability not as resting on any **general** conception of agency, but as a form of liability *sui generis* ('of its own kind'; 'the only one of its kind') developed by the courts to meet the exigency of the moment.

The rule was described by du Parq LJ in *Hewitt* v *Bonvin* [1940] 1 KB 188, in the following words:

> The driver of a car may not be the owner's servant and the owner will nevertheless be liable for his negligent driving if it be proved that at the material time he had authority, express or implied, to drive on the owner's behalf. Such liability depends not on ownership, but on the delegation of a task or duty.

In this case a son borrowed his father's (the defendant's) car to take home two girlfriends, who were injured as a result of the son's negligent driving. The father was found not to be vicariously liable for the negligent driving, for no purpose of his was being served by his son at the time.

In *Ormrod* v *Crosville Motors* [1953] 1 WLR 409, however, the driver was taking the defendant's car from Birkenhead to Monte Carlo so that the defendant could use it there on holiday. On the journey an accident was caused by the driver's negligent driving. The defendant, the owner of the car, was found to be vicariously liable to the plaintiff, who had been injured in the accident.

Morgans v *Launchbury* [1972] 2 All ER 606, is the leading authority on this issue. The decision places great emphasis on the requirement that the **owner's** 'purposes' or 'interests' are the paramount factor in such cases.

The defendant, a wife, owned and insured the family car which her husband used often for work and pleasure. With her consent he took the car on a journey round some pubs (a 'pub crawl') having entrusted the driving to a friend. The plaintiff was injured when the friend, who was not insured, drove negligently and crashed the car.

The plaintiff sued the wife in her capacity as principal of her husband who was alleged to have been acting as her agent at the time of the crash. The House of Lords held the defendant not liable. Lord Wilberforce said: '. . . if the husband was, as he clearly was, using the car for his own purposes, I am unable to understand how his undertaking to delegate his right to drive to another can turn the driver into the wife's agent in any sense of the word.'.

In many cases, drivers are themselves insured and, as you will see in **Chapter 8**, *Monk* v *Warbey* [1935] 1 KB 75 suggests that the owner of the vehicle may be liable for breach of statutory duty where he allows an uninsured person to drive his vehicle (see **8.3.4.3**). Thus *Morgans* is not the only route for a plaintiff to follow in search of money.

You will also see in **Chapter 2** that insurance must now be taken out for liability to passengers. In *Morgans*, however, the plaintiff was a passenger in a **bus**, with which the negligent driver in this case had collided.

1.4.4   CONTRIBUTION AND INDEMNITY

The provisions of the Civil Liability (Contribution) Act 1978, which are dealt with below, may enable the employer or principal, as the case may be, to recover some, or all, of the damages from his employee or agent. Also, at common law, a servant will be liable to compensate the master for the amount of damages paid by him. This matter is dealt with in **Chapter 8**.

1.5 Contributions between Tortfeasors

A plaintiff may have suffered damage at the hands of **more** than **one** tortfeasor, and where this is the case we need to distinguish between **different groups** of **tortfeasors**. In effect, tortfeasors may fall into **one** of **three** groups:

(a) joint tortfeasors;

(b) independent tortfeasors;

(c) several concurrent tortfeasors.

We shall examine each of these groups in turn.

1.5.1 JOINT TORTFEASORS

Joint tortfeasors are two, or more, tortfeasors who are **jointly** responsible to the same plaintiff for causing him the same damage. In other words, tortfeasors here are liable on the same facts.

Each of the tortfeasors can be sued for the full amount of the loss, although a plaintiff cannot recover his damages more than once. The apparent problem is solved by means of 'contributions between tortfeasors', which we examine below.

This joint liability can occur in several ways:

(a) one tortfeasor can **incite** the other(s) to commit a tort;

(b) they may commit a joint breach of a duty owed by each of them;

(c) they may have an **express** or **implied** common design or purpose (for example, such a purpose would be **implied** in cases of **vicarious** liability);

(d) where **employers** are vicariously liable for the torts of their **employees**, or **principals** are vicariously liable for the torts of their **agents**, or **employers** are liable for the torts of their **independent contractors** (in those exceptional cases where employers are said to have a 'non-delegable duty').

1.5.2 INDEPENDENT TORTFEASORS

The legal description applied to these tortfeasors is 'several' tortfeasors, i.e. liability is **separate**: the tortfeasors act on an **independent** basis, to inflict **different** items of damage on the same plaintiff. In **this** case there are, therefore, **separate** and **distinct** torts involved, each tortfeasor being responsible only for his 'own' damage.

1.5.3 SEVERAL CONCURRENT TORTFEASORS

This form of liability again involves **separate, independent** acts (or torts) against the same plaintiff but on this occasion the torts **combine** to cause the **same** damage, i.e. the plaintiff does not suffer different items of damage.

In this case each tortfeasor is severally (i.e. separately) liable for the whole damage, but the plaintiff can recover only **one** set of damages.

1.5.4 DIFFERENCES BETWEEN THE DIFFERENT GROUPS OF TORFEASOR

At the outset, we can eliminate 'independent' tortfeasors: each independent tortfeasor is responsible only for the **separate** item of damage his tort has inflicted upon the plaintiff. There are no **special** rules applicable in such cases.

Any problems in the present context, that of **contribution** between tortfeasors, will be encountered in relation to

- joint tortfeasors, and
- several concurrent tortfeasors

because, obviously, tortfeasors belonging to both groups have caused the **same** damage to the plaintiff; the only difference between them being, in broad terms, that whereas joint tortfeasors have acted together, in concert, in pursuance of some common purpose or goal, independent tortfeasors have 'combined' to cause damage quite by chance.

Today, the issue of **contribution** between tortfeasors, whether they are of the 'joint' or 'several concurrent' variety, is governed by the rules laid down in the Civil Liability (Contribution) Act 1978. We will be examining those rules below, but first a brief mention of the position of these tortfeasors at common law will help to put the matter into perspective.

Originally, there were two main differences between joint and several concurrent tortfeasors at common law:

(a) if a court judgment was obtained against a **joint** tortfeasor, any **later** action by the plaintiff against the other joint tortfeasors was barred, even where the judgment debt was never paid by the joint tortfeasor against whom judgment had been obtained; and

(b) where the plaintiff agreed to **release** a **joint** tortfeasor, this had the effect of releasing **all** the joint tortfeasors. (A 'release' simply means giving up, or discharging, or renouncing any rights or claims against another person.)

These rules applied **only** to joint tortfeasors.

The first rule has been abolished by s. 3 of the Civil Liability (Contribution) Act 1978, which provides that where a plaintiff receives his compensation in a judgment '. . . recovered against any person in respect of any . . . damage . . .' this will **not** be a bar '. . . to an action, or to the continuance of an action, against any other person who is (apart from any such bar) jointly liable with him in respect of the same . . . damage.'.

This is not, however, the end of the story. If the plaintiff **does** bring a later action against **either** a joint or a several concurrent tortfeasor, s. 4 of the 1978 Act provides that the plaintiff will not get his costs in the later action(s) **unless** he can satisfy the court that there were reasonable grounds for bringing such later action(s).

The second common law rule, concerning 'release', has been left untouched by legislation but its importance, in **practical** terms, has been much diminished by **judicial interpretation**.

Today, 'release', which is executed in a formal way, is distinguished from an 'agreement not to sue' (a mere declaration of consent) made with a joint tortfeasor. In the case of an agreement not to sue, which is the more common of the two, the **overall** obligation is **not** extinguished: the plaintiff is prevented merely from going against the joint tortfeasor with whom he made the agreement. A 'release' still operates to release all the joint tortfeasors. In addition, however, to the distinction which has been developed between 'release' and 'agreement not to sue', in cases of doubt the courts are somewhat reluctant to interpret an 'agreement' as a 'release', and so in practice the release is less important than it used to be.

You will be interested to know, however, that even where there **is** a release the **overall** cause of action survives where there is an express or implied **reservation** of the right of action against the other joint tortfeasors.

There is today little difference in practical terms between joint and several concurrent tortfeasors.

1.5.5 THE RULES OF CONTRIBUTION BETWEEN JOINT AND SEVERAL CONCURRENT TORTFEASORS

1.5.5.1 The general rule

Section 1(1) of the 1978 Act provides: 'any person liable in respect of any damage suffered by another person may recover contribution from any other person liable in respect of the same damage (whether jointly with him or otherwise).'.

1.5.5.2 Eligibility to make a claim

Having stated the **general** position, the Act goes on to provide in s. 1(6): 'References in this section to a person's liability in respect of any damage are references to any such liability which **has been** or **could** be established in an action brought against him in England or Wales by or on behalf of the person who suffered the damage.'.

Thus, the person who is looking for a contribution must either have **actually** been found liable in respect of the relevant damage or could **potentially** have been liable for that damage if sued.

If he could not have been liable because, for example, a statutory limitation period had expired, he will not be able to claim a contribution.

However, a tortfeasor who settles the action against him by admitting liability and paying the plaintiff in full, may still seek a contribution from the other tortfeasor(s) if, in the words of s. 1(2) of the 1978 Act, 'he was liable immediately before he made or was ordered or agreed to make the payment in respect of which contribution is sought'.

By virtue of s. 1(4) of the 1978 Act, where a tortfeasor settles with the plaintiff but does **not** admit liability, he can still seek a contribution from the other tortfeasor(s), but he will have to show that he was legally liable for the relevant damage.

Section 1(4) says:

> A person who has made or agreed to make any payment in bona fide [i.e. in good faith, without any fraud or collusion in wrongdoing] settlement or compromise of any claim . . . shall be entitled to recover contribution . . . without regard to whether or not he himself is or ever was liable in respect of the damage, provided, however, that he would have been liable assuming that the factual basis of the claim against him could be established.

We must next consider **who** is **liable** to **contribute**.

1.5.5.3 Liability to a contribution action

Reference must again be made to s. 1(1) of the 1978 Act (see **1.5.5.1**): 'any other person liable in respect of the same damage' can be the subject of contribution proceedings.

Section 1(3) says that such a person can still be liable to make a contribution even though he is no longer liable to the plaintiff: '**unless** he [the tortfeasor against whom contribution is sought] ceased to be liable by virtue of the expiry of a period of limitation or prescription which extinguished the right on which the claim against him in respect of the damage was based.'. [emphasis supplied]

This proviso, or qualification to s. 1(3) does **not** apply to the majority of limitation periods in tort because they do not extinguish the 'right'; they only bar the remedy. Thus, in most cases the proviso does not apply.

Unfortunately, however, we have to consider s. 1(5) of the 1978 Act, which appears to be in **conflict** with s. 1(3). Section 1(5) says:

A judgment given in any action . . . by or on behalf of the person who suffered the damage in question against any person from whom contribution is sought . . . shall be conclusive in the proceedings, for contribution as to any issue determined by that judgment in favour of the person from whom the contribution is sought.

The effect of this provision, according to *Winfield* (p. 631) is that if the action by the **plaintiff** against the tortfeasor liable to make a contribution is dismissed by the court on its **merits** (i.e. there is no legal basis at all to the case) that tortfeasor is not liable to make any contribution to any other tortfeasor(s). If, however, the plaintiff fails on a **procedural** point, for example, because of expiry of time via the statutory limitation period, s. 1(5) does not apply and the tortfeasor is open to a claim for contribution from the other tortfeasor(s). All turns on the interpretation of the word 'issue' in s. 1(5) and on this view, **procedural** matters are not caught by it.

Successive proceedings by plaintiffs against joint or several concurrent tortfeasors are not common; contribution proceedings are in practice dealt with in the **original** action brought by the **plaintiff**, **either** because the plaintiff will sue **all** the tortfeasors at the **same** time **or** the tortfeasor who is sued alone will use third party procedures to 'join' the other tortfeasor(s) as defendants in the action brought by the plaintiff.

Finally, two further matters of importance must be noted:

(a)   liability to contribute in the present context is **not** limited to those who are liable only in **tort** for the same damage. A person is 'liable' for present purposes, whether his liability arises from '. . . tort, breach of contract, breach of trust or otherwise' (s. 6(1) of the 1978 Act);

(b)   there is a limitation period within which a claim for contribution must be brought. By virtue of s. 10 of the Limitation Act 1980, this period is two years from the date when the right to claim contribution accrued. This date is the date of the judgment or settlement of the plaintiff's claim, as the case may be.

1.5.5.4   How much will the contribution be?

According to s. 2(1) of the 1978 Act:

the amount of contribution recoverable from any person shall be such as may be found by the court to be just and equitable having regard to the extent of that person's responsibility for the damage in question.

Section 2(3) provides, however, that if a limit was set, by contract or statute or the operation of the rules of contributory negligence, to the amount which the plaintiff could have recovered from the second defendant, then the first defendant cannot recover from the second defendant a sum by way of contribution in excess of that limit.

When assessing the second defendant's 'responsibility for the damage' the court must consider all the circumstances of the case, including degrees of blameworthiness and causation.

Subject to s. 2(3), s. 2(2) gives the court power to exempt the second defendant from having to contribute, or to order the second defendant to pay an indemnity.

We should note that:

(a) apportionment is made only on the basis of the degree of fault and causative potency of the conduct of the **parties before the court**; and

(b) the Act does not direct the court to apportion on the basis of equality amongst the tortfeasors.

You will find a good example of the liability of several concurrent tortfeasors in *Fitzgerald* v *Lane* [1987] 2 All ER 455, which is discussed at **4.4**.

The 1978 Act is set out in *Cases and Materials* (**1.2**).

1.6 Summary

Chapter 1 is concerned with the basic elements of the law of torts, i.e. **capacity to commit a tort**, **vicarious liability** and **contributions** between tortfeasors. These matters can be relevant in any problem involving torts, though in practice conventional torts examination questions do not generally raise issues involving bankrupts, aliens, the Post Office and other, more esoteric, capacities. Crown capacity and similar issues are usually the concern of constitutional law.

Capacity to **commence** proceedings, i.e. to **sue** in tort can also be a complicated issue in some contexts, but for our purposes it is enough to know that minors will sue through their 'next friend', persons under a mental disability can be represented by the Official Solicitor or a guardian *ad litem* and corporations (i.e. artificial legal 'persons') can sue in their own names, though not all torts are capable of being committed against such bodies: thus, for example, corporations cannot be falsely imprisoned, though they may be defamed and have their property damaged as the result of negligence.

It is always dangerous to generalise in these circumstances, but it is probably the case that 'capacity' is less important in general terms than contributions between 'tortfeasors' and 'vicarious liability': these are matters which cannot be ignored in any tortious context. 'Contribution' and 'vicarious liability' are not, of course, **inevitably** relevant issues in **all** circumstances, but they are concerns of common occurrence.

You should acquire a working knowledge of the provisions of the Civil Liability (Contribution) Act 1978, and **distinguish** them **carefully** from the provisions of the Law Reform (Contributory Negligence) Act 1945, which regulate the **defence** of contributory negligence. This defence is dealt with in **Chapter 2**.

Vicarious liability is the most important topic of all in the present context, and attracts the greatest proportion of our attention in this chapter. We are concerned with vicarious liability at common law, and not with any form of special liability that might be imposed by statute. When someone is found to be vicariously liable, he is being made responsible for the act(s) of another person and, though that **other** person will remain **personally** liable for whatever form of liability he is guilty of (usually the tort of **negligence**), the one who is **vicariously** liable will be **strictly** liable, i.e. **his** liability is not personal **fault** of any kind.

Vicarious liability is commonly associated with the liability of an employer for the tort(s) of his employee, committed in the course of the latter's employment. Indeed, we focus on that form of liability; but it is very important to appreciate that this form of liability is **not limited** to such relationships; or for that matter to the law of torts: it can be found, for example, in the law of **partnership** and **agency**.

We cannot escape the influence of the concept of 'agency' in tort; it is a convenient device for imposing liability in appropriate circumstances, the circumstances being determined according to the reality of the commercial situation or on grounds of policy.

The law of agency is an aspect of commercial or business law, and can only be touched upon in the present context. In the commercial world **agents** are commonly appointed by **contract** to negotiate deals for their **principals**; the agent's authority may be 'actual', 'implied', or 'ostensible' (i.e. 'apparent') and many legal disputes turn on the question of whether the agent's authority extended to the particular transaction in question and whether, as a consequence his principal is liable for his acts. In the law of tort the idea of agency is often used, as *Winfield* (p. 613) puts it, on an *ad hoc* (i.e. 'for this purpose') basis; in other words, not as part of a consistent application of the 'commercial' concept of agency. In any case, there will not often be a **contract** of agency in existence between the parties, thus it is usually a matter of **implying** an agency relationship in the circumstances of the case.

The vicarious liability of **vehicle owners** for the negligence of drivers can be explained on this basis; according to Lord Wilberforce in *Morgans* it is based on the conclusion that the 'principal' **ought** to pay in the circumstances.

This concept of *ad hoc* agency, if we may borrow that expression, can be used to extend vicarious liability wherever it is thought by the courts to be appropriate. It seems, in some cases at least, to be based on the idea of 'control' and 'direction'. Thus, the hirer of another's employee could be vicariously liable on this basis. You may recall the case of *Watkins* (see **1.4.1.3**) in which the Court of Appeal found that the schoolboy was not the employee of the education authority in the circumstances. The court discussed, also, the question of whether he was the defendant's agent.

It was decided that he was not, but an interesting observation was made on what would have been within the scope of his authority had he been an agent. (We call this an *obiter dictum*, i.e. 'a saying by the way', because it was not an issue which **required** a **decision** from the court, therefore it is not a binding precedent.) Buckley LJ said that the school's prohibition, issued to the children against toys being removed from the central depository for such items, would have effectively restricted the boy's authority as an agent; and by leaving the cycle in the corridor he would have exceeded his authority to act. If, however, he had been an **employee** of the defendants, that factor would not have so affected his work as to take him outside the course of his employment. If correct, this view suggests that a broader approach may be taken to the definition of 'course of employment' than is taken to the definition of 'scope of authority'.

In any context, it is always important to distinguish between a person's **primary** liability and his **vicarious** liability, and nowhere is this point made more clearly than in the relationship of employer and employee.

The vicarious liability of an employer ('master') for the tort(s) of his employee ('servant') is the classic instance of this form of liability. In general, the relationship of employee and employer is a contractual one, based on financial reward for service, and in practice this is the type of relationship we encounter in the cases.

SAQ 8

Have you ever looked up the word 'employee' in a dictionary? Pause for a moment in your studies and please do so, if your answer is in the negative.

Write down the definition you have found.

You might be interested to know that the latest edition of *Chambers English Dictionary* defines 'employee' as: 'a person employed'. The dictionary defines the word 'employ' as: 'to occupy the time or attention of; to use as a means or agent; to give work to'.

It may be suggested that an 'employee', for the purposes of **vicarious liability** in **tort**, need not be the one who is paid for his service, particularly in view of the use made in the cases of the concept of implied agency.

In *Rose* v *Plenty* (see **1.4.2.3**) the plaintiff succeeded, to some extent, because he was benefiting the defendant, and it may be that that approach is another way of looking at the same problem. He was suing the defendant in vicarious liability for the negligence of the milkman who had engaged him to help with the milk round; but suppose that the **plaintiff** had committed a tort in pursuance of this objective. The question might have then arisen of whether the defendant could have been found vicariously liable for **his** behaviour.

ACTIVITY 2

Please read about the decision in *Ilkiw* v *Samuels* **[1963] 2 All ER 879** in *Cases and Materials* **(1.1.2.3)**. Write down the reasons for the Court of Appeal's decision in that case.

The Court of Appeal in *Ilkiw* held that either:

(a) the lorry driver was negligent in allowing the person to drive the vehicle; or

(b) that the lorry (truck) was driven negligently whilst it was under the control of the lorry driver;

and in **either** case, that the negligence arose in the course of the lorry driver's employment.

(See also *A & W Hemphill Ltd* v *Williams* [1966] 2 Lloyd's Rep 10 and *Kay* v *ITW Ltd* [1967] 3 All ER 22 in *Cases and Materials* (**1.1.2.3**).)

In connection with an **employer's** vicarious liability for the **torts** of his employee, we have seen that there are essentially two potential areas of difficulty:

(a) is the person in question an 'employee' (or 'servant') or an 'independent contractor'?

(b) was the tort(s) committed in the course of the employee's employment?

You will have gathered by now that neither of these issues is amenable, in the present context, to any 'scientific' or systematic analysis. We can only sum up the situation in the phrases, beloved of lawyers: 'each case turns on its own facts'; and 'it all depends on the circumstances of the case'.

As Lord Mansfield put it, in another context, in *Fisher* v *Prince* (1762) 3 Burr 1364; 'The reason and spirit of cases make law; not the letter of particular precedent.'. This is true of the law generally; it is especially true of the law of tort as a whole, dependent as it is on such a vast body of case law; but to focus even more narrowly on the two issues before us, i.e. 'employee' and 'course of employment', we see more than ever that the 'law' often lies in the 'interstice', i.e. in the gap between decisions; or, to put it another way, is often found by reading 'between the lines' of the 'black letters' of the law.

We have seen that an employer may be liable even for the acts of an independent contractor. This is the case where the employer is personally liable in some way, because of his negligence in choosing an incompetent contractor or because of the operation of the doctrine of 'non-delegable duties'.

The liability in relation to choice of contractor is well-established, and independent of the 'neighbour principle' in *Donoghue* v *Stevenson* [1932] AC 562 (which you will read about in **Chapter 3**) although that authority could provide the foundation for a case based on the notion of 'proximity'.

You can read about a leading case on liability for independent contractors *Salsbury* v *Woodland* [1969] 3 All ER 863 in *Cases and Materials* (**1.3**).

The Court of Appeal, in *Rowe* v *Herman, The Times*, 9 June 1997, followed this case. In *Rowe* occupiers of land engaged independent contractors who, after leaving the site, left some metal plates on the public footpath adjacent to the land. The plaintiff tripped over these plates and was injured. It was held that the principle that an employer is not liable for the negligence of an independent contractor is subject to two exceptions *viz.* (i) where the work involves extra-hazardous activities and (ii) where danger is created by work on the highway. Since neither exception applied on the facts, the defendant occupiers were not liable. They were not to be treated as if they were occupiers of the highway.

There is no closed list of non-delegable duties; new ones are being developed all the time.

In *Rogers* v *Nightriders* [1983] RTR 324, the defendant ran mini-cabs and contracted to hire one to the plaintiff, using an independent contractor to drive the vehicle. At first instance, the defendant was found not liable on the ground that an employer of a contractor was not vicariously liable for the torts of that contractor. The Court of Appeal, however, held that since the defendant had contracted with the plaintiff to provide a vehicle, and injury to the plaintiff was foreseeable if the vehicle was defective, the defendant owed a **personal, non-delegable** duty of care to the plaintiff to see that the vehicle was in a reasonable state of repair. It was a legal obligation which could not be delegated to a contractor, though its performance could be. If, however, the contractor neglected to fulfil his part of the bargain, the employer remained **personally** liable where that negligence caused injury to a third party. The contractor in such a case will, of course, **also** be liable to the injured plaintiff in negligence.

'Course of employment' is very much an issue in which the facts are paramount. As *Winfield* (p. 601) puts it: '. . . it contains no criteria to decide when or why an act is within or outside the scope of employment and no single test is appropriate to cover all cases.'.

It is evident that the courts in general take a broad view of what **is** and is **not** within the course of a particular employee's employment. We have seen that the cases have laid down some very general lines of guidance, but these provide only a sense of direction; they do not give us any firm guidance on the solution that the court is likely to arrive at in any given case.

The fact, for example, that the employee was guilty of some intentional wrong may, as we have seen, be a deciding factor. There is a tendency away from 'course of employment' where such behaviour is involved.

We have seen, however, that if intentional wrongs have a sufficient connection with the employee's duties, they may be regarded as coming within the course of his employment.

In *Racz* v *Home Office* [1994] 1 All ER 97, the House of Lords held that the Home Office could be vicariously liable for the (alleged) deliberate mistreatment of a prisoner by prison officers. The issue before the House was an argument on the **pleadings**, i.e. whether the plaintiff's statement of claim disclosed an arguable legal point for resolution by the court. Their Lordships decided that the alleged mistreatment of the plaintiff by the officers, the result of the commission of the tort of misfeasance in public office, could be an unauthorised mode of performing their authorised duties, provided there was a sufficient nexus between the unauthorised acts and the officers' official duties. This was a matter which could only be resolved by hearing the evidence at a trial, therefore the House remitted the case back to the court of first instance for determination.

The following extract from the speech of Lord Jauncey sums up the position:

> My Lords, in my view, striking out para 6 of the claim could only be justified if the inevitable result of proof of the averments therein was that the unauthorised acts of the prison officers were so unconnected with their authorised duties as to be quite independent of and outside those duties. Mr Sankey invited your Lordships to draw inferences from the averments in the statement of claim, but only if such inferences were absolutely unavoidable and inescapable could he succeed. Mr Harris, on the other hand, in argument and in his written case, pointed out that it is likely to be a question of fact and degree whether the prison officers were engaged in a misguided and unauthorised method of performing their authorised duties or were engaged in what was tantamount to an unlawful frolic of their own. My Lords, I consider that there is substance in Mr Harris's submission. I am in no doubt that it is impossible to determine the precise character of the actions of the prison officers upon which will depend the liability or otherwise of the defendants for their acting from a perusal of the pleadings alone and that this can only be done after the facts have been established. It follows that, there being no compulsitor [Scots law — 'a means of compelling'] to strike out para 6 by reason of *Hague's* case, the case must go to trial on the whole pleadings as they stand.

The tort of misfeasance in public office is committed where a public official in effect abuses his official position, by maliciously misusing his office in such a way as to cause loss to the plaintiff.

An **express** prohibition issued by the employer against certain acts is not conclusive of the issue; the prohibition must restrict the **scope** of employment, not merely the way of performing the job.

In **Chapter 7** we discuss *Stone* v *Taffe* [1974] 3 All ER 1016, which is concerned principally with the question of 'occupiers' liability', but an argument on vicarious liability is also involved in the decision. The licensee of the pub, its manager, who was an employee of the owners of the pub, had been told quite clearly **not** to entertain customers after drinking hours. He ignored this instruction, however and, in so doing, was acting illegally when he continued his nocturnal activities. Due to this disobedient employee's negligence in failing to light some steps, the plaintiff (a visitor on the premises) fell to his death one night after leaving one of the illicit drinking sessions. (The action in tort for damages was brought by representatives of the deceased's estate.)

It was held by the court that the employer's prohibition did not in the circumstances limit the scope of the employee's employment; it only limited the **mode** of performance of his work, and the employers were vicariously liable for the death. The court took into account the following factors:

(a)   the plaintiff was not aware of the employer's order;

(b)   the plaintiff could not have avoided the danger created by the employee (although his damages were reduced by 50 per cent for contributory negligence: see **Chapter 2**);

(c)   there was no evidence that the plaintiff was likely to have known of the order.

The main problem in legislating for the determination of the course of employment issue is the plain fact that there is such a wide diversity of jobs, occupations, pursuits, callings, professions, etc, that it is virtually impossible to do anything more than decide each case essentially on its own facts.

You will have seen that the factors of time and place are often of importance in these cases. Yet 'time' in the present context may mean something different; it might be less crucial for a salaried employee than for an employee paid on a piece-rate or bonus-rate basis. The same is true of the factor, 'place'.

You have read about some of the so-called 'driving' cases in which these factors have played their part. Yet not **all** drivers' terms of employment are the same; the 'course of employment' of a long-haulage truck driver, for example, for the purpose of determining whether a detour is an entirely new and independent journey from his authorised route, or only a 'momentary' deviation which can be overlooked, may not be the same as that, say, of a van driver who is engaged only on local deliveries.

The range of employed **drivers** alone is immense including, for example, coach and bus drivers, travelling salespersons, to name but a few.

It will not be necessary to remind you that decisions in this field turn often on fine distinctions. In *Storey* v *Ashton* [1869] LR 4 QB 476, the employee was a deliveryman of wine. After making a delivery, he was returning to his employer's premises with some empty flagons, when he made a detour to collect the belongings of a fellow employee, who was with him on the job, and take them elsewhere. His negligent handling of his horse and cart during this unofficial journey (no purpose of his employers was being furthered by it) resulted in injuries to the plaintiff. On the facts, his employers were found not to be vicariously liable for his negligence because the detour was too substantial to be within the course of his employment.

In broad terms, the determination of the issue must depend on whether or not it can be said that the employee was still engaged substantially enough on what he was expressly or impliedly employed to do.

Thus, in *Harvey* v *O'Dell* [1958] 1 All ER 657, the employee who had agreed to put his 'combination', i.e. motor-cycle and sidecar, into the service of his employer, was driving from a place he had been sent to by his employer, to perform a task, to a nearby café some miles away for a meal, when he caused an accident due to his negligent driving.

The plaintiff was injured in this accident. The employee's temporary workplace did not have a canteen, and his journey in search of food was found to be within the course of his employment. *Jones* says (p. 277): 'Mealbreaks seem to produce particular problems'. Much seems to depend on what is authorised, and what can be impliedly authorised.

In line with the **general** position concerning travelling **to** and **from** work, there being a duty upon the employee to get to work which is independent of his course of employment, **authorised** meal breaks **themselves** may be outside the course of employment on the authority of *Crook* v *Derbyshire Stone Ltd* [1956] 1 WLR 432. Presumably, the same must be true of implied meal breaks. It could be said that the employee in *Harvey* was on his **way** to a meal break, and not actually engaged in the meal break itself at the time of the accident. No doubt, the same reasoning could be true of other types of rest breaks.

We have seen, however, that the courts usually take as broad a view as possible of this matter, and, for example, if some benefit or advantage to the employer can be found in any of these situations, it may be enough to bring the event into the employee's course of employment.

In *Smith* v *Stages* [1989] 1 All ER 833 (see *Cases and Materials* (**1.1.2**)), an employee was paid travelling time to get to a site some distance away from his usual place of work; he was acting in the course of his employment during that journey.

We should always remember to distinguish carefully between a person's **primary** liability and their **vicarious** liability. In one of the 'hospital cases', *Cassidy* v *Ministry of Health* [1951] 2 KB 343, Denning LJ suggested that the hospital authorities could be liable personally to an injured patient for their own negligence in providing inadequate hospital facilities, as an alternative to being liable vicariously for the negligence of, say, an employed doctor or nurse.

Support for this view can be found in the judgments of Browne-Wilkinson V-C in the Court of Appeal in *Wilsher* v *Essex Area Health Authority* [1986] 3 All ER 801, and of Slade LJ in *Bull* v *Devon Area Health Authority* [1993] 4 Med LR 117 (CA). In *Bull* Slade LJ said that the Authority owed a personal duty of care to their patients. On the facts, this was a duty to provide for the safe delivery of a baby and the health of both mother and baby.

In some cases, of course, a plaintiff may have a **contractual** relationship with the doctor who is treating his private patient on the hospital premises; or there may be a contract with **both** hospital **and** doctor. The **tortious** duty owed by a hospital would seem to be of the non-delegable kind, therefore the hospital would not escape liability by merely employing a doctor or nurse, for example, who were independent contractors: *Street* (pp. 493–4).

A further illustration of the distinction between **primary** and **vicarious** liability can be found in *Nahhar* v *Pier House (Cheyne Walk) Management* (1984) 270 EG 329. The landlords of a block of flats operated a system whereby absent tenants left their keys with a porter, who was employed by the landlord. During a stay in hospital the plaintiff duly left his key with the porter, who used it to gain entry to the plaintiff's flat and steal some jewellery. The landlords, the defendants, were not aware that the porter had a weighty criminal record. It was held that the defendants were liable (a) **personally**, in the tort of negligence, because they should have checked thoroughly the porter's background (the **deposit** of keys was not a negligent system); and (b) **vicariously** for the act of the porter in the course of his employment.

1.7 Further Reading

Hepple, B.A., and Matthews, M.H., *Tort: Cases and Materials*, 5th edn, London: Butterworths, 1996, Chapters 17 and 18.

Jones, M., *Textbook on Torts*, 5th edn, London: Blackstone Press, 1996, pp. 268–289.
Markesinis, B.S., and Deakin, S.F., *Tort Law*, 3rd edn, Oxford: Oxford University Press, 1994, pp. 134–43, 496–522.
Rose, F.D., 'Liability for Employee's Assaults' (1977) 40 MLR 420.
Salmond and Heuston on the Law of Torts, 21st edn, London: Sweet & Maxwell, 1996, Chapters 20 and 21.
Street on Torts, 9th edn, London: Butterworths, 1993, Chapters 15, 27, 31.
Weir, T., *Casebook on Tort*, 8th edn, London: Sweet & Maxwell, 1996, Chapters 6 and 7.
Winfield and Jolowicz on Tort, 14th edn, London: Sweet & Maxwell, 1994, Chapters 21, 22, 25.

1.8   End of Chapter Assessment Question

Chris lends to his friend, Ray, a van driver, Geoff, as a temporary replacement for Ray's own driver who is ill. While making deliveries in Ray's van one day, Geoff decides to pull in for lunch at a café, and in so doing negligently knocks down and injures Liz. He is so upset by this that he drives to a pub some miles away and proceeds to get drunk. At the pub he meets Michelle and offers to drive her home, but on the way he negligently collides with another vehicle and Michelle is injured.

Advise Liz and Michelle on any claims they may have for damages in the law of tort.

See *Cases and Materials* (1.5) for a specimen answer.

CHAPTER TWO

GENERAL DEFENCES

2.1 Objectives

By the end of this chapter you should be able to:

■ understand the principles of the following **general** defences:

(a) *volenti non fit injuria*

(b) illegality

(c) necessity

(d) contributory negligence

(e) mistake

(f) inevitable accident

(g) act of God

(h) statutory authority

(i) duress

(j) self-defence

(k) defence of property;

■ distinguish them from each other;

■ apply them to factual situations, where relevant.

2.2 Introduction

General defences, like **parties** (which are the subject of Chapter 1) are one of the (few) general, unifying and universal features of this often disparate collection of legal actions that go together under the heading 'Law of Tort'. It is for this reason that **general defences**, as well as **parties**, are dealt with at the beginning of this book.

'Defences' is a topic which the learner should have in mind **throughout** a study of the law of tort, and always have at the ready when attempting to solve a problem.

In general, the burden of proving a defence is on the **defendant**. The general defences in the law of tort are as follows:

(a) *volenti non fit injuria*

(b) illegality/*ex turpi causa non oritur actio*

(c) necessity

(d) contributory negligence

(e) mistake

(f) inevitable accident

(g) act of God

(h) statutory authority

(i) duress

(j) self-defence

(k) defence of property.

In this chapter we shall **concentrate** on *volenti*; **illegality**; **necessity**; **contributory negligence**. First, however, we will examine briefly **mistake**; **inevitable accident**; **duress**; **self-defence**; **defence of property**.

Act of God (if it exists) and, particularly, **statutory authority**, are of more importance in the context of some of the named, or 'nominate', torts, such as nuisance, and some forms of trespass. Accordingly, you will find discussion of these defences, where relevant, in later chapters.

It is also the case that:

■ further references to the 'main' general defences occur throughout this work;

■ the same is true of the more 'minor' general defences;

■ reference will be made in specific contexts to specific defences, for example, fair comment in relation to defamation;

■ **causation** is raised by **defendants**, therefore it is in reality a form of defence (see **Chapter 4**).

2.2.1 MISTAKE

It is probably more accurate to state that there is **no general** concept of mistake as a defence *per se* in tort. Mistake can be pleaded, however, by a defendant in **appropriate** circumstances as a means of escaping liability.

Thus, some torts require no intent beyond a voluntary act. That is the case with **trespass**, for example. In *Baseley v Clarkson* (1681) 3 Lev 37, it was said that if X walks on to Y's land under the honest mistake that he thinks it is his, or that he has a right to be on it, his mistake will be no defence. It seems to follow, therefore, that mistake is no **defence** where liability is strict.

It can be stated, therefore, as a general proposition that in those torts where liability is strict, for example, **trespass** and **conversion**, a defendant is liable **irrespective** of any mistake or negligence on his part.

Can you guess what the position is in the case of other types of tort? Write down your answer on a piece of paper.

Where liability depends on **intent**, or **motive**, or **unreasonable behaviour**, mistake **is** a factor taken into account in determining liability. In the tort of **deceit**, for example, the plaintiff must prove the **dishonesty**, or **fraud**, of the defendant and obviously the question of honest mistake will be relevant in such cases. The tort of **negligence** is based on the behaviour of the 'reasonable man' and the question may arise as to whether this hypothetical being would have made the mistake made by the defendant.

Any mistake pleaded by a defendant must be one of **fact**, because of the principle summed up in the Latin expression '*ignorantia juris neminem excusat*', i.e. ignorance of the law is no excuse. This principle is of universal application in law, and is, of course, not restricted to the law of tort.

2.2.2   INEVITABLE ACCIDENT

If a defendant pleads 'inevitable accident' he is really saying that a 'reasonable man' in his position at the time of the accident could not have avoided doing what he did in the circumstances, taking into account any precautions that would have been expected from the reasonable man.

According to *Winfield* (pp. 746–7) inevitable accident has no place in the tort of negligence, or any other tort based on fault, because it is the **plaintiff's** task to prove that the defendant was at fault, **not** for the defendant to exonerate himself. The learned author contends that it is equally irrelevant in torts of strict liability, simply because the defendant's fault in those cases is not in issue.

It may, however, have a role to play in those cases of negligence where *res ipsa loquitur* applies. In these cases some burden of exculpation is placed on a defendant. This is a topic dealt with in **Chapter 3**.

By the same token, 'inevitable accident' may be relevant in any other tortious situation in which the **defendant** is expected to extricate himself from an inference of liability. *Winfield* suggests this may be the case with highway authorities' liability for injury resulting from the state of the highway (p. 747, note 84).

2.2.3   DURESS

Can you think of the forms 'duress' might take? Please draw up a list of any forms of duress that spring to mind.

You might have written that 'duress' can take the following forms:

  (a) threats of force, violence or unlawful acts;

  (b) physical compulsion;

  (c) 'economic' duress.

The balance of opinion amongst academic writers seem to be that only **actual physical compulsion** will suffice for the **defence** of duress.

It seems that duress may also negative the defence of **consent**. Consent is dealt with later in this chapter.

2.2.4 SELF-DEFENCE

It is well-established defence for a defendant to plead that the damage complained of by the plaintiff is inflicted by way of self-defence, certainly of the defendant's own person and possibly of the person of a third party. A 'third party' defence would probably be all the stronger if the defendant had a duty to protect that third party.

Take a break from your reading for a moment and please attempt an answer to the following question.

Would a defendant be allowed to plead that he had a right of self-defence because he acted under the mistaken, but honest, belief that he could so act?'

In *Rigby v Chief Constable of Northants* [1985] 2 All ER 985, it was held that the defence cannot be based solely on such a basis. There must be an objective case for self-defence in the circumstances.

You may care to note, however, the point made by Street in connection with defence of property; see **2.2.5**.

There are three main characteristics of the defence (though each case must be assessed in the light of its factual circumstances):

  (a) the response of the defendant must be reasonable in the circumstances; and

  (b) the defensive measures must be proportionate to the harm threatened;

  (c) the defensive measures may be taken **before** any physical contact occurs; in other words, the defence can be activated as soon as an attack is threatened.

It must be the case that where the defendant has responded to a **threat**, as distinct from actual contact, he will have to show that the plaintiff was likely to carry out the threat. This will include the **ability** of the plaintiff to do so.

You will find it helpful to refer to **Chapter 9** which deals with **trespass to the person**; in particular, the section on **assault** and **battery** will assist you on the question of threats.

Standards of reasonableness differ, according to the values and practices of society at the relevant time. Thus, in *Fraser* v *Berkeley* (1836) 7 C & P 621, Lord Abinger said: 'If an author is to go and give a beating to a publisher who has offended him, two or three blows with a horse-whip ought to be enough to satisfy his irritated feelings.'. His Lordship may have had his tongue in his cheek when he said that, but it would certainly not reflect modern views on the matter.

Any response by a defendant must be **proportionate** to the threat, or damage inflicted upon the defendant. This requirement is evident even in earlier authority.

In *Cockroft* v *Smith* (1705) 2 Salk 642, for example, during an altercation in court, an attorney moved his hand towards the eyes of a clerk attending the court; it was held that the clerk could not justify biting off one of the attorney's fingers.

Can you think of any typical situation in which the issue of self-defence might be of particular relevance?

You might have had in mind a **fight** between two or more people (**not** a regulated boxing match, in which the question of consent might arise; consent is dealt with below).

According to Lord Oaksey in *Turner* v *MGM* [1950] 1 All ER 449, 'If you are attacked by a prize fighter you are not bound to adhere to the Queensberry Rules. It is clear, however, that even in the lowest of brawls any force used in self-defence must be both reasonable and proportionate to the threat of, or actual, force offered by the plaintiff.'.

In *Lane* v *Holloway* [1968] 1 QB 379, the Court of Appeal found that in a fight between a man aged 64, who was drunk at the time, and a man aged 27, a 'savage' blow struck by the latter upon the former was out of all proportion to the more feeble attempt of violence on the part of the older man. In other words, a light blow struck by the older man did not justify a savage blow in response by the younger man.

In *Barnes* v *Nayer, The Times*, 19 December 1986, the Court of Appeal weighed the defendant's response against the behaviour of his victim and her family. The defendant had attacked a woman with a machete, killing her in a most hideous way. He was convicted of manslaughter, but a civil claim for damages in trespass to the person was brought against him by her estate. Although he claimed that the dead woman and her family had made life a misery for him and his family, and had encouraged the sons of both families to fight each other, and had made more violent threats to one of his sons, it was found that his deadly attack was out of all proportion to anything offered by the deceased.

This case was not concerned with self-defence; in fact it was concerned with a plea by the defendant that the defences of *volenti, ex turpi causa* and contributory negligence applied. The court found that these defences, which we examine below, could not be sustained in the light of the defendant's response with the machete.

Although it is not concerned with self-defence, *Barnes* can be used by way of **analogy** in this connection on the issue of 'reasonableness' and 'proportion'.

'There may be some difficulty in determining just when the parties were engaged in an "ordinary fight with fists" and which blows are in proportion, but this will be treated as a question of fact.' *Jones* (p. 348).

The Court of Appeal decision in *Revill* v *Newbery* [1996] 1 All ER 291 offers a further illustration of this defence (see **Chapter 7**).

Please read about *Murphy* v *Culhane* [1976] 3 All ER 533, in *Cases and Materials* (2.1.1). Write down details of the issue before the Court of Appeal and the outcome of the appeal.

The question to be answered by the court was whether the defences of *ex turpi causa*, contributory negligence, and *volenti* applied in a claim for trespass to the person. The question was answered in the **affirmative**.

2.2.4.1 Provocation

Before proceeding to **defence of property**, it is necessary to consider the question of whether **provocation** can be considered a defence in tort, because it can be closely linked to the issue of self-defence.

Provocation does not appear to be a defence in the usual sense, but it may operate as a **mitigating** factor. In *Gray* v *Barr* [1971] 2 QB 554, Lord Denning said: '. . . [the court] can take into account [in awarding damages] not only circumstances which go to aggravate damages, but also those which go to mitigate them.'. This is authority for the proposition that provocation may well affect the **amount** of damages awarded.

In *Lane* v *Holloway* (see **2.2.4**), it was said that provocation could eliminate any **exemplary** damages but would not affect any general (**compensatory**) award. The plaintiff's conduct in this case was, however, regarded as trivial in comparison with the defendant's retaliatory action, and the defendant was treated as being solely responsible for the plaintiff's damage. The retaliatory response of the defendant was the result of the plaintiff's description of the defendant's wife as 'a monkey-faced tart'.

In *Barnes* v *Nayer* (see **2.2.4**) May LJ seemed to agree with the point on mitigation of exemplary, but not compensatory, damges, but said that a person who provokes someone else is still entitled to full compensation if the response to the provocation is out of all proportion to what has been offered by the other side.

2.2.5 DEFENCE OF PROPERTY

On the whole, this defence, though apparently recognised in principle, is not so readily accepted as self-defence, and is, therefore, harder to justify than that defence. It seems to overlap with necessity, which is dealt with below; indeed, the same is true of self-defence. This point will be taken up again, when we deal with the defence of necessity at **2.3.3**.

As Street puts it (p. 90): 'One may use reasonable force to defend land or chattels in one's possession against any person threatening to commit or committing a trespass to the property.'.

The author futher indicates (at p. 88) that as in the case of

> . . . defence of the person, if the defendant has a reasonable belief that force is essential to end the trespass, he may use it although he is mistaken in thinking it to be necessary, but if he mistakenly believes that the plaintiff is a trespasser, he has no defence.

In relation to self-defence we saw that the question of whether **reasonable** force had been used was a matter of fact in each case, and the same is true in the present context. No doubt, violence can be met with **proportional** force; non-violence will require an equally appropriate response.

In *Collins* v *Renison* [1754] Say 138, the plaintiff, a trespasser, was on a ladder in the defendant's garden and refused to descend when requested to do so by the defendant. The defendant's plea, that he '. . . gently shook the ladder . . . and gently overturned it and gently threw the plaintiff from it upon the ground' was rejected by the court.

It was found that the defendant's use of force was disproportionate to the plaintiff's resistance and he was liable in damages in trespass to the person.

The issue of an occupier's liability to trespassers upon his land, including the question of **deterrent** and **retributive** measures taken against such entrants, is discussed in **Chapter 7**.

It may be that there is a defence of defending the property of other persons from one's own household, according to *Street* (p. 90) quoting Blackstone (an 18th century jurist).

2.3   The Remaining Major Defences

We now have to deal with the general defences *volenti non fit injuria*; illegality; necessity; contributory negligence.

2.3.1 *VOLENTI NON FIT INJURIA*

We are concerned here with a defence of **general** application in the law of tort, which is also a **complete** defence, i.e. a defendant who is successful in his plea of *volenti non fit injuria* ('no injury is done to one who consents') will escape liability completely.

It is usually encountered in cases of **personal injury**, though it **could** apply to damage to property.

This is a defence of considerable antiquity, and it embraces the whole spectrum of 'acceptance', by the plaintiff, of the defendant's tortious, or potentially tortious conduct. *Volenti* embraces **three** forms of 'acceptance', which are not always sufficiently articulated:

(a)   consent

(b)   exclusion of liability

(c)   voluntary assumption of risk.

Rather than use *volenti* indiscriminately, as is often the case, it is preferable, and avoids obfuscation, to **differentiate** between each of the three elements of acceptance.

Jones (p. 387) puts the point well:

> *Volenti non fit injuria*, the plaintiff's voluntary assumption of risk, is a defence that is in a state of some confusion. This is partly due to a considerable overlap with other conceptual techniques employed to limit or reduce a defendant's liability, such as the **exclusion** of liability, contributory negligence, and the standard of care in negligence. The *main* problems, however, stem from the indiscriminate use of the word 'consent' in different contexts and for different purposes.

2.3.1.1   Consent

This expression is best understood as conveying the defence for **intentional** torts; the majority of writers seem to be agreed on this point: for example, *Salmond*, *Street* and *Winfield* hold this view. There is 'consent' to something **specific**; it is commonly encountered in cases involving **trespass to the person**, a form of liability dealt with in **Chapter 9**.

Consenting to a surgical operation, or other medical procedure, or to a fair rather than foul, tackle in a rugby match, are only some examples of consent to interference with the person in the form of assault and battery. Consent in these contexts, and others, is dealt with as appropriate throughout this book. The **general** nature of consent is our concern at **this** stage of study.

You will find details of a number of interesting cases on consent in the medical context, and on the question of obtaining the consent of minors and others who are incapable, mentally, of giving their consent in *Cases and Materials* (**2.2.1.1**).

In **these** cases it is said that the effect of the permission, or consent, is to prevent conduct, which would otherwise be actionable, from being tortious. To put it another way, consent prevents a duty in tort arising at all; it legalises what would otherwise be tortious.

An occupier's permission to enter premises, or land, for instance, makes entry legal that would otherwise be a trespass (unless the entrant can plead statutory or other legal authority or justification). As *Winfield* (p. 823) says this sort of permission, or consent, is usually described as the plaintiff's 'leave' or 'licence'; but this is, in essence, only a matter of nomenclature: the **legal effect** is the same.

Please pause for a moment, and consider whether consent can be implied from a plaintiff's conduct.

Although consent is commonly said to be 'express', i.e. the plaintiff has specifically addressed his mind to the issue, for example, giving written consent to a surgical operation (oral consent would perform the same function, though problems of **evidence** might then arise), consent may be implied from the circumstances.

Taking part in a sporting activity provides an example of such circumstances. A participant in such an activity is taken to have consented, within the rules of the game, to bodily contact with other participants that might otherwise amount to trespass to the person. In particular, you may wish to refer to the decision in *Condon* v *Basi*, which is discussed in **Chapter 3**.

Implied consent can also be used to justify emergency medical treatment, though the defence of **necessity** probably offers a more plausible rationale for the doctor's, or other medical worker's, immunity from suit in such circumstances. The defence of necessity is discussed below, but we may note here that necessity cannot be used where the defendant knows that the plaintiff does not wish to have the treatment.

In *Arthur* v *Anker* (1996) 146 NLJ 86, the Court of Appeal held that a plaintiff who had parked his car on private land without permission, but who had seen a notice to the effect that vehicles would be clamped and subject to a release charge, had impliedly consented to the terms of the notice. The court emphasised that motorists in such circumstances must have seen a suitably-worded notice, the release fee must be reasonable and easily payable, and the release of the vehicles must be prompt.

2.3.1.2   Exclusion of liability/agreements not to sue

This is sometimes referred to as 'express' *volenti* but it is submitted that this is a misnomer. Exclusion of liability is better understood as a defence *sui generis* ('of its own kind') **separate** from consent, as discussed above, and voluntary assumption of risk, which is discussed below.

At common law a defendant, could, by means of contract or other agreement or notice, either **exclude** or **restrict** any duty in tort which he would otherwise owe the plaintiff.

Issues may arise in these cases involving the incorporation of terms, and the bringing of conditions to the notice of the plaintiff. This topic is considered in **Chapter 7**, which deals with **occupiers' liability**; that discussion will, however, also sufficiently illustrate the **general** point now being made.

The essential point to grasp here is that the **terms** of the agreement will govern the question of whether the defendant is able to escape liability. There are, however, certain general limitations on a party's ability to **exclude** or **restrict** his liability.

In the case of **business contracts**, the Unfair Contract Terms Act 1977 imposes some important limitations on a party's power to exclude or restrict liability. You will find more detailed discussion on this matter in **Chapter 7**. Again, although the matter is discussed there in relation to **occupiers'** liability, what is said is also illustrative of the position in tort **generally**. It may be noted that the 1977 Act applies not only to attempts at **exclusion** of liability; attempts to **restrict** liability are also caught by the Act. The 1977 Act is set out in *Cases and Materials* (**2.2.1.2**).

It is likely that the common law rule relating to incorporation of terms in contracts, and the *contra proferentem* rule of construction are applicable here. These are matters concerning the law of contract and works on that subject should be consulted for further information.

You will be interested to learn that s. 29 of the Public Passenger Vehicles Act 1981 provides that an operator of public service vehicles cannot, by contract, negative or restrict liability for personal injury or death to his passengers.

Under s. 149 of the Road Traffic Act 1988, any attempt by the user of a private motor vehicle to exclude or restrict the duty of care owed to a passenger by 'any antecedent agreement or understanding between them' is void.

On the authority of *Pitts* v *Hunt* [1990] 3 All ER 344, s. 149 **also** catches voluntary assumption of risk (see **2.3.2.1**).

In some cases, for example, attempts to avoid safety legislation, the courts will 'strike out' exclusion notices which are 'repugnant to statute'. This point is taken up in **Chapter 8**.

The legal effect of 'exclusion' or agreement not to sue is the same as for consent and it is obvious that there can, ultimately, be no distinct and irrefutable dividing line between the two forms of defence. Exclusion or agreement can, and does, however, extend to liability for negligence and the plaintiff must be a party to the agreement.

In contrast, 'consent' is traditionally associated with 'intentional' torts, and can arise by implication.

Furthermore, where consent and, as we will see, voluntary assumption of risk are concerned, the defence turns on the question of whether the plaintiff has **actually** consented or agreed to accept the risk of injury, whereas exclusion or restriction of liability pivots merely on the question of whether the defendant has effectively brought the term to the notice of the plaintiff. In short, 'has the defendant effectively disclaimed liability?'.

It will not avail the plaintiff to plead that he has not read or taken note of the excluding term if he ought to have done so in the circumstances.

You will find *Norwich City Council* v *Harvey* [1989] 1 All ER 1180 in *Cases and Materials* (**2.2.1.2**). This is an interesting case, involving the effect of contractual terms on third parties.

2.3.1.3   Voluntary assumption of risk

This is sometimes known as '**implied** assumption of risk' (*Winfield*, p. 730) as contrasted with '**express** assumption of risk'. It has just been argued, however, that **express** assumption of risk, where it takes the form of some contractual undertaking or agreement not to sue, is best regarded as a free-standing defence. In the case of some **non-contractual agreement**, on the other hand, it may be correct to describe it as a form of **express** assumption of risk.

Can you think how voluntary assumption of risk might differ from 'consent' and 'exclusion of liability' or 'agreement not to sue'?

It differs from 'consent' in that it has reference to the **risk** of injury occurring; consent refers to the **certainty** of some **particular** interference.

It differs from 'exclusion' or 'agreement not to sue' in that it is a waiver of liability **implied** in the circumstances.

Voluntary assumption of risk is usually associated with the tort of negligence, although it is conceivable that a plaintiff could assume the risk of some intentional or deliberate interference, where his conduct is such that the defendant is led to the conclusion that he has consented to the interference. Support for this contention can be found in the judgment of Sir John Donaldson MR in *Freeman* v *Home Office (No. 2)*. This case is discussed in **Chapter 9**.

In contrast, 'consent' is usually associated with intentional torts, whilst 'exclusion' has universal application.

Risk

It is meaningless in legal terms to inquire whether a plaintiff has impliedly assumed a risk, where that risk is not even remotely tortious in nature. Much confusion can arise when, for example, even judges will sometimes refer to the fact that everyone runs the risk of injury when using the highway. Although modern traffic conditions **are** dangerous, it is only where someone is guilty of **tortious** behaviour that the question of whether the injured party has waived his right to sue arises. The same is true, for example, in relation to the ordinary, usual and incidental risks that spectators have to face at dangerous sporting activities.

The defence is only relevant where either:

(a) it is established that the defendant is in breach of his duty to the plaintiff, i.e. has **committed** a **tort** against him. In this case, the effect of assumption of risk is to negate the breach of duty; or

(b) the waiver of his right to sue by the plaintiff prevents any duty arising in the first place. Of course, a duty can only arise in relation to conduct that could be tortious: for example, if a traffic accident would have occurred **however** carefully a vehicle driver had conducted himself, the defence is hardly relevant. In the tort of negligence, the duty of a vehicle driver is to observe the standard of care of a reasonable man acting in the circumstances of the particular case.

Agreement

'Voluntary assumption of risk' is usually concerned with **negligent** behaviour on the part of a defendant.

SAQ 15

You have not yet studied the tort of negligence, which is discussed in Chapter 3, but can you guess any difficulties that might be encountered with a defence based on the implied waiver by a plaintiff of his legal right to sue if he is injured as the result of the defendant's negligence?

You might have guessed that the tort of negligence is of such a nature that in many cases the **form** the negligent behaviour takes is not known until after the relevant events have taken place, i.e. liability is based on an *ex post facto* inquiry. In other words, liability is fixed **retrospectively**, by posing the question 'how would a reasonable man have conducted himself in the circumstances of the defendant?'. The driver of a car, for example, owes a duty to take care for the safety of all other road users; but the breach of duty can take a number of forms, because driving involves many functions of the brain and limbs.

In the absence of some **express** provision, or consent, how can a court determine the **extent** of the plaintiff's waiver?

Unless care is taken in its application, assumption of risk can easily become a licence to commit negligence, and it is unlikely that the courts would allow that situation to develop.

As *Winfield* (p. 730) puts it: '. . . a quite extraordinary situation would have to exist for the court to be justified in holding that the plaintiff had consented **generally** to lack of reasonable care by the defendant.'.

Thus, there is considerable authority for the proposition that even where implied assumption of risk is concerned, something in the nature of an **agreement** between the parties is a necessary pre-condition for the defence. It is essential that the plaintiff has a detailed awareness of the particular risk(s) in question.

SAQ 16

Can you think of another reason why an agreement is thought to be necessary?

We will see, shortly, that acceptance of risk must be **freely** given; it must be a full, free and unfettered acceptance, therefore an agreement will be good evidence that this is in fact the case.

Jones (p. 388) defines *volenti non fit injuria* 'as . . . a voluntary agreement by the plaintiff to absolve the defendant from the legal consequences . . . of harm created by the defendant, where the plaintiff has full knowledge of both the nature and extent of the risk [involved in the particular case]'.

The decision in *Nettleship* v *Weston* [1971] 3 All ER 581, which is discussed in **3.7.1**, is strong authority for the proposition that an agreement between the parties is necessary. You will find an extract from the judgment of Lord Denning MR in this case, in *Cases and Materials* (**2.2.1.3**). On the other hand, some judges are prepared to accept implied assumption of risk **without** the need for an 'agreement'.

In *Morris* v *Murray* [1990] 3 All ER 801, the plaintiff and the pilot of an aircraft had met in a pub and together consumed a **large** volume of alcohol. It was agreed after some hours of drinking that they would take a trip together in the aircraft.

As a result of the negligence of the drunken pilot, the aircraft crashed. The pilot was killed and the plaintiff was badly injured in the accident. The plaintiff brought an action for damages against the pilot's estate.

At first instance, the defendant's alternative plea of contributory negligence was accepted, the plaintiff's damages being reduced by 20 per cent, and the defence of voluntary assumption of risk was rejected.

The Court of Appeal, however, **reinstated** the plea of voluntary assumption of risk and the deceased pilot's estate escaped liability completely. Fox LJ, in delivering the judgment of the court, said that the drunken escapade

> was fraught with danger from the start. If the plaintiff had been sober at the time he must be taken to have accepted fully the risk of serious injury. The danger was both obvious and great . . . [he must have known] that the deceased . . . was [not] capable of discharging a normal duty of care.

Although the plaintiff had himself been drinking 'he was certainly not "blind drunk" and was capable of appreciating the risks involved in what was merely a form of "entertainment".' According to his Lordship this flight served no useful social purpose and there was no need or compulsion for the plaintiff to join in. By embarking upon the flight the plaintiff implicitly waived his rights in the event of injury consequent on the deceased's failure to fly with reasonable care. He accepted the risks and implicitly discharged the deceased from liability.

The possibility of a plaintiff being able to plead that drunkenness prevented him from 'consenting' was left open, though it may be doubted if a court would accept such a plea.

In rejecting the possibility of contributory negligence, on the facts, his Lordship said that the wild irresponsibility of the venture was such that the law should not intervene to award damages. Flying with a drunken pilot was great folly. He pointed out that the defence of voluntary assumption of risk had been abrogated by statute in relation to passengers in motor vehicles covered by insurance, although there did not exist any similar enactment relating to aircraft and therefore applicable to the present case.

The Court of Appeal in *Morris* did not, it is obvious, see any merit at all in the plaintiff's claim, and was loath to allow the defence of contributory negligence, because to do so would have given the plaintiff **some** compensation.

According to Fox LJ, the plaintiff had implicitly waived his rights by 'embarking upon the flight', which means in legal terms, that he had thereby abandoned his legal remedy against the defendant. A crucial issue in *Morris* was the fact that the deceased pilot was very drunk indeed and incapable of performing the complex task of piloting an aircraft, and that the plaintiff must have been well aware of this state of affairs.

If this is a correct line of reasoning, it would seem to follow that it might only be **contributory negligence** on the part of the plaintiff to take a trip in an aircraft piloted by someone who was only **slightly** under the influence of alcohol. On this basis, the distinction to be made in such situations would be between **degrees** of foolhardiness on the part of a plaintiff: the greater the state of intoxication of the pilot, the greater the risk the plaintiff would be taking with his safety.

Morris seems to suggest that there comes a point at which the plaintiff must have abandoned all thought of self-preservation; or at least is being recklessly indifferent to the matter. At this juncture voluntary assumption of risk is appropriate as a defence.

With respect, it must be dangerous to fly with someone who is subject to **any** degree of intoxication; no doubt, the greater the state of drunkenness the greater the danger of an accident. In which case, the defence of **contributory negligence**, to be discussed shortly, offers the court a means of judging the degree of a plaintiff's lack of care for his own safety.

The true situation in *Morris* is that the court did not want to award the plaintiff any compensation at all, on the ground that he had, in the circumstances, taken an **unreasonable risk** with his own safety. Unfortunately that is also the basis of the defence of contributory negligence, as we will soon discover, and it may be argued that the decision in *Morris* does little to clarify the distinction between the two defences.

A court cannot, however, according to the decision in *Pitts* v *Hunt* (see **2.3.2.1**) find a plaintiff to be 100 per cent to blame under the legislation governing the defence of contributory negligence.

There is another reason for the dilemma in which the Court of Appeal found itself in *Morris*. Can you guess what it might be?

Contributory negligence applies where the plaintiff is **partly** to blame, **with the defendant**, for his own injury. In *Morris*, although there was no doubt that the plaintiff had been extremely careless for his own safety, it could not be said that the defendant was not also to blame. In fact, in this case, both parties were *in pari delicto*, i.e. equally to blame. They were engaged, jointly, in a grossly hazardous activity.

Do you think that the court would feel justified, if the defence of contributory negligence was applied, in finding that the plaintiff in this case was more to blame for his injury than the defendant? Probably not, hence the recourse to voluntary assumption of risk. In a case like this the court's power to **reduce** the plaintiff's damages for contributory negligence is very limited.

It is submitted, however, that to define voluntary assumption of risk in such a way is to turn it into a blunt instrument of policy and to sever any link it has with the idea of consent. The defence, in this way, becomes very like the defence of illegality (see **2.3.2**) which is a true creature of judicial policy.

The court in *Morris* side-stepped the 1945 legislation which applies where the plaintiff and the defendant are each partly responsible for the plaintiff's injury. The Law Reform (Contributory Negligence) Act 1945 is discussed at **2.3.4**. *Morris* is not, however, the only case in which a court has expressed willingness to consider the use of voluntary assumption of risk as an instrument of policy to block completely the attempt of a 'willing' plaintiff to obtain compensation.

In *Kirkham* v *Chief Constable of Greater Manchester* [1990] 3 All ER 246 (see also **Chapter 4**) the Court of Appeal accepted an argument that voluntary assumption of risk might have been available as a defence, had the deceased not been suffering from mental illness at the time of his injury. The deceased had hanged himself whilst in custody, and his estate sued the police for negligence, i.e. for failing to inform the prison authorities of the deceased's suicidal tendencies, contrary to official procedure.

In *Kirkham* there did not exist even the **possibility** of an **implied** agreement, which *Winfield* (p. 731) argues ought to be enough for the defence to operate, thus the view that the availability of voluntary assumption of risk is based on an 'agreement' between the parties is by no means accepted universally.

The court in *Kirkham* contemplated the possibility of a plea of *volenti non fit injuria* where a person of **sound** mind should commit suicide, or be injured in the attempt. As Lloyd LJ put it:

I deal first with *volenti non fit injuria*. Where a man of sound mind injures himself in an unsuccessful suicide attempt, it is difficult to see why he should not be met by a plea of *volenti non fit injuria*. He has not only courted the risk of injury by another; he has inflicted the injury himself. In *Hyde* v *Tameside Area Health Authority, The Times*, 16 April 1981 the plaintiff, who had made an unsuccessful suicide attempt, brought an action for damages against the health authority alleging negligence on the part of the hospital staff. Lord Denning MR doubted whether a defence of *volenti non fit injuria* would be available in such a case seeing that '[the plaintiff] did not willingly injure himself. He wanted to die.' I find that reasoning hard to follow. Any observation of Lord Denning MR is, of course, entitled to great weight; but the observation was *obiter*, since the court held that the hospital staff had not been negligent. Moreover we were told by counsel for the plaintiff, who happened to have appeared for the plaintiff in that case, as well, that the point was never argued.

So I would be inclined to hold that where a man of sound mind commits suicide, his estate would be unable to maintain an action against the hospital or prison authorities, as the case might be. *Volenti non fit injuria* would provide them with a complete defence. There should be no distinction between a successful attempt and an unsuccessful attempt at suicide. Nor should there be any distinction between an action for the benefit of the estate under the Law Reform Act and an action for the benefit of dependants under the Fatal Accidents Act. In so far as Pilcher J drew a distinction between the two types of action in *Pigney* v *Pointer's Transport Services Ltd* [1957] 2 All ER 807, [1957] 1 WLR 1121, I would respectfully disagree.

But in the present case Mr Kirkham was not of sound mind. True, he was sane in the legal sense. His suicide was a deliberate and conscious act. But Dr Sayed, whose evidence the judge accepted, said that Mr Kirkham was suffering from clinical depression. His judgment was impaired. If it had been a case of murder, he would have had a defence of diminished responsibility due to disease of the mind.

I have had some doubt on this aspect of the case in the light of Dr Sayed's further evidence that, though his judgment was impaired, Mr Kirkham knew what he was doing. But in the end I have been persuaded by counsel for the plaintiff that, even so, he was not truly *volens*. Having regard to his mental state, he cannot, by his act, be said to have waived or abandoned any claim arising out of his suicide. So I would reject the defence of *volenti non fit injuria*.

It may be observed that even a **sane** person cannot be in full control of his faculties at the time of the suicide or attempted suicide, and therefore cannot be truly *volens*. In any event, it might be preferable to block a claim for damages in these cases simply on the basis that the plaintiff caused his own injury.

You will find a discussion on 'causation' in **Chapter 4**. However, while this approach may offer a solution in **some** cases involving suicide, it hardly offers a convincing explanation for finding against the plaintiff where the defendant is under a duty to prevent the plaintiff's act in the first place.

There is in **general**, as you will discover in **Chapter 3**, no duty of care in negligence placed upon anyone to prevent harm to others, least of all in those circumstances in which the harm is self-inflicted. Suicide, as one form of self-inflicted harm, is, after all, in literal terms self-murder; therefore the circumstances in which someone, or some organisation, will owe a duty to take steps to prevent such behaviour will have to be rather special.

The circumstances in *Kirkham* were of a special kind, there was very close proximity between the parties and **official procedures** recognised the potential dangers inherent in those circumstances. Suicide committed in prison is a known risk of which the authorities are well aware. In this regard, a mentally unstable prisoner with known suicidal tendencies is a greater risk than the allegedly 'sane' prisoner with the same tendencies.

It may be the case that where a prisoner is not mentally ill there is simply nothing of an external nature to put the authorities on their guard. The circumstances may well be different, however, where a 'sane' prisoner has in the past exhibited suicidal tendencies; there must surely be a duty on the part of the authorities to take appropriate action on those facts.

In *Kirkham* the defendant was in **close** supervision of the potential suicide, and it is arguable in common sense terms that **anyone** who is contemplating suicide is probably in an unbalanced state of mind at the time, even if they are clinically 'sane'. It must, therefore, be very difficult, if not impossible, to distinguish between suicides or attempted suicides according to the state of mind of the actors.

If a duty is imposed, it is discharged (see **Chapter 3**) by the exercise of **reasonable** care in the circumstances of the case; in other words, the plaintiff will have to show that the defendant was **negligent** on the facts. As you will discover, the courts are allowed a considerable measure of discretion in fixing the standard of care. In the case of suicide, or attempted suicide, committed in custody it will be a matter of 'the greater the risk the greater the care needed', and the degree of care required will, no doubt, be assessed in terms of the individual prisoner's circumstances.

According to the Annual Report of the Police Complaints Authority for 1994–95, the PCA supervised investigations into 48 deaths in custody during 1994–5, compared with 27 in 1993. There were 25 deaths in police stations, of which 15 were by hanging, and the Authority expressed particular concern at the design of prison cells, because many prisoners apparently hanged themselves from the open hatch in the cell door. In 1997 there were 70 suicides in prison.

Even if there **is** a duty, **and** that duty has been breached, it is still incumbent on the plaintiff (or his estate or dependants where death results) to prove **cause** and **effect**. In some circumstances, it may well be impossible for the plaintiff to convince the court that the most reasonable of precautions, if taken by the defendant, would have prevented the suicide or attempted suicide: *a fortiori* in the case of the 'sane' plaintiff. In **that** case, the court is free to conclude that the deceased or injured plaintiff was wholly responsible for his own injury.

The defence of contributory negligence arising under the 1945 Act (see **2.3.4**) may also be available in appropriate circumstances.

It is suggested, with respect, that the approach of Farquharson LJ is to be preferred, though even here a distinction is made between the 'sane' and the 'insane' suicide. His Lordship said:

> Dr Sayed, who gave evidence for the plaintiff at the trial and was well acquainted with Mr Kirkham's medical history, agreed under cross-examination that Mr Kirkham's suicide was a conscious and deliberate act. In those circumstances it is argued that the defendant could rely on the maxim *volenti non fit injuria*. In one sense there can be no better evidence of Mr Kirkham being *volens* than the fact that he died by his own hand. In my judgment this defence fails on two grounds. It is clear that Mr Kirkham was disturbed at the time of his death: quite apart from his recent medical history there was his behaviour at home immediately before his arrest, and his shouting at the magistrates in court, when they remanded him in custody to Risley, that if he was sent there he would never come back. Dr Sayed gave evidence that Mr Kirkham was, at the time of his death, suffering from clinical depression. I have already cited his opinion that Mr Kirkham was desperate and wanted to do away with himself. In the light of those facts and that evidence, it seems to me quite unrealistic to suggest that Mr Kirkham was truly *volens*. His state of mind was such that, through disease, he was incapable of coming to a balanced decision even if his act of suicide was deliberate. The second ground is that the defence is inappropriate where the act of the deceased relied on is the very act which the duty cast on the defendant required him to prevent.

If in such circumstances the defendant could raise this defence, as counsel for the plaintiff submits, no action would ever lie in respect of a suicide or attempted suicide where a duty of care could be proved.

The Court of Appeal was given a further opportunity to consider these issues in *Reeves* v *Commissioner of Police for the Metropolis, The Times*, 20 November 1997. In this case an action in negligence was brought by the **estate** of a man who had committed suicide whilst in police custody.

At first instance, it was found that the relevant police officers owed a duty of care to the deceased because they were aware that he was a suicide risk. Furthermore, these officers were found to have been negligent on the facts, i.e. they were in breach of their duty of care. It was held, however, that there was no liability in negligence because the defences of contributory negligence, *novus actus interveniens* and *volenti non fit injuria* were available to the defendants. Apparently, the court was also willing to accept a plea of *ex turpi causa non oritur actio* from the defendants but it was not found necessary to pursue this point.

By a majority, the Court of Appeal followed the reasoning of Farquarson LJ in *Kirkham* (above) and held that these defences did not apply at all in the circumstances. Buxton LJ was of the opinion that no distinction should be made between 'sane' and 'insane' detainees for present purposes; indeed, the judge at first instance had not proceeded on that basis and so was unable to apply the defences of *volenti*, etc., against the plaintiff since the deceased had carried out the very act that the defendants were under a duty to prevent in the first place.

Lord Bingham CJ, however, disagreed with Buxton LJ on the applicability of contributory negligence. His Lordship was of the opinion that the Law Reform (Contributory Negligence) Act 1945 was wide enough to cover such cases as the present one, in order that a court could use its discretion to reduce any damages awarded in proportion to the deceased's share of responsibility. In the instant case, his Lordship said had he been sitting on his own (i.e. had he been the sole judge in the case) he would have reduced the plaintiff's damages by 50 per cent.

In his dissenting judgment, Merritt LJ agreed with the majority decision **only** on the issue of *ex turpi causa non oritur actio*. His Lordship was of the opinion that the other defences operated to defeat the plaintiff.

He agreed, in particular, with the finding of the trial judge that the deceased was contributorily negligent to the order of 100 per cent. (On the issue of 100 per cent contributory negligence, see **2.3.4.2** below).

As *Jones* says (p. 391): 'The very notion of implied consent represents a policy decision about the types of conduct that should defeat a claim in tort.'

Standard of care

Obfuscation is created in some cases of negligence where the courts are in fact setting appropriate standards of care, but the language of *volenti* is used to justify the decisions.

These decisions concern mainly injuries sustained by spectators and competitors at sporting and similar events. It is evident that spectators and competitors attending and participating in such events run the risk of injury; the more dangerous the event, the more likely the injury, or the likelihood of serious injury.

It could hardly be the case that injured parties in such circumstances would be able to claim compensation from either the competitors or the organisers of the events. If, however, the injuries sustained were caused by the **tortious** behaviour of such persons, the question of compensation and, therefore, **defences** would arise. Defences presuppose tortious behaviour or behaviour that would **otherwise** be tortious but for the existence of a defence. We have seen that *volenti* can operate in both ways, i.e. to negate the effect of a breach of duty or to prevent the duty arising in the first place.

The problem in the present context is that judges often talk of a plaintiff's willing acceptance of the risk **inherent** in some dangerous event or competition. With respect, if these risks are not the result of **tortious** behaviour it is pointless to express any exemption from liability in terms of 'acceptance'.

A tennis ball or soccer ball hit into the crowd, quite accidentally, during the normal course of play is not connected with any tort, so what is the point of claiming that the spectators take the risk of injury in such a case? A similar point has been adduced, earlier in this chapter, in relation to road accidents.

The following statement, by Sellers LJ in *Wooldridge* v *Sumner* [1963] 2 QB 43, is typical of this approach: 'There would, I think, be a difference, for instance, in assessing blame which is actionable between an injury caused by a tennis ball hit or a racket **accidentally** [*emphasis added*] thrown in the course of play into the spectators . . . and a ball hit or a racket thrown into the stands in temper or annoyance when play was not in progress.'.

In similar vein is the observation of Diplock LJ in the same case: 'A person attending a game or competition takes the risk of any damage caused to him by any act of a participant done in the course of and for the purposes of the game or competition notwithstanding that such an act may involve an error of judgment or a lapse of skill, unless the participant's conduct is such as to evince a reckless disregard for the spectator's safety.'.

By 'reckless disregard' his Lordship must have meant 'negligence'. You will see in **Chapter 3** that negligence is not based on recklessness, but if his Lordship meant trespass to the person, discussed in **Chapter 9**, which can be committed recklessly, he would merely be saying that a participant in the event could be liable in trespass in such circumstances. Since the action of the plaintiff was pursued in the tort of negligence, his Lordship must have had that form of liability in mind. This case has been interpreted as laying down a 'heat of the moment' standard of care for **competitors**, lower than might otherwise be expected.

In *Wooldridge* the plaintiff was a photographer at a horse show. He was taking some close-up photographs at a horse-jumping event, when he was struck by a horse ridden by the defendant, who had, according to the plaintiff, been negligent in the handling of his steed. It was found that the defendant had not, in fact, been negligent, because he had kept within the rules of the competition and had observed the standard of care appropriate to a competitor in such an event.

The Court of Appeal in *Wilks* v *Cheltenham Home Guard Motor Cycle and Light Car Club* [1971] 2 All ER 369, did not adopt an acceptance of risk approach but proceeded on the basis simply of what would be an appropriate standard of care for a competitor going all out to win. The event in question was a motor cycle scramble, and a spectator, the plaintiff, was injured when one of the cycles got out of control. An action was brought in negligence against the organisers of the event and the motor cycle rider who had lost control. The trial judge found that the organisers had fenced the track perfectly adequately and had not been negligent, but he found **against** the second defendant, the competitor. The finding **for** the first defendant, the organisers, was not challenged, but the second defendant appealed and the Court of Appeal had to consider the question of his liability.

The court found that a competitor going all out to win in such a competition could not be expected to observe the standard of care of a careful, prudent driver of an ordinary vehicle in use on the public highway. In the circumstances, the defendant had observed the standard of care expected of him, within the rules of the event, and had not been negligent. It is interesting to note that whilst Lord Denning MR preferred to apply the 'reckless disregard' test from *Wooldridge*, Edmund Davies and Phillimore LJJ adopted a simpler 'negligence' approach, albeit adapted to the circumstances of the case. For their Lordships it was merely a question of whether this competitor had observed the standard of care expected of him in the circumstances.

These cases involve the duty of care, in negligence, owed by a competitor to a spectator. In *Harrison* v *Vincent* [1982] RTR 8, discussed in **3.7.1**, the plaintiff was a fellow participant of the defendant in the event, which was a race for motor cycles with sidecars. The 'normal' negligence standard was said to be applicable to the **maintenance** of the vehicle, for which the defendant was responsible, but the 'reckless disregard' test was found to be appropriate to the **riding** of the machine.

The approach of Edmund Davies and Phillimore LJJ in *Wilks* (above) is preferable to this 'dual standard' analysis. It is difficult to see what 'reckless disregard' adds to the standard of care in negligence; it suggests merely that the court must adjust the standard according to the circumstances of the case. Standard of care in the tort of negligence is discussed in **Chapter 3**.

In *Condon* v *Basi* [1985] 2 All ER 453, discussed in **3.7.1**, the question of liability in negligence between competitors was also relevant, and you may wish to refer to that decision at this stage. Sir John Donaldson MR observed, in that case:

> I have cited from those two judgments [from the Australian case of *Rootes* v *Shelton* [1968] ALR 33] because they show two different approaches which, as I see it, produce precisely the same result. One is to take a more generalised duty of care and modify it on the basis that the participants in the sport or pastime impliedly consent to taking risks which would otherwise be a breach of the duty of care . . . [the other approach suggests that the general *Donoghue* v *Stevenson* (discussed in **Chapter 3**) standard of care applies, adapted to the circumstances] . . .

His Lordship preferred the latter approach, but went on to say

> . . . I do not think it makes the slightest difference in the end if it is found . . . that the defendant failed to exercise that degree of care which was appropriate in all the circumstances, or that he acted in a way to which the plaintiff cannot be expected to have consented. In either event, there is liability.

With all respect, the end does not always justify the means and the ordinary standard of care approach is much simpler than the implied consent approach. We have so far considered cases in which spectators have sued competitors, and competitors have sued fellow competitors, but the *volenti* approach has also been taken in cases where spectators have sued the **organisers** of the event.

Thus, for example, in *Murray* v *Haringey Arena Ltd* [1951] 2 KB 529, the plaintiff was six years old and a spectator at an ice hockey match held on the defendant's premises. He was injured when a puck was hit into the crowd. His claim for damages failed, and it was said to be because the organisers were not liable for risks ordinarily incidental to the game since spectators willingly accepted those risks. This decision must really be based on the fact that there was simply no negligence behind the incident, because it is hardly satisfactory to assert that such a young plaintiff had waived his legal right to sue.

As *Jones* says (p. 393):

> This is not an application of *volenti non fit injuria*. It is true that in a sport which necessarily involves some physical content the players can be taken impliedly to consent those contacts which occur within the ordinary performance of the game. But this consent negatives what would otherwise be a battery, it is not consent to negligence by other competitors. Similarly, spectators do not assume the risk of negligence simply by being present at the event.

In truth, the **consensual** relationship between the parties in these cases determines the relevant standard of care. In **this** sense, it may be said that the plaintiff's consent as a matter of policy can set the relevant standard of care, appropriate to the circumstances; though 'consent' can hardly explain the decision in *Murray* (above).

You will find the decision in *Phillips* v *Whiteley* [1938] 1 All ER 566 discussed in **3.7.1**. In this case the language of *volenti* was not employed, yet the plaintiff was only entitled to the standard of care expected of a **jeweller**, when piercing ears; she had consensually accepted a low standard of care. It could also be claimed, by analogy, that in *Morris* v *Murray* the plaintiff had accepted, and was only entitled to, the standard of care expected from a drunken pilot.

Ultimately, it is a question of policy whether consent determines the standard of care in any given set of circumstances.

Please note the following general points:

(a)   competitors may also sue the organisers of the event (see **Chapter 7**);

(b)   occupiers' liability may be relevant (see **Chapter 7**);

(c)   exclusion of liability by way of contract may be relevant in some cases;

(d)   the provisions of the Unfair Contract Terms Act 1977 may also be relevant.

We are now in a position to consider the remaining general features of *volenti non fit injuria*.

2.3.1.4   The consent or agreement must be real

It is a cardinal feature of the defence that mere knowledge of a risk or danger is itself not enough. Although knowledge is **evidence** of acceptance, a plaintiff must be shown to have waived his legal remedy. Section 2(3) of the Unfair Contract Terms Act 1977, says 'where a contract term or notice purports to exclude or restrict liability for negligence a person's agreement to or awareness of it is not of itself to be taken as indicating his voluntary acceptance of any risk'.

You will notice that the Act implicitly recognises a defence of *volenti* **separate** from exclusion of liability by contract. Please see the discussion above, and in **Chapter 7**.

Employment cases

The acceptance of risk must be voluntary, so it will very rarely succeed in an action by an employee against his employer because the economic reality is that few employees have any real choice.

In *Smith* v *Baker* [1891] AC 325, the plaintiff was a quarryman working below a crane carrying loads of stone, and in *Burnett* v *British Waterways Board* [1973] 1 WLR 700, he was a lighterman working a barge, with knowledge of a notice purporting to exclude the defendant from liability for injuries. The plea of *volenti* failed in both cases, because the plaintiffs, who were employees of the defendants respectively, had no real choice in the matter. They had to accept their working conditions.

A plea of *volenti* by an employer was successful in *ICI* v *Shatwell* [1965] AC 656, but the circumstances in that case were somewhat exceptional. You can read about the decision in **Chapter 8**.

It may be possible for an employer to use *volenti* where an employee has **specifically** agreed to undertake a particular task, fraught with danger, for extra payment, so-called 'danger money'. Consent would, however, as in **all** cases of *volenti* have to be **specific**; consent must relate to the risk or danger which occurs and not to some interference of a general nature.

This is especially so where consent precedes an act of negligence, because it cannot always be certain what form the negligence will take. As Diplock LJ said in *Wooldridge* (above) the relevant consent 'is not consent to the risk of injury but consent to the lack of reasonable care that may produce that risk . . . [and] the plaintiff at the time [he gave his consent must have] full knowledge of the nature and extent of the risk that he ran.'.

His Lordship went on to say that even if a danger, created by the defendant, was in existence at the time the plaintiffs decided to run the risk (having full knowledge of the risk) the court would still enquire whether it was reasonably foreseeable by the defendant whether the plaintiff 'would so act in relation to [the danger] as to endanger himself'.

SAQ 18

Do you think that the test of knowledge of the danger, and its nature and extent, is subjective or objective?

The test is subjective, i.e. what the plaintiff actually knew, **not** objective, i.e. what he ought reasonably to have known.

It follows that the plaintiff must be **capable** of understanding the nature and extent of the risk in question. The decision in *Kirkham* (above) illustrates this point; and drunkenness was no excuse for the plaintiff in *Morris* (above).

If a plaintiff **ought** to have known of a danger, the appropriate defence is **contributory negligence**.

Duress or fraud may vitiate consent where it affects the very nature of the interference to which the plaintiff has consented.

In *Hegarty* v *Shine* (1878) 4 LRIr 288, the plaintiff contracted venereal disease from her lover. It was held that there was no battery (trespass to the person) on the facts, because the **sexual intercourse** which had taken place was not obtained by deceit (fraud). The plaintiff knew full well the nature of the physical interference; she had not been deceived as to the nature of the act itself. The defendant's false statement that he did not have the disease did not affect the nature of the act of intercourse. Of course, had there been fraud she could have also sued in the tort of deceit. This Irish authority must be treated with caution on its facts, because the court based its decision partly on the **illegality** of the plaintiff's conduct; but it can still be used as authority to illustrate the basic point about the nature of consent.

Illegality is examined at **2.3.2**, and you can read about trespass to the person in **Chapter 9**.

There arises also the question of consent to an illegal act. Although in criminal law consent may be no bar to proceedings, as in *R* v *Brown* [1993] 2 WLR 556, in which the House of Lords held, by a majority, that participants in certain sado-masochistic practices could be criminally liable for their mutual infliction of harm, in spite of each person's willingness to undergo the physical abuse, it was held in *Murphy* v *Culhane* (see **2.2.4**) that consent can block a claim for damages in the civil law.

Rescue

Volenti has also been rejected in the so-called 'rescue cases'.

If, as a result of the pressures of the moment, whether these pressures be legal or moral, a person is injured in rescuing, or attempting to rescue, someone else who has been put in peril as the result of the defendant's wrongful behaviour, that injured person (the 'rescuer') has an **independent** cause of action in tort against the defendant. In short, if rescue is foreseeable in the circumstances, and danger invariably invites rescue, a duty of care is owed directly to the rescuer, i.e. the defendant's obligation to the rescuer is not based on any breach of duty to the person imperilled. It is not necessary that the person placed in danger should have been **hurt** or even that he was actually in danger, provided that the rescuer's conclusion that danger did exist was reasonable at the time of the emergency.

This duty **to** rescuers is firmly established in the law, although there is no **general** legal obligation upon anyone to attempt a rescue.

ACTIVITY 4

Please consider the decision in *Videan* v *British Transport Commission* **[1963] 2 All ER 860**, in *Cases and Materials* **(2.2.1.4)**. What is the main point emerging from this case?

The decision emphasises the **independent** nature of the duty owed to the rescuer. It was held that the defendant was in breach of its duty to the plaintiff, who had rescued a person (a trespasser on the defendant's premises; for the duty owed by an occupier of premises to trespassers, see **Chapter 7**) to whom at that time the defendant did not owe any legal duty. It was enough that the **rescuer's** presence on the premises was foreseeable at the relevant time; indeed it was sufficient that **some** emergency was foreseeable in the circumstances, not necessarily the actual emergency which materialised.

Although a duty to rescuers had earlier been recognised in other jurisdictions, notably that of the USA, it was not until the decision of the Court of Appeal in *Haynes* v *Harwood* [1935] 1 KB 146, that such an obligation became firmly established in English law.

The court cited with approval the following opinion of Cardoza J expressed in *Wagner* v *International Railway Co.* (1921) 133 NE 437:

> Danger invites rescue. The cry of distress is the summons to relief. The law does not ignore those reactions of the mind in tracing conduct to its consequences. It recognises them as normal. It places their effects within the range of the natural and probable. The wrong that imperils life is a wrong to the imperilled victim; it is a wrong also to his rescuer.

In *Haynes*, a horse and cart took off along a busy street because the horse had been frightened as a result of a young boy thowing a stone; all this was put down to the defendant's negligence. The plaintiff, a policeman, was injured when he stopped the horse, so preventing injury to members of the public. He was awarded damages, as a rescuer, against the defendant.

Haynes v *Harwood* was followed in *Baker* v *Hopkins and Son Ltd* [1958] 3 All ER 147, in which a doctor went to the rescue of workmen endangered by their employer's negligence. The men were working at the bottom of an open shaft, and had been overcome by carbon monoxide fumes leading from a faulty compressor unit. Unknown to anyone at the time, the men were dead, but the doctor insisted on being lowered down the fume-filled shaft, secured only by a rope tied round his waist. No breathing apparatus was available, in fact firemen were waiting for it to arrive.

The doctor, like the men, succumbed to the fumes and his widow was awarded damages against the men's employer, the defendant, for breach of its duty to the doctor as a rescuer.

SAQ 19

Do you think that a person who places himself in danger may owe a duty to a foreseeable rescuer?

The answer is 'yes'. The point was discussed in *Baker* (above) and an **affirmative** opinion expressed in the Court of Appeal and at first instance; in *Harrison* v *British Railways Board* [1981] 3 All ER 679, it was applied to the facts.

ACTIVITY 5

Please read about *Harrison* in *Cases and Materials* (2.2.1.4). Can you write down two features of this case which are of importance in the present context?

Two important conclusions were drawn by the judge in this case:

   (a)   a person who puts **himself** in danger can be liable to his rescuer;

   (b)   a rescuer, the plaintiff in *Harrison*, can be met by the plea of **contributory negligence**.

It may be that a rescuer, who bungles the attempt, could make matters worse, in which case the rescuer might find himself sued by the rescuee. No doubt, on the basis of ordinary *Donoghue* v *Stevenson*, 'neighbour' principles (see **Chapter 3**), the rescuer could well owe a duty of care in negligence to the rescuee. The rescuee would then have to prove breach of duty, i.e. negligence on the facts. Presumably, the relevant standard of care would be that of the reasonable man attempting a rescue, perhaps in extremely hazardous conditions, therefore the standard expected **in the circumstances** would reflect the court's assessment of the merits of the rescuer's action. The courts are not keen to find against a rescuer.

'Standard of care' in negligence is discussed in **Chapter 3**.

The decision in *Horsley* v *MacLaren* ('*The Ogopogo*') [1971] 2 Lloyd's Rep 410 (Canada) can be found in *Cases and Materials* (**2.2.1.4**). It illustrates a number of important matters concerning the 'rescue relationship', including the point relating to a bungled rescue.

It is now established that:

(a) rescuers can claim damages for 'nervous shock'. You can read about *Chadwick* v *British Railways Board* and *Wigg* v *British Railways Board* in **Chapter 6**; at **6.3.2** and **6.3.4.3** respectively.

(b) 'professional rescuers' can claim damages in appropriate cases. You can read about *Ogwo* v *Taylor* in **Chapter 7**.

SAQ 20

Why do you think it relevant that the duty owed to rescuers should be discussed in the present context?

'Rescue' is dealt with here because rescuers are **volunteers**. There is no **general** duty to rescue, therefore it might be said that rescuers can be met with a plea of *volenti*. This has been rejected in genuine rescue cases, because rescuers are not acting 'freely'; they are acting under the compulsion of the moment. They are not, in that sense, free agents.

You may also be interested to learn that defendants have sometimes, for example see *Baker* v *Hopkins* (above), argued that *novus actus interveniens* (intervening act, coming between the defendant's wrong and the plaintiff's damage) applies in rescue cases, i.e. the rescuer's voluntary act causes his own damage. This argument can only be sustained where the rescuer's behaviour amounts, in the opinion of Willmer LJ in *Baker*, to a 'wanton disregard for his own safety'.

In *Harrison* v *British Transport Commission* (above) the finding of 20 per cent contributory negligence on the part of the rescuer was arrived at only very reluctantly, and the courts will be slow generally to accept criticism of a rescuer's behaviour from the person who created the emergency in the first place.

You can read about the decision in *Crossley* v *Rawlinson* [1981] 3 All ER 674 in **Chapter 4** at **4.5.1.2**.

It is true, however, that a 'rescuer' may not succeed at all where he intervenes after the danger has gone, because his conduct may be regarded as unreasonable in the circumstances. In *Cutler* v *United Dairies (London) Ltd* [1933] 2 KB 297, the plaintiff went into a field to calm the defendant's restive horse and was injured in so doing. The court accepted that he was a mere 'volunteer', because there was no real danger to person or property.

The duty to rescuers extends to those who attempt to, or actually save property and goods, whether they belong to himself or other persons. In *Hyatt* v *Great Western Railway Co.* [1948] 1 KB 345, the court said the ruling in *Haynes* (above) applied also to the rescue of property.

It may be, however, that a plaintiff/rescuer would not be justified in taking the same risks in relation to property that would be acceptable in 'saving' persons. Each case will, no doubt, be determined on its own facts.

A final point on 'rescue' concerns the essential nature of the duty itself. It is often dealt with in the context of the tort of negligence, and is expressed in terms of the defendant's 'negligence' towards the rescuer; it is considered as an example of duty of care in negligence. The leading cases do not, however, turn on an application of *Donoghue* v *Stevenson* and, whilst a defendant's negligence is often the reason for an emergency arising in the first place, the duty owed to the rescuer is, as we have seen, not dependent on any duty owed to the victim.

In view of the fact that a defendant may be liable to a rescuer where he places himself in danger, a would-be suicide attempt would probably attract rescue.

This is hardly the usual 'stuff' of **negligence** (see **Chapter 3**). The duty to rescuers, in fact, seems to be based on **simple** foreseeability of rescue in the circumstances: the defendant does not need to be 'at fault' beyond the requirement that 'danger invites rescue'.

2.3.2   ILLEGALITY

This general 'defence' is often expressed by reference to the Latin maxim *ex turpi causa non oritur actio*. In English, this means that an action in law cannot be founded on an illegal act.

2.3.2.1   Comparison with *volenti*

Illegality, like *volenti*, is a **complete** defence; i.e. if the defendant is successful in his plea the plaintiff gets **nothing** at all; **and** both defences are based very much on policy. Thus, success in either defence is very hard to predict, although *ex turpi causa* is probably the more difficult defence in that regard.

The two defences are, therefore, very close, as the following words of Fox LJ in *Morris* v *Murray* (see **2.3.1.3**) indicate (he was referring to *volenti*): 'It seems to me . . . that the wild irresponsibility of the venture is such that the law should not intervene to award damages and shall leave the loss where it falls.'.

The cases indicate, it is submitted, that these defences will be accepted whenever the court feels that the claim of the plaintiff is without merit, in spite of the defendant's clear culpability.

The rationale for 'illegality' is that the **plaintiff's** cause of action is tainted with crime or immorality or will excite public distaste or opprobrium, or is an 'affront to the public conscience' (see *Kirkham* v *Chief Constable of Greater Manchester* discussed at **2.3.1.3** and **Chapter 4**). It rests on the premise that the court should not provide a forum for legal action in the particular circumstances of the case. *Volenti*, on the other hand, is based on the plaintiff's **consent** to injury.

Nevertheless, the sentiment expressed by Fox LJ in *Morris* does seem to explain the reasoning behind the application of **both** defences in some cases. In any event, it could be argued that the parties in *Morris* were engaged in an illegal joint enterprise, they were *in pari delicto*. It must be illegal for an aircraft to be flown in the circumstances of that case. If a stranger to the venture, on the ground at the time, had been injured in the accident, would that person not have had a cause of action against **both** plaintiff and defendant in *Morris*?

Megaw LJ in *Nettleship* v *Weston* [1971] 2 QB 691 (see **3.7.1**) suggested that someone who went willingly on a journey with the drunken driver of a motor car could be regarded as *in pari delicto* with the driver, in terms of aiding and abetting the illegal behaviour, and could be met with a plea of *ex turpi causa* should he be injured in an accident caused by the driver's negligence. It would not be sufficient, however, **merely** to be present or carried in a vehicle driven by such a person, or to be in an unroadworthy vehicle or in a vehicle which was not taxed and/or uninsured.

Another leading case on *volenti*, *ICI* v *Shatwell* (discussed in **Chapter 8**) could also be explained on the basis of illegality. The brothers were obviously engaged in a joint, and deliberate, flouting of the law.

It must be stressed that illegality, as such, was not pleaded in either *Morris* or *ICI* and Megaw LJ was expressing an *obiter* opinion in *Nettleship*.

Please consider the decision in *Pitts* v *Hunt* [1990] 3 All ER 344, in *Cases and Materials* (2.2.2.1). Why was *volenti* not relevant in that case?

That defence was not relevant, because of the provision in s. 149 of the Road Traffic Act 1988 prohibiting exclusion of liability. According to the Court of Appeal that provision catches **implied** *volenti*, as well as agreements, etc. Thus, the defendant in *Pitts* had to have recourse to *ex turpi causa*, which is unaffected by the 1988 Act.

In the absence of a provision such as that contained in the Road Traffic Act 1988, the opinion of Fox LJ in *Morris* v *Murray* should leave us in no doubt that *volenti* could well have been applicable in *Pitts*.

You will observe that the reasons given by the Court of Appeal in *Pitts* for finding that *ex turpi causa* applied differed. Thus, Dillon LJ found that the plaintiff's action arose directly *ex turpi causa*; Balcombe LJ held that the courts cannot set a standard of care for the circumstances where the parties are engaged in a joint criminal enterprise; and Beldam LJ said that public policy prevented the plaintiff from receiving compensation.

2.3.2.2 Illegality

Authority on the subject is scanty and each case seems to be decided on its merits. This defence is based on public policy, i.e. the courts will not help a plaintiff where it would be 'an affront to the public conscience' (see Lloyd LJ in *Kirkham*) to do so and might encourage him or others to engage in illegal activities.

In *Ashton* v *Turner* [1981] QB 137, for example, two burglars were in a 'get away' car. The plaintiff was the passenger and was injured by the defendant's negligent driving.

The court refused to recognise a duty of care between participants in a crime, in relation to an act done in **connection** with the commission of that crime. This, said the court, was a matter of public policy.

Of course, the device of refusing to set a duty of care will only work where the tort of negligence is involved. In other cases, for example trespass to the person, *ex turpi causa* must be faced as a defence to a cause of action which has already formed. Again, where **negligence** is involved, some courts have said they will not set a **standard of care** for criminal activity, rather than set a lower standard. In *Pitts v Hunt* the court said it was 'impossible' to set such a standard, though that factor seems to have been a reason (or excuse?) for a **reluctance** to distinguish between **degrees** of illegality.

Factors taken into account in these cases are as follows, though none can be regarded as conclusive:

(a)   were the parties *in pari delicto*?

(b)   was the tort an integral part of the illegal activity?

(c)   in the opinion of Bingham LJ in *Saunders v Edwards* [1987] 2 All ER 651, the illegality must probably arise directly and not be **incidental** to what would otherwise be a genuine cause of action. His Lordship said he preferred to take a **pragmatic** approach to the solution of such problems;

(d)   current moral standards must play a part in some situations;

(e)   it may be relevant that a plaintiff has to rely on an illegal contract;

(f)   causation will be important (see **Chapter 4**) and matters of time and space will play their part.

Thus, if the illegality is totally unconnected with the tort it may be ignored. In *National Coal Board* v *England* [1954] AC 403, Lord Asquith said:

If A and B are proceeding to the premises which they intend burglariously to enter, and before they enter them B picks A's pocket and steals A's watch, I cannot prevail upon myself to believe that A could not sue in tort.

In general, the more serious the offence, and the stronger the causal link between the offence and the tort, the more likely it is that *ex turpi* will apply.

In *Saunders* v *Edwards* (above) the plaintiffs entered into a contract (lease) with the defendant which was designed to avoid stamp duty, i.e. to defraud the Inland Revenue. Afterwards, the plaintiffs sued the defendant in the **tort** of **deceit** (which is another name for fraud) when they found that the lease did not include a roof terrace which the defendant had promised would be part of the rented premises.

The Court of Appeal held that the plaintiffs were not barred from bringing an action in the **tort** of deceit by the *ex turpi* defence, because they did not have to rely on the illegal contract in order to prove their case in tort. The claim in deceit was an **independent** course of action, which merely incidentally materialised during an illegal transaction. The plaintiff's deceit on the Inland Revenue did not affect the deceit of the defendant. The moral culpability of the defendant greatly outweighed that of the plaintiffs. The court had to steer a middle course between aiding people seeking to pursue or enforce an illegal object, or agreement, and refusing assistance to a deserving plaintiff on the first indication of any unlawfulness.

It was held in *Marshall* v *Osmond* [1983] QB 1034, that police in pursuit of someone who has wrongly taken and driven away a vehicle do owe a duty of care in negligence to that person, but it is a duty to take such care as is appropriate in the circumstances. Thus, by analogy with sporting activities discussed above, in relation to *volenti*, the court will be able to adjust liability according to the facts of the case. In the *Nottingham Evening Post* of 29 March 1990, it was reported that a motor-cyclist injured in 'a high speed chase' had been awarded £13,500 damages against the police, although the plaintiff's damages had been reduced because of his contributory negligence. Reference should also be made to *Revill* v *Newbery* (see **Chapter 7**).

Of course, the reason for the court's reluctance to aid the plaintiff may not, as we have seen, be the involvement of a crime or 'offence'; illegality can, for example, be based on an 'affront to public conscience'.

2.3.3   NECESSITY

This general defence may be described as the deliberate or intentional commission of what might otherwise be **tortious** conduct, in order to avoid some greater evil, there being no reasonable alternative. However, its precise boundaries are unclear and there is some overlap with other defences such as defence of property and self-defence.

According to *Street* (p. 90), the difference between these defences '. . . is that self-defence or defence of property pre-supposes that the **plaintiff** is *prima facie* a wrongdoer: the defence of necessity contemplates the infliction of harm on an innocent plaintiff.'.

It is unlikely that necessity will provide a defence to actions for **negligence**, because the issue in such a case will simply be whether the person was negligent or not in the circumstances.

2.3.3.1   Protection of the realm

In the *Saltpetre case* (1606) 12 Rep 12, it was said that entry upon another's land by officers of the State in order to defend the realm, by the construction of earthworks, would be protected 'but after the danger is over, the trenches and bulwarks ought to be removed . . .'.

The extent to which this protects an **ordinary individual** seeking to utilise the defence, however, and whether the *status quo ante* (i.e. the state in which things were) should be restored, or compensation paid as of right is doubtful.

In *Rigby* v *Chief Constable of Northamptonshire* [1985] 2 All ER 985, the police in using CS gas to get a psychopath out of the plaintiff's premises set them on fire. It was found that necessity protected the police from the plaintiff's action in **trespass** (to land), but there was liability in **negligence** because the police conducted the operation without the support of adequate fire prevention facilities.

2.3.3.2   Protection of the person

In *Esso Petroleum Co. Ltd* v *Southport Corporation* [1956] AC 218, it was said that jettisoning goods or, as in this case, discharging oil (which polluted the corporation's beaches) from a ship which was in danger of sinking in order to save those on board could be justified by necessity. The action in trespass to land failed.

Again, in *Leigh* v *Gladstone* (1909) 26 TLR 139, it was held that necessity justified the forcible feeding of the plaintiff, a suffragette who was on hunger strike in prison. The plaintiff's action in trespass to the person (battery) failed.

2.3.3.3   Protection of property

In principle, necessity is available in this context, but it is not so readily acceptable as in protection of the person. In *Cope* v *Sharp (No. 2)* [1912] 1 KB 496, the defendant was held not liable for having set fire to the plaintiff's land in the reasonable, though mistaken, belief that it was the only way to prevent a larger fire from destroying the defendant's employer's pheasant shoot. He had acted reasonably **at the time**, although it later transpired that the fire would not have spread.

In the earlier case of *Kirk* v *Gregory* (1876) 1 Ex D 55, however, the defendant removed a deceased person's valuables 'against the remote chance' that they might be stolen by servants who were having a 'jubilant feast', and his plea of necessity failed. It was also held by the Court of Appeal in *Southwark London Borough Council* v *Williams* [1971] Ch 734, that the defence could not be used as a 'mask for anarchy' by homeless squatters who were defending an action in trespass to land for occupying unoccupied council premises.

In this form of defence, i.e. protection of property, it is arguable that compensation might be sought, for the effects of an act of necessity, on quasi-contractual grounds: *Winfield* (pp. 753–4).

In all cases of necessity there must be no reasonable alternative open to the defendant. Thus, it was said in *Esso* v *Southport* (above) that if he brought about the need for intervention by his own negligence, his plea must fail. There must **be** a danger (or what seems to be one in the perception of the reasonable man) **and** the action taken must be reasonable in the circumstances.

In *R* v *Bournewood Community and Mental Health NHS Trust, ex parte L* [1998] 3 All ER 289, (this was a **judicial review** case) the applicant, L, who was autistic, could not speak and needed 24-hour care. It was clear that he could neither consent to nor refuse medical treatment. During one of his weekly visits to a day centre he became disturbed and, in the absence of his carers, was admitted informally into hospital without time limit. The question of the lawfulness of his detention came to be considered by the Court of Appeal and the hospital authorities pleaded necessity, on the basis that treatment was in L's best interests.

It was held that the only legal justification for detaining L was to be found in s. 131 of the Mental Health Act 1983, which allows informal admission and treatment with a patient's consent. Since L lacked the capacity to consent it followed that his detention amounted to false imprisonment in the circumstances, and the common law defence of necessity could not be used to justify this. (False imprisonment is a form of **trespass to the person** and is dealt with in **Chapter 9**.)

The House of Lords, however, reversed the decision of the Court of Appeal. It was held that the common law principle of necessity had **not** been displaced by the 1983 Act. A mentally disordered person without any capacity to consent **could** be admitted under s. 131 of the Act, and necessity provided the justification for this admission. Necessity, where proved, would justify actions which would otherwise be tortious.

2.3.4   CONTRIBUTORY NEGLIGENCE

The burden of proof is on the defendant to show that the plaintiff did not take reasonable care of himself and contributed, by this want of care, to his own injury. This defence has no relevance to claims between **co-defendants**; these claims are governed by the provisions of the Civil Liability (Contributions) Act 1978, which have been discussed in **Chapter 1**.

According to *Fookes* v *Slaytor* [1979] 1 All ER 137, the defendant must specifically plead the defence.

An issue of contributory negligence is, in essence, an issue of **fact**, to be determined according to the circumstances of the case. Damages are **apportioned** according to the degrees of fault of the **plaintiff** and **defendant**.

The law is laid down in the Law Reform (Contributory Negligence) Act 1945, as interpreted in the cases. The Act is set out in *Cases and Materials* (**2.2.3**).

The rules, according to s. 4 of the Act, are not confined to the tort of negligence. In s. 4, 'fault' is defined as : 'negligence, breach of statutory duty or other act or omission which gives rise to a liability in tort, or would, apart from this Act, give rise to the defence of contributory negligence'.

In *Murphy* v *Culhane* (see **2.2.4**) it was held that the defendant could plead this defence to a claim made in trespass to the person, which is a form of liability based on *intentional* interference.

You can read about the interesting case of *Corporacion Nacional Del Cobre De Chile* v *Sogemin Metals Ltd* [1997] 2 All ER 917 in *Cases and Materials* (**2.2.3**).

In *Gran Gelato Ltd* v *Richcliff (Group) Ltd* [1992] 1 All ER 865, the Court of Appeal held that the 1945 Act applied where there was **concurrent** liability in contract and tort on the part of the defendant, though the duty in tort had to be identical with the contractual obligation.

2.3.4.1 Apportionment

Section 1(1) of the Law Reform (Contributory Negligence) Act 1945 provides that:

> Where any person suffers damage as the result partly of his own fault and partly of the fault of any other person or persons, a claim in respect of that damage shall not be defeated by reason of the fault of the person suffering the damage, but the damages recoverable in respect thereof shall be reduced to such extent as the court thinks just and equitable having regard to the claimant's share in responsibility for the damage.

At common law, before 1945, contributory negligence was a **complete** defence.

The court is given a **discretion** by the Act to do what is 'just and equitable' in the circumstances of the case. The courts have not laid down rigid rules on this matter: they do not want to fetter their discretion unduly. Thus, there is no single principle governing apportionment in these cases.

In *Capps* v *Miller* [1989] 2 All ER 333, a motorcyclist, injured in a collision caused by the defendant's negligence, was wearing a crash helmet at the time of the accident, but he had not fastened the chin strap properly. It seems that had his helmet stayed on, the extent of his injuries would probably have been some 'incalculable degree less'. The trial judge found against contributory negligence because of the defendant's 'gross' negligence, and the fact that the plaintiff's responsibility was less than 10 per cent.

The Court of Appeal held that the plaintiff's carelessness **should** be taken into account, bearing in mind that he had committed a criminal offence, and breach of statutory duty, in failing to secure his helmet. Accordingly, the Court of Appeal ordered a 10 per cent reduction in his damages.

2.3.4.2 Plaintiff's contribution

It is essential that the plaintiff **and** the defendant have contributed to the former's injury; both parties must be to blame. This is essentially a matter of establishing that the plaintiff's conduct had causative potency: you may wish to refer to **Chapter 4**, which deals with the general issue of 'causation'.

In *Stapley* v *Gypsum Mines Ltd* [1953] AC 663, a foreman instructed Stapley and another coal miner, X, to make the roof of a mine safe. They could not do so but agreed to carry on working. The roof collapsed on Stapley, killing him. The House of Lords had to decide whether the accident was solely Stapley's fault, or partly X's fault.

It was held that the court must discriminate between those faults which are too remote and those which are not. One test was whether there was 'sufficient separation of time, place or circumstances' between the respective negligence, in which case it was **not** contributory negligence, or whether X's fault was 'so much mixed up with the state of things brought about by Stapley that, on a common sense view, it must be regarded as having contributed to the accident.'. These words are taken from Lord Reid's speech. In this case it was found that X's negligence **had** contributed to the accident, but the damages would be reduced by 80 per cent because of Stapley's negligence.

Apportionment under the 1945 Act is not automatic. On grounds of legal causation, the court may find a plaintiff to be **wholly** at fault and that he must therefore himself bear the **whole** loss. Indeed there has been much debate about whether a plaintiff can be found 100 per cent to blame under the 1945 Act. The balance of opinion is probably against this view, and it does not seem to accord with the wording of the Act, which speaks in terms of apportionment of blame between the parties.

In *Pitts* v *Hunt* (see **Activity 6**) Beldam and Dillon LJJ expressed the opinion that there should be an apportionment of 50 per cent contributory negligence in the case of a joint illegal enterprise. It was said that the provisions of the 1945 Act apply only where the plaintiff is **partly** to blame, and that a finding of 100 per cent contributory negligence would not be appropriate.

In *Froom* v *Butcher* [1976] 1 QB 286 the Court of Appeal considered the consequences of a failure to wear a seat belt in a motor vehicle. The defendant's negligence was the **sole** cause of an accident involving the plaintiff's car, and the plaintiff suffered injuries which would have been avoided had he worn a seat belt, whilst an injury to his finger would have occurred even if he had been wearing a seat belt.

It was held that, apart from cases where injury would not be eliminated by the wearing of a belt, and cases where wearing a belt might be dangerous in itself, for example, where an occupant of a vehicle was pregnant or obese, damages for injuries to the occupants of seats in the front of cars should be reduced, where no seat belt was worn though one was provided. The reduction should be 25 per cent where a seat belt would have prevented the injury, and 15 per cent where it would have reduced the severity of the injury. Reversing the decision of Nield J, at first instance, the Court of Appeal reduced the plaintiff's overall damages by 20 per cent.

It was emphasised by the court that the plaintiff need not have contributed to the accident; it was enough that he had contributed to the damage caused by the accident. As Lord Denning MR said: 'The accident is caused by the bad driving. The damage is caused in part by the bad driving of the defendant, and in part by the failure of the plaintiff to wear a seat belt.'.

In *Condon* v *Condon* [1977] RTR 483, it was held that where the plaintiff suffered from a phobia of being shut in, this was a sufficient reason for not wearing a seat belt.

It may be noted that since 1973 statutory regulations have provided that protective headgear must be used when riding motorcyles and, since 1981, it has been compulsory to use seat belts in the front seats of cars. Special provisions concerning seat belts relate to children under fourteen, and there are some exemptions relating to the use of headgear and seat belts. The use of seat belts in the rear seats of cars has, since 1989, also been compulsory in certain circumstances.

Observance or non-observance of these regulations by a plaintiff would be evidence for or against the existence of contributory negligence, as the case may be.

In *Clifford* v *Drymond* [1976] RTR 134, the Court of Appeal made a 20 per cent reduction in the plaintiff's damages where, in contravention of Rule 13 of the Highway Code, he used a zebra crossing in such a way that he was struck by a car.

In *Gregory* v *Kelly* [1978] RTR 426, the plaintiff's damages were reduced by 40 per cent, for not wearing his seat belt and knowing, from the start of the journey, that the foot brake in the vehicle was inoperative.

There are a number of cases in which plaintiffs have had their damages reduced for contributory negligence in accepting lifts from drunken motorists.

In *Owens* v *Brimmell* [1977] QB 859, for example, the plaintiff and the defendant went on a 'pub crawl' and got drunk. The defendant drove the plaintiff home and crashed the car. The plaintiff's damages were not reduced for his failure to wear a seat belt, because the defendant could not prove that such failure had made any difference to his injuries, but a reduction of 20 per cent was made for his contributory negligence in riding with a drunken driver.

Conduct which in the case of an adult would be regarded as contributory negligence is not necessarily so regarded when committed by a child. The test of competence, partially subjective, is 'did the child conform to the normal standard expected from his age group?'.

According to Salmon LJ in *Gough* v *Thorne* [1966] 1 WLR 1387, the child should be: 'not a paragon of prudence, nor a scatterbrained child'. In this case, a girl aged 13 was found not to be contributorily negligent in crossing the road without looking, when signalled to do so by a lorry driver unaware that he was being overtaken. The same reasoning was applied in *Jones* v *Lawrence* [1969] 3 All ER 267, to a boy aged seven, who ran out into the road without looking and was hit by a motor cyclist travelling at 50 mph in a 30 mph zone. In *Minter* v *D & H Contractors, The Times*, 30 June 1983, the defence was applied to a boy aged nine, when riding his bicycle in a busy street.

On the authority of *Oliver* v *Birmingham and Midland Motor Omnibus Co. Ltd* [1933] 1 KB 35, a child, an aged or infirm person, is not prejudiced by being 'identified' with the negligence of the person in whose charge he happens to be at the time of the defendant's negligent act. In this case a young child was crossing the road in the charge of his grandfather whose negligence, together with the bus driver's, caused the child's injuries. It was found that the child's damages would not be reduced because of the grandfather's negligence.

Where a plaintiff is faced with an emergency, or 'dilemma', as a result of the defendant's tort, he will not be contributorily negligent, even if, with hindsight, he did not make the best decision, provided that he acts reasonably **at the time** of the emergency or dilemma. This is the case for example, where the plaintiff is exercising some right and the question arises whether he acted reasonably in doing so in spite of the situation of danger created by the defendant.

As Patteson J put it, in *Clayards* v *Dethick* (1848) 12 QB 439: 'The whole question was, whether the danger was so obvious that the plaintiff could not with common prudence make the attempt.'.

The injury suffered by the plaintiff must also be within the broad scope of risk created by his negligence.

In *Jones* v *Livox Quarries Ltd* [1952] 2 QB 608, the plaintiff, contrary to express instructions, rode on the back of a quarry vehicle. A dumper vehicle driven by another employee collided with the rear of the quarry vehicle, crushing the plaintiff. It was held that the injury was caused partly by the plaintiff's dangerous position on the vehicle. The argument that the plaintiff's negligence related to the foreseeable risk of falling off, but not to the risk of being crushed was rejected. His injury was within the scope of the risk which the plaintiff's conduct had created.

Very often the plaintiff owes a duty of care in negligence to the defendant, in other words, there is reciprocity of duty, for example, in the case of two motorists who collide. It is not necessary, however, that the plaintiff owes such a duty.

As Bucknill LJ put it in *Davies* v *Swan Motor Co. (Swansea) Ltd* [1949] 2 KB 291: 'It is not necessary to show that the [plaintiff's] negligence constituted a breach of duty to the defendant. It is sufficient to show lack of reasonable care by the plaintiff for his own safety.'.

2.3.4.3   Nature of 'damage'

'Damage' in s. 4 of the Law Reform (Contributory Negligence) Act 1945 is couched in terms wide enough not only to include 'loss of life and personal injury', but also damage to property.

In *Drinkwater* v *Kimber* [1952] 1 All ER 701, the word 'damage' was found not to include liability to pay damages to a third party.

The court in *Maes Finance Ltd* v *A L Phillips and Co., The Times*, 25 March 1997, had to consider whether contributory negligence could be raised for the **first** time at the **assessment of damages stage**, i.e. **after** the court had delivered its judgment. It was held that much would depend on the issues settled in the judgment. Thus, if the judgment had settled an issue on which a claim of contributory negligence would depend, the defence could only be pleaded if the judgment itself was set aside. If no such issue had been settled, e.g. where a defendant alleged that the plaintiff had himself caused a particular loss, contributory negligence could be raised at the assessment of damages stage.

2.4   Summary

The general defences are dealt with in **Chapter 2** because:

(a)   they provide a unifying link between the torts;

(b)   they are important features of all cases, and the learner should be **constantly** aware of their potential importance **whenever** a problem has to be tackled; in any event some questions require advice to be given to a potential **defendant**;

(c)   they colour and shape the torts to which they apply; indeed, they are an **integral** component of the torts.

This last feature is evident in the tort of battery where, in some cases, it is claimed that far from the defendant having the burden of proving consent on the part of the plaintiff, it is for the plaintiff to show that the physical interference with his person was committed without his consent. It was so found in *Freeman* v *Home Office* [1983] 3 All ER 589. This case, and others are discussed in **Chapter 9**, which deals with **trespass to the person**.

Consent may also affect certain aspects of the tort of **negligence**. Often, there is some confusion about whether the plaintiff's 'consent', or 'agreement', exempts defendants from any liability at all, in the sense that consent prevents any duty of care arising, or whether it simply negates the defendant's breach of his duty of care, or whether it is used to set a standard of care appropriate to the circumstances of the case.

In the first and second situations, the effect of consent will be the same, i.e. the defendant will escape liability, whereas in the third situation he will remain under an obligation, but if a lower standard of care is set than might otherwise be the case, his obligation will not be as onerous as it might have been. The defendant, in other words, may seek to use a plaintiff's consent to his advantage in several contexts in the tort of negligence.

This is the case, for example, in sporting and similar events, where the rules of the game may determine the outcome of litigation for both competitors and players alike. In some cases of negligence, for example, *Phillips* v *Whiteley* [1983] 1 All ER 566, discussed at **3.7.1**, a plaintiff's willingness to accept a lower standard of care is inferred without recourse to 'consent', or *volenti*.

Many defences are dealt with in the context of particular torts, for example, **statutory authority** in relation to **nuisance** and **justification by law** (or **lawful authority**) in relation to **trespass to the person**. The Police and Criminal Evidence Act 1984 confers powers of arrest, which may be used as a defence in cases of **false imprisonment**, and assault and battery.

There are also a number of defences which relate to the **criminal** law which might be of relevance in some situations involving tortious conduct. Thus, for example, reasonable force may be used to resist unlawful criminal interference, although this is probably merely self-defence; in certain circumstances citizens are, at common law, entitled to take reasonable steps to prevent a breach of the peace; under s. 3 of the Criminal Law Act 1967, reasonable force may be used in the prevention of crime or apprehension of offenders, suspected offenders, or those 'unlawfully at large'.

This chapter focuses on the main general defences, though many of these are themselves the subject of further treatment in subsequent chapters. The chief general defences are:

(a) illegality;

(b) *volenti non fit injuria*;

(c) contributory negligence.

It is only contributory negligence, in fact, which is widely used. It is a versatile defence, in that it applies to most, if not all, torts, where appropriate, and it offers the courts a means of 'sharing the blame' between the parties.

Illegality has always been an unpredictable and uncertain defence: the learner will appreciate by now the contentious basis on which it is predicted. 'Public policy' is, one judge said many years ago, 'an unruly horse'. Illegality is, however, brought back to life from time to time, as the decision in *Pitts* v *Hunt* (see **Activity 6**) demonstrates. The defence invariably turns on such factors as:

(a) the seriousness of the offence involved;

(b) the parties' culpability in the crime;

(c) connection with the crime which can involve difficult questions of causation;

(d) an 'affront to the public conscience', which appears to be based on the notion that the public would not be happy to see the courts helping or encouraging plaintiffs in the pursuit of their illegal conduct; it might also encourage others were the courts to assist such plaintiffs.

The Court of Appeal in *Kirkham* v *Chief Constable of Greater Manchester* said, *obiter*, that the public might dislike the idea of a 'wholly sane' suicide or attempted suicide attracting compénsation. You will find extracts from the judgments in *Kirkham* in *Cases and Materials* (**2.3**). See also *Reeves* v *Commissioner of Police of the Metropolis* (above).

The conflict of opinion in these cases may require resolution by the House of Lords.

In *Euro-Drain Ltd* v *Bathurst* [1988] 2 All ER 23, Kerr LJ said:

> The *ex turpi* defence ultimately rests on a principle of public policy that the courts will not assist a plaintiff who has been guilty of illegal (or immoral) conduct of which the courts should take notice.

You can see that the involvement of a criminal act is **not** a pre-requisite for this defence.

Kirkham is only one of several cases, heard in the Court of Appeal in fairly recent times, in which there has been some sort of reference to the effect on the 'public conscience' if the courts should provide a forum for actions tainted with illegality. It is, at best, a vague notion and it is unclear how the public reaction is to be gauged in any particular instance. Apart from the question of **degree**, it is uncertain whether emotional reactions or feelings of retribution on the part of the public should be incorporated in the 'test'.

This 'public conscience' approach is criticised in *Pitts* v *Hunt* and received a disapproving analysis in the House of Lords in *Tinsley* v *Milligan* [1993] 3 WLR 126. In *Tinsley*, Lord Goff expressed the opinion that the 'public conscience' test in effect amounted to nothing more than a statement by the court that it had a **discretion** 'whether to grant or refuse relief'. You will find an extract from Lord Goff's speech in *Tinsley* in *Cases and Materials* (**2.3**). This discretion, it is submitted, lies behind all the reasons given by the courts when refusing to assist the plaintiff on grounds of illegality.

The court will sometimes refuse to set a duty where illegal activity is involved. This approach incorporates the factor of illegality into the argument on whether or not a duty of care ought to be imposed in particular circumstances. We have seen that *volenti* is often used in this way and that that distorts the picture of what is really happening. In both cases, i.e. of illegality and *volenti*, their pivotal roles as **defences** is obscured in such cases. In any event, this approach can only work where the tort of negligence is involved, because the duty is **fixed** in other torts. We have seen, however, that consent may be part of the duty equation in some cases of battery.

This is also true of the standard of care rationale: the court will refuse to get involved in assessing degrees of illegality. It can only work where the standard has to be set in the particular circumstances of the case; that means it only applies where negligence or fault of some kind has to be proved.

It is also claimed that the courts must not be seen to encourage the plaintiff and others in illicit activities. This is a difficult claim to substantiate because the **deterrent** effect of a refusal to assist the plaintiff is of dubious substance, particularly where, as is often the case, the issue before the court is essentially one of negligence.

As you will see in **Chapter 3**, the courts' categorisation of a person's behaviour as 'negligent' is invariably the result of an *ex post facto* ('retrospective') inquiry, and it would be difficult to substantiate a claim of any deterrent effect where it is only known **after** the event that the law has been broken.

Illegality bears strong resemblances to *volenti non fit injuria* (or *volenti* for short). You will also see that lawyers will often say that a plaintiff was *volens*, this is merely another way of referring to *volenti*.

Both defences are based on public policy. *Volenti* is said to be based on the **consent** of the plaintiff, but the determination of that 'consent' by the courts is often influenced by considerations of policy as, for example in *Morris* v *Murray* and *ICI* v *Shatwell*. Both defences are **complete** defences and both defences are based on the merits of the plaintiff's claim.

Volenti, for reasons that will now be apparent to you, is not a widely-used defence. In the opinion of Fleming, *An Introduction to the Law of Torts*, 2nd edn, Oxford: Oxford University Press, 1985, the defence is 'moribund', for two main reasons:

(a) the difficulty of proving consent, as Fleming puts it (at p. 140): 'The life-cycle of the defence, indeed, is marked by the progressive displacement of *imputed* consent by nothing short of *real* consent as the basic requirement'; and

(b) the rise in popularity of contributory negligence, which has eclipsed *volenti*.

Whilst it is true that genuine cases of *volenti* are rare, we must remember the 'standard of care' cases discussed above and such isolated instances as *ICI* v *Shatwell* (which you can compare with *Stapley* v *Gypsum Mines*) and *Morris* v *Murray*.

Most confusion, in fact, occurs in the **implied** (or imputed) *volenti* cases. The expression *volenti non fit injuria* embraces the whole range of consent or agreement and whatever form it takes, it may be said that it all boils down to consent or no consent, but it has been suggested that:

(a) consent, which may be express or implied, should be restricted to intentional torts (any specific consent given to an intentional interference, for example, the tort of battery, would not extend to an act of negligence);

(b) contractual consent or similar agreements should be regarded as a form of defence *sui generis*, which can embrace both intentional torts and the tort of negligence;

(c) the term 'voluntary assumption of risk' best expresses the notion of **implied** consent to negligence (**express** consent to negligence is best dealt with in terms of contractual, or **similar** agreements).

It is this last form of *volenti* which causes most difficulty, and which is often obscured by the 'standard of care' cases. On principle, the courts are reluctant to accede to its use, because it can so easily become a licence to commit negligence in those cases where the consent precedes the act of negligence.

This reluctance was behind the decision in *Dann* v *Hamilton* [1939] 1 KB 509, in which the plaintiff accepted a drunken driver's offer of a lift in his car. The plaintiff was found not to be *volenti*.

This decision was distinguished in *Morris* v *Murray* on the ground that the aircraft trip in that case 'served no useful social purpose'. In *Dann* the female plaintiff needed to get home, late at night, after a party.

Can you say why the dispute in *Dann* v *Hamilton* would not arise today?

The argument on *volenti* would be superfluous, because of s. 149 of the Road Traffic Act 1988.

The defence of contributory negligence was not raised in *Dann* and, in any event, at that time it would have been a complete defence, but *Owens* v *Brimmell* (and other cases) suggest that that defence might now succeed on such facts.

Contributory negligence, which is based on the premise that the plaintiff either knew or **ought** to have known of the relevant danger, must be distinguished from *volenti* which is based on the plaintiff's **full** knowledge of the nature and extent of the risk, and both defences must be distinguished from *novus actus interveniens* and *nova causa interveniens*, the doctrine of intervening causes, which is discussed in **Chapter 4**. In practice, however, it may often be difficult to find the precise dividing line between them all, as cases like *Morris* v *Murray* demonstrate.

All are means of defence, and the courts' task, in the final analysis, is to strike a balance between the interests of the litigants, taking into account, too, the public interest.

2.5   Further Reading

Hepple, B.A., and Matthews, M.H., *Tort: Cases and Materials*, 5th edn, London: Butterworths, 1996, Chapter 7.
Jones, M., *Textbook on Torts*, 5th edn, London: Blackstone Press, 1996, Chapter 14.
Salmond and Heuston on the Law of Torts, 21st edn. London: Sweet & Maxwell, 1996, Chapter 22.
Stanton, K.M., *Modern Law of Tort*, London: Sweet & Maxwell, 1994, Chapter 5.
Street on Torts, 9th edn, London: Butterworths, 1993, Chapters 6 and 15.
Weir, T., *Casebook on Tort*, 8th edn. London: Sweet & Maxwell, 1996, Chapter 5.
Winfield and Jolowicz on Tort, 14th edn. London: Sweet & Maxwell, 1994, Chapter 26.

2.6 End of Chapter Assessment Question

Rex, and his fiancée, Portia, after drinking alcohol at lunchtime, stole a car for a joyride. Portia, not wearing her seat belt, drove the car at speed along a cliff top road, skidded on a bend and the car crashed into a boulder before coming to a stop hanging precariously over the edge of the cliff. Rex was injured but managed to get out of the car.

Sam, a passing motorist, stopped at the scene of the accident and, together with Rex, climbed into the car to help Portia. The car tipped up under the combined weight of them all and fell down the cliff. Rex and Sam were seriously injured and Portia was killed, but it transpired that she would in any event probably have died from her initial injuries.

Discuss the tortious issues arising from these events.

See *Cases and Materials* (2.5) for a specimen answer.

CHAPTER THREE

NEGLIGENCE

3.1 Objectives

By the end of this chapter you should be able to:

■ state the basic requirements for liability in the tort of negligence;

■ appreciate the degree of overlap between the three elements of liability;

■ understand the significance of the term 'duty of care' and acknowledge the role played by **policy** in determining its existence;

■ appreciate those areas of potential liability which are of a contentious nature;

■ explain the significance of the term 'breach of duty';

■ establish an acquaintance with the mechanisms whereby the courts determine the requisite standard of care appropriate to the circumstances of each case.

3.2 Introduction

In the law of tort the word 'negligence' has **two** meanings: first, a **descriptive** meaning, e.g. one person may **negligently** libel another (the relevant **tort** being that of **libel**); secondly, a **specific form** of liability, which originated as such early in the nineteenth century. In its modern form, it dates from *Donoghue* v *Stevenson* [1932] AC 562.

The second meaning is the more important one, and it is **this** form of negligence which is the subject of our attention in this chapter.

As a **tort**, negligence is said to consist of three elements:

(a) a legal **duty**;

(b) a **breach** of that duty;

(c) **damage** suffered as a consequence of that breach.

However, these elements **overlap**: they are **not** discrete in terms of jurisdiction. As the cases are examined in more detail, you will see that the courts often regard them as different ways of tackling the **same** problem. The problem is one of controlling liability and the judges tackle it in a pragmatic fashion.

Thus, in practice 'duty', 'breach' and 'damage' are often 'telescoped'. In *Lamb* v *Camden LBC* [1981] QB 625 Lord Denning reminds us, in effect, that we are not here dealing with watertight compartments. His Lordship points out that **duty, breach** and **damage** 'continually run into one another'; they are also 'devices' used by judges to control liability.

You may be surprised to learn that in *Hedley Byrne* v *Heller* [1964] AC 46 Lord Pearce said that he often found it useful to **start** with 'damage' and **work his way back** to 'duty'.

In this chapter we examine each element **separately**, but throughout your study of the topic it is important that you bear in mind the preceding observations on the nature of all three elements.

3.3 Duty

This is probably the **most significant** of the control devices referred to above.

The **plaintiff** must prove that a duty of care was owed by the plaintiff in the **circumstances** of the **particular** case. This issue raises points both of 'law' **and** 'fact'. This means that **first** a duty must exist in **principle**, and then the plaintiff must seek to justify the application of the 'law' to the actual 'facts' of the case.

The law will recognise a duty of care in negligence only where the relationship between the parties is seen as giving rise to that duty: there can never be a duty 'in the air', so to speak. Each case must therefore be examined in the light of its own facts, but in general terms the 'duty criteria' i.e. foreseeability, proximity and just and reasonable may be more easily established, at least on a *prima facie* basis, where the parties **already** stand in some relationship to each other. This could be the case where there is a contractual or statutory relationship between the parties, or where they are fellow users of the highway or have some analogous relationship.

Furthermore, a plaintiff will generally have a less difficult task in establishing a duty where there is precedent in the case law on the point in issue. Much will depend here on the strength and relevance of the authority.

A plaintiff will have the greatest difficulty where the case is of a novel nature i.e. is what lawyers call 'a hard case'. Here, the argument must be based simply on the applicability of the 'duty criteria' to the facts of the case.

Today a legal duty of care in negligence must satisfy the **'neighbour' principle** formulated by Lord Atkin in *Donoghue* v *Stevenson*. He said (at p. 579 of the law report):

> You must take reasonable care to avoid acts or omissions which you can reasonably foresee would be likely to injure your neighbour . . . ['neighbours' being]: persons who are so closely and directly affected by my act that I ought reasonably to have them in contemplation as being so affected when I am directing my mind to the acts or omissions which are called in question.

Consider carefully this definition. Is a defendant to be liable merely on the basis that his victim was 'foreseeable' in the circumstances?

The Atkinian 'test' has always been seen as a **necessary** requirement in the 'duty' equation, but very rarely, if ever, has it been regarded as a **sufficient** determinant of liability *per se*, otherwise there might be **unbridled** expansion of liability. To the requirement of 'foreseeability' the courts have since 1932 added the condition of 'proximity'. Together, these requirements can be said to comprise the 'neighbour' test. However, some judges insist that it is 'proximity' which is synonymous with 'neighbour-hood'. It is probably impossible to offer a completely satisfactory explanation of the expression 'proximity': all we can say is that it seems to mean some sort of 'nearness' between the parties; this could be **physical** proximity, in terms of **spatial** and **geographical** limitations; or **legal** proximity in that, for example, there might already exist a contractual relationship between the parties.

In *Alcock* v *Chief Constable of the South Yorkshire Police* [1992] 1 AC 310 Lord Oliver said (at p. 411) '. . . the concept of *proximity* is an artificial one which depends more on the court's perception of what is the reasonable area for the imposition of liability than upon any logical process of analogical deduction.'.

Some 40 years earlier, a Canadian judge, MacDonald J had made much the same point. In *Nova-Mink* v *Trans-Canada Airlines* [1951] 2 DLR 241, he said (at p. 254):

> When . . . *a court holds that the defendant was under a duty of care [it] is stating as a conclusion of law what is really a conclusion of policy as to responsibility for conduct involving unreasonable risk* . . . There is always a large element of judicial policy and social expediency involved in the determination of the duty problem, however it may be obscured by the traditional formulae.

(By 'traditional formulae' the judge meant the familiar concepts of **foreseeability** and **proximity**.)

SAQ 23

Please look again at the words in italics in the quotation from *Nova-Mink*. In one sentence only, please explain what they mean.

You should have said something along the following lines: 'A court will first determine what is good public policy in relation to the scope of a proposed duty of care before reaching a decision on the facts of the case'.

In *Home Office* v *Dorset Yacht Co.* [1970] AC 1004, four law lords based their decision that a duty was owed by the Home Office on the requirements of the public interest.

Bingham LJ suggested in *Caparo Industries plc* v *Dickman* [1989] 2 WLR 316 (CA) that the imposition of a duty is ultimately a question of **fairness** and depends upon:

(a) the relationship of the parties;

(b) the nature of the risk involved;

(c) public interest in the matter.

Thus a duty of care might be too onerous on a party if it renders them liable for an indeterminate amount of care for an indeterminate time to an indeterminate class of people. As a matter of policy, however, it might be fair to impose a duty of care on a defendant who voluntarily exercises professional skills if that duty arises from another pre-existing duty, e.g. in contract, or perhaps if a duty of care would promote some socially desirable objective.

In *Peabody Donation Fund* v *Parkinson* [1985] AC 210 Lord Keith said that the Atkinian test should not be treated as if it were definitive; in all cases, as well as establishing both foreseeability and proximity, it must also be **just and reasonable** to impose a duty.

We will see at **3.3.2** that this decision also marked the beginning of a sustained attack on Lord Wilberforce's dictum for determining the existence of a duty of care, formulated in *Anns* v *Merton LBC* [1978] AC 728.

You should also consider the view expressed by Lord Goff in *Smith* v *Littlewoods Organisation* [1987] AC 241 (at p. 248): '. . . the broad principle of liability for foreseeable damage is so widely applicable that the function of the duty of care is not so much to identify cases where liability is imposed as to identify those where it is not . . .'.

3.3.1 THE NEIGHBOUR TEST AS A GENERAL PRINCIPLE OF LIABILITY

Please read the extracts from the speeches of Lord Reid in *Dorset Yacht* and Lord Wilberforce in *Anns* in *Cases and Materials* (3.1.1) What points are being made by their Lordships?

A number of judges in subsequent cases followed the lead of Lord Reid in *Dorset Yacht* and Lord Wilberforce in *Anns* in regarding the Atkinian formulation as a **statement of principle**. The importance of this from our point of view is that the foreseeability test was raised to a greater prominence with regard to the **general** development of the tort of negligence; the Atkinian test was regarded more in terms of **ratio** than **obiter**. In particular, Lord Wilberforce's approach seemed to suggest that a plaintiff who succeeded in establishing an Atkinian relationship with the defendant had succeeded in showing a *prima facie* duty of care in law i.e. a **presumptive** duty had arisen. The following cases are examples of this approach: *Ross* v *Caunters* [1980] Ch 297; *JEB Fasteners* v *Marks Bloom* [1983] 1 All ER 583; *Junior Books* v *Veitchi Co. Ltd* [1983] 1 AC 520. (These three cases will be the subject of our attention in **Chapter 5**.)

3.3.2 A DIFFERENT VIEW

However, this more principled approach (represented by the 'Wilberforce approach' from *Anns* v *Merton* and the 'Reid approach' in *Dorset Yacht*) became the subject of a conservative reaction. Lord Keith in *Peabody* was critical of Lord Wilberforce's dictum:

he was especially concerned that the Wilberforce approach might lead to a situation in which the authority of common law precedent could be undermined. (See *Cases and Materials* (3.1.2).)

In *Leigh and Sillavan Ltd* v *Aliakmon Shipping Co. Ltd* [1986] AC 786 Lord Brandon said that Lord Wilberforce's view was intended to be applied only in novel situations and not across the board in negligence so as to influence areas where clearly established authority can be found.

Lord Donaldson MR in the Court of Appeal (in the same case) expressed the contrary view (shared by some other judges) that the Wilberforce dictum enabled a court to override established authority if it thought policy dictated that result.

It is in fact this latter interpretation of the Wilberforce dictum which has fuelled much of the reaction to that approach. Many judges in more recent cases have voiced disquiet about courts embarking on voyages of discovery in the development of policies without reference to established authority: for example, Lord Brandon and Lord Oliver in *Leigh and Sillivan*.

Lord Keith renewed his attack on the *Wilberforce* approach in *Yuen Kun Yeu* v *A-G for Hong Kong* [1988] AC 175.

ACTIVITY 8

Please read the extract from the speech of Lord Keith in *Yuen Kun Yeu* v *A-G for Hong Kong* in *Cases and Materials* (3.1.2). Please explain the point he is making.

In Lord Keith's opinion the Wilberforce test in its second stage, the qualification of the foreseeability stage, was too vague and ineffective as a control mechanism. Its terms of control were of an 'indefinable' nature. His Lordship thought it preferable to develop new duties incrementally and by analogy with established categories of duty. Indeed, the Wilberforce test had been 'elevated [in later cases] to a degree of importance greater than it [merited]'.

Lord Bridge in *Curran* v *NI Co-Ownership Housing Association Ltd* [1987] AC 718 said that *Anns* v *Merton* represented the 'high-water mark' of a trend in the law of negligence towards the 'elevation' of the Atkinian principle into one of general application from which a duty of care could always be derived unless there were clear countervailing considerations to exclude it. 'The trend should be resisted.'

His Lordship returned to this theme in *Caparo Industries plc* v *Dickman* [1990] 1 All ER 568 (HL), a case which is regarded as a leading authority on 'duty of care' in negligence generally. (He also said the expressions 'foreseeability', 'proximity' and 'just and reasonable' were **not** definitions; they were merely **'labels'** attached to conclusions reached by the judges after considering the policy issues at stake in any given situation.)

You may find some extracts from the various speeches, including that of Lord Bridge, of interest in the present context: see *Cases and Materials* (**3.1.2**).

Recent authority, i.e. cases decided **after** *Caparo*, in other words, judges in later cases, have **interpreted** *Caparo* in this way. The decision itself suggests that searching for a single 'test' is a fruitless exercise, yet recent authority has in **effect** created a **three-stage** 'test' for determining a duty of care: to the familiar requirements of 'foreseeability' and 'proximity' the courts have added the requirement that it must be 'just and reasonable' to impose a duty in the circumstances. Unfortunately, each requirement overlaps with the others: they cannot be seen as forming discrete conditions of liability.

The decision in *Caparo* itself does, however, emphasise that any 'test' or approach to the issue of 'duty' must operate within an **incremental** framework, i.e. in general the law should develop on a **case by case** basis. Cases involving **personal injury** and/or **actual damage to property** will, however, rarely, if ever, cause difficulty in terms of the establishment of a duty of care. This was the position taken for example by Lord Denning in *Nettleship* v *Weston* (see **3.7.1**) and Lord Oliver in *Caparo*. The House of Lords in *Marc Rich & Co.* v *Bishop Rock Marine* [1995] 3 All ER 307 has, however, held that the three-stage test must be applied in **all** difficult cases regardless of the type of damage suffered. Their Lordships said there was no logical distinction between 'physical' damage and so-called 'pure economic loss': in both types of case damages could only be awarded in terms of **financial compensation**. The decision in *Page* v *Smith* (see **Chapter 6**) has arguably diminished the distinction between 'mental' and 'physical' damage.

You should read the extract from *Weir's Casebook* and the decisions in *Topp* v *London Country Bus* [1993] RTR 279, *Skinner* v *Secretary of State for Transport*, *The Times*, 3 January 1995, *Elguzouli-Daf* v *Commissioner of the Metropolis* [1995] 1 All ER 833, *Olotu* v *Home Office and Another* [1997] 1 All ER 385 and *Barrett* v *Ministry of Defence* [1995] 3 All ER 87 in *Cases and Materials* (**3.1.2**) before proceeding any further.

SAQ 24

Do you think there might be any other major problems to be considered in connection with the 'duty' issue in negligence?

Major problems are likely to be encountered in the contexts of the relationship between contract and tort (see **3.4**), the liability of public bodies (see **3.5**) and certain specific issues i.e. omissions, 'pure' economic loss, 'nervous shock' and the unborn child (see **3.6**).

3.4 Liability in Contract and Tort

At this point we need to consider the following *obiter* opinion of Lord Scarman in *Tai Hing Cotton Mill Ltd* v *Liu Chong Hing Bank* [1986] AC 80 (PC):

> Their Lordships do not believe that there is anything to the advantage of the law's development in searching for a liability in tort where the parties are in a contractual relationship . . . their Lordships believe it to be correct in principle and necessary for the avoidance of doubt to adhere to the contractual analysis.

Traditionally, a plaintiff who has a contract with the defendant has often been able to choose whether to sue in contract **or** tort: the choice would depend on which cause of action gave the better result. For example, the rules governing remoteness of damage differ between the two causes of action; different limitation periods apply; and contributory negligence is not a defence in contract.

Concurrent liability in this sense has long been recognised, particularly in professional relationships, for example, that of solicitor and client. More recently, however, the courts have been less willing to allow plaintiffs this freedom, insisting that the law of tort cannot be used to create liability where none exists in contract. *Greater Nottingham Co-operative Society* v *Cementation Piling and Foundations Ltd* [1989] QB 71 (CA) which is examined in some detail in **Chapter 5** (at **5.4.2**), illustrates this. In many of these cases Lord Scarman's opinion has been cited in support of this approach.

The House of Lords, in *Henderson and Others* v *Merrett Syndicates Ltd and Others* [1994] 3 All ER 506 has held, however, that a pre-existing contractual relationship between the parties did not **of itself** preclude a concurrent liability in tort. A plaintiff in such a case could choose which remedy produced the best results, unless the contract provided otherwise.

Lord Goff agreed with the Master of the Rolls in this case that the *Tai Hing Cotton Mill* case was concerned only with the question of establishing a duty wider in scope than provided for by the terms of the contract between the parties. That is, Lord Scarman's dictum did not apply to a duty in tort which was **conterminous** with the pre-existing contractual obligation. *Henderson* is considered in more detail in **Chapters 5** and **13**.

In *Holt* v *Payne Skillington, The Times*, 22 December 1995, the Court of Appeal held that a duty of care in negligence arising between the parties to a contract could impose wider obligations than those imposed by the contract. Hirst LJ said there was no reason in principle why a *Hedley Byrne* (see **Chapter 5**) duty could not arise in an overall set of circumstances where, by reference to certain limited aspects of those circumstances, the parties entered into a contract which imposed more limited obligations than those arising in tort. In such a case the duties arising in tort and contract would be concurrent but not coextensive. His Lordship, who delivered the judgment of the court, said that the tort duty would be imposed by the general law whilst the contractual obligations were the result of the parties' common intention. He pointed out, however, that there would have to be no term in the contract precluding or restricting the wider obligations in tort.

ACTIVITY 9

Please read the extract from *Johnstone* v *Bloomsbury Health Authority* [1991] 2 All ER 293 (*Cases and Materials* (3.2)). Consider why an action in tort was brought instead of in contract.

The plaintiff sued in tort in order to enlist the employer's common law duty of care (see **Chapter 8**) which contains an obligation to safeguard the employee's health — something to which his contract of employment made no specific reference.

Further reading on this topic can be found in Dolding, L. and Fawlk, C., 'Judicial Understanding of the Contract of Employment' (1992) 55 MLR 562.

3.5 Public Bodies and Negligence

Public authorities do **not** enjoy a **general** immunity from suit in negligence, but on the whole the courts have traditionally taken a cautious approach to the development of the law in this context. The reasons for this include:

(a) the fact that **public** duties are often involved;

(b) **Parliament** has given the authorities concerned a considerable amount of statutory discretion to formulate policies and the courts are reluctant to interfere with this discretion;

(c) there is sometimes a statutory remedy available, such as a right of appeal; and

(d) the courts have developed remedies against public bodies by means of **judicial review**.

The issue in this section is whether public bodies should be governed by the same criteria in terms of liability in the tort of negligence. In *Dorset Yacht* and in *Anns* it was said that in order to find a public body liable in respect of the negligent exercise of its statutory powers there had to be established, in addition to the usual requirements for the tort of negligence, two factors:

(a) an *ultra vires* (this means 'beyond the powers of') exercise of the power in question; and

(b) the existence of a decision taken at the 'operational' rather than the 'policy making' level.

See the extracts from the speeches of Lord Diplock in *Dorset Yacht*, Lord Wilberforce in *Anns* and Lord Hoffman in *Stovin* v *Wise* [1996] 3 All ER 801 which refer to the issue of the negligent exercise of statutory powers (**Cases and Materials** (**3.1.1** and **3.3**)).

What do you take to be the difference between the 'operational ' and 'policy-making' levels of a public body?

A decision arrived at by a public body **within** the terms of its statutory discretion is, according to this approach, a decision taken at the policy-making level. On the other hand, a decision taken in the context of **implementing** a policy is made at the **operational** level.

Haydon v *Kent County Council* [1978] QB 343 (CA) provides a good example of this dichotomy. The issue here was whether the plaintiff could succeed against the defendants for the consequences of their failure to grit footpaths in icy weather, the plaintiff having slipped and suffered personal injury. In essence, a public spending decision was involved: the council had decided to give priority to gritting the highways in preference to treating footpaths. This decision by the council was regarded as coming within the ambit of the council's **statutory**, **discretionary**, i.e. **policy-making** powers and was therefore not amenable to an action in tort. (If the council had decided to spend money on gritting footpaths, it would have been an **operational** error to have performed the task negligently.)

This distinction, between decisions taken at the **policy** and **operational** levels is not accepted as all that important by some authorities. Thus, in *Rowling* v *Takaro Properties* [1988] AC 175 (PC) Lord Keith warned against over-reliance on this 'operational/policy' distinction. He advocated an essentially **pragmatic** approach in cases involving negligence by public authorities. You will find an extract from his speech in *Cases and Materials* (3.3). His Lordship took a similar approach in *Murphy* v *Brentwood District Council* [1990] 2 All ER 908 (HL).

According to Foulkes, *Administrative Law*, 7th edn, 1990: '[The] distinction [between operational and policy decisions] was always acknowledged to be difficult in application and it has now been largely disregarded'.

The House of Lords in *M* v *Newham LBC* and other cases heard with *M* (see **Activity 10** below), however, accepted as legitimate an argument based on the distinction between 'policy' and 'operational' decisions. You will also find it referred to in a number of other cases.

In *Jones* v *Department of Employment* [1988] QB 1 the Court of Appeal reviewed the authorities and Glidewell LJ was **content** merely to ask the question: 'whether [in all the circumstances] it is **just and reasonable** that the adjudication officer should be under a duty of care at common law to the claimant to [social security] benefit'.

The court found that an adjudication officer (whose job is to determine social security claims) did not owe a duty of care in negligence to the plaintiff who was claiming social security benefits, in relation to his conduct of the case. It was indicated that the claimant's only remedy would lie in **judicial review**.

According to Slade LJ in *Calveley* v *Chief Constable of Merseyside* [1988] 3 All ER 385 (CA):

> The court [in *Jones*] answered [the] question in the negative, having regard to the nature of the adjudication officer's responsibilities and, in particular, to the fact that the statutory framework provided a right of appeal . . .

> His Lordship said that if a common law duty of care had been found in *Jones*, disappointed claimants would have '. . . an alternative route . . . to appeal against the adjudication officer's decisions'. Furthermore, it was doubtful if Parliament had intended that the adjudication officer should be under the threat of an action in negligence should he err in his determination of a claim.

Lord Donaldson said in this case that the relationship between an investigating officer and a police officer under investigation (the subject matter in *Calveley*) is not dissimilar to the relationship between an adjudication officer and a claimant. In the performance of their duties, both the investigating officer and the adjudication officer derive their authority from, and are controlled by, statute. Both are performing non-judicial duties, but duties calling for judgment and due regard for rights. In both cases there are **statutory routes of appeal** backed up by the public law supervisory function of the High Court (**judicial review**).

In *Hill* v *Chief Constable of West Yorkshire* [1989] AC 53 it was found that the police did not owe a duty of care in relation to the conduct of an investigation into the murders by the 'Yorkshire Ripper' (Peter Sutcliffe). The plaintiff was the mother of one of the victims who, it was alleged, would not have died at the hand of Sutcliffe had the police exercised an appropriate degree of care. The court said that foreseeability of harm was not of itself sufficient to form the basis of a duty of care. (See the speech of Lord Keith in *Cases and Materials* (3.1.2).)

SAQ 26

Please consider briefly other possible reasons for not imposing a duty of care on the police to a member of the public or a police officer under investigation.

Lord Donaldson in *Calveley* identified another ground for finding against the existence of a common law duty of care in the present circumstances: the public interest in the free and fearless investigation of such complaints. He agreed with Lord Keith's observation in *Hill* that whilst the existence of such a duty in relation to some activities might be in the public interest because it might lead to higher standards of care, this could not be said of police activities. It was also Lord Donaldson's opinion that if the investigating officer were to owe a duty of care to a police officer under investigation, it might be argued that he should owe a similar duty to the person who had complained about the conduct of the officer under investigation and whose complaint had led to the investigation in the first place. (Where such a person had been convicted in a criminal court he might appeal not only against conviction but he might also try an action in negligence against the investigating police officers should the appeal fail. 'It is an unattractive prospect.')

The decision of the Court of Appeal, that no duty of care should be imposed because it would be contrary to the public interest to impose such a burden on the police, was upheld on appeal ([1989] AC 1228).

We need to note something of very great importance within the context of actions involving public authorities: this is the availability of **judicial review** for the purpose of challenging the legality of decisions made by such bodies in purported exercise of their statutory powers. This form of review is governed by s. 31 of the Supreme Court Act 1981 and RSC Order 53.

In *Cocks* v *Thanet District Council* [1983] 2 AC 286 (HL) a **further** distinction was drawn. The case involved a claim that a local housing authority was in breach of its duty to provide accommodation to the plaintiff under the terms of the Housing (Homeless Persons) Act 1977 (which is now Part III of the Housing Act 1985). The court said there now existed 'a dichotomy between a housing authority's public and private law functions'. The question of whether the plaintiff satisfied the statutory conditions for eligibility was a **public** law issue; the authority's obligation to provide accommodation once the conditions were satisfied was, on the other hand, a matter of **private** law.

This approach was followed in the High Court in *R* v *Northavon DC, ex parte Palmer, The Independent*, 22 February 1994.

It was found in *Lonrho plc* v *Tebbitt and Another* [1992] 4 All ER 280 that a negligent decision given by a minister of the Crown which is categorised as an **operational** rather than a **policy** decision may give rise to a private law duty of care. However, where it is impossible on the pleadings to determine the considerations relevant to the exercise by the minister of the statutory power, it is not appropriate on a striking-out application to decide whether the exercise of the power gave rise to a duty of care. This is because the question of whether a duty of care in fact exists will depend on the facts determined at the trial.

By exercising certain powers under the Fair Trading Act 1973 the Secretary of State for Trade and Industry and the Department of Trade and Industry prevented Lonrho from bidding for shares in the House of Fraser plc. The Court of Appeal found that the plaintiff, Lonrho, was entitled to make a claim in **private** law (i.e. **tort**) against both the Secretary of State and the Department. (See also *Cases and Materials* (**3.1.2**).)

In several recent actions against local authorities, and their advisors in some instances, by parents and children, alleging liability arising in the tort of negligence and a breach of statutory duty (Child Care Act 1980 and Children Act 1989), the courts have been reluctant to allow the claims to go forward. Much emphasis has been placed on alternative methods of redress, such as the public law remedies: *M* v *Newham LBC* and other cases heard with it (see **Activity 10**).

Please read the extracts from *Rowling, Wood* v *The Law Society, The Times*, 30 July 1993, *M* v *Newham LBC; X* v *Bedfordshire CC and other appeals* [1995] 3 All ER 353 and *Stovin* v *Wise* [1996] 3 All ER 801 in *Cases and Materials* (**3.3**).

Consider the arguments put forward by the courts against finding liability in the tort of negligence and in one sentence identify the main factor common to all three cases.

The main common factor to be found in these cases is that the claims for damages in negligence were all made against **public bodies**. *Stovin* v *Wise* also places some **emphasis** on the notion of '**particular and general reliance**'.

You can read about decisions concerning liability of the **police** in negligence in *Alexandrou* v *Oxford* [1993] 4 All ER 328, *Osman* v *Ferguson* [1993] 4 All ER 344 and *Ancell* v *McDermott* [1993] 4 All ER 355 and of the **fire authorities** in *Capital and Counties plc* v *Hampshire County Council and others* [1997] 2 All ER 565 and *Daly* v *Surrey County Council, The Times,* 25 October 1997, in *Cases and Materials* (**3.8**). In **3.3** you will also find details of other cases involving public bodies as defendants. The courts in some of these cases have applied the decision in *X* v *Bedfordshire CC* (above).

Murphy v *Brentwood District Council*, discussed in **Chapter 5**, is also a 'public authority' case.

3.6 Specific Issues in Relation to Duty

We also need to take special note of the following issues in the context of 'Duty'.

3.6.1 OMISSIONS

The common law traditionally distinguishes between liability for **misfeasance** and **non-feasance** (or **positive** act(s) and **omissions** to act): in general terms, there is a marked reluctance to impose liability for **omissions**. The following extract from the speech of Lord Goff in *Smith* v *Littlewoods Organisation* [1987] 1 All ER 710 (at p. 729) makes this position clear:

> Why does the law not recognise a general duty of care to prevent others from suffering loss or damage caused by the deliberate wrongdoing of third parties? The fundamental reason is that the common law does not impose liability for what are called pure omissions. If authority is needed for this proposition, it is to be found in the speech of Lord Diplock in *Home Office* v *Dorset Yacht Co. Ltd* where he said: 'The very parable of the Good Samaritan (Luke 10:30) which was evoked by Lord Atkin in *Donoghue* v *Stevenson* illustrates, in the conduct of the priest and of the Levite who passed by on the other side, an omission which was likely to have as its reasonable and probable consequence damage to the health of the victim of the thieves, but for which the priest and Levite would have incurred no civil liability in English law.'

See also Lord Hoffmann in *Stovin* v *Wise* [1996] 3 All ER 801 in *Cases and Materials* (3.3).

3.6.2 'PURE' ECONOMIC LOSS

See **Chapter 5**.

3.6.3 'NERVOUS SHOCK'

See **Chapter 6**.

3.6.4 THE UNBORN CHILD

The Congenital Disabilities (Civil Liability) Act 1976 confers a limited right of action upon a child born disabled as a result of pre-birth injury, but this is restricted to plaintiffs born **after** 22 July 1976, which is the date of the Act's commencement. A corresponding **common law** duty of care caters for plaintiffs born **before** that date: *Burton* v *Islington Health Authority* [1992] 3 All ER 833 (CA). You will find further details in *Cases and Materials* (3.4.1).

In *McKay* v *Essex Area Health Authority* [1982] 2 WLR 890, the Court of Appeal rejected (on grounds of public policy) a claim for 'wrongful birth' ('or life') by the plaintiff who had been born disabled, allegedly as a result of the failure of a doctor to diagnose rubella in the plaintiff's mother when she was pregnant with the plaintiff. It was claimed that had the doctor not been negligent, the mother would have aborted the plaintiff, who would not then have been born in a handicapped condition. See now the 1976 Act (above). There is, however, nothing to prevent **parents** suing doctors for failing to inform them that their children will be born handicapped – on the basis that otherwise an abortion would have been considered and carried out: *Rance* v *Mid-Downs Health Authority* [1991] 1 All ER 801.

3.6.5 ADVOCACY

It has been decided by the House of Lords in *Rondel* v *Worsley* [1969] AC 191 and in *Saif Ali* v *Mitchell* [1980] AC 198 that advocates do not at common law owe a duty of care to their clients with regard to the way in which they conduct **court** proceedings and in respect of any **pre-trial** work which is tantamount to a preliminary decision affecting the presentation in court.

The position may be different, however, under the terms of s. 62(1) and (2) of the Courts and Legal Services Act 1990. Read the extracts from this Act in *Cases and Materials* (**5.4**).

In *Kelly* v *Corston* [1997] 4 All ER 466 (CA) it was held that an advocate's immunity from liability in negligence extended to a barrister who, at '**the door of the court**', negotiated and advised his client to accept a **settlement** of the action which could only be effective **if approved by the court**.

3.7 Breach of Duty

3.7.1 GENERAL OBSERVATIONS

'Breach' is the **essence** of negligence; it describes the defendant's **behaviour** which actually injures the plaintiff; 'breach' is often treated in practice as synonymous with 'negligence' and it is **this** which probably most people would regard as 'negligence'. The question for us here is whether the defendant has measured up to the **standard of behaviour** in the particular circumstances of the case. The defendant's behaviour at the relevant time must conform in general to the standard of the hypothetical 'reasonable man'. The question with which we are concerned is 'what would the reasonable man have done, or not have done, in the circumstances of the case?'.

The standard of care is constant, though the actual 'quantum' or amount of care required varies from case to case. What do you think this statement means?

It means that in formal terms the standard, of the 'reasonable man', is constant and objective but in practice the relevant standard will have to be determined in **each** case, according to the **circumstances** of that case, judged in the light of the reasonable man test. It is thus inevitable that the standard eventually set will contain elements of the subjective.

3.7.1.1 Capacity

For that reason it is often important to identify the **capacity** in which the defendant was acting at the relevant time. Let us imagine that the defendant was a competitor in a dangerous sport, such as motorcycle racing. He may owe a low quantum of care as a competitor **going all out to win** and as such he will be entitled to take risks which would not otherwise be justified, but that will not protect him from liability if his negligent act in fact arises from his capacity as a person obliged to maintain his machine in a reasonably safe condition (see *Harrison* v *Vincent* at **2.3.1.3**).

3.7.1.2 Consent

We should also take account of the fact that a plaintiff's **consent** may affect the degree of care expected in certain situations as, for example, in the Court of Appeal decision in *Condon* v *Basi* [1985] 2 All ER 453 (approving the approach taken in the Australian case of *Rootes* v *Shelton* [1968] ALR 33). The issue here was the standard of care expected in a **sporting** activity in which the parties have agreed to abide by the rules of the game. In a game of football, for instance, 'serious and dangerous foul play' would be negligence, but that would not be true of every technical infringement of the rule because in the normal course of events accidental infringements of the rules are likely. In addition, more in the way of care (according to Sir John Donaldson MR) is required in the First Division than in a local league game. (See *Cases and Materials* (**3.5.1.1**) for *Condon* and details of a case which followed it — *Smolden* v *Whitworth*, *The Times*, 23 April and 18 December 1996. See **3.5.1** also for *McCord* v *Swansea City AFC*, *The Times*, 11 February 1997.)

3.7.1.3 Experts

It seems, also, that the foresight of the **ordinary** reasonable man is not appropriate in situations involving defendants who actually possess or hold themselves out as possessing special skills or expertise. Defendants in such cases are judged by the appropriate professional or 'expert' standard of care which, in the medical context, for example, is known as the '*Bolam*' standard.

'[W]here you get a situation which involves the use of some special skill or competence, the test as to whether there has been negligence or not is not the test of the man on the top of a Clapham omnibus because he has not got this special skill. The test is the standard of the ordinary skilled man exercising and professing to have that special skill': McNair J in *Bolam* v *Friern Hospital Management Committee* [1957] 1 WLR 582.

The judge went on to say '. . . he [the defendant, a doctor] is not guilty of negligence if he has acted in accordance with a practice accepted as proper by a responsible body of medical men skilled in that particular art'.

The 'Bolam Test', was approved in *Whitehouse* v *Jordan* [1981] 1 WLR 246 [HL] in which a surgeon was found not liable for brain damage allegedly caused during forceps delivery at the plaintiff's birth.

In *Matrix-Securities Ltd* v *Theodore Goddard (a firm)*, *The Times*, 13 November 1997, it was held that the duty of solicitors and counsel practising in a **specialised** field is to exercise such skill and care as would be exercised by a reasonably competent practitioner in the **relevant sector** (i.e. the **specialised** field) of those professions. 'Field' in this context means **area of work**.

SAQ 28

What ought to occur to the 'reasonable man' in special situations?

A defendant who has **claimed** to possess some special skill or expertise will normally be regarded as having 'held himself out' as possessing that skill or expertise, and will be judged accordingly.

Thus, *Cattley* v *St John's Ambulance Brigade* (1988) QBD (unreported) (but to which you will find reference in LEXIS and 53 *MLR* 255) involved an allegation of negligence against two members of the St John's Ambulance Brigade. The judge applied the *Bolam* test: 'has the defendant exercised the ordinary skill of an ordinary competent man exercising that particular art?'. He found that a volunteer administering first aid would be negligent if he did not observe the standards of 'the ordinary skilled first aider exercising and professing to have that special skill of a first aider'. No negligence was found on the facts because the volunteers had observed the procedures laid down in the Brigade's *First Aid Manual*.

We must distinguish, however, other situations, for example, where a layman renders first aid in an emergency. Such a person will not be expected to show the dexterity of a brain surgeon for he is not usually regarded as holding himself out as possessing any special skill.

In *Wells* v *Cooper* [1958] 2 QB 265 a householder performing the ordinary household task of screwing on a door knob was expected to observe the standard of a 'reasonably competent carpenter', but was not required to exhibit the competence of a carpenter working in a **professional** capacity.

According to *Phillips* v *Whiteley* [1938] 1 All ER 566 a jeweller who pierces ear-lobes will not be regarded as having purported to be anything other than what he is. (But do you suppose that a jeweller piercing ear-lobes today would be expected to have an increased awareness of the risks of infection, e.g. the HIV 'Aids' virus, through blood or other body fluids?)

On the other hand, you will not be surprised to learn that one who carries out electrical rewiring (*Green* v *Fibre Glass Co.* [1958] 1 QB 245), or electro-convulsive treatment (*Bolam* v *Friern Hospital* [1957] 1 WLR 582) will be expected to come up to professional standards even if he is not in fact possessed of them. In *Nettleship* v *Weston* [1971] 2 QB 691 it was held that a learner driver owes even to his passenger instructor the same degree of skill which would be expected from a qualified driver. In *Wilsher* v *Essex Area Health Authority* [1986] 3 All ER 801 (CA) it was held that an inexperienced doctor is expected to observe the standard of a reasonably competent doctor of the relevant grade. The standard of care was said to be related to the job undertaken **not** to the individual's experience.

SAQ 29

Do you think other considerations might be taken into account by the reasonable man?

The cases show that there is **no exhaustive** list of factors indicating breach of duty, but they also show that certain **common factors** are considered by the courts in setting the standard of care appropriate for the circumstances of the particular case. **These factors** are identified by most authorities (for example Street, *Law of Torts*, Chapter 13.2, 9th edn, 1993) as follows.

3.7.1.4 The usual practice in the trade, profession or calling in question

If the defendant has followed the normal pattern of care to be expected in his trade or profession, this raises a presumption that there was no breach of duty. In *Morris* v *W Hartlepool Navigation Co.* [1956] AC 552, however, the plaintiff was injured because a ship's hatch was left open and unfenced at sea. The evidence showed that the normal practice had been followed. According to Lord Cohen (at p. 579) 'when the court finds a clearly established practice "in like circumstances" the practice weighs heavily in the scale on the side of the defendant and the burden of establishing negligence, which the plaintiff has to discharge, is a heavy one'. On the facts, it was held that the plaintiff had discharged this burden because the general practice was so manifestly unsafe and unnecessary.

On the other hand, in *Gold* v *Haringey Health Authority* [1987] 2 All ER 888 (*Cases and Materials* (3.5.1.2)) a doctor did not warn his patient of the failure rate for sterilisation, but he was found not to be negligent **although experts said they would have warned the plaintiff**, because there was still a considerable number of doctors (possibly 50 per cent) who would **not** have issued a warning.

Conversely, the fact that the defendant has not followed the normal practice is evidence, but not proof, that he or she was negligent. According to *Salmond on Torts* (20th edn, 1992, p. 240) 'many advances in medical science have been due to such deviations'.

There is an argument that the courts in **medical** cases given **undue** emphasis to the 'normal practice' factor – usually in favour of the medical profession. See the brief extracts from the journal, *Professional Negligence* and Jones, *Textbook on Torts* in *Cases and Materials* at **3.5.1.2**. You can also read at that point about the decision in *Bolitho* v *City and Hackney Health Authority* [1997] 4 All ER 771: this is an important recent decision of the House of Lords.

3.7.1.5 The magnitude of the risk

In *Bolton* v *Stone* [1951] AC 850, the House of Lords found that the risk of anyone outside a cricket ground being injured from within was so remote that the defendant was not liable in negligence.

3.7.1.6 Importance of the defendant's objective

If the defendant is under some compulsion, legal or moral, to act, say, in an emergency, he may be expected to be less careful than otherwise. In *Watt* v *Hertfordshire CC* [1954] 1 WLR 835 (CA) firemen, in a hurry to rescue a woman trapped under a vehicle, failed properly to secure a heavy jack on the back of their lorry (the vehicle properly equipped for such a task being unavailable). The jack slipped and injured the plaintiff, one of the firemen. In the circumstances it was found that the fire authorities had **not** been negligent. Lord Denning indicated that the decision might have gone the other way had the defendants been engaged in ordinary commercial pursuits.

3.7.1.7 The seriousness of any likely injury to the plaintiff

In *Paris* v *Stepney BC* [1951] AC 367, a one-eyed workman, engaged on work underneath vehicles, was blinded in his remaining eye by a metal splinter. The House of Lords held that though his disability, which was known to the defendant (his employers), did not increase the likelihood of injury, it made any such injury much more serious than in the case of an ordinary employee and negligence was found on the facts.

3.7.1.8 The state of technical or scientific knowledge

This factor played a very important role in *Roe* v *Minister of Health* [1954] 2 QB 66, in which the plaintiff was admitted to hospital for treatment, including a spinal injection of nupercaine. The drug had to be stored in ampoules kept in a sterilising solution of phenol. Unknown to medical science generally, phenol could percolate through microscopic cracks in the ampoules. Thus the plaintiff came to be injected with carbolic acid and became paralysed from the waist down. It was held that the defendant was not liable for the actions of the doctors involved. As Denning LJ said: 'Nowadays it would be negligence not to realise the danger, but it was not then'.

You could compare *Roe* with the decision in *McGhee* v *National Coal Board* [1972] 3 All ER 1008. The plaintiff caught dermatitis from working in a brick kiln without the provision of adequate washing facilities by the defendant, his employer. The House of Lords held that the defendant was liable even though medical science could not show how exactly these conditions caused the ailment: it was sufficient that they were known to cause it.

3.7.1.9 The practicalities of taking precautionary steps

If safety measures are comparatively easy to take, the balance may weigh in favour (though not necessarily conclusively) of the plaintiff. In *Haley* v *London Electricity Board* [1965] AC 778 the defendant's servants 'roped off' a hole they had been digging in the road, blocking the entrance by a single bar, near the ground, to deter pedestrians. The plaintiff, a blind man, fell into the hole and was injured. It was held that because the presence of a blind person was foreseeable, and adequate precautions would have been simple to take, the defendant was liable.

On the other hand, in *Bolton* v *Stone* (see **3.7.1.5**), there was a distance of one hundred yards between the plaintiff and the batsman, and a seventeen-foot fence in between. In view of the slight risk, it was difficult to see what further precautions could have been taken.

3.7.2 SOME CONCLUSIONS

It would be a mistake to conclude that this list of 'relevant factors' is exhaustive (this has been indicated at **3.7.1**) and there may well be overlap between them. One important lesson which you should have drawn is that each case must turn on its own facts.

You may well find the following extract from Weir's *Casebook* (at p. 188) instructive in this respect:

> This decision [*Qualcast* v *Haynes* [1959] AC 743, which emphasised the importance of **the facts of the case** in **breach** problems] should deter counsel from citing decisions on breach as authority for the case in hand, and dissuade the student faced with a problem from hunting down cases 'on all fours', like a housewife seeking a matching thread in a haberdashery. But the student may have to read a good many cases in order to gain vicariously the experience which lies at the root of sound judgment. Despite the best efforts of the higher courts, however, counsel (who are paid by the day) continue to cite enormous numbers of case (see *Lambert* v *Lewis* [1982] AC 225) and county court judges (who are paid to use their judgment) continue to apply decisions on breach as if they laid down fixed rules ('inching forward into traffic isn't negligence', *Worsfold* v *Howe* [1980] 1 All ER 1028).
>
> Another effect of the principal decision [i.e. *Qualcast*] is to emphasise that the proper form of question, when one is dealing with breach of duty, is 'Did the defendant take reasonable care?' One must not pick on some feature of the defendant's acts and say: 'Was he under a duty not to do that?' (see also *A.C. Billings & Sons* v *Riden* [1958] AC 240, 264, per Lord Somervell of Harrow). Of course, the plaintiff must normally identify what it was in the defendant's behaviour that he finds objectionable — e.g. that he omitted to give a signal before turning right on the highway. But the question remains 'Did the defendant drive with reasonable care, considering that he gave no signal?' and does not become 'Was the defendant under a duty to give a signal?' Matters of detail are to be treated as part of the question of breach, not as raising sub-duties with a specific content.

Perhaps, however, we should leave the last word on this issue with James (*General Principles of the Law of Torts*, 4th edn): 'To say that conduct is "careless" or "negligent" is not to define, but to evaluate it; and evaluation can only be made in the light of some measure or "norm" which the evaluator has in mind.'.

See also *Cases and Materials* (**3.5.2**) for further decisions which illustrate the fixing of an appropriate standard of care in the circumstances of the case. One of these cases, *Mullin* v *Richards* [1998] 1 All ER 920 (CA), is of particular importance because it concerns the standard of care appropriate for 15-year-old schoolchildren.

3.7.3 BURDEN OF PROOF OF NEGLIGENCE ON THE FACTS

The burden of proving any allegation against the defendant lies on the **plaintiff**; the evidence being assessed on the so-called '**balance of probabilities**' and **not** on the basis of beyond all reasonable doubt (the higher standard applied in criminal law).

Read the extract from s. 11, Civil Evidence Act 1968 in *Cases and Materials* (3.5.3), and in one paragraph describe the implications for the law of tort.

The Civil Evidence Act 1968, s. 11, reverses the common law rule that a conviction may not be used as evidence in civil proceedings. The effect of the section is that if a person is proved to have committed an offence, he shall be taken to have committed that offence until the contrary is proved. Thus, for example, proof of a conviction of an offence involving negligence places the burden of disproving negligence on the defendant.

In **Chapter 4** you will find a discussion of two cases, *McGhee* v *NCB* and *Wilsher* v *Essex Area Health Authority* (see **4.4**). These decisions are also important authorities concerning the **plaintiff's burden of proof**.

Do you think circumstantial evidence can ever be used by a plaintiff? Consider the maxim *res ipsa loquitur*.

In some cases a plaintiff cannot point exactly to the person(s) to blame for his or her injury; a typical example would be of a plaintiff waking up after an operation in hospital to find a swab inside his or her body. It is in such situations that a court might be persuaded (after the plaintiff has made out an **outline** or **prima facie** case) to **infer** negligence by the defendant, unless the defendant can offer an acceptable explanation of the circumstances. Such a situation is summed up in the maxim *res ipsa loquitur* (in English this means 'let the thing/situation speak for itself').

Three conditions must be satisfied for the application of the maxim *res ipsa loquitur*. They are as follows:

(a)   that the defendant had a right to control of the thing or event; and

(b)   that the accident should be something which could not, in the normal course of events, have happened without **someone's** negligence; and

(c)   that there should be **no known facts** on the basis of which the accident can be explained in terms of the negligence of the defendant, thus excluding the operation of *res ipsa loquitur*).

When the maxim **does** apply (and this is a matter of law for the judge to decide) we should assess its **legal** effect, that is, we have to consider here whether:

(a)   any burden of proof shifts to the defendant; or

(b)   the proof burden remains with the plaintiff. In this case, the formal burden would stay with the plaintiff, but the defendant would have to cope with the evidential burden. In other words a prima facie inference of negligence is raised by the plaintiff, which must be displayed by evidence adduced by the defendant. If the defendant's story is capable of belief, the 'ball' is back with the plaintiff, by analogy with a game of tennis, in which the ball is constantly moving between the players. Here, each player will be hoping that his or her opponent will be put 'on the spot' in dealing with the delivery.

ACTIVITY 12

Please read the extracts from the cases *Henderson* v *Henry E. Jenkins & Sons* [1969] 3 All ER 756, *Ward* v *Tesco Stores Ltd* [1976] 1 All ER 219 and *Ng Chun Pui* v *Lee Chuen Tat* [1988] RTR 298, and Weir's *Casebook*, in *Cases and Materials* (3.5.3) and consider the following questions in the context of *res ipsa loquitur*:

(a)   whether an effect similar to strict liability is achieved in some negligence cases by its use;

(b)   does it mean that a defendant can be found liable on circumstantial evidence?

(c)   does the formal burden of proof remain with the plaintiff?

(a) It can be argued that the effect of the 'doctrine' of *res ipsa loquitur* is to produce in some negligence cases a form of strict liability. *Henderson* provides an example of such a decision.

(b) In effect, a defendant can be found liable on circumstantial evidence.

(c) It is said that the effect of the application of the 'doctrine' is that the plaintiff is entitled to judgment unless the defendant can exonerate himself. However, it is only a *prima facie* inference and if the defendant can produce some evidence to displace the inference the burden of proof remains with the plaintiff.

There is, however, authority for the proposition (*Henderson*, for example) that the effect of applying *res ipsa loquitur* is to reverse the burden of proof, i.e. the plaintiff, having made out a *prima facie* case of negligence, can expect the burden to pass to the defendant who will then be liable if he cannot prove that he was not negligent. The Privy Council, in *Ng Chun Pui*, however, has approved the former view, i.e. that a plea of *res ipsa loquitur* raises only a *prima facie* inference of negligence, and the burden of proof remains ultimately with the plaintiff.

See also *Cases and Materials* (3.5.3) for further important decisions concerning *res ipsa loquitur* and commentary by Wright and Milner.

3.8 Damage

In common with many other torts, such as nuisance, negligence requires proof of damage. It is for the plaintiff to prove that he or she has suffered '**damage**' *and* that **that** damage was **caused** by the defendant's tort(s). This matter is discussed in **Chapter 4**.

3.9 Summary

This chapter deals with the basic concept of the common law tort of negligence, though the issue of 'damage' is dealt with in **Chapter 4**. It is duty and breach of duty which we have examined at this stage.

All torts are composed of duty and breach; many of them also require damage and even where **a tort** is actionable *per se* (that is without proof of actual damage) for example, as in **trespass to the person**, **actual** damage will have to be established if the plaintiff wishes to receive **compensation**. Negligence, however, is of such an **open-ended** nature that **special** attention has to be paid to those elements.

In 'hard' cases (or novel situations) where there is little, if any, established authority on the issues raised, the courts have to have some means of setting boundaries for duty situations: there can never be negligence 'in the air'. In the words of Lord Keith in *Yuen Kun Yeu* (see **3.3.2**) '. . . Otherwise there would be liability in negligence on the part of one who sees another about to walk over a cliff with his head in the air, and forbears to shout a warning.'.

The Atkinian approach, the 'neighbour 'test', based on reasonable foreseeability, has formed the basis since 1932 for determining the existence of a duty of care especially in hard cases; though foreseeability **alone** has never been sufficient. 'Proximity' has for long also been required; and **policy** has always played a crucial role in this context.

It is true that, as a result principally of the views expressed by Lord Reid in *Dorset Yacht* and Lord Wilberforce in *Anns*, 'foreseeability' for a while was given a more prominent part to play; but a reaction set in to the more liberal approach that these opinions seemed to herald, mainly because it was felt that insufficient emphasis was being given to established authority.

Today, a three stage test (the 'Caparo test') is in vogue for deciding whether a duty of care should be imposed:

(a)   reasonable foreseeability must exist;

(b)   proximity must be present;

(c)   it must be 'just and reasonable' for a duty to be imposed in the circumstances of the case.

Furthermore, an **incremental** development of the law is favoured. This means that duties will be worked out on a case-by-case basis, by analogy with **established** categories of duties.

It is interesting to note that the main message emerging from the speeches in *Caparo* is that a 'test' approach to the question of 'duty' is undesirable and should therefore be avoided. If anything, *Caparo's* emphasis is on a 'just and reasonable'/incremental approach to the question of 'duty' or 'no duty'. The 'Caparo test' referred to today is thus the creation of judges and lawyers, pursuing some element of 'certainty' in post-*Caparo* cases.

On first acquaintance the notion of 'duty' in the present context suffers from a lack of definition, in terms of form and content. There is, undoubtedly, no magic formula available which will enable you to instantly recognise this somewhat amorphous concept. A duty will not appear simply as a result of someone chanting 'foreseeability, proximity and just and reasonable' as though those expressions formed some mantra (see Winfield — Preface to 14th ed.).

'Foreseeability' is sometimes said to be an issue of **fact** (the so-called 'factual duty') in that the court at this stage is enquiring into the question of whether the plaintiff has been **unreasonably** (note the emphasis on the last word) put at risk by the defendant: i.e. this is an enquiry into **probability.** Nevertheless, one should always be aware of the influence of **policy** considerations in this context. In other words, the enquiry into 'foreseeability' is not always the simple 'factual' exercise that it appears to be: foreseeability is a plastic concept which can be used by the courts to achieve **normative** ends.

For example, in 'nervous shock' cases (**see Chapter 6**) it is interesting to consider why it is that claims of 'rescuers' are favoured, whilst claims by 'bystanders' are not. Surely, in terms of **factual** foreseeability, bystanders at accidents are often at least as foreseeable as rescuers.

In **practice**, 'foreseeability' embraces both 'fact' and 'law' (concepts which are themselves 'adaptable' when used by a skilled and creative lawyer or judge). But, for purposes of **formal** argument, commentators generally regard the legal, policy issues as more appropriately arising at the 'proximity' and 'just and reasonable' stages of the enquiry.

'Proximity', unfortunately, is something which is generally more difficult to pin down than foreseeability' – yet it lies close to the heart of the modern tort of negligence. It is a **companion** of foreseeability: the two notions must not be regarded as **synonymous**.

Indeed, 'proximity' is meant to signify **something more** than mere closeness in terms of temporal or spatial relationships, though these factors of time and space are often of great practical significance. In some cases proximity may be established at least partly, by reference to **statutory and contractual** relationships existing between the parties.

In essence, 'proximity' describes (it does **not define**) the **legal** relationship existing between the parties once foreseeability has been established. Lord Atkin, in *Donoghue* v *Stevenson* itself, put it in the following terms:

Acts or omissions which any moral code would censure cannot in a practical world be treated so as to give a right to every person injured by them to demand relief. In this way, rules of law arise which limit the range of complainants and the extent of their remedy.

He made it clear, later in his speech, that the **general** governing factor in this context would be the 'neighbour principle'. We must, however, for purposes of formal argument, be careful to separate the 'foreseeability' element in the neighbour principle from the 'proximity' element: the notion of Atkinian neighbourhood is made up of these two elements.

In *Caparo* v *Dickman* Lord Oliver regarded 'proximity' as something which could not be defined: it was, in his Lordship's opinion, 'a **description** of circumstances from which pragmatically the law concludes that a duty of care exists' (emphasis added). In other words, a court uses 'proximity' merely to describe a conclusion which the court has reached on the basis of appropriate considerations, i.e. 'proximity' cannot indicate what the court's conclusion should be.

Caparo appears to base considerations pertinent to 'proximity' upon the **incremental** approach. With regard to novel situations, their Lordships approved the approach advocated by Brennan J in *Sutherland Shire Council* v *Heyman* (see **5.5.7**). 'Proximity', therefore, is established by referring to, and applying, existing case law.

At the proximity stage it is clear that legal policy will play a leading role, in that the manipulation and application of existing case law is a creative process: the court must decide whether or not to extend/adapt the law to meet new demands. If a new case is, to use a traditional legal expression, 'on all fours' (i.e. more or less alike) with previously decided authority then usually the result is something of a foregone conclusion; but often there may be argument about the applicability of an earlier authority to the facts of the new case. The precise scope of the earlier authority may be debatable because, for example, the judges in that case disagreed or a judgment may be somewhat obscure or did not consider factors which the later court regards as crucial to the issue.

In short, the application of the established law is invariably **not** straightforward: a position highlighted when a case is presented for consideration which is at the opposite end of the spectrum from the 'all fours' case, the **novel** case, i.e. the sort of case which earlier authority has not yet resolved **at all**. Here the court must decide whether to **extend** the existing law to an entirely new situation. Cases involving **'pure' economic loss, public authorities, psychiatric damage** and **omissions**, for example, are contentious and likely to be prominent in this context.

It is to the 'fair, just and reasonable' stage of the enquiry that such a case must be taken. The resolution of the case will thus depend on what might be called considerations of **naked** policy. Considerations of fairness, justice and reasonableness apply to **all** cases, however: they are not applied exclusively to the novel situation. Indeed, the House of Lords in *Marc Rich and Co. AG* v *Bishop Rock Marine Co. Ltd*, *'The Nicholas H'* (see **5.5.11**) said that **every** case, whatever the nature of the damage involved, had to satisfy the 'fair, just and reasonable' test. In other words, even where 'proximity' is clear an inference of duty may be rebutted by use of the 'fairness' test. Presumably, where there is a strong line of established authority on some issue it will be easier to satisfy that test than it would be, for example, in a novel situation where existing law has not addressed the issue, i.e. where existing authority is scanty or practically non-existent, and the court must appeal to first principles.

You should bear in mind that what you have just read is an attempt to describe the **formal** state of affairs in relation to the duty of care problem. It is this formal approach which you **must** take yourself whenever the question of whether or not a duty of care arises in relation to any problem you may encounter. In practice, however, the matter is less clear-cut.

Lord Oliver, in *Caparo* v *Dickman* said: 'The three requirements of proximity, justice and reasonableness and degree of foreseeability might be regarded as facets of the same thing.'. Lord Bridge, in the same case (see **5.5.7**) described the three stages as 'labels' rather than as **definitions**.

In other words we might say, to use a homely analogy, that a label bearing the words 'Tomato Relish' and listing the ingredients on a jar containing some edible concoction will tell the reader nothing of any substance about how that product has been put together.

Foreseeable risk was the predominant factor in the decision of the Court of Appeal in *Margereson and Hancock* v *J W Roberts Ltd* (**two cases heard together**), *The Times*, 17 April 1996. Over a number of years the appellants, who used asbestos in their manufacturing processes, deposited lots of asbestos dust outside their factory premises. Both plaintiffs, as young children (they were now of late middle-age), played in and with the dust. The plaintiffs, now suffering from mesothelioma (this disease of the lungs has a recognised scientific link with exposure to asbestos), claimed damages in the tort of negligence: the appellants argued that the potential dangers from exposure to asbestos did not come to their knowledge until 1933. The court, in dismissing the appeal, found that sufficient, material, knowledge was common long before that date and the test to be applied here was whether the appellants should have reasonably foreseen a risk of **some** pulmonary (i.e. lung) injury – not **necessarily** mesothelioma.

A sense of judgment is the only 'answer' here; this will develop only with time and perseverence. A sense of judgment will materialise in a gradual and incremental way, once **the whole of negligence, including established areas of liability** e.g. misstatements, has been encompassed.

You should look back on this topic after reading **Chapters 5 and 6** and think a little about the matter. The cases discussed and referred to in those chapters will help you in gaining insight and a feeling of 'judgment'.

It will be seen that although the existence of a duty cannot be divorced from the facts of each case i.e. in formal terms a duty can only be owed to an individual plaintiff on the facts, the courts are also involved in making normative decisions i.e. imposing value-judgments.

You can read extracts from Weir's Casebook and Howarth's Textbook in *Cases and Materials* (3.6).

Once a duty of care is established, the plaintiff must show that there has been a **breach** of that duty. The question of whether or not there has been a breach of duty turns on the relevant **standard of care** to be observed in the particular circumstances of the case.

We have seen that the relevant standard is that of the hypothetical reasonable man; the question posed in each case is 'how would the reasonable man have acted in the circumstances?'. Whilst this in formal terms consists of an **objective** approach to the problem, it is evident from the cases that subjective elements will inevitably influence any decision.

As with the 'Duty' issue in negligence, policy plays an active role in determining the standard of care issues too.

Finally, the operation of the maxim *res ipsa loquitur* has been noted. This is an aid available to plaintiffs in certain situations for getting cases off the ground. Without it they would not get very far at all because they are, in these special circumstances, unable to say precisely what went wrong and who is to blame. In a sense, plaintiffs are enabled to set proceedings rolling merely by pointing a reasonable finger of suspicion at the defendant.

3.10 Further Reading

Convery, Jane: 'Public or Private? Duty of Care in a Statutory Framework – *Stovin* v *Wise* in the House of Lords' (1997) 61 MLR 559.

Hepple, B.A., and Matthews, M.H., *Tort: Cases and Materials*, 5th edn, London: Butterworths, 1996, Chapters 2 and 5.

Jones, M., *Textbook on Torts*, 5th edn, London: Blackstone Press, 1996, Chapters 1, 2 and 3.

Markesinis, B.S., and Deakin, S.F., *Tort Law*, 3rd edn, Oxford: Oxford University Press, 1994, Chapters 1 and 2 (pp 65–162).

Salmond and Heuston, *Law of Torts*, 21st edn, London: Sweet and Maxwell, 1996, Chapters 2 and 9.

Stanton, K.M., *The Modern Law of Tort*, London: Sweet and Maxwell, 1994, Chapters 1, 2 and 3.

Street on Torts, 9th edn, London: Butterworths, 1993, Chapters 1, 11 and 13.

Weir, T., *A Casebook on Tort*, 8th edn, London: Sweet and Maxwell, 1996, Chapters 1 and 2.

Winfield and Jolowicz on Tort, 14th edn, London: Sweet and Maxwell, 1994, pp. (v)–(ix) and Chapters 1, 2 and 5.

3.11 End of Chapter Assessment Questions

1 '. . . the well known passage in Lord Atkin's speech [in *Donoghue* v *Stevenson*] should I think be regarded as a statement of principle. It is not to be treated as if it were a statutory definition. It will require qualification in new circumstances. But I think that the time has come when we can and should say that it ought to apply unless there is some justification or valid explanation for its exclusion.' (*Home Office* v *Dorset Yacht Company*, per Lord Reid.)

Discuss.

2 Mandy was driving her car home one night, when a tyre punctured as a result of an invisible structural defect in its wall. She attempted to change the wheel, but without success. Nick, a passing motorist, saw her plight and offered his assistance. He changed the wheel but forgot to tighten the wheel-nuts. As a result the wheel came off soon afterwards, the car crashed and Mandy was injured.

Advise her on any claim she may have in tort against Nick. Would your answer be different if Nick were an AA patrolman, whom Mandy had summoned to help her?

NB: **two** questions are given here because questions on duty of care in negligence often take the form of **essay** questions; and **Chapter 3** covers **breach** of duty, as well as duty.

See *Cases and Materials* (3.8) for specimen answers.

CHAPTER FOUR

CAUSATION AND REMOTENESS OF DAMAGE

4.1 Objectives

By the end of this chapter you should be able to:

■ appreciate the theoretical distinction between 'causation in **fact**' and 'causation in **law**';

■ assess critically the so-called **'but for'** test, assessing its utility in connection with the determination of 'factual' issues of causation;

■ assess the state of the case law on 'factual' causation **and**, in particular, appreciate the significance of the expressions (defences) *novus actus interveniens* and *nova causa interveniens*;

■ appreciate the two 'tests' for determining issues of 'remoteness' of damage ('causation in law'); as well as the significance of the so-called 'egg-shell skull' principle.

4.2 Introduction

You will find it convenient to deal with this topic immediately after studying the tort of negligence, since most of the case law deals with issues arising in that form of liability; but please try to bear in mind from the outset that **problems of causation and remoteness arise in all torts**: they are **not** restricted to the tort of negligence.

We will be examining in detail two topics in this chapter: they are called **causation** and **remoteness** but you may find it instructive to consider first the general nature of these topics.

In formal, theoretical terms we should be prepared to distinguish between **causation** and **remoteness**. We should always consider, however, what Lord Denning has told us on several occasions, see, for example his judgment in *Lamb* v *Camden LBC* [1981] 2 All ER 408, and that is that these two concepts **cannot** be separated in **practical** terms.

See also *Cases and Materials* (**4.1**) for extracts from Lord Denning's judgments in *Roe* v *Minister of Health* [1954] 2 All ER 131 and *Spartan Steel Ltd* v *Martin Ltd* [1972] 3 All ER 557.

What do you think the theoretical difference might be between causation and remoteness?

The cases seem to show that the difference lies in the following: causation refers to the chain of causation between the tort(s) and the damage; the plaintiff must establish an unbroken connection between his damage and the defendant's wrongful conduct. Causation is concerned with consequences and non-consequences in a **factual** sense. The issue is one of cause and effect.

Thus, for example, in the well-known case of *Barnett* v *Chelsea Hospital* [1969] 1 All ER 428, a patient, the deceased, had been admitted to hospital with severe vomiting and the doctor concerned failed, negligently, to diagnose the man's condition. The medical evidence showed that the patient would have died anyway, from poisoning as a result of ingesting arsenic, irrespective of the negligence in diagnosis, which was not an operative cause of the death. (The decision is an example of the application of the 'but for' test, which we will return to later in this chapter; see, e.g. **4.3**.)

In each case the basic issue to be determined is whether the defendant has **materially** contributed to the damage; his tort need not be the **only** cause of the injury.

On the other hand, remoteness is relevant at the stage following the establishment of a factual connection between tort and damage. It **is** concerned with consequences; but these are said to be legal rather than factual consequences, though it must be admitted that it is not always easy to draw a satisfactory distinction between factual and legal in this context. Remoteness is said to be concerned **only** with the question of **which** of the **established** consequences is to be the subject of compensation. Thus, for example, in **negligence** liability exists in general **only** for those consequences of a **reasonably foreseeable** type or kind.

NB: in this chapter, D1 means the first defendant and D2 means the second defendant.

4.3   Causation

In general, the courts approach this matter in a **pragmatic**, **common sense** way; considerations of strict logic and philosophy are eschewed by the judges and policy often plays an important role in the determination of difficult issues. Judges frequently emphasise the importance of common sense in this context, as, for example, Stephenson LJ in *Knightley* v *Johns* [1982] 1 All ER 851, a case which is discussed at **4.4.1**.

The **'but for' test** is usually employed in the investigation of causative links between the tort(s) and the damage. This test involves asking the simple question: 'would the plaintiff have incurred the damage "but for" the defendant's tort?'. A **negative** answer to this question means that it is likely that the defendant's wrong factually caused the plaintiff's damage.

If the damage would have been sustained **anyway**, **irrespective** of the defendant's wrong, there will be no liability: *Barnett* v *Chelsea Hospital* is a clear example of such a situation. This test is, however, a somewhat crude device and does not in every case provide a satisfactory solution, at least in more complex cases.

SAQ 32

Can you think of any situations in which the 'but for' test might be an inadequate device for settling disputes concerning causative links?

Amongst such situations are the following:

First, where there are **several** concurrent causes of the damage, each of them being sufficient on its own to produce the end result. Here, the 'but for' test would cancel out each cause; in strict, logical terms the damage **would** have occurred irrespective of cause A, because the **other** cause(s) would produce the result; so it would be with cause B, etc.

In such a case common sense would be applied (see, for example Stephenson LJ in *Knightley* v *Johns*) and the court would assess the share of blame as best it could in the circumstances. If, for example, **two** causes could be identified in a particular situation then, all things being equal, blame might be apportioned on a 50/50 basis. No doubt **policy** would be a factor to consider in such a context and, of course, each case will always turn on its facts.

Secondly, where there are **successive** acts/events causing damage. Thus, in *Cutler* v *Vauxhall Motors* [1974] 1 QB 418 the plaintiff grazed his right ankle in an accident caused by the defendants. The injury caused an ulcer to form and, because the plaintiff had been suffering for some time from varicose veins in both legs, an immediate operation was necessary. He claimed damages from the defendants for the **pain and discomfort of the operation** but the Court of Appeal held that since the plaintiff would very probably have needed a similar operation within five years in any case, the defendant's negligence could not be regarded as the cause of the **operation**.

However, in *Baker* v *Willoughby* [1969] All ER 1528, the defendant negligently injured the plaintiff's leg. He was later shot in that leg by X and the leg had to be amputated and an artificial one fitted in its place. The House of Lords held that the second injury did not make the defendant liable only for the plaintiff's disability until the time the leg was removed. As a matter of **policy** it was found that there was causal connection betweeen the defendant's negligence and the plaintiff's disability **after** the operation. If the first tortfeasor were released from further liability after the amputation and the second tortfeasor liable only for causing the removal of an already damaged leg, the plaintiff would receive less compensation than he deserved. It was decided that there was no practical difference between a permanently disabled natural leg (from the point of view of general disablement) and an artificial one. On that reasoning the defendant's liability was not decreased by the supervening act of X, whose own liability would be limited to the consequences of injury to an already disabled leg (here including the consequences of the necessary amputation). (The person responsible for the supervening act was a bank robber, who could not be traced; even if found he might prove to be a 'man of straw' and unable to meet any judgment made against him.)

A different approach was taken in *Jobling* v *Associated Dairies* [1982] AC 794 (see *Cases and Materials* (4.2)) in which the supervening event was a 'natural' one, i.e. a disease, which caused further injury to the plaintiff. The defendant was found liable by the House of Lords only up to the point at which the disease (it effectively ended the plaintiff's working life) took over. The court said that the later event must be taken into account in limiting the amount of damages awarded; the defendant was entitled to a 'discount'. (In general, the courts make a deduction for the 'vicissitudes of life'; these cannot be ignored where they have occurred by the date of the trial.)

In *Jobling, Baker* was criticised in terms of its general approach (though it was not declared to be wrong on its facts). Thus the law **may** recognise a distinction between a supervening **tort** and a supervening **natural event**. See the extract from Hepple and Matthews, *Tort: Cases and Materials*, in *Cases and Materials* (4.2).

You may have noticed that it is only in the most straightforward of circumstances that the 'but for' test will provide a ready answer. It is really only a starting-point in the process of establishing causation.

Thus in *Baker* and *Jobling* there were **supervening** events (or causes) to consider and the court in each case was obviously of the opinion that justice and fairness would not be achieved were there to be a simple application of the test to the facts. It is clear that a more pragmatic and policy-based solution was the aim in these circumstances. The same is true of *Cutler* except that the defendant's negligence in this case brought forward a future possibility.

Performance Cars v *Abraham* [1962] 1 QB 33 illustrates a rather different set of circumstances in which the 'but for' test was insufficient. There were two defendants in this case. The **first** one had negligently damaged the plaintiff's expensive car; later the **second** defendant collided with the car and the question of **his** liability for a paint respray arose. The court found that since this was **already** essential because of the damage sustained in the **first** accident, the **second** defendant was **not** liable for this part of the plaintiff's claim.

4.4   Proof of Causation

The legal burden of proof in this regard is on the **plaintiff**, on the basis of the **balance of probabilities**, i.e. that it is for the plaintiff to show that it is more likely than not that the defendant's wrong caused the loss.

This is difficult where the damage **might** also be due (as well as to the defendant's tort) to some non-tortious cause. The plaintiff must prove that the damage is due, at least substantially or materially, to the tort.

In *McGhee* v *NCB* [1972] 3 All ER 1008 (see *Cases and Materials* (4.3)) the plaintiff had contracted dermatitis through working in some brick kilns belonging to his employers. He claimed that they had been negligent in not installing showering facilities. The state of medical knowledge concerning dermatitis at the time meant that the court could not determine whether the taking of showers after work would have prevented the plaintiff from contracting the disease. The lower courts found the remployers to be in breach of statutory duty, by not providing adequate washing facilities, but said there was no tortious liability for the disease because the plaintiff could not show that the breach of duty had caused his injury. Nevertheless, the House of Lords held the defendants liable.

The House refused to distinguish between materially increasing the risk of injury by failure to provide showering facilities and materially contributing to injury.

 SAQ 33

What do you think is the effect of this decision on the law in general terms?

This decision raised the possibility that there had been a change in the fundamental obligation placed on a plaintiff in such cases, from proof of factual causation to one merely of proving breach of duty. In view of the state of medical knowledge at the time, and thus the uncertainty of the cause, the 'but for' test was jettisoned and the court applied what might be called a 'probably for' test.

McGhee was applied in two Court of Appeal cases in 1987. In *Fitzgerald* v *Lane* [1987] 2 All ER 455 the difficulty in proof of causation was not due to any deficiencies in the state of medical knowledge. The plaintiff, whilst crossing a road, was struck first by D1's car and then by D2's car. His damage included a neck injury. D2 claimed that the impact with **his** car was not a cause of the plaintiff's tetraplegia (the result of the neck injury). The plaintiff and D1 relied on *McGhee* and the question for the court was this: 'had the impact with D2's car caused or contributed to the tetraplegia by inflicting a blow to an uninjured neck, or had it increased the harm to an already injured neck?'. The Court considered that in such a case as this there was clearly a risk (on the evidence, even if the neck was already injured through impact with D1's car, further damage 'must' have been caused by D2, there was a dented bumper and broken number plate, for instance) that the plaintiff's head would be harmed in a way which could result in tetraplegia.

See also *Kay* v *Ayrshire and Arran Health Board* [1987] 2 All ER 417, *Page* v *Smith* [1996] 3 All ER 272 and *Hill* v *Tomkins, The Guardian*, 18 October 1997 in *Cases and Materials* (4.3).

Again, in *Hotson* v *East Berkshire Health Authority* [1987] 2 All ER 909 (*Cases and Materials* (4.3)) the plaintiff suffered from an injured leg from which there was a chance of a full recovery. However, his leg was permanently damaged after negligent medical treatment and his chances of recovery were reduced to somewhere between zero and 25 per cent. The House of Lords held, **reversing the** decision of the Court of Appeal, that there is no principle in tort which would allow a percentage of a full financial recovery based on probabilities. A plaintiff's claim could only be worked out on an 'all or nothing' basis.

Hotson involves the question of recovery for 'loss of chance' in **tort** : in the context of the case this concerned loss of chance of medical recovery.

You can read extracts from 'A Lost Chance for Compensation in the Tort of Negligence by the House of Lords' (1991) 54 MLR 511 and 'Causation in Medico-Legal Practice: A Doctor's Approach to the "Lost Opportunity" Cases', (1992) 55 MLR 521 in *Cases and Materials* (4.3).

You should know that the decision in *Hotson* was reversed on the ground that the plaintiff had failed to discharge the burden of proof placed on him, i.e. to show that there was a sufficient causative link between his condition and the defendant's negligence. The House of Lords left open the question of recovery for loss of chance in tort.

In *Allied Maples Group Ltd* v *Simmons* [1995] 4 All ER 907, the Court of Appeal, in a non-medical context, held that where a plaintiff's loss flowed from the defendant's negligence but was dependent upon the hypothetical behaviour of some independent third person, issues both of causation and quantification of damages could arise. First, in terms of causation, the plaintiff had to prove that he acted to obtain a benefit or avoid a risk. He was not required to prove in that sense that the third person would have so acted. At the second stage it was then sufficient for the plantiff to establish that there was a **substantial chance** (and not just a **speculative** one) that the third person would have acted in favour of the plaintiff. The assessment of a substantial chance was not a matter of causation, i.e. an issue to be determined according to the balance of probability, it was a matter of quantification of damages: ranging from the **barely real** or **substantial** to the **near certainty.**

The court approved the following observation of Lord Lowry in *Spring* v *Guardian Assurance plc* (see **Chapters 5** and **8**):

> [O]nce the duty of care is held to exist and the defendant's negligence is proved, the plaintiff only has to show that by reason of that negligence he has lost a reasonable chance [of employment — this was a case of a negligent reference] which would have to be evaluated and he thereby suffered loss . . . He does not have to prove that but for the negligent reference [the prospective employers] would have employed him.

The Court of Appeal in *First Interstate Bank of California* v *Cohen Arnold and Co., The Times,* 11 December 1995, confirmed that the evaluation of a substantial chance is a matter to be considered by the court when it is quantifying the amount of damages to be awarded. The defendant firm of chartered accountants reported negligently to the plaintiff bank that their client, X, a property developer, was a person of wealth. Consequently, the bank lent to X a sum of money well above their normal lending for the particular type of deal. X defaulted on the loan and the bank lost heavily. At first instance, the bank was awarded damages of £2.7m against the defendants.

On appeal, the Court of Appeal held, applying *Allied Maples*, that the judge at first instance, who had found that at the time the tort took effect the best price reasonably obtainable for the property was £3m, should have estimated the chance of selling it at that price in a falling market. That chance was two to one so the award would be reduced to £2m.

It must be remembered that *Ross* v *Caunters*, *White* v *Jones* and *Spring* v *Guardian Assurance plc* are 'loss of expectation' cases. See the extract from the article by Charles Lewis in *Cases and Materials* (4.3).

Please turn to *Cases and Materials* (4.3) and consider *Wilsher* v *Essex Area Health Authority* [1988] 1 All ER 871, paying particular attention to Lord Bridge's opinion expressed in that case. What was the outcome of this decision in relation to the ruling in *McGhee*?

The decision in *Wilsher* means that *McGhee* may only be helpful to a plaintiff where a single 'agent' (per Lord Bridge) or cause is involved, and the question is whether there has been a material increase in a clearly identifiable risk. There is room for discussion whether a material increase in risk is identical with a material contribution to an injury (Jones, pp. 112–18).

4.4.1 INTERVENING CAUSES

A defendant may seek to establish a break in the chain of causation by introducing arguments based on a *novus actus interveniens* (act of a stranger) or a *nova causa interveniens* (intervening incident). The resolution of such an argument will depend on **the facts of each case**, as interpreted by means of such guiding principles as are available to the judges, and the requirements of policy.

A useful starting-point is the decision of the Court of Appeal in *Knightley* v *Johns* [1982] 1 All ER 851. In this case the first defendant, Johns, had caused an accident in a road tunnel within which operated a one-way traffic system. A police inspector, who was in charge of the situation, realised that he had failed to close the tunnel to on-coming traffic and ordered two constables (one of whom was the plaintiff) to go back against the on-coming traffic in the tunnel to remedy his mistake. The plaintiff was injured when he collided with a car; the motorist was not negligent. In acting as they did both the inspector and the plaintiff had broken police standing orders. The plaintiff claimed damages from Johns, the police inspector and the chief constable (as being vicariously liable for the negligence of the inspector).

It was found by the Court of Appeal that though the plaintiff had added to the danger by his behaviour, not having acted in a wanton or foolhardy way, he was not guilty of negligence and therefore was not responsible for his own injuries. Thus the appeal was heard on the issue of whether the inspector had been negligent, and whether that negligence was a *novus actus interveniens* (see below) breaking the chain of causation between Johns' negligence and the plaintiff's injuries.

The court held that:

(a) the inspector **had** been negligent;

(b) in considering whether a *novus actus interveniens* had occurred it was necessary to ask the question 'was the damage the natural and probable, i.e. reasonably foreseeable, result of the defendant's negligence?'. Put another way, 'was something similar likely to happen?' (**not** a mere possibility which would not occur to a reasonable man; or if it did would be discounted by him as being so remote that no precautions were required). If the answer was 'yes', no event in the sequence of events was a *novus actus interveniens*. Common sense, rather than logic would show what was and what was not reasonably foreseeable;

(c) the inspector's negligence in the present case was the real cause of the plaintiff's injuries; it was a new cause and not a concurrent cause with the negligence of Johns. It broke the chain of causation between the latter's negligent act and the plaintiff's injuries.

Thus, the inspector and the chief constable were liable to the plaintiff.

In these cases, said Stephenson LJ, it was always helpful, though not necessarily decisive, to determine which events were deliberate choices to do positive acts; which events were omission or failures to act; which acts/omissions were innocent or mere miscalculations; and which acts/omissions were negligent. Deliberate/negligent acts were more likely to break the chain of causation than conduct which was not; positive acts would more easily break the chain than mere inaction; mistakes/miscalculations were more to be expected of human beings in a crisis.

The authorities suggest that in those situations where the supervening act/event is a 'natural and probable' consequence of the defendant's wrongful behaviour, the chain of causation is **not** broken.

In *Haynes* v *Harwood* [1935] 1 KB 146, Greer LJ said that a defendant may be liable for the consequences of the act of a third party where that act is 'the very kind of thing which is likely to happen if the want of care which is alleged takes place'.

You may find it instructive to compare the following two cases by way of illustration:

The plaintiff in *Wieland* v *Cyril Lord Carpets* [1969] 3 All ER 1006, was unable to use her bifocals (spectacles) properly, because of a neck injury caused by the defendant's negligence, and as a result fell down some stairs, suffering further injury. It was held that the defendant was liable for the fall as well as the neck injury. The plaintiff had acted reasonably in descending the stairs in the circumstances: it was necessary that she should go about her business and she had taken all possible care.

However, in *McKew* v *Holland* [1969] 3 All ER 1621 the plaintiff's legs were liable to give way without warning owing to an injury caused by the defendant's negligence. One day the plaintiff descended some stairs, felt his legs weaken, jumped to avoid a fall and broke his ankle. The House of Lords found that the chain of causation was broken; the defendant was not liable at all for the broken ankle. The plaintiff had acted unreasonably in the circumstances and was the **sole** author of his misfortune because he had not taken all reasonable care in the circumstances.

SAQ 34

Do you find it possible to reconcile these two decisions?

Wieland and *McKew* are difficult cases difficult to reconcile, other than on the basis that *McKew* is a classic case of contributory negligence (the **partial** defence under the Law Reform (Contributory Negligence) Act 1945); and that it was on **this** basis that the case should have proceeded rather than on a finding that the plaintiff was **wholly** to blame for his own injury. This defence is examined in **Chapter 2**.

A further authority will remind you of the importance of considering each case on its facts and the role played by policy in these decisions. In *Lamb* v *Camden London Borough Council* [1981] 2 All ER 408 (*Cases and Materials* (**4.3.1**)) the defendants conceded that they had committed a nuisance (and admitted negligence) by breaking a water main, which caused the plaintiff's house to be flooded so that it had to be vacated until it could be made safe. Squatters moved in and caused further damage to the property. The Court of Appeal held that the damage caused to the house by the squatters was too remote, and the defendants were therefore not liable for it. Lord Denning said that although it might be arguable that the damage caused by the squatters was reasonably foreseeable (the trial judge had found the damage unforeseeable and too remote: no one familiar with the house and locality would have regarded such invasions as 'likely'), as a matter of **policy** it was not a recoverable **form** of damage; the plaintiff could have insured against such risks (so spreading the risk through the community). Watkins LJ thought that a 'robust and sensible' approach should be taken to such matters. Although the damage might be 'reasonably foreseeable' the approach he favoured would often produce an 'instinctive' feeling that the damage (as in the present case) was too remote.

See also *Ward* v *Cannock Chase DC* [1985] 3 All ER 537 in *Cases and Materials* (**4.3.1**).

Salmond and Heuston, *The Law of Torts*, describes the decision in *Lamb* as an illustration of 'Common Sense and the Law' and you can read appropriate extracts from this book and Weir's *Casebook* in *Cases and Materials* (4.3.1).

4.4.1.1 Acts of third parties

In some instances the actions of third parties may be foreseeable and lead to liability on the part of the defendant.

In *The Oropesa* [1943] P 32, the persons in charge of the defendant's ship were responsible, as a result of their negligent navigation, for a collision with another ship. The master of this other ship put to sea in a lifeboat in order to discuss the possibility of salvaging his vessel. This action was found to be reasonable in the circumstances and therefore a foreseeable result of the collision. The personal representatives of the plaintiff, who was in the lifeboat and who drowned when it capsized, recovered damages from the defendant in negligence.

In *Stansbie* v *Troman* [1948] 2 All ER 48 the plaintiff, a householder, enlisted the services of the defendant, a painter. The plaintiff had to be absent from his house for a while and he left the defendant working there alone. Later, the defendant went out for two hours leaving the front door unlocked. He had been warned by the plaintiff to lock the door whenever he left the house. Whilst the house was empty someone entered it by the unlocked front door and stole some of the plaintiff's possessions. The defendant was held liable for the plaintiff's loss for, although the criminal action of a third party was involved, the possibility of theft from an unlocked house was one which should have occurred to the defendant.

Do you think it might make any difference if the third party is not fully responsible for his or her actions?

Many decisions have turned on this factor. The defendant will be liable for damage caused by such a person in those circumstances where he should have reasonably foreseen the third party's lack of responsibility.

In *Shiffman* v *Order of St John* [1936] 1 All ER 557 children playing in Hyde Park brought down a flag-pole insecurely erected there by the defendants, thus injuring the plaintiff. The defendants were held liable in negligence to the plaintiff. Also, in *Thomas* v *Bishop* [1976] CL 1872, the defendant was held liable when a loaded pistol which he had put on top of a cupboard was obtained by a child of two, who shot the plaintiff with it. It was found that the defendant ought reasonably to have foreseen that something of the sort might occur.

You should consider also the decisions in *Meah* v *McCreamer* [1985] 1 All ER 367 and [1986] 1 All ER 953 (Woolf J). The plaintiff sustained head injuries in an accident caused by the defendant's negligent driving. As a result, he underwent a marked personality change and subsequently committed crimes of violence against several women. Prior to the accident he had had a history of petty crime and a poor employment record, but he had had a number of relationships with women and there was no evidence of his being violent towards them. The plaintiff argued that without the accident he would not have committed these offences because there would have been no personality change. There was medical evidence to the effect that the plaintiff was in **any event** a 'criminally aggressive psychopath' and that he was someone who had 'underlying tendencies to sexual aggressiveness', but the judge regarded him as a person who was not committed to violent crime prior to his accident; it was due to the accident that his inhibitions had been reduced and he had given vent to his feelings.

The judge found in his favour and awarded him damages for his imprisonment, subject to a discount for his free board and his poor employment record; and for his criminal tendencies, which would probably have resulted in him spending some periods in prison. His damages were also reduced for his contributory negligence in accepting a lift from the defendant, knowing him to be drunk at the time.

You may be interested to know that the plaintiff was sued in trespass to the person, successfully, after his first action by two of the women he had attacked, and in the **1986** proceedings he claimed from the defendant **these** amounts of money. This claim was unsuccessful, being too remote; it would also be contrary to public policy, said the judge, to allow such a claim.

In *Lawrence* v *Osborne, The Times*, 8 November 1997, the plaintiff, an accountant, suffered brain damage in a motoring accident caused by the (admitted) negligence of the defendant. (The legal argument in this case concerned **size of damages**).

The accident had not impaired the plaintiff's intelligence, indeed his intelligence had possibly been enhanced as a result of the incident, according to the evidence. What the accident had done, however, was to turn the plaintiff into a 'helpless flirt' who was unable to stop proposing to women. In short, the accident had left the plaintiff with an impaired memory and a change of personality caused by damage to those parts of the brain governing behaviour, emotion and control. He was now a voluntary patient whose financial affairs were administered by the Court of Protection.

According to May J: 'In so far as Peter's [the plaintiff] present problems of disinhibition and temper are exacerbations of characteristics that he had before the accident, the essential difference is that before the accident they were under control and were not significant personal and social impediments, whereas now they are.'. His Lordship awarded the plaintiff £950,000 in damages.

Cornell v *Green, The Guardian*, 13 February 1998, is a decision of the Court of Appeal to much the same effect. On this occasion, however, the accident left the plaintiff a 'better person' who was 'too nice' to be employable in his old job as an insurance salesman. The accident (again, legal argument related only to **size of award**) had robbed the plaintiff of his thrusting and aggressive personality, essentially of his cunning characteristics, which had made him so good in his job. Stuart-Smith LJ said that as a result of the accident the plaintiff was unemployable in 'a reputable sales force'. The court awarded the plaintiff damages totalling £320,000.

4.4.1.2   Acts of the plaintiff

You will have noticed that we have already considered several cases in which the causative effect of the plaintiff's own behaviour has been at issue, namely *Wieland*, *McKew* and *Meah*. Would you consider it relevant that the plaintiff has committed suicide?

The authorities suggest that it is only another factor to weigh in the circumstances of each case.

Thus, in *Pigney* v *Pointer's Transport* [1957] 1 All ER 1121 the plaintiff committed suicide some years after he had received an injury to his head caused by the defendant's negligence. It was held that the suicide was the result of an acute anxiety neurosis and depression brought on by the head injury. Pigney's widow was successful in her claim against the defendants for damages for his death, because the original injury was still operating on Pigney so as to make him not entirely responsible for his actions. (In *McKew* v *Holland* for instance, the original injury did not prevent the plaintiff from taking proper care of himself.)

Lord Denning, however, in *Hyde* v *Tameside Area Health Authority, The Times*, 16 April 1981, denied that liability would lie for either an attempted or a successful suicide. He adopted a policy approach to the problem, basing his argument on the familiar 'floodgates of litigation' consideration and the fact that suicide is a crime in **ecclesiastical** law.

Watkins LJ and O'Connor LJ, unlike Lord Denning, said they found it unnecessary to consider the issue of causation, though Watkins LJ thought the plaintiff's attempt at suicide was not foreseeable in the circumstances and O'Connor LJ said:

> I do not think that the fact that a patient commits suicide or attempts suicide will necessarily break the chain of causation . . . It all depends on the circumstances of an individual case. In the present case applying *The Wagon Mound* [below] I do not think that the injury . . . can be connected to the breach of duty suggested against the hospital.

The finding of the court, in favour of the defendants, was a simple one, i.e. that there was just no negligence on the facts. To put the matter another way, the plaintiff had failed to establish a breach of duty by the defendant.

To take a further example, in *Kirkham* v *Anderton (Chief Constable of Greater Manchester)* [1990] 3 All ER 246 the Court of Appeal held that where the police fail to inform the prison authorities, in contravention of a code of practice, that a prisoner on remand has suicidal tendencies, that increases the risk that the prisoner might attempt suicide and the police are liable in negligence where the prisoner commits suicide. It would seem that in appropriately 'close', proximate circumstances a defendant can owe a duty to a plaintiff to protect the plaintiff from injuring himself by informing a third party of the potential danger.

4.4.1.3 Duty approach

You will find some cases in which the problem of acts of a third party is treated as a **duty** issue. In *Perl* v *Camden LBC* [1984] QB 342 it was held that the defendant council did not in the circumstances owe a duty to the plaintiff to secure their premises to such an extent that thieves could not gain access via these premises to the plaintiff's dwelling. The court said that there was no special relationship as in *Dorset Yacht* (see **Chapter 3**), and *Stansbie* v *Troman* (see **4.4.1.1**) was distinguished on the ground that in that case there existed a contract between the parties and there was an element of reliance by the plaintiff on the defendant.

A similar problem faced the Court of Appeal in *King* v *Liverpool City Council* [1986] 3 All ER 544. The plaintiff was the tenant of a council flat, and the flat directly above her was unoccupied. She informed the council, the defendants, of the unoccupied flat and the fact that it was not protected against vandals. Nothing was done and vandals entered the empty flat, ripping out water-pipes etc. The plaintiff's flat was flooded. More complaints were made by the plaintiff and the defendants took some measures, but they were by no means extensive and vandals entered on two more occasions. There was more flooding of the plaintiff's flat. She claimed that the council had been negligent and were therefore liable to her in both negligence and nuisance. It was held (affirming the decision at first instance) that since there was little that was available to the defendants in the way of effective deterrent measures, they owed no duty of care to the plaintiff. The court emphasised that there must be a **duty** in such cases to prevent harm from the actions of third parties.

Of course, each case turns on its facts and it does **not** follow that the existence of a duty of care **always** depends on whether the defendant could have taken precautions where the risk is foreseeable.

Finally, in *Smith* v *Littlewoods Organisation* [1987] 1 All ER 710 (***Cases and Materials*** (**4.2.1**)) the House of Lords found that the owners of a disused cinema were not liable for damage to neighbouring properties caused by a fire started by trespassers at the cinema; on the facts, the owners had no knowledge of any fire risk arising from the state of the cinema. A duty of care to prevent that damage was the only duty alleged on Littlewoods and unless they were bound reasonably to anticipate and guard against that danger, they had no relevant duty of care requiring them to inspect the premises.

According to Lord Mackay, while it was probably the case that children might attempt to break into the cinema, that by no means established that it was a probable consequence of its being 'vacated and not lockfast' that it would be set on fire. No one anticipated any adverse consequences arising from the cinema. His Lordship drew a distinction between a fire hazard on premises and the 'ordinary case' of theft, where the thief used one set of premises to gain access to other premises from which he intended to steal; there was no similar hazard (to fire) on the first proprietor's land in such a case. Neighbours could take steps against theft in a way not possible with fire.

Lord Goff said there was no **general** duty of care to prevent third parties from causing damage, and there was nothing in the circumstances of the present case to put the defendants under any particular obligation.

4.4.1.4   Intervening medical negligence

What we have to consider here is the issue of intervention: 'does supervening human behaviour **necessarily** operate so to break the chain of causation?'. In **general** terms it is **likely** that supervening negligence by a third party will be unforeseeable, and therefore will break the causative link between the original wrong and the damage.

Problems are often encountered where later damage is inflicted by negligence: for example, where original injuries are aggravated or further (i.e. new) damage is caused by later **medical** negligence. In this situation the court must decide whether the first cause was still operative at the time of the later negligence.

The House of Lords in *Hogan* v *Bentinck Collieries* [1949] 1 All ER 588, a case concerned with Workmen's Compensation Acts (now repealed) held that medical **negligence** interrupted causation. Lord Normand said: '[However] an operation prudently advised and skilfully and carefully carried out should not be treated as a new cause, whatever its consequences may be'.

It has been held, in a **non-medical** context, that a person who tortiously creates a dangerous situation in the **highway** is not exonerated from liability for further consequences only on the basis that someone else comes along and **negligently** exacerbates matters.

SAQ 37

Just pause at this point and write down a set of facts which might illustrate such circumstances.

You might have been thinking about the sort of circumstances that occurred in *Wright* v *Lodge and Shepherd* [1993] 4 All ER 299, where the Court of Appeal exonerated from blame, for subsequent events, the driver of a car who had negligently failed to get her car off the road when the vehicle broke down at night. The road was unlit, the weather was foggy and the second defendant, a lorry driver, collided with the car injuring a passenger. **Both** the car driver **and** the lorry driver were found liable to the **passenger**; but the lorry driver **alone** was liable to **other** road users when his vehicle overturned on the **opposite** side of the dual carriageway. The court came to this second conclusion because the lorry driver was guilty of **reckless** driving, and this **recklessness** effectively broke the chain of causation (it was a *novus actus interveniens*) between the first driver's negligence and the injuries to the **other** road users. According to the evidence, this **second** batch of damages would not have occurred had the lorry driver been only **negligent**.

The question to be answered in **all** these cases where the issue of intervening causes is raised is: 'what is within the scope of the risk created by the original defendant's negligence?'.

ACTIVITY 14

Consider the extract from the judgment of Beldam LJ in the decision of the Court of Appeal in *R* v *Cheshire* [1991] 3 All ER 670 in *Cases and Materials* (4.3.1.2). What guidance does this give on the issue of causation in the law of tort?

You will find that his Lordship emphasises the different policies behind the criminal law and the law of tort. In the **latter**, it may be more likely that the chain of causation will be broken because the law is concerned primarily with liability to pay **compensation**, rather than with the question of deterrence.

4.4.1.5   Action taken by the plaintiff to minimise his/her loss

In general, it is unlikely that a plaintiff will break the chain of causation when performing their general legal obligation to **mitigate** the loss. The Court of Appeal in *Spartan Steel & Alloys Ltd* v *Martin & Co. (Contractors) Ltd* [1973] 1 QB 27 seemed to have been of this opinion, but presumably the plaintiff's performance of this obligation will have to be reasonable in the circumstances. (*Spartan Steel* is the subject of study in **Chapter 5**.)

4.4.1.6   Reflex action

A 'natural' reflex action on the part of a third party or the plaintiff is probably something which a defendant will have to accept as 'likely to happen'. In *Carmarthenshire County Council* v *Lewis* [1955] AC 549 (HL) a motorist swerved instinctively to avoid a young boy who dashed across the road after escaping from school as a result of the defendants' negligence. The motorist was injured, and received damages from the defendants.

The decision in *Lewis* was based on the special relationship that exists between a school authority and the children in its care. This relationship is something like that which exists between children and their parents, although a school authority will usually have a **contractual**, or **statutory** relationship with the child or his or her parents as the case may be. Parents, teachers and school authorities, and social workers and social services authorities are expected to exercise the standard of care of the 'prudent parent' with regard to the behaviour of children in their care, and may be held **personally, not** vicariously, liable for that behaviour in appropriate circumstances.

This behaviour may, due to lack of appropriate control in the circumstances, be a causative factor in accidents affecting third parties, as in *Lewis*. It may also lead to liability on the part of the person in charge for theft and damage caused intentionally by the child. In *Vicar of Writtle* v *Essex County Council* (1979) LQR 656, a local authority, in its statutory capacity as **social services authority**, was found liable in negligence for theft and damage caused by a young person in its care. (You will recall that *Dorset Yacht*, a case encountered in **Chapter 3**, is a case which proceeds on similar lines. Note, also, the decision in *Jauffer* v *Akhbar*, which you will find discussed in **Chapter 7**).

The 'person in charge' may also be liable where **the child** is injured, due to lack of adequate supervision. Thus, in *Barnes* v *Hampshire County Council* [1969] 3 All ER 746, a teacher, for whom the local education authority was **vicariously liable**, negligently allowed a young child to wander off into a nearby busy road, after classes had finished; as a result the child was injured.

In English law, however, the issue of **parental** liability is a moot point. It is thought that the courts would, in general, be reluctant to find liability on the part of a parent in negligence for injury caused to a child through lack of adequate supervision, on the policy ground that such litigation would be harmful to the family relationship.

There are, nevertheless, some circumstances in which the law **may** allow claims; typically, these are situations, in which there exists **insurance** cover. In *Parnell* v *Duguid*, *The Guardian*, 22 July 1997, a 13-year-old boy sued his mother for acute burns he suffered as a baby. He was burned after playing with matches when his mother, the defendant, left him in her car whilst shopping. Kay J approved a **settlement** of damages with the mother's insurers, but, whilst **negligence** (i.e. breach of duty) was not admitted, it appears that the existence of a duty of care was not contested.

Occupiers' liability (see **Chapter 7**) is another area of liability in which insurance plays a very active role, and actions by children against their parents as **occupiers** of premises are unlikely to conflict with any policy concerning family relationships. **Settlements** with insurers are, in general, more likely than litigation.

You should, at this point, look back to **Chapter 3** and the discussion on 'duty of care' and 'breach of duty' contained therein.

4.5   Remoteness

There are two main tests of remoteness which are applied in **tort**, namely **direct** consequences and **foreseeable** consequences.

ACTIVITY 15

Try to write down what you think each of these terms means and what is the essential difference between them.

4.5.1   DIRECTNESS

The leading authority is *Re Polemis* [1921] 3 KB 560. As a result of the negligence of stevedores, who were servants of the defendant, a plank fell into a ship's hold containing petrol in metal containers. The impact of the plank as it hit the floor of the hold caused a spark, and petrol vapour was ignited. The ship was destroyed. Arbitrators found that the spark could not have been reasonably foreseen, though **some** damage was foreseeable from the impact.

The Court of Appeal held, unanimously, that the defendant was liable since the plaintiff's loss (the consequence of the defendant's servants' negligence) was a direct, though not reasonably foreseeable, result. Unfortunately 'directness' was not defined, and there is still doubt as to whether 'direct' damage is confined to damage suffered by plaintiffs which is foreseeable in a **general** sense, or to damage to the **particular** interest of the plaintiff which was likely to be affected.

The ruling by the court appears to be this: provided **some** damage is foreseeable, liability lies for **all the natural and direct** consequences flowing from the breach of duty. Obviously, the decision is based on a **broad** approach to the definition of 'kind' of damage.

4.5.1.1   Reasonable foreseeability

The leading authority is *The Wagon Mound (No. 1)* [1961] AC 388 (*Cases and Materials* (**4.4.1.1**)).

The defendant carelessly discharged oil from a ship in Sydney Harbour, and the oil floated on the surface of the water towards the plaintiff's wharf. The plaintiff's servants, who were welding on the wharf, continued their work after being advised (**non-negligently**) that it was safe to do so. Sparks from the welding equipment first of all ignited cotton waste mixed up in the oil; then the oil itself caught fire. The plaintiff sued for destruction of the wharf by fire.

The defendant was found not liable in negligence, because it was not reasonably foreseeable that the oil might ignite on water in these circumstances. Damage by **fouling** was foreseeable; damage by **fire** (the case here) was **not** foreseeable. This approach was felt to be fairer to defendants, on the argument that the *Re Polemis* test was insufficiently precise and likely to lead to an unfair burden being placed on tortfeasors. Furthermore, it had the effect of ensuring that foreseeability governed **all three** stages of negligence.

The Privy Council declared that as far as the tort of negligence was concerned *Re Polemis* was no longer good law and liability would lie only for foreseeable damage of the **kind** or **type** in fact suffered by the plaintiff.

Do you suppose that the ruling in *The Wagon Mound* resulted in a big change in the law?

There is authority for the proposition that a **broad** approach should be taken in interpreting 'kind' or 'type', at any rate as far as **personal** injury is concerned. After all, there will be **practical** significance in 'kind' or 'type' only if precision is required in their interpretation. The difference between *Polemis* and *Wagon Mound* turns on how the two cases define 'kind of damage'. Some cases decided since 1961 suggest that the courts have not departed significantly from *Polemis*. Let us have a look at them.

Thus, for example, in *Bradford* v *Robinson Rentals Ltd* [1967] 1 All ER 267, the plaintiff, an employee of the defendant, was sent on a 500 mile journey in a van with no heater in extremely cold weather, despite his protests. The defendant argued that damage by way of pneumonia or chilblains was foreseeable; but not the plaintiff's actual injury, which was frostbite. It was held that the plaintiff's injury was of a foreseeable type (injury from cold), so he succeeded.

A more precise approach was taken in *Tremain* v *Pike* [1969] 3 All ER 1303, however. The plaintiff, an employee of the defendant, caught leptospirosis (Weil's disease) through coming into contact with the urine of infected rats on the defendant's farm. It was alleged that the farm was overrun by the rodents because of the defendant's negligence.

Payne J said: 'This, in my view, was entirely different in kind from the effect of a rat bite or food poisoning by the consumption of food or drink contaminated by rats.'. He went on to find that the plaintiff's damage was too remote. The judge in this case evidently gave a **strict** interpretation to the words 'kind' or 'type'.

Although the decision in *Tremain* probably accords more with the letter of the law in *Wagon Mound*, it is in **practice** the approach taken by the judge in *Robinson* which more accurately reflects the attitude of the courts to 'kind' or 'type', at least in **personal injury** cases. *Tremain* is probably out of line with general authority. With regard to **property** damage (including **pure economic loss**) the position is less clear. According to Markesinis and Deakin (p. 189): '. . . the test of remoteness for property damage . . . is more strict . . . The precise limits to recovery can probably only be established on a case-by-case basis.'. See also the extracts from McKendrick and Stanton in **Cases and Materials** (**4.4.1.1**).

You may be interested to learn that on the **facts** of the case, i.e. on the evidence, *Tremain* might well in any event be decided differently today. In *Campbell* v *Percy Bilton, The*

Guardian, 17 February 1988, it was held that where an employee of the defendants contracted Weil's disease through coming into contact with water infected by rats' urine (he was employed on a building site where he came into contact with pools of infected water in crevices in steel girders, etc.), he was entitled to damages in view of the incidence of the disease (it was greater than in 1969) and the available knowledge of this hazard in that particular working environment.

4.5.1.2 The way in which the damage occurs

According to *Hughes* v *Lord Advocate* [1963] 1 All ER 705 (***Cases and Materials*** (**4.4.1.2**)) **the whole complex of events** leading to the injury (which must **itself** be of a foreseeable 'type' or 'kind') does not need to satisfy the foreseeability test.

Post Office engineers left a hole in the road covered by a tent and marked by oil lamps. The plaintiff, a boy of eight, was badly burned when he entered the tent and dropped an oil lamp into the hole, which contained explosive gas. It was held that injury by burning (touching a hot lamp) was foreseeable, and injury by explosion was 'by burning'. Lord Guest said: '. . . it is sufficient if the accident which occurred is of a type which should have been foreseeable.'. According to Lord Reid the 'precise concatenation of circumstances' need not be foreseeable.

You should, however, compare with this decision the approach taken by the Court of Appeal in *Doughty* v *Turner Manufacturing Co.* [1964] 1 All ER 98 (***Cases and Materials*** (**4.3.1.2**)). The defendant's servant knocked a loose asbestos-cement cover into a cauldron of sodium cyanide which was at a temperature of 800°C. The plaintiff moved closer to see inside it, since there had been no reaction. A few minutes later there was an explosion and he was injured.

Do you think he would be awarded damages?

In the event, he was **not** awarded damages.

It was held that only a **splash** was foreseeable: '. . . it would be quite unrealistic to describe this accident as a variant of the perils from splashing' (per Pearce LJ).

There seems little doubt that *Doughty* does not follow the *Hughes* line of reasoning. Indeed, *Doughty* appears to proceed on the same interpretation of *Wagon Mound* as *Tremain*. You may care to know that *Doughty* was decided at a time when asbestos was thought to be safe and unlikely to behave in this fashion. It has already been pointed out that *Tremain* might be decided differently today.

Much will depend on the assessment by the court (on the evidence led) of the risk involved in each case. Thus, for example, a broad view of **fire** risk was taken by Woolf J in *Salmon* v *Seafarer Restaurants Ltd* [1983] 3 All ER 729 and Lord Bridge in *Ogwo* v *Taylor* [1988] AC 431: '. . . [the plaintiff fireman] has no time to reflect on the precise nature and extent of the risks he is running'.

By way of contrast, in *Crossley* v *Rawlinson* [1981] 3 All ER 674, it was found that an injury to a would-be rescuer was not foreseeable because the injury was suffered **on the way** to the dangerous state of affairs. In the court's opinion the plaintiff's injury had come about in an unforeseeable way.

The decisions on *Wagon Mound* seem to raise the question of whether **quantum** or amount) of risk is relevant at the **remoteness** stage, as opposed to the **duty** stage, where it clearly is relevant; at the **remoteness** stage of the argument only foreseeability of **consequences** (**not** of risk) needs to be established. **If it is** relevant, and the cases suggest a **positive** answer, it might be claimed that the *Wagon Mound* test is one of **risk** or **hazard** rather than precise foreseeability of damage, and therefore more appropriate to the **duty** stage. However, since foreseeability is now relevant at **each** of the **three** stages of inquiry in negligence, perhaps the issue is one only of **academic** significance.

4.5.1.3 Extent of harm

According to *Vacwell Engineering* v *BDH Chemicals* [1971] 1 QB 88, foreseeability as to **extent** of damage is **not** necessary. In this case it was held that an **explosion** was foreseeable in the circumstances and that that was sufficient for liability: it was irrelevant that the explosion that in fact occurred was unforeseeably **large**.

You may find it helpful at this stage to stop reading for a little while and write a short paragraph, outlining the case for and against the notion of foreseeability (as opposed to directness) in relation to remoteness of damage.

Foreseeability is a more flexible concept than that of directness, and helps the courts to arrive more easily at policy decisions. It is also said to achieve fairer results for defendants, where their liability depends on 'fault'. On the other hand, whilst this may be a desirable state of affairs in some respects it is also the case that foreseeability entails a large measure of unpredictability. Its unpredictability in relation to the duty of care issue has been noted in **Chapter 3**. The role of the concept in connection with remoteness is, however, much more in the nature of a touchstone of liability than is the case with duty and is therefore of much greater significance in the present context, because it determines more precisely the **extent** of the defendant's liability for what is by now his or her established negligence.

You will find discussion on this point by *Dias* in the *Cambridge Law Journal* [1962] CLJ 178. An extract from this article appears in *Cases and Materials* (**4.3.1.1**).

4.5.1.4 Relative nature of foreseeability

You may find the decision in *The Heron II* [1969] 1 AC 350 of interest in this context; indeed, those of you who have studied the law of contract will probably remember the case as an important authority in that subject.

The House of Lords, in emphasising the difference between the rules of remoteness in contract and in tort, gave to the word **foreseeable** a meaning different from **probable** or **likely**. Lord Reid said that the rule in **tort** imposes a much wider liability than that in contract:

> . . . the defendant will be liable for any **type** [or kind] of damage which is reasonably foreseeable as liable to happen even in the most unusual case, unless the risk is so small that a reasonable man would in the whole circumstances feel justified in neglecting it.

'Foreseeability is a **relative**, not an **absolute** concept' [*emphasis added*]: *Winfield* p. 161.

ACTIVITY 17

Please turn to *Cases and Materials* (4.4.1.4) and consider the *Wagon Mound (No. 2)* [1966] 2 All ER 709 (Privy Council). After considering the facts of the case and the extract from Lord Reid's speech, write down a summary of its significance in relation to remoteness of damage.

Lord Reid considers that a risk is foreseeable to the 'reasonable man' even in what might seem to be 'improbable' cases, i.e. it can be a 'real' risk for present purposes even though it is only a **small** risk. He also said the tort of nuisance, as well as the tort of negligence, was governed by the *Wagon Mound* test of remoteness.

You will find in **Chapter 10**, that the House of Lords in *Cambridge Water Co.* v *Eastern Counties Leather plc* [1994] 1 All ER 53, has confirmed Lord Reid's finding on nuisance (see **10.4.3**).

In essence, he reiterated this view in *The Heron II* (above), though that case does **not** deal with the torts of negligence and nuisance: the point of debate concerned remoteness of damage in contract and tort **generally**.

See also *Slatter* v *British Railways Board* [1966] 2 Lloyd's Rep 395 in *Cases and Materials* (**4.4.1.4**).

4.5.1.5 The jurisdiction of foreseeability as a test of remoteness of damage

You do need to consider, at some stage, the question of whether 'foreseeability' is restricted to the law of negligence as a governing factor in 'remoteness'. All the evidence points to the conclusion that its jurisdiction **extends beyond** the boundaries of the tort of negligence.

The *Wagon Mound (No. 2)* (above) is authority for the proposition that the tort of **nuisance** is subject to the same test of remoteness as negligence, and the House of Lords has held in *Cambridge Water Co.* v *Eastern Counties Leather plc* [1994] 1 All ER 53 that this is **also** the case for liability arising under the rule in *Rylands* v *Fletcher*, which imposes **strict** liability at common law. (Nuisance and *Rylands* v *Fletcher* are covered in **Chapters 10** and **11**.)

'There now seems every likelihood that foreseeability will be held to be the test of remoteness in some other torts as well, whether or not it [foreseeability] is the test of liability.' (*Winfield* pp. 158–9.)

It may not apply to **deceit** (*Winfield* p. 289) or any tort where liability turns on proof of intention or recklessness; the action for breach of statutory duty may also be exempt from the influence of foreseeability. The position with the tort of defamation is not abundantly clear.

4.6   Sensitive Plaintiffs

 SAQ 39

Do you think it possible that some plaintiffs get special treatment? Can you think of a sensitive plaintiff?

It is at this point that we should consider the effect of the so-called 'egg-shell skull' rule, i.e. the defendant must '**take his victim as he finds him**'. According to this rule, once reasonably foreseeable damage occurs (of course it must be of the right 'kind' or 'type') the defendant is liable for the **full** extent of that damage, even where that extent would not normally be expected.

In *Smith* v *Leech Brain* [1962] 2 QB 405 for example (approved in *Wagon Mound (No. 1)*) the plaintiff was splashed and slightly burned on the lip by molten metal, due to the defendant's negligence. Through the plaintiff's predisposition to cancer, the burn became malignant and the plaintiff died. The defendant was found fully liable, although a 'normal' person would not have suffered the cancer and death in those circumstances.

Again, in *Robinson* v *The Post Office* [1974] 2 All ER 737, the defendants negligently lacerated the plaintiff's leg, and a doctor was negligent in carrying out the test dose procedure for allergy reaction to anti-tetanus serum. As a result of the doctor giving the plaintiff an anti-tetanus injection, the plaintiff contracted inflammation of the brain, because he was allergic to the injected serum. The defendants were found wholly and solely liable for the plaintiff's damage, including the complications suffered as a result of the allergic reaction. It was shown that the plaintiff would have suffered the same harm whether or not the doctor had been negligent, and the defendants had to 'take their victim as they found him', with his allergy.

You may also find the following observation of Eveleigh J in *Wieland* v *Cyril Lord Carpets* (see **4.4.1**) of interest:

> I do not regard the *Wagon Mound* as dealing with the extent of the original injury or the degree to which it has affected the plaintiff. Still less do I regard it as requiring foreseeability of the manner in which that original injury has caused harm to the plaintiff. Indeed the precise mechanics of the way in which the negligent act results in the original injury do not have to be foreseen.

His Lordship is here affirming the 'egg-shell skull' rule and the validity of *Hughes* (see **4.5.1.2**).

In relation to **property**, to paraphrase Scrutton LJ in *The Arpad* [1934] P 189, if one injures a horse which happens to be the Derby winner one cannot claim that one thought it to be only 'an old nag'. However, *Winfield* (p. 164) says:

> [It is more uncertain, however] where the loss claimed is not 'intrinsic' [but is due to the fact that the plaintiff cannot, as a result of the damage,] **earn profits** [from the property]. (*Emphasis added*)

(There is authority both ways, i.e. that foreseeability **is** relevant and that it is **not** relevant in such circumstances.)

In *Parsons* v *Uttley Ingham* [1978] QB 791 (CA) a **contract** case involving injury to pigs, and in which Lord Denning regarded the test of remoteness in contract as being the same as in tort, it was said that as long as **some** kind of illness/injury (to the pigs) was foreseeable it did not matter that it eventually took the form of an unforeseeably rare kind of illness/injury.

You should be aware that there is much disagreement with Lord Denning's view on remoteness in contract and tort. We can see that it does not accord with Lord Reid's view in *The Heron II* (see **4.5.1.4**).

You may care to know, however, that in **assessing monetary damages** (i.e. in awarding compensation) the court will take into account the fact that an 'egg-shell skull' victim is at greater risk from the ordinary vicissitudes of life than a 'normal' person, and might well award him or her less than would be given to a 'normal' plaintiff.

You should distinguish from this 'egg-shell skull' rule, the principle that in assessing the amount of monetary compensation to which a plaintiff is entitled, the plaintiff's 'worth' or 'value' (the same is true of his or her property) cannot be subject to foreseeability reasoning. Thus, it is a defendant's bad luck if he or she happens to injure the chairperson of a privatised utility (invariably a high-earner) rather than a vagrant.

4.6.1 IMPECUNIOSITY

The Liesbosch [1933] AC 449 (also known as *The Edison*) is a leading authority on this point. The defendant's ship, *The Edison*, sank *The Liesbosch*, a dredger, belonging to the plaintiff. The plaintiff was held entitled to recover the following for the defendant's negligence:

(a) the cost and delivery of a similar dredger at market price, which was foreseeable;

(b) the cost of a pecuniary guarantee to a harbour authority, payable for breach of contract caused by the sinking of the dredger (economic loss flowing from the plaintiff's physical loss); but **not**

(c) the extra expense incurred in hiring at a very high rate, instead of buying, a substitute dredger, for this was caused by the plaintiff's own impecuniosity; the plaintiff's financial loss had been aggravated only by his **own** lack of resources.

Thus, the plaintiff's poor financial state was **his** own bad luck and he could not claim any loss that could be attributed to that factor.

The decision in *The Liesbosch* was strongly influenced by considerations of policy (e.g. see the speech of Lord Wright) and appears to be out of accord with the principle that the defendant must 'take his victim as he finds him' (both physically and financially).

The Liesbosch has been distinguished by the Court of Appeal where extra cost was incurred in delaying repairs to a damaged car pending the approval of the plaintiff's insurer (in *Martindale* v *Duncan* [1973] 1 WLR 574) and to a damaged building where the delay was reasonable on commercial grounds (in *Dodd Properties (Kent) Ltd* v *Canterbury City Council* [1980] 1 All ER 928). However, in *The Borag* [1981] 1 WLR 274, CA, the plaintiffs incurred interest charges on overdrafts in order to provide a guarantee to secure release of their ship which had been wrongfully arrested. The loss was held to be too remote.

It was also distinguished in *Perry* v *Sidney Phillips* [1982] 3 All ER 705 (CA). (In this case it was found that an action in negligence and an action in contract can exist concurrently;

the two actions may be available for the benefit of the same person.) The plaintiff bought a defective house; and was also made redundant in his employment. He had, in the normal course of events, put in an offer for the house subject to contract and satisfactory surveyor's report. The defendant surveyors had reported that the house was in a satisfactory state, but on the plaintiff moving in various serious defects were discovered. The plaintiff obtained another surveyor's report, and estimates from builders for remedial work. He was involved in much expense and trouble.

The question arose as to whether the plaintiff had done anything to **mitigate** his loss. Apparently he had not carried out any major repair work for several reasons: (i) he could not afford the expense (a second mortgage was not available); (ii) repairs might hide the serious defects; (iii) the intransigence of the defendants. He had, however, carried out a few small repairs himself and had obtained advice about a damp course and the eradication of woodworm, etc.

The defendants were held liable for the negligent performance of their contract to survey the house. Damages for inconvenience and vexation were included, though cost of repairs over and above the fall in value of the house (the plaintiff did not intend to effect the repairs) were not. In such cases a plaintiff is entitled, basically, to the difference between market value and what was paid for the house.

It was found that *The Liesbosch* did not apply to **mitigation**. In relation to mitigating his loss, the plaintiff had acted reasonably in the circumstances.

Mattocks v *Mann* [1993] RTR 13 (CA) provides another interesting illustration of the limits of the ruling in *The Liesbosch*. The plaintiff's car was damaged and she made a claim against the third party's insurers, who failed to provide her with the money for the repairs (as agreed) but she could not herself pay the cost of the work. The repairers refused to release the car until they were paid, so she carried on hiring a car until the insurers paid up. It was found that she could claim against the third party (and therefore their insurers) for **that** part of the hire period (as well as for the rest of the period). In the 'varied web' of affairs after an accident only in 'exceptional circumstances' was it possible or correct to isolate a plaintiff's impecuniosity as a separate cause and as terminating the consequences of a defendant's wrong. It could be contemplated, clearly, in such circumstances that where repair costs were substantial the source of that cost would be the insurers. It had made clear that the insurers would indemnify the third party and they had instructed an engineer to negotiate. In reliance on this the plaintiff had given instructions to the repairers to go ahead with the work.

4.7   Intention/Recklessness

Consequences (as opposed to **acts**) which the defendant **intends** or about which he is **reckless** may involve liability for **more extensive consequences**. In such cases it may be that the court will **presume** that the defendant intended the 'natural and probable consequences' of his behaviour. You may care to consider this point further when you come across the example, in **Chapter 10**, of the ruling in *Wilkinson* v *Downton* [1897] 2 QB 57 (see **10.6.2.2**).

4.8   Summary

'Causation' and 'remoteness' are issues which may be of crucial importance in **any** context within which tortious liability is in question. In this book, however, they are dealt with immediately after the treatment of 'Negligence' because most difficulties are in practice encountered in this form of liability.

In conventional, formal, terms 'causation' and 'remoteness' represent different stages in the process of linking the defendant's breach of duty with the plaintiff's damage.

'Causation' is all about the 'factual' link, i.e. there must be an unbroken chain of causation between breach and damage; once that issue is settled, there remains the question about consequences in the 'legal' sense, i.e. 'is the defendant liable for all or only some or for none of the results of his or her tort?'.

Although, in the final analysis, there is probably only one, single problem of 'remoteness of damage' (it is certainly dealt with in that fashion by some leading writers and see Lord Denning in *Lamb* v *Camden Borough Council* (see **4.4.1**)), this book deals with the matter under separate headings for the reason that this provides you, the learner, with a clearer introduction to the complexities of the subject.

The 'but for' test, you will have found, provides an answer to the problem of 'causation in fact' in straightforward cases, but in more complex situations the court must feel its way to a solution as best it can. It is said that the approach of the 'ordinary' person imbued with the virtue of 'common sense' is the one adopted by the courts: we saw this, for example, in *Knightley* v *Johns*. Various assumptions (for example, *Cutler* and *Jobling*) are made, but broader 'policy' reasoning can produce results like *Baker* v *Willoughby* and *McGhee*.

In **general** terms 'foreseeability' is the ruling factor in causation cases; this is clear from the authorities on *novus actus interveniens* and *nova causa interveniens*, as we saw, for example, in *Haynes* v *Harwood* and *Stansbie* v *Troman*.

It is important for you to remember that the burden of proving the causative link is on the plaintiff, and the House of Lords has fairly recently gone to the trouble in *Wilsher* to make this point abundantly clear.

The plaintiff must also be prepared to justify his or her case on the issue of remoteness of damage or 'legal' consequences, because a defendant will not necessarily be liable for all the consequences that flow from his or her tort.

In negligence (and some other torts, such as nuisance) the *Wagon Mound* test applies, and a defendant will only be liable where the plaintiff has actually suffered damage of the 'kind' or 'type' which was foreseeable in the circumstances; or, rather, **reasonably** foreseeable in the circumstances: Oliver LJ in *Lamb*. You will have read that the *Wagon Mound* test replaced the *Re Polemis* 'direct consequences' test, though that approach is probably still in vogue in some contexts, such as deceit.

You will have noted that there is some controversy, at least in academic circles, concerning the difference between the *Polemis* and *Wagon Mound* tests. In **practice**, there seems little to choose between them bearing in mind the decisions in *Hughes*, the 'egg-shell skull' cases, and personal injury cases generally. There is room for debate as to whether the rather benign approach taken in personal injury cases to the exact requirements of 'kind' or 'type' applies to property damage.

We have seen that *The Liesbosch* says the 'egg-shell skull' rule does not apply to **impecunious** plaintiffs, i.e. a defendant does not have to take his or her plaintiff's 'poverty' as he or she finds it. This rule has, however, been qualified in more recent cases such as *Mattocks* v *Mann*.

In overall terms, policy plays a crucial role in all aspects of 'causation' and 'remoteness'. You will by now find that statement unsurprising.

See also the extracts from Jones, Fleming, Markesinis and Deakin, and Winfield in *Cases and Materials* (4.5).

4.9 Further Reading

Hepple, B.A., and Matthews, M.H., *Tort: Cases and Materials*, 5th edn, London: Butterworths, 1996, Chapter 6.

Jones, M., *Textbook on Torts*, 5th edn, London: Blackstone Press, 1996, Chapter 4.

Markesinis, B.S., and Deakin, S.F., *Tort Law*, 3rd edn, Oxford: Oxford University Press, 1994, pp 163–192.

Salmond and Heuston, *Law of Torts*, 21st edn, London: Sweet and Maxwell, 1996, pp. 521–540.

Stanton, K.M., *The Modern Law of Tort*, London: Sweet and Maxwell, 1994, Chapter 4.

Street on Torts, 9th edn, London: Butterworths, 1993, Chapter 14.

Weir, T., *A Casebook on Tort*, 8th edn, London: Sweet and Maxwell, 1996, Chapter 4.

Winfield and Jolowicz on Tort, 14th edn, London: Sweet and Maxwell, 1994, Chapter 6.

4.10   End of Chapter Assessment Question

David leaves an old paraffin lamp burning in his garden shed, where there is a strong draught. As a result fire starts, and spreads rapidly. This fire combines with another fire, the source of which is unknown, and the fire produced by this combination threatens Penny's house, which is located a quarter of a mile away. Penny is holding a garden party at the time, and a general panic ensues. Richard, the butler, drops a tray containing rare antique glasses, one of which cuts the arm of Fay, a haemophiliac, who bleeds to death before hospital treatment can be obtained. Penny's house is destroyed in the conflagration.

Advise David, on his liability in tort, if any.

See *Cases and Materials* (4.7) for a specimen answer.

CHAPTER FIVE

NEGLIGENCE: 'PURE' ECONOMIC LOSS/NEGLIGENT MISSTATEMENT

5.1 Objectives

By the end of this chapter you should be able to:

■ state the law concerning claims for 'pure' economic loss in the tort of negligence;

■ appreciate the evolution of the law regarding liability for negligent **'misstatements'** and its apparent **separation** from the position concerning liability for negligent **'acts'**;

■ appreciate the significance of the decisions in *Hedley Byrne* v *Heller* and *Caparo* v *Dickman* and of the special relationship requirement established in the former case, as interpreted in the later authority;

■ apply the law relating to third party claims in cases of negligent misstatements and appreciate the significance of the decisions in *Ross* v *Caunters* and *White* v *Jones* in connection with the relationship between contract and tort.

5.2 Introduction

In historical terms claims for 'pure' economic (or financial) loss have **generally** been **unsuccessful** in the tort of **negligence.** The law of tort in general is mostly concerned with **physical** loss and economic loss consequential upon that physical damage. Loss of a purely economic nature is recoverable elsewhere, however, for example in the law of **contract** and, indeed, in some **torts,** such as **deceit, conspiracy and interference with contractual relations**.

At common law the traditional position is that where negligence leads to so-called **'pure' economic** loss, i.e. financial loss which is not the **direct** result of **physical** loss, that loss may well **not** be recoverable. **Consequential** loss, i.e. financial loss which is the **direct** result of physical damage (whether to person or property) is generally recoverable.

Thus, in *Cattle* v *Stockton Waterworks* (1875) LR 10 QB 453, the plaintiff had contracted with a landowner to build a tunnel under his land and was unable to recover extra expenses incurred in finishing the work after the defendant (a waterworks) had negligently flooded the land. The decision went against the plaintiff because his 'only' loss was connected to his liability under the contract to finish the job on time. No tangible property of his had been damaged; nor had he suffered any personal injury. Any financial loss flowing from either kind of damage **would** have been recoverable.

This decision has been confirmed in a long line of later decisions, for example *SA de Rémorguage à Hélice* v *Bennetts* [1911] 1 KB 243 (a tug company was unable to recover the towing fee lost when the defendant sank its tow); *Weller* v *Foot and Mouth Disease Research Institute* [1966] 1 QB 569 (auctioneers failed to recover profits from cattle auctions cancelled owing to an outbreak of foot and mouth disease (caused by the defendant's negligence) amongst cattle in the surrounding area); *Electrochrome Ltd* v *Welsh Plastics Ltd* [1968] 2 All ER 205 (a case involving similar facts to *SCM* and *Spartan Steel* (below) except that the interruption of supply to the plaintiff's factory was of water, i.e. interruption of mains water supply caused by a damaged fire hydrant).

In *British Celanese* v *Hunt* [1969] 2 All ER 1252 the defendant negligently allowed metal foil strips stored on his land to blow on to a power line, cutting the supply to the plaintiff's factory. **Machines were damaged** and economic loss resulted. The plaintiff was awarded full damages because the economic loss flowed from tangible damage to property, in other words both the physical damage to the machines caused by molten metals solidifying therein, and the resultant economic loss, were recoverable. A similar decision was arrived at in *SCM* v *Whittall* [1971] 1 QB 337, where the defendant cut an underground cable supplying electricity to the plaintiff's factory.

Please read the facts of *Spartan Steel & Alloys Ltd* v *Martin & Co. (Contractors) Ltd* [1973] 1 QB 27 in *Cases and Materials* (5.1). In one paragraph, describe the outcome of this case.

The Court of Appeal, by a majority, held that only the first two heads were redressable: the third was pure economic loss not flowing from the plaintiff's own physical loss. Lord Denning said this decision was dictated by **policy**: an admittedly arbitrary line had to be drawn somewhere, otherwise liability would rocket out of control. He pointed out that the plaintiff could insure against such a risk, so spreading the cost throughout the community. It would be an unfair burden to place liability on 'one pair of shoulders' in such circumstances.

Edmund Davies LJ (**dissenting**), admitting that his view did not accord with tradition, said that he would have allowed the third head **as well**, since it was a foreseeable and direct consequence of the defendant's negligent act. (Lord Roskill in *Junior Books* (below) gave some support to this view.)

You should make a point of remembering that this case is an authority on **remoteness of damage**; it is **not** a 'duty' case.

You should read a case on manufacturer's liability arising under the 'narrow' rule in *Donoghue* v *Stevenson* (an important part of **negligence**, though it is dealt with in **Chapter**

13) called *Aswan Engineering Establishment Co.* v *Lupdine Ltd* [1987] 1 All ER 135 (*Cases and Materials* (**5.1**)). It illustrates well the distinction between 'mere' economic loss and economic loss caused by damage to property.

By way of conclusion, you may care to take note of the following observation made by Lord Diplock in *Lambert* v *Lewis* [1981] 2 WLR 713:

> where the economic loss suffered by a distributor in the chain between the manufacturer and the ultimate consumer consists of a liability to pay damages to the ultimate consumer for physical injuries sustained by him, or consists of a liability to indemnify a distributor lower in the chain of distribution for his liability to the ultimate consumer for damages for physical injuries, such economic loss is not recoverable under the *Donoghue* v *Stevenson* principle from the manufacturer.

His Lordship was referring to the so-called 'narrow' rule in *Donoghue*, which imposes a duty of care on manufacturers to their ultimate consumers. This branch of negligence is dealt with under Product Liability in **Chapter 13**.

The innocent reader may be surprised to learn that the other judges in the House of Lords held, however, that such a loss **may** be recoverable. This decision (which forms a **special** situation in the tort of negligence) shows how difficult it is to predict in advance how the courts will classify claims for financial loss.

In line with this decision it was found in *Virgo Steamship Co.* v *Skaarup Shipping Corporation* [1988] 1 Lloyd's Rep 352 that a claim for pure economic loss may be actionable where it forms part of a chain of claims which **originated** in a claim for physical damage.

In this chapter we will trace the development of the law regarding 'pure' economic loss in **traditional** terms, i.e. according to the vector of production; that is to say on the basis of whether the financial loss was caused by a negligent **act** or a negligent **misstatement**. It will be seen that where loss is suffered as a result of reliance on a **misstatement**, that loss is recoverable, provided the conditions of recovery are satisfied. We will attempt to show later, however, that it may be misleading to separate loss caused by 'acts' from loss caused by 'misstatements'.

5.3   Acts: the Principle

SAQ 40

From what you have just read in 5.2, do you think it the case that there exists a general rule, subject perhaps to exceptions, that damages for 'pure' economic loss cannot be recovered in the tort of negligence?

The answer to this question is as tentative as the issue is confusing!

In traditional terms the answer seems to be 'yes'. 'As a general rule "pure" economic loss is irrecoverable in the tort of negligence': Stanton (p. 332).

On this view of the law, it seems that in order to succeed in a claim for pure economic loss a plaintiff must bring his or her case within some recognised exception to the general rule. The authorities discussed in **5.2** certainly give considerable support to this view.

It is submitted, however, that the true answer is 'no'. As Lord Oliver said in *Murphy* v *Brentwood District Council* [1990] 2 All ER 908 (a case which will be discussed in **Chapter 7**):

> It does not, of course, at all follow as a matter of necessity from the mere fact that the only damage suffered by a plaintiff in an action for the tort of negligence is pecuniary or 'economic' that his claim is bound to fail. It is true that, in an uninterrupted line of cases since 1875, it has consistently been held that a third party cannot successfully sue in tort for the interference with his economic expectations of advantage resulting from injury to the person or property of another person with whom he has or is likely to have a contractual relationship (see *Cattle* v *Stockton Waterworks Co.* (1875), *Simpson & Co.* v *Thomson* (1877), *SA de Rémorquage à Hélice* v *Bennetts* (1911)). That principle was applied more recently by Widgery J in *Weller & Co.* v *Foot and Mouth Disease Research Institute* (1965) and received its most recent reiteration in the decision of this House in *Leigh and Sillivan Ltd* v *Aliakmon Shipping Co. Ltd* (1986). But it is far from clear from these decisions that the reason for the plaintiff's failure was simply that the only loss sustained was 'economic'. Rather they seem to have been based either on the remoteness of the damage as a matter of direct causation or, more probably, on the 'floodgates' argument of the impossibility of containing liability within any acceptable bounds if the law were to permit such claims to succeed. The decision of this House in *Morris Steamship Co. Ltd* v *Greystoke Castle* (1946) demonstrates that the mere fact that the primary damage suffered by a plaintiff is pecuniary is no necessary bar to an action in negligence given the proper circumstances (in that case, what was said to be the 'joint venture' interest of shipowners and the owners of cargo carried on board) and if the matter remained in doubt that doubt was conclusively resolved by the decision of this House in *Hedley Byrne & Co. Ltd* v *Heller & Partners Ltd* (1963) where Lord Devlin convincingly demonstrated the illogicality of a distinction between financial loss caused directly and financial loss resulting from physical injury to personal property.

> The critical question, as was pointed out in the analysis of Brennan J in his judgment in *Sutherland Shire Council* v *Heyman* (1985) is not the nature of the damage in itself, whether physical or pecuniary, but whether the scope of the duty of care in the circumstances of the case is such as to embrace damage of the kind which the plaintiff claims to have sustained (see *Caparo Industries plc* v *Dickman* (1990)).

In the same case Lord Keith expressed the contrary view, that recovery for pure economic loss is possible **only** if the plaintiff falls within some recognised exception (such as liability for negligent misstatement, discussed below) to the general rule, which forbids recovery.

It is submitted that there is, in fact, little difference in substance between the views expressed by Stanton and Lord Keith on the one hand, and Lord Oliver on the other: once any 'exception' to the 'general rule' is recognised, the reality is that 'pure' financial loss is recoverable.

5.4   The Decision in *Junior Books* v *Veitchi*

Please read about *Junior Books Ltd* v *Veitchi Co. Ltd* [1982] 3 All ER 201 in *Cases and Materials* (5.2). What was the outcome of that case? Write down your answer in one paragraph.

It was decided in **preliminary** proceedings (no ruling on actual liability was made by the House of Lords) that the defendants probably did owe a duty of care in the **tort of negligence** to the plaintiffs; certainly there was a case to argue and the matter was referred back to the court of origin (in Scotland) for resolution of the issue.

You should note that there was no action available in contract against X (the **plaintiffs** had chosen the defendants) and the plaintiffs' architect had not been negligent.

5.4.1   POST-*JUNIOR BOOKS* DEVELOPMENTS

In terms of conventional wisdom this decision had enormous implications. Was not the plaintiff's claim one for **contractual** liability, though framed in **tort**? It is as though the plaintiffs had claimed a breach of **warranty** by the defendants, a warranty of care and skill. Lord Brandon, dissenting, certainly thought so. He pointed out the difficulties inherent in assessing the facts relating to quality in tort: unlike contract, the law of tort does not have a body of established criteria for tackling this problem.

The majority reasoning, however, was based on the very special circumstances of the case: it was obvious that the parties were **extremely** close in terms and proximity and foreseeability. The plaintiff was claiming on an **individual** basis, not even as a member of a closely defined class of potential plaintiffs.

The general interpretation given to this decision in **later** cases is a **restrictive** one. No doubt this reaction will not surprise you, in view of the cautious approach taken to the **general** development of the tort of negligence. *Junior Books* has been interpreted by a number of judges as turning on the plaintiffs' 'reliance' on the skill of the defendants.

The House of Lords in *Leigh and Sillavan Ltd* v *Aliakmon Shipping Co. Ltd* [1986] 2 All ER 145, held that a shipowner owed no duty of care to a buyer of goods which, it was claimed, had been damaged due to faulty storage whilst they were in the defendant's care; at the relevant time the buyer had neither title to nor possession of the goods. It was pointed out that there was already a settled line of cases on the point, and that authority should not be undermined by arguments based merely on foreseeability and proximity.

Doubt was expressed on the importance of 'reliance' in limiting liability for pure economic loss in cases where there had been no express **misstatement** by the defendant. We will see later that there may be liability for pure economic loss where the plaintiff has relied on a **misstatement** made by the defendant.

In effect, the court refused to give to the plaintiff a remedy in tort where none existed in contract.

You may be interested to know that in the **Court of Appeal** Goff LJ **did** find that a duty of care existed but also found that there had been no **breach** of that duty.

In *Tate and Lyle* v *GLC* [1983] 1 All ER 1159, *Junior Books* was equated to a case in which damage to property had actually **occurred,** though this does seem difficult to accept. In *Junior Books* the floor had not been damaged; its **quality** was defective.

5.4.2   CONTRACTUAL RELATIONSHIPS

The existence of a **contractual** framework underlying the issue of liability has been put forward in some cases as the reason for not allowing an action in **tort**.

In *Candlewood Navigation Corporation Ltd* v *Mitsui OSK Lines Ltd* [1985] 2 All ER 935, the Privy Council held that a plaintiff with no proprietary or possessory rights to goods, but only a contractual claim over them, could not claim damages in **tort** for economic loss suffered when those goods were damaged by the defendant. The law of tort could not be used, it was said, to provide a remedy where none existed in contract. Lord Fraser (who was in the majority in *Junior Books*) said that though *Junior Books* 'may be regarded as having extended the scope of duty somewhat' it was 'not in point' here.

ACTIVITY 20

Please read about *Muirhead* v *Industrial Tank Specialities* [1985] 3 All ER 750 in *Cases and Materials* (5.2.1). How does the view of Goff LJ differ from that of the other judges in the Court of Appeal?

In the opinion of Goff LJ the facts of *Junior Books* showed 'the parties had deliberately structured their contractual relationship in order to achieve the result . . . no direct liability inter se'. He thought it 'safest' to regard *Junior Books* as authority for liability on the basis of 'a very close relationship between the parties' on its particular facts, and chose not to stress the element of **reliance** emphasised by the other judges.

In *Greater Nottingham Co-operative Society Ltd* v *Cementation Piling and Foundations Ltd* [1989] QB 71 (CA), it was held that the Society's claim in the **tort** of negligence for foreseeable economic loss caused by the mode of performance of the defendant's contractual obligations could not be sustained, because there was **actual** privity of contract between the plaintiff and defendant. This contract was silent with regard to the way in which the defendant was to carry out its work. Purchas LJ said there should be borne in mind the fact that the parties had an 'actual opportunity to define their relationship by means of contract and took it'. Woolf LJ indicated that 'for the time being at any rate' the courts were against any expansion of liability for pure economic loss beyond what was 'strictly required' by binding authority.

5.4.3 GENERAL POINTS

The following **general** observation on *Junior Books* by Lord Goff in *Smith* v *Littlewoods Organisation* [1987] 1 All ER 710 (HL), will also be of some interest to you: '. . . in *Junior Books* . . . some members of your Lordships' House succumbed, perhaps too easily, to the temptation to adopt a solution based simply on proximity.'.

In **Chapter 7** you will find discussion of two important House of Lords cases, *D & F Estates* v *Church Commissioners for England* [1989] AC 187 and *Murphy* v *Brentwood District Council* [1990] 2 All ER 908. Their Lordships in these cases regarded *Junior Books* as turning on its own special facts, in other words liability was based on a relationship of a **unique** nature.

It is submitted that the authorities on liability for pure economic loss inflicted by negligent acts do **not** demonstrate beyond doubt that recovery is denied in such cases because of a general **rule** to that effect. *Junior Books* is not said to be **wrongly** decided; rather, it is said to be of **limited application**, which is another matter. The courts are **reluctant** to impose liability for pure economic loss caused by acts, but a policy is not quite the same as a general rule, and a court should impose such liability where it is fair, just and reasonable to do so.

No doubt you will by now feel inclined to agree with Hepple and Matthews (p. 152) who say that we are dealing here with '. . . [a] conceptual morass'.

Please note that a number of the cases in **Chapter 7**, which is concerned with liability in connection with **premises,** are also concerned with 'pure' economic loss. *D & F Estates* and *Murphy* are leading cases on economic loss, but they are discussed in detail in that chapter because they are best understood in the context of 'premises'.

5.5 Misstatements

Liability for negligent misstatements causing pure economic loss lies in ordinary common law negligence: it is **not** a separate tort. Thus the usual requirements of duty, breach and damage have to be proved. The special treatment is necessary because:

(a) the plaintiff must also establish extra factors under the head of 'duty';

(b) the cases are difficult;

(c) there is an overlap with the law of contract; and

(d) a duty has only been fully recognised since the decision of the House of Lords in *Hedley Byrne and Co.* v *Heller and Partners* [1963] 2 All ER 575.

The law of negligence in **this** respect has developed more slowly and restrictively than liability for negligence generally.

What do you think may be the reasons for this cautious development of the law?

There appear to be two main reasons for this state of affairs:

(a) people are generally less careful in what they say than in what they do, particularly when expressing opinions on social or informal occasions, rather than in their business or professional capacity; and

(b) in the words of Lord Pearce in *Hedley Byrne* '. . . words are more volatile than deeds, they travel fast and far afield, they are used without being expended.'.

5.5.1 LIABILITY IN OTHER SITUATIONS

Before we proceed to an examination in detail of liability arising under the case of *Hedley Byrne*, you may care to note that economic loss caused by misstatements may be the subject of claims in contexts **other** than in the general law of negligence: for example where there is a **fiduciary relationship** (such as solicitor and client); and under **statute**, for example the **Misrepresentation Act 1967** (liability arises here in contract **and** tort, see below).

The **Financial Services Act 1986** imposes liability for loss caused by untrue or misleading statements made in connection with the 'listing particulars' or prospectus issued by a company concerning the issue of shares, debentures or other securities. In such a case the defendant is obliged to show that he had reasonable grounds to believe that his statements were true or not misleading: a burden of proof favourable to the plaintiff.

You may also wish to note the effect of the **Data Protection Act 1998**. This Act gives individuals new rights in respect of information which is recorded on computer ('personal data'). This Act, which implements the EU Data Protection Directive (Directive 95/46, OJ 1995 L281/31) came *partly* into effect on 16 July 1998.

Please consider the provisions of the Misrepresentation Act 1967, s. 2(1) in *Cases and Materials* (5.3.1). Under what circumstances may a plaintiff sue and what might be the advantages to him in so doing?

The cause of action conferred by the Act differs from the common law action under *Hedley Byrne* in that, amongst other factors, the plaintiff must have been induced by the defendant's misrepresentation to enter into the contract; the plaintiff does not have to establish a duty of care; and it is for the defendant to show that he believed on reasonable grounds that his statement was true, rather than for the plaintiff to prove negligence.

The Court of Appeal in *Howard Marine* v *Ogden* [1978] QB 574 held that s. 2(1) provides an action in **tort** for misrepresentation. According to *Royscot Trust Ltd* v *Rogerson* [1991] 3 All ER 294, damages are assessed in **tortious** terms and **remoteness** of damage is determined as in the tort of **deceit**.

5.5.2   LIABILITY ARISING UNDER *HEDLEY BYRNE*

Hedley Byrne and Co. v *Heller and Partners* [1963] 2 All ER 575 (HL) (*Cases and Materials* (5.3.2)) is universally regarded as a landmark decision in the field of pure economic loss, at any rate with regard to liability for negligent **misstatements**. This has been so for more than 30 years, and the case is **still** of central importance in this context.

An advertising agency (the appellants) wished to know whether they could safely do work on credit for some clients. Accordingly, they asked **their** bank to obtain a credit reference from the **clients'** bank, the respondents. The respondents negligently supplied a favourable reference, but they gave it '**without responsibility**'.

The appellants were never paid by their clients, who became insolvent. They had no money, having been in a poor financial condition for some time and the respondent bank ought to have known of this situation.

You guessed correctly: the appellants sued the respondents for negligence, in an attempt to get compensation for their loss.

On the **facts**, their Lordships decided that the respondents did **not** owe the appellants a duty of care, but **only** on the basis that the 'without responsibility' disclaimer effectively acted as an exclusion of liability clause. It was their Lordships' opinion that **without** that statement there could well have been a duty to take care.

Favourable reference was made in *Hedley Byrne* to a vigorous **dissenting** judgment of Denning LJ in *Candler* v *Crane Christmas and Co.* [1951] 1 All ER 426 (CA). According to his Lordship the defendants in that case, a firm of accountants, owed a duty of care in negligence not only to the client for whom they prepared accounts; they also owed a duty to any third parties they knew would be shown the accounts and who would be likely to rely on them.

In strict terms, *Hedley Byrne* is authority only on the basis that it contains strongly persuasive **obiter dicta**; yet this view has for so long been taken as representing English law on the point that it would be pedantic in the extreme to insist that the case is not of **binding** authority.

Their Lordships made it clear that in finding, for the first time in English law, that a duty of care could arise for negligent misstatements, **mere** foresight of harm should not be enough.

SAQ 42

Can you think of a more stringent test to determine liability for careless misstatements than mere 'foreseeability'?

Any test will probably have to be based on **very close proximity** between the parties involved because of the fear of **indeterminate** liability, i.e. liability towards an indeterminate number of people, for indeterminate amounts of money. Their Lordships in *Hedley Byrne* hit upon the idea of a **special relationship**.

This requirement of a 'special relationship' has become an accepted feature of the law, as you will see. But it is at best a vague notion, as the various attempts to define it in *Hedley Byrne* demonstrate. It is more of a 'sum total of its parts' rather than a coherent 'whole'.

In the words of Lord Morris:

> If in a sphere in which a person is so placed that others could reasonably rely on his judgment or his skill or on his ability to make careful inquiry, a person takes it on himself to give information or advice to, or allows his information or advice to be passed on to another person who, as he knows or should know, will place reliance on it, then a duty of care will arise.

His Lordship went on to say that he thought a special relationship followed from proof that the defendant assumed responsibility for his advice. Lord Hodson agreed with him on this point.

Lord Devlin felt that a special relationship resembled a contractual relationship without any consideration.

It is submitted that this 'definition' from Lord Devlin comes closest to the necessary relationship which must exist between the parties, though we will see later that 'assumption of responsibility' is assuming an increasingly important role in more recent case law.

You may feel after reading the material which follows that Denning LJ in the earlier case of *Candler* (above) could have been defining the special relationship when he said: '. . . it [the duty of care owed by the defendants in his opinion] appears to be limited to cases where the information or advice is given in response to an enquiry for the guidance in question.'.

What is the consequence of this view?

'[The special relationship signifies] little more than that the standard *Donoghue* v *Stevenson* foreseeability test cannot be used [in the context of negligent misstatements]': Stanton, p. 341.

5.5.3   SUBSEQUENT DEVELOPMENTS

It is only by examining later cases, in which the courts have been given the opportunity to consider the ramifications of *Hedley Byrne*, that we can hope to draw a clearer picture of the law.

In *Mutual Life and Citizens' Assurance Co. Ltd* v *Evatt* [1971] AC 793, the majority of the Privy Council narrowed the ambit of 'special relationship' by confining it to cases where the defendant **either** was in the **business** of supplying information or advice, **or** had **claimed to possess** the necessary skill to give it and the preparedness to take care in giving it. Thus, it was held that no duty of care was owed by an employee of a life assurance company in giving advice to a life policy holder about the wisdom of investing in a company associated with the employee's company.

There were two dissenting opinions in this case. They were delivered by Lords Reid and Morris (two of the judges in *Hedley Byrne* (above)) who argued for a wider duty than that suggested by the majority. They said that a duty existed not only in the circumstances stated by the majority, but **also** where advice was sought or given by someone in **the usual course of business**. Their Lordships stressed that **social** or **casual** occasions must be ruled out.

There is some doubt, however, whether the majority view in *Evatt* represents English law. Indeed, in *Esso* v *Mardon* [1976] QB 801 both Lawson J at first instance, and the Court of Appeal clearly preferred the reasoning of the **minority** in *Evatt*.

In *Esso*, M entered into a contract with E to lease to M a petrol filling station. He did so on the strength of a negligent misrepresentation by E's expert that the 'through-put' would reach 200,000 gallons per year, about double the realistic figure. M suffered considerable financial loss, despite all his strenuous efforts. The Court of Appeal held that E was liable to pay substantial damages, not only for breach of warranty but also for the tort of negligence, in respect of the loss suffered in the first year up to the renewal of the tenancy agreement (to which Lawson J had confined his assessment), the capital put into the business, the overdraft and loss of future earnings for a number of years.

On the other hand, in *Argy Trading Development Co. Ltd* v *Lapid Developments Ltd* [1977] 3 All ER 785 the defendant, who was the plaintiff's landlord, allowed fire insurance cover for the demised premises to lapse without informing the plaintiff. The defendant was found not liable because there was no 'holding out', no statutory duty, no sufficient business relationship between the parties, no 'financial interest' on the part of the defendant and no inquiry by the plaintiff coupled with advice or information given by the defendant; in short, there was no 'special relationship' between the parties.

SAQ 44

What main factors do you think the plaintiff will be expected to establish in order to show the existence of a special relationship?

Over the last 30 years the following features of the necessary special relationship have emerged from the case law:

(a)   reliance by the plaintiff;

(b)   gratuitous advice or information may lead to liability;

(c)   assumption of responsibility by the defendant;

(d)   the *Hedley Byrne* 'rule' encompasses statements/advice/notices/omissions, etc.

We will examine the first three features in detail; the fourth feature is self-explanatory, though we ought to note the fact that liability for **any** omission is always more difficult to establish than liability for a 'positive' act (see **Chapter 3**).

5.5.4   RELIANCE

The defendant must be someone on whose advice, skill, etc., the plaintiff can **reasonably** and foreseeably expect to rely. Thus, for example, in the Canadian case of *Klein* v *Canadian Propane* (1967) 64 DLR (2d) 220, it was held that advice given by the driver of a propane gas tanker as to the source of a gas smell was not such as to make him liable for the results of an ensuing explosion.

Again, it must be obvious that the parties' relative position to each other must be a crucial factor in many cases. If the person seeking advice or information has manifestly more skill or knowledge in the matter than has the defendant, it is less likely that the latter will be under any duty of care to the former.

The decision in *Briggs* v *Gunner* (1979) 129 NLJ 116 offers a good illustration of the point being made. (See *Cases and Materials* (5.3.3).)

Please read about the decision in *Luxmoore-May* v *Messenger May Baverstock* [1990] 1 All ER 1067 (CA) in *Cases and Materials* (5.3.3) and consider in what way it might be linked with reliance.

Both *Briggs* and *Luxmoore-May* illustrate the difficulties inherent in establishing a duty of care and reliance; they also indicate that a plaintiff may experience considerable problems in convincing the court of the appropriate **standard of care** which a defendant is expected to observe.

This issue of **standards** was the **central** feature in *Luxmoore-May*.

You can read an important decision of the House of Lords on 'reliance' in *Cases and Materials* (5.3.3). The case is called *Williams* v *Natural Life Health Foods* [1998] 2 All ER 577.

Finally, we should always remember that reliance is a factor which can arise in any context of misstatement; it can, for instance, lead to problems of **causation**. A lack of a causative link was the ground on which the Court of Appeal overturned the trial judge's finding in *JEB Fasteners Ltd* v *Marks Bloom and Co.* [1983] 1 All ER 583 (see **5.5.8.3**). Problems concerning negligent misstatement may also arise in the context of causation where it is alleged that the plaintiff has been **contributorily** negligent. The **defence** of **contributory negligence** has been discussed in **Chapter 2**.

5.5.5 GRATUITOUS ADVICE, ETC.

What is the advantage about paying for advice?

In **principle** it does not matter that the advice or information is given free of charge, though it is always going to be easier for a plaintiff to establish the necessary relationship with the defendant where the latter is paid for his services, or at least has received some discernible benefit or advantage in the circumstances.

In *Chaudhry* v *Prabhaker* [1988] 3 All ER 718 the Court of Appeal held that the standard of care applicable to the duty of care owed by an unpaid agent to his principal was an objective one and such as to be reasonably expected of him in all the circumstances. Thus, a friend was found liable for loss suffered when, in breach of his duty, he recommended to the plaintiff the purchase of a second-hand car which turned out to be both unroadworthy and valueless.

The defendant **accepted** that he owed a duty of care to the plaintiff, claiming only that he had discharged his duty by observing the standard of care required of him in law. The case proceeded on the basis that there existed a gratuitous relationship of principal and agent between the parties and thus any question of liability arose in tort. The court accepted, however, that liability could also arise under the *Hedley Byrne* principle: logically the standard of care expected in this context should be the same as that required of an unpaid agent.

May LJ, whilst concurring in the judgment against the defendant, said 'In the light of the more cautious approach taken in recent cases . . . [e.g. *Yuen Kun Yeu*; see **5.5.6**] it is doubtful whether the defendant's concession [as to the existence of a duty of care] has been rightly made in law'. He did not find 'entirely attractive' the proposition that one had to impose on a family friend looking out for a first car for a 'girl of 26' a *Donoghue* v *Stevenson* duty of care. 'Neither can one apply the *Hedley Byrne* principle to the first defendant's answer to the plaintiff's inquiry about the car's history, since to do so would make social relations and responsibilities between friends unnecessarily hazardous. However, the concession has been made . . .'.

5.5.6 ASSUMPTION OF RESPONSIBILITY

In *Lambert* v *Lewis* (above) it was found that a special relationship is not created between defendant and plaintiff **merely** as a result of the defendant having said something which he seriously intended another or others to act upon. Liability does not arise in respect of a **volunteered** misstatement; the misstatement must be made in **response** to an **inquiry** from the plaintiffs.

An 'assumption of responsibility' is required in all cases, to distinguish merely casual or 'social' advice (for example, a solicitor giving casual advice to a fellow-passenger on a train) from that given in a professional or business context. Even if advice or information is given in a situation which can be categorised as 'formal', however, it does not follow **necessarily** that an assumption of responsibility will be found.

In *Tidman* v *Reading Borough Council, The Times*, 10 November 1994 it was found by Buxton J that liability under *Hedley Byrne* did not arise where council officials gave advice to a member of the public who had made an 'informal' inquiry about a matter concerning planning permission on land that he was trying to sell.

Can you think of the reasons which might be given by the judge for reaching this conclusion? Write them down before you proceed with your reading of this text.

His Lordship gave the following reasons:

(a)   the council owed a **public** duty (under the relevant legislation) to apply the planning law; an overriding obligation to advise individuals would be inconsistent with the public interest;

(b)   the plaintiff's approach to the council was by way of an informal telephone call; the advice was given on very little information available from the plaintiff. To impose liability in such a case would, in any event, deter local authorities from giving advice of this nature, and that would be contrary to the public interest;

(c)   the plaintiff could be reasonably expected to seek **independent** advice before acting in such circumstances.

Think back to *Hedley Byrne*. What did we say there was the basis of liability?

The basis of liability was a 'special relationship'.

Lord Goff in the House of Lords in *White* v *Jones* [1995] 1 All ER 691 (which we examine at **5.5.8.3**) claimed that the *Hedley Byrne* principle was 'founded upon an assumption of responsibility'. There is, however, some inconsistency in the cases concerning the **nature** of this assumption.

Some judges regard **voluntary** assumption of responsibility as a requirement for recovery of damages in **every** case of pure economic loss, see, for example, Dillon LJ in *Simaan General Contracting Co.* v *Pilkington Glass (No. 2)* [1988] 1 All ER 791 at **5.6**.

On balance, though, it seems that a defendant may be regarded in **law** (even though not in fact) as having assumed responsibility to the plaintiff. 'Voluntary' assumption is only a **fiction**.

Lord Keith in *Yuen Kun Yeu* v *A-G For Hong Kong* [1988] AC 175 (PC) said that liability depends **not** on 'voluntary' assumption of responsibility; it depends on a sufficient **degree of proximity** between the parties: thus **voluntary** assumption of responsibility is merely an **example** of a particular factual situation leading to 'proximity'. It is the **directness** and **closeness** of the relationship between the parties which is the crucial factor.

The Court of Appeal, in *Banque Keyser Ullman SA* v *Skandia (UK) Insurance Co. Ltd* [1989] 2 All ER 952, approved of his Lordship's opinion. You can read about the *Keyser Ullman* case in *Cases and Materials* (**5.3.4**).

Lord Griffiths in *Smith* v *Bush; Harris* v *Wyre Forest DC* [1989] 2 All ER 514 (*Cases and Materials* (**5.3.4**)) said it was sufficient for the law to **deem** responsibility.

In *Smith* and *Harris*, heard together, it was found that surveyors acting for mortgagees owed a duty of care to house purchasers, i.e. the plaintiffs, the mortgagors, who relied on negligent reports issued by the surveyors. In *Smith* the surveyor acted for a building society and his report was shown to the plaintiff. In *Harris* the mortgagees were a local authority and the surveyor was a member of their own staff; his report was not shown to the plaintiff but the court said that he was entitled to assume from the local authority's offer of a mortgage that the property had been professionally valued. In both cases the plaintiff paid the surveyor's fees.

Their Lordships discussed the duty of care owed by a valuer to (a) the party instructing him (usually the mortgagee) and (b) any other party likely reasonably to rely on the valuation report (usually the purchaser). It was held that a dual responsibility exists in such cases.

The plaintiffs had **not** employed independent surveyors to survey the properties. In many cases, however, it **will** be necessary to do this or at least opt for a **full** report on the structure, from the building society surveyor, because mortgage valuations at the basic level are of only a cursory nature. The lender is interested in the property only to the extent that the resale value will equal the loan. In the **present** cases, however, it was reasonable to rely on the basic reports (though they did not amount to full structural surveys) because the properties involved were of a standard nature and not expensive; it was common practice amongst buyers at this end of the housing market to rely simply on the mortgage valuation report.

According to Lord Templeman 'in both appeals . . . the existence of such a dual duty is tacitly accepted and acknowledged because notices excluding liability for breach of duty to the purchaser were drafted by the mortgagee and imposed on the purchasers'.

It is worth noting that a duty of care was found without any formal attempt to apply the principal authority, i.e. *Hedley Byrne*. There was, in any event, disagreement on the effect of that decision.

Whilst Lord Templeman and Lord Jauncey said that it was necessary for the defendant in such cases voluntarily to have assumed responsibility to the plaintiff, Lord Griffith thought otherwise; according to him it was enough for the law to **deem** assumption of responsibility.

Again, on the question of whether it was necessary to have a relationship equivalent to contract Lord Griffith expressed no opinion, Lord Templeman and Lord Jauncey thought the answer was 'yes' and Lord Brandon and Lord Keith agreed with them.

The attempts to exclude liability were held, in each case, to be caught by ss. 2(2) and 11(3) of the **Unfair Contract Terms Act 1977**.

Under the 1977 Act defendants acting in the course of business cannot exclude liability for negligence causing death or personal injury. In relation to any **other** damage, as in *Smith* and *Harris*, the test of reasonableness must be satisfied. Reasonableness is assessed on the facts of each case.

After reading about *Harris* and *Smith* you should look at the earlier decisions in *Anderson* v *Rhodes* [1967] 2 All ER 850 and *Yianni* v *Evans* [1982] QB 438, in **Cases and Materials** **(5.3.4)**.

Having read about **Briggs v Gunner** in *Cases and Materials* **(5.3.3)**, please state, in one sentence, the general conclusion of Foster J concerning the circumstances in which the law will imply a duty of care.

In *Briggs* Foster J said that the law will imply a duty of care where someone with a special skill is entrusted to exercise that skill and he knows, or ought to know, that reliance will be placed on his skill and judgment.

It is clear that assumption of responsibility (coupled of course with reasonable reliance) lies at the heart of liability under *Hedley Byrne*. In *Lonrho plc* v *Fayed* [1988] 3 All ER 464, for example, it was found that the defendants (who were business advisers) had not assumed responsibility towards their clients' business competitors in respect of representations made by them, on behalf of their clients, to the Monopolies Commission.

The Court of Appeal in *Van Oppen* v *Clerk to the Bedford Charity Trustees* [1989] 3 All ER 889 found that a school had no general duty to take out personal accident insurance cover for its pupils or to advise parents of the desirability of such cover. An argument that there was a duty to have regard to the economic welfare of pupils, arising naturally from the relationship of school and pupil, was also rejected. There was no evidence of a voluntary assumption of responsibility by the school; in any case there was no evidence that any parent had relied on the school. It might have been prudent to advise parents to insure, but all carelessness could not be elevated into a tort: there must be a legal duty not to be careless and it would be neither just nor reasonable to impose on the school a greater duty than that which rested on a parent.

The standard of care involved in such a case (**where any duty of care existed**) was said to be that of the reasonably careful parent, subject to the conditions of school life and numbers of pupils involved. The question of whether a prudent parent had a duty to take out accident insurance was raised. O'Connor LJ thought that if a school decided that all pupils were to be covered by personal accident insurance under a block policy and then failed negligently to renew the policy, an injured pupil would have a good claim against the school.

More recently, the House of Lords in *Henderson and Others v Merrett Syndicates Ltd and Others; Arbuthnott and Others v Feltrim Underwriting Agencies Ltd and Others; Deeny and Others v Gooda Walker Ltd and Others* [1994] 3 All ER 506, found that a duty of care, in *Hedley Byrne* terms, arose on the **facts simply because**:

    (a)   there was an assumption of responsibility to provide professional/quasi-professional services;

    (b)   there was someone who relied on those services.

The cases concerned the liability of managing agents at Lloyd's of London (the epicentre of the insurance business) to 'names' who were, at the relevant time, members of syndicates managed by the agents. Those agents gave advice to the 'names' on the risks involved in underwriting insurance and on questions concerning reinsurance.

It was said that the agents held themselves out as having special skills and the names relied implicitly on that expertise. Authority was given to the agents to bind the names to contracts of reinsurance, etc. The relationship between the parties (we must not lose sight of the fact that the parties were bound together by **contract**) was **sufficient on its own** to justify the imposition of a duty of care under *Hedley Byrne*.

We have already seen in **Chapter 3** that this case is authority for the proposition that a pre-existing contractual relationship between the parties, at least in a case like the present one where professional/quasi-professional services were involved, did not **of itself** preclude concurrent liability in tort. A plaintiff could choose which remedy produced the best results, unless the terms of the contract provided otherwise.

The decision was applied, at first instance, in *Aiken and others v Stewart Wrightson Members' Agency Ltd and others* [1995] 3 All ER 449, in which the liability of a Lloyd's underwriting agent towards 'names', and the liability owed by members' agents and managing agents, in connection with entering into a run-off reinsurance contract with a reinsurer on behalf of Lloyd's syndicates, fell to be considered. Again, issues relating to both tort and contract were involved.

SAQ 48

Having read in Chapter 3 about the 'three-stage' test for determining the existence of a duty in difficult cases of negligence generally, has the thought crossed your mind that this test might be regarded by the judges as being of especial importance in the context of negligent misstatement?

Whether or not you have applied your mind to this issue, you will find that the answer is 'yes'. You may wish at this point to refer back to **5.5**.

5.5.7   A STRICTER TEST

The decision of the House of Lords in *Caparo Industries plc v Dickman* [1990] 1 All ER 568, (**Cases and Materials** (5.3.5)) confirms that this is the case. It is authority for the proposition that the parties must be **very close together** indeed before there can be any question of a duty of care arising from the facts: a high **degree** of **proximity** is required.

In *Caparo* the plaintiffs were considering a take-over bid for a company in which they held shares and, as shareholders, they received a copy of the company's audited accounts. Acting in reliance on these accounts, which showed a profit made by the company, the plaintiffs bought more shares in it and eventually took it over. It later emerged that due to the auditors' (the defendants) negligence, the accounts had been wrongly audited; the company had, in fact, made a loss.

How would you defend the action?

The judge at first instance found that the defendants did not owe the plaintiffs, as shareholders and potential investors, any duty of care. By a majority, however, the **Court of Appeal** allowed the plaintiffs' appeal. In the first place, it was reasonably foreseeable that the plaintiffs would rely on the audited accounts; secondly, there existed sufficient proximity between the parties and the defendants had voluntarily assumed responsibility directly to *Caparo*; thirdly, it was just and reasonable to impose a duty in this case. The duty, it should be noted, was found in favour of *Caparo* **not** as potential investors in and take-over bidders for the company; it was owed to the plaintiffs only as an individual existing shareholder in the company. In reaching this conclusion the court clearly regarded 'special relationship' as inseparable from 'proximity' and 'justice'; 'reasonable reliance' did not alone define the 'scope' of the 'special relationship'; 'just and reasonable' was likened to the second stage of the Wilberforce test (see **3.3.2**).

You should also read about the decision in *Al Saudi Banque* v *Clarke Pixley* [1989] 3 All ER 361, in *Cases and Materials* (**5.3.5**).

In *Caparo* the House of Lords, in **overturning** the decision of the Court of Appeal, ruled as follows. Auditors of a public company owe no duty of care:

(a) to a member of the public who relies on the accounts to buy shares (there was insufficient proximity because of the potential liability of the auditors); or

(b) to an individual shareholder in the company who desires to buy more shares (such a person is in no better position than a member of the public in the present context).

The auditors' statutory duty to prepare accounts was owed only to the shareholders as a body, to enable them to make informed decisions concerning the running of the company; the purpose of this duty, said their Lordships, was not to enable individual shareholders to buy shares with an eye on profits.

This decision is also important for the views expressed on the general criteria required for a duty of care in negligence, as well as the discussion concerning the specific requirements for liability in the context of negligent misstatements. It offers further evidence that the case-by-case, or incremental, approach to the development of the tort of negligence is now fully in favour. (See **Chapter 3**.)

According to Lord Bridge, notions such as 'fair, just and reasonable', 'neighbourhood' and 'proximity' are mere labels; they 'are not susceptible of any such precise definition as would be necessary to give them utility as practical tests'. He said:

> traditionally the law finds the existence of the duty in different specific situations each exhibiting its own particular characteristics. In this way the law has identified a wide variety of duty-situations, all falling within the ambit of the tort of negligence, but sufficiently distinct to require separate definition of the essential ingredients by which the existence of the duty is to be recognised.

His Lordship felt that the law has moved away from the difficulty of using a single general principle to determine whether a duty of care is owed and had 'now moved in the direction of attaching a greater significance to the more traditional categorisation of distinct and recognisable situations as guides to the existence, the scope and the limits of the varied duties of care which the law imposes.'

Lord Oliver felt that the most that could be attempted was a 'broad categorisation of the decided cases according to the type of situation in which liability has been established in the past'; to pursue a general test of liability was to chase a 'will-o'-the-wisp'.

Lords Roskill, Ackner and Jauncey agreed with this reasoning.

Approval was given by the House to the views of Brennan J in the High Court of Australia in *Sutherland Shire Council* v *Heyman* (1985) 60 ALR 1, where he rejected the use of Lord Wilberforce's two stage test (see **3.3.2**):

> It is preferable in my view that the law should develop novel categories of negligence incrementally and by analogy with established categories, rather than by a massive extension of a *prima facie* duty of care restrained only by indefinable considerations which ought to negative, or to reduce or limit the scope of the duty or the class of persons to whom it is owed.

As with all seminal cases it is necessary to examine subsequent case law in order to gauge the impact of the principal case.

In *Al Nakib (Investments) Jersey Ltd* v *Longcroft* [1990] 3 All ER 321, Mervyn Davies J, in a case which involved an application to strike out part of the plaintiff's claim, held that whilst company directors owed a duty of care to those who bought shares in **a rights issue** after relying on the company prospectus, they did **not** owe any duty to **shareholders** or **anyone else** relying on the prospectus to buy shares in the company through the **stock market**. In other words, the duty was limited specifically to purchasers of shares in the **particular rights issue**.

A qualified approach to the establishment and terms of a duty of care can also be seen in *Mariola Marine Corp* v *Lloyd's Register of Shipping ('Morning Watch')* [1990] 1 Lloyd's Rep 547. The main issue here was whether Lloyd's owed a duty of care in negligence not to cause economic loss to persons (other than the owners of the vessel) foreseeably likely to rely on a survey of *'Morning Watch'* before the ship was put on the market. Phillips J found against such a claim, because the main purpose of the classification of vessels for Lloyd's Register of Shipping was the **physical** safety of persons and property while at sea.

In *Morgan Crucible Co.* v *Hill Samuel Bank Ltd* [1990] 3 All ER 330, the court had to consider a take-over bidder's claim against the directors, advisers and accountants of the 'target' company, that financial representations made by the company to its shareholders during take-over tussles were misleading and negligent. It was claimed that the announcement of the bid distinguished the case from *Caparo*, and put it into the ambit of *Smith* and *Harris* (see **5.5.6**). Thus, there was sufficient proximity between the parties.

SAQ 50

How would you decide this case?

Hoffmann J refused leave to amend the plaintiff's statement of claim, on the argument that the defence documents (like the audit certificate in *Caparo*) had a regulatory background, in the present case it was the *City Code on Takeovers, etc*. The purpose of the circulars issued by the defendants was to advise **shareholders**; they were not directed to **bidders** for the company. His Lordship felt that there was an even stronger case for denying a duty of care in the present circumstances than in *Caparo*, i.e. in a contested bid the interests of the shareholders and bidders conflicted.

On appeal, however, the Court of Appeal, [1991] 1 All ER 148 allowed modification of the plaintiff's statement of claim. It was found that the issue should be allowed to go to trial because there was an **arguable** case that the representations were made with a view to influencing the bidder's conduct, so creating a duty of care not to mislead the bidder.

You will find an interesting extract from the judgment of Slade LJ in this case in *Cases and Materials* (**5.3.5**).

In *Kuwait Asia Bank EC* v *National Mutual Life Nominees Ltd* [1990] 3 WLR 297 (PC) the court had to consider, in the context of the New Zealand rules concerning service of process outside the jurisdiction, the claims that a shareholder or other person who was concerned with the appointment of a director of a company owed a duty of care to the company's creditors, to see that the director acted diligently and competently. The Privy Council found against such a duty, and also said that a director does not owe a duty to creditors of the company merely because of his **status as director**, though a director could take on a **special** duty to creditors.

ACTIVITY 24

Please consider carefully the Court of Appeal decision in *James McNaughton Paper Group Ltd* v *Hicks Anderson and Co.* [1991] 1 All ER 134, in *Cases and Materials* (**5.3.5**) and write down answers to the following questions:

(i)   What was the outcome of the case?

(ii)   Neill LJ produced a check-list of factors to consider in such cases. Without
       looking at the list, which is given at the end of the report in *Cases and
       Materials*, what do you think might be in it?

The plaintiffs in *James McNaughton* wished to take over a company and asked the
defendants, who were accountants to the subject of the takeover bid, to prepare some
draft accounts of their clients' affairs as quickly as possible for use in the takeover
negotiations. It was found that the defendants owed no duty of care to the plaintiffs. The
Court of Appeal regarded it as important that the plaintiffs were experienced in business
and, in any event, they could have brought in their own accountants.

See also *Minories Finance Ltd* v *Arthur Young* [1989] 2 All ER 105 and *Mills* v *Winchester
Diocesan Board of Finance* [1989] 2 All ER 317 in *Cases and Materials* (5.3.5).

In two sentences, please state the general effect of *Caparo* and later decisions in which
it has been applied.

It seems that as a result of *Caparo*, which emphasises the application of the 'three-stage'
test and an incremental development of the law, the scope of *Hedley Byrne* has been
considerably narrowed. Mere foreseeability of reliance by the plaintiff is not enough; the
defendant must be actually **aware** of:

(a)   the **plaintiff** (either as an individual, or as a member of an identifiable class of
       persons, to whom the advice or information will be communicated);

(b)   the **purpose** for which the advice or information has been sought; **and**

(c)   the fact that the plaintiff is **likely to rely** on the advice or information for **that**
       purpose.

As you are aware, negligence requires proof of damage: therefore it will always be necessary for a plaintiff to prove, in addition to satisfying any other conditions of liability, that he **acted** on the advice or information to his **detriment**.

You can read about two important decisions in *Cases and Materials* (**5.3.5**). The decisions are called *South Australia Asset Management Corporation* v *York Montague Ltd* [1996] 3 All ER 365 (HL), and *Bank of Credit and Commerce International (Overseas) Ltd* v *Price Waterhouse, The Times*, 4 March 1998 (CA).

5.5.8 THREE PARTY RELATIONSHIPS

The problem here concerns those situations in which A makes a negligent misstatement to B who relies on it to C's detriment. At first sight this situation cannot easily be accommodated under *Hedley Byrne*, because liability arising from that authority is based on the plaintiff **himself** relying on the misstatement, and suffering a detriment in so doing.

5.5.8.1 Statute

In *Ministry of Housing* v *Sharp* [1970] 2 QB 223 the defendant was required by statute to keep an official register of local land charges. The defendant's servant negligently omitted the plaintiff's land charge from a list of charges relating to land about to be purchased. The omission meant that the plaintiff's charge was lost. The defendant was found liable for the plaintiff's loss (though he would not be now: Land Charges Act 1972, s. 10(6)). The Court of Appeal regarded the case as consistent with the principle established in *Hedley Byrne*.

In *Sharp* the defendant made his statement, not to the plaintiff, but to the purchaser, a third party. Thus, the question arises whether the notion of a 'special relationship' applies equally to **three**-party as well as to **two**-party relationships.

It may be that the decision is restricted to its own, statutory context; it does not fit into any established category of negligence. Lord Denning alone based his judgment squarely on the claim that *Hedley Byrne* applied in the circumstances. Salmond LJ thought that the principal case (i.e. *Hedley Byrne*) did not apply in the present context precisely, whilst Cross LJ was hesitant in finding for the plaintiff, but was prepared to follow his more experienced brethren.

5.5.8.2 Contract

The defendant's breach of contract can be seen in terms of a negligent **act**.

Sharp was approved and relied upon by Megarry VC in *Ross* v *Caunters* [1979] 3 All ER 580, though it was held in **this** case that liability was more appropriately based on the principle laid down in *Donoghue* v *Stevenson* than on *Hedley Byrne*.

This approach, based on the notion that *Hedley Byrne* was merely 'illustrative' of liability for 'pure' economic loss, i.e. it was **not** 'definitive' of such liability, seemed to indicate that in the **long term** the law about misstatements might be assimilated into the general law dealing with negligent acts. It must be said, however, that his Lordship relied heavily on the now discredited 'Wilberforce test' (see **3.3.2**). We will **return** to this more general issue later; it may be that we are now witnessing the **beginnings** of that assimilation, albeit by means of a different route.

In *Ross*, solicitors who, in breach of **contract**, negligently omitted to warn a testator that spouses of intended beneficiaries should not attest his will, were held to be in breach of duty in **tort** to an intended beneficiary (with whom they had no contractual relationship) whose spouse had attested it with the result that the gift to that beneficiary was void. The judge said:

There are at least two ways in which *Hedley Byrne* may be regarded. First, it may be regarded as establishing a special category of case in which alone, by way of exception from the general rule, purely financial loss may be recovered in an action for negligence. Second, it may alternatively be regarded as establishing that there is no longer any general rule (if there ever was one) that purely financial loss is irrecoverable in negligence.

Do you consider that the negligence complained of in *Ross* could be categorised other than in terms of a misstatement? Please express your answer in the form of a single sentence.

It would be **more** appropriate to regard the solicitors' negligence in *Ross*, at least from the plaintiff's point of view, as an **act**, i.e. a **breach** of contract to a third party.

5.5.8.3 Others

The plaintiff in *JEB Fasteners* v *Marks Bloom* [1981] 3 All ER 289, was not an identified individual. Woolf J based his reasoning principally upon 'foreseeability', applying dicta of Lord Wilberforce in *Anns*, and side-stepping the restrictive formula laid down in *Hedley Byrne*. *Hedley Byrne*, and subsequent authorities, were seen as merely **illustrative** and not definitive of liability for negligent misstatement. This reasoning is similar to that of the judge in *Ross* (see **5.5.8.2**). The defendants in *JEB Fasteners* were company auditors, and had audited the accounts of a company which was now in financial difficulties. It was found to be reasonably foreseeable on the facts that these certified accounts might be relied upon by persons considering taking over the company. The court held that the defendant accountants owed a duty of care to the plaintiffs, who had taken over the company.

On appeal, the Court of Appeal at [1983] 1 All ER 583, found that the defendants' negligence, i.e. breach of duty, had not **caused** the plaintiffs' loss sustained as a result of the takeover because the plaintiffs' main purpose in taking over the company was to acquire the services of its two directors. The decision at first instance was reversed, but only on the issue of **causation**.

In *Lawton* v *BOC Transhield Ltd* [1987] 2 All ER 608, the judge found that a special duty of care was owed, in the context of negligent misstatement, where a reference was given by a former employer for a former employee who was on probation with his new employer. It was found that the defendant (former employer) knew or ought to have known that the plaintiff (former employee) would lose his new job if an unfavourable reference was given. There was said to be close proximity between the parties; *Hedley Byrne* was mentioned, but a *Ross* v *Caunters* approach was taken to the existence of a duty of care. (You will have noted that the reference was given to and relied upon **by the new employer**, to the detriment of the plaintiff.)

The defendant was found not liable on the facts because there was no negligence on its part, in other words, there was no **breach** of duty.

In *Spring* v *Guardian Assurance plc* [1993] 2 All ER 273 the Court of Appeal overruled *Lawton*. It was held that a person writing a reference does not owe a duty of care in negligence to the 'subject of the reference'. The only duty to that person it was said arises in the torts of **defamation** and **malicious falsehood**.

ACTIVITY 25

Please turn to *Cases and Materials* (5.3.6.1) and read the House of Lords decision in *Spring* [1994] 3 All ER 129. What is the result of that decision and how did their Lordships arrive at it?

You will find that the Court of Appeal's decision was **reversed** and the result in *Lawton* reinstated, though **not** on the same grounds. It was held that employers **did** owe a duty of care in relation to the giving of character references for past and present employees, but this liability was not based on grounds of **mere** foreseeability. Whilst it is true that some of their Lordships (Lords Lowry, Slynn and Woolf) relied on a general conception of negligence liability, *Hedley Byrne* was also applied (Lords Goff and Lowry). Others based their reasoning on the special duty of care owed by employers to their employees (Lords Goff, Slynn and Woolf). Accordingly, we will return to *Spring* in **Chapter 8**. Lord Keith delivered a dissenting speech.

We must ask whether the decisions in *Sharp* and *Ross* represent anything more than isolated attempts to produce a remedy in rather special circumstances. The subsequent case law suggests that an **affirmative** answer must be given to this question.

According to Jones (p. 65) 'The rather special facts [of *Sharp*, *Ross* and *Lawton*] (involving reliance by a third party) make it difficult to derive any general principle from them . . .'.

Oliver LJ (in the Court of Appeal decision) in *Leigh & Sillivan Ltd* v *Aliakmon Shipping* (see **5.4.1**) thought that '*Ross* [stood] on its own': damage resulted from a transaction with a third party, there was loss of **expectation of profit** to the plaintiff, and it was doubtful if there was any damage suffered by the third party (the testator). Goff LJ in the same case (in the Court of Appeal decision) 'assumed' *Ross* v *Caunters* was correctly decided.

In *Clarke* v *Bruce Lance and Co.* [1988] 1 All ER 364 the Court of Appeal refused to extend *Ross*, and found that a testator's solicitors did not owe a duty of care to a potential beneficiary under a will, to advise the testator that a particular transaction which the testator had entered into was likely to harm the potential beneficiary's interest. Reference was made to the decision in *Yuen Kun Yeu* (see **5.5.6**) and it was said that

(a) there was a lack of close proximity between the plaintiff and the defendants;

(b) if the defendants owed a duty to a potential beneficiary of the property, it could not be owed to the plaintiff alone; it would be owed (per Balcombe LJ) to the whole indeterminate class of potential donees or beneficiaries;

(c) another effective remedy existed if the defendants were negligent in their advice to the testator, i.e. the testator (or his personal representatives, as the case might be) had a cause of action in contract. If the plaintiff also had a cause of action in tort, the defendants were at risk of having to pay damages twice over.

The Court of Appeal in *White* v *Jones* [1993] 3 All ER 481 however, affirmed the **essential** correctness of the ruling in *Ross*. It was found that *Ross* was unaffected by the decision of the House of Lords in *Murphy* v *Brentwood DC* (see **5.3** and **7.3.2**) since it formed one of the recognised exceptions to that decision.

In *White* solicitors had failed, negligently, to draw up a will as agreed with the testator (the solicitors were dilatory in doing the job) resulting in a loss of legacy to the plaintiffs, who were beneficiaries under the will. The defendant solicitors were negligent in delaying the preparation of a new will to replace an earlier one which the testator had decided to revoke, and he died before the new will was prepared. The plaintiffs received **nothing** under the first will, which was **unrevoked** and **effective**, but would have benefited under the proposed new will. The defendants were found liable in the tort of negligence to the **beneficiaries**, i.e. the plaintiffs.

SAQ 53

You have just read that the 'essential correctness' of *Ross* was confirmed in *White*, and might be wondering about the meaning of this somewhat enigmatic expression. What do you think it means?

It means that the Court of Appeal agreed with the learned judge in *Ross*, that the solicitors **ought** to be liable on the facts of that case, and that that was the position in the **present** case.

You will recall that the judge in *Ross* did not attempt to extend the principle of *Hedley Byrne* to the facts of the case before him, **rather** he found for the plaintiff on the basis of the ordinary 'neighbour' principle in *Donoghue* v *Stevenson*. In this approach he prayed in aid the Wilberforce test from *Anns* (see **3.3.2**).

The Court of Appeal in *White* rejected argument that *Ross* had been implicitly overruled by *Caparo* and *Murphy* v *Brentwood DC* [1990] 2 All ER 908 (HL) (a case which is dealt with in **Chapter 7**) and found that *Ross* was correctly decided, because it was in a category of its own, a view suggested by Lord Oliver in *Caparo*. '. . . in truth *Ross* v *Caunters* was a policy decision in the sense that the circumstances were such that the law ought to grant a remedy': Farquharson LJ in *White*.

It was found in *White* that the solicitors **did** owe a duty of care in negligence to the plaintiff, in that *Ross* could be extended **incrementally** to provide a remedy. The court said that otherwise a person who had suffered real damage, the beneficiary in such cases, would be without an effective remedy because of the doctrine of privity of contract. Only the testator or his personal representatives could sue on the contract for the will; or in tort as an **alternative** because a duty of care in negligence would without doubt be owed to the testator.

> . . . The will takes effect upon the testator's death. The testator cannot sue. The executor cannot sue because the estate is not diminished by the negligence: it is only the distribution of the estate that is altered . . . the breach of [the duty of care owed to the testator] will result in an award of nominal damages in the sum of £1 . . . it seems just and reasonable that the law should provide a remedy . . . There is either a remedy in tort or there is no remedy.

(Farquharson LJ in *White*.)

In **this** way the **testator's** intention could be fulfilled.

All the judges in *White* went out of their way to make it clear that the ruling in that case was made to provide **justice in a particular context**. The decision is no authority for a **general** remedy against solicitors because they basically owe obligations only to their clients. The courts are extremely reluctant to open the door too far for claims regarding 'loss of expectation'.

Please read *Parker-Tweedale* v *Dunbar Bank PLC (No. 2)* [1990] 2 All ER 588 and *McCullagh* v *Lane Fox, The Times*, 25 January 1994 and *The Times*, 22 December 1995, in *Cases and Materials* (5.3.6.1).

Perhaps mindful of the potential dangers, of 'opening the floodgates', inherent in any extension of *Ross* v *Caunters* the House of Lords declined to apply it on appeal in *White* v *Jones* [1995] 1 All ER 691. Their Lordships in fact found in favour of the beneficiary, as had the Court of Appeal, but disagreed with that court on the precise legal route leading to that conclusion.

SAQ 54

Can you think of any other way of finding for the beneficiary in *White*?

In the House of Lords any solution based on *Ross* was rejected; it was found that the defendant solicitors had 'assumed responsibility' under *Hedley Byrne* for their negligence, and **that assumption of responsibility** to the testator should be extended so to include 'the intended beneficiary [of the testator] who, as the solicitor could reasonably foresee, might, as a result of the solicitor's negligence, be deprived of his intended legacy in circumstances in which neither the testator nor his estate would have a remedy against the solicitor' (Lord Goff).

Lord Goff, who delivered the main speech in *White*, said this approach not only produced 'practical justice' for the parties concerned; it also resulted in the following benefits:

1. There is no unacceptable circumvention of established principles of the law of contract.

2. No problem arises by reason of the loss being of a purely economic character.

3. Such assumption of responsibility will be subject to any term of the contract between the solicitor and testator which might exclude or restrict the solicitor's liability to the testator under the principle in *Hedley Byrne*, although such a term would be most unlikely to exist in practice.

4. Since the *Hedley Byrne* principle is founded upon an assumption of responsibility the solicitor might be liable for negligent omissions as well as negligent acts of commission.

5. Damages for loss of an expectation are not excluded in cases of negligence arising under the principle in *Hedley Byrne* simply because the cause of action is classified as tortious. Such damages might in principle be recoverable in cases of contractual negligence and there is, for present purposes, no relevant distinction that can be drawn between the two forms of action.

His Lordship rejected the *Ross* v *Caunters* approach to the resolution of such a problem in the following words: 'an ordinary action in tortious negligence on the lines proposed in *Ross* v *Caunters* is inappropriate because it does not meet any of the conceptual problems which have been raised.'.

You should read the extracts from the speeches of Lord Goff, and others, in *Cases and Materials* (5.3.6.1).

It is submitted, with respect, that the view of the dissenting minority is to be preferred in this decision of the House of Lords. To apply *Hedley Byrne* in such a situation, in which the key element of **reliance** (by the plaintiff) is missing, is to risk straining the notion of a special relationship to breaking point. On this view it would be far better and would accord more with principle to apply *Ross* to the present facts. In this way a **special** duty of care in negligence owed by solicitors to beneficiaries can be recognised and controlled. As Steyn LJ put it in the Court of Appeal:

While I recognise that there may be difficult problems to be considered in future, it does not seem to me that *Ross* v *Caunters* created an uncontrollable principle. In my view the requirements of foreseeability, proximity and justice, which are needed to establish a duty, together with the concepts of breach, causation, loss and remoteness, are adequate to contain liability of the *Ross* v *Caunters* type within acceptable limits. And in my judgment the recognition of a duty of care in such a case, which involves very special considerations, will not assist arguments on the recoverability of other heads of economic loss. I would rule that *Ross* v *Caunters* was correctly decided.

See also the extract from Weir and the cases of *Penn* v *Bristol and West BS, The Times*, 19 June 1995 and *Goodwill* v *British Pregnancy Advisory Servie* [1996] 2 All ER 161 in *Cases and Materials* (5.3.6.1).

In *Esterhuizen* v *Allied Dunbar Assurance plc, The Times*, 10 June 1998, it was held that the duty of care imposed on solicitors in *White* v *Jones* extended to persons other than solicitors who offered will-making services.

5.5.9 OMISSIONS AND ACTS

There are two other special features of *White* which you ought to consider. First, the solicitors were negligent by way of **omission** rather than by way of commission (or **positive** act) because they **failed to act** in time. This problem can, however, be accommodated under either *Ross* or *Hedley Byrne*.

As Steyn LJ said in the Court of Appeal: 'While as a matter of fact negligence in failing to act may often be more difficult to establish than negligence in the drafting or executing of a will, there ought in principle to be no distinction between commission and omission in this particular field.'.

It is the **second** factor which may cause more difficulty. The solicitors were guilty of breach of contract (to the testator) by failing to **act**; they did not utter a misstatement (or fail to warn) in classic *Hedley Byrne* terms. As a result of *White* it would seem that **acts** as well as misstatements are covered by *Hedley Byrne*. *Ross* did not raise the same problem because the decision in **that** case was based on ordinary *Donoghue* v *Stevenson* principles, whereas *Hedley Byrne* has invariably been regarded only as a **misstatement** case.

SAQ 55

Can you see a way out of this difficulty?

Your attention has already been drawn to the views expressed in *Ross* and *JEB Fasteners* that *Hedley Byrne* can be viewed as authority for the proposition that there is no **general** rule against recovery for 'pure' economic loss in the tort of negligence; in other words, that *Hedley Byrne* is not **definitive** of liability in this field, but is only **illustrative** of such liability. The decision in *White* seems to add strength to this argument, by applying *Hedley Byrne* to **acts**. If *Hedley Byrne* applies only to **misstatements** it might be a genuine exception to the so-called general 'rule', limited perhaps by the notion of 'assumption of responsibility'. (If, though, this 'assumption of responsibility' can be stretched as it has been in *White*, that would make it a control of dubious quality.)

In any event, **earlier** authority can be found for the view that *Hedley Byrne* applies to acts. The decision in *Junior Books* has been explained in terms of *Hedley Byrne* 'reliance' by Lord Bridge and Lord Keith in *Murphy* v *Brentwood DC*; and solicitors were found liable under *Hedley Byrne* for failing to register the plaintiff's interest in a piece of land as a land charge in *Midland Bank Trust Co. Ltd* v *Hett, Stubbs and Kemp* [1979] Ch 384. Lord Keith said in *Murphy*:

> . . . In *Pirelli General Cable Works Ltd* v *Oscar Faber & Partners (a firm)* (1983), it was held that the cause of action in tort against consulting engineers who had negligently approved a defective design for a chimney arose when damage to the chimney caused by the defective design first occurred, not when the damage was discovered or with reasonable diligence might have been discovered. The defendants there had in relation to the design been in contractual relations with the plaintiffs, but it was common ground that a claim in contract was time-barred. If the plaintiffs had happened to discover the defect before any damage had occurred there would seem to be no good reason for holding that they would not have had a cause of action in tort at that stage, without having to wait until some damage had occurred. They would have suffered economic loss through having a defective chimney on which they were required to expend money for the purpose of removing the defect. It would seem that in a case such as the *Pirelli General Cable Works* case, where the tortious liability arose out of a contractual relationship with professional people, the duty extended to take reasonable care not to cause economic loss to the client by the advice given. The plaintiffs built the chimney as they did in reliance on that advice. The case would accordingly fall within the principle of *Hedley Byrne & Co Ltd* v *Heller & Partners Ltd* (1964). I regard *Junior Books Ltd* v *Veitchi Co. Ltd* (1982) as being an application of that principle.

Lord Oliver in *D & F Estates* also expressed a similar opinion, i.e. that *Junior Books* can be seen as an application of *Hedley Byrne*:

> There is, therefore, a strong argument that *Hedley Byrne* has **always** had the potential as a form of liability **not** restricted to misstatements; that it opens up liability for pure economic loss in a **general** sense, being limited only by the requirements of the 'special relationship'. If *Junior Books* is to be explained in terms of *Hedley Byrne*, and if that authority applies to acts as well as misstatements, it is difficult to see *Hedley Byrne* as an 'exception' to a general 'rule'; indeed, it would seem to have the quality of a vector of change, of assimilating 'acts' with 'misstatements', of forming a 'general' 'rule' **for** liability for 'pure' economic loss.

5.5.10   PHYSICAL DAMAGE

Liability for a careless misstatement resulting in **physical** damage was imposed in *Clayton* v *Woodman* [1962] 2 QB 533. An architect was found liable to a bricklayer for careless misstatements about how to conduct building work. The bricklayer suffered physical injury as a result of relying on the architect's assurances.

Please read *Clay* v *Crump and Sons* **[1964] 1 QB 533** in *Cases and Materials* **(5.3.7). What was the outcome of the case, and what is the legal basis of the decision?**

The Court of Appeal in *Clay* found in favour of liability for a negligent misstatement causing personal injury in a three-party relationship (that is, where someone **else** relied on the defendant's assurance to the plaintiff's detriment) on the basis of the *Donoghue* v *Stevenson* 'neighbour' principle.

There was a 'neighbour' relationship between the parties, based on the very close proximity existing between a professional person, such as the defendant in this case, and someone very likely to be affected by his careless assurances on safety matters.

You might think that this separate strand of liability for careless misstatements causing **physical** damage could exist quite happily with *Hedley Byrne*, complementing that authority's jurisdiction in pure economic loss.

See also *Sharpe* v *Avery* [1938] 4 All ER 85 in *Cases and Materials* **(5.3.7)**.

In *T (a minor)* v *Surrey County Council and Others* [1994] 4 All ER 577, however, the court applied *Hedley Byrne* in a case of **physical** damage. The plaintiff, suing through his mother as his next friend, claimed damages in the following circumstances. His mother had been told by the local authority's child-minding adviser that there was no reason why she should not place her infant son, under one year old at the time, with X, who was a child-minder registered with the local authority under the Nurseries and Child-Minders Regulation Act 1948. A few months earlier, however, another young infant had been injured whilst in X's care, it was thought as a result of violent shaking, though X was not convicted of any offence and it appears that the local authority could not decide whether X was responsible. The child-minding adviser did, though, advise X that she should think about taking care of older children.

T's mother placed him with X and he subsequently sustained brain damage as a result of an incident similar to that involving the other infant. T, as plaintiff, sued the local authority for breach of statutory duty (because there was a failure to de-register X), negligence in failing to cancel X's registration and the child-minding adviser's negligent misstatement. T also sued X for negligence, trespass to the person and breach of contract.

The claim for breach of statutory duty failed because the judge ruled that no private law right of action for breach of this statutory provision had been conferred by the 1948 Act. It was said that the issue of a duty of care in negligence in respect of the local authority's use of its powers under the 1948 Act 'ran on parallel lines' to the question of breach of statutory duty; it followed, therefore, that this claim must also fail.

It was held, however, that there was liability for negligent misstatement arising under *Hedley Byrne* because T's mother would not have put him into X's care had she known the full facts. X was also found liable under all three heads of T's claim.

Please read the extract from the judgment of Scott Baker J in *T (a minor)* v *Surrey CC*, in *Cases and Materials* (5.3.7), and take from it four important features. Write them down on a piece of paper.

Four important features of this case are as follows:

(a)   there is no mention of assumption of responsibility;

(b)   the point is not taken that it was not the **plaintiff** who relied on the misstatement, but his mother;

(c)   the judge makes the point that it is easier to recover for physical damage than for economic loss;

(d)   although the report does not say so, it is presumably the case that the local authority was found **vicariously** liable for its adviser's negligent misstatement. (Vicarious liability is the subject of treatment in **Chapter 1**.)

The lack of attention to the question of assumption of responsibility is surprising in view of the importance attached to this requirement in other cases; this factor must weaken the judgment in *T*.

There is no argument on the question of 'third party' relationships under *Hedley Byrne*; in the past that has been a point of contention in some cases and the courts have had to find ways **round** the difficulty: for example, in *Ross* and *White* (see **5.5.8.2** and **5.5.8.3**).

It is curious that the judge should consider a plaintiff to have a stronger case when claiming compensation for physical damage rather than mere economic loss under *Hedley Byrne*. Is it not the case that this form of liability was developed to meet claims for mere economic loss?

The judgment in *Clay* was not cited in *T*, yet it provides a ready-made basis for finding in favour of the plaintiff; it suggests an approach which meets the difficulties suggested. *T* is yet another example of the extension of liability under *Hedley Byrne*, an expansion of jurisdiction which appears to be based solely on pragmatic considerations rather than on the basis of an orderly and principled development, in keeping with the incremental approach (see **Chapter 3**).

Finally, you may care to consider the following important authority on pure economic and physical loss **generally**.

5.5.11   GENERAL

In *Marc Rich Co. AG and Others* v *Bishop Rock Marine Co. Ltd and Others* [1994] 3 All ER 686 the Court of Appeal had to consider the following facts.

The plaintiffs were owners of cargo carried in a ship which went down at sea as a result of a cracked hull. This fault had developed during the earlier part of the voyage and at one point the ship put into port and temporary repairs were carried out. The defendants, who were surveyors of ships, had inspected the vessel after the repairs were done, and had passed it as sea-worthy. It sank after resuming its journey.

It is important to understand the status of the defendants, because *Marc Rich* is one of the so-called 'hard' cases referred to in **Chapter 3**. In shipping terms the defendants are known as a 'Classification Society'; these societies (the defendants being one of the biggest in the world) provide services, for example in surveying, to those shipowners who register with them. They set standards of safety, etc., and are therefore very important to shipowners in connection with insurance and matters concerning governmental regulation. Shipowners must abide by the rules set by the society with which they are registered, but the society can only make recommendations to the shipowners, who are not forced to follow the recommendations. The only sanction which a society can apply is the suspension or withdrawal of classifications.

The plaintiffs in the present case had sued the shipowners, the head charterers of the ship and, in tort, the defendants. In the event, the action against the shipowners was settled out of court for a proportion of the loss and proceedings against the head charterer were dropped. This left proceedings in the tort of negligence against the defendants to be determined.

It was alleged that the defendants had a duty of care to avert the consequences of the shipowners' breach of duty. The plaintiffs also contended that where **physical** damage was involved it was incumbent on a plaintiff to show only foreseeability of damage; in other words, where only **physical** damage was involved it was not necessary in seeking to establish a duty of care, to satisfy the three-stage test (referred to in **Chapter 3**).

How would you defend this action?

The court held that there is in principle no legal distinction between physical damage, whether to person or property, and pure economic loss. All claims for loss in negligence are matters of **financial** compensation and it followed that the three-stage test must be satisfied in **all** cases.

On the facts, the bills of lading (contracts of carriage) imposed a non-delegable, contractual duty on the shipowners to exercise 'due diligence' to ensure the seaworthiness of their vessel. These contracts incorporated the Hague Rules, an international code of practice drawn up between carriers and cargo owners, which benefited both sides. If a duty in negligence had been imposed on the defendants it would be virtually identical to the duty owed by the shipowners (under the contract) but without the benefit of the Hague Rules: therefore, it would not be 'just and reasonable' to impose a duty of care on the defendants in these circumstances. After all, there were no 'dealings' at all between the plaintiffs and the defendants in this case. As Balcombe LJ put it:

> Although the judge [at first instance, in the present case] rightly accepted that physical damage and foreseeability were not enough to establish a duty of care, and that it was

necessary to establish proximity, he seemed to be of the view that 'fair, just and reasonable' was not a necessary criterion in physical damage cases (see [1992] 2 Lloyd's Rep 481 at 499) and that the 'incremental' approach by Brennan J in the Australian case of *Sutherland Shire Council* v *Heyman* (1985) does not apply to physical damage cases at all. It was here in my judgment that the judge fell into error. Since this is not a case of direct physical damage where it is self-evident that a duty of care exists, then in my judgment it is necessary to consider the matter in the light of the criteria mentioned by Lord Bridge in the *Caparo Industries* case.

For my part I doubt whether the words 'fair, just and reasonable' impose a test additional to that of 'proximity': in my judgment these are criteria to be adopted in considering whether the necessary degree of proximity exists. As Lord Oliver of Aylmerton said in *Murphy* v *Brentwood DC* (1990): 'The essential question which has to be asked in every case, given that damage which is the essential ingredient of the action has occurred, is whether the relationship between the plaintiff and the defendant is such, or, to use the favoured expression, whether it is of sufficient "proximity", that it imposes on the latter a duty to take care to avoid or prevent that loss which has in fact been sustained.'.

This is essentially a question of policy.

This decision was affirmed by the House of Lords at [1995] 3 All ER 307 (see *Cases and Materials* (**5.3.8**)).

At first sight, *Marc Rich* suggests that at long last the courts have recognised the fact that there is no proper distinction between the different forms of damage. This decision has the potential for bringing *Hedley Byrne* closer than ever to *Donoghue* v *Stevenson*, particularly in the light of developments already discussed in this chapter.

Past experience suggests, however, that the courts will continue to treat pure economic loss as a different form of damage. As Scott Baker J says in *T* (see **5.5.10**) '. . . the courts are more ready to find a duty of care owed where the consequence of a breach is personal injury rather than damage to property and still less mere economic loss.'.

Read the extract from the judgment of Potts J in *Burton* v *Islington Health Authority* [1991] 1 All ER 825, in *Cases and Materials* (**5.3.8**), on the general position concerning 'physical' and other damage in connection with 'duty of care' in negligence. The decision in this case was affirmed by the Court of Appeal at [1992] 3 All ER 833. See also *Nitrigin Eireann Teoranta* v *Inco Alloys Ltd* [1992] 1 All ER 854 in *Cases and Materials* (**5.3.8**).

Marc Rich was distinguished by the Court of Appeal in *Perrett* v *Collins, The Times*, 23 June 1998. The plaintiff was a passenger in an aircraft owned, built and flown by D1 and he was injured when the plane crashed. D2 was an inspector employed by D3 (the statutory authority responsible for airworthy certificates). D2 had issued a certificate of fitness for flight under s. 3 of the Civil Aviation Act 1983, and the question for the court to decide was whether D2 and D3 owed the plaintiff a duty of care in negligence. It was held that a duty owed by D2 and D3 would not duplicate D1's liability, because D2's role was an independent and 'critical' one: the aircraft could not take off without a certificate from D2. A passenger in an aircraft was entitled to assume that it had met the appropriate safety standards and that those involved had taken proper care in discharging their obligations.

5.6 Summary

Liability for negligently inflicted economic loss has always been a difficult problem to fathom. Where the economic loss flows from physical damage to person and/or property little difficulty, beyond the actual measurement of the loss suffered, is encountered. It is 'pure' economic loss, where nothing is hit but the 'wallet', which poses the problem; loss which is not the direct result of physical damage.

'Loss of expectation', as it is sometimes called, is seen in traditional terms as more of a **contractual** problem; it is regarded as an inappropriate claim for the law of **tort**. We have traced, briefly, lines of reasoning, from many cases, which support the *status quo* although opinions differ on whether or not this is due to a general 'rule' to this effect.

The decision in *Hedley Byrne*, however, changed all that. It can be seen as a bridge between tort and contract in that it recognises a claim in **tort** for 'loss of expectation'. *White* may be seen as confirming this role for *Hedley Byrne*. Since 1963 it has been necessary to distinguish between pure economic loss caused by negligent 'acts', and such loss flowing from negligent 'misstatements'. *Hedley Byrne* became established as **the** authority for negligent misstatements causing 'pure' financial loss, and was seen conventionally as forming the 'exception' to the **general** 'rule' that such loss was irrecoverable in the tort of negligence.

According to **another** viewpoint, however, *Hedley Byrne* is not **definitive** of liability in this field; it is merely **illustrative** of a certain **type** of liability. In other words, it does not have **exclusive** jurisdiction in relation to liability for negligently inflicted 'pure' economic loss.

In accordance with this interpretation, liability was imposed in *Junior Books* **and** *Ross*. Ironically, these developments have themselves fallen victim to a wider application of *Hedley Byrne*. By extending the scope of 'reliance' and 'assumption of responsibility', chiefly the latter, the courts have widened the jurisdiction of *Hedley Byrne* in recent times:

(a)   it now encompasses 'acts', as well as misstatements, because *Junior Books* is seen in the opinion of eminent judges to be explicable only in its own terms; in any case *Hedley Byrne* has been **applied** to 'acts' in *Midland Bank Trust Co. Ltd*, and *White*;

(b)   it embraces 'omissions', as well as 'acts'

(c)   it covers three-party relationships;

(d)   it extends to cases of physical damage.

Lord Goff, in *Henderson*, said that the law of tort provides the **general** framework for the law of obligations but the law of contract can be used to **avoid** or **displace** tortious obligations. Where, however, the parties have carried on business within the context of **contract and sub-contract**, i.e. where there is a contractual 'chain' which has been designed to prevent privity of contract arising between the plaintiff and defendant, the law can regard that 'chain' as being **inconsistent** with an **assumption of responsibility** – which can be used by the court to **short-circuit** 'the contractual structure so put in place by the parties'. In other words, the law of tort may be used, in appropriate circumstances, to create a relationship resembling a contract.

Henderson **itself** may be regarded as turning on its own special facts; it is the **potential** of the views expressed in that case which provide food for thought, and the promoters of this view, principally Lord Goff, give little insight on **when** an assumption of responsibility will short-circuit a contractual claim. His Lordship seemed to think that the court might well infer an **agreement** to **exclude** or **modify** tortious obligations in the case of an **ordinary, everyday** sub-contract in the building/construction context, but that is just about the limit of his specific guidance on this matter.

In *Henderson* the 'names' had a relationship with the managing agents, but the contractual framework was designed in such a way that the 'names' only had **formal** contractual rights against their own, **members'** agents; in turn, the **managing** agents were liable to the **members'** agents, under the terms of the sub-agency contract between the agents as a whole. Thus, in conventional terms, there was no (direct?) privity of contract between the plaintiffs (the **names**) and the defendants (the **managing** agents).

However, their Lordships in *Henderson* regarded the facts therein as **unusual**, and took the view that in **this** case the agreements were **neither** inconsistent with the defendants' assumption of responsibility to the plaintiffs, **nor** did the contractual framework provide for obligations which were less onerous than those provided for by the law of tort, i.e. the respective obligations were **conterminous**. Thus, the plaintiffs were free to choose whether to sue in contract or in tort.

That is the key to **this** particular decision viz. the **co-extensive** nature of the contractual and tortious obligations of the defendants.

Henderson, however, is, as we have already observed, authority for the **general** proposition that the law of tort is not complementary to the law of contract: on the contrary, tort law is the **fundamental** one, although contract can be used, where appropriate, to modify tortious obligations. That is, tortious obligations **stay in place** unless they are so inconsistent with a contract that it can only be concluded that the parties intended to **conclude** or **limit** the tortious obligations. This might be the case where a contract laid down duties which were of a **lesser** nature than those provided for in the law of torts – although, in the **appropriate** context (see above) an agreement would always have to be consistent with a defendant's (must he be a **professional** or **specialist**?) basic tortious obligation of an 'assumption of responsibility'.

Henderson and *White* v *Jones* are authorities for the proposition that 'assumption of responsibility', a concept of the law of tort, can be used to **transcend** the conventional tort/contract 'boundary'; to create a legal relationship equivalent to contract but without consideration (see Lord Devlin in *Hedley Byrne*) although the parties have **refrained** from entering into a **formal** contractual relationship. It may be thought that *White* v *Jones* goes further than *Henderson*, because there was no contractual chain in the **former** case.

Lord Goff said in *Henderson* that *Hedley Byrne* applied to the performance of duties (professional/specialist?) **other than** the giving of advice or information, but the full implications of *Henderson* and *White* v *Jones* remain uncertain. For example, would *Junior Books*, if decided today, be based upon an 'assumption of responsibility' by the sub-contractors? If so, would that be a more satisfactory way of circumventing the doctrine of privity than the utilisation of the Wilberforce test? Is it acceptable to use *Hedley Byrne* to 'trump' privity's hand?

It is submitted, therefore, that *Hedley Byrne* has ceased to be an 'exception' (if it ever was) to the general 'rule' about pure economic loss in negligence, restricted to liability for misstatements, and has metamorphosed into **the** all-embracing form of liability for negligently inflicted pure economic loss. This result may be applauded, although it may have been achieved in a pragmatic and piecemeal fashion, for three important reasons:

(a) it recognises the illogical distinction between 'economic' and 'physical' loss (an illogicality emphasised in *Marc Rich*);

(b) it mitigates the often artificial distinction between 'acts', 'statements' and 'omissions';

(c) it further relieves, as did *Donoghue* before it, in relation to 'manufacturer' and 'consumer', the harsh results which flow from the doctrine of **privity of contract**.

There remain, however, a number of difficulties with this enlarged jurisdiction of *Hedley Byrne*. First, are only **professional** acts caught by 'assumption of responsibility'? Is it merely a question of asking whether the defendant has 'engaged his **professional** responsibility' for the task in hand? It is uncertain whether, for example, in a situation similar to that in *Simaan* (see above) there would be an 'assumption of responsibility' for a contractual obligation by A (subcontractor) (B is the main contractor with whom A has his contract) to C (the developer/owner of a building, etc.).

In *Simaan* the defendant supplied glass panels under a contract to a subcontractor employed by the main contractor to install the panels in a building being erected for X. The main contractor, the plaintiff, suffered 'pure' economic loss when X rejected the panels as defective and withheld payments under the main contract. On the facts, the Court of Appeal thought it would be unjust and unreasonable to impose a duty of care in negligence on the defendant (in favour of the plaintiff) since to find for the plaintiff would not be in accord with the contractual arrangements which existed between the parties. The imposition of such a duty on the defendant would be tantamount to the imposition of a legal obligation on the defendant which the parties, via their contractual negotiations, had taken steps to avoid. See also the cases discussed in **5.4.2** above.

Secondly, it will be seen in **Chapter 7**, which deals with liability for dangerous premises, that developers, builders, etc., and local authorities, are not responsible in the tort of negligence for the provision of defective premises **unless** those defective premises cause damage to person or property. **Professional** people such as surveyors on the other hand, may be liable **irrespective** of whether damage is caused to other property, or to persons, by the defective structure. In other words, **their** liability, in tort, extends to defects in **quality**, which is in **effect** liability of a contractual nature, embracing as it does the cost of repair.

Thirdly, it is clear that cases like *Ross* and *Junior Books* represent an assault on the doctrine of privity of contract. *White* continues this attack, albeit from a different direction. It remains to be seen whether this develops into something more than a mere skirmish.

Finally, is it the case that *Hedley Byrne* was intended to cover liability for **physical** damage sustained by means of a negligent misstatement? There is authority, in *Clay*, for the proposition that liability for this form of damage is already accommodated under the general neighbour principle of *Donoghue*.

On the other hand, we have seen that distinctions between 'physical' damage and 'economic' damage are illogical **and** that there is **recent** authority in which the distinction has been criticised. Furthermore, to extend the scope of *Hedley Byrne* rather than adopt a wider approach to the development of the law is in keeping with the *Caparo* line of **incremental** reasoning.

The only problem with this line of argument is whether the law can give up its preoccupation with the distinction between 'physical' and 'economic', and whether the *Hedley Byrne* 'rule' is capable of the extensions it is being made to bear.

See also *Cases and Materials* (**5.4**) for further decisions in this area. You will also find there an extract from the Courts and Legal Services Act 1990.

In *Abbott* v *Strong, The Times*, 9 July 1998, A Ltd sent a circular to its shareholders inviting subscriptions for new shares (a 'rights' issue). Included in the circular was a profit forecast, supported by a letter from B, a firm of accountants, and the plaintiffs (the shareholders) alleged that this forecast was misleading. The court had to decide whether B owed a duty of care to the plaintiff with regard to the advice given to A Ltd, i.e., a duty **beyond** that owed to the plaintiffs flowing from the letter included in the circular. It was held that where X makes a statement or gives advice to Y, **to help Y to make representations to Z**, X does not owe a duty of care to Z where Z is **unaware** of X's assistance to Y.

5.7   Further Reading

Allen, T., 'Liability for References: The House of Lords and *Spring* v *Guardian Assurance*' (1995) 58 MLR 553.

Cane, P., *Tort Law and Economic Interests*, Oxford: Oxford University Press, 1991, pp. 511–518.

Cooke, R., 'An Impossible Decision' (1991) 107 LQR 46.

Craig, P.P., 'Negligent Misstatements, Negligent Acts and Economic Loss' (1976) 92 LQR 213.

Fleming, J. G., 'Requiem for *Anns*' (1990) 106 LQR 525.

Hepple, B.A., and Matthews, M.H., *Tort: Cases and Materials*, 5th edn, London: Butterworths, 1996, Chapter 4.

Jones, M., *Textbook on Torts*, 5th edn, London: Blackstone Press, 1996, pp. 58–100.

Kaye, T., 'Acts Speak Louder than Statements, or Nine into One Will Go' (1995) 58 MLR 574.

Lorenz, W., and Markesinis, B., 'Solicitors' Liability Towards Third Parties' (1993) 56 MLR 558.

Markesinis, B.S. and Deakin, S.F., *Tort Law*, 3rd edn, Oxford: Oxford University Press, 1994, pp 76–118.

Martin, R., 'Categories of Negligence and Duties of Care: *Caparo* in the House of Lords' (1990) 53 MLR 824.

Salmond and Heuston, *Law of Torts*, 21st edn, London: Sweet and Maxwell, 1996, pp. 210–219.

Stanton, K.M., *The Modern Law of Tort*, London: Sweet and Maxwell, 1994, Chapters 14 and 16.

Street on Torts, 9th edn, London: Butterworths, 1993, pp. 206–217.

Weir, T., *Casebook on Tort*, 8th edn, London: Sweet and Maxwell, 1996, pp. 29–83.

Winfield and Jolowicz on Tort, 14th edn, London: Sweet and Maxwell, 1994, pp. 93–118 and Chapter 11.

5.8   End of Chapter Assessment Question

Doubledeal set up a tax consultancy service in 1985. The business has thrived. Apart from tax matters Doubledeal has, over the years, given advice to his clients concerning investments. He admits that this policy has helped to expand his business.

Harold goes to Doubledeal in order to consult him about his tax problems. In consequence of the advice given, Harold buys some rare works of art in order to escape inheritance tax. He also asks Doubledeal for his opinion as to the prospects of Unitechnics Ltd, a new company which has been set up to retrain displaced university staff. He invests £40,000 in Unitechnics Ltd, acting on Doubledeal's assurance that the company is in a healthy financial condition.

The conversation then goes on to more mundane matters, but just as Harold is about to leave Doubledeal says: 'By the way, if you have any spare capital in these bad times, Ranchland Ltd (an American-owned real-estate firm operating in Snowdonia) is a good bet'. Two weeks later Harold invests £50,000 in this company.

Some weeks later, Harold learns that he has been wrongly advised concerning his inheritance tax position, and also that Unitechnics Ltd and Ranchland Ltd are just about to go into liquidation, having been in grave financial difficulties for six months. He also receives a bill from Doubledeal: 'For advice re Inheritance Tax'.

Advise Harold on any claim he may have in tort against Doubledeal.

See *Cases and Materials* (5.6) for a specimen answer.

CHAPTER SIX

NEGLIGENCE: NERVOUS SHOCK/PSYCHIATRIC DAMAGE

6.1 Objectives

By the end of this chapter you should be able to:

- appreciate the differences, if any, between 'physical' and 'mental' injury;

- appreciate the distinction made in the cases between 'grief', 'sorrow', etc. and **'psychiatric injury'** ('nervous shock');

- analyse the **categories** of plaintiffs entitled to recover damages;

- assess critically the **general** nature of the 'special relationship' which plaintiffs in this context have to establish, paying **particular** attention to 'foreseeability' and 'proximity'.

6.2 Introduction

'Nervous shock', the traditional description for **psychiatric** damage, may be the subject of a claim for damages in **its own right** within the tort of negligence, and not merely as an **incidental** item in some general claim for personal injury. 'Shock' is regarded generally in modern law merely as another type of **harm to the person**.

Lord MacMillan in *Bourhill* v *Young* [1943] AC 92 (HL) said:

> The crude view that the law should take cognisance only of physical injury resulting from actual impact has been discarded, and it is now well recognised that an action will lie for injury by shock sustained through the medium of the eye, or the ear without direct contact. The distinction between mental shock and bodily injury was never a scientific one, for nervous shock is presumably in all cases the result of, or at least accompanied by, some physical disturbance in the sufferer's system.

Again:

> . . . in the case of mental shock there are elements of greater subtlety than in the case of ordinary physical injury, and these elements may give rise to debate as to the precise scope of legal liability.

ACTIVITY 28

Look up the words 'nervous' and 'shock' in a dictionary. Try to combine their meanings into a working definition. We will compare it with what the judges have said, at the end of this chapter (see 6.6).

6.2.1   INTENTIONAL INTERFERENCE

It is important at the outset that we distinguish between liability arising under *Wilkinson* v *Downton* [1897] 2 QB 57, which lies for **'intentionally'** causing harm (including 'shock'); this is dealt with, in **Chapter 10**, within the context of **harassment** (see **10.6.2**). In **this** chapter we are concerned only with nervous shock inflicted **negligently**.

6.2.2   GRIEF, SORROW AND ANXIETY

Liability does **not** lie for anxiety, grief, etc. on their own, although the position is different in **contract** and in the tort of **deceit**. The Protection From Harassment Act 1997 allows claims for 'anxiety': s. 3(2).

These conditions may, however, be the subject of compensation in the tort of negligence where they result from some **physical** injury, as the court said, for example, in *Kralj* v *McGrath* [1986] 1 All ER 54. You can read about this case in *Cases and Materials* (6.1.1).

Nevertheless, in *Whitmore* v *Euroway Express Coaches, The Times*, 4 May 1984, the judge at first instance, whilst accepting the traditional distinction drawn between worry, grief, etc. and 'nervous shock', refused to find against the plaintiff, who had seen her husband badly injured as a result of the defendant's negligence, only on the ground that she had not suffered 'medical' shock or psychiatric disorder (the generally accepted definition of 'nervous shock').

He awarded the plaintiff damages for what he regarded as shock in its 'ordinary everyday meaning'. It was not possible, he said, to define such shock to any greater extent than that; but it was a 'concept which everyone understood'. His Lordship said he was in as good a position as any doctor or psychiatrist to judge whether the plaintiff had suffered 'ordinary shock'; he eschewed the expression 'nervous shock'. It was the court's duty in personal injury cases to exercise common sense and reasonableness and apply tests shared by ordinary people.

It is submitted that this decision is out of line with authority.

Authority in general favours the 'medical' approach with regard to the nature of 'nervous shock', in other words the courts look for **medically** defined damage. Lord Denning said this in *Hinz* v *Berry* [1970] 2 QB 40. Lord Bridge, in *McLoughlin* v *O'Brian* [1982] 2 All ER 298, favoured the expression **'psychiatric illness'**; and in *Attia* v *British Gas* [1987] 3 All ER 455, Bingham LJ thought that the expression 'nervous shock' was **misleading** and **inaccurate**; he preferred **'psychiatric damage'** because that term was more capable of embracing **mental illness, neurosis** and **personality change**.

In *A and Others* v *P & O Ferries*, *The Independent*, 5 May 1989 (arbitration proceedings concerning the *'Herald of Free Enterprise'* Zebrugge ferry claims), post-traumatic stress disorder and pathological grief were said to be recognised psychiatric illnesses. The arbitrators acknowledged that the 'odd legal phrase "nervous shock" did not connote shock in the sense in which it was often used in ordinary conversation'. Grief, distress or any other normal emotion was not enough: a plaintiff had to establish a **positive psychiatric illness**.

Physical consequences of psychiatric damage are compensable: e.g. *Galt* (**6.3.2**).

6.3   The Legal Cause of Action

Liability for psychiatric illness inflicted negligently has developed in a way analogous to liability for negligent misstatements, which we studied in **Chapter 5**. That is to say, the law has been applied over the years in a more cautious and guarded way than has been the case in some other areas of liability in negligence.

Why do you suppose it is that liability for psychiatric illness has been approached in this way?

The reason for this caution is the fear of bogus claims, based on the unreliability of medical evidence, and difficulties in proof of causation. As the medical profession has expanded its knowledge and expertise in this field, however, so the courts have in more recent times been more willing to expand legal liability for this type of damage.

It is evident, though, that the judges are still concerned to keep liability within what they would regard as reasonable limits. The 'floodgates of litigation' argument is still an important factor in this context, and many arbitrary decisions can be explained satisfactorily only by reference to judicial policy.

A plaintiff must establish the **usual** ingredients of the tort of negligence **and** meet a number of special requirements. We will be looking at these special conditions of recovery later (see **6.3.2** to **6.3.5.1**), but we will first take a brief look at the history of liability for 'nervous shock' in order to prepare ourselves for an examination of the modern authorities.

6.3.1   THE HISTORY OF THE CLAIM

At first, liability was limited to 'shock' suffered as a result of the plaintiff being placed by the defendant's negligence in a situation in which they feared for their **own** physical safety. In *Dulieu* v *White* [1901] 2 KB 669, the plaintiff, a pregnant barmaid, suffered shock when the defendant negligently drove his horse-drawn van through the wall of a public house.

Kennedy J said: 'A has, I conceive, no legal duty not to shock B's nerves by the exhibition of negligence towards C or towards the property of B or C.'. He found in favour of the plaintiff.

This became known as the 'Kennedy proviso'; it was rejected in *Hambrook* v *Stokes Bros* [1925] 1 KB 141. In this case it was said that a plaintiff could recover because of fear for the safety of **relatives**. A mother suffered shock after she saw a runaway lorry pass the spot where her children had just been walking, though she may not have feared for her own safety. She died of a heart attack, and her estate recovered damages from the defendants for their negligence.

However, in *King* v *Phillips* [1953] 1 QB 429, a mother, seventy yards from where a taxi was slowly backing over her child's tricycle, was held to be outside the 'area of risk' and her claim for shock was dismissed. In both cases the plaintiffs did not actually **see** their children to be in danger.

You may care to consider whether *King* would now be decided differently in view of the decision in *McLoughlin* v *O'Brian* (below).

You will discover that *McLoughlin* introduced the idea of recovery of damages for shock where the plaintiff witnesses the 'immediate aftermath' of an accident, and the plaintiff in *King* might well have come within the terms of the 'aftermath' approach.

6.3.2   ELEMENTS OF THE CLAIM

In *Hambrook* the Court of Appeal said that a plaintiff must suffer, or experience, the shock by means of his or her own **unaided** senses; in other words it is not enough merely to be **told** of an incident.

This requirement was confirmed in *Boardman* v *Sanderson* [1964] 1 WLR 1317, in which a father, out of sight, but within 'earshot' of a car backing over his son's foot, was allowed to recover from the driver, the defendant. However, it is not essential that the plaintiff sees or hears the incident itself: it is enough if he sees its immediate effects. The Court of Appeal in *Boardman* distinguished *King* (above) on the ground that in the instant case the defendant knew of the plaintiff's presence in the vicinity; this therefore, meant there was a close proximity between the parties. A contention that it was necessary for the plaintiff to be actually on the scene at the time of the accident was rejected. The defendant owed a duty not only to the boy 'but [also] to the near relatives of the boy who were, as he knew, on the premises within earshot, and likely to come upon the scene if any injury or ill befell that boy' (Omrod LJ).

In *Hinz* v *Berry* [1970] 2 QB 40, parents and their children were picnicking in a lay-by. The plaintiff, the mother, and one child crossed the road to pick flowers and from a safe position saw the rest of the family injured from having been hit by the defendant's negligently driven vehicle. She was awarded £4,000 damages for nervous shock. The Court of Appeal confirmed that damages are not awarded in these cases for sorrow, grief or anxiety.

The decision in the Australian case of *Benson* v *Lee* [1972] VR 879 is instructive. A mother recovered damages for shock suffered partly as a result of having been told of her child's death, and partly because of the effect on her of having accompanied the child in the ambulance to hospital. Lush J doubted whether the 'rule' that the plaintiff must perceive the accident had survived *Wagon Mound (No. 1)* [1961] AC 388 and argued that 'If within the limits of foresight something is experienced through direct and immediate perception of the accident, or some part of the events constituting it, which imparts shock, that is, I think, all that the law requires.'.

You can read about the decision in *S* v *Distillers Company (Biochemicals) Ltd* [1969] 3 All ER 1412 in *Cases and Materials* (**6.2.1**).

SAQ 58

Please pause for a moment. Do you think it possible that non-relatives may recover damages for psychiatric illness?

In some cases this is precisely what has happened.

Thus, for example, in *Chadwick* v *British Railways Board* [1967] 1 WLR 912 a serious train crash was caused by the defendant's negligence. The plaintiff suffered nervous shock from the horror of the incident after coming to render assistance. Walter J held the defendant liable because it was foreseeable that someone would suffer shock from the defendant's negligence; a duty was owed to **rescuers**; and shock caused by fear for the safety of others was remediable. The plaintiff had a history of psychiatric trouble, but the medical evidence showed that he had been cured of his previous illness. (You may wish to refer to **Chapter 2**, **General Defences**, in which the duty to rescuers is discussed at **2.3.1.4**.)

In *Pearson* v *British Midland*, *The Times*, 10 February 1998, the plaintiff, who was the first person to rescue passengers from the Kegworth air disaster was awarded £57,000 for what Garland J described as the 'recurring nightmare' which had blighted his life. The plaintiff suffered severe post traumatic stress disorder (PTSD) for over six years after helping victims from the wreckage of the aeroplane which crashed on to an embankment of the M1 motorway in 1989, killing 47 people.

On the night of the disaster the plaintiff and his wife were travelling north on the M1. His wife, who was driving the car, managed to stop at the scene after avoiding debris from the aircraft which was strewn across the motorway. The plaintiff went to see what assistance he could give and was first on the scene; he spent three hours comforting the injured occupants of the aeroplane.

Out of the total award £17,000 was for general damages to compensate the plaintiff for his suffering. This award was in line with similar PTSD payments ordered by the courts, although previous awards were made to persons who suffered because they were accident victims or professionals called to the scene of the accident in the course of their duty.

In two cases plaintiffs have recovered for shock caused by fear for the safety of **workmates**. The first is *Dooley* v *Cammell Laird and Co. Ltd* [1951] 1 Lloyd's Reports 271. The plaintiff, who was an employee of the defendants, suffered shock when the sling on the crane he was working snapped and the load fell into the open hold of a ship. Some of his colleagues were working in the hold at the time, and he feared for their safety. His claim for damages was successful. (He obtained judgment against his employer for **breach of statutory duty**; and against a **second** defendant, the owner of the defective sling, in **negligence**.

In the second case, *Galt* v *BRB* (1983) 133 NLJ 870, the plaintiff, a train driver, was driving his train when he came suddenly upon two fellow employees working on the track ahead, the train having just rounded a bend. He could not stop quickly and thought the men would be killed (in fact they managed to escape). At first instance he was awarded damages for nervous shock, and those damages included an award for increased injury due to a pre-existing disease. He suffered from a pre-existing, but symptomless, condition which predisposed him to a heart attack (myocardial infarction) in such circumstances.

You may have observed that there was very close proximity between the parties in both cases; and in each instance the plaintiff was operating machinery which could have seriously injured the workmates who had been placed in danger.

At this stage it might be helpful if you took stock of the general development of liability for shock inflicted negligently. In particular, you could consider:

  (a)   the people who are entitled to sue for damages;

  (b)   the circumstances in which they can sue.

According to what we have read **so far**, only those persons who can establish **recognised** psychiatric illness need consider legal action. If they can do that, it seems they must next show the shock was caused as a result of fear for their own safety, for the safety of relatives or the safety of working colleagues.

Please read about the decision in *Attia* v *British Gas plc* [1987] 3 All ER 455, in *Cases and Materials* (6.2.1). What do you consider to be the main point about this case?

The main point about the case is that the Court of Appeal considered it perfectly feasible for a plaintiff to argue that psychiatric damage was a reasonably foreseeable result of witnessing damage to his or her **property**.

6.3.3   DUTY OF CARE

We have not yet, however, examined the **general** basis of the duty of care in these cases. As we saw earlier, the usual ingredients of negligence have to be established by the plaintiff and 'duty' is probably the main problem area here.

According to *Bourhill* v *Young* [1943] AC 92 (*Cases and Materials* (**6.2.2**)), the plaintiff may have to show that he or she was in the 'area of risk', or 'disaster area' as others have called it. The plaintiff, who was pregnant at the time, **heard** the sound of an accident caused by the defendant, who was killed in the incident. (The action was brought against his estate.) However, she **saw** nothing of the **immediate** event as she stepped off a tram; the accident had occurred about 50 yards away from her. She very soon afterwards made her way to the scene of the accident and suffered shock because of what she saw. As a result of this shock she lost her baby, but her claim for damages failed.

Can you think of the reasons that led to this decision? Write down your answer before you read what follows.

In the House of Lords, three judges said she was not entitled to recover because she was not within the area of **impact**. This reasoning seems to be at odds with earlier authority, such as *Hambrook*. The other judges found against her on **another** ground, i.e. that since she had no relationship with the person injured in the accident, shock to her was not foreseeable. Furthermore, it was held that a pregnant plaintiff was abnormally sensitive to shock in such circumstances. Lord Porter said:

> The driver of a car or vehicle is entitled to assume that the ordinary frequenter of the streets has sufficient fortitude to endure such incidents as may from time to time be expected to occur in them, including the noise of a collision and the sight of injury to others, and is not to be considered negligent towards one who does not possess the customary phlegm.

The 'phlegm and fortitude' approach, suitably adapted to meet the case of a person who can show some 'special relationship', as a test of reaction to circumstances may still hold good, as we will see later. The test of the susceptibility of a normal person has for long been regarded as the touchstone, although the **reverse** is probably true with regard to the nature of the accident itself.

In appropriate cases, however, it is submitted that a duty may be owed to a plaintiff with peculiar characteristics, by analogy with *Haley* v *London Electricity Board* [1965] AC 778. In *Haley* the defendants had made some excavations in the highway and the plaintiff, who was blind, fell into one of the holes and was injured when walking on the pavement. It was found that the defendants were liable in negligence to the plaintiff, for failing to take **special** precautions to warn blind people of the dangers inherent in the works. Having listened to evidence about how many blind inhabitants there were in the area, the court concluded that a duty of care was owed to the plaintiff as a member of a foreseeable class of persons likely to be affected by the defendant's activities.

The ordinary principles of liability for injury do not apply without qualification in this context.

List the possible reasons for this state of affairs.

This state of affairs is due to a number of factors:

(a) the risk of a great number of actions;

(b) the risk of fraudulent claims;

(c) the problem of putting a monetary value on such damage, for example, see the *P & O Ferries* arbitration case (at **6.2.2**); and

(d) the difficulty in some cases of proving the link between the defendant's conduct and the plaintiff's shock.

To apply literally the ordinary concept of foreseeability could well produce what the courts might see as excessive litigation, although we will see later that two cases, *McLoughlin* v *O'Brian* and *Wigg* v *British Railways Board* have been influenced by *Anns*. It is foreseeable, for example, that the relations of an accident victim will be told of his death or injury, and that they may suffer shock simply on being given this news; but it may be doubted whether the courts would allow a claim for damages in such a case.

In *Schneider* v *Eisovitch* [1960] 2 QB 430, the plaintiff and her husband were injured in a vehicle accident caused by the defendant's negligence. Upon recovering consciousness, some time later in hospital, she was told of her husband's death and suffered shock as a result. At first instance, it was found that she could add a claim for this damage to her claim for her physical damage.

Can you think what the judge's reasons for giving this decision might have been?

The decision stands alone; it has not been overruled, but it is difficult to reconcile the ruling with later authority other than on the point that the plaintiff was herself injured physically in the accident itself, and it may be that the claim for shock was allowed to 'piggyback' on the claim for physical damage.

It seems that there must be some special limitation to the extent of liability for 'nervous shock', but there appears to be little agreement as to the nature and scope of this limitation. Winfield, for example, has suggested that there must exist some 'special relationship' in the circumstances of each case. Some judges have used the concept of remoteness of damage, for example Denning LJ in *King* v *Phillips*, but usually the concept of duty of care is more popular.

Few, if any, clear principles emerge from the majority of the cases. In *King* Denning LJ suggested that had the plaintiff been physically injured she could have recovered damages. It does not follow, however, that there is necessarily a duty not to inflict nervous shock merely because the plaintiff is within the area of physical impact; nor does it follow that a plaintiff's absence from that area is fatal to his claim for damages. The soundness of the 'impact theory', which we encountered in *Bourhill* v *Young* (above) may be doubted, particularly in view of the decision in *McLoughlin* v *O'Brian*, as we will see later.

In *King* v *Phillips* Denning LJ said that the test adopted in *Bourhill* v *Young* (above) '. . . was not foreseeability of physical injury, but foreseeability of emotional shock'. This was approved by the Privy Council in *Wagon Mound (No. 1)* (examined in **Chapter 4**). It was said in *Jaensch* v *Coffey* (1984) 54 ALR 417 (Australia) (a case in which the plaintiff succeeded on similar facts *to McLoughlin*; see **6.3.4**) that the specific illness suffered by the plaintiff need not be foreseeable; it was enough to show reasonable foresight of a recognised psychiatric condition brought on by shock. You should also consider the decision in *Page* v *Smith*, which is dealt with at **6.3.7**. It was held in this case that foreseeability of psychiatric illness is not the correct test where the plaintiff is directly involved in the accident and well within the range of foreseeable physical injury. Here, the plaintiff is to be regarded as a 'primary' rather than a 'secondary', victim of the accident. The duty of care owed in such a context is the same duty not to cause 'personal injury' – which applies in cases of physical harm. (This decision was applied in *Young* v *Charles Church*, which you will find in *Cases and Materials* **(8.2.3.1)**.)

6.3.4   A PERIOD OF EXPANSION?

Please read about the decision in *McLoughlin* v *O'Brian* [1982] 2 All ER 298, in *Cases and Materials* **(6.2.3)**. What was the result of the appeal to the House of Lords?

The House of Lords, however, rejected the policy argument and found unanimously in favour of the plaintiff. Liability was extended to the 'immediate aftermath' of an accident.

6.3.4.1   The speeches

It is instructive to examine the salient features of the speeches in this case. All their Lordships agreed that it was incumbent upon the plaintiff to establish that the shock which in fact she suffered was a reasonably foreseeable result of the defendant's careless driving. Lords Scarman and Bridge found that once causation was established (the defendants had admitted negligence in respect of the collision) this was all that the plaintiff need show and that it was not for the courts to limit, on policy grounds, a right to recover for reasonably foreseeable damage caused by a defendant. Lord Scarman suggested that, apart from special cases, policy was not justiciable (i.e. where common law principle dictated the result, as in the present case) and it was the function of Parliament, not the courts, to set limits on grounds of policy. He thought that the result in the present case **might** be socially undesirable; there was a powerful case for legislation such as that enacted in New South Wales and the Australian Capital Territories.

You will find an extract from an Australian Ordinance of 1955 in *Cases and Materials* (**6.2.3.1**).

Do you think that Lord Scarman's view of the role played by policy in these cases might have found favour with his brethren in *McLoughlin*?

You would be right to conclude that the answer is 'No'.

Lords Wilberforce, Bridge and Russell regarded policy as having a much more important role to play in judicial deliberations; reasonable foreseeability of shock to the plaintiff is a necessary, though not necessarily sufficient, condition of liability and policy may legitimately restrict the range of liability. (It may be noted that Lord Wilberforce did not employ his two-stage test and argued on the basis of a 'logical progression' in the cases, i.e. he adopted an approach reminiscent of the 'incremental approach' to the duty of care issue in negligence discussed in **Chapter 3**.) The present case, it was said, came within the current boundaries of the law.

According to the speeches, these 'boundaries' can be set out as follows:

(a) no relief for mere grief or sorrow;

(b) no need to show direct impact or fear of immediate personal injury for oneself;

(c) shock suffered as a result of injury to, or fear for the safety of, a near relative was compensable;

(d) apart from *Boardman* v *Sanderson* (above) there was no English case in which a plaintiff out of sight and earshot of an incident involving a near relative had recovered damages for shock;

(e) a rescuer could recover damages.

6.3.4.2 The elements of a claim

The House of Lords said that three elements had to be considered in these cases: the 'class' of persons whose claims should be recognised; their proximity to the accident; and the means by which the shock was caused. We will now consider each of these elements in turn.

'Class of persons'

The existing law recognised the claims of those with close family ties at one end of the range of protected persons and denied the claims of ordinary bystanders at the other end of the range. This was either because such persons were expected to show sufficient fortitude to cope with the ordinary vicissitudes of life, or because defendants could not be expected to compensate the world at large.

Proximity

On proximity to the accident, it was obvious that it must be close in both time and in space; it must be proved that the defendant's negligence has caused the nervous shock. The 'immediate aftermath' fell within the required degree of proximity.

If you have read about the *Distillers* case, in **Cases and Materials** (6.2.1), you will have noticed that it does not come within the usual type of 'accident' case encountered in the context of 'shock'.

Communication

As to communication, there was no case in which compensation had been awarded for shock brought about by a third party. The shock must come through sight or hearing of the event or of its immediate aftermath.

Can you see a problem with this kind of limitation?

According to Lord Wilberforce the courts would have to consider at some time whether the equivalent of sight or hearing, e.g. 'simultaneous television', would suffice.

Lord Bridge said a defendant's duty must depend on reasonable foreseeability and must be adjudicated on a case by case basis. If asked 'where the thing was to stop' his answer would be 'where in the particular case the good sense of the judges, enlightened by progressive awareness of mental illness, decided'. His Lordship explained a hypothetical example of an hotel fire. He said it was logical to suppose that a mother who reads a newspaper report of a fire at a hotel where she knows her children are staying and who later learns of their death would have a claim against the person responsible for the fire: imagination rather than direct perception would link together the defendant's behaviour and the shock for purposes of causation.

It may interest you to know that *McLoughlin* was an important influence in the Australian case of *Jaensch* v *Coffey* (1984) 54 ALR 417. In this case the plaintiff went to hospital and there saw her husband in great pain from his injuries, both before and between emergency operations. She was awarded damages for shock.

6.3.4.3 Nature of the accident

It was also said in *McLoughlin* that the **nature** of an **accident** or its **immediate aftermath** (for example, its particularly horrific nature) may well be an important factor in these cases. Not surprisingly *McLoughlin*, like any other case, is a child of its era and the decision was no doubt influenced by *Anns*; though it is debatable whether it can be described accurately as an 'application' of the Wilberforce test. It is true, however, that the judge at first instance in *Wigg v British Railways Board, The Times*, 4 February 1986 regarded *McLoughlin* as freeing the law from the shackles of policy considerations.

In *Wigg*, the plaintiff, a train driver, succeeded in his claim for shock and trauma suffered when he came upon the body of a person very soon after it had been struck down by an open door on the plaintiff's train as it left a station. The plaintiff had left his cab to search for the victim.

The judge found that it was reasonably foreseeable by the defendants that the driver would behave as he did, that there was a risk he might suffer nervous shock as a consequence, and that they were in breach of the duty of care they owed him. The guard on the train had been negligent regarding the open door and BRB were vicariously liable for his negligence.

It was found that *McLoughlin* v *O'Brian* enabled the court to decide each case on its own merits rather than on policy considerations and that the fundamental question in each case was one of reasonable foreseeability. His Lordship rejected the defendants' claim that it was not foreseeable that train drivers of **reasonable** fortitude would have suffered nervous shock (the plaintiff had had two previous experiences of death on the track in 1979 and 1980). It was also found that the plaintiff had done more than the ordinary disinterested bystander would have done: he had searched for and found the victim and offered him words of comfort as well as staying with him. (Unknown to the plaintiff, the victim was already dead.)

Although the plaintiff could be described as a rescuer it was, said the judge, unnecessary so to find because the nervous shock suffered by the plaintiff was reasonably foreseeable.

All of this must now be read in the light of subsequent developments.

6.3.5 *ALCOCK* v *CHIEF CONSTABLE OF THE SOUTH YORKSHIRE POLICE* (1991)

In *Jones and Others* v *Wright (Chief Constable of South Yorkshire)* [1991] 1 All ER 353, Hidden J upheld claims by eight plaintiffs whose close relatives were victims of the Hillsborough football tragedy in April 1989. They witnessed the disaster unfold on television, knowing that their relatives were at the game. The claims were made against the South Yorkshire police in negligence for nervous shock.

It was held that watching live television coverage of an accident satisfied the requirement of 'proximity'. Siblings as well as parents were entitled to make successful claims; there was 'no basis in logic or law' why brothers and sisters should not be able to recover damages. Not all the victims died in the disaster: two were injured and one escaped unhurt. One plaintiff lost her case because she was the fiancée of the victim, and not a relative.

Another plaintiff succeeded who watched television in a coach parked outside the football ground as his son died; as did a plaintiff who was sitting in the stand above the Leppings Lane terrace, as his two brothers were killed.

According to the judge a television viewer saw the same image that he would see if he were standing in the position of the camera, and would be aware that the pictures were coming live from Hillsborough football ground: 'Just as a store detective [watching on a TV monitor] sees goods put into the pocket and not in the basket, although he is not present at the scene, so does the TV watcher see the crowd surge forward in pen three of the Leppings Lane stand, though he is not present.'.

The defendants argued that a finding for the plaintiffs would open the floodgates of litigation.

SAQ 65

What do you suppose the judge's reaction was to this claim?

Rejecting the claim that his ruling would open the floodgates for claims from the millions of people who watched the disaster on television, his Lordship said claimants had to meet three requirements: a medically diagnosed psychiatric illness (in these cases 'post traumatic stress disorder'); being at the match or witnessing it live on television; being a mother, father, brother or sister of a victim.

Presumably, his Lordship would have included **spouses** in the list of those eligible to claim. Established case law would support that view.

Damages were claimed also by the families of three of the victims for pre-death suffering, under the provisions of the Law Reform (Miscellaneous Provisions) Act 1934. Hidden J, rejecting the claim, said that this was not 'a route the Court should take'. (Claims for this head of damages were successful in out-of-court settlements in connection with the disaster at King's Cross Underground station, which is referred to at **6.3.8**, and the Zeebrugge disaster, which is referred to at **6.2.2**.)

The Court of Appeal, however, at [1991] 2 All ER 88, overturned the decision of Hidden J.

Their Lordships limited liability to those persons in a **parent-child relationship**, which could include grand-parents, and **spouses**. Even in relation to close relatives such as these, the court said liability does not extend to those who witnessed the events only by watching or hearing 'live' (or simultaneous) television broadcasts, or who identified a body in the mortuary afterwards. This was not regarded as coming within the *McLoughlin* 'aftermath'.

It was held that 'everyday' simultaneous television broadcasts do not, because of the television industry's code of ethics, portray **recognisable suffering** individuals; therefore this form of communication did not satisfy the test of 'sight' or 'hearing' of the event or its immediate aftermath.

Parker LJ said: 'The vast majority of people do not suffer psychiatric illness from this sort of shock.'. He thought that a television viewer was not sufficiently close and directly connected with the police negligence in this case.

According to Nolan LJ, nervous shock as used in the decided cases connotes a reaction to 'an immediate and horrifying impact' and this factor was missing in the present case. His Lordship did not, however, rule out the possibility or recovery for **some** television viewers. He said:

> If a publicity-seeking organisation made arrangements for a party of children to go up in a balloon, and for the event to be televised so that their parents could watch, it would be hard to deny that the organisers were under a duty to avoid mental injury to the parents as well as physical injury to the children, and that there would be a breach of that duty if through some careless act or omission the balloon crashed.

It is clear that his Lordship intended this to be only an **example** of a **special** 'live' broadcast that might be an **acceptable** means of communication of psychiatric illness.

Plaintiffs 'actively' involved in the event(s) need not, it was said, establish their relationship with the primary victim. **Rescuers** would be included here. Both Stocker and Parker LJJ explained *Dooley* (see **6.3.2**) as turning on the fact that the plaintiff in that case took an **active** part in the course of events, because he was working the crane at the time of the accident. He was the **servant** of the defendant at the relevant time.

As you will see, all this was accepted by the House of Lords, although a rather different approach was taken to the issue of qualifying relationships. Their Lordships adopted a more flexible categorisation than the Court of Appeal of those eligible to sue for damage of this kind, though the formula which emerged from the House is still of a restrictive nature.

In a second judgment the court also dismissed appeals for damages for 'pre-death' suffering brought by one parent on behalf of his two daughters and by James Wafer on behalf of his brother.

On appeal to the House of Lords, reported as *Alcock v Chief Constable of the South Yorkshire Police* [1991] 4 All ER 907, the appeals of the relatives from the Court of Appeal decision were unanimously dismissed. Their Lordships applied the *McLoughlin* 'aftermath' test: the plaintiff must **experience** the incident or its immediate aftermath by **seeing** and/or **hearing** it. **Throughout** this case the Chief Constable admitted a duty of care and breach of that duty, but argued that this was owed only to those who died or were injured.

Can you predict the reasons for this result? Write down your answer before you read what follows.

It was held that a plaintiff who relied on shock suffered for the plight of others had to satisfy **two** basic conditions:

(a)   it must be reasonably foreseeable that he or she would sustain psychiatric injury due to his or her close bond of love and affection with the victim; and

(b)   there must be proximity in terms of **time** and **space**.

The House of Lords said that none of the claimants had witnessed the actual injury to their loved ones, seeing the disaster on a live television broadcast was not equivalent to being at the ground within actual sight or hearing of the event and its immediate aftermath. Watching such scenes on television could not in **law** give rise to shock, though it might be different in **medical** terms. The court also rejected the claims of two persons who were actually at the event (an FA Cup semi-final), namely a man whose brothers died and a man who lost a brother-in-law, because they failed to prove a sufficiently close bond with the victims.

The plaintiffs included a wife, parents, sisters, brothers, uncles, a grandfather, a brother-in-law, a fiancée and a friend. In the case of **parents** and **children** or **spouses** there is a rebuttable **presumption**, said their Lordships, that the relationship between the victim(s) of the tragedy and the claimant(s) is of the closest bond of love and affection. It will, of course, be for the **defendant** to **rebut** this presumption.

In the case of **other** relationships it will be for the **plaintiff** to **establish** love and affection.

There was general agreement that there was no need to limit a right of action to parents and spouses but, whilst Lords Ackner and Jauncey would require the plaintiff to establish a relationship **akin** to that of parent or spouse, Lords Keith and Oliver would merely require the plaintiff to establish close ties of love and affection. According to Lord Keith such ties may be stronger between engaged couples than others married for many years.

Lord Oliver said that it would be 'inaccurate and hurtful' to suggest that grief was made any less real by a more gradual realisation of loss, but the law should not be extended to cover such cases.

Alcock says that the shock must be the result of a **sudden** incident. There must be, as some judges put it, a 'shocking **event**' causing the immediate psychiatric illness: a gradual build-up of illness is not acceptable.

It was also said by the House that attendance at a temporary morgue to identify a relative, no earlier than nine hours after the tragedy, was not participation in the immediate aftermath.

None of their Lordships was prepared to rule out the possibility of a 'mere' spectator or 'bystander' recovering damages if the circumstances were sufficiently **horrific**.

6.3.5.1   *Alcock* and beyond

It is clear that the House of Lords in *Alcock* took a very cautious approach to the question of recovery for psychiatric injury. The line taken by Lord Wilberforce in *McLoughlin* ' which, in contrast to his now discredited expansionist formula in *Anns*, was of an **incremental** nature, was said to represent the law on shock.

The **full** implications of the ruling in *Alcock* will only emerge over the years, but it is important that we attempt a summary of its **immediate** effects. However, before we do that it is necessary to consider several matters of considerable importance; matters which have to be taken into account in our summary.

See also the extract from Napier and Wheat in *Cases and Materials* (6.2.4.1).

Please read the decisions in *Hevican* v *Ruane* [1991] 3 All ER 65, and *Ravenscroft* v *Rederiakiebolaget Transatlantic* [1991] 3 All ER 73; [1992] 2 All ER 470, CA in *Cases and Materials* (6.2.4.1), and consider how they stand in relation to *Alcock*.

An interesting feature of both these cases is that they turn on issues of **remoteness** and **causation**; in both cases the defendants admitted negligence.

It is clear, however, that their effect is at odds with *Alcock*. In *Hevican* the plaintiff was not present at the immediate aftermath of the accident and in *Ravenscroft* the mother was even further 'removed', in *Alcock* terms, from the accident, not having even seen the body of her son.

6.3.6   PROPERTY

You will by now have read about *Attia* in *Cases and Materials* (**6.2.1**), and learned that it is authority for the proposition that a plaintiff may in appropriate circumstances recover damages for shock suffered as a result of concern for his or her property. It is submitted that this decision may have to be reconsidered in the light of *Alcock*, which requires the plaintiff to have established either a special relationship with the victim of the defendant's negligence; or to have been in fear for his or her own safety; or to be a member of a recognised class of claimant, such as a rescuer.

Attia was cited, but not considered by their Lordships in *Alcock*.

Can you think of a special factor, which might distinguish *Attia* from other authorities?

You might have thought about the possibility of a **contractual** relationship existing between the plaintiff and defendant. If you had done so you would have hit upon something which might well be a distinguishing feature of the case. The parties **did** have a contract and, whilst it is true this made no provision for the recovery of damages for shock should the defendants be negligent, they were therefore in very close proximity indeed.

In *Perry* v *Sidney Phillips and Son* (see **4.6.1**) the plaintiff was awarded damages for the worry and distress he suffered because of the physical inconvenience of living in a house with severe defects which the defendants had negligently failed to report.

6.3.7   THE PLAINTIFF'S REACTION

Claimants for damages must exhibit sufficient 'phlegm and fortitude'; they must not be over-sensitive or receptive to shock. In *Bourhill* this test was applied to a bystander, but apparently **all** plaintiffs must clear this hurdle, although it may be that a mere witness may have to show a 'stiffer upper lip' (that is, such a person may have to be more robust in this respect) than, for example, a close relative.

In *Ravenscroft* Ward J said: 'Both psychiatrists agree that she is not a lady of undue sensitivity, but is **of reasonable fortitude**.'.

The 'egg-shell skull' rule, however, applies to **extent** of injury: i.e. if the ordinary person would have suffered shock, the particularly susceptible may be able to succeed even though the consequences are more severe.

Thus, in *Malcolm* v *Broadhurst* [1970] 3 All ER 608, Lane J said: 'The defendant must take the wife [the plaintiff] as he finds her and there is no difference in principle [between] an egg-shell skull and an egg-shell personality'.

The plaintiff and her husband were injured in a car accident caused by the negligence of the defendant. She claimed damages for:

(a) her physical injuries;

(b) intensification of her pre-existing nervous condition (see the 'egg-shell skull' rule, above);

(c) her psychological injuries suffered because of her husband's injuries;

(d) loss of her wages flowing from (a), (b) and (c);

(e) loss of her wages caused by the termination of her husband's one-man business (which had employed her) due to his death from his injuries.

It was held that all but (e) (pure pecuniary loss) were redressable. Head (c) was recoverable because the damage was for a foreseeable type and 'the fact that it arises or is continued by reason of an unusual complex of events does not avail the defendant'.

In *Brice* v *Brown* [1984] 1 All ER 737, the plaintiff was severely neurotic and the court held that the defendant did **not** have to take her as he found her. The plaintiff and her young daughter were involved in a motor accident caused by the defendant's negligence; in this accident the daughter was only slightly injured, but the plaintiff suffered considerable psychiatric damage through fear for her safety. Applying the test of what would have been the reaction of someone of ordinary phlegm and fortitude, it was found that the plaintiff should recover nothing.

If someone of ordinary phlegm **would**, in the circumstances of the case, have suffered shock the plaintiff would in fact have been compensated for the **full** extent of her psychiatric damage, because she would have benefited from the application of the 'egg-shell skull' rule.

Alcock confirms the requirement of 'phlegm and fortitude'.

Please read *Page* v *Smith* [1994] 4 All ER 522 (CA) and [1995] 2 All ER 736 (HL) in *Cases and Materials* (6.2.5). What was the outcome of this case?

In *Page*, the plaintiff was involved, but not physically injured, in a traffic accident caused by the defendant's negligence. The plaintiff claimed that his myalgic encephalomyelitis ('ME') from which he had suffered for some 20 years, but which, at the time of the accident was in remission, had been aggravated by this incident. He claimed compensation for psychiatric damage.

The Court of Appeal dismissed his claim because it was not reasonably foreseeable that someone of 'customary phlegm' would sustain any psychiatric injury due to a road accident in which he suffered no physical injury. A 'frightening experience' is not enough. (There was no claim by the plaintiff of fear for his own safety or fear for anyone else's safety.)

In the House of Lords, however, it was held, by a majority of three to two, that foreseeability of **physical** harm was enough to enable a plaintiff, who was **directly** involved in an accident caused by the defendant's negligence, to claim damages for 'shock'. It was **not** necessary that the plaintiff should be physically harmed.

The issue was, however, sent back to the Court of Appeal to determine the issue of **causation**, i.e. did the plaintiff's experience in the accident cause his condition? In the meantime, the £162,153 damages awarded to the plaintiff by the High Court in 1992 was withheld until the Court of Appeal arrived at a decision.

In *Page* v *Smith (No. 2)* [1996] 3 All ER 272 the court ruled that the test applicable in causation cases (determined on the 'balance of probabilities') was whether the defendant's negligence had caused or materially contributed to the development or the prolongation of the plaintiff's symptoms. A 'material' cause was one which was **more than** 'minimal' or 'trivial' or 'insignificant'. On the present facts, the **balance** of medical opinion regarded the defendant's negligence as a factor that could have materially contributed to the re-emergence of the plaintiff's condition and 'converted it from a mild and sporadic state to one of chronic intensity and permanence' (Sir Thomas Bingham MR, with whom Morritt and Auld LJJ agreed). The court found that since the trial judge, who had listened to all the evidence, was satisfied (**in the plaintiff's favour**) on this issue it would not be appropriate to disagree with him. The defendant's appeal was accordingly **dismissed**.

6.3.8 'PROFESSIONAL' RESCUERS

Alcock recognises that rescuers may be in a privileged position with regard to claims for nervous shock, but it does not deal specifically with the position of professional rescuers, such as fire officers and police officers. The court left this point open. It would seem, however, that there should be no problem in principle with such claims; indeed claims by professional rescuers might well be more foreseeable than claims by other rescuers in some situations.

In *Hale* v *London Underground* (1992) 11 BMLR 81, a fire officer, who had taken part in the rescue operations at the King's Cross fire disaster, was awarded damages for the psychiatric illness he suffered as a result of what he had experienced during that rescue. The defendants had admitted liability, but disputed the size of the damages. Other fire officers involved in this incident have received out-of-court settlements.

It was widely reported in the press during the early part of 1995 that 14 police officers, present on the terraces of the football ground at Hillsborough, had reached favourable out-of-court settlements with the Police Authority's insurers for shock suffered during the performance of their duties at that event. These reports also indicated that some of the unsuccessful plaintiffs in *Alcock* had been angered by these settlements.

In a consultation paper, published on 29 March 1995, the Law Commission recommended wider rights for disaster victims' families to claim damages for psychiatric illnesses, such as post-traumatic stress disorder, induced by their loved ones' deaths. It described the decision in *Alcock* as 'unnecessarily restrictive' and called for a new statute to clarify and liberalise the law. The commission said:

> For the law to distinguish the claims for shock-induced psychiatric illness of one mother present at the scene of her son's death or its immediate aftermath from that of another mother who was not present at the scene but came across the aftermath several hours later, or who heard about the incident from a friend or saw it on television, might justly give rise to accusations of arbitrary and insensitive line-drawing.

The commission also sought views on whether 'professional rescuers' should be entitled to compensation for psychological trauma. It expressed no view, but questioned whether there was any justification for distinguishing between physical and psychological injuries. It also noted that excluding professional rescuers would allow off-duty policemen and firefighters involved in rescues to claim, while barring those doing the same acts on duty.

In *Frost and Others* v *The Chief Constable of the South Yorkshire Police*, *The Times*, 3 July 1995 it was held at first instance that six police officers, who brought test cases on behalf of 23 officers, were 'bystanders' who played too peripheral a part in the Hillsborough disaster to be awarded damages for their severe psychological trauma. The plaintiffs were **not** on the **terraces** at the time, they dealt with fans on the **pitch**; they performed mouth-to-mouth resuscitation, sorted bodies on the pitch, and stripped bodies at the mortuary.

The judge said that a bystander of a horrific incident was not entitled to claim damages for psychiatric damage, and the officers fell into that category. In any event, he said, police officers should be more able to deal with traumatic events than ordinary bystanders 'being persons of extraordinary phlegm'. It was also necessary to observe that an event might be less traumatic for someone who helped rather than watched it helplessly.

On the facts of the case only one of the police officers was a 'rescuer' in relation to the immediate aftermath of the accident, but he was not doing anything which suggested that it would be just and reasonable to regard him as proximate when an ordinary spectator of the 'horrific scene' would not qualify as proximate.

You should **now turn** to *Cases and Materials* (**6.2.6**) and read the extracts from the two leading judgments in the Court of Appeal at [1997] 1 All ER 540. It will be observed that the Court's finding was to the effect that police constables who suffered post traumatic stress syndrome either **in the course of their duty** as constables or as rescuers were entitled to damages. (As 'professional' rescuers police constables would, no doubt, regard rescue as one facet of their contracts of employment.)

In *Scholfield* v *Chief Constable of West Yorkshire*, *The Times*, 15 May 1998, the plaintiff, a police officer, accompanied a colleague, X, to a house in which four guns had been found. X suddenly fired one of the guns into some bedding material but the plaintiff, quickly realising what was about to happen, had moved to protect the persons who had reported the presence of the guns. The plaintiff later developed post traumatic stress disorder and claimed damages from the Chief Constable for X's negligence (this was an action for **vicarious** liability). The Court of Appeal held that the relationship between the plaintiff and X, as colleagues engaged in the same task in the course of their employment, was sufficiently proximate to make the plaintiff a **participant** in the incident rather than a mere bystander. It was enough that she was involved in the **event** during which the negligent act took place: the plaintiff was directly involved in the incident **and** at risk of physical injury (see *Page* v *Smith*). It was clear that X knew or ought to have known that the plaintiff was a risk of physical injury and that she might sustain psychiatric harm as a consequence.

In cases outside the employer/employee relationship the courts have found it necessary to distinguish between 'primary' and 'secondary' victims, and to apply special limiting criteria (the '*Alcock*' criteria) to the claims of these 'secondary' victims.

You may also read about the decision of the Court of Appeal in *Duncan* v *British Coal Corporation*, which was heard at the same time as *Frost*, in **Cases and Materials (6.2.6)**.

6.3.9 BYSTANDERS

What do you see as the main problem in the way of recovery for bystanders?

Mere witnesses, or bystanders, who suffer shock as a result of experiencing an accident in which a stranger has been injured or placed in danger through the defendant's negligence, have long been in a difficult position regarding claims for shock. In *Alcock* such claims were not ruled out entirely, at least in those situations where the circumstances of the accident were particularly horrific. This requirement, of gruesome circumstances, indicates that bystanders will more often than not be defeated in their claims for damages by the 'phlegm and fortitude' condition.

As Lord Keith said in *Alcock* 'The case of a bystander . . . is difficult. Psychiatric injury to him would not ordinarily . . . be within the range of reasonable foreseeability, but could not perhaps entirely be excluded from it if the circumstances of a catastrophe occurring very close to him were particularly horrific.'.

Lord Ackner also observed '. . . while it may be very difficult to envisage the case of a stranger, who is not actively . . . involved in a disaster or its aftermath, other than in the role of rescuer, suffering shock induced psychiatric injury by the mere observation of . . . injury of a third person . . . I see no reason in principle why he should not, if in the circumstances, a reasonably strong nerved person would have been so shocked.'.

Please turn to *Cases and Materials* (6.2.7), and read *McFarlane* v *EE Caledonia Ltd* [1994] 2 All ER 1. What do you consider to be the effect of this decision on the argument that bystanders may recover damages for shock in certain, limited circumstances?

We find that the Court of Appeal has rejected **altogether** the claim of the mere witness on the ground that a plaintiff, who is outside the recognised exceptions of the colleague or rescuer, must have ties of love and affection with the victim.

This ruling is inconsistent with *obiter* opinions expressed in the House of Lords in *Alcock*; evidently the issue awaits resolution.

In the meantime, we may record the decision in *Frost* (see **6.3.8**) where police officers succeeded in their action because they were classed as employees/rescuers.

You can also read about the interesting decisions in *Hegarty* v *EE Caledonia Ltd* [1997] 2 Lloyds Rep. 259, and *Hunter* v *British Coal Corp. and Another* [1998] 2 All ER 97 in *Cases and Materials* (**6.2.7**).

6.3.10 POST-*ALCOCK* DECISIONS IN GENERAL

Two cases indicate that the courts have adopted a restrictive approach to the definition of 'immediate aftermath'.

In *Taylor* v *Somerset Health Authority* [1993] PIQR 262, the plaintiff's husband died in hospital as a result of the defendant's negligence; she was told of this and saw his body about an hour later. The judge held that the plaintiff had not witnessed the immediate aftermath, as in *McLoughlin*, for the following reasons:

(a) the plaintiff went to the hospital only to settle her mind;

(b) the visit was not to identify the body;

(c) her husband's body was not in an 'injured' state.

Again, in *Taylor* v *Shieldness Produce Ltd* [1994] PIQR 329, the plaintiffs were told that their son had been involved in an accident and went to the hospital straight away, but did not see him. However, they followed the ambulance to another hospital where they caught a brief glimpse of him on his way to intensive care. They saw blood on his face. The father saw him afterwards in intensive care, and his mother saw him the following day. They stayed with him for two days, and then he died. The Court of Appeal said that the 'immediate aftermath' of this accident, which had happened at 10.45am on the day that the plaintiffs were told of their son's involvement in it, could not be extended to cover the next two days while he was in hospital.

You can read about the decision in *Sion* v *Hampstead Health Authority* [1994] 5 Med LR 170 in *Cases and Materials* (**6.2.8**).

We are now in a position to attempt an evaluation of the general effect of *Alcock*.

Please pause here, get hold of a sheet of paper (A4 size) and a pen, and jot down a summary of the main features of the present law on negligently inflicted psychiatric injury.

Amongst the features you might have listed there should appear the following:

(a) someone who is injured **physically** and is shocked as a result may recover damages;

    (b)   someone who suffers shock because of fear for their own physical integrity may recover damages (provided the shock is medically recognised);

Other cases are difficult; a plaintiff may recover for shock suffered through fear for the safety of others (it is not necessary that the victims be **actually** injured) but:

    (c)   the plaintiff must establish a recognised psychiatric illness;

    (d)   the plaintiff must experience the event or its 'immediate' aftermath, and therefore suffer shock, by means of his or her own unaided senses: it is not enough to be simply **told** of an event;

    (e)   a gradual development of psychiatric illness is not acceptable, there must be a **sudden** shock to the psyche;

    (f)   the plaintiff must exhibit appropriate 'phlegm and fortitude';

    (g)   it is necessary for the plaintiff to show that he or she had close ties of love and affection with the victim(s); in some instances this is presumed, but in others the plaintiff must establish the tie;

    (h)   if the plaintiff is a rescuer or workmate of the victim it will not be necessary to establish the tie of love and affection;

    (i)   watching an event on television is not acceptable (because it is not sufficiently 'instantaneous') unless, perhaps, **either** a **special** transmission is involved (for example, where it is like the example given by Nolan LJ in *Alcock*; see **6.3.5**) **or** the Broadcasting Code of Ethics has been broken and the victims are recognisable as individuals, in which case any action would be against the broadcaster, rather than the person responsible for the event;

    (j)   a 'mere' bystander might recover if the event is horrific enough;

    (k)   a person may be entitled to recover for shock suffered in connection with their property, though the authority for that proposition is of a special nature;

    (l)   the 'egg-shell skull' rule applies to psychiatric damage.

The Court of Appeal in *Taylor* v *Shieldness Produce Ltd* found that there was no 'shock' in that case. Not all judges, however, take the same strict approach to this issue of 'shock'.

In *Frost* Henry LJ said: '[W]hat matters is not the label on the **trigger** for psychiatric damage, but **the fact and foreseeability** of psychiatric damage by **whatever process**. . . . Clearly the law should accept PTSD rather than exclude it whether it is caused by sudden shock (properly defined) or **not**.' [emphasis added].

Nevertheless, it may be that whilst this view could appeal to more judges, some of them, at least, might be prone to take this more relaxed approach only where so-called 'primary' victims were involved.

It was reported in *The Guardian*, 28 November 1996, that 21 parents had received **out-of-court settlements** of compensation claims brought against Lincolnshire NHS Trust for post traumatic stress disorder suffered as a result of their children having been either killed or injured by Nurse Allitt whilst they were patients in the Trust's hospitals. This is noteworthy because the Trust decided to **settle** with claimants to whom it probably owed no legal obligations: *Alcock* suggests that the parents fell outside the range of legal proximity because none of them actually witnessed either the actual infliction of harm upon their children or experienced the immediate aftermath of the relevant incidents.

6.3.11 STATEMENTS

In principle it may be that shock suffered as a result of reliance upon a negligent misstatement is recoverable from the misrepresentor. There is, however, a paucity of English authority on the point.

A New Zealand court in *Furniss* v *Fitchett* [1958] NZLR 396, found the defendant, who was medical adviser to both the plaintiff and the plaintiff's husband, liable for having given the husband a certificate alleging negligently that the plaintiff was a paranoiac; the husband used this certificate in evidence in proceedings brought by the plaintiff against him for maintenance. The plaintiff suffered shock on disclosure of the certificate's contents and recovered damages from the defendant.

There is no doubt that the parties in *Furniss* were in very close proximity indeed; presumably a **very** 'special relationship' will have to be established by a plaintiff who hopes to succeed for shock caused by a misstatement.

In *Guay* v *Sun Publishing Co.* [1953] 2 SCR 216, a Canadian case, the defendants published negligently in their newspaper an untrue report that members of the plaintiff's family had been killed. The court denied recovery for shock caused to the plaintiff by this report, holding that the defendants owed only a duty to publish in good faith.

It may be that a plaintiff who can establish an assumption of responsibility by the defendant, by analogy with developments in *Hedley Byrne* liability noted in **Chapter 5**, could succeed in recovering damages for shock caused by a negligent misstatement. We have seen, at **5.5.10**, that *T* v *Surrey CC* is authority for the proposition that *Hedley Byrne* extends to cases of physical loss.

An even more problematic case would be one where the 'story' was true, but the plaintiff alleged that the defendant was negligent in the **way** that news was relayed. In other words, is there a duty to break bad news gently? The matter awaits resolution.

You can read about the decisions in *A and Others* v *Tameside and Glossop Health Authority and Another, The Times*, 27 November 1996, and *Powell* v *Bolady, The Times*, 26 November 1997 in **Cases and Materials (6.2.9)**.

6.3.12 PRE-DEATH TRAUMA

In *Hicks* v *Wright* [1992] 2 All ER 65, the House of Lords unanimously rejected a claim of damages for trauma suffered by two females (sisters aged 19 and 15 at the time) before they were crushed to death on 15 April 1989, at the Hillsborough disaster. Lord Bridge said:

> No one can feel anything but the greatest sympathy for the relatives of those who died. The anguish of parents caused by the death in such a horrifying event of sons and daughters on the very threshold of life must indeed have been almost unbearable. However, the medical evidence indicated that someone unable to breathe through crushing of the chest, as the girls were, would lose consciousness within seconds and die within five minutes.

The parents had argued that there was a gradual build-up of pressure, causing increasing breathlessness, discomfort and pain for twenty minutes. His Lordship said: 'both the High Court and Court of Appeal had concluded that the evidence did not establish any injury before the fatal crushing injury, and it was impossible to say they were wrong. Fear itself, of whatever degree, was a normal human emotion for which no damages could be awarded. Those trapped in the crush who escaped injury had no claim for the distress suffered in what must have been a truly terrifying experience.' It followed that the families acting on behalf of the estates of those who died, could not claim damages in relation to fear of impending death.

The parents of the deceased received only £3,500 **bereavement damages** for the daughter aged 15, and nothing for the elder daughter because she was over 18 years of age. (The **fixed** sum is now £7,500 but the increase has not been made retrospective.)

6.4   Summary

The law on liability for **psychiatric** damage inflicted negligently, the time-honoured expression 'nervous shock' now being less popular than it used to be, is, to put it crudely, 'in a mess'. Lord Oliver in the leading case of *Alcock* said he did not regard the present state of the law as '. . . logically defensible'.

It is true that a body of law, of sorts, has been put together since the late nineteenth century; the law has, to a considerable extent, followed medical advances in the recognition of psychiatric illness. In *Victorian Railway Commissioners* v *Coultas* (1888) 13 App Cas 222 (Privy Council) a claim for shock was denied on the ground that the courts would be swamped by a flood of bogus claims; the medical evidence available was regarded as unreliable.

Since then, as we have seen, various claims have been recognised, ranging from fear for the plaintiff's own safety to fear for the safety of the plaintiff's property. In *Vernon* v *Bosley (No. 1)* [1997] 1 All ER 577 (CA), the plaintiff saw his two daughters and their friend drowned when their nanny, the defendant, accidentally drove the family car into a river. The defendant admitted liability but disputed **minutely** the plaintiff's claim for damages, which took 70 days to hear. In the event, at first instance, he was awarded a record £1,178,000 (reduced on appeal to £622,000: 30 March 1996) for having been left by the accident, as Sedley J put it, 'a helpless and dependent shadow of his former self'.

The plaintiff and his wife 'watched helplessly' from the river bank while the emergency services tried to save the children 'not knowing whether they were alive or dead'.

According to Sedley J the plaintiff had, before the accident, been a successful business-man, but his business collapsed and his marriage 'fell apart' after the accident. The effect of seeing the accident had been 'to destabilise for good a previously insecure but manageable personality, provoking chronic reactive anxiety and depression which have now become permanent features of his mental state. (This included features of post-traumatic stress disorder and of pathological grief but 'was not a textbook example of either'.)

'Witnessing the accident was not the sole cause, but it was the initiating cause of an uneven but perceptible sequence of mental deterioration and personality collapse in an already vulnerable individual'.

In the Court of Appeal the defendant's (i.e. her insurers) appeal was dismissed, by a majority. Evans LJ, with whom Thorpe LJ agreed, confirmed that damages for 'mere' grief and suffering **alone** (see e.g. *Hinz* v *Berry*) were not recoverable. The question for the court to decide, however, was whether such heads of claim had to be 'discounted', i.e. **subtracted** from the **psychiatric** damage for which damages were recoverable.

You will have already discovered, from your earlier reading, that damages are recover-able in the tort of negligence even where that negligence is only **a** cause (although it must be a **substantial** cause) of the plaintiff's damage. Thus, on the present facts, even though the plaintiff had suffered grief, etc., because of **bereavement** the plaintiff could recover for this provided he could show recognised psychiatric damage caused wholly or partly by the defendant.

The court said it would be 'unrealistic and artificial' to engage in an exercise to dissect the plaintiff's state of mind into those bits which had been influenced by **psychiatric** damage and those bits which had been influenced by ordinary grief and sorrow. In the judgment of Evans LJ the plaintiff had satisfied the court that he had **in substance** sustained recognised mental injury as a result of the defendant's negligence and he should recover in full.

It is significant, however, that his Lordship made much of the fact that there were no **policy** reasons for limiting the damages recoverable by the plaintiff. To put it another way, there was nothing in the present circumstances to justify the court in denying to the plaintiff the benefit of the all-or-nothing principle which lies behind the law of tort, viz. where there was no damage, there would be no recovery of compensation, whereas there would be full recovery even though there was only some damage.

On the other hand, Stuart-Smith LJ, in his dissenting judgment, said that the plaintiff had failed to discharge the legal burden placed upon him to prove that his mental illness was caused by his witnessing the aftermath of the accident.

Understandably, the courts still entertain doubts in this area of liability, and in *McLoughlin* were quite explicit about the policy issues. This openness about policy was continued into *Alcock,* but the problem lies in the rationalisations which the judges have felt constrained to make in order to keep liability in check. These rationalisations lead to logically inconsistent and arbitrary decisions. You have seen six points made about:

(a) the definition of 'immediate aftermath';

(b) watching events on television;

(c) 'phlegm and fortitude';

(d) ties of 'love and affection' (which may involve the unedifying spectacle of defendants seeking to show the absence of such ties even between close relatives, or of plaintiffs seeking to show such ties in relationships where they are not presumed);

(e) being told of an event and not otherwise experiencing it (Lord Bridge in *McLoughlin* attempted to show that it is perfectly natural for the mind to make the required connection between tragedy and 'shock');

(f) the problem of the 'mere bystander' (the Court of Appeal in *McFarlane* refused to be drawn into the dispute of what constitutes sufficient 'horror').

In *McCarthy* v *Chief Constable of the South Yorkshire Police and Others, The Times,* 12 December 1996, a half-brother of one of the Hillsborough victims who actually witnessed the incident, being present in the football stadium at the time, was awarded damages for his psychiatric damage because he established the strongest of ties of love and affection with the deceased.

It is difficult to disagree with Lord Scarman in *McLoughlin,* and Lord Oliver in *Alcock,* when they say that it is time for **legislative** intervention.

6.5 Reform

The decision in *Page* v *Smith* introduced the vexed vocabulary of 'primary' and 'secondary' victims into the context of liability for negligently inflicted psychiatric damage. (Lord Oliver in *Alcock,* whose speech is often referred to by judges who use these labels, including, in *Page,* Lord Lloyd, the progenitor of the distinction, did not actually employ the words, although he did identify different categories of claimant.)

In the words of the Law Commission Report No. 249, *Liability for Psychiatric Illness*, at para. 5.45: 'We have seen that in recent cases the courts have thought it important to distinguish between primary and secondary victims; and that there is confusing inconsistency as to where and why that distinction is being drawn.'

These words, 'primary' and 'secondary', often seem to mean different things to different judges, but the Commission identified at least two different classifications of 'primary' victim, viz. the 'narrow' and the 'broad' classifications. (Although not entirely free from doubt, there seems to be more agreement about the meaning of 'secondary' victims, i.e. they are those persons who only **witness others** being injured or exposed to injury. It is **these** claimants who will have **most** difficulty in establishing the special proximity requirements laid down in *Alcock*.)

The 'narrow' classification was based on Lord Lloyd's classification in *Page* v *Smith* and would embrace as primary victims only those persons within risk of reasonably foreseeable **physical** injury.

However, the Commission was not convinced that these claimants should receive special consideration in law for three reasons, viz. (i) medical opinion was against it; (ii) psychiatric injury can often be suffered (e.g. stress at work) although no one is seen being put at risk of physical injury; and (iii) earlier authority (e.g. *Hambrook* v *Stokes Bros.*) has rejected any distinction between plaintiffs who have suffered fear for their own safety and those who have feared only for the safety of others.

The 'broad' classification of 'primary' victim (e.g. of the sort that Lord Oliver had in mind in *Alcock*, though he did not actually use the **label**, 'primary') would be based on persons who had **participated** in the accident. This would be more flexible than the narrow approach, and would include those plaintiffs who can show proximity either via actual **participation in the event** as primary victims **or** in terms of their relationships to the immediate victim(s) and their perception of the accident or its immediate aftermath as secondary victims.

In the Commission's view, though, whilst a 'broad' approach would be preferable to the 'narrow' one because the latter is too exclusive of deserving cases, it is not without its ambiguities and uncertainties because it offers 'little guidance as to where the line between primary and secondary should be drawn'. Difficulties can be encountered with definitions of 'direct involvement' and 'event', for example; there is also the question of deciding upon the requisite **degree** of participation (see e.g. *Frost* in which **some** claimants succeeded as 'employees' but not as 'rescuers', whilst **one** of them succeeded as a 'rescuer' but not as an 'employee'!).

What of the plaintiff in *Attia* or the plaintiff who complains of negligent communication of bad news? As the Commission says, these are cases in which the claimants could well be described as 'primary' victims, yet theirs would be 'prime' examples of claims upon which the courts would probably seek to impose 'special restrictions'.

On the whole, the Commission saw the distinction (between 'primary' and 'secondary' victims) as being 'more of a hindrance than a help' and recommended that the courts should 'abandon attaching **practical** significance' [**emphasis added**] to the distinction, but its use might well be helpful for **descriptive** purposes. Certainly, in the Commission's opinion 'the distinction is being given a policy importance which it does not merit.' (Report paras. 5.45–5.54; see also paras. 2.52–2.60).

The use of the distinction in *Hunter* v *British Coal Corp.* [1998] 2 All ER 97 (***Cases and Materials*** (**6.2.7**)) is of particular interest.

In the law report, it is stated that the appeal was heard from Sheffield County Court, where the plaintiffs action in 'negligence' was dismissed. There is no reference to whether this is negligence in *Donoghue* v *Stevenson* terms or in *Wilsons and Clyde Coal Co.*

v *English* terms; indeed there is no reference whatever in the report to the latter authority so, presumably, the case proceeded on the basis of liability for breach of a *Donoghue* v *Stevenson* type of duty rather than the special duty owed by employers to their employees, as in *English*.

In that event the application of *Alcock*, and associated authorities, to the facts of *Hunter* would be unremarkable, but **if** it was the *English* type of **duty** that was under consideration in *Hunter* (in relation to the action against *Cementation*, because, of course, there was no contractual relationship between the plaintiff and the British Coal Corp.) it is arguable that **that** duty contains within itself its own control of liability criterion; viz. proximity is determined by reference to the fact that the duty is based on the **contractual** relationship between the parties, and there is no need to employ *Alcock* controls.

It is true that Brooke LJ does say, in *Hunter* at p. 106: 'If one puts on one side questions which may arise out of Mr. Hunter's **contractual** relationship with Cementation . . .' [**emphasis added**]; and, at p. 109, 'In my judgment it would be quite wrong for this court to push forward the frontiers of liability in the way advocated by Mr Berrisford, [counsel for the plaintiff] **particularly as the case was not very fully argued**, [**emphasis added**] at a time when the Law Commission . . . has just completed a major review of this area of the law.' However, the point is then lost in a familiar discussion of *Alcock* and *Page* v *Smith* arguments concerning 'primary' and 'secondary' victims, etc.

The dissenting judgment of Hobhouse LJ (see **Cases and Materials 6.2.7**) does, it is submitted, get nearer to the point being made. The decisions in *Frost* and *Duncan* are also nearer the mark on this issue.

Unfortunately, *Hunter* seems to go even further by applying the *Alcock* and *Page* v *Smith* criteria to **the action for breach of statutory duty**. There is absolutely no meaningful discussion at all on this matter; yet it is reported that the judge at first instance found the defendants to have been in breach of s. 83 of the Mines and Quarries Act 1954.

It is submitted that the apparent subsuming of the *English* duty and, apparently, **the action for breach of statutory duty**, under the *Alcock* formula creates the risk of these actions being placed within the *Donoghue* v *Stevenson* relationship.

This is not, it is argued, a distinction based on form rather than substance, because the action for breach of statutory duty is not a form of negligence; and the *English* type of duty, though a form of negligence, is based firmly on the contractual relationships between the parties. The latter duty, though sharing some common characteristics with the 'neighbour' (*Donoghue*) duty, viz. standard of care and remoteness of damage, arguably obtains its **proximity** from contract and should be argued in those terms, particularly in view of the **incremental** approach to the development of the law favoured in *Caparo* and subsequent authority.

On the matter of **statutory duty**, the Law Commission (paras. 2.41–2.44), Brooke LJ himself in *Hegarty*, and Rose J in *Francis Aston* v *Imperial Chemical Industries Group* (unreported, 21 May 1992 – cited in the Law Commission's Report at p. 27, note 124) were of the opinion that this cause of action contained its own control mechanisms regarding proximity. The decision in *Hunter* therefore appears to be at odds with principle, on this issue at least.

You should have this case in mind when you study the material in **Chapter 8** (*Learning Text* and *Cases and Materials*).

Policy problems are to the fore where the defendant is himself his **own** 'victim'. In other words, 'Does X owe a duty of care to Y not to cause psychiatric damage to Y by injuring **himself** or placing **himself** in danger of injury?'. The problem may be more acute where there is a clear *Alcock* relationship between X and Y, e.g. that of spouses.

In *Bourhill* v *Young* the defendant was his own 'victim', but the point was not dealt with since the case proceeded on another basis. There are, however, dicta of Lord Robertson in the Scottish Court of Session in that case (1941 CS 395, at 399) denying liability on the argument that the line of liability for negligence must be drawn somewhere.

Similar dicta of Deane J in *Jaensch* v *Coffey* was referred to, with apparent approval, by Lord Oliver in *Alcock*. The Law Commission, in its Consultation Paper No. 137 (para. 5.47) came to the same conclusion, though its reasoning was based on the argument that to impose a duty of care in such cases would place an unreasonable restriction on a person's right of self-determination. (This might be of particular importance where a person actually committed **suicide** or attempted to do so – suicide or attempted suicide being legally acceptable under the terms of the Suicide Act 1961.)

The Law Commission, in its Report No. 249, recommends that a right of action be available against a defendant who imperils himself: see *Cases and Materials* (**6.3**).

6.6   Further Reading

Hepple, B.A. and Matthews, M.H., *Tort: Cases and Materials*, 5th edn, London: Butterworths, 1996, pp. 118–131.
Jones, M., *Textbook on Torts*, 5th edn, London: Blackstone Press, 1996, pp. 100–113.
Markesinis, B.S., and Deakin, S.F., *Tort Law*, 3rd edn, Oxford: Oxford University Press, 1994, pp 118–129, 204–208.
Napier, M., and Wheat, K., *Recovering Damages for Psychiatric Injury*, London: Blackstone Press, 1995.
Nasir, K.J., 'Nervous Shock and *Alcock*: The Judicial Buck Stops Here' (1992) 55 MLR 705.
Salmond and Heuston, *Law of Torts*, 21st edn, London: Sweet & Maxwell, 1996, pp. 219–223.
Stanton, K.M., *The Modern Law of Tort*, London: Sweet & Maxwell, 1994, pp. 203–210.
Street on Torts, 9th edn, London: Butterworths, 1993, pp. 180–181, 197–203.
Weir, T., *A Casebook on Tort*, 8th edn, London: Sweet & Maxwell, 1996.
Winfield and Jolowicz on Tort, 14th edn, London: Sweet & Maxwell, 1994, pp. 49–124.
Weller, M., 'Post-traumatic Stress Disorder' (1993) 143 NLJ 878.

6.7   Answer to Activity 28

The following definitions of 'nervous' and 'shock' are taken from *Chambers English Dictionary*, 7th edn, 1988:

■ **nervous** *adj* having nerve; sinewy: strong, vigorous, showing strength and vigour; pertaining to the nerves: having the nerves easily excited or weak, agitated and apprehensive (often with *of*): shy: timid: in a jumpy state.

■ **shock** *n.* a violent impact, orig. of charging warriors: a dashing together: a shaking or jarring as if by a blow: a blow to the emotions or its cause: outrage at something regarded as improper: a convulsive excitation of nerves, as by electricity: the prostration of voluntary and involuntary functions caused by trauma, a surgical operation, or excessive sudden emotional disturbance: a stroke of paralysis *(coll.)*. — *v.t.* to meet or assail with a shock: to shake or impair by a shock: to give a shock: to shake or impair by a shock: to give a shock to: to harrow or outrage the feelings of: to affect with abashed and horrified indignation. — *v.i.* to outrage feelings: to collide with violence.

You may care to compare these definitions with those you have looked up, where they come from different sources.

If we take 'nervous' as simply referring to the senses, 'shock' does seem to convey the meaning of damage as recognised by the judges; it emphasises the sudden assault or attack upon the plaintiff's 'nerves' that judges say is necessary. Could it be, however, that by adopting the expression '**psychiatric** damage', which suggests a somewhat broader approach, the law will eventually recognise **progressive** illness in this context?

To adopt another dictionary approach (see *Chambers*, above), **psychiatry** is concerned with the medical treatment of diseases of the mind.

6.8   End of Chapter Assessment Question

Dahlia takes her daughter, Primrose, to a funfair owned and operated by Nigel. Primrose wants a ride on the big dipper so Dahlia, who does not like high speeds, leaves her in the queue and goes for a ride on the big wheel which is about 80 yards away. While Dahlia is watching from the big wheel, the carriage in which Primrose is riding flies off the rails of the big dipper, due to a loose bolt in the framework, and plummets 60 feet to the ground. Primrose is badly injured, and Dahlia is at first hysterical, and later suffers from recurrent feelings of anxiety, and from insomnia.

Sage, who is also on the big wheel at the time of the accident, is so shocked at what he sees that he later suffers from catastrophic neurosis, and is unable to work for 15 months. Some 10 years earlier Sage had been a voluntary patient at a mental hospital, where he had been treated for a neurotic condition.

Primrose's father, Chrys, sees pictures of the accident on the television news that evening, and is so shocked that he suffers a heart attack.

Discuss any potential liability in tort on the part of Nigel towards Dahlia, Sage and Chrys.

See *Cases and Materials* (6.5) for a specimen answer.

CHAPTER SEVEN

LIABILITY FOR DANGEROUS PREMISES AND LAND

7.1 Objectives

By the end of this Chapter you should be able to:

■ establish an acquaintance with all the different ways in which liability may arise for injury sustained **on** premises;

■ have a detailed knowledge and understanding of the provisions of the **Defective Premises Act 1972**, the liability of **builders, developers, architects** (and others in a similar position) and **local authorities** at common law;

■ have a detailed knowledge and understanding of the law governing the liability of an **occupier** to his or her lawful **'visitors'** under the **Occupiers' Liability Act 1957**;

■ have a detailed knowlege and understanding of the law governing the liability of an **occupier** to his or her **'non-visitor'** entrants (e.g. **trespassers**) under the **Occupiers' Liability Act 1984**.

7.2 Introduction

This chapter deals with the liability of persons who are concerned in some way with premises, but only with regard to damage suffered, in the main, **on** those premises. Nuisance, and other forms of tortious liability which are **also** concerned with responsibility for premises, but involve claims for damage sustained **off** premises, are dealt with **elsewhere** in this text (see **Chapters 10** and **11**).

You will find that:

(a) 'premises' includes 'structures';

(b) the range of persons who may be responsible is wide;

(c) people can be responsible in **different capacities**;

(d) we are concerned **mainly** with the question of liability arising under **three** statutes, i.e. the Occupiers' Liability Acts of 1957 and 1984 and the Defective Premises Act 1972.

We will examine first the liability in **negligence** of various defendants in connection with premises, before proceeding to liability arising under the Defective Premises Act 1972 and **occupiers' liability** under the 1957 and 1984 Acts. You will find all three Acts set out in **Chapter 7** of *Cases and Materials*.

7.3 Liability Arising in Various Capacities in Negligence

7.3.1 VENDORS AND LESSORS

A buyer or tenant, or visitor of the tenant, who suffers personal injury or injury to separate property as a result of the defect, may sue in tort a vendor or lessor with regard to defects pre-existing the sale or lease.

In *Cavalier* v *Pope* [1906] AC 428 the House of Lords decided, however, that a 'bare' **landlord** could not be sued in the tort of negligence in respect of such defects; later, in *Bottomley* v *Bannister* [1932] 1 KB 458 **vendors** were also given immunity from suit in such circumstances. The defendant in this case had built premises on his land and then sold the premises. Curiously, even at that time, he **would** have owed a duty of care in negligence had he constructed the building on someone else's land. *Bottomley* is now of **historical** interest only because, as we will see in *Rimmer*, a vendor or lessor who is also a builder can be liable in negligence. This point was established in *Dutton* and confirmed in *Murphy* (see **7.3.2**).

Defects must usually be **latent** (**and**, as you will see in *Murphy*, cause injury to **separate** property or to the person) **or** it must be unreasonable to expect the plaintiff to abate the danger and reasonable for the plaintiff to have exposed himself to the risk of damage (that 'damage' must, again, be damage to separate property or injury to the person). This is similar to the position regarding defective **goods** under the 'narrow' rule in *Donoghue* v *Stevenson* (1932) which you will read about in **Chapter 13**.

The Court of Appeal, in *McNerny* v *Lambeth LBC* (1988) 21 HLR 188 held that the rule in *Cavalier* v *Pope* was still binding authority. Thus, a local authority was found not liable (as 'bare' landlord) in negligence for damage caused by condensation in premises which were not in a state of disrepair.

In *Rimmer* v *Liverpool City Council* [1984] 1 All ER 930, however, the local authority was both **architect and builder as well as landlord**. The plaintiff, a tenant of the defendants, was injured when he fell through some 'dangerously thin' glass in a wall panel on the premises. Complaints from the plaintiff and other tenants about the potential danger had been ignored. The defendants were found by the Court of Appeal to owe a duty of care under the *Donoghue* v *Stevenson* neighbour principle.

Apart from the case where the defendant is responsible in some capacity other than 'bare' landlord, the rule in *Cavalier* does not apply to **furnished** lettings.

You may care to note, **briefly** because it is not the concern of **this** text to look closely at such matters, that **statute** and **common law** may imply certain terms into the **contract** of tenancy between **landlord** and **tenant**. For example, ss. 11 to 13 of the Landlord and Tenant Act 1985 impose on a landlord (by implying into his contract with the tenant) a duty to repair and maintain the structure and exterior of and certain installations in a dwelling-house in a lease for less than seven years. This was extended by s. 16 of the Housing Act 1988 to the exterior and structure of a building of which the demised premises form part and, subject to certain exceptions, to shared parts of any such buildings.

In *Barrett* v *Lounova [1982] Ltd* [1989] 1 All ER 1 the Court of Appeal held that where a tenancy agreement imposed an express obligation on the tenant to repair the inside of the premises, but said nothing about repairs to the outside, and the tenant's obligation was enforceable throughout the tenancy and could not be performed properly unless the outside was kept in repair, the **common** law could imply an obligation by the landlord to repair the outside in order to give business efficacy to the agreement.

Of course, **vendors** (or 'sellers') will **also** be open to liability in contract, including defendants in such cases as *Bottomley*, i.e. builders who are also vendors. The same is true of builders who are also **lessors**.

There may also be liability, in **appropriate circumstances**, in the tort of **deceit**. (Third parties will not be able to sue on the contract, nor will they be able to sue in deceit, because **they** will not have **relied** on the fraudulent misstatement.)

SAQ 70

Why do you suppose that 'bare' landlords and vendors enjoy a special privilege in relation to claims made against them in negligence?

It is because of the old common law policy of 'let the buyer (or lessee) be aware', *caveat emptor*, that the property is to be taken with all its faults, fraud apart. Sellers or lessors of realty (real property, i.e. land) have been traditionally placed in a privileged position in comparison with the vendors of personalty (personal property, i.e. 'goods').

In more recent years, however, inroads have been made into this immunity of **builders** who are **also vendors** or **lessors**, notably by the Defective Premises Act 1972, which we examine at **7.4**. You will have already read about the decision in *Rimmer* (above) which also makes this point.

7.3.2   ARCHITECTS AND OTHERS

Liability may be imposed on persons such as architects, designers, building inspectors and local authorities, **as well as builders**, under the *Donoghue* v *Stevenson* 'neighbour' principle.

You will now be taken through a line of cases which imposed a wide duty of care upon such parties, particularly so with local authorities. All the cases have been overruled on their facts, but their legacy of **a basic duty of care remains**; they are no longer of specific authority because they imposed liability for 'pure' economic loss. One of them, *Anns* v *Merton LBC* [1978] AC 728, will be familiar to you.

The cases are still of importance for the reason that they established **clearly** the basic duty of persons such as builders, developers and local authorities, but you must always remember what you will soon learn, i.e. that the liability these cases established has been much curtailed in the cases of *D & F Estates* (below) and *Murphy* (below).

The first case is *Dutton* v *Bognor Regis UDC* [1972] 1 QB 373, in which the defendants, a local authority, had statutory powers to inspect the foundations of new buildings to ensure that they were adequately constructed, before giving approval for the buildings to be completed. A builder wished to build a house on the site of an old rubbish tip. The defendants' surveyor approved the foundations and the builder was able to proceed to build the house up to damp-course level. This stage was also approved by the surveyor and the house was completed at the end of 1959. The builder had not provided adequate foundations for the type of land and the defendants' surveyor did not notice this fact, having failed to make a competent inspection. The builder sold the house to X early in 1960, and in December 1960 X sold it to the plaintiff. The plaintiff did not employ a surveyor to check the house before purchase because it was new, and the court accepted evidence that even had she employed a surveyor, he could not have discovered the hidden defect in the foundations. The plaintiff's building society surveyor passed the house. Soon after the plaintiff moved into the house in January 1961, very serious structural defects appeared due to the subsidence of an internal wall caused by the inadequate foundations. The defects worsened and, in 1963, a surveyor employed by the plaintiff discovered that the house had been built on a rubbish tip. In 1964 the plaintiff sued the builder and the defendants for negligence, claiming damages of £2,740 (i.e. £2,240 for the cost of repairing the house and £500 for diminution in its market value). The claim against the builder was settled out of court for £625, because it was accepted by the plaintiff that he was exempt from liability for negligence.

As **a matter of record**, the court said that the builder **did** in fact owe a duty of care in such circumstances and would have found against him had the case proceeded to trial. This was, of course, an **obiter** opinion because the case against the builder had already been settled. Lord Denning said that a vendor or lessor who was also a builder did not enjoy immunity from suit in negligence:

> [otherwise] . . . it would mean that a contractor who builds a house on another's land is liable in negligence in constructing it, but that a speculative builder, who buys land and himself builds on it for sale, and is just as negligent as the contractor, is not liable. That cannot be right. Each must be under the same duty of care and to the same persons.

The Court of Appeal unanimously held the defendants liable, affirming the decision of the lower court. The defendants, through their building inspector (a matter of vicarious liability) owed a duty of care to the plaintiff to ensure that the inspection of the foundations was properly carried out, and to ensure that the foundations were adequate. You will find further details of the this case in *Cases and Materials* (5.3.7).

The Court of Appeal then held in *Batty* v *Metropolitan Property Realisations* [1978] QB 554, that the same duty may be owed by a **developer** who has not taken reasonable care to see that his land is suitable for building.

Finally, in *Anns* the House of Lords held that failure by a **local authority** to inspect building foundations properly or not to inspect at all (i.e. there is a breach of the Building Regulations) could result in liability at common law if the authority's power to inspect (under the then Public Health Act 1936) had been carried out otherwise than in the bona fide exercise of its discretion (i.e. *ultra vires*) **and negligently**.

Accordingly Merton LBC was held to be under a duty of care at common law in respect of a block of flats for which it had approved plans and which later came to have serious structural faults. It was found that no actual physical damage need be shown by the plaintiff, it was enough that the defect in the building was such as to create, according to Lord Wilberforce, 'present or imminent danger to the health and safety of persons occupying it'.

Health and safety are relevant here because of the background legislation, i.e. the Public Health Act 1936.

Have you noticed a common thread running through these three cases?

In none of the cases was there any actual physical damage to person or property. Damages for 'pure' economic loss, i.e. **cost of repair**, to make good the defect, which need not have caused actual physical damage, were recoverable. It is true that the decisions were explained away on a number of occasions as being cases of physical damage, i.e. damage **to** the relevant building caused by the defects(s), but they remained as something of an anomaly until they were re-examined by the House of Lords in *D & F Estates* and *Murphy*.

In *D & F Estates* v *Church Commissioners for England* [1988] 2 All ER 992, the plaintiffs occupied a flat, and had to pay out extra money in order to repair defective plastering work which had been carried out by sub-contractors of Wates, the builders of the flats. Since there was **no contract** between the plaintiffs and the defendants, the claim had to be brought in **tort**. The House of Lords had to decide two issues:

(a) were Wates Ltd, the main building contractors, liable for the negligence of their sub-contractor who carried out the defective plastering work?

(b) if so, was the cost of replacing the plaster work recoverable?

It was found, confirming the general position, that a main contractor is not normally liable for the negligence of his sub-contractor. He has a duty to appoint a competent sub-contractor and exceptionally there could be circumstances in which it would be obvious that a sub-contractor was doing his work negligently, thus imposing on the main contractor a duty to intervene.

As Lord Bridge put it: 'A main contractor is **not** under a general non-delegable duty to ensure that a building [is] free from dangerous defects . . .'. This finding will be of interest to you in connection with 'vicarious liability', which is dealt with in **Chapter 1**.

Their Lordships also held, more importantly in the present context, that the cost of repairing a defect in a building is recoverable in negligence only if the defect has actually caused personal injury or physical damage to **other** property.

Anns was interpreted as imposing a duty on **local authorities** but **not** on others, such as **builders**, in respect of **the harm or threat of harm** (due to non-observance of Building Regulations) to occupiers of the buildings in question.

Lord Bridge, however, said that in the case of 'complex structures' (a house as opposed to a simple wall, for instance) one part of the structure might be regarded as distinct from another part of the structure, so that damage to one part caused by a defect in another part might arguably be regarded as damage to 'other property': for example, defective foundations of a building might cause damage to **other** parts of the building. *Anns* was said to be a case of that kind, and *D & F Estates* was **not**. He did not confine his discussion to buildings; his Lordship made a number of references to defective **products** in general.

In contrast, Lord Oliver thought that *Anns* turned on the issue of a statutory duty, and *D & F Estates* did not; thus, there was no duty of care in the present case.

In *Murphy* v *Brentwood District Council* [1990] 2 All ER 908 (*Cases and Materials* (**7.1.1**)), the defendant local authority had a statutory power, under s. 64 of the Public Health Act 1936, to approve or reject building plans. Acting on the negligent advice of an independent contractor, a firm of consulting engineers, the defendants approved plans for the foundations of a house; these plans contravened Building Regulations.

It was found by the Court of Appeal that the authority were in breach of their duty of care in so acting, and when the house became imminently dangerous to the health or safety of the occupier they were liable to pay damages either to avert that danger or, if repairs were impracticable, to meet the fall in the value of the house on resale (though for an amount not exceeding the cost of the repairs). *Anns,* as interpreted in *D & F Estates* was applied.

It was also found that the council were liable for the negligence of the independent contractors, because s. 64 of the 1936 Act imposed a duty on the council to ensure that houses were properly built, so that injury to the safety or health of occupiers was avoided; this duty could not be discharged by delegating its performance to the engineers. (It was said to be a 'non-delegable duty', the concept of which is discussed in the context of vicarious liability in **Chapter 1**.) The damage suffered by the plaintiff was such that there was a risk of soil and gas pipes breaking and causing an imminent risk to health and safety. According to Nicholls LJ the cause of action accrued when there was a 'present' or 'imminent' danger to health and safety.

The court found that damages were not restricted to repairing the physical results of the defective foundations, for example, cracked wall, but also included the cost of remedying the underlying defect, so to ensure that the house was not dangerous to health and safety. If it was not practicable to do the remedial work, the owner/occupier could claim the amount of the fall in value of the house. Furthermore, it was said, if a plaintiff was awarded damages for necessary remedial work, plus costs, he or she could claim any fall in value of the house due to the attitude of purchasers/mortgagees towards repaired properties.

It is somewhat difficult to reconcile the decisions in *Anns* and *D & F Estates*, since it would place local authorities in an anomalous position in comparison with defendants such as builders. *D & F Estates* left an apparent anomaly because **a builder** could not be sued for the cost of repair of a defective house, but a **local authority** could be liable in those circumstances.

On appeal, the House of Lords adopted the *D & F Estates* approach to the question of liability in tort for present or imminent danger to the safety and health of owners/occupiers, resulting from damage to buildings. The decision of the Court of Appeal in *Murphy* was reversed; *Anns* was overruled on its facts. It was found that the local authority did **not** owe a duty of care to prevent damage to buildings in these circumstances; the loss was of a 'pure' economic kind, which was irrecoverable in these circumstances. *Murphy* is authority only for the proposition that a local authority is not responsible for 'pure' economic loss, since the cost of repairing the defective building was loss of that kind. The decision leaves open the question of whether a local authority might owe a duty of care with regard to **physical** damage.

The House of Lords in *Murphy* held that a local authority, when performing its statutory function of controlling building work, was not liable in negligence to the occupier or owner of a building, for the cost of rectifying a dangerous defect in the building caused by the negligent failure to see that the building was built, or designed, according to the statutory standards. This would be the case where the defect was discovered **before** it caused physical injury, to the person or to 'other property', i.e. it was a **patent** rather than **latent** defect.

Have you noticed an important general feature of *D & F Estates* and *Murphy*?

In both cases the plaintiffs could not succeed in contract, which is the traditionally appropriate means of obtaining damages for the cost of repairing defective items, and so they tried the law of tort. The courts, however, would not allow this. (We have already discussed the reasoning behind such decisions in **Chapter 5**.)

It is interesting to note that Lord Bridge showed less enthusiasm for the 'complex structures' theory (an idea imported from the USA) in *Murphy*. His Lordship seemed to think that it had limited scope, and might be useful only in situations where **separate** items were supplied to a building, for example, a central heating boiler, which exploded, damaging the building. The supplier of the boiler could be liable, where the accident was due to his negligence, or liability might be imposed on him by the Consumer Protection Act 1987, discussed in **Chapter 13**.

In *Richardson* v *West Lindsay DC* [1990] 1 All ER 296, it was found that it would not normally be either just or reasonable to impose upon a local authority a duty to the owner of a building to see that he complied with appropriate Building Regulations; this was 'regardless of whether the loss suffered by the building owner as a result of failing to comply with the regulations was physical or economic'. The plaintiff, the owner in the present case, had a statutory duty to comply with the regulations in question and was in breach of them and suffered loss as a result of faulty construction work. The local authority had an obligation to ensure that a building owner complied with the regulations, but could reasonably expect the owner to obtain competent advice and assistance in order to discharge his duty and carry out the work in a satisfactory manner.

The Court of Appeal confirmed the finding of the judge, treating the matter as a preliminary issue, that the council was not in breach of statutory duty, and did not owe the plaintiff a duty of care at common law.

Stovin v *Wise* (see **Chapter 3**) and the notion of 'reliance' introduced in that case may have potential for development in the *Murphy* and other public authority contexts. As enunciated by Lord Hoffmann – in *Stovin*, it is, however, a somewhat vague notion – although it may only be in its embryonic stage at present.

You will find the extracts from some of the speeches in *Murphy*, and the decision of the House of Lords in *Department of the Environment* v *Thomas Bates and Son Ltd* [1990] 2 All ER 943 in *Cases and Materials* (**7.1.1**). See also *Cases and Materials* (**7.1.1**) for the important decision in *Targett* v *Torfaen Borough Council* [1992] 3 All ER 27, the Latent Damage Act 1986, *Invercargill City Council* v *Hamlin* [1996] 1 All ER 756 and *Nitrigin Eireann Teoranta* v *Inco Alloys Ltd* [1992] 1 All ER 854 (*Cases and Materials* (**5.3.8**)).

7.3.3 INDEPENDENT CONTRACTORS

Independent contractors working on premises may be liable in terms of the *Donoghue* v *Stevenson* 'neighbour' principle.

In *Billings* v *Riden* [1958] AC 240, the House of Lords allowed a claim for damages by an elderly lady who was injured by following a 'safe route' advised by contractors working at the house she was visiting. In the words of Lord Reid: '[There was] a duty to take such care as . . . was reasonable . . .'.

In *Buckland* v *Guildford Gas Light and Coke Co.* [1944] 1 KB 410, contractors were found liable in negligence to a **trespasser**: the plaintiff was electrocuted when she came into contact with an electricity cable passed through the branches of a tree she had just climbed. The trespasser's presence, however, must be foreseeable in such circumstances. Presumably this liability would also extend to activities on premises.

If contractors possess enough 'control' over the premises, they will presumably be 'occupiers', and their liability will depend on the terms of the 1957 Act or those of the 1984 Act, as the case may be. Occupiers' liability is dealt with at **7.5**.

7.3.4   GENERALLY

An occupier may be liable generally in negligence under the *Donoghue* v *Stevenson* neighbour principle.

In *Cunard* v *Antifyre* [1933] 1 KB 551 the plaintiff was a sub-tenant in the defendant's block of flats. Guttering fell from the roof, a part of the building retained by the defendant, through the glass roof of the plaintiff's kitchen, damaging his goods and injuring his wife. The roof was not covered by the lease, therefore no claim was possible in respect of repairing covenants, etc; and the plaintiff's wife could not sue in the tort of nuisance, considered in **Chapter 10**, because she had insufficient interest in the property.

Talbot J said: 'The plaintiff's true cause of action is for negligence, for failure by an occupier to take reasonable care to see that his property does not get into such a state as to be dangerous to adjoining property or persons lawfully thereon'.

There would, it was said, be liability if the guttering fell on a passer-by in the street, provided the negligence were proved; indeed, it would probably be a case of *res ipsa loquitur*. It was held that there was an equivalent liability in negligence to the tenant and his lawful visitors, therefore the plaintiff and **his wife** could sue in negligence.

It is important for you to **note** that this liability is separate from the obligation placed upon an occupier by the 1957 and 1984 Acts, and that encountered in s. 4 of the Defective Premises Act 1972. All **three** Acts are considered below.

7.3.5   INJURIES TO FIREFIGHTERS

In *Ogwo* v *Taylor* [1987] 3 All ER 961 the plaintiff was a fireman and he was injured whilst attending a fire at the defendant's house. The fire had been started by the defendant using a blowlamp to burn off the paint on the fascia board under the guttering of the roof, thereby causing the roof timber to catch fire. The plaintiff went into the roof space to tackle the fire and was seriously injured by steam generated by water poured on to the fire. It was not suggested that the contents of the roof space were unusually combustible or that there was any special danger from hidden cause. The plaintiff brought an action in ordinary negligence (the 'neighbour principle') claiming that because the fire was started negligently, and he had been injured as a result, he was entitled to damages.

The Court of Appeal, reversing the judge at first instance, found for the plaintiff and this decision was confirmed by the House of Lords. It was said that someone, whether occupier, contractor, licensee or trespasser, who started a fire negligently may in the absence of special circumstances not known to the fireman be liable to him when he was injured in fighting that fire. Foreseeability of injury was regarded as the crux of the matter.

Approval was given to the decision in *Salmon* v *Seafarer Restaurants Ltd* [1983] 3 All ER 729 where Woolf J held that the defendants were liable to a fireman, who was called out to attend a fire started negligently by the defendants, and injured fighting the blaze. His Lordship considered whether there was any basis for limiting the duty owed to firemen, since they are specially trained to deal with the dangers inherent in any outbreak of fire:

> Where it can be foreseen that the fire which is negligently started is of the type which could, first of all, require firemen to attend to extinguish that fire, and where, because of the very nature of the fire, when they attend they will be at risk even though they exercise all the skill of their calling, there seems no reason why a fireman should be at any disadvantage, when the question of compensation for his injuries arises.

The 'rescue' principle was also applied in these cases. This principle is discussed in **Chapter 2**.

7.3.6 LANDLORDS

A landlord might be liable, in negligence, where he is in breach of an obligation to repair or maintain: the contract itself may provide for this obligation, or statute or common law may imply it into the contract.

This form of liability differs from that discussed at **7.3.1** in that it concerns **landlords only**, not vendors; it applies only where there is an obligation to repair or maintain; and it includes cases where the defect appears **after** the start of the lease. The Landlord and Tenant Act 1985 applies: see **7.3.1**.

Section 4 of the Defective Premises Act 1972, replacing s. 4 of the Occupiers' Liability Act 1957, provides that a landlord who is under an obligation to repair:

> owes to all persons who might reasonably be expected to be affected by defects in the state of the premises a duty to take such care as is reasonable in all the circumstances to see that they are reasonably safe from personal injury or from damage to their property caused by a relevant defect. [The] said duty is owed if the landlord knows (whether as a result of being notified by the tenant or otherwise) or he ought in all the circumstances to have known of the relevant defect.

In *Clarke* v *Taff Ely Borough Council* (1983) 10 HLR 44, the plaintiff who was a visitor of the tenant in a council house, was injured when she fell through rotten floor boards. The house, built before the Second World War, was of a type known to have a potentially dangerous floor construction. The defendants, who were held liable, admitted that rot was foreseeable in the circumstances, and it was said that notice is unnecessary where a defect is obvious on a reasonable inspection. (It is, however, advisable to put the landlord on notice wherever possible.)

The duty in s. 4 is owed to all persons within the 'area of risk', and not merely to tenants and visitors. Thus, it could be owed to a trespasser in appropriate circumstances. By s. 4(4) the same duty is owed where the landlord, rather than being under an obligation to repair or maintain, reserves expressly or impliedly, a right or power to enter and repair; but he will **not** be liable to the tenant if the defect is due to a failure to repair something which the tenant himself has expressly agreed to maintain.

In *Smith* v *Bradford Metropolitan Council, The Times,* 22 June 1982 the tenant of a house was injured as a result of a defective patio installed by an earlier tenant. The defendant landlords knew of the defect, and it was held by the Court of Appeal that their power to enter the premises was the equivalent, for present purposes, of an obligation to repair. The patio was regarded as part of the premises in the circumstances.

An **alternative** claim was put forward by the tenant in *Barrett* v *Lounova* (see **7.3.1**) for breach of the terms of s. 4. It was alleged that as a result of the disrepair there had been extensive water penetration causing damage to the interior of the house. In the circumstances this claim was not pursued, but Kerr LJ thought that in principle there was no reason why an injunction to enforce the statutory obligation could not issue in a proper case.

Please turn to *Cases and Materials* (7.1.2), where you will find *McAuley* v *Bristol City Council* [1992] 1 All ER 749. It provides another interesting illustration of the operation of s. 4.

7.4 Liability Arising under the Defective Premises Act 1972

Under s. 1 of this Act a vendor or lessor owes a **strict** duty of care if he is in the business of, or in the exercise of any statutory power makes arrangements for, the provision of dwellings or installations in dwellings. The duty is 'to see that the work which he takes on is done in a workmanlike or, as the case may be, professional manner, with proper materials and so that as regards that work the dwelling be fit for habitation when completed'. The duty is owed **by**:

(a)   those engaged in erection, conversion, or enlargement of dwellings, as well as by

(b)   those who in the course of business or in the exercise of statutory power, engage others in the work.

The duty is owed **to**:

(1)   anyone ordering the work and

(2)   anyone who acquires a legal or equitable interest in the dwelling.

ACTIVITY 35

Please find a piece of paper and on it jot down a list of the most important features of s. 1, as you see them.

Amongst these features you might have noted the following:

(a)   liability is **strict**, i.e. negligence need not be proved;

(b)   s. 1 contains language relating to 'quality', redolent of **contract** language;

(c)   damages may therefore be claimed for the cost of repair, though the defect(s) in quality must make the property **not fit for habitation** on completion;

(d)   only **dwellings** are included within the ambit of the Act;

(e)   not only builders may incur liability here; people **such as architects** are also included.

You will find the Act set out in *Cases and Materials* (7.2).

One interesting result of the decisions in *D & F Estates* and *Murphy* (see 7.3.2) has been to increase the potential importance of the 1972 Act, by diminishing the role of the common law in these buildings cases. Indeed, in *Murphy* some of their Lordships said the very existence of the Act, and the absence of any discussion on it in *Anns*, were reasons for overruling that decision.

Strength is given to s. 1 by s. 3 of the Act, which provides for the **survival** of a duty of care **after disposal** of the premises in question. It says:

> where work of construction, repair, maintenance or demolition or any other work is done on or in relation to premises, any duty of care owed, because of the doing of the work, to persons who might reasonably be expected to be affected by defects in the state of the premises created by the doing of the work shall not be abated by the subsequent disposal of the premises by the person who owed the duty.

The section does not, however, impose liability for negligent **omissions** to effect repairs (though s. 4 at **7.3.6** may be effective in this respect).

This provision applies to **any** duty of care coming into effect before disposal and 'disposal' includes leasing as well as selling. You will perhaps have noted that much the same result was achieved in such cases as *Dutton* (see **7.3.2**) where there was an attempt to abolish the builder/vendor's or builder/lessor's immunity from negligence.

You may have concluded by this stage that the 1972 Act is quite a radical piece of legislation. If that is what you have been thinking, prepare yourself for a surprise. Can you think what this surprise might be?

It is, if you have not already guessed as much by now, the 'let-out' in the Act. This is to be found in s. 2:

> No action for a breach of duty under s. 1 may be brought if there is in existence a scheme or document approved by the Secretary of State conferring rights in respect of defects in the dwelling.

The 'scheme' or 'document' referred to is some arrangement between the defendant and the plaintiff, like the 'guarantee' that is often given with new houses, which confers on the latter certain rights against the former. For example, the National House Builders' Protection Scheme (operated by the National House Building Council) whereby the builder warrants the proper construction of the dwelling and takes out insurance which will cover any claim against the builder. You will, no doubt, have noted that the Secretary of State must **approve** the scheme in question.

However, after changes made to the scheme by the NHBC, the Secretary of State has agreed with the NHBC that the Approved Scheme Order of 1979 is not to be effective. This means that currently no Approved Scheme exists and effectively s. 1 is not excluded by s. 2 (see I. N. Wallace QC (1991) LQR 228 at 242–3).

7.5 Occupiers' Liability to Lawful Visitors

We will now consider liability arising under the Occupiers' Liability Act 1957. This will be done by examining each of the major provisions of the Act (*Cases and Materials* (7.3)).

7.5.1 ACTIVITIES

At common law, before 1957, the duty owed by an occupier of premises to his lawful
entrants, with respect to the **static** condition of those premises, for example a hole in a
floor, varied according to whether the visitor entered by contract, or as invitee or
licensee. It was based on a **special** line of cases, **not** on the *Donoghue* neighbour principle.
This duty was **certainly** abolished by the **Occupiers' Liability Act 1957**, which replaced
it with the 'common duty of care'. But there was **another** duty at common law owed by
occupiers **and** non-occupiers, covering **current activities** carried out on premises, and it
is arguable that this old, **separate** line of authority based on *Donoghue*, that is, the 'activity
duty', remains at **common law** despite the Act.

In brief, a distinction was made in the law between different types of activity. On the one
hand, activities which rendered the premises unsafe, i.e. created some danger of a
continuing nature, would come within the terms of the occupancy duty; whereas
activities which did not affect the condition of the premises as such would, on the other
hand, be determined by reference to the duty arising in ordinary common law negligence. It is the latter type of activity, sometimes called current activities, which is the
concern of our discussion here and in **7.6.4.2**.

Furthermore, the activity duty may be unaffected by s. 1(3)(b) of the **Unfair Contract
Terms Act 1977**, which applies only to **occupation** of premises used for business
purposes. We will return to the 1977 Act at **7.5.7**.

The problem arises because of the apparent conflict between two parts of the 1957 Act:

(a) s. 1(1), which says the Act only applies 'in respect of dangers due to the state of
     the premises **or to things done or omitted to be done on them**' (*emphasis added*).
     The part emphasised would seem to be clear on the point that activities **are**
     covered by the Act;

(b) s. 1(2) which unfortunately says that the Act shall 'regulate the nature of the duty
     imposed by law in consequence of a person's **occupation or control** of premises'
     (*emphasis added*).

You may think that the spirit of the Act is to include current activities but words are
words to lawyers and there have certainly been arguments going **both** ways in the past.
According to *Winfield*, **13th** edn, at p. 208 the Act covers only the **'occupancy'** duty; in
the **14th** edition of this work, at pp. 226–7, this point is confirmed. A further point,
however, is made in the later edition: 'Defects in the premises which were not created
by the occupier but which he has failed to remedy must be within the Act and the Act
alone if there is no other relationship between him and the plaintiff . . .'. An 'intermediate' case is identified: '[this] is where the defendant by some positive act creates a danger
affecting the condition of the premises and here the matter is probably covered both by
the Act and by the law of negligence.'.

Salmond at p. 267 identifies both arguments, but says the weight of academic opinion
follows the *Winfield* line that '. . . activities wholly unrelated to the particular land in
question, but which just happen to be carried on there, are governed by ordinary
Atkinian negligence as far as non-trespassers are concerned.'.

Lord Keith in *Ferguson* v *Welsh* [1987] 3 All ER 777 took the view that the distinction
between the occupancy duty and the activity duty had disappeared as a result of the
passing of the 1957 Act, relying on the words emphasised in s. 1(1) above. See also the
robust agreement of D. Howarth, *Textbook on Tort*, London: Butterworths, 1995 at p. 369.

However, Lord Goff in the same case came to the opposite conclusion, relying on the
words '. . . the premises' for the purposes for which he is invited or permitted by the
occupier to be there' in s. 2(2) of the 1957 Act (see **7.5.5**).

Whichever view is correct, it seems that this matter can only be one of academic interest. In practice, whether the ordinary duty of care in negligence or the 'common duty of care' under the 1957 Act is applied to 'current activities', the result will be much the same. As you will see soon, the standard of care applied under the Act is very similar to that applied at common law.

In any event, there is authority in the cases for the *Winfield* argument. In *Jauffur* v *Akhbar*, *The Times*, 10 February 1984 a boy aged 14 was negligent in his home; there was an incident with a lighted candle, which caused a fire. The plaintiff, a visitor, was badly burned as a result of the boy's behaviour and she sued the boy together with his father, in negligence. It was alleged that the father owed a duty to instruct his son, a minor, in the handling of lighted candles and to supervise his activities in the house. The boy admitted negligence, and the father was found liable because he had failed to give his son any instructions or warning about the use of candles, knowing that there were some of these items in the house.

The plaintiff also alleged breach of the common duty of care, imposed by the 1957 Act, on the father's part, but the judge doubted whether the Act applied to such a case as this and gave judgment in negligence only.

There is opinion in the Court of Appeal in *Ogwo* (see **7.3.5**) that the fire in that case did not come within the terms of the 1957 Act.

See also **7.6.4.2** where the matter is discussed further, with particular reference to the duty owed by occupiers to trespassers.

Clearly, apart from the question of the 'activity' duty, where an occupier owes a duty (whether at common law or under statute) which is independent of his duty as **occupier**, he may be sued either under the independent duty or under the 1957 Act, or both. Thus, for example, an employee injured on his employer's premises may rely either on the 1957 Act, or on the common law duty owed by a master to his servant, or on an action for breach of statutory duty (where appropriate). The master's duty to his servant, and the action for breach of statutory duty are dealt with in **Chapter 8**.

7.5.2 PREMISES

According to s. 1(3) they include land and buildings and 'any fixed or moveable structure, including any vessel, vehicle or aircraft'. In *Bunker* v *Brand* [1969] QB 480, it was said that this definition included pylons, grandstands, lifts and even tunnels. According to *Wheeler* v *Copas* [1981] 2 All ER 405 even a ladder may be 'premises' for present purposes.

7.5.3 OCCUPIER

It is provided by s. 1(2) that:

The rules so enacted shall regulate the nature of the duty imposed by law in consequence of a person's occupation or control of premises and of any invitation or permission he gives (or is to be treated as giving) to another to enter or use the premises, but they shall not alter the rules of the common law as to the persons on whom a duty is so imposed or to whom it is owed; and accordingly for the purpose of the rules so enacted the persons who are to be treated as an occupier and as his visitors are the same (subject to subsection (4) of this section) as the persons who would at common law be treated as an occupier and as his invitees or licensees.

By s. 1(3) that:

the rules so enacted in relation to an occupier of premises and his visitors shall also apply, in like manner and to the like extent as the principles applicable at common law to an occupier of premises and his invitees or licensees would apply, to regulate –

(a)   the obligations of a person occupying or having control over, any fixed or moveable structure, including any vessel, vehicle or aircraft; and

(b)   the obligations of a person occupying or having control over any premises or structure in respect of damage to property, including the property of persons who are not themselves his visitors.

By s. 1(4) that:

a person entering any premises in exercise of rights conferred by virtue of an access agreement or order under the National Parks and Access to the Countryside Act 1949, is not, for the purposes of this Act, a visitor of the occupier of those premises.

We must turn to the **common law** for guidance on this matter. 'Occupier' is a term which means a person with **control** of the premises; sometimes this may even include an independent contractor. There may also be more than one occupier of the same premises at the same time.

You can read about *Harris* v *Birkenhead Corporation* [1976] 1 All ER 341 in *Cases and Materials* (**7.3.1**). It illustrates a particular facet of 'control'.

The occupier is responsible, because he normally supervises and controls the premises, and decides who shall and who shall not enter.

In *Bunker* (see **7.5.2**) the defendants, who were engineers, were found to be still in control of a machine roller, even though a specialist contractor had been called in to modify the machine.

The House of Lords in *Wheat* v *Lacon* [1966] AC 552, approved the following observation of Lord Denning in the Court of Appeal: 'If a person has any degree of control over the state of the premises it is enough [to make him an occupier]'.

Thus, there may be more than one 'occupier', and *Wheat* v *Lacon* in fact is an example of this. The defendants, who were brewers, owned a public house in which they employed a manager. Part of the private accommodation upstairs was used with their consent as a boarding house. The manager and his wife occupied this part of the premises, though there was **no** tenancy agreement with the brewers. The plaintiff and his wife, who were paying lodgers of the manager, one night used outside stairs on the premises and the plaintiff fell from the stairs. This unlit staircase was the only way up to the first floor; the staircase was in darkness because someone had stolen the bulb from the electric light fitting. The plaintiff died, and it was alleged that his death was the result of a breach of the common duty of care under the 1957 Act.

The House of Lords held that both the brewers and the managers were occupiers. It was not essential, said the court, that an occupier should have exclusive control so long as he retained **some** responsibility. As it happened, the claim failed because there was insufficient evidence of negligence on the facts. The defendants were not responsible for the act of the unknown person who had taken the bulb, and the stairs were safe in normal circumstances.

In *Fisher* v *CHT Ltd* [1966] 2 QB 475 Crockfords arranged for independent contractors to run the restaurant in their gaming club. The independent contractors employed a third party to redecorate the restaurant. An employee of the third party was injured when an electrician employed by the independent contractors switched on the electricity without warning.

The Court of Appeal found both Crockfords and the independent contractors liable as **occupiers,** though the contractors were three times as culpable as Crockfords and therefore liable in that proportion. The plaintiff's employers (the 'third party') were found most responsible because as **employers** they had not provided a safe system of working. They were sued as **employers,** not occupiers, under their **special** common law duty owed to their employees, discussed in **Chapter 8.** All three parties were therefore held responsible in different proportions: Crockfords 10%, the independent contractors 30% and the third party 60%. The independent contractors were insolvent, however, and Crockfords were liable finally for 25% and the third party 75%. This is an example of the apportionment of damages under what is now the Civil Liability (Contribution) Act 1978 (which is dealt with in **Chapter 1**). You can see from this case that there may be several parties owing **different** duties of care in relation to premises.

In *AMF International Ltd* v *Magnet Bowling Ltd* [1968] 2 All ER 789 an independent contractor and the owner were found to be occupiers of a building, although part of it was separated by a screen and the contractor only went to the other side of it to see to the heating and lighting.

Stop reading at this point and consider whether 'control', for the purposes of identifying an 'occupier', has to be exclusive. Is it a matter of 'law' or of 'fact'?

At one time it was the case that a person could only be regarded as an 'occupier' if he or she possessed the actual power to control entry to the premises, but since *Wheat* v *Lacon* it has not been necessary for this. As Lord Denning said, in the Court of Appeal:

Wherever a person has a sufficient degree of control over premises that he ought to realise that any failure on his part to use care may result in injury to a person coming lawfully there, then he is an 'occupier' and the person coming lawfully there is his 'visitor'.

Presumably, the same test, but with 'non-visitor'/'trespasser' substituted for 'visitor', would be used to determine occupation for purposes of the 1984 Act (see **7.6.4**).

It is also clear from *Wheat* v *Lacon* (the leading case) that control does **not** have to be exclusive and the question, in any case, of whether control is sufficient is one of fact to be determined on the evidence presented. Each case will turn on its facts, but as a **general** guide:

(a) even if an occupier engages an independent contractor to do work on his premises, the occupier will usually still retain sufficient control;

(b) if the owner of land **licenses** someone to be on his land, but retains a right to enter for purposes of repair, the owner will have enough control to be an 'occupier'; and a landlord (i.e. where land is **leased** by him to others) may let part of premises, but keep other part(s) (an obvious example is **common parts** of blocks of flats, such as staircases) and then he will be an occupier of those other part(s);

(c) in the case of **leased** premises, the landlord will normally have given up control
and the occupier will be the **tenant**.

7.5.4 'LAWFUL VISITOR'

We must now consider the question of **who** exactly is a 'lawful visitor'. Again, reference
should be made to s. 1(2), (3) and (4) which has been examined in **7.5.3** in relation to the
issue of 'occupation'. This is one of the trickier problems encountered in occupiers'
liability. Again, we must turn to the **common law** to find the answer to our question.

In brief terms, 'visitors' for the purposes of the 1957 Act are those persons who would
have been lawful entrants at common law before the Act came into operation. Such
persons are invitees, licensees, and entrants under contract; and those who enter **as of
right**, in other words they are lawful entrants by force of law, it does not matter whether
they have the occupier's permission to be on the premises or not (see s. 2(6) of the 1957
Act). Those entrants 'as of right' obtain their authority to be present from various
statutes, for example policemen, meter-readers and postmen.

Where an entrant claims to have the **express** authority of the occupier to be present, any
dispute will turn merely on the entrant's ability to prove the fact of permission. Much
more in the way of a problem is likely to be encountered where **implied** permission is
in issue, and it is to that form of permission that we now turn our attention.

7.5.4.1 Implied permission

It is for the person who claims the existence of the implied permission to **prove** on the
facts that it exists. The burden is not a light one, because it is not enough to show mere
tolerance.

To quote Lord Dunedin, in *Addie (Robert) and Sons (Collieries) Ltd* v *Dumbreck* [1929] AC
358:

> Permission must be proved, not tolerance, though tolerance in some circumstances
> may be so pronounced as to lead to a conclusion that it was really tantamount to
> permission; a mere putting up of a notice 'No Trespassers Allowed' or 'Strictly Private',
> followed when people often come, by no further steps, would, I think, leave it open
> for a judge or jury to hold implied permission. There is no duty on a proprietor to
> fence his land against the world under sanction that, if he does not, those who come
> over it become licensees.

Thus, in *Lowery* v *Walker* [1911] AC 10, members of the public had used a short cut across
the defendant's land, to get to a railway station, for nearly 35 years, but he had never
instituted legal proceedings against them, because many of the people concerned were
his customers. On these facts, it was held that the entrants were **licensees**, and when one
of them was injured by a wild horse, which the defendant had put into the field without
warning, he was able to recover damages as a **licensee** from the defendant.

In *Edwards* v *Railway Executive* [1952] AC 737, however, the House of Lords warned
against finding in favour of plaintiffs for sympathetic reasons, and said that it is not
enough to show that the occupier knows of the entrant's presence or has failed to take
the necessary steps to prevent his entry. In Lord Goddard's words: '. . . repeated trespass
of itself confers no licence. There must be evidence either of express permission or that
the landowner has so conducted himself that he cannot be heard to say that he did not
give it.'.

Take a rest from reading the text at this juncture, and have a guess as to why it might be helpful to an entrant to establish *implied* permission. Also, why should the House of Lords in *Edwards* (above) refer to 'sympathy' in decision-making?

If an entrant can establish that he or she is an implied licensee, then today that would make the entrant a 'visitor' for the purposes of the 1957 Act. Before 1957, the entrant would have been a member of a class of entrants for which a special line of authority had been developed at common law, to confer on them a right to a fairly stringent duty of care from the occupier.

The alternative would be to be classed as a 'trespasser'; trespassers were, as we will see later, entitled at common law under the rule in *Addie* (above) only to a **minimal** degree of protection from an occupier. Today, the 1984 Act applies to such relationships and, when we examine its provisions later, it will be seen to offer considerable protection to a trespasser.

There is the clue to the second question: since trespassers were entitled to much less protection at common law in the old days, courts on occasion were inclined, especially in the case of trespassing children, to find implied licences rather than brand the plaintiff a trespasser.

Canvassers and similar entrants

It is said that 'common usage' can confer an implied licence on such people as canvassers, deliverers of 'free' newsheets, those who have lost their way and are seeking directions, and entrants of similar ilk. (That is so unless the entry of such persons is expressly forbidden. A notice seen recently on the gate to a private residence read: 'No hawkers, peddlers or evangelists'. The purport behind the notice seems reasonably clear.)

In *Dunster* v *Abbot* [1953] 2 All ER 1572 a canvasser was, on this basis, considered to be a licensee and not a trespasser. The court said he could become an **invitee** (this case was decided before the 1957 Act came into effect) if the occupier did business with him. The canvasser left the defendant's premises in the dark, and was injured. The plaintiff claimed that the occupier had switched off the outside light too soon; he had insufficient time to leave the premises safely. The court found no negligence on the part of the occupier.

More recently, in *Robson* v *Hallett* [1967] 2 QB 939, Diplock LJ said:

> . . . when a householder lives in a dwelling house to which there is a garden in front and does not lock the gate of the garden, it gives an implied licence to any member of the public who has lawful reason for doing so to proceed from the gate to the front door and back door and to inquire whether he may be admitted and to conduct his lawful business.

His Lordship went on to say that if the licence was withdrawn the entrant would not be a trespasser during a reasonable period of time which he needed in order to leave the premises.

Overstepping the mark

Even though there may be permission or authority to enter, it will on occasion be necessary to consider whether the entrant has **abused** that permission or authority. As Scrutton LJ put it in *The Carlgarth* [1927] P 93: 'When you invite a person in your house to use the staircase you do not invite him to slide down the banisters.'.

Thus, an occupier may not be liable to an entrant who goes to a part of the premises where the occupier has expressly or impliedly told him not to go, by notice or otherwise. Again, an entrant may be injured on a part of the premises where he could not **reasonably** be expected to go.

The 1957 Act itself makes it clear that an occupier will not be liable where an entrant uses the premises for some purpose(s) unconnected with the invitation or permission. Therefore, if a meter-reader, for example, who enters by right should steal contents from the premises he will have abused his permission.

SAQ 76

What do you think happens to the legal status of the entrant where he makes a wrongful use of the premises?

He becomes a trespasser on those premises, although there is authority for two propositions.

(a) Permission to enter one piece of land may by implication be extended to another adjoining piece.

In *Pearson* v *Coleman Bros* [1948] 2 KB 359 a child wandered from a circus to an adjoining zoo in the process of looking for a lavatory. At the zoo she was injured; the court found that she was a licensee at the zoo and said that an occupier must indicate clearly that the visit (the girl was under the old law an invitee at the circus) is limited in terms of time and place.

Your attention is drawn to the point made earlier, about sympathy for the plight of entrants who might be regarded as trespassers, at a time when the law governing the liability of occupiers to unlawful entrants was much harsher than it is today. Even *Pearson* should, perhaps, be read in that light.

(b) A person who is a lawful entrant to begin with will probably not lose that status where it is the fault of the occupier that causes him to 'step out of line'.

In *Braithwaite* v *South Durham Steel Co.* [1958] 1 WLR 986 due to the occupier's negligence a lawful entrant was forced to move out of the area where he had permission to be, into an area outside the remit of that permission. It was held that he was still a lawful entrant.

We have seen that it is possible for a person to become a trespasser, although that person was a lawful entrant initially, because he goes on to some part(s) of the premises the occupier did not intend him to enter or because he uses his permission for some wrongful purpose. It may also be the case that **time** is the enemy of the lawful entrant.

Please consider the following scenario.

X attends a party held by the manager of a public house, after licensing hours, and falls down some stairs outside the pub on emerging from the building. He dies and his widow sues the local brewery, which owns the pub. The defendants say he was a trespasser at *that* time, but he was not aware of the fact that the manager was only allowed to have a private party outside the pub hours if he first obtained permission from the defendants (the brewery company) *and* informed the police. The manager had not satisfied either of these two conditions.

Would you find the deceased a trespasser at the relevant time?

These are the facts of *Stone* v *Taffe* [1974] 3 All ER 1016 in which the Court of Appeal decided that the dead man was **not** a trespasser, as alleged by the defendant, because an occupier who wants to impose a time limit on the permission given to an entrant must make this condition **clear** to the entrant. Here, this had not been done and the deceased was a lawful entrant at the relevant time.

Persons who enter premises in pursuance of a public or private right of way

The law is in something of a confusing state with regard to **public** rights of way. Entrants in this case are disowned specifically by the 1984 Act, in s. 1(7).

According to the Court of Appeal in *Greenhalgh* v *British Railways Board* [1969] 2 QB 286 neither are they 'visitors' for the purposes of the 1957 Act. It may be that the *Herrington* doctrine of 'common humanity' would apply in such cases. We will see later that the ruling in this case, which was replaced for 'mainstream' trespassing by the 1984 Act, may still be valid for cases falling outside the Act.

There is also an old common law form of liability applicable to public rights of way, but it only covers negligent misfeasance, i.e. positive acts and not negligent nonfeasance, i.e. failure to act. If, however, the public right of way is maintained at **public** expense the highway authority may be liable, under the Highways Act 1980, for **both** forms of negligence.

In *McGeown* v *Northern Ireland Housing Executive* [1994] 3 All ER 53 the House of Lords confirmed that the owner of land over which a public right of way passes is not liable for negligent nonfeasance towards members of the public using it. A person exercising a public right of way is, as such, neither the licensee nor the invitee of the occupier of the soil over which the right of way runs. Furthermore, said their Lordships, if a licence to use the pathway was granted by the landowner before it became a public right of way, that licence becomes merged in that right of way and is thereby extinguished.

The position regarding **private** rights of way is more straightforward. By virtue of s. 1(1)(a) of the Occupiers' Liability Act 1984, persons using such a right of way are owed a duty of care under **that** Act. This is also the case for those exercising rights of access under the National Parks and Access to the Countryside Act 1949.

Finally, you should read about the House of Lords case *Ferguson* v *Welsh* [1987] 3 All ER 777 in *Cases and Materials* (**7.3.2.1**). It illustrates the point that in those circumstances where there are several occupiers, the entrant may be a 'visitor' vis-à-vis one occupier and a trespasser with regard to another occupier.

7.5.5 THE 'COMMON DUTY OF CARE'

This is defined in s. 2(2) of the Occupiers' Liability Act 1957 as follows:

> The common duty of care is a duty to take such care as in all the circumstances of the case is reasonable to see that the visitor will be reasonably safe in using the premises for the purposes for which he is invited or permitted by the occupier to be there.

It will be seen that s. 2(3) is also of importance in this respect; its provisions are considered later on. That is also the case with s. 2(4).

At common law, before the 1957 Act came into operation, there were, as we have already seen, **several duties** of care owed to entrants; today that number has been much reduced. As far as **lawful** entrants were concerned the different duties each had their own standard of care so that, for example, a licensee might be owed a different standard of care from an invitee.

The 1957 Act, by providing a single duty of care owed to **all** lawful visitors, has reduced the various **standards** of care to **one**, i.e. the **common** duty of care. This common duty of care is, in essence, a duty to act without **negligence** with regard to the safety of the visitor, and the same sort of considerations that are relevant in an action for common law negligence will be relevant here.

Initially, two points may be made concerning this statutory obligation:

(a) as Mocatta J put it in *AMF* v *Magnet Bowling* (see **7.5.3**) an occupier is **not** an insurer against all the risks; he is expected in general to take only **reasonable** care;

(b) the Act refers to the safety of the visitor, not necessarily the safety of the premises. Thus a visitor may be 'safe' on 'unsafe' premises, provided the occupier has taken adequate precautions in the circumstances: for example, by providing adequate warning of some danger on the premises. It is a question of evidence, on the facts of the case, whether the common duty of care has been observed which means, of course, that it **may** be necessary in some situations for the occupier actually to make the premises safe in order to ensure the safety of the visitor.

It would be useful if you were at this point to refer to **Chapter 3** to look at the factors taken into account when considering what the 'reasonable man' would or would not have done for the purposes of determining the standard of care at common law (see **3.7.1**).

SAQ 77

Why not get a piece of paper right now, and write down on it a list of factors which might well be taken into account by a court when deciding whether or not an occupier has discharged his or her obligation(s) under the common duty of care.

In your list you may well have included the following factors:

(a) if there is more than one occupier, it could be that each one will be expected to observe a different standard of care;

(b) the likelihood of the injury occurring in the circumstances;

(c) the nature of the danger itself;

(d) the steps necessary to avert the danger: here the practicalities of taking pre-cautions will come into account, for example, cost, extent and for how long the state of affairs has existed;

(e) was a warning necessary in the circumstances of the case?

7.5.5.1   General observations

The Act itself makes **specific** provision for some special cases, but before we look at them there are two cases worthy of note; they help to explain further the general nature of the common duty of care.

In s. 2(2) there is reference to the visitor being 'reasonably safe in using the premises for the purposes for which he is invited or permitted by the occupier to be there.'.

Lord Goff, in *Ferguson* v *Welsh* (see **7.5.4.1**) claimed that the plaintiff's injuries did not come within the wording of s. 2(2) because he had been injured as a result of the way in which he did his work on the premises. On the other hand Lords Keith, Brandon and Griffith were of the opinion that the sub-section applied to dangers due to the state of the premises (Lord Goff's point) **and** known dangers arising from things done or allowed by the occupier to be done on the premises. According to this, majority, view the plaintiff **did** come within the terms of the Act; his claim failed simply because there was no breach by the occupier of his 'common duty of care'.

In *Cunningham* v *Reading Football Club Ltd* [1992] PIQR 141, the Club, who were occupiers of a football ground, were found responsible for the injuries sustained by policemen on duty at the ground when supporters of a playing team broke off pieces of concrete steps and started throwing them. The concrete was in a poor state due to lack of maintenance, and the club knew that pieces of it had been used by fans for this wrongful conduct on previous occasions.

You may care to contrast this decision with the earlier case of *Simms* v *Leigh Rugby Football Club* [1969] 2 All ER 923. The plaintiff was playing, as a member of a visiting football team, in a match at the defendants' ground. A concrete wall ran alongside the touchline and its position complied with bye-laws of the Rugby Football League governing body. The plaintiff was tackled near the wall, thrown towards it and injured. The evidence was uncertain on the point whether he had come into contact with the wall. There being no evidence of a similar incident in the past, it was held on the balance of probabilities that the plaintiff's injury was not caused by contact with the wall. Furthermore, this injury (a broken leg) sustained in a tackle was an accepted risk in playing rugby football. Thus, on the facts the defendants were found not liable. In any event, said the judge, the risk of injury in the circumstances though foreseeable was so improbable that the defendants could not be expected to take steps to prevent it.

In *Cunningham*, it was found that the defendants knew that it was 'very probable' that lumps of concrete would be thrown.

Res ipsa loquitur, discussed in **Chapter 3**, will apply in appropriate circumstances. It was used successfully by the plaintiff in *Ward* v *Tesco Stores Ltd* [1976] 1 WLR 810, where she slipped in a pool of yoghurt on a supermarket floor. However, Ormrod LJ would not accept that a prima facie case of negligence (this action was brought in ordinary negligence and not under the Act) on the part of the supermarket staff could be inferred because the fact that the yoghurt was there, on the floor, did not show that it had been present for any **significant** period of time. (You will by now appreciate fully that length of time is a crucial factor in any claim for negligence.)

7.5.5.2   Special cases

We now come to the special cases provided for in the Act itself.

Can you guess what these special provisions are?

There are **two** 'special cases'.

In s. 2(3) the Act says:

> The circumstances relevant for the present purposes include the degree of care, and of want of care, which would ordinarily be looked for in such a visitor, so that (for example) in proper cases –
> (a)   an occupier must be prepared for children to be less careful than adults; and
> (b)   an occupier may expect that a person, in the exercise of his calling, will appreciate and guard against any special risks ordinarily incident to it, so far as the occupier leaves him free to do so.

Let us deal first with children. Evidently, each case will turn on its own facts; the question must always be: 'has the occupier discharged his common duty of care in the circumstances?'. The age of the entrant and the nature of the danger will be the two crucial factors to consider in such cases.

In *Titchener* v *British Railways Board* [1983] 3 All ER 770, it was held that older children (a 15-year-old in this case) should be regarded as adults in the present context; but in other cases it is, in broad terms, a matter of special care.

As Hamilton LJ put it in *Latham* v *R Johnson and Nephew Ltd* [1913] 1 KB 398: 'In the case of an infant, there are moral as well as physical traps. There may accordingly be a duty towards infants not merely not to dig pitfalls for them, but not to lead them into temptation.'.

The courts have developed a doctrine of 'traps' and 'allurements' with regard to children. Occupiers must be aware that young entrants are likely to 'go where the attraction is', as it were.

In *Glasgow Corporation* v *Taylor* [1922] 1 AC 44, a child, aged seven, picked some berries off a bush in a public park. He died after eating what were in fact poisonous berries. The defendants were found liable because this bush, with its attractive fruit resembling blackberries, was an 'allurement' to a young child who could not be expected to be as aware of the danger as an adult. There was no warning of the danger and the bush had not been cordoned off.

A boy of seven was also involved as plaintiff in another leading case, *Liddle* v *Yorkshire (North Riding) County Council* [1934] 2 KB 101. The defendant council had left a pile of soil next to a wall and it was possible, by climbing up the pile to reach the top of the wall. The plaintiff, whilst playing with his friends, got on to the wall in this way and fell off, injuring himself. He lost his case against the council because the danger here was obvious, there was no 'trap' or 'allurement', even to the plaintiff. However, he had been warned off on previous occasions and was regarded as a **trespasser**.

This case says the idea of an 'allurement' is applicable only where the child is a lawful visitor in the first place, but moves to a part of the premises where he or she should not go. The notion of allurement, in other words, cannot turn a child trespasser into a lawful entrant. Nevertheless, in the past children have successfully used 'allurement' to persuade the courts to create implied licences.

We have seen that the courts were willing to do this in order to mitigate, by avoiding, the rule in *Addie* v *Dumbreck*. Now that the 1984 Act has introduced, as we will see, a much more flexible formula for the resolution of disputes between occupiers and trespassers it is debatable whether allurement will be as important in this context in the future.

In general as far as minors are concerned, and this is the final observation on the topic of child entrants, most people would agree that there are few situations which would not pose some degree of danger to very young children. They may be so young that they cannot appreciate even the most obvious of dangers. In such cases the courts will consider all the circumstances, to decide whether occupiers could have reasonably expected adults to be accompanying the children.

Devlin J in *Phipps* v *Rochester Corporation* [1965] 1 QB 450, considered the nature of an occupier's obligation towards a child who has not yet reached the age of 'reason'. The plaintiff was aged five, and engaged on a blackberrying expedition with his sister, aged seven, on the defendant's building site. He fell into a ditch, which was an obvious danger, because he was too young to get across it safely. The court found that the defendant had acquiesced in the presence of members of the public and the children were licensees, but he was entitled to expect very young children to be accompanied by an adult and was therefore not liable for such an obvious danger. The accident would not have happened to an older child, or to the plaintiff if he had been in the care of an adult, as the defendant could have reasonably expected in the circumstances.

The Court of Appeal gave its approval to this line of reasoning in *Simkiss* v *Rhondda Borough Council* [1983] 81 LGR 460. On the defendant's land there was a slag heap, near to flats and houses, and local children often used blankets and trays as makeshift sleds to slide down this heap. The plaintiff, a girl of seven, was injured when doing this and sued the council. Since there was no hidden danger, and no duty to fence in those circumstances, the only danger here was the slag heap itself. It was found that the defendants could rely on parents to exercise some control over their children, and to tell them not to play in dangerous places, or even **prevent** very young ones from doing so. In the circumstances, the defendant was expected to exercise only the care of a careful and prudent parent. It seems that the child's father thought the place in question was not dangerous.

In *Jolley* v *London Borough of Sutton* [1998] 3 All ER 559, the defendant occupied land on which an abandoned boat had lain for at least two years. Whilst the occupier accepted the argument that the boat was both an allurement and a trap to children, it claimed that it was only liable for reasonably foreseeable injuries, i.e. those suffered by children who played on the boat and which were caused by the attractiveness of the boat to children, and by its dangerous condition. The plaintiff was injured when he jacked up the boat in order to repair it, and the boat fell on him. He was aged 14 at the time. The Court of Appeal agreed that the defendant was not liable, because it was not **reasonably foreseeable** that children would jack up the boat in order to repair it. Lord Woolf, delivering the judgment of the court, said the case was **distinguishable** from *Hughes* v *Lord Advocate* (see **Chapter 4**) because the accident was of a different type and kind from anything which the defendant could have reasonably foreseen in the circumstances.

We can now consider the position of those entrants with a special calling or skill. An occupier is, under the Act, quite justified in expecting those entrants to exercise their special skill and to take care to guard themselves against any risks or danger of which they ought reasonably to be aware.

Lord Goddard said in *Bates* v *Parker* [1953] 2 QB 231: 'Where a householder employs an independent contractor to do work, be it of cleaning or repairing, on his premises, the contractor must satisfy himself as to the safety or condition of that part of the premises on which he is to work.'.

In *Roles* v *Nathan* [1963] 1 WLR 1117, Lord Denning said: 'When a householder calls in a specialist to deal with a defective installation on his premises, he can reasonably expect the specialist to appreciate the need to guard against the dangers arising from the defect.'. In this case, two chimney-sweeps were killed by inhaling carbon monoxide fumes, while attempting to seal up a 'sweep hole' in the chimney of a coke-fired boiler which was alight at the time, and which was a special risk ordinarily incidental to the calling of a sweep.

It was held that the occupier could expect the deceased to take special care to guard against danger from flues; there was no liability on his part on these facts. **Warnings** about the danger had also been given to the sweeps and this was taken into account by the court in arriving at its decision.

We have already seen (at **7.3.5**) in *Salmon* and *Ogwo*, the cases involving firemen injured on premises, that it is not enough for an occupier to plead simply that an entrant is skilled and that liability lies only in respect of exceptional risks or dangers. The two cases decide that there is no difference in such circumstances between 'ordinary' and 'exceptional' risks because the issue is simply whether or not the injury is reasonably foreseeable. *Ogwo* tells us, however, that an occupier can reasonably expect a firefighter not to take unnecessary risks by being foolhardy, and to follow standard practice in doing his job.

7.5.5.3 Warning notices

An occupier may seek to discharge his or her common duty of care by exhibiting a **warning** notice. In s. 2(4) we find the following provision:

> In determining whether the occupier of premises had discharged the common duty of care to a visitor, regard is to be had to all the circumstances, so that (for example) –
> (a) where damage is caused to a visitor by a danger of which he had been warned by the occupier, the warning is not to be treated without more as absolving the

occupier from liability, unless in all the circumstances it was enough to enable the visitor to be reasonably safe; and

(b) where damage is caused to a visitor by a danger due to the faulty execution of any work of construction, maintenance or repair by an independent contractor employed by the occupier, the occupier is not to be treated without more as answerable for the danger if in all the circumstances he had acted reasonably in entrusting the work to an independent contractor and had taken such steps (if any) as he reasonably ought in order to satisfy himself that the contractor was competent and that the work had been properly done.

Section 2(4)(b) is considered **separately** at **7.5.5.4**. It is included **here** only for purposes of **continuity**.

'Without more' means without more **evidence of other** circumstances, or measures taken, for example, such as roping off a source of danger. Thus the notice must be **exceptionally** clear and unambiguous if the occupier is to rely on it **alone**. **Each** visitor must be given the opportunity to avoid **the danger in question**. Of course, **a notice can** be used in **conjunction** with **other** methods of protecting a visitor, for example roping off an area of danger; in such a case the precise wording of the notice might not be quite so crucial.

SAQ 79

Can you think of an example of a suitably worded warning notice?

All cases will depend on their **own facts**, but an appropriate notice might read as follows:

'WARNING TO ALL ENTRANTS ON THESE PREMISES. TAKE CARE. ENTRY TO THIS ROOM IS EXPRESSLY FORBIDDEN. THE FLOOR IS LIABLE TO GIVE WAY WITHOUT ANY WARNING.'

Another notice might read: 'DANGER. CLEANING IN PROGRESS. THIS FLOOR IS SLIPPERY WHEN WET.'.

A visitor is thereby assisted in coping safely with the danger.

It seems that the Act approaches the matter in a **subjective** way; in other words it is the effect of the notice on the **individual** visitor that matters. Thus, it is necessary that the **particular** visitor should fully understand the warning; it may, therefore, be useless to rely on a written or visual warning where a blind entrant is concerned. As the Act says, the notice must be enough to make the visitor reasonably safe in the circumstances of the case.

You may have realised by now that an occupier, by referring to a danger in his warning is making it perfectly clear that he is fully aware of its existence, therefore the burden on him to show that his warning alone is sufficient is an onerous one.

The occupier in *Roles* v *Nathan* (see **7.5.5.2**) convinced the majority of the Court of Appeal that his unwritten warning was adequate. The deceased were told on several occasions not to stay too long in the flue **and** that the boiler should not be lit until the access-opening ('sweep hole') had been closed. Actually, agents of the occupier **themselves** turned the boiler on in contravention of the warnings; for this reason Pearson LJ regarded the warnings as inadequate.

We have seen, however, that the sweeps were regarded as persons with a special calling, who ought to have appreciated and guarded against the danger.

Finally, warning notices as such must be distinguished from **exclusion** or **restriction** of liability notices and 'risk' notices, whereby a visitor's attention is drawn **generally** to the risk of danger. This is an attempt to raise the defence of **voluntary assumption of risk**.

Both types of notice are dealt with below, but can you think at this point in your learning of appropriate forms of wording for them?

As far as **exclusion** of liability is concerned, a common expression is 'The management accept no liability for any accident howsoever caused.'.

In the case of risk, **a notice** might read: 'All patrons enter entirely at their own risk.'.

7.5.5.4   Independent contractors

Section 2(4)(b) is relevant here. It is set out in **7.5.5.3**.

In effect this provides a defence to occupiers; it offers a means of establishing that the common duty of care has been discharged on the facts. The burden of proof is on the occupier as to whether he has acted reasonably in the circumstances. He will have to show that he has done all that **reasonable** care requires in the circumstances.

The obligation can be split up into its component parts as follows.

(a)   The occupier must take reasonable steps to ensure that the contractor is competent. As far as the 'man in the street' is concerned, this begs the question as to the means of checking on technical competence. Each case must turn on its facts, but enquiring of trades or professional or technical organisations or local authorities, etc., may suffice.

(b)   Where the nature of the work involved allows it, the occupier is expected to see that the work has been properly done.

It was said in *AMF International Ltd* v *Magnet Bowling* (see **7.5.3**) that in the case of the re-wiring of a building, for example, an occupier could trust a contractor, but much depends on the circumstances of the case. Thus in some cases it might be necessary to see that the contractor's work is supervised by an architect or other professional person where the work is especially complex or potentially dangerous, for example, the construction of a large building. Mocatta J said that the negligence of the architect or other person would not itself involve the occupier in liability; otherwise, in technical cases, the common duty of care would become equivalent to the obligation of an insurer.

Much will depend on the occupier's own knowledge and, presumably, resources. Our 'man in the street' would not normally be expected to know of defective technical work.

(c) It must be reasonable in the circumstances for the occupier to give the work to an independent contractor. In general terms this is probably the case where the job needs specialist knowledge and/or equipment (indeed in such cases it **may** be wrong for an occupier **not** to employ a contractor and to attempt the work himself) or where it is usual commercial practice to do so.

You may well find that a few illustrations from the case law will help to make these points clearer. As you will be aware by now, pre-1957 cases can be used for this purpose.

In *Haseldine* v *Daw* [1941] 2 KB 343, the plaintiff was injured when the defendant's lift failed as a result of the negligence of a firm of contractors employed by the defendant to repair the lift. The defendant had employed competent contractors to maintain the lift, therefore he was not liable. Scott LJ said:

the landlord of a block of flats, as occupier of the lifts, does not profess as such to be either an electrical or, as in this case, a hydraulic engineer. Having no technical skill he cannot rely on his own judgment, and the duty of care . . . requires him to obtain and follow good technical advice. If he did not do so, he would, indeed, be guilty of negligence. To hold him responsible for the misdeeds of his independent contractor would be to make him insure the safety of his lift. That duty can only arise out of contract . . .'

By way of contrast, in *Woodward* v *Mayor of Hastings* [1954] KB 74, the plaintiff slipped on an icy step at the defendant's school. The step had been left wet in frosty conditions by a negligent cleaning contractor. The defendant was found liable. The Court of Appeal **distinguished** *Haseldine*, which involved the maintenance of a lift, requiring technical knowledge. This was not the case in *Woodward*, which concerned merely the cleaning of a snow-covered step. As Du Parcq LJ put it: '[The] craft of the charwoman may have its mysteries, but there is no esoteric quality in the nature of the work which the cleaning of a snow covered step demands.'.

In *Wells* v *Cooper* [1958] 2 QB 265, it was held that a householder may undertake an ordinary domestic repair, for example, the fixing of a new door handle. He will have discharged his duty if he does the work with the care and skill of a reasonably competent carpenter. The court said this was not a case where the technical nature of the work required the occupier to employ an independent contractor.

Finally, it was held in *Cook* v *Broderip*, *The Times*, 15 March 1968, that the occupier of a flat was not liable to his domestic help who was injured because a contractor had negligently installed a new switch fuse in the flat. The occupier was entitled to trust the contractor.

We have not yet finished with the problem of independent contractors in relation to s. 2(4)(b) of the 1957 Act. In fact, we need to consider three issues:

(a) the expression 'without more' which appears in the sub-section;

(b) the issue of 'demolition', i.e. is work of demolition included?

(c) in s. 2(4)(b), the phrase 'any work of construction, maintenance or repair' may cause difficulty **apart** from the issue of whether it can embrace 'demolition'.

First, the words 'without more'. They seem to mean that there may be evidence of the occupier's complicity in events which will not allow him to hide behind the contractor. In *Coupland* v *Eagle Bros Ltd* (1969) 210 Estates Gazette 581, the plaintiff was electrocuted by a live wire because the contractor had not switched off the current while carrying out electrical work. The occupier knew that the wire was dangerous and had not warned anyone. It was held that the 'without more' provision did not absolve him from liability; he was **concurrently** negligent with the contractor.

Next, we have to consider the word 'demolition'. Section 2(4)(b) refers to 'work of **construction, maintenance** or **repair**' (*emphasis added*). On the face of it, 'demolition' does not easily fit into this formula. Lord Keith, however, in *Ferguson* v *Welsh* (see **7.5.4.1**) expressed the opinion that a 'purposive' approach to the interpretation of the 1957 Act might suggest work of demolition **would** be included.

Stop reading for a while and concentrate on the interpretation of this sub-section. Do you favour such a broad approach? What result would a more literal, 'technical' approach produce?

A 'narrower' view suggests that a simple demolition job is not included within this wording. You may care to consider the view of E. McKendrick, *Tort Textbook*, 6th edn, London: HLT Publications, 1992, p. 209:

> With the greatest respect to his Lordship [Lord Keith] it is difficult to see how construction can encompass demolition; demolition is the very opposite of construction. Where a contractor is employed to demolish a building prior to constructing a new one it is conceded that such demolition work should be caught by s. 2(4)(b) but the same reasoning should not apply where, as in *Ferguson*, the contractors were employed only for the purpose of demolition.

Finally, the question can arise as to what other sort of work comes within the sub-section. For example, in *Gaffney* v *Aviation and Shipping Co. Ltd* [1966] 1 Lloyd's Rep 249, it was held not to cover careless stowage by stevedores.

As with the word 'demolition', much will depend on whether a 'broad' or a 'narrow' interpretation is given to the wording. According to the 'purposive' view, the purpose behind the Act must be considered and the legislation has to work in practice.

In *AMF International* v *Magnet Bowling* (see **7.5.3**) the plaintiff company had a contract with the defendant company to supply and install bowling equipment in the defendant's bowling alley whilst it was being built. The building contractors, at a certain stage in the construction, negligently said the plaintiff could go ahead with its work. As a result of heavy rain the site was flooded and the plaintiff's equipment was damaged. The defendant should have checked the work of the contractors before allowing the plaintiff to enter the premises, but the defendant argued that the contractor's failure to prevent flooding was not 'faulty work'. It was held, however, that in order to give sensible meaning to s. 2(4)(b) **incidental** work came within it; in the present case this consisted of a failure by the contractors to ensure that flooding did not take place whilst the building was being constructed. On the facts, the contractors had sufficient control of the premises to make them occupiers too.

7.5.6   ENTRY BY CONTRACT

We must here deal with **two** sections of the 1957 Act.

Section 5(1) of the Act provides that persons entering or bringing goods on premises under a contract are owed the common duty of care 'insofar as the duty depends on a term to be implied in the contract by reason of its conferring' the right concerned. There is therefore in the case of contractual visitors or licensees an implied common duty of care.

An express provision of the contract will negative the duty. The contract itself is the final determinant of the duty (**subject** to the provisions of the Unfair Contract Terms Act 1977, which we examine at **7.5.7.1**) but in the absence of provision to the contrary the common duty of care applies. The contract can provide that a **higher** duty than the common duty of care is to apply.

Liability here lies in **contract** and/or **tort** (under s. 2 of the Act). You can read about *Sole v WJ Hallt Ltd* [1973] 1 QB 574 in *Cases and Materials* (**7.3.3**). It illustrates this dual liability.

Section 3 deals with the position of persons who enter premises in pursuance of a contract to which they are not parties.

Section 3(1) provides that where an occupier is bound by contract to permit strangers to the contract to enter or use the premises, the occupier cannot by that contract exclude or restrict the common duty of care owed to them. This is an exception to the general rule that rights and duties may be modified by contract and the reason is that the stranger should not be adversely affected by the provisions of a contract to which he is not a party. The stranger is entitled to the benefit of any obligations undertaken by the occupier in the contract, insofar as they go beyond the common duty of care, subject to any provision of the contract to the contrary.

Can you write down, in one short paragraph, the general effect of this provision?

Where the occupier is bound by contract to permit third parties, who are strangers to the contract, to enter or use the premises, the duty owed to them cannot be restricted or excluded by the contract, but (unless the contract states otherwise) the third party can take advantage of any term of the contract which confers protection in excess of the common duty of care. For example, if an occupier permits his tenant and a friend of the tenant to use his premises by a contract that provides that the premises are to be lit at night (not **specifically** required under the common duty of care), the tenant's friend may sue the occupier for injury caused by his failure to light the premises.

A third party is therefore in a specially protected position if he enters as a result of a right conferred by contract. This provision frequently protects the employees of contractors working on the premises.

You may care to record further provisions of s. 3:

By s. 3(2) an occupier who has taken all reasonable care is not responsible for the defaults of an independent contractor unless the contract expressly provides otherwise.

Section 3(4) provides that:

> where by terms or conditions governing any tenancy (including a statutory tenancy which does not in law amount to a tenancy) either the landlord or tenant is bound, though not by contract, to permit persons to enter or use premises of which he is the occupier, this section shall apply as if the tenancy were a contract between the landlord and the tenant.

7.5.7   EXCLUSION OF AN OCCUPIER'S LIABILITY UNDER THE 1957 ACT

Exclusion or **modification** of the duty must be **distinguished** carefully from **warning** and **risk** notices. Warning notices have already been dealt with, and voluntary assumption of risk is examined at **7.5.8**.

Section 2(1) provides that the common duty of care is owed by the occupier to all his visitors, 'except in so far as he is free to and does extend, restrict, modify or exclude his duty . . . by agreement or otherwise'.

Evidently, the Act acknowledges that the occupier's freedom in this respect may be limited.

Can you attempt a brief list of restrictions on the occupier's ability to limit his liability?

You might have written down the following list of restrictions:

(a)   liability to those persons who enter as of right under s. 2(6);

(b)   liability to third parties cannot be excluded or restricted by contract with someone else, by virtue of s. 3;

(c)   there may be some **special** statutory provision prohibiting exclusion or modification of liability, for example the Public Passenger Vehicles Act 1981 and the Road Traffic Act 1988 (both Acts are dealt with, briefly, in **Chapter 8**);

(d)   the Unfair Contract Terms Act 1977 may apply.

We will now proceed to examine the effect of the 1977 Act on occupier's liability under the 1957 Act. You may have studied the 1977 Act in detail within the context of the law of contract; in that case you will be acquainted with the Act's terms and general effect. In addition, reference has been made in **Chapter 5** to the Act's effect on exclusion clauses with regard to liability arising under *Hedley Byrne*.

Only a basic, and necessarily brief, treatment of the 1977 Act can be given here. You will find the Act set out in *Cases and Materials* (**2.2.1.2**).

7.5.7.1   'Business liability'

The Unfair Contract Terms Act 1977 applies in both **contract** and **tort**, but only in relation to things done or to be done, in the course of a business. 'Business liability' includes liability arising from the occupation of business premises.

This provision is found in s. 1(3) of the 1977 Act. Section 2 of the Occupiers' Liability Act 1984 extends the meaning of 'business liability'. It says that the following words are to be added at the end of s. 1(3) of the 1977 Act:

> but liability of an occupier of premises for breach of an obligation or duty towards a person obtaining access to the premises for recreational or educational purposes, being liability for loss or damage suffered by reason of the dangerous state of the premises, is not a business liability of the occupier unless granting that person such access for the purposes concerned fall within the business purposes of the occupier.

This was done to provide for those situations in which fees are charged for entry to premises but the money goes to charity.

'Business' is defined, in broad terms, in s. 14: it includes, of course, what one would expect in terms of ordinary business or commercial activities; but it goes beyond that to cover the activities of the professions, central and local government and other public authorities. It does not include contracts of a casual and occasional nature, say where A agrees to dig B's garden for reward during A's Easter vacation. Beyond this, the 1977 Act gives us no better definition of business.

It must also be remembered that the Act applies **only** to **exemption** clauses in contracts, i.e.:

(a)   those which attempt to **exclude** or **restrict** liability; or

(b)   impose onerous conditions on enforcement of liability; or

(c)   restrict the right to a remedy; or

(d)   restrict or exclude rules of evidence or procedure; or

(e)   attempt to modify the contractual obligation.

7.5.7.2   Negligence

Section 2(1) of the 1977 Act provides as follows:

> A person cannot by reference to any contract terms or to a notice given to persons generally or to particular persons exclude or restrict his liability for death or personal injury resulting from negligence.

List the features of this provision that relate most strongly to the present discussion.

You might have listed the following features:

   (a) not only contract terms are covered; 'notices' are included too, therefore the Act must also extend to **tort** ;

   (b) only liability in relation to **death** and **bodily injury** are mentioned;

   (c) it is restricted to damage caused by **negligence**.

Thus, whether it is contract **or** tort that is involved, the relevant behaviour of the defendant must be 'negligence'. Not all torts are based on negligence, and many contracts involve strict liability, therefore s. 2 does not apply in such cases. (Where contracts do not contain obligations to take reasonable care or to exercise reasonable skill, the 1977 Act only applies to exemption clauses where one party is a 'consumer' or the contract is based on 'written standard terms of business'.)

Having established that s. 2 is not restricted to exemption clauses in contracts, but applies also in tort, we now need to know what 'negligence' means in the present context. This is defined in s. 1 to mean breach of an obligation to take reasonable care or to exercise reasonable skill arising out of the **express** or **implied** terms of a **contract**, or existing at common law in **tort**, or arising out of the Occupiers' Liability Act 1957.

The absolute ban on exemption of liability for negligence is restricted to cases of **death or bodily injury**. In the case of liability for other loss or damage s. 2(2) says that exclusion **is** possible where the term or notice passes the 'reasonableness' tests set out in s. 11. The burden of proving 'reasonableness' is on the person who wants to rely on the exemption clause or notice.

7.5.7.3   Notice

In those cases of tort where liability **may** be excluded the task can be achieved by a non-contractual 'notice', because s. 2(1) of the 1957 Act uses the expression 'by agreement or otherwise'. By this means the Act gave effect to the decision of the Court of Appeal in *Ashdown* v *Samuel Williams and Son Ltd* [1957] 1 QB 409.

The defendants had put up a number of notices on their land to the effect that all entrants were present at their own risk, and that they would have no claim against the defendants for any injury whatsoever. It was held that the defendants had taken all reasonable steps to bring the conditions contained in the notices to the plaintiff's attention. The plaintiff could not therefore recover when she was injured as a result of the negligent shunting of railway trucks by the defendants.

Today, the 1977 Act would outlaw such an exemption notice on its **facts**, but the case stands as authority for 'notice' where the defendant **is** free to 'restrict, modify or exclude' his liability under the 1957 Act. It is authority for the proposition that **actual** notice of the condition is not necessary, provided **reasonable** steps have been taken to bring it to the attention of the plaintiff. In other words, **constructive** notice will do. This may lead to difficulty in the case of children and the illiterate.

You may care to read about another Court of Appeal case which followed *Ashdown*; it is called *White* v *Blackmore* [1972] 3 All ER 158 (see *Cases and Materials* (7.3.4.1)).

7.5.7.4   A minimum standard of care

Winfield (at pp. 240–1) argues that the original (we will examine at **7.6.4** the **modern** duty of care) duty owed by occupiers to **trespassers**, representing as it does a **minimum** obligation, should be owed to **lawful** entrants in **all** cases. In other words, **no** occupier should be able to exclude **this** duty of care. The old duty, not to injure the entrant deliberately or recklessly cannot be excluded 'for A cannot lawfully license B to inflict a wilful injury upon him'. 'If it be objected that a lawful visitor [who enters premises subject to the occupier's terms] may therefore be worse off than a trespasser entering without notice of the occupier's terms [the 1984 Act imposes a considerably higher standard of care than the original duty] it may be replied that at least the visitor is, or ought to be, aware of these terms.' Jones (at p. 195) argues that it is the duty laid down in the 1984 Act which applies to lawful visitors in these circumstances.

7.5.8   *VOLENTI NON FIT INJURIA*

You may recall this defence, of 'voluntary assumption of risk', which was discussed in **Chapter 2**, as one of the traditional **general** defences in the law of tort.

This defence applies to liability arising under the 1957 Act, by virtue of s. 2(5), which says there is no liability for 'risks willingly accepted as his by the visitor'.

The Unfair Contract Terms Act 1977 preserves the defence, but does say in s. 2(3) that someone's agreement to or awareness of an exemption condition or notice does not 'itself' indicate that person's voluntary acceptance of the risk. Apart from this, the usual conditions for the defence will apply. For example, there must be **full, free** and **unfettered** consent.

Although there is some apparent element of overlap between them, it is important to distinguish between 'volenti', 'warning' and 'exemption of liability'. Your attention has already been drawn to this.

In *Simms* (see **7.5.5.1**) it was found that the plaintiff had willingly accepted the risk, by virtue of s. 2(5), of playing on a football field which, as far as the distance of the wall from the touchline was concerned, complied with the Rugby Football League's bye-laws.

Would you care to summarise the main differences between these three concepts?

The main differences between the three ideas are as follows:

(a) a warning merely informs a visitor of a danger which he can guard against if he wishes. It will be a question of fact in each case whether the warning is enough on its own to make the visitor reasonably safe, so discharging the occupier's duty of care;

(b) knowledge of a risk, whilst not **enough** on its own, may be evidence that a visitor has willingly accepted the risk, so absolving the occupier from liability;

(c) an exemption clause or notice, provided it has been adequately brought to the visitor's attention, is a condition of entry; it simply says 'you can come in, on condition that I am not liable for any damage you suffer whilst you are on the premises.'.

The end result will be the same, in all three cases, i.e. an absence of liability on the part of the occupier.

7.5.9 CONTRIBUTORY NEGLIGENCE

Knowledge may also be evidence of contributory negligence on the part of the visitor. This, again, is a **general** defence in tort which you will have encountered in **Chapter 2**. The provisions of the Law Reform (Contributory Negligence) Act 1945 apply to liability arising under the 1957 Act. Thus, for example, in *Stone* v *Taffe* (see **Activity 36**) the visitor's damages were reduced because of his contributory negligence.

7.5.10 DAMAGE

Under s. 1(3) of the 1957 Act this covers personal injury (**presumably** this would include nervous shock), damage to the visitor's goods and consequential financial loss. The sub-section goes on to say that damage to 'property' includes 'the property of persons who are not themselves his visitors'. *Winfield* says (at p. 242) that would '. . . seem to allow an action by an owner who is not a visitor'. Unfortunately, however, the 1957 Act imposes its duty of care in favour of the visitor and much would depend on how a court would see the purpose, if a purposive interpretation were taken, of the Act. North, in 'Occupiers' Liability' (1957) argues that a third party **cannot** sue directly under the 1957 Act for damage to his property in the possession of a visitor. The visitor would technically be a bailee of the third party's goods and, whether the bailment was for reward or was of a gratuitous nature, the visitor would be liable to account over to the third party with regard to any damages received for damaged goods. In any case, the third party could sue the occupier **directly** under the Torts (Interference with Goods) Act 1977: under s. 1 of that Act 'negligence' is a form of interference with goods. You may wish at this point to refer to **Chapter 9**.

Please read about *Smith* v *Vange Scaffolding Ltd and Another* [1970] 1 All ER 249 in *Cases and Materials* (7.3.5), and write down a brief summary of the decision in that case.

Not only was the plaintiff successful in his claim against his employers. He succeeded also against the second defendants under the Occupiers' Liability Act 1957, and for their vicarious liability as well as their breach of certain statutory regulations pertaining to safety on building sites.

7.6 Occupiers' Liability to Entrants other than Visitors coming within the Terms of the 1957 Act

In practice this means liability towards 'trespassers', though we have seen it is not only these entrants who fall outside the protection of the 1957 Act. The Occupiers' Liability Act 1984 (*Cases and Materials* (7.4)) is the main focus of our attention at this stage, though it will be helpful generally to trace briefly the history of liability to trespassers and, indeed, essential in particular to understand the duty which the 1984 Act replaced, because that earlier duty will apply to cases not included within the terms of the 1984 Act.

7.6.1 TRESPASSERS

We will, however, first refresh our memories as to the definition of a 'trespasser'. What is important is not what is in the mind of the entrant, because one can trespass quite innocently. Honest mistake is no defence and liability **for** the tort of trespass to land on the part of the entrant in that sense is 'strict'. **Voluntary** movement is all that is required; there is no necessity for the entrant to intend to trespass. It is the intention of the occupier of the land in question that is important.

In *Addie* v *Dumbreck* [1929] AC 358 Lord Dunedin defined a trespasser as a person 'who goes to the land without invitation of any sort and whose presence is either unknown to the proprietor, or, if known, is practically objected to'.

Thus, the term 'trespasser' includes the 'guilty', as well as the 'innocent'. Someone who enters without permission is a trespasser; in **this** sense, there is no difference between a burglar or a person out for a walk in a field.

We will see, however, that the nature of the duty owed by the occupier may differ according to the nature of the trespasser. In any case, although all trespassers are guilty of illegal acts, i.e. the wrongful entry, trespassers such as burglars are likely to be met with the plea of *ex turpi causa non oritur actio*. You will recall this defence from **Chapter 2**.

Curiously, *ex turpi causa non oritur actio* is not pleaded against all trespassers; probably because modern law will not countenance a departure from an irreducible minimum of protection even for illegal entrants. It may also be the case that even burglars are protected against the infliction of intentional harm, the setting of traps or the creation of retributive dangers such as electrified fences. The application of force to illegal entrants can only in some cases be justified on grounds of self-defence or defence of others. It is long settled law that only 'reasonable' force can be used to eject trespassers. Indeed, occupiers may well find themselves facing criminal charges where unlawful force is used.

See also **7.6.4.2**.

7.6.2 THE ORIGINAL DUTY TO TRESPASSERS

Intentional harm inflicted on a trespasser was actionable unless it was reasonably necessary to protect the property from trespassers.

In *Bird* v *Holbrook* (1828) 4 Bing 628, an occupier of land set a trap for trespassers viz. a spring-gun, on his land. The plaintiff, a trespasser on the land, was injured by the device and the occupier, the defendant, was found liable under a principle of the common law to the effect that it is unlawful to inflict harm upon the person of another in an **intentional** and **indirect** way.

It is noteworthy that the course of action is not restricted to the context of occupation of land; and it is not a form of trespass to the person – thus proof of damage is essential. The decision in *Wilkinson* v *Downton* (see **10.6.2.2**) illustrates the application of a similar principle.

It became accepted that **deterrent** measures could reasonably by adopted by occupiers to discourage trespassers, but they were distinguished from measures which could be classed as **retributive** dangers. These measures of retribution gave rise to liability at common law.

It was a question of fact in each case whether a measure would be classified as 'deterrent' or 'retributive'. In general, dangers likely to do serious harm would be 'retributive'. An occupier could also be liable for injury inflicted **recklessly** on a trespasser.

In both cases, the occupier had to know of the trespasser's presence although it might be enough if a trespasser's presence was extremely likely. The leading case was *Addie* v *Dumbreck* [1929] AC 358.

7.6.3   THE DUTY OF COMMON HUMANITY

In *British Railways Board* v *Herrington* [1972] AC 877, the House of Lords rejected *Addie*. Their Lordships said a new duty was needed in the light of modern society: not only were there more children, but their parents had less control over them and they had fewer places in which to play. Furthermore, modern technology had produced greater dangers for them.

A six-year-old boy, the plaintiff, was playing with his friends on land bounded by an electrified railway line. He got through a fence in poor repair and fell on to a live line. The stationmaster had been warned of the condition of the fence and, despite his knowledge that children frequented the area, the fence had not been repaired.

The Court of Appeal found the defendants liable. The decision was based on the old test of reckless disregard for the safety of the trespasser.

The House of Lords held that, although the general rule remained that a person trespassed at his own risk, an occupier's duty was not limited to not harming the trespasser intentionally or recklessly. Where an occupier knew that there were, or were likely to be, trespassers on his land and that the **condition** of his land **or** an **activity** on it was likely to injure the trespasser, he must take reasonable steps to enable the trespasser to avoid that danger. This duty arose only where the probability of the danger was such that the occupier ought to act in 'common humanity'.

It was held that the Railways Board were in breach of this duty. They had brought on to their land an allurement, i.e. an electrified rail, and had not taken reasonable steps to prevent harm to the plaintiff.

Herrington introduced a duty of a very flexible nature; nowhere was 'common humanity' closely defined, their Lordships preferring a pragmatic approach which would enable the court to fashion the duty to fit the circumstances.

Lords Reid and Wilberforce said that the duty would vary 'according to [the] knowledge, ability and resources' of the occupier. It was a question of whether a conscientious, humane man with **this** occupier's knowledge, skill and resources, could reasonably have been expected to do something which would have avoided the accident. Their Lordships appeared to have a **subjective** test in mind. Lord Reid also said:

> [the occupier] might often reasonably think, weighing the seriousness of the damages and the degree of likelihood of trespassers coming against the burden he would have to incur in preventing their entry, or making his premises safe, or curtailing his own activities on his land, that he could not fairly be expected to do anything. But if he could at small trouble and expense take some effective action, again I think that most people would think it inhumane and culpable not to do that.

Lord Diplock said the 'kind of trespasser' (for example a burglar, vandal or child) could be an important factor, as was 'the degree of expectation that a trespasser will come...'. Lord Wilberforce mentioned 'the nature and degree of the danger'.

The *Herrington* duty was not developed exclusively for trespassing children.

Please leave your main reading for a little while and concentrate on the Court of Appeal decision in *Pannett* v *McGuiness and Co. Ltd* [1972] 3 All ER 137 in *Cases and Materials* (7.4.1). What do you think was the court's interpretation in this case of the ruling in *Herrington*?

The Court of Appeal appeared to reject any distinction of substance between 'common humanity' and 'reasonable care' in ordinary negligence. Lord Denning, in particular, seemed to equate the *Herrington* duty with the idea of duty in the tort of negligence.

According to Neill LJ in *Revill* v *Newbery* [1996] 1 All ER 291 (CA), *Herrington* enabled a trespasser to recover damages in negligence. (See **7.6.4.2.**)

The *Herrington* cases may today be used not only in those circumstances where the 1984 Act does not apply; they may also be helpful for **illustrative** purposes (only) in connection with arguments concerning liability imposed by the 1984 Act.

You will find that there is a paucity of case law authority on the terms of the 1984 Act.

7.6.4 LIABILITY ARISING UNDER THE OCCUPIERS' LIABILITY ACT 1984

7.6.4.1 Entrants to whom a duty is owed

Section 1 of the 1984 Act says it replaces the rules of the common law governing the duty of an occupier of premises to 'persons other than his visitors'. These persons are trespassers, those who enter under private rights of way or by virtue of s. 60 of the National Parks and Access to the Countryside Act 1949.

7.6.4.2 The duty arising under the Act

The Act says, in s. 1(1) that its objective is to determine:

(a) whether any duty is owed by a person **as occupier of premises** to persons other than his visitors in respect of any risk of their suffering injury on the premises by reason of **any danger due to the state of the premises or to things done or omitted to be done on them**; and

(b) if so, what that duty is. (*emphasis added*)

It can be seen from the language used that so-called current activities may not be covered by this Act (see **7.5.1**). There, are however, *obiter* opinions in the House of Lords in *Herrington* (above) that there was no distinction in the doctrine of common humanity between the occupancy duty and activities, but this case could only be used as a **persuasive** authority in the context of liability arising under the 1984 Act.

In an earlier case, *Videan* v *British Transport Commission* [1963] 2 All ER 560 (see **Activity 4**), which was concerned with the *Addie* v *Dumbreck* duty (see **7.6.2**), Pearson LJ expressed the opinion that current activities came within the terms of the then occupiers' duty.

The Law Commission in its 1976 Report (see below) agreed with the view that the 1957 Act (see above) did not extend to activities, which came within the terms of common law negligence. It was also the Commission's view that the 1984 Act should not embrace activities. It was said that the liability of an occupier under statute should relate only to something which made the premises unsafe, because not all activities or omissions occurring on premises were concerned with the safety of premises as such. In that sense the occupier in relation to activities would be in the same position as a non-occupier who had injured someone on premises:

> Thus, if a person (whether an occupier or not) while shooting rabbits injures another person (whether a trespasser or not), whether he is liable will depend on the ordinary principles of negligence at common law (para. 26).

In *Revill* v *Newbery* (see below) Neill LJ agreed with this line of reasoning. As his Lordship acknowledged, however,

> This solution [that an occupiers' liability for current activities should be determined by reference to the ordinary principles of common law negligence] may give rise to difficulties. Thus, it would seem that if an occupier of land arranges for a party to shoot on his land and one of the party negligently injures a trespasser, the occupier might be liable under s. 1 of the 1984 Act if the conditions set out in s. 1(3) are fulfilled. On the other hand, if he goes out shooting alone his liability, if any, would be determined under the common law of negligence.

We will return to this matter of current activities when we examine the decision in *Revill* (below).

The duty imposed by the 1984 Act is set out in s. 1(4) as follows:

> Where, by virtue of this section, an occupier of premises owes a duty to another in respect of such a risk, the duty is to take such care as is reasonable in all the circumstances of the case to see that he does not suffer injury on the premises by reason of the danger concerned.

This is a duty of a flexible nature, adaptable to widely varying circumstances. It has to be of this nature, to cope with the range of entrants it covers. Not only trespassers are protected by this legislation, as we have seen; but trespassers themselves are a mixed bunch, ranging from the wandering child to the rampaging burglar and beyond. It is stating the obvious to point out that a **negligent** act, as well as an **intentional** one could come within the terms of this duty.

There is, however, a problem with this duty.

Look at the wording carefully. Can you spot the difficulty?

The point to be made is this: there is no 'automatic' duty. Section 1(4) says **'where, by virtue of this section** [a duty is owed] **in respect of such a risk** . . .'. There is no doubt that there is a reference here to some pre-conditions. These are to be found in s. 1(3) which provides as follows:

> An occupier of premises owes a duty to another (not being his visitor) in respect of any such risk as is referred to in subsection (1) above if –
> (a)   he is aware of the danger or has reasonable grounds to believe that it exists;
> (b)   he knows or has reasonable grounds to believe that the other is in the vicinity of the danger concerned or that he may come into the vicinity of the danger (in either case, whether the other has lawful authority for being in that vicinity or not); and
> (c)   the risk is one against which, in all the circumstances of the case, he may reasonably be expected to offer the other some protection.

You must be aware that the duty imposed by the Act arises **only** if these three conditions are satisfied.

This provision is potentially confusing, because it seems to consist of a mixture of **subjective** and **objective** tests. We have seen that *Herrington* imposed an arguably **subjective** test: 'What could reasonably be expected of **this** occupier in the circumstances?'.

The Law Commission, on whose Report entitled 'Liability for Damage or Injury to Trespassers and Related Questions of Occupiers' Liability' (Report No. 75, Cmnd 6428), 1976, the 1984 Act was based intended that the replacement duty for *Herrington* should be of an objective nature: 'What could be expected of a reasonable person in those circumstances?'. It is debatable whether that purpose has been achieved.

As E. McKendrick, *Tort Textbook*, London: HLT Publications, 1992 (p. 214) puts it:

> The words 'he knows' suggest a subjective test, but the words 'has reasonable grounds to believe' suggest an objective test.

He further points out that it is perhaps intended:

> that the Act shall apply to the situation where the occupier knows or is aware of the primary facts but fails to draw the reasonable inference from the known facts . . . It is

difficult to see how the Act could apply to the situation where the occupier is unaware of the primary facts in circumstances where the reasonable occupier would have been so aware.

On the other hand, according to *Winfield* (p. 244):

> In some respects this approach [in the 1984 Act] is very close to that of the common duty of care and the ordinary negligence duty: in particular, the occupier incurs liability where he does not know but **ought** to know the facts which would signal to a reasonable man the presence of a trespasser or of the danger to him; and the standard appears to be objective and not conditional by the occupier's own resources . . .

It cannot be denied, however, that there appears to be a conflict in the wording between s. 1(3) and s. 1(4); in other words, whilst it is clear that the standard of duty laid down in s. 1(4) is of an objective nature, it is not so clear that the same can be said of the standard laid down in s. 1(3) which must be satisfied before that duty arises.

There is authority going both ways in the Court of Appeal in *White v St Albans City and District Council, The Times*, 12 March 1990. In this case, the plaintiff easily got through an inadequate fence (though it was not in disrepair) on the defendant's land in order to take a short cut. He was injured when he fell into a trench which he could not have been expected to see. This was a danger of which the defendant was actually aware, so there was no argument on that point. What was in issue was knowledge of someone's presence in the vicinity of the danger (s. 1(3)(b)). It was found that there was no evidence that the land was used as a short cut, and there was no reason for the defendant to believe that there would be anyone in the vicinity of the danger. This was said to be a matter of fact in each case. The plaintiff's argument that it was sufficient to satisfy s. 1(3)(b) on the present facts to show that the occupier had fenced his land, thereby establishing that there was reason to believe that someone was likely to come into the vicinity of the danger, was not accepted by the court. The court said that each case had to be looked at according to the actual state of affairs on the land at the time of the injury.

In *Swain v Puri* [1996] PIQR P442, the Court of Appeal had to consider a claim by a **trespasser** under s. 1 of the Occupiers' Liability Act 1984. A boy aged nine fell from the roof of a disused factory and claimed damages for his injuries from the occupier. It was argued for the plaintiff that he was owed a duty of care under the Act, i.e. that at the time of the trespass there had been **reasonable grounds** for **believing** that children would trespass for the purposes of s. 1(3)(b) of the Act.

The court found **against** a duty of care on the facts. Although the fences round the premises were by no means 'intruder proof', they were of a substantial nature and there was no evidence of earlier trespass – thus the occupiers had **no** 'reason to believe' that children would climb on to the roof. 'Reasonable grounds to believe' in the context of s. 1(3)(b) meant that the occupier must have either **actual** knowledge of the relevant facts or **know of** facts which would provide **evidence** of 'grounds to believe' that a certain state of affairs existed. **Constructive** knowledge (based on an argument that the occupier 'ought to have known') was insufficient for the purposes of s. 1(3)(b).

In *Revill v Newbery* [1996] 1 All ER 291, the plaintiff and another person trespassed on the defendant's premises by attempting to break into a shed on his allotment. At the time, the defendant, aged 76, was sleeping in the shed in order to guard his belongings from the depredations of thieves and vandals. He was wakened by the sounds of the attempted entry and picked up his shotgun, firing it through a small hole in the door of the shed. His shot hit the plantiff, wounding him in the arm and the chest.

At first instance, the defendant was found liable to the plaintiff in common law negligence which, in the circumstances of the case, was coterminous with the terms of s. 1 of the Occupiers' Liability Act 1984. The defences of self-defence and *ex turpi causa non oritur actio* were rejected, but the plaintiff was found to be two-thirds contributorily negligent under the terms of the Law Reform (Contributory Negligence) Act 1945.

Neill LJ delivered the main judgment in the Court of Appeal. It was his Lordship's opinion that the defendant's conduct in the present case fell within the terms of a current activity, and that if he were to be liable to the plaintiff it would have to be on the basis of an application of the principles of common law negligence; the defendant could not be liable *qua* (as) occupier under s. 1 of the 1984 Act.

His Lordship quoted from the Law Commission's 1976 Report (see below):

> It seems clear that the wording [of the Occupiers' Liability Act 1957 — see **7.5.1**] is apt to cover conduct on the premises which causes a continuing source of danger, thereby rendering it unsafe. It is less clear whether the words have the effect of bringing within the scope of the 1957 Act all claims for injuries on the occupiers' premises arising from every kind of activity or omission on them irrespective of whether they are connected with the safety of those premises as such . . .

He agreed with the view expressed by the Commission that so-called activities were not caught by either the 1957 Act or the 1984 Act (both Acts use much the same wording in this respect, as we have already seen above and at **7.5.1**) and concluded that s. 1 of the 1984 Act applied only to an occupier **as occupier**:

> Section 1 is concerned with the safety of the premises **and** [emphasis added] with the dangers due to things done or omitted to be done on the premises. [It will be noted that his Lordship uses the connecting word 'and' rather than 'or' which is the word in the relevant legislation; 'or' being a word which introduces alternatives. Presumably this is an error in transcription.] In concluding whether Mr Newbery is liable on the facts of this case, the fact that he was the occupier is irrelevant. Accordingly . . . [the liability of the defendant is to be considered] in the same way as one would have examined the liability of a third person, for example a friend of Mr Newbery who was staying in the hut, if that third person had fired the shot.

It was his Lordship's opinion, however, that although the 1984 Act did not apply to current activities it was necessary to look at the duty laid down by the Act in order to determine the content of the common law duty of care in negligence which did apply to current activities.

Thus, on the facts of the present case, since the defendant was engaged in an activity rather than playing the role of occupier as such, his liability would be determined at common law and the parameters of that liability would be set by reference to the provisions of the 1984 Act.

The conditions set out in s. 1(3) were to be satisfied and s. 1(4) defined the relevant standard of care. For example, the 'danger' referred to in s. 1(3)(b) was the gun which was about to be discharged. This was not a mere warning shot, said his Lordship, it was a shot likely to hit anyone in the vicinity of the door to the shed.

Neill LJ agreed with the finding at first instance, and found that the defendant was liable by applying principles of law similar to those set out in s. 1 of the 1984 Act.

Evans LJ said:

> I agree . . . with Neill LJ that it is not necessary to decide in the present case whether the statutory duty owed by an occupier under s. 1 of the 1984 Act includes activities which he engages in personally on the premises. I therefore express no concluded view in that issue. With the sole reservation, I entirely agree with his judgment.

This is an interesting observation, because Neill LJ appeared to agree with the view that activities did *not* come within the ambit of the 1984 Act and proceeded accordingly. His Lordship found that the defendant was liable under the terms of the activity duty, determined by reference to the 1984 Act. It is not clear, therefore, which source of liability Evans LJ has in mind.

Millett LJ, like Evans LJ, agreed with Neill LJ in dismissing the appeal: 'For the defendant's conduct was clearly dangerous and bordered on reckless . . .'.

If the reasoning of Neill LJ is correct it has two important effects on the law. First, it means that the 1984 Act is *in effect* extended to cover current activities and, secondly, it has the effect of extending that Act to cover the liability of non-occupiers in relation to activities. It may be that his Lordship intended only occupiers' activities to be determined by reference to the provisions of the 1984 Act, though this point is not explicit in the judgment.

With regard to the defendant's plea of *ex turpi causa non oritur actio* (see **2.3.2**), Neill LJ considered whether the plaintiff's criminal conduct made it impossible for the court to set a standard of care in the circumstances of the case. He said that the existence of s. 1 of the 1984 Act makes it clear that Parliament is of the opinion a burglar cannot be treated as an outlaw, and the Law Commission in its 1976 Report was in favour of some duty being owed, even to a trespasser 'engaged in a serious criminal enterprise'. In his Lordship's opinion the liability of a person in the defendant's position was to be decided according to a test 'similar to that set out in s. 1(4) of the 1984 Act'.

> There is in my view no room for a two-stage determination whereby the court considers first whether there has been a breach of duty and then considers whether notwithstanding a breach the plaintiff is barred from recovering by reason of the fact that he has engaged in crime.

Evans LJ agreed that a trespasser/criminal is not an outlaw, and is owed a minimal duty. In the present case there was no illegal transaction or criminal joint enterprise involved.

On self-defence, pleaded by the defendant, his Lordship concluded that the defendant had used unjustified violence towards the plaintiff, which exceeded that permitted for self-defence.

Millett LJ said:

> . . . The assailant or intruder may be met with reasonable force but no more; the use of excessive violence against him is an actionable wrong. It follows . . . that there is no place for the doctrine *ex turpi causa non oritur actio* in this context. If the doctrine applied, any claim by the assailant or trespasser would be barred no matter how excessive or unreasonable the force used against him.

The Court of Appeal upheld the decision at first instance, in which the defendant was found liable in common law negligence, although the plaintiff's damages were reduced by two-thirds for his contributory negligence (under the terms of the Law Reform (Contributory Negligence) Act 1945).

A final point concerning this case can be made; Rougier J at first instance (*The Times*, 1 December 1994), said:

> [*Ex turpi causa* applied only where] . . . the injury complained of was so closely interwoven in the illegal or criminal act as to be virtually a part of it or if it was a direct uninterrupted consequence of that illegal act.

> The discharge of a shot gun towards burglars who are not displaying any intention of resorting to violence to the person is, in my judgment, out of all proportion to the threat involved, even making all due allowance for the agony of the moment, and therefore any injury, sustained by such discharge cannot be said to be an integral part nor a necessarily direct consequence of the burglary.

Volenti non fit injuria

Section 1(6) embodies this defence. It says:

> No duty is owed by virtue of this section to any person in respect of risks willingly accepted as his by that person (the question whether a risk was so accepted to be decided on the same principles as in other cases in which one person owes a duty of care to another).

Obviously, the usual conditions pertaining to the defence will apply: you may care to refer to **Chapter 2**, in which the general defences in tort, including *volenti*, are discussed.

In the present context, the issue of whether *volenti* applies may be even more problematic than it is in general. We have already seen that the 1984 Act embraces both unlawful non-visitors (i.e. trespassers) as well as lawful non-visitors (i.e. those entering under private rights of way, as well as those entering by authority of the National Parks and Access to the Countryside Act 1949). That, however, is not the only problem because not even all trespassers are the same, and so it is evident that the **factual** interpretation of the duty of care laid down in the 1984 Act is likely to vary enormously between different entrants, not least between different 'types' of trespasser.

It would not be unreasonable to suggest that this will also be the case with the application of *volenti*.

Jones (p. 204) argues, for example, that where **trespassers** are concerned (and by this he seems to mean **adult** trespassers, though he does not make the point explicit) the courts take an **objective** approach to the question of 'agreement' (necessary for all *volenti* cases) 'so that it is possible to argue that knowledge of **a** risk plus entry on to the land renders a trespasser *volenti*'. He says it would be more difficult to sustain this argument in the case of a **lawful** non-visitor.

Warnings and other measures bringing dangers to the attention of the entrant

According to s. 1(5):

> Any duty owed by virtue of this section in respect of a risk may, in an appropriate case, be discharged by taking such steps as are reasonable in all the circumstances of the case to give warning of the danger concerned or to discourage persons from incurring the risk.

Clearly, warning notices and other measures are envisaged in this context.

Have a close look at the wording of this sub-section (i.e. s. 1(5) of the 1984 Act) and compare it with the provision concerning 'warning' in s. 2(4)(a) of the 1957 Act. Write down any differences you can see between the two provisions.

There are two differences to note here:

(a)   in the 1957 Act a warning is not sufficient 'without more', unless

(b)   it is enough in all the circumstances to make the visitor reasonably safe.

These conditions are absent from the 1984 Act provision, suggesting that it may be easier for an occupier to discharge his duty under s. 1(5) than would be the case under s. 2(4)(a) of the 1957 Act. In other words, a warning may have much more 'bite' under the 1984 Act.

It is true that more than a mere notice may be required in the case of children, especially perhaps where 'allurements' are concerned. The notion of allurement was an important factor in *Herrington* (see **7.6.3**). Other measures may be needed in such cases.

In this context, 'deterrent' and 'retributive' measures may be of importance. You may recall that this matter was the subject of our earlier attention.

Section 1(5) does refer to 'the danger' and 'the risk' and it is therefore arguable that any warning ought to make it reasonably clear that there is some particular danger or risk for the entrant to avoid. A simply worded notice, for example saying 'Keep Out. Private' might not be enough, because it would do no more than inform the entrant that he would be a trespasser if he entered. Of course, some dangers are pretty obvious, even behind closed doors, and such a notice might be sufficient in an appropriate case with regard to **those** dangers.

It is quite common today for building sites to have, in addition to such measures as fencing and hoarding, notices displayed at strategic points warning of general danger. A notice observed recently stated:

NOTICE

WARNING TO PUBLIC. This building site is private property. No unauthorised persons allowed. Liability will not be accepted by the builder for any injury sustained by trespassers.

NOTICE TO PARENTS. Parents are especially requested to warn children of the dangers and consequences of trespassing on this site.

This is an obvious attempt to activate s. 1(5), although the notice is couched in **general** terms and it may be thought that it would not be sufficient to warn of specific dangers.

Pause here for a little while. Can you think of any good reason why someone might not be too specific in their warnings about dangers on their premises, other than ignorance of or uncertainty about the law?

You might have thought that a warning which **was** specific in this sense could, in some situations, make it easier for an entrant to establish liability because it could trigger s. 1(3) of the 1984 Act.

Notices like the one detailed above raise another point. This can be expressed in the question: 'can an occupier expect very young trespassers to be accompanied by an adult?'. In other words, 'does the principle of *Phipps* v *Rochester Corporation* (see **7.5.5.2**) apply also to trespassing children?'

To pose another question, 'is the warning notice given above appealing for prudent parents, and if it is will it have any legal significance?'.

There seems to be no good legal reason why *Phipps* should not also apply in the context of trespass. Both Jones (p. 203) and *Winfield* (p. 244) are of this opinion.

Exclusion of liability

We have to deal here with two points, the second of which awaits resolution.

First, the Unfair Contract Terms Act 1977 does not apply to the duty laid down in the 1984 Act: the 1977 Act refers only to common law duties, and the common duty of care under the 1957 Act. (There is doubt, however, whether the doctrine of 'common humanity' formulated in *Herrington* comes within the terms of the 1977 Act.)

Secondly, the 1984 Act makes no reference at all to the question of exclusion of liability, although the Law Commission (Cmnd 6428) did recommend that occupiers should be able to exclude their liability. It seems to be the general opinion amongst writers that occupiers cannot, as a matter of public policy, avoid their statutory obligations in the absence of clear words allowing them to do so. In any event, it is also argued, the standard of care laid down to trespassers (whether it is the original common law standard, or that of common humanity, or that laid down in the 1984 Act) consists of an **irreducible minimum** which public policy dictates cannot be excluded.

Jones, however, argues (p. 205) that Parliament cannot have intended that occupiers should be in a worse position *vis-à-vis* non-visitors than they are in relation to their lawful visitors. Thus, it may be that the duty laid down in the 1984 Act **can** be excluded. (It will be recalled that the 1957 Act allows liability to be excluded, in certain circumstances.) If this argument is correct, he continues, occupiers should be free to exclude their liability under the 1984 Act but **not** liability for an irreducible minimum, which would be liability for intentional or reckless conduct, i.e. the 'original' common law duty. He would draw a distinction, however, between trespassers and those who enter under a private right of way or the 1949 Act (see **7.6.4.1**): liability towards **these** entrants should not be excludable at **all**.

Finally, Jones says (p. 195) that if there is a minimum standard which cannot be excluded in the case of trespassers the argument must apply with even more force to lawful visitors in those cases where the 1957 Act duty can be excluded.

7.6.4.3 Damage

Liability under the 1984 Act is limited to **personal injury**, although that is defined quite widely. The Act says, in s. 1(8) and (9):

> (8) Where a person owes a duty by virtue of this section, he does not, by reason of any breach of the duty, incur any liability in respect of any loss of or damage to property.

> (9) In this section –
> 'highway' means any part of a highway other than a ferry or waterway;
> 'injury' means anything resulting in death or personal injury, including any disease and any impairment of physical or mental condition; and
> 'moveable structure' includes any vessel, vehicle or aircraft.

It seems that an injured entrant could not also claim for loss even of his clothes under the 1984 Act. Any claim for loss of or damage to 'property' must be brought under some appropriate common law principle.

Can you think of any appropriate common law action?

You might have listed the following:

(a)   presumably, the doctrine of 'common humanity' might apply, but this was developed **principally** for personal injury;

(b)   the ruling in *Addie* v *Dumbreck* (see **7.5.4.1**);

(c)   if *Tutton* v *AD Walter* [1986] QB 61, a case you have encountered in **Chapter 3**, is good authority the ordinary law of negligence may be used in such circumstances. Liability in negligence towards 'trespassing' bees was imposed on an occupier in that case.

7.7   Summary

Liability for dangerous premises and land comes in many guises and is of a labyrinthine nature. We are concerned with its **tortious** aspects, but it is impossible to ignore the **contractual** and **statutory** aspects of the subject. It is not possible to avoid these different aspects of the subject because at many points they impinge upon and overlap with one another.

It is clearly the case that on many occasions an aggrieved person will find it more advantageous to sue in contract, or bring proceedings under some special statutory provision relating to housing conditions, rather than sue in tort. Often, statutes imply into contracts of letting terms favourable to tenants, so strengthening the cause of action in contract. That leads to another point: much may depend in these 'premises' cases on **who** is suing and **who** is being sued. In many instances, there will be no contractual relations between the parties and in others there may be some obstacle in the way of an action in contract; it is here where **tortious** liability has to be considered.

In tort, a wide range of **potential** defendants is available, e.g. builders, local authorities, vendors, architects, surveyors, structural engineers, designers, developers and occupiers. It is our **main** concern to examine liability arising under the Defective Premises Act 1972, and that of occupiers, indeed this subject is often called simply 'occupiers' liability', but we cannot restrict our attention to these topics. Accordingly, we begin by looking at liability arising under the general law of negligence, and it is here where we find such a potentially wide range of persons who might be liable to a fairly restricted range of plaintiffs.

At this point we are concerned principally with the line of cases beginning with *Dutton* and ending with *Murphy*. We have seen, of course, that these are not only 'premises' cases; they are also important authorities on the question of recovery for 'pure' economic loss, as well as having standing on the general issue of 'duty of care' in negligence.

D & F Estates and *Murphy* have severely restricted liability for premises in the general tort of negligence, in fact *Murphy* finally overruled *Anns* itself. In **broad** terms, since very few rules are completely watertight, liability is limited to cases where defective premises produce **latent** defects which cause **actual physical** damage to the person and/or **separate** property.

Liability for the condition of premises may arise through **the rules of a club**. In *Robertson* v *Ridley* [1989] 2 All ER 474 the plaintiff, a member of a club (an unincorporated association) was injured on club premises. He fell off his motor cycle when leaving the premises as a result of failing to see a pothole in the driveway. He sued the chairman and secretary (the club officers), arguing that since the club's rules provided that they had legal responsibility for the conduct of the club a duty was owed to him to keep the premises in a reasonable state of repair and safety. It was found that there was no express provision in the rules concerning the condition of the premises, therefore there was no duty of care owed to the plaintiff in the terms claimed. The common law rule that no liability existed between an unincorporated association (or its members) and individual members applied in the present circumstances.

The Defective Premises Act 1972, however, not only imposes liability of a wider nature; it also imposes **strict** liability in s. 1. Other liability is provided for elsewhere in the Act. This Act contains features of both tortious and contractual liability, though the cause of action lies in tort. It replaces s. 4 of the Occupiers' Liability Act 1957 with a new s. 4 of its own; this section imposes a wide duty of reasonable care, towards his tenants and **others**, upon a landlord of premises.

Then we come to the Occupiers' Liability Act 1957, which imposes a duty upon 'occupiers' of 'premises' to take reasonable care for the safety of their '**lawful** visitors'; in other words the Act imposes a 'negligence duty'. All these expressions, and others including the 'common duty of care', can and do raise problems of interpretation which have to be resolved where possible by reference to **case law**.

The Unfair Contract Terms Act 1977 is involved in relation to the liability of 'business' occupiers.

Traditionally, the law has offered more protection from liability to occupiers where entrants have been trespassers, rather than lawful visitors. Today, the main body of law on this topic is contained in the Occupiers' Liability Act 1984.

There is a big difference between the law governing liability to trespassers as it used to be and the present-day duty. The 1984 Act duty is of a very flexible nature, and is quite capable of including an act of negligence on the part of an occupier. That would, at one time have been quite unthinkable: the original duty to trespassers was limited to **intentional** or **reckless** behaviour. This was later changed, though not until 1972 in *Herrington*, to the duty to act with 'common humanity' which is itself flexible enough to embrace negligence.

It must be said, however, that although both Occupiers' Liability Acts impose standards of care which are very close, it is evident that the 1984 Act is a very different creature from the 1957 Act. In the case of the former Act, certain difficult conditions, **three** in number, have to be satisfied before the duty can be activated.

The 1957 Act deals with what might be termed, relatively at least, a homogeneous class of entrant, i.e. the lawful visitor. Under the 1984 Act, not only does the problem of a wide range of **trespassers** have to be faced, from the 'deprived' to the 'depraved', but there is also the fact that some **lawful** entrants only get protection under the Act, i.e. those entering under a private right of way and under the National Parks and Access to the Countryside Act 1949. Inevitably, any decision made on the facts under the 1984 Act must reflect this state of affairs.

Unfortunately, there is a distinct lack of case law on the interpretation of this Act. Both Acts deal with the **safety** of the premises in question, and therefore even 'activities' (if they are caught by the legislation) must relate to that issue. It is arguable that where the occupier is engaged in some pursuit which is not directly connected with **this** sort of safety, for example, injury is sustained as a result of the negligent shooting of pigeons by the occupier on his land, liability would lie in ordinary negligence.

Finally, whilst the 1957 Act covers damage to goods as well as personal injury, the 1984 Act imposes liability **only** for **personal injury**. The latter Act, however, offers a wide definition of 'personal injury', to include 'disease' or 'impairment of a mental condition'. This might include 'nervous shock'. It would be surprising if the 1957 Act could not be interpreted in similar fashion.

7.8   Further Reading

Hepple, B.A., and Matthews, M.H., *Tort: Cases and Materials*, 5th edn, London: Butterworths, 1996, Chapter 9.
Jones, M., *Textbook on Torts*, 5th edn, London: Blackstone Press, 1996, Chapter 6.
McKendrick, E., *Tort Textbook*, 6th edn, London: HLT Publications, 1992, Chapter 17.
Markesinis, B.S., and Deakin, S.F., *Tort Law*, 3rd edn, Oxford: Oxford University Press, 1994, pp. 280–307, 325–343.
North, P.M., *Occupiers' Liability*, London: Butterworths, 1971, generally.
Salmond and Heuston, *Law of Torts*, 21st edn, London: Sweet & Maxwell, 1996, Chapter 11.
Spencer, J.R., 'The Defective Premises Act 1972 — Defective Law and Defective Law Reform' (1974) 33 CLJ 307.
Stanton, K., *Modern Law of Tort*, London: Sweet & Maxwell, 1994, pp. 193–203.
Street on Torts, 9th edn, London: Butterworths, 1993, Chapter 16.
Winfield and Jolowicz on Tort, 14th edn, London: Sweet & Maxwell, 1994, Chapter 9.

7.9   End of Chapter Assessment Question

Lax, a students' law society, has organised a dance for its members only at Isadora's, a local nightspot. At the time of the dance the management of Isadora's are in the process of having a new lighting system installed by Flashers Ltd, electrical contractors, and a notice at the entrance to the club reads, 'Beware. Electrical Work in Progress'. Art and Bart, two members of Lax, and Catherine, Bart's 15-year-old girlfriend, turn up for the dance and are admitted on producing tickets which state, 'Valid to Lax members only'. Art is injured when he trips over a trestle left by Flashers in the foyer, which is dimly lit. Bart is injured when a revolving light falls on his head as he is dancing. Catherine goes in search of a toilet through a door marked 'private' and is electrocuted when she feels for a light switch and touches some bare electric wires left by Flashers Ltd.

Discuss the tortious issues, if any, arising in these circumstances.

See *Cases and Materials* (7.6) for a specimen answer.

CHAPTER EIGHT

THE ACTION FOR BREACH OF STATUTORY DUTY AND THE EMPLOYERS' COMMON LAW DUTY OF CARE TO THEIR EMPLOYEES

8.1 Objectives

By the end of this chapter you should be able to:

■ understand the principles governing the common law action for breach of statutory duty;

■ assess, in particular, the conditions that a plaintiff must establish in order to succeed in an action for breach of statutory duty;

■ appreciate the nature and application of the employer's common law duty of care to his employee;

■ distinguish between the two causes of action.

8.2 Introduction

In this chapter you will be reading about **two distinct** causes of action in tort:

(a) the action for breach of statutory duty; and
(b) the employer's common law duty of care to his employees.

The former cause of action is based on somewhat tenuous propositions and is replete with policy considerations. It is not unlike the 'duty of care' issue in the tort of negligence. On the other hand, the common law duty to employees is much more straightforward: it is a corollary of the **contractual** relationship which exists between the parties. Although this action lies in **negligence**, it is a special form of that liability and is **not** the result of an application of the *Donoghue* principle.

You might well be wondering why the two torts are being treated together. If this question **is** running through your mind you will have identified a very important practical point. In practice, many plaintiffs are injured at the workplace and bring actions under **both** torts.

Naturally, they will use the employer's common law duty; but they are also able to point to a wide range of **statutes** which have been passed over the years to regulate safety at work, and there is a lot of accumulated case law establishing the availability of the action for breach of statutory duty.

It must not be thought, however, that this latter action is available only to employees who are injured at work. You will see, later, that the cause of action theorectically applies in **any** appropriate set of circumstances. Thus, in that sense, it has a much wider jurisdiction than the employer's duty of care at common law.

The employment relationship is further complicated in that the principle of **vicarious** liability is often brought into play. (Vicarious liability is dealt with as a topic in **Chapter 1.**) It is quite common, in fact, for an employee to sue his employer **vicariously** for the tort of **another employee and** sue the employer for breach of his **own, primary** duty (i.e. the common law duty outlined above) **and** sue the employer for breach of some statute, for example the Factories Act 1961.

We will now consider in detail the two causes of action.

8.3   The Action for Breach of Statutory Duty

Some statutes have been passed **specifically to provide a remedy in tort**: for example the Nuclear Installations Act 1965 and the Occupiers' Liability Act 1984. New torts may be created by statute, such as the tort concerning illegal eviction, provided for in the Housing Act 1988.

Many statutes, such as the Occupiers' Liability Act 1957, **consolidate** the previous common law, or provide special schemes of compensation, for example, the Vaccine Damage Payments Act 1979.

Other statutes contain sections **specifically** preventing action in tort, when their provisions are breached.

Can you guess what the next point is going to be?

The next point is that whilst no problems are encountered with statutes such as those mentioned, it is a different matter where statutes are **silent** on the question of civil liability in **tort**. In other words, the whole problem here is concerned with legislation which says **nothing** about claims for compensation in tort. As *Winfield* (p. 189) puts it:

What it [the chapter] is concerned with is when a court will conclude that a statute which is primarily regulatory or criminal in its purpose should be treated as giving rise to a civil action at the suit of a person who is injured as a result of non-compliance with it. Fundamentally, the question is one of interpretation of the particular statute but enough case law has accumulated around the subject to require treatment in a book on torts.

It is **this** type of statute on which we focus our attention in this chapter, although we also speak of an 'action for breach of statutory duty' when referring to an action brought under, for example, the Occupiers' Liability Act 1957.

8.3.1   HOW IS IT DONE?

The law reports are full of cases in which plaintiffs have been successful in their claims for damages for breaches of statutory duty, although the statutes themselves have made no apparent provision for this. There are also many cases where such claims have failed miserably. Why should this be so? Is it all a matter of luck? Why should some claims be regarded as meritorious, whilst others are dismissed?

It is apparent that the answer depends on the interpretation placed upon the statute(s) in question by the court, in the particular case. Since 'statutory interpretation' is involved, the 'Mischief Rule' and other guides to statutory interpretation will be important, and you should refer to your earlier studies on this topic, or consult **either** or **both** of the following:

Cross, R., *Statutory Interpretation*, 3rd edn (Bell, J. and Engle, G.), London: Butterworths, 1995.
Miers, D.R. and Page, A.C., *Legislation*, 2nd edn, London: Sweet & Maxwell, 1990.

An action may be brought in tort for damage sustained as a result of the breach of a statutory duty, if the true construction of the statute establishes that it was the intention of the legislature that such a remedy should be available. It is the express or presumed intention of the legislature that determines whether there is a civil action for breach of statutory duty. Put in these terms the issue looks deceptively simple, but in truth the litigant who decides to bring such an action is often entering a legal minefield.

Salmond puts the matter into perspective: 'It is doubtful . . . if any general principle can be found to explain all the cases on the subject'. Again, at p. 252, '. . . much depends in each case upon the context of the statute and the court's perception of the policy considerations involved'.

Lord Denning in *Ex parte Island Records Ltd* [1978] 1 Ch 122, went so far as to say that the court might as well 'toss a coin' to decide the issue. He was referring to certain 'presumptions' which have become established guides for the courts, in helping them to determine whether or not a civil action in tort is available in a difficult case. In his Lordship's opinion, there was so much conflict between the presumptions that he found them singularly unhelpful.

However, whilst Lord Denning would simply reject them and decide each case on its 'facts' or 'merits', these presumptions, through the force of precedent, seem to be firmly established in the law and we must examine them in some detail in order to see 'how it is done'.

Before we do that, it will be helpful to take a brief look at the historical development of the action for breach of statutory duty.

8.3.2   BACKGROUND TO THE ACTION

Actions for breach of statutory duty are as old as the statute of Westminster II of 1285, but the modern action on the case dates from *Ashby* v *White* (1703) 2 Ld Raym 938, in which a cause of action in tort was held to apply in respect of an interference with the plaintiff's statutory right to vote.

Indeed there are some old cases which assert that **wherever** a statutory duty exists, so the common law should allow a claim in tort to a person who can show he has suffered damage as a result of a breach of that duty.

This is not the modern approach. As Salmond says (p. 251): 'The modern approach is to limit the extent of liability by treating the question in each case as one relating to the intention of the legislature in creating the duty'.

As Lord Simonds said, in *Cutler* v *Wandsworth Stadium Ltd* [1949] AC 398: 'The answer must depend on a consideration of the whole Act and the circumstances, including the pre-existing law, in which it was enacted'.

Each statute tends to contain its own rules and peculiarities. Therefore, the golden rule in this context is that whether the plaintiff has a remedy in tort depends upon a construction of the particular statute.

As Lord Diplock said, in *Boyle* v *Kodak Ltd* [1969] 2 All ER 439: 'The statutes say nothing about civil remedies for breaches of their provisions. The judgments of the courts say all'. (His lordship was, of course, referring to the 'silent' statutes to which reference has been made.)

It is against this background that we now examine the 'presumptions' that Lord Denning found so difficult to apply in *Ex parte Island Records* (see **8.3.1**), in the context of the confusing and conflicting case law on the subject.

8.3.3 THE PRESUMPTIONS

It is generally accepted that the following statement by Lord Tenterden in *Doe d. Murray, Lord Bishop of Rochester* v *Bridges* (1854) 1 B & AD 847 is the starting point:

> where an Act creates an obligation, and enforces the performance in a specified manner, we take it as a general rule that performance cannot be enforced in any other manner . . . but [if] no mode of enforcing its performance is ordained, the common law may, in general, find a mode suited to the particular nature of the case.

It must **always** be the case, of course, that the relevant legislation places an obligation upon the defendant in the first place. The decision in *Harrison* v *National Coal Board* [1951] AC 639 provides a good illustration of this point. It was held in this case, by the House of Lords, that where statutory duties relating to safety in mines were imposed on the mine owner, and duties relating to shotfiring were imposed on the shotfirer, the mine owner was not liable for breach of statutory duty regarding injuries caused by the shotfiring.

We will now examine each of the presumptions outlined in Lord Tenterden's speech (above).

8.3.4 A SPECIAL REMEDY

Where a special remedy is provided in a statute, it is presumed in the absence of indications to the contrary to be the sole remedy, and to exclude a right of action in tort.

SAQ 91

At this point you may care to consider the set of facts given below, and then write down your opinion on the likely interpretation that would be given to them by a court. Do not be shy, you stand a 50-50 chance of being 'right'. *Cover up* 8.3.4.1 before you start.

The Waterworks Clauses Act 1847 required the defendants to maintain a certain pressure of water for the purpose of extinguishing fires. The statute provided that a failure to perform this duty should be an offence punishable by a fine of £10; it said nothing about any civil remedy. The defendants failed to maintain the pressure and the plaintiff's house caught fire and was burned down. He sued for damages for breach of statutory duty.

8.3.4.1   The answer

The facts you have just considered are taken from *Atkinson* v *Gateshead Waterworks Co.* (1877) 2 ExD 441. In this case the Court of Appeal held that, although the destruction was caused by the defendant's breach of statutory duty, the statute intended that the fine should be the sole remedy available and no action in tort could be entertained.

8.3.4.2   The special remedy approach qualified

However, Lord Diplock, in *Lonrho Ltd* v *Shell Petroleum Co. Ltd (No. 2)* [1981] 2 All ER 456, identified **two** exceptions to the case of a **criminal penalty**:

(a) where on the true construction of the Act it is apparent that the obligation or prohibition was imposed for the benefit of a particular class of individuals;
(b) where the statute creates a public right and an individual member of the public suffers particular, direct and substantial damages other and different from that which is common to the rest of the public.

In this case, the British Government had prohibited trade with Rhodesia (the former British colony, now Zimbabwe) under certain statutory powers, which provided for penalties of a criminal nature in the event of non-compliance with the prohibition. One oil company, Lonrho, which had complied with the sanctions and incurred heavy financial losses, sued competitors, who had breached the sanctions, for breach of their statutory obligations.

It was held that Lonrho did not come within either exception, because sanctions against Rhodesia were intended to create only **public** rights for **Rhodesian** citizens.

8.3.4.3   Benefit of a class

The first exception given by Lord Diplock is not new. It has long been the case that a plaintiff must usually show he is within the class of persons whom the statute was intended to protect.

According to Lord Diplock, in *Lonrho*, if a statute prescribes a duty for the protection of a class of the community, it is deemed, in the absence of evidence of a contrary intention, to confer a corresponding right of action on any member of the class who may suffer damage as a result of a breach of the duty.

It does not, however, follow **necessarily** that a plaintiff will be without a civil remedy merely because the statute can be shown to be a measure for protecting **only the public**. Of course, the burden on the plaintiff to prove that the statute has created a private right will be lighter where the duty is imposed for the benefit of a particular class of persons, of which he is a member.

In *Phillips* v *Britannia Hygienic Laundry Co.* [1923] 2 KB 832, Atkin LJ said:

> . . . the question is not to be solved by considering whether or not the person aggrieved can bring himself within some special class of the community or whether he is some designated individual. The duty may be of such paramount importance that it is owed to all the public. It would be strange if a less important duty, which is owed to a section of the public, may be enforced by an action, while a more important duty owed to the public at large cannot. The right of action does not depend on whether a statutory commandment or prohibition is pronounced for the benefit of the public or for the benefit of a class. It may be conferred on anyone who can bring himself within the benefit of the Act, including one who cannot be otherwise specified there as a person using the highway.

This dictum has been applied in many subsequent cases, and it indicates clearly that the 'protection of a class' test is not conclusive. The balance of authority, see *Lonrho* for example, suggests, however, that something in the nature of an overwhelming case would have to be shown by a person who could not bring himself within an appropriate 'class'.

In *Phillips* it was held that, although a major purpose of the Motor Cars (Use and Construction) Order 1904 was to prevent damage from unroadworthy vehicles to other property on the highway, a breach of the Order did not give rise to an action in tort at the suit of an individual.

A statutory duty may be so expressed as to limit the classes of persons for whose benefit it was designed, and in such a case it will depend on the construction of the relevant statutory provision whether the plaintiff is a member of the protected class.

In *Knapp* v *Railway Executive* [1949] 2 All ER 508, a statute provided that gates must be erected at level crossings and supervised and maintained by the railway authorities. A motorist attempted to stop his car at a crossing but, due to faulty brakes, the car hit the gate. The gate had not been maintained, and swung back and injured the train driver.

The court held that there was no remedy under the statute available to the train driver, against the railway authorities because the purpose of the statute was to protect **road users** against danger from the railway.

Again, in *Hartley* v *Mayoh & Co.* [1954] 1 QB 383, a fireman was electrocuted whilst attending to a fire at the defendants' factory. There existed statutory regulations for the protection of 'persons employed'. It was held that since firemen did not come within the description, his widow must fail in her action for breach of statutory duty by the defendants.

In *Keating* v *Elvan Reinforced Concrete Co.* [1968] 1 WLR 722, the court, as one of its reasons for holding that the Public Utilities Street Works Act 1950 gave no right of action to individuals, cited provisions in the Act creating **civil liabilities** in **favour** of **public authorities**.

In *Coote* v *Stone* [1971] 1 WLR 279, the Court of Appeal decided that the defendant's breach of a statutory regulation prohibiting the parking of a car on a 'clearway' did not give rise to a civil action by the plaintiff, who had collided with the defendant's parked car. The court classified the duty imposed by the regulations as being owed to the public and not to any class or individual.

The court reviewed some of the earlier traffic statutory duty cases, and gave as examples of breaches of public duties not giving rise to civil actions: parking on double yellow lines; failure to show rear lights during the hours of darkness; parking opposite double white lines.

As examples of breaches of such duties which did give rise to civil actions, as being not merely public duties but having also been designed to prevent injury to a class of persons, the court referred to *Monk* v *Warbey* (below); and breach of pedestrian crossing regulations.

Cases like *Coote* emphasise the important element of 'public' duties.

In general a statute creating public duties, and not affecting the rights of private persons, is enforceable only by criminal prosecution; or the Attorney-General may apply for an injunction; or application may be made for judicial review.

As Salmond puts it (p. 251): '[T]here is no civil remedy if a statute merely prohibits or makes conduct criminal without imposing a duty to a specific class.'.

We will return to the question of **public** duties later in this chapter at **8.3.6**. The next issue we have to address concerns legislation, and there is much of it, passed to protect employees in the workplace. You will recall that a claim was made at **8.2** to the effect that actions for breach of statutory duty are common in this context; they are also generally more successful than actions brought in other contexts.

Actions against employers

These cases illustrate the argument that whatever the first of Lord Tenterden's presumptions may say about the law in **general** terms, in **practice** (at any rate where **fines** are imposed on **employers** for breaches of safety legislation passed for the protection of their employees) there seems to be no bias against civil claims.

Salmond (p. 253) argues that this is true **wherever** the remedy laid down in the Act or Regulation is a **fine**. It is submitted, with respect, that the only clear and extensive authority for this proposition can be found in the Factories Act cases.

These 'industrial' cases, it is further submitted, are easier 'targets' for the 'class' approach, because the safety legislation can **only** have been passed for an easily ascertainable class, i.e. employees. Indeed, Lord Diplock, in arguing for the 'class' approach in *Lonrho*, took his analogy from the '. . . case of the Factories Act and similar legislation'.

'Industrial' cases may be rather special, and it could arguably be potentially misleading to use them to extend the 'class' argument (and to support the point made by Salmond on fines). Employees are **clearly** a homogenous group of persons with, in this context, only **personal safety** as their interest. It will be seen later that the **nature** of the interest to be protected by the action for breach of statutory duty may well influence the outcome of a case.

Furthermore, the genesis of **this** cause of action occurred in the late nineteenth century when the courts were plainly reacting somewhat to the earlier raw, *laissez-faire* philosophy governing attitudes to the safety of employees. Since then, a huge body of **precedent** has been built up on the topic, and account must be taken of that fact.

Is 'like' being compared with 'like'? It is submitted that the answer is 'No'.

The courts have, for a long time now, favoured employees claiming that statutes passed for their protection give them rights of action for breaches of statutory duty. This 'bias' is firmly entrenched by a wealth of precedent.

The 'class' test was applied in *Groves* v *Lord Wimborne* [1892] 2 QB 402, which is an early example of this approach. The defendant's servant was injured as a result of the failure of the defendant to fence dangerous machinery as required by statute, the Factory and Workshop Act 1891 (see now the Factories Act 1961). It was held that the statute, which imposed only a fine on the defendant for the breach, created a duty for the benefit of a specified class of persons, i.e. employees, and must be presumed to give a remedy to a member of that class injured in consequence of a breach of the duty. The fine of £100 was regarded as inadequate.

Many other examples can be found in the 'industrial' case law, but only one further instance is given here. In *Westwood* v *Post Office* [1974] AC 1, Westwood was a Post Office employee who, whilst trespassing in a part of the telephone exchange at which he worked, fell to his death through a defective floor over a lift shaft. The plaintiff, his widow, suing on behalf of his estate, under the Offices, Shops and Railway Premises Act 1963, succeeded, in spite of the fact that Westwood had been outside the course of his employment at the time. The House of Lords said that the Act covered the safety of all those 'employed' at the premises, regardless of whether they were actually doing their job at the time.

It is submitted that care should be taken in using decisions from the 'industrial' cases as authority for propositions in favour of civil claims in **other** statutory contexts.

Other classes

The courts do not **generally** favour construing penal statutes so as to create torts.

Thus, for example, in *Badham* v *Lambs Ltd* [1946] KB 45, it was held that a vendor of a vehicle who contravened a provision of the then Road Traffic Act (see now the Road Traffic Act 1988) as to the condition in which the car sold could legally be put on the road, and which imposed a fine for any contravention, was found not liable to a third party injured in an accident caused by the condition of the car.

This decision is more typical of the **general** position concerning penal legislation, although it is true that occasionally cases like *Monk* v *Warbey* [1935] 1 KB 75, have to be considered. It is submitted, however, that such cases are exceptional.

In *Monk* the statute concerned, the Road Traffic Act 1930 (see now the Road Traffic Act 1988), which provided a penalty for breach of the provision concerned, was held also to give a right of action in tort to a person injured as a result of a breach of duty. The defendant lent his car to a friend, although he was not insured against third party risks unless he was driving himself. This was a breach of s. 35 of the Act. The friend injured the plaintiff, who was unable to recover against the insurance company, which had not covered such an accident. It was held that this was the very kind of case which the Act was passed to discourage, and that the statutory penalty should not be deemed to exclude an action in tort by a party aggrieved. The plaintiff recovered damages from the defendant.

Monk was followed in *Martin* v *Dean* [1971] 3 All ER 279. The plaintiff was injured by a vehicle being driven by X, who had borrowed it from the owner, the defendant. The owner's insurance did not cover the vehicle whilst it was being driven by X. The plaintiff successfully claimed damages against X on the ground of his negligence.

The plaintiff also claimed against the owner, who was in breach of his duty under the replacement for s. 35 of the 1930 Act, s. 201 of the Road Traffic Act 1960 (see now the

Road Traffic Act 1988). It was held that the owner was in breach, and that such breach did give rise to a civil action, but in such circumstances as these the damage caused by the owner's breach was dependent upon the driver's ability to satisfy the judgment made against him. If the driver was well able to satisfy the judgment, the owner's breach caused no damage but where, as here, the driver was unable, because of his limited means, to make prompt payment, judgment could be made against the owner for the full loss.

Cases such as these are now dealt with under an agreement (which has the force of law) between the Motor Insurers' Bureau and the Department of the Environment, whereby the Bureau (which is maintained by the insurance companies) will pay out in the event of damage caused by uninsured drivers of vehicles on the public highway, provided there is, in the circumstances, a legal obligation to take out insurance. Thus, *Monk* and *Martin*, on their facts, are important only for purposes of illustration.

Can you identify the policy reasoning behind *Monk* (and *Martin*)? Write it down, in two short paragraphs, on a piece of paper.

It is one of the **universal** features of the action for breach of statutory duty that, unless there are clear words to the contrary in the Act in question, the courts will not favour a plaintiff's claim where to do so would **subvert** or **supplant** the existing common law. If, however, to allow the claim would **supplement** the common law, that objection would have no relevance and the court might more readily find in the plaintiff's favour.

On the facts, at that time, *Monk* **supplemented** the existing action in common law negligence, by allowing a claim for damages directly against a person who was not liable in negligence, but who had the funds available to pay compensation. This argument is advanced by *Winfield* (p. 197) as the real explanation for the decision in *Monk*, and it is an attractive proposition; but the 'class' approach is the **stated** basis for the decision. It is, perhaps, significant that the decision was given at a time when there was no Motor Insurers' Bureau.

You will recall that in both *Monk* and *Dean* it was the **drivers** only who were liable in the tort of negligence.

Road users have not been generally favoured as a **class** in the context of the action for breach of statutory duty. *Winfield* (p. 197) says this is due to the fact that 'isolated pockets of strict liability' (many of the statutes concerned impose **strict** liability, i.e. liability in which the defendant's **fault** need not be proved) would thereby be introduced into an area of liability which is based on common law negligence.

Another factor is surely the **size** of the class in this case, and the question of how heavy the burden will be on the defendant if liability is imposed.

It will be found in **Chapter 10** that road users, as a class of persons, may have certain claims in **public nuisance**. They can also bring claims for personal injury or damage to property, in certain circumstances, concerning the condition of the highway, against the highway authority under the Highways Act 1980.

According to *Wentworth* v *Wiltshire County Council* [1993] QB 654, the action under the 1980 Act is not available to someone who has a business next to the highway, and who suffers pure economic loss due to the fact that access to his premises is denied to vehicular traffic because of the highway's condition. Furthermore, the 1980 Act contains a special method of enforcement in such a case. Of course this legislation, unlike the legislation which is the subject matter of our study here, **actually** confers a civil remedy upon road users.

Lonrho says little about **how** a class is to be ascertained in any given situation, though of course the answer may be pretty obvious in some instances (for example, employees or, as in *Ex parte Island Records Ltd*, musical performers).

In fact, this issue can be likened to the duty of care problem in the tort of negligence, where policy invariably plays a pivotal role in 'hard cases'.

Pause here and consider the following question: 'Do you think that the class protection approach provides the conclusive answer, in all cases?'

As an experienced student you will probably have answered this question in the negative. If that is so, you would be absolutely correct.

Not only is the question 'is a particular statute passed for the benefit of a "class" of persons?' often a difficult one to answer, influenced as it is by policy considerations; even in a case where a court accepts the plaintiff's argument that legislation **was** passed with the intention to confer upon a class of persons some benefit, it does not **follow** that an action for **breach** of statutory duty will be recognised.

Thus, the House of Lords, in *R v Deputy Governor of Parkhurst Prison, ex parte Hague* [1992] 1 AC 58, found that the Prison Rules 1964 did not confer upon prisoners an action in tort for damages, in the event of their breach by the prison authorities. The plaintiff's claim was based on a breach of Rule 43, concerning the segregation of prisoners by the prison authorities.

It was held that a court cannot escape its duty to determine the intention of Parliament. The existence of a clearly defined class of persons cannot be the sole determinant of the issue. On the facts, the court said, the Prison Act 1952 and the Rules made thereunder were intended **only** for the governance of prisons, including the control of prisoners.

Please read the House of Lords case, *Calveley v Chief Constable of Merseyside* [1989] 1 All ER 1025 in *Cases and Materials* (8.1.1.1). What was the reason given by Lord Bridge for the decision in this case? Write down your answer in two sentences.

The reason given by his Lordship was that although the legislation certainly gave to the plaintiff (a police officer) a benefit, it was not one for monetary compensation. In fact, the benefit was the protection of fairness in procedural matters where the officer was under investigation, after a complaint had been made against him.

There are a number of other matters of which we must take note, for example the question of 'public' duties mentioned above, and the position where the remedy provided by the statute is **not** a criminal sanction. Before we do that, however, we have to direct our attention to the **second** 'exception' outlined by Lord Diplock in *Lonrho*.

Can you remember what that 'exception' is?

The **second** exception is the case where a statute has created a **public** right and an **individual** suffers different damage from that sustained by the rest of the public. Please note that this is not the 'public **duties**' issue referred to above.

8.3.4.4 Public rights and particular damage

Lord Diplock's second exception here is remarkably similar to the concept of 'special damage' in public nuisance, which you will learn about in **Chapter 10**.

This exception suffers from even greater vagueness than the 'class exception' given in *Lonrho*.

Both exceptions are obviously open to considerable judicial interpretation, but at least 'class' is rather less opaque than the notion of particular damage coupled to public rights. It is the 'public rights' aspect of this exception which causes the problem of definition.

According to Lord Diplock in *Lonrho* a public right is some right which is available to the Queen's subjects where they wish to enjoy it. His Lordship drew a distinction, however, between those Acts which create public rights (i.e. statutes which create **crimes**) and those which simply prohibit the public generally from doing something which they could otherwise do legally ('mere prohibitions' do **not** create any public right in the present context). There is therefore a distinction, for this purpose at least, between 'crimes' and 'prohibitions'. In *Lonrho* itself the sanctions provisions came into the second category.

His Lordship seemed to be at a loss to explain his reasoning much beyond this. Jones (at p. 296) says this is simply asserting that some criminal legislation is actionable in the present case, whilst some is not.

You should consider the extract from *Winfield* and *Dear v Newham LBC, The Times*, 24 February 1988, both to be found in *Cases and Materials* (8.1.1.2).

ACTIVITY 40

Please consider the Court of Appeal decision in *Richardson* v *Pitt-Stanley and Others* [1995] 1 All ER 460 in *Cases and Materials* (8.1.1.2), and write down the points of significance which emerge from the judgments. You will need a large sheet of paper.

Amongst the matters of importance which you might have listed are the following:

(a) existing remedies at common law were regarded as adequate;

(b) it was considered to be significant that the plaintiff's loss was 'economic';

(c) also of significance was an alleged distinction between a statute which creates merely a criminal offence, and one which declares that certain conduct is 'unlawful' and **then**, separately, imposes a criminal sanction. It is claimed that it is easier to infer a civil remedy in the **latter** case, i.e. where conduct is made generally unlawful (rather than being classified simply as a criminal offence, as in the **former** case);

(d) the Act in question imposed 'very substantial' fines for breaches of its provision;

(e) Parliamentary debates were considered and *Hansard* consulted;

(f) although a clearly definable class was involved (there was considerable reference to Lord Diplock's judgment in *Lonrho*) this was not regarded as conclusive by the majority;

(g) the **dissenting** judge, however, referring to the first exception in Lord Diplock's speech (above) regarded the class factor as being **overwhelmingly** in favour of inferring a civil remedy. The statutory duty imposed was not, he said, an 'entirely general' duty, owed to 'the world at large'; it was a duty owed to a clearly definable class of persons of which the plaintiff was one;

(h) Sir John Megaw, the dissenting judge, also thought it significant that the duty was not of an 'absolute' nature. On the contrary, it required proof of fault on the part of the defendant.

There are still two issues of **general** importance to consider; these include the issue of 'public' duties referred to above. Since they are concerns which are germane to the topic as a **whole**, we will leave discussion of them until after we have dealt with some **special matters**. i.e.:

(a) where the special remedy provided by the statute is **not** a **criminal** sanction;
(b) the second presumption laid down by Lord Tenterden in *Doe d. Murray* (see **8.3.3**).

8.3.4.5 Where the statutory remedy is not a criminal sanction

Lord Diplock in *Lonrho* said: 'Where the only manner of enforcing performance for which the Act provides is prosecution for the criminal offence of failure to perform the statutory obligation or for contravening the statutory prohibition which the Act creates, there are two classes of exception to this general rule'. He then went on to specify the two exceptions which we have already examined. By his words, 'this general rule' his Lordship was referring to the first of Lord Tenterden's presumptions.

It is clear, from the cases we have considered in the context of 'class' interests, that it is not always sufficient for a plaintiff to bring himself within the benefit of a class. This is so, even where the statute imposes a criminal sanction. Where the means of enforcement is some **other** method, the class argument is correspondingly weaker. Lord Tenterden's first presumption has greater force in such circumstances.

Lord Diplock has made it clear that his 'exceptions' to the general rule are applicable to the case of the **criminal** sanction, but this does not mean that the class argument is never likely to appear elsewhere. The 'general rule' is based only on a **presumption** after all; this case can be rebutted in appropriate cases by argument, but it will need to be a **strong** argument.

In *Wyatt* v *Hillingdon London Borough Council* (1978) 76 LGR 727, the Chronically Sick and Disabled Persons Act 1970 had placed a duty on social services authorities to provide for the needs of a class of persons, i.e. disabled persons; the plaintiff was clearly a member of this class and there was no doubt on the question of whose benefit the statute had been passed to promote.

The 1970 Act, however, in common with a number of other social services measures, was subject to s. 36 of the National Assistance Act 1948, which contained a 'default' procedure, empowering the Secretary of State for Social Security to apply for a court order where social services authorities, including the defendant council, were failing to perform their statutory duties. In spite of the fact that this procedure had at that date never been activated, the Court of Appeal found that the existence of the procedure impliedly excluded an action for damages at common law.

Cases involving methods of enforcement other than criminal sanctions are likely to be similar to this one. It is not suggested that the procedure will be the same, but **similar**, i.e. some **administrative** form of relief; it might, for instance, be on **appeal** to some tribunal.

Sometimes provision is made for an appeal to a court. In any event, where decisions of public bodies are concerned judicial review (see **3.5**) may be available.

In short, where there are available, as a means of enforcing the statute, a number of alternatives to the action for breach of statutory duty, this factor may militate against a finding of a civil remedy in tort.

Can you guess what the policy reasons might be behind the decision in *Wyatt*?

There are several policy reasons for this decision (and indeed for **similar** decisions), because a public authority was involved:

(a) Jones (pp. 296–7) claims that whilst there is no 'specific' presumption applying to public authorities, the courts are generally reluctant to find a civil remedy if liability is likely to be extensive. Jones refers to public 'utilities', but we can include public authorities generally here;

(b) where public duties are involved, and this point will be raised again under 'public duties' (see **8.3.6**) the obligation is invariably expressed in wide, general terms which give the public body concerned considerable discretion. This is especially so in cases where the expenditure of public money is involved concerning, as it does, issues of policy-making on the part of the public body in question. The issue may be felt to be too 'political' for the court to intervene, and on the facts of *Wyatt* it was felt intervention would be better left to the Secretary of State.

Salmond (at p. 254) speaking **generally** says '. . . provisions which are highly specific and detailed in laying down the precise content of the duty are more likely than others to lend themselves to enforcement by way of an action for damages.'.

(c) The fact that the Secretary of State was given the special power of enforcement may have confirmed the essentially 'public' nature of the local council's obligation under the statute.

8.3.5 WHERE THE STATUTE IS SILENT ON THE QUESTION OF ENFORCEMENT

This is where we have to consider the **second** of Lord Tenterden's presumptions. According to his Lordship, in such cases '. . . the common law may, in general, find a mode suited to the particular nature of the case.'.

The **discretion** given to the court in such cases may be noted in the wording of Lord Tenterden's speech. It is often said that the courts will more readily read into such a statute a cause of action in tort. As in **all** cases, it is assumed that Parliament and the parliamentary draftsman know the case law, and the ways of the judges, and so where nothing is said at all about means of enforcement it is assumed that will be no objection to a civil remedy.

In *Thornton* v *Kirklees Borough Council* [1979] QB 626 Megaw LJ said: 'where an Act imposes a duty . . . for the benefit of a specified category of persons but prescribes no special remedy for breach of that duty, it can normally be assumed that a civil action for damages will lie.'.

Whilst no doubt this is a correct statement of principle, it should in **general** be regarded only as a strong **starting** point.

Please remember that in **any** context of breaches of statutory duty, that is of the type under discussion in this chapter, there are so many considerations to take into account in determining the so-called 'intention of Parliament'. Thus, the absence of a specific remedy in the Act in question cannot be regarded as **conclusive** of whether or not a civil remedy in tort is available.

In *Thornton*, the issue involved was the duty owed by local authorities, as **housing** authorities, to homeless persons under the then Housing (Homeless Persons) Act 1977 (now the Housing Act 1985 Part III).

SAQ 96

Can you think of any particular legal obstacles there might be in way of establishing *civil* liability cases such as *Thornton*? Get hold of a piece of writing paper and jot down these 'obstacles'.

Amongst the obstacles facing a litigant in such cases, you might include the following:

(a) whilst an easily discernible class was involved in *Thornton*, the **size** of it and the **extent** of potential liability could be a problem;

(b) the wording of the duty itself could be a problem. How much discretion and policy-making power does it confer on the body involved?

(c) there might well be some alternative method available of enforcing the obligation, such as judicial review.

Where a statute makes no provision at all for enforcement, a court might look favourably on an argument that the **only** way of enforcing the statute is by way of an action in tort; otherwise the law would never be activated. That is in **general**, however, unlikely to be the case, because there will probably be another remedy in existing law. (This point is taken up in **8.3.7**.) Thus, in **practice** the argument is likely to revolve around the adequacy of some already existing remedy or procedure.

Public duties, and alternative methods of enforcement are taken up below, in rather more detail. We will deal first with public duties.

8.3.6   PUBLIC DUTIES

The observations made here are relevant to the action for breach of statutory duty **generally**. It has already been noted that it is Jones's contention that public utilities stand in a special position in the present context, i.e. that there is a marked reluctance on the part of the courts to infer an action for breach of statutory duty where liability is likely to be extensive. He suggests that *Atkinson* (see **8.3.4.1**) can be explained on this basis. Where public bodies have failed to observe duties imposed on them by statute the courts, on the whole, are not in favour of allowing an action in tort.

ACTIVITY 41

Please re-read the House of Lords decision in X *and Others* v *Bedfordshire County Council (and Other Appeals)* [1995] 3 All ER 353 in *Cases and Materials* (3.3). What is the basis of the decisions in these cases?

The reasoning in these cases, behind the decision that no action in tort for breach of statutory duty was available, is twofold:

(a) the duty flowing from the Children and Young Persons Act 1969, the Child Care Act 1980 and the Children Act 1989, is expressed in very general terms; and

(b) local social services authorities, who owe the duty, are given extensive discretion to act under the terms of the duty.

In any event, where public bodies are concerned, the distinction between 'public' law and 'private' law may have to be considered. We have looked at this in **Chapter 3**, in relation to actions in negligence, but we must also note its importance in the **present** context.

8.3.6.1 'Public' law and 'private' law proceedings

The common law action, in tort, for breach of statutory duty is concerned with the question of a plaintiff seeking damages for breach of duty; it is **not** concerned with efforts to obtain a declaration or an order of mandamus or some other administrative (or public) law remedy. That is a matter of 'public' law, which involves judicial review proceedings, via s. 31, Supreme Court Act 1981 and Order 53 of the Rules of the Supreme Court, in the High Court. An action in tort, a matter of 'private' law, is started via a writ or an originating summons.

In *Cocks* v *Thanet District Council* [1983] 2 AC 286, the plaintiff sought a declaration that the council were in breach of duty under the Housing (Homeless Persons) Act 1977 (see now Part III, Housing Act 1985) but the council, on a preliminary point, claimed that he should have sought judicial review. It was held in the House of Lords, following *O'Reilly* v *Mackman* [1983] 2 AC 237, that a 'dichotomy [now exists] between a housing authority's public and private law functions', thus the decision as to whether the plaintiff satisfied the statutory criteria was a 'public' law deliberation by the council. However, once the authority were satisfied on this count, any obligation to provide housing under the Act was a matter of 'private law', via the action of breach of statutory duty.

This makes it clear that a plaintiff may have no choice but to institute proceedings for judicial review in respect of some decisions. The possibility of an action for breach of statutory duty in tort can only arise at the **second** stage. It is not only cases arising under housing legislation which are caught by this ruling: *Cocks* only follows *O'Reilly*, which is of **general** application.

The position is further complicated by the fact that it is possible to obtain **damages** in Order 53 proceedings, **as well as** other remedies such as an injunction and declaration, where an infringement with a private right can be shown. Therefore, there might be a tendency in **these** cases to force plaintiffs to use Order 53 throughout.

It is not suggested that it is impossible in 'public' law cases to establish a cause of action in tort, merely that it may be more difficult to do so than is the case in other contexts.

No doubt *Thornton* (see **8.3.5**) will have to be reconsidered in the light of *Cocks*.

In *R* v *Northavon District Council ex parte Palmer*, *The Times*, 22 February 1994, it was held at first instance that a housing authority's breach of duty arising under Part III of the Housing Act 1985, to conduct inquiries where applications were made for accommodation by persons who claimed to be homeless or threatened with homelessness, did not give rise to any private law action in tort for damages.

The 1985 Act, in s. 62, imposes a duty upon a housing authority to conduct inquiries where application is made for help under the Act. In ss. 63 and 65 a duty to secure accommodation is imposed on the authority where it is satisfied that the application meets the statutory criteria, qualifying the applicant for help under the Act. It is the purpose of the inquiries to discover whether these conditions are met by the applicant. The judge said:

> Inquiries by a local authority under section 62 are part of its decision-making and therefore public law functions. The proper conduct of these inquiries is a matter concerning not only the applicant. It affects the public purse and the general community and those people already on the housing list. The duties of a local authority under section 62 are duties in public law and do not afford any individual a cause of action in private law.

> The alternative claim for damages for breach of statutory duty under sections 63 and 65 can only arise once a local authority has reached a decision, in the exercise of its public law functions, that the conditions necessary to give rise to a duty to secure accommodation under either section are satisfied. Once the existence of a duty to provide accommodation has been established, an action for damages for breach will lie. The council is not in breach of any private law duty to the applicant under section 63 and 65.

8.3.7 THE STATE OF THE PRE-EXISTING LAW, INCLUDING THE COMMON LAW

We have already touched on this issue, when it was pointed out that the courts tend to look at the possibility of **alternative** remedies being available to the plaintiff, i.e. alternatives to a cause of action for breach of statutory duty.

Of course, the existence of some remedy in the statute itself is a factor, as we have seen. In this respect there may be a distinction between criminal penalties and other methods of enforcement.

Traditionally, where a crime is involved there is perhaps more hope of success because the sanction may not be regarded as adequate in the circumstances. An analogy may be made with the common law crime of public nuisance and the special action available in tort in that case. As you know, nuisance is dealt with elsewhere in **Chapter 10**.

According to the majority view, led by Lord Denning, in *Ex parte Island Records* (see **8.3.1**) a civil action would be avilable to any person whose private rights were infringed as a result of criminal conduct. This very broad approach, however, is now subject to the 'Diplock qualification' imposed in *Lonrho* (see **8.3.4.2**). In *Island Records* **injunctive** relief was sought, not damages.

Just pause for a moment. Why might it be significant that the plaintiff wanted an injunction in *Island Records*, and not damages (other than incidental costs)?

The significance lies in the fact that the injunction is a discretionary remedy, whilst the remedy of damages is a **right** available to a plaintiff once a wrong has been established. Thus, it might be thought that the *Island Records* view would not 'open the floodgates' too much, since the courts would not **have** to award the remedy, even if a wrong were established, where an injunction was sought.

It appears, however, that the *Lonrho* ruling applies whatever the form of relief sought by the plaintiff.

In *Rickless* v *United Artists Corporation, The Times*, 17 June 1985, in an action brought under the Dramatic and Musical Performers Protection Act 1958, it was held that the Act was passed primarily to protect the economic interests of **performers**, so that to construe the Act as ceasing to apply after the performer was dead would be partly to frustrate and not fulfil its purpose. Thus, unless the Act conferred civil remedies a well as imposing criminal sanctions the performer's protection was inadequate. Civil remedies would include, said Hobhouse J, a right to apply for an injunction to restrain potential criminal actions.

In *Lonrho*, said the judge, Lord Diplock drew a distinction between language in a statute which created a legal right and language which created a mere prohibition (a distinction criticised often for its vagueness); he recognised that statutory prohibitions could give rise to civil remedies as well. It was a matter of examining the purpose of the legislation. If it was legislating for the protection of a particular class, then *prima facie* the statute should be construed as giving a right to a civil remedy to the members of that class. The decision was confirmed by the Court of Appeal at [1987] 1 All ER 679.

You may be interested to know that the law on the technical point involved has now been changed by the Copyright, Designs and Patents Act 1988, but *Rickless* can still be used for purposes of illustration and example in the general context of the action for breach of statutory duty.

The existence of some alternative remedy, and its adequacy is, however, a factor taken into account in **all** cases. It may, of course, have more importance where the statute in question does not provide a specific remedy, but that itself, i.e. the absence of a special remedy, is only another factor to be weighed by the courts in these cases. As Lord Simonds said, in *Cutler* v *Wandsworth Stadium Ltd* [1949] AC 398:

> The only rule which in all circumstances is valid is that the answer must depend on a consideration of the whole Act and the circumstances, including the pre-existing law, in which it was enacted.

Thus, the adequacy of the pre-existing common law may be considered.

In *Phillips* v *Britannia Hygiene Laundry Co.* (see **8.3.4.3**) a lorry in use on the public highway had a defective axle, which was in breach of certain statutory regulations relating to the construction and use of vehicles on the roads. It was held that there was no right to a civil action in tort for breach of statutory duty available to the owner of another vehicle damaged in consequence of the breach. The existing law of negligence, the court said, was sufficient to provide a remedy.

The authorities are not, however, consistent on this point in the sense that the existence of an adequate common law remedy can sometimes be given as the reason for finding against an action for breach of statutory duty, although it is debatable as to how **conclusive** such a factor is. On the other hand, the **absence** of an alternative common law remedy is not necessarily fatal to a claim for redress.

There is also the vexed question of 'adequacy'. How is that to be assessed? We have already seen that *Winfield* argues, for example, that policy considerations may well enter the equation at this point. The learned author suggests that all might be well where the statute in question supplements rather than supplants the common law. Does the statute fit into the existing common law basis of liability?

Jones (p. 292) suggest that a plaintiff's task might be easier where the standard of care set in the statute 'more or less corresponds to a common law duty'.

We have seen in **Chapter 3** that English judges are not, on the whole, keen supporters of strict liability, and many statutes impose such a standard. That factor, however, has not prevented judicial willingness to infer actions for breach of statutory duty in industrial safety cases, so it, too, cannot be regarded as a conclusive consideration.

The **adequacy** of the **statutory** means of enforcement, where one exists, may also be raised by the plaintiff in support of his or her argument for an action in tort.

Groves v *Wimborne* (see **8.3.4.3**) proceeded on this basis, though it may be wrong to regard this decision as a strong **general** authority, as we have already seen. Indeed, as many commentators have pointed out, there was an alternative common law remedy available to the plaintiff, i.e. an action for breach of the special duty an employer owes to his employee. We will be looking at that duty later in this chapter.

As is the case with 'class', the interpretation of 'adequate remedy' is open to policy considerations and can only be regarded as one factor to be considered in all the circumstances of the case.

In 'public' duties cases, as we have seen, the existence of an appeal procedure laid down in the statute, or the availability of judicial review, may be taken into account in determining the question of an adequate alternative remedy. This factor may be relevant in such cases whether the statute lays down some 'alternative' remedy or makes no provision at all for a remedy.

ACTIVITY 42

You will find details of the decision both at first instance and in the Court of Appeal in *West Wiltshire District Council* v *Garland and others* **[1993] 4 All ER 246 and [1995] 2 All ER 17**, in *Cases and Materials* **(8.1.2)**.

Please consider these details and write down a list of the findings. Also please answer the question: 'what exactly were the plaintiffs trying to establish in this case?' You will need a big sheet of paper.

In your list of the findings you should have the following:

(a)   the purpose of external audit was to protect the **local authority** and **not** its officers. Thus, since the proximity between the auditors and the officers only came about because of the operation of the **statute**, it would be 'unfair, unjust and unreasonable' to hold that a duty of care in negligence was owed by the auditors to the officers;

(b)   the lack of any other effective remedy against the auditors meant that 'Parliament could be taken to have intended an action for breach of statutory duty to be available to the local authority';

(c)   there was no reason why, where a plaintiff had available an action for breach of statutory duty for a negligent performance of that duty, he could not **also** have

> an action for common law negligence in respect of the same act of negligence. In principle there was no reason why the two should not co-exist. That cause of action in negligence was, however, only available to the local authority and not its officers.

The defendants in this case, who were officers of the local authority and who had been criticised by the district auditor in his report on the council's accounts, were being sued by their employer, the council, for breach of contract and breach of fiduciary duty relating to the payment of certain moneys. In this case they were invoking a High Court **procedure** by which defendants may bring other persons into the litigation as third parties. The defendants were here trying to bring in as third parties the district auditors on the basis that they had advised the defendants as to the legality of the payments in question. Obviously, to do this, they had to establish some tort(s) on the part of the auditors, hence the claims for breach of statutory duty and common law negligence.

You will find it useful to read the decisions in *Ministry of Housing* v *Sharp* [1970] 1 All ER 1009 (this case was considered in relation to 'pure' economic loss in **Chapter 5**) and *CBS Songs Ltd* v *Amstrad Consumer Electronics plc* [1988] AC 1013 in *Cases and Materials* (**8.1.2**).

8.4 The Elements of the Cause of Action for Breach of Statutory Duty

The burden is on the plaintiff to establish each of these elements. We will now examine them.

(a) there must first be an obligation placed by the statute on the defendant. We have dealt with the point at **8.3.3**: *Harrison* v *National Coal Board* illustrates the point;

(b) the statute must 'intend' an action in tort. This is the foundation of all that has been said in the chapter so far;

(c) the plaintiff must come within the protection of the statute. Again, this issue has been dealt with in the discussion on 'class';

(d) there are three other factors to consider:

   (i) the defendant must have breached the statute (see **8.4.1**);

   (ii) the defendant's breach of duty must have caused the damage (see **8.4.2**);

   (iii) the harm suffered is within the scope of the general class of risks at which the statute is directed (see **8.4.3**).

8.4.1 THE DEFENDANT MUST HAVE BREACHED THE STATUTE

The standard of care is set in the **statute itself**, thus each case must be looked at on its own facts; though a body of precedent builds up over the years on commonly used expressions, and that factor must not be overlooked. This is particularly so in industrial injuries cases, where there has been so much litigation. In many instances liability is **strict** (the word 'absolute' is often used instead of 'strict') as, for example, under the Factories Act 1961 where one comes across the expression '[some part of machinery] shall be securely fenced'.

In *John Summers* v *Frost* [1955] AC 740, s. 14(1) of the Factories Act 1961 required that every dangerous part of a machine be fenced. The plaintiff won damages for injury to his thumb caused by contact with a grinding wheel, despite the fact that putting a guard over the only unfenced part of the wheel would have rendered it unusable.

Frequently, the duty is to protect workers, operators and others 'so far as is reasonably practical', or words to that effect.

In *Larner* v *British Steel plc* [1993] 4 All ER 102, the plaintiff brought an action for a failure on the part of his employer to see that his workplace was 'made and kept safe', 'so far as it was reasonably practicable to so'. The duty on the employer to do this was imposed by s. 29(1) of the Factories Act 1961.

The plaintiff gave evidence that reasonable steps could have been taken, but the defendant submitted no evidence. It denied liability, but did not **specifically** plead that it was not reasonably practicable to make the workplace safe.

The trial judge found for the defendant, and the plaintiff appealed. His point of appeal was that the defendant could only claim, within the terms of s. 29(1), that it was not reasonably practicable to do something if the matter was actually **pleaded** and **proved** by the defendant.

It was contended by the defendant, however, that 'safe' in the present context meant 'safe from a reasonably foreseeable danger'; therefore the plaintiff, in order to prove that the workplace was unsafe, had to show that the danger in question was reasonably foreseeable by the defendant.

The Court of Appeal agreed with the plaintiff that s. 29(1) made **no** reference to foreseeability, thus foreseeability was not relevant to liability here. To imply such a test, said the court, would limit a claim for breach of statutory duty to a situation where negligence would also succeed.

This decision shows that while a 'reasonably practicable' standard is not as strict as a 'shall do' standard, it is still stricter than a negligence standard.

Where a duty is qualified, whether or not it has been complied with will depend on all the circumstances. If the regulation requires 'reasonably practicable' (or similar) precautions, then the risk has to be measured against the availability and practicability of those precautions, and the general practice must be considered, as in common law negligence.

In *Adsett* v *K & L Steelfounders* [1953] 1 WLR 773, Singleton LJ declared: 'In deciding whether all the practicable measures were taken one must have regard to the state of knowledge at the material time, particularly, to the knowledge of scientific experts.'.

8.4.1.1 Statute and negligence

Each statute must be carefully construed to see whether it was the intention that the duty should be strict or that it is dependent on wrongful intent or negligence. The term 'statutory negligence' has been used in some cases to refer to statutory standards based on **negligence**. However, although there may be resemblances, in some cases, between the common law action for negligence and the tort of breach of statutory duty, the modern tendency is to keep the two causes of action separate. As Lord Wright said, in *London Passenger Transport Board* v *Upson* [1949] AC 155:

> . . . a claim for damages for breach of a statutory duty intended to protect a person in the position of the particular plaintiff is a specific common law right which is not to be confused in essence with a claim for negligence. The statutory right has its origin in the statute, but the particular remedy of an action for damages is given by the common law in order to make effective, for the benefit of the injured plaintiff, his right to the performance by the defendant of the defendant's statutory duty. It is an effective

sanction. It is not a claim in negligence in the strict ordinary sense . . . whatever the resemblances, it is essential to keep in mind the fundamental differences of the two classes of claim.

The decision in *Bux* v *Slough Metals* [1973] 1 WLR 1358, shows that the torts of breach of statutory duty and negligence are separate and distinct. In actions for breach of statutory duty the existence and nature of the duties depend on a proper interpretation of the relevant statutes; in claims for negligence the matters are determined by reference to the well-established principles of the common law. Where both statutory and common law duties exist, an action for negligence may succeed where an action for breach of statutory duty may fail, since the nature of the statutory duty may be very different from the reasonable care required by the common law.

In this case, the plaintiff, who worked in a foundry, was splashed with molten metal and as a result lost the sight of an eye. For the protection of such workers certain statutory regulations provided that 'There shall be provided . . . suitable goggles or other suitable eye protection'. The plaintiff sued the defendants, his employers, for breach of that duty and of the common law duty of care owed by a master to his servant. (We deal with the common law duty of care at **8.6**.)

After working for the defendants for a year the plaintiff, along with his fellow-workers, had been provided with goggles. He found that, when used, they soon misted over and he had constantly to wipe them clean. This interfered with the speed of his working and, because he was paid on a piece-work basis, limited his earnings. In common with the other workers, he stopped using the goggles after using them for only a few days.

The defendants had issued this type of goggles only after testing various other types and obtaining the advice of the British Safety Council. It seems, however, that they simply acquiesced in their employees' practice of not using the goggles.

The Court of Appeal held that the defendants had 'provided suitable goggles' and that therefore the claim for breach of statutory duty failed. There was no duty laid down in the regulations to see that the goggles were **used**.

The defendants then argued that the regulations provided a complete safety code, and compliance with that code made it impossible to say that there had been any failure to show reasonable care. Therefore the claim for common law negligence must also fail.

The court rejected this argument. The statutory duty was the limited one of 'providing'. The defendants had failed to take reasonable care for the safety of their employees; it was not enough to provide the goggles and then stand by while the men did dangerous work with their eyes wholly unprotected. Whilst the plaintiff succeeded in his claim for negligence, he was held to be 40 per cent to blame and apportionment was made under the Law Reform (Contributory Negligence) Act 1945.

Whilst failure to conform to a standard imposed by statute may be a breach of statutory duty, it is not in itself conclusive evidence of negligence; it may, however, sometimes be *prima facie* evidence of negligence.

Thus, there **is** an element of overlap between the two torts, where a plaintiff makes a claim in both causes of action

Differences between the action for breach of statutory duty and an action in negligence

(a) A defence of *volenti non fit injuria* may be available in the common law action for negligence but invalid for breach of statutory duty. This point is taken up at **8.5.1**.

(b) Moreover in most cases arising under statutes the statute defines the standard of care and the defendant is liable if he fails to show that standard of care. In negligence at common law, however, the standard of care is determined by the court, not by the legislature.

You should consider two cases to be found in *Cases and Materials* (8.2.1.1). They are *Austin Rover* v *HM Inspector of Taxes*, *The Times*, 15 August 1989, and *Dexter* v *Tenby Electrical Accessories Ltd*, *The Guardian*, 22 February 1991. Both cases involve **criminal** prosecutions, i.e. for breach of s. 4(2) of the Health and Safety at Work Act 1974, in the *Austin Rover* case, and for breach of s. 29(1) of the Factories Act 1961 in *Dexter*. In a criminal case the standard of proof, i.e. 'beyond all reasonable doubt', differs from the tortious standard, which is proof on the 'balance of probabilities'.

The illustrations given so far concern **industrial** relationships, but actions for breach of statutory duty and actions for negligence occur in **other** contexts. It is regarded as axiomatic that the two actions go hand-in-hand, and whenever a statutory duty arises it follows that there will be a possibility of liability in negligence. In other words, the statutory duty creates 'proximity' for the purposes of negligence.

Your attention is drawn to *West Wiltshire DC* v *Garland* (see **Activity 42**) which illustrates this point. *M* v *Newham LBC*, and *E* v *Dorset CC*, both of which appear in *Cases and Materials* (3.3), may also be referred to for guidance on the relationship between these two causes of action.

Bux illustrates the action for breach of statutory duty **and** the **special** duty of care in negligence owed by an employer to his employee.

8.4.2 THE DEFENDANT'S BREACH OF DUTY MUST HAVE CAUSED THE DAMAGE

As in all other torts, the plaintiff must prove legal causal connection between the breach and his injury. In Lord Reid's words, in *Bonnington Castings* v *Wardlaw* [1956] AC 613: 'at least on a balance of probabilities [that] the breach of duty caused or materially contributed to his injury'. This case involved liability for inhalation of silica dust, due to inadequate ventilation in breach of the Factories Act.

In *McWilliams* v *Arrol* [1962] 1 All ER 623, a steel erector fell to his death because he was not wearing a safety harness. The defendants had broken a statutory duty in failing to provide a safety harness, but the evidence did not establish that the deceased would have worn the harness even if one had been provided. Indeed the reverse seemed likely, because the defendants were able to show that the deceased, and his workmates, rarely ever used safety harnesses. The practice was common in the construction industry.

The House of Lords held that the plaintiff had not discharged the burden of proving that the death was caused by the breach of statutory duty and therefore the defendants were entitled to succeed, since it was 'probable' that the deceased would not have used the safety equipment. There was no duty on the defendant to see that the harness was **worn**. It is now over 30 years since the decision in *McWilliams* and, in that time, a much more rigorous safety regime has been developed under the Health and Safety at Work Act 1974. Thus, these facts are unlikely to be repeated. See the extract from Lord Devlin's speech in *Cases and Materials* (8.2.2)

8.4.2.1 Who owes the duty?

The statute must impose the duty on the defendant himself. It is a question of interpreting the Act, or regulation, to see on whom the burden is imposed. In some cases the duty may be imposed, in effect, on the plaintiff. This issue has arisen most frequently in actions by employees against their employers. Once the statute has been interpreted to impose a duty on the defendant, the general principle is clear, i.e. the obligation is **personal** to the defendant and he cannot escape liability by delegating its performance to someone else. As Lord Warrington said in *Lochgelly Iron Co.* v *M'Mullan* [1934] AC 1, a case involving an action by an employee against his employer: '. . . the owner cannot relieve himself of his obligation by saying that he has appointed reasonably competent persons and that the breach is due to negligence on their part. . .'.

This rule applies whether the 'reasonably competent person' is an employee or an independent contractor.

Stop reading for a while, and please consider the following question: 'Is it possible for a *plaintiff* to put the defendant in breach of statutory duty?'

In some cases, the act or omission of the plaintiff himself has the legal result that both plaintiff and defendant are in breach of the same duty.

Thus, in *Ginty* v *Belmont Building Supplies* [1959] 1 All ER 414, the plaintiff was an experienced employee employed by the defendants, who were roofing contractors. Statutory regulations, binding on both parties, required that crawling boards should be used for work done on fragile roofs. Although the defendants provided such boards, the plaintiff did not use them and consequently fell through a roof, sustaining serious personal injury. Both parties were, in law, in breach of their statutory duties, but the judge held that the only wrongful act was that of the plaintiff. Pearson J said:

> . . . it would be absurd if, notwithstanding the employer having done all he could reasonably be expected to do to ensure compliance, a workman, who deliberately disobeyed his employer's orders and thereby put the employer in breach of a regulation, could claim damages for injury caused to him solely by his own wrong-doing.

If, however, the plaintiff establishes the defendant's breach of duty, and that he suffered injury as a result, he establishes a prima facie case against the defendant, who will escape liability only if he can rebut this by proving that the only act or default which caused the breach was that of the plaintiff himself. Thus, where some fault can be attributed to the defendant, e.g. an employer fails to provide adequate instructions or supervision, the plaintiff will recover some damages. They may, of course, be substantially reduced for his contributory negligence.

In *Ross* v *Associated Portland Cement Manufacturers Ltd* [1964] 2 All ER 452 (*Cases and Materials* (8.2.2)), the deceased, a charge-hand steel erector and two colleagues, had to repair a safety net which was situated some 22 feet above ground level in the employer's factory. He was simply left to get on with the work as he thought best and without any proper equipment. The evidence showed that the deceased could use any equipment he could find, and could also ask the chief engineer for advice or equipment, though no encouragement was given with regard to the latter possibility, in spite of the fact that he was a newcomer to the job and the task was of an unusual nature for a steel erector. Whilst using a ladder (according to the evidence a movable platform should have been used) the deceased met his death.

His widow sued (under what is now the Fatal Accidents Act 1976) and it was first held that the employer was in breach of its statutory duty, under s. 29(1) Factories Act 1961, but the sole cause of the accident was the deceased's own negligence in using the ladder.

In the House of Lords it was found that the employer was partly responsible (66 per cent) because it had not provided proper equipment and kept the place of work as safe as was reasonably practicable; in particular it was important that the deceased's decision to use the ladder was forced upon him because of the absence of appropriate equipment for the job.

Lord Reid referred to the judgment of Pearson J in *Ginty* v *Belmont Building Supplies* [1959] 1 All ER 414 (in which the test of causation was said to be, 'Whose fault was it?') and said:

> If the question is put in that way one must remember that fault is not necessarily equivalent in this context to blameworthiness. The question really is whose conduct caused the accident . . . That approach appears to me to avoid the difficulty which has sometimes been felt in explaining why an employer, put in breach of a statute by the disobedience of his servant, can escape liability to that servant for injuries caused by the breach. If the employer exercised all due diligence, and the breach and resultant injuries were solely caused by the servant's conduct, the employer is liable vicariously for injuries sustained by a third party just as he would be for injuries caused solely by his servant's common law negligence: but he can say to the disobedient servant that his conduct in no way caused or contributed to that servant's injuries.

According to Lord Donovan there was no evidence that Ross (the deceased) was an expert or specialist at repairing safety nets suspended between aerial ropeways; there was no evidence that he had done this kind of work before. '[In] *Ginty* . . . suitable appliances **were** provided by the employer but the man refused or neglected to use them.'

8.4.3   THE HARM SUFFERED IS WITHIN THE SCOPE OF THE GENERAL CLASS OF RISKS AT WHICH THE STATUTE IS DIRECTED

In *Gorris* v *Scott* (1874) LR 9 Ex 125, a statute required animals on board ship to be penned in. In breach of the statute sheep were not penned in and were washed overboard. The court held that an action for breach of statutory duty would fail because the statute was intended to prevent the spread of disease, not to prevent animals from drowning.

Evidently, the plaintiff's damage must come within the terms of the statute concerned; and it is likely that the stricter the duty imposed by the legislation, the stricter the court will be in requiring the plaintiff to keep within the letter of the law.

Thus, in *Chipchase* v *British Titan Products Co.* [1956] 1 QB 545, a workman fell off a platform 9 inches wide and 6 feet above the ground. Certain statutory regulations, which applied to all platforms 6 feet 6 inches or more above the ground, required that platforms should be 34 inches wide. The plaintiff tried to argue that as his case was so nearly within the regulations they ought to be taken into account by the court. The court would not accept this argument, and there was no liability for breach of statute.

In *Close* v *Steel Co. of Wales* [1962] AC 367, the House of Lords had to consider s. 14 of the Factories Act 1961, which imposes a duty to see that dangerous parts of machinery 'shall be securely fenced'. The plaintiff, an employee of the defendants, was injured when a dangerous piece of machinery flew out of a machine and hit him. It was held that he could not recover by basing his claim on s. 14.

An employee can, therefore, rely on a breach of s. 14 only where he comes into contact with the dangerous part of the machine; an injury caused in a different way is not covered.

Again, in *Hands* v *Rolls-Royce* (1972) 69 LSG 504, the plaintiff, who was injured when a defective lavatory seat came adrift from the pan, was found to have no remedy under s. 7 of the Factories Act 1961, because that section related only to the spread of infection.

It must be said, however, that the **general** approach to the application of *Gorris* is somewhat less strict.

In *Grant* v *National Coal Board* [1958] AC 649, the House of Lords approved that decision, although in this case the statute was held to cover the damage suffered. The plaintiff was employed in the defendants' mine. The Coal Mines Act 1911 provided that 'the roof and sides of every travelling road . . . shall be made secure'. The accident occurred because a bogie on which the plaintiff was travelling was derailed as a result of a fall of stone from the roof. It was held that the protection of the statute was not limited to direct falls from the roof but covered accidents caused indirectly by such falls. This case illustrates the modern tendency not to apply the decision in *Gorris* too strictly.

In *Donaghey* v *Boulton and Paul Ltd* [1968] AC 1, a statutory regulation was designed to prevent employees from falling off roofs on which they were working. The House of Lords held that it made no difference that the plaintiff fell through a hole in the roof rather than through fragile roofing material.

Lord Reid said that provided the plaintiff's damage is of the kind that the statute was designed to prevent, it is irrelevant that it occurred in a way not contemplated by the statute.

The problem with risk in the present context is the same as in the tort of negligence. In both torts the risk, or danger, must be foreseeable (or within the Act(s) in the case of statutory duties) but the exact way in which the accident occurs need not be so.

8.4.3.1   Common law duty

You should always remember that there may be a right of action for the common law tort of negligence in general, or the employer's **special** duty of care where relevant, even although there is no breach of a statutory duty, or although the breach of the duty does not give a right of action in tort.

No statute will be construed to exclude an existing common law duty unless it says so, expressly or by necessary implication.

Please consider *Pickering* v *Liverpool Daily Post and Echo Newspapers plc* **[1991] 2 AC 370** in *Cases and Materials* **(8.2.3.1). What was the outcome of this case? Write down your answer in** *one* **sentence.**

You might have expressed yourself in terms similar to the following: even a member of a class of persons for whose benefit a statute has been passed will not succeed unless the injury suffered is of a kind or type recognised by the law as sounding in damages.

You will have seen that the plaintiff was, in effect complaining of an invasion of privacy. This is not yet recognised as a tort in its own right.

An interesting case on psychiatric damage, *Young* v *Charles Church (Southern) Ltd, The Times*, 1 May 1997 (CA) can be found **Cases and Materials (8.2.3.1)**.

8.5   Defences

Apart from the usual arguments that a defendant can put forward to counter the plaintiff's case, for example in relation to **causation**, two of the **general** defences discussed in **Chapter 2** fall to be considered in the present context.

8.5.1   *VOLENTI NON FIT INJURIA*

It is arguable that public policy does not allow this defence to be used by an employer who is in breach of his statutory duty to the plaintiff, at least where the duty is of a strict (or 'absolute') nature. The reasoning for this argument rests on the claim that Parliament cannot have intended defendants to 'contract out' of their statutory responsibilities.

In *ICI* v *Shatwell* [1965] AC 656, two employees were injured in an explosion caused by their **own** failure to observe safety precautions required by statutory regulations in the interests of their own safety. One of them sued the employer, alleging that the employer was **vicariously** liable for the other employee's share of the responsibility for the accident. The House of Lords found as follows:

   (a)   where employees are themselves under a statutory duty, and jointly do something in breach of that duty, the employer is not vicariously liable;

   (b)   each employee in this case could plead *volenti* against the other, thus the defence was available to the employer when sued as being **vicariously** liable for their torts;

   (c)   it would be otherwise if the duty concerned had been a statutory duty placed on the employer or if the wrong had been that of a superior whose orders the plaintiff had been bound to obey.

Thus, where the duty has (perhaps even only partly) been broken by the employer or a 'superior' servant, the defence cannot be raised.

You can read extracts from some of the speeches in this case in *Cases and Materials* (**8.3.1**).

8.5.1.1   Other cases

The *ICI* decision is clear authority for the proposition that in actions by employees against their employer for breach of statutory duty it is only where the employer is sued **vicariously** for the breach of a statutory obligation **on the part of an employee** that the employer can plead *volenti*.

It is not clear whether the defence is available in **other** cases of breach of statutory duty. That is, in cases not involving claims by employees against their employers.

Winfield (p. 203) argues that the defence does apply in other contexts, subject to contrary provision in the legislation itself. *Street* (p. 411) suggests that it might be contrary to public policy **generally** to allow someone to avoid their statutory duty.

You may be surprised to learn that such an important point awaits resolution by the courts. It is submitted that it cannot be the case that Parliament intended the defence to apply generally to statutory obligations.

8.5.2   CONTRIBUTORY NEGLIGENCE

In general terms the rules provided by the Law Reform (Contributory Negligence) Act 1945 apply.

The only qualification is that since the object of statutes like the Factories Act 1961 is to protect workers from acts of inattention, slight inadvertence tends to be ignored, even though such a slip by the servant might be enough to make the master vicariously liable to an injured third party. As Stable J put it in *Carr v Mercantile Produce Ltd* [1949] 2 KB 601:

> The Factories Act [the predecessor of the 1961 Act] is there not merely to protect the careful, the vigilant and the conscientious workman but, human nature being what it is, also the careless, the indolent, the inadvertent, the weary and even, perhaps, in some cases, the disobedient.

For example, in *Mullard v Ben Line* [1970] 1 WLR 1414, the plaintiff, an experienced ship repairer, fell through a hatch left open by the defendant in breach of statutory duty. The Court of Appeal, reducing the assessment of the plaintiff's share of the blame from 50 per cent to 33 per cent, held that an employee should not be blamed too severely for a momentary error.

In *Ryan v Manbre Sugar Ltd* (1970) 114 SJ 492, Lord Denning MR found that pure inadvertence (slipping down factory steps known to be slippery) could not amount to contributory negligence.

The standard of care is that of the ordinary prudent worker (or other person protected by the statute) assessed in all circumstances of the case.

There are a number of decisions in which plaintiffs have failed owing to their contributory negligence, but that has been where the plaintiff was 'fantastically wrong' or where 'it was a crazy thing to do'. The courts favour the employee where he is injured as a result of his employer's breach of statutory duty, at least where that duty was imposed for the protection of the employee. The courts, it seems, will find an employee guilty of contributory negligence only in cases where that negligence is very clearly established as the part cause of the injury.

It may be that in the context of statutory duties (at any rate in the industrial sphere) a more subjective approach is taken to the issue of contributory negligence.

You will find two cases on contributory negligence in *Cases and Materials* (8.3.2).

Please read the account of the decision in *Westwood v Post Office* [1974] 3 All ER 184 in *Cases and Materials* (8.3.2). Write down, in one short paragraph, the result of their Lordships' deliberations.

It appears from the decision of the majority of the Law Lords in *Westwood* that no reduction in damages for contributory negligence will be made where the plaintiff's 'conducive folly' has taken the form of disobedience (the plaintiff was suing his employer for breach of statutory duty) rather than of negligence.

8.5.2.1 Experience

As we have seen, an employer who is put in breach of a statute solely by an employee's default can claim, where the circumstances allow, that the injury and breach of duty have been caused by the **employee**.

It may be, although this is on the whole more true where the common law duty of care is involved (see **8.6**), that in some circumstances a competent and experienced person can be expected to look after himself. Much depends on the circumstances of the case.

Thus, in *Norris* v *Moss* [1954] 1 WLR 346, the plaintiff began to repair some scaffolding in a way described as 'fantastically wrong' and was held solely responsible for his consequent injuries.

On the other hand, in *Boyle* v *Kodak Ltd* [1969] 2 All ER 439, the House of Lords held that once the plaintiff has established that there was a breach of statute imposing strict liability on the employer, and that the breach caused the accident, he need do no more. The employer has a good defence, however, if he can prove that it was only the act or default of the plaintiff himself which caused or contributed to the non-compliance,

In this case, the relevant statutory obligation was imposed on **both** the employer and the employee. It was held that the employers had not proved that they had instructed the plaintiff, who was inexperienced, on how to comply with the regulations; therefore their breach of statutory duty was a cause of the damage. The plaintiff's damages were reduced by one half, since he was also in breach of the statutory duty.

The House said, however, that if the duty had been imposed solely on the employer the plaintiff's damages would not have been reduced although performance of the duty was delegated to him, unless the employer proved that he had been contributorily negligent in accordance with the terms of the 1945 Act.

8.5.3 GENERAL OBSERVATIONS ON DEFENCES

We have seen that there is uncertainty about the application of *volenti* to breach of statutory duty in cases other than those involving employers and employees.

You will also have noticed that the cases discussed in relation to contributory negligence are all employment cases. It is important not to lose sight of the fact that the defence applies to the action for breach of statutory duty **generally**. The cases quoted can be taken to illustrate, *mutatis mutandis* (i.e. the necessary changes in the factual circumstances being made) relevant, **non-employment**, issues of causation.

It has been suggested that the courts tend to take a more subjective approach to the question of contributory negligence where employees are concerned, and this factor should be taken into account when considering the use of these authorities for purposes of argument by analogy.

SAQ 99

This is a suitable point at which to pause and take stock of the action for breach of statutory duty. List the elements of the cause of action; elements which have to be established by the plaintiff.

In order to bring a civil action the plaintiff must prove that:

(a) there was an obligation on the defendant;

(b) the statute intends to allow an action in tort;

(c) he was one of the class of persons protected by the statute;

(d) the harm suffered by him is within the scope of the general class of risks at which the statute is directed;

(e) the defendant has breached the statute;

(f) the breach caused the damage.

The learner must always bear in mind, of course, that all of this relates only to those statutes which do not *prima facie* confer a civil cause of action in tort for their breach, because they are **silent** on the point. Statutes such as the Occupiers' Liability Act 1957 exist only to give such an action, whilst **others** state expressly that no action in tort is available.

Some more recent statutes, however, whilst not created **solely** for this purpose, do state that an action in tort is available for their breach.

The Consumer Protection Act 1987 provides an example of this type of legislation. Section 41 of that Act provides that breaches of **consumer safety regulations** (a matter for criminal sanctions) made under Part II of the Act are enforceable by actions in tort for breach of statutory duty. This provision must not be confused with Part I of the Act, which imposes strict liability in tort for defective products and which is discussed in **Chapter 13**.

The Health and Safety at Work Act 1974, is a further example of this more modern approach. This is, in the main, a piece of legislation concerned with the imposition of criminal offences and does not provide for compensation in the civil law.

In s. 47 of the 1974 Act it is provided that a breach of the **general** duties arising under the Act, which is a criminal offence, is not actionable in civil law. A breach of regulations, made under the Act, will, however, be actionable in tort **unless** the regulations **themselves** provide otherwise.

An example of regulations made under the 1974 Act are the Construction (Design and Management) Regulations 1994 (SI 1994 No. 3140), which came into force on 31 March 1995. In s. 22 of the Act, 'Enforcement', it is provided as follows:

> Breach of a duty imposed by those Regulations, other than those imposed by regulation 10 and regulation 16(1)(c), shall not confer a right of action in any civil proceedings.

The Act will eventually replace legislation such as the Mines and Quarries Act 1954, the Factories Act 1961, and the Offices, Shops and Railway Premises Act 1963, with an appropriate safety regime. Central to the scheme are the Management of Health and Safety at Work Regulations 1992.

In broad terms, the 1974 Act provides for **general duties**, laid down in the Act; for **regulations**, to be made under the Act; and for **codes of practice**, to be made under the Act.

This statutory scheme is administered by the Health and Safety Executive, and is now substantially complete, having been given fresh impetus in recent years by a spate of European Community Directives.

Please turn to *Cases and Materials* (8.3.2) and consider the decision in *Hewett* v *Alf Brown's Transport Ltd* [1991] ICR 471. Write down the result in *one* paragraph.

It was found that there existed a foreseeable risk of injury to families of the defendant's employees but, on the facts, the plaintiff's husband had **not actually** been exposed to the risk of lead contamination whilst removing waste from the site. Thus, the defendant was not liable for breach of statutory duty to the husband, nor was it liable for breach of its common law duty (see **8.6**) to him. Therefore, there could be no liability to the plaintiff because the degree of exposure to contamination of her husband was minimal and not culpable.

8.6   An Employer's Liability at Common Law

8.6.1   INTRODUCTION

In less modern terms, this is the 'master's common law duty to his servant'. You will recall the words 'master' and 'servant', from your study of vicarious liability in **Chapter 1**.

At the outset, you would do well to remember that in actions brought by employees against their employers it is common to sue for breach of the duty we are about to examine, **as well** as for breach of statutory duty, **and** vicarious liability.

An employer owes a **personal** duty of care in common law negligence to his employees. According to Lord Herschell in *Smith* v *Baker and Sons* [1891] AC 325:

> . . . [T]he contract between employer and employed involves on the part of the former the duty of taking reasonable care to provide proper appliances, and to maintain them in a proper condition, and so to carry on his operations as not to subject those employed by him to unnecessary risk.

The duty of care in tort is therefore based on the **consensual** relationship between employer and employee, it is a corollary of the contractual obligation and is therefore influenced by the terms of the contract.

Although it might be said to be a *Donoghue* type of duty, it is **independent** of the 'neighbour' principle. It follows, therefore, that:

(a)   it is an obligation arising in **both** contract and tort;

(b)   this is an issue quite **separate** from that of vicarious liability.

The leading case is the House of Lords decision in *Wilsons and Clyde Coal Co.* v *English* [1938] AC 57, in which it was held that the 'master' must use reasonable care and skill for the safety of the 'servant'. This is simply **one** facet of a **single** duty of care, but that duty may be divided into three aspects:

(a)   an obligation to provide reasonably competent supervisors and workmates;

(b)   an obligation to provide premises, plant and materials;

(c)   an obligation to furnish a safe system of work.

It is a **single** duty, but of a manifold nature. You will have noticed by now that there is overlap between the three aspects.

The duty is personal and non-delegable by the employer. As Lord Wright put it in *Wilsons*: 'It is the obligation which is personal to him (the master) and not the performance.'. So if the employer does delegate the duty, he himself remains responsible.

If you turn to *Cases and Materials* (**8.4.1**), you will find a more recent illustration of the duty in *McDermid* v *Nash Dredging and Reclamation Co. Ltd* [1987] 2 All ER 878.

8.6.2   GENERAL NATURE OF THE DUTY

Before we proceed to examine the three aspects of the duty, we will look at the duty's general characteristics.

This duty is a branch of the law of negligence; a duty of care developed to fit the relationship between master and servant. The burden of proof rests on the plaintiff.

The plaintiff's task in this regard may be easier where the employer is also in breach of some statutory duty, and the ambit of each duty coincides with the other. You will remember from your studies in **Chapter 3** that s. 11 of the Civil Evidence Act 1968 provides that a **conviction** for a criminal offence is admissible in civil proceedings as evidence that the person so convicted committed the offence. (This provision may, of course, also assist a plaintiff who is suing in tort for breach of a statutory duty.)

We have to take note of the effect on the duty of the Employers' Liability (Defective Equipment) Act 1969, which is dealt with at **8.6.4**, but in general this duty, owed by an employer to his employee (**not** to his **independent contractor**) is one of **reasonable** care.

This is not a liability imposed regardless of fault. The obligation is fulfilled by the exercise of due care and skill:

(a) a mere omission may be enough, actual knowledge on the employer's part of a danger is not necessary if he **ought** to have known of it;

(b) evidence of conformity to the common practice of those engaged in the activity in question is important in showing due care, as it is in any area of negligence;

(c) whether there has been a breach of the duty is a question of **fact**, as in all cases of negligence.

In *Harris* v *Bright's Asphalt Contractors Ltd* [1953] 1 All ER 395, Slade J said that this was:

a duty not to subject an employee to any risk which the employer can reasonably foresee and which he can guard against by any measure, the convenience and expense of which are not entirely disproportionate to the risk involved.

For example, in *Richardson* v *Stephenson Clarke Ltd* [1969] 1 WLR 1695, the plaintiff was left to choose his own equipment. He was careless in his choice, and suffered injury as a result. The defendant was not negligent in the circumstances, because the plaintiff was an **experienced** worker, who could safely be left to select his equipment from that offered by his employer. The equipment **itself** was safe.

Finally, a more recent illustration can be found in *Smith* v *Scott Bowyers Ltd* [1986] IRLR 315. The plaintiff, an employee of the defendant, was aged twenty and had been employed for nineteen months. He was injured through slipping on a greasy factory floor. The defendant knew of this risk and had issued its employees, including the plaintiff, with wellington boots which had diamond ridge soles. These boots could be replaced on request.

The plaintiff's injury was due to the fact that he had not asked for new boots to replace his current ones (themselves replacements) which were worn out and dangerous. At first instance it was found that the defendant was liable for breach of duty because it had not emphasised the danger nor conducted safety checks of the boots. The plaintiff's damages were reduced by one third for contributory negligence.

The Court of Appeal, however, allowed the defendant's appeal. There was no obligation on the employer in this instance to instruct its employees to wear the boots, or to inspect the condition of the soles from time to time. The plaintiff's own lack of care, in failing to renew the wellingtons, was **the** cause of his injury.

SAQ 100

Pause here for a moment or two. What are the *three* elements of the employer's special common law duty?

These elements are:

(a)   an obligation to provide reasonably competent supervisors and colleagues;

(b)   an obligation to provide proper premises, plant and materials;

(c)   an obligation to provide a safe system of work.

We are now in a position to consider each of the three aspects of the employer's common law duty, but at the outset we must be careful to remember that it is a **single** duty, of a manifold nature, and that its three 'aspects' overlap with each other.

8.6.3   REASONABLY COMPETENT SUPERVISORS AND COLLEAGUES

This facet of the duty is no longer as important since the abolition, by the Law Reform (Personal Injuries) Act 1948, of the doctrine of 'common employment'. According to this **common law** doctrine, an employee was understood to have agreed to bear the risk arising from the negligence of fellow employees for the purpose of **vicarious** liability. As we have seen in **Chapter 1**, because of this reform many actions that are today brought in vicarious liability would previously have been pursued in employer's liability.

The employer's special duty may still be useful, however in respect of employees given to bullying, practical jokes and similar behaviour.

Please stop reading for a moment. Why should this duty be more useful in such situations than vicarious liability?

If you think back to **Chapter 1** and to vicarious liability, the problem is one of bringing such behaviour within the employee's 'course of employment'.

In *Hudson* v *Ridge Manufacturing* [1957] 2 QB 348, the employee, described as 'not over intelligent', had a **four-year record** of practical joking at work. The plaintiff, a fellow employee, was injured by one of the miscreant's 'jokes', and was held entitled to damages from the employer for breach of the special duty of care. The employer had been negligent in not controlling the activities of the joker, who could have been **dismissed** for misconduct.

However, in *Smith* v *Crossley Bros* (1951) 95 SJ 655, there was no liability on the employer for severe injuries to a sixteen-year-old employee, caused when two fellow employees played a cruel and highly dangerous prank on him, because this was not a reasonably foreseeable event in the circumstances. There was no record of misdeeds, as in *Hudson*, therefore the employer was not negligent. The incident was an isolated one.

You may be interested to know that actions in vicarious liability were unsuccessful in **both** cases, because the acts in question were not within the employee's course of employment.

SAQ 102

Can you think of any *other* circumstances in which an employer might be liable for this aspect of his duty?

Where there is no fault on the part of the other employee, but an injury is caused by negligent staffing, i.e. the employer hires an insufficiently qualified person, the employer may be liable. In *Black (or Butler)* v *Fife Coal Co. Ltd* [1912] AC 149, a colliery manager was employed who had no experience of carbon monoxide in a pit where its presence was a possible danger. The employer was found liable to the plaintiff, who was injured as a result, for negligent choice of supervisor.

The obligation at this point also requires the employer to instruct the employee on the operation of any tools or equipment used in the work involved.

'Bullying in the workplace' is, today, a high-profile issue and should be considered as a future source of litigation. You should also consider the applicability of **vicarious** liability of an employer in this context (see **Chapter 1**), though difficulties may be encountered in satisfying the requirements of 'course of employment', bearing in mind that bullying will invariably involve **intentional** behaviour on the part of the offending colleague.

Bullying, by whatever means, is essentially harassment and is thus discriminatory in terms of employment law. Employers who fail to curtail it may find themselves liable with the perpetrator(s). In the case of *Harrison* v *Lawrence Murphy & Co., The Chartered Secretary*, 1 March 1998, a female employee was subjected to several months of bullying and sexual harassment by a senior legal executive, whose actions were witnessed by the senior partner who did nothing in response. The firm **settled** the case for £50,000.

8.6.4   THE PROVISION OF ADEQUATE PLANT, MATERIALS, AND PREMISES

This aspect of the employer's duty covers the provision of appropriate equipment, including safety devices and protective clothing, as well as the maintenance of existing equipment.

At **common law** the ordinary principles of negligence apply. Thus, in *Davie* v *New Merton Board Mills* [1959] AC 604, it was held by the House of Lords that where the plaintiff had been injured by a defective metal 'drift' (a type of tool) which splintered in use, his employer was not liable in negligence if all reasonable care had been taken in:

(a)   buying a reputable make of tool;

(b)   from a reputable source; and

(c)   the defect was of a **latent** nature, i.e. was not discoverable upon reasonable inspection.

The court took the view that the employer had not delegated performance of his obligation to the manufacturer, because the latter is not someone for whom the employer is responsible.

Later cases limited *Davie* to its own facts, but the general position was felt to be unsatisfactory in that an employee could in some cases be without a remedy merely for the fact that he could identify the manufacturer.

Today, however, s. 1(1) of the Employers' Liability (Defective Equipment) Act 1969, provides that:

> where . . . an employee suffers personal injury in the course of his employment in consequence of a defect in equipment provided by his employer for the purposes of the employer's business; and the defect is attributable wholly or partly to the fault of a third party (whether identified or not), the injury shall be deemed to be also attributable to negligence on the part of the employer . . .

Read the passage from the 1969 Act, and draw up a list of its important features.

In your list you might have included the following:

- the Act applies to **employees**
- who suffer **personal injury**
- in **the course of their employment**
- because of a defect in **equipment**
- **provided by** the **employer**
- for the **employer's business**
- the defect must be due to the **fault** of a **third** party
- who **need not** be identified
- the injury is **deemed** to be **also** due to the **employer's** negligence.

It follows, therefore, that: 'employee' does **not** include **a self-employed person**, i.e. an independent contractor; liability on the part of the **employer** is **strict**.

The employer may recover from the manufacturer, where appropriate: by suing in contract; by claiming on an indemnity (where he has been indemnified by the manufacturer); by seeking a contribution under the Civil Liability (Contributions) Act 1978 (dealt with in **Chapter 1**).

The employee is not prevented from proceeding **directly** against the **manufacturer**.

Can you identify the basis of such a claim?

The employee can sue for breach of the manufacturer's duty (the so-called 'narrow' rule) in *Donoghue* v *Stevenson*; or breach of obligation under Part II of the Consumer Protection Act 1987. The former requires proof of negligence and the latter involves strict liability. Both causes of action are dealt with in **Chapter 13**.

The advantage to the employee of suing under the 1969 Act is that if he can show, on the balance of probabilities, there must have been fault on the part of some third party (say, the manufacturer) because of the nature of the defect in the equipment provided by the employer, the employer is liable whether or not he was at fault. The injury must have been caused by the defect.

You can read the Act, and two cases relating to it, namely *Coltman* v *Bibby Tankers Ltd* [1987] 3 All ER 1068 and *Knowles* v *Liverpool City Council* [1993] 4 All ER 321 in *Cases and Materials* (8.4.2).

8.6.4.1   Plant and premises

The duty at common law is to provide and maintain safe plant and safe premises. In *Toronto Power Co.* v *Paskwan* [1915] AC 734, Channell J said:

> It is true that the master [employer] does not warrant the plant, and if there is a defect on reasonable examination, or if, in the course of working, plant becomes defective and the defect is not brought to the master's [employer's] knowledge and could not by reasonable diligence have been discovered by him, the master [employer] is not liable, and further, a master [employer] is not bound at once to adopt the latest improvements and appliances.

In the case of plant, mere temporary failure of maintenance might not be enough to breach the duty although regular inspection is probably necessary in the case of complex or dangerous machinery.

The duty includes a failure to provide obviously necessary equipment, or that which a reasonable employer ought to regard as needed. It covers necessary safety devices on dangerous machinery, and the provision of protective equipment where necessary.

You should remember, however, that the employer's obligation is one of **reasonable** care in the circumstances, not a warranty of the safety of plant and equipment. In some cases it may be sufficient to rely on the employee himself rectifying simple defects in the equipment used by him.

Please stop what you are doing for the moment, and consider whether there is any qualification to be made to the requirement of reasonable care in relation to plant and equipment.

There is the effect of the Employers' Liability (Defective Equipment) Act 1969 to be accommodated . This, as we have already seen, imposes strict liability upon an employer in certain circumstances, where equipment is supplied by the employer for use in his business.

As far as 'premises, or 'place of work' is concerned, the employer is expected to make the place, and the access to that place, as safe as reasonable care and skill will allow.

Thus, in *Latimer* v *AEC Ltd* [1953] AC 643, the plaintiff was one of four thousand employees at the defendant's factory; he slipped, at night, on the factory floor, the surface of which was oily. The floor had been flooded as the result of a very heavy thunderstorm, and when the flood subsided it left an oily film on the surface. The House of Lords held, overruling the trial judge, that it was not unreasonable for the defendants to put on the night-shift rather than close the factory until the oily surface had been rendered safe. In the circumstances there was insufficient evidence of want of reasonable care.

It follows from this reasoning that danger caused by some fleeting, or temporary, or exceptional condition **might** not invoke liability; but each case must always be considered on its **facts**.

Premises of a third party

Liability may extend, in effect, to the premises of some third party; it may also cover a third party's plant and equipment. It all depends on the circumstances of each case; it is an issue of a **pragmatic** nature.

In *Wilson* v *Tyneside Window Cleaning Co.* [1958] 2 QB 110, Pearce LJ said:

> Whether the servant [employee] is working on the premises of the master or on those of a stranger, that duty is still the same; but as a matter of common sense its performance and discharge will probably be vastly different in the two cases. The master's own premises are under his control: if they are dangerously in need of repair he can and must rectify the fault at once if he is to escape the censure of negligence. But if a master sends his plumber to mend a leak in a private house, no one could hold him negligent for not visiting the house himself to see if the carpet in the hall creates a trap. Between these extremes are countless possible examples in which the court may have to decide the question of fact. Did the master take reasonable care so to carry out his operations as not to subject those employed by him to unnecessary risk? . . . So viewed, the question whether the master was in control of the premises

ceases to be a matter of technicality and becomes merely one of the ingredients, albeit a very important one, in a consideration of the question of fact whether, in all the circumstances, the master took reasonable care.

The employee is entitled to be protected against sources of danger created by anyone who should reasonably have him in contemplation, including another contractor working on the premises.

Whether a warning of danger is sufficient in any of the above cases is a matter to be decided in the light of the facts. The question to be answered in this context is: 'was reasonable care taken to protect **this** employee in the **particular** circumstances?'.

In some situations the employer may have to take positive action to protect the employee, whilst in others the fact that the employee knowingly incurs the risk may be evidence of his contributory negligence.

You will by now be aware that *volenti non fit injuria* is a difficult defence to establish in employment cases.

Can you think of another cause of action that might be available to an employee, who is injured whilst working on the premises of a third party?

Where someone is employed to work on the premises of a third party, he is a lawful visitor of the **occupier**, who owes him the common duty of care under the Occupiers' Liability Act 1957.

You can read the interesting decision in *Square D Ltd* v *Cook* [1992] IRLR 34 in *Cases and Materials* (**8.4.2.1**).

We now come to the third facet of the employer's common law duty to his employee.

8.6.5 THE PROVISION OF A PROPER SYSTEM OF WORKING AND EFFECTIVE SUPERVISION

This is of a two-fold nature, namely the **putting in place** of a system **and** its **continuing operation**.

In *Wilsons and Clyde Coal Co.* (see **8.6.1**) Lord Justice Clerk Aitchison (a Scottish judge) said that there is no responsibility on the employer for 'isolated or day-to-day acts of the servant of which the master is not presumed to be aware and which he cannot guard against'. He is responsible for 'the practice and method adopted in carrying on the master's business of which the master is presumed to be aware and the insufficiency of which he can guard against.'.

In *Wilsons* the employer had placed dangerous cutting machinery in a narrow mine passage, and employees used this opening on a frequent basis. It was held that this amounted to an unsafe system of work.

This case was considered in *Speed v Thomas Swift and Co. Ltd* [1943] KB 557, in which the plaintiff was engaged in loading a boat from a barge. He was injured when a hook on a winch caught in the boat's rail. These were special circumstances, on the facts, not having occurred on any previous occasion. Lord Greene, agreeing with Lord Justice Clerk Aitchison's description of 'system of work' in *Wilsons*, said:

> It may include the physical lay-out of the job – the setting of the stage, so to speak – the sequence in which the work is to be carried out, the provision in proper cases of warnings and notices, and the issue of special instructions.

> A system may be adequate for the whole course of the job or it may have to be modified or improved to meet circumstances which arise. Such modifications or improvements appear to me equally to fall under the head of systems.

Write a short statement, setting out what you think was the outcome of this case.

You might have said that the system of work, used on previous occasions, should be modified for this one operation. Any required modification would be part of the system. The employer was found liable for negligence because the failure to modify meant there was no safe system of work on this one occasion.

Thus a normally safe system may be made dangerous in a particular situation, which never recurs, yet there can be an obligation on the part of the employer to see that appropriate modifications are made to the original scheme.

In many instances employees do not follow approved schemes of work, ignoring measures established for their own safety. The reasons for this state of affairs cover a wide spectrum, ranging from wilful disregard, through inexperience, mere inattention, annoyance, to getting in the way of work.

The employer is always under a duty to take reasonable precautions for his employee's safety, but he is not an insurer of safety, nor is his relationship to his employee similar to that of a schoolteacher to his pupil. In appropriate circumstances, no doubt, an employer can rely on the good sense of a skilled worker to avoid danger of which he has been warned. In general, however, a master cannot expect his servants to lay down and operate a system for themselves.

In *General Cleaning Contractors v Christmas* [1953] AC 180, the plaintiff was cleaning outside windows. He opened a window slightly, and held onto the ledge to balance. As he did so, the bottom sash moved; he fell and was injured.

It was held by the House of Lords that it is not up to workmen to devise and take safety precautions. It is the duty of the employer to consider the situation, devise a suitable system, instruct the men what they must do and supply any necessary equipment, for example, window wedges in this case. Lord Oaksey said:

> An employer must take into account that workmen may have disregard for their own safety. This means they must minimise the danger of a workman's own carelessness and take reasonable care to ensure that employees comply with necessary safety precautions.

At this point, it would be helpful if you paused for a while and thought about the employer's duty in general terms. Set out your answer in one written paragraph.

The duty of care is that of an ordinary, prudent employer. It will normally suffice for the defendant to show that he has provided the protection which accords with the standard practice in the enterprise or undertaking concerned; or that he has complied with the terms of any relevant statutory provisions.

In *Clifford* v *Charles H Challen & Son Ltd* [1951] 1 KB 495, protective cream was provided in the defendant's factory to protect workmen against dermatitis. But the foreman, a 'superior servant', of supervisory status, made known to workmen his dislike of the cream and encouraged slackness regarding its use.

It was held that the employers were liable to the plaintiff who contracted dermatitis. The employers had not taken reasonable care for the safety of workmen.

However, in *Woods* v *Durable Suites Ltd* [1953] 1 WLR 857, the facts were similar to *Clifford* but in this case the employers not only provided cream, they also posted warnings in the factory about the consequences of not using it. It was held that the employers had taken reasonable care, and were therefore not liable.

It must always be borne in mind, however, that the duty is of a personal nature, i.e. personal to the **employer** and personal to the **employee**. The duty is personal to the employer in that it is **non-delegable**, which means that though **practical** performance of the duty can be delegated to another, **legal responsibility** for its performance cannot.

As far as the employee is concerned, the employer's obligation is of a personal nature in that it is owed to **him**, or **her**, as an **individual**. Thus, there may be circumstances of which the employer is aware, or ought to be aware, making an individual employee a more likely victim of injury than another worker in the same situation.

In *Paris* v *Stepney Borough Council* [1951] AC 367, the House of Lords said that in considering whether employers are negligent, regard must be had to their knowledge of the physical characteristics of a particular employee. In this case the employer had not taken reasonable care to protect the particular employee by providing him with safety goggles when they knew he was one-eyed. A two-eyed employee doing the same job would not have needed the same protection, because the risks in **general** were not too high.

You will, of course, know by now that each case turns on its facts, and we can contrast with this decision *Withers* v *Perry Chain Co.* [1961] 1 WLR 1314. The plaintiff contracted dermatitis at work, and she was offered 'safer' alternative employment. This she willingly accepted, yet dermatitis recurred. She sued for damages, contending that since her weakness was known to her employer, she should not have been involved in any work which exposed her to the risk of dermatitis. The Court of Appeal held that her employer had acted reasonably in the circumstances, the only alternative was to dismiss her.

Bux v *Slough Metals*, a case referred to at **8.4.1.1**, is an example of a finding of an unsafe system because of the individual characteristics of the employee in question. You may recall that the employer had not taken any steps to persuade the employee to use the safety equipment.

You will find the following cases in **Cases and Materials** (**8.4.3**). They provide further illustrations of this aspect of the employer's duty of care: *Charlton* v *Forrest Printing Ink Co. Ltd* [1980] IRLR 331; *White* v *Holland Precision Castings* [1985] IRLR 215; *Pape* v *Cumbria County Council* [1991] IRLR 493; *Mulcahy* v *Ministry of Defence* [1996] 2 All ER 758 (CA); *Williams* v *British Coal Corporation, The Times*, 24 January 1998; *Tarrant* v *Ramage* [1998] 1 Lloyd's Rep 185.

8.6.5.1 Safe system on premises of a third party

The employer's duty of care extends, where appropriate, to the provision of a safe system of work on the premises of third parties.

In *General Cleaning Contractors Ltd* (see **8.6.5**) the defendants were found liable for failing to provide a safe system of window-cleaning on a customer's premises.

In *Morris* v *Breaveglen Ltd* [1993] IRLR 350, it was held that where an employer sent an employee to work on a site under the direction and control of the main contractor, he remained liable to that employee if the system of work was unsafe. (The employee was sent under a labour only sub-contract.)

Furthermore if, in the past, he had allowed his employee to operate plant for which he had no proper training, the employer would be liable for his employee's injuries caused by the lack of training when the employee was using the main contractor's plant. *Wilsons and Clyde Coal Co.* and *McDermid* (see **8.6.1**) were applied.

The court also found that the employer was liable in tort for breach of statutory duty: the relevant plant had been used in breach of regulation 3 of the Construction (General Provisions) Regulations (SI 1961 No. 1580).

SAQ 109

There is a 'hidden' point to note in *Morris* v *Breaveglen*. Can you spot it?

The employee was found to be under the 'direction and control' of the main contractor, i.e. the latter could, where appropriate, be **vicariously** liable for that employee's torts committed in the course of his employment with the main contractor. Yet the defendant was still under an obligation to the employee to see that a safe system of work was in operation.

8.6.6   CONTRACT AND TORT

In *Johnstone* v *Bloomsbury Health Authority* [1991] 2 All ER 293, in which the plaintiff brought proceedings for a judicial declaration, it was held by the Court of Appeal that a doctor who is required by his employers to work so much overtime that injury to his health is reasonably foreseeable, may sue his employers in tort. The plaintiff claimed damages for clinical depression.

You will recall this case from **Chapter 3** on duty of care in negligence. It is, of course, concerned with the employer's duty of care, and provides a good illustration of how the terms of the contract underpinning the relationship of employer and employee impinge on the tortious aspects of that relationship.

The Health Authority, the doctor's employer, contended that the doctor's contractual commitment to work for up to an average of 88 hours per week, as required, either qualified or negated the employer's duty to take reasonable care for the doctor's health. Whilst two judges saw merit in this argument, the Court found, on balance, that the employer could only require the employee to work in line with the employer's duty to take reasonable care for the physical integrity of his employee.

SAQ 110

You may be wondering, after the Court of Appeal hearing in 1991, and the decision of that court discussed above, why there should now, in 1995, be an 'out-of-court settlement'. Can you think of the reason for this state of affairs?

The reason for this situation is that the Court of Appeal and other hearings were only concerned with the so-called **preliminary issue** of whether there was a case to argue at all. All argument was on the pleadings, and what sort of case they presented. In fact *Johnstone* was due to begin, as a full hearing, in the High Court in early May 1995.

On 26 April 1995, wide coverage was given in the press, and elsewhere, to the fact that Dr. Johnstone had received £5,000 in an out-of-court settlement from his employer. Estimated costs to date of £150,000 were also to be met by the employer. The dispute had been active for some six years and had involved ten court hearings.

8.6.7   NEW TYPES OF DAMAGE

Johnstone raises the possibility that the employer's duty may extend beyond care for the employee's mere physical safety. In the past, only **physical** safety seems to have been in issue. The case itself was concerned clearly with illness of a 'physical' **and** 'nervous' sort, i.e. stress and sleep deprivation.

In *Walker* v *Northumberland County Council* [1995] 1 All ER 737, it was held that the employer's duty of care to provide a safe system of work extended to a case where it was reasonably foreseeable that the employee might suffer psychiatric damage, due to stress brought on by the **amount** or **nature** of the work expected from the employee. You will find more detail on this important case in *Cases and Materials* (8.4.4).

In *Pocock* v *North East Essex Mental Health NHS Trust*, *The Guardian*, 3 March 1998, a widow accepted £25,000 in **settlement** of her claim that her husband, a mental health nurse, was driven to suicide by the stress of his job. The Trust denied negligence in failing to act when it became clear that the deceased was becoming ill as a result of the pressures on him: it claimed that it had done all that could have been reasonably expected. Popplewell J approved the **settlement**, which was for half the sum claimed.

However, the injury in question must be of a recognised kind, and fall within the established terms of the employer's duty of care. Thus, in *Mughal* v *Reuters Ltd*, *The Times*, 10 November 1993, the plaintiff, an employee of the defendant, claimed damages for injury suffered as a result of repetitive work, i.e. 'repetitive strain injury'. It was alleged that the employer had failed to provide a safe system of work in relation to the use of a VDU (Visual Display Unit).

It was held that repetitive strain injury is not in itself a condition known to medical science and, in any event, there was no known safe method of fitting or posture for individual employees. Therefore it was not reasonable to expect an employer to provide a safe system of work in such circumstances, because the knowledge required for setting one up was simply not available.

This may prove to be a myopic view, however; recent research indicates that repetitive strain injury (RSI) may well 'exist' as a recognised medical condition. A scientific study conducted for the charity **Action Research**, which focused not on muscles and joints but on the sensory nerves in the hand, found reduced sensitivity to vibration not only among RSI sufferers but also among office workers who had not developed the condition. The study is published in the International Archives Occupational and Environmental Health (*The Guardian*, 12 February 1998).

In the *Cumberland 'Times and Star'* 24 January 1997, it was reported that 'Lilliput Lane', a manufacturer of hand-painted model buildings, had **agreed** to a settlement of £29,568 damages plus costs in an action brought by an employee for failing to advise her about the risks of RSI. The plaintiff had been employed by the defendants as a model painter and had to work with very thin brushes; this meant repetitive wrist movements over long periods. She had been medically retired in 1992 because of the condition of her hands and elbows.

The House of Lords has, however, recently implicitly recognised RSI. In *Pickford* v *Imperial Chemical Industries plc* [1998] 3 All ER 462, the plaintiff alleged that she had suffered RSI as a result of her employment as a typist with the defendant. Her claim failed for the following reasons:

(a)   she could not prove that her cramp was caused by her typing work, as opposed to being merely associated with it;

(b)   RSI was not reasonably foreseeable in **her** case;

(c)   the defendant was not negligent in failing to warn of the risk of such a condition arising in **her** case.

It is submitted that where it can be shown that the claim comes within the ambit of the employer's duty of care, for example, there is an unsafe system of work, claims such as that made in *Dooley* (discussed in **6.3.2**) could be accommodated within the terms of **this** duty rather than the one formulated in *Alcock* (see **6.3.5**).

Looked at in those terms, it can be argued that professional rescuers, for instance, could in some cases expect their employers to provide a safe system of work on the premises of a third party. It is, after all, reasonably foreseeable, that if proper methods of crowd control are not established in advance, police officers at events like the Hillsborough disaster may well suffer psychiatric damage.

It may be, of course, that the establishment of a 'safe system' would not be regarded as feasible in such circumstances as Hillsborough. It is at least **conceivable**, however, that such a claim could be based on the employment of incompetent fellow employees, etc.

The decision in *Frost*, in the Court of Appeal, was based partly on the obligations of an employer to his employees. *Frost* is discussed in **Chapter 6**.

ACTIVITY 46

Please consider the decision of the Court of Appeal in *Reid* v *Rush and Tomkins* [1989] 3 All ER 228 in *Cases and Materials* (5.4). In one sentence, write down the result of this case.

In *Reid* it was held that the employer's duty of care in tort does not embrace an obligation either to provide, or advise the employee himself to obtain, insurance cover for special risks when working abroad, where the contract of employment is silent on the point.

You will see that *Reid* is a 'pure economic loss' case, and can be considered together with the authorities in **Chapter 5**.

In that chapter at **5.5.8.3** you were asked to consider *Spring* v *Guardian Assurance plc and Others* [1994] 3 All ER 129. The House of Lords in *Spring*, like the court in *Reid*, also had to decide whether an employee could recover damages for pure economic loss, but on this occasion the issue before the court was whether an employer owed a duty of care in negligence with regard to the giving of a character reference for a past or present employee.

In finding that an employer **did** owe such a duty, some of their Lordships said that the duty rested on an implied term in the contract of employment to that effect.

This decision provides an interesting contrast with *Reid*, in which the Court of Appeal refused to follow that line of reasoning in respect of insurance cover.

Litigation in relation to 'passive' smoking (tobacco) allegedly causing injury to employees at work is almost certainly another issue which will have to be faced by employers. Thus, in *Bland* v *Stockport Borough Council, New Law Journal*, 12 February 1993, the plaintiff claimed damages from the defendant, her employer, for injury to her health caused by exposure to cigarette smoke at work. Without accepting liability, the defendant **settled** the action for £15,000.

It is worthy of note that s. 7 of the Offices, Shops and Railway Premises Act 1963 requires the effective and suitable provision for securing and maintaining the ventilation of every work room by the circulation of adequate supplies of fresh or artificially purified air. An action for breach of statutory duty (see **8.3**) may also be possible in this context.

In *Connelly* v *RTZ Corporation* [1997] 4 All ER 335, the House of Lords ruled that the plaintiff, who had developed throat cancer after working in the defendant's uranium mine in Namibia and who claimed that due to the defendant's negligence he had been exposed to high levels of radioactive uranium and silicia dust, could sue his former employers in England. Their Lordships said that legal aid was not available in Namibia (his English legal team was said to be willing to work on a 'conditional fee' basis, i.e. no win no fee); nor was highly professional representation from legal and scientific experts available in that country. These were cogent reasons for finding that the case could be tried in England.

(This decision may open the door for other multi-national companies with headquarters in England to be sued in the United Kingdom for the negligence of their overseas subsidiaries.)

8.6.8 COMPULSORY INSURANCE

The Employers' Liability (Compulsory Insurance) Act 1969 places an obligation on employers to take out insurance against liability to their employees for personal injury sustained in the **course of their employment**. This obligation is not limited to insuring against liability arising under the employer's common law duty, it extends to appropriate cases of breaches of statutory duty.

You will find the Act in *Cases and Materials* (8.4.5).

8.6.9 DEFENCES

8.6.9.1 Contributory negligence

An employer may plead the contributory negligence of the employee, under the provisions of the Law Reform (Contributory Negligence) Act 1945, where appropriate. The defence is accepted more readily than it would be in actions, say, under the Factories Act 1961, but where the conduct of the employee, alleged to be negligent, is the result of an effort to get on with his job for the benefit of the employer, the courts will be slow to find contributory negligence. 'Nonetheless, in practice, contributory negligence is often successfully invoked as a defence': Jones (p. 183).

The general provisions of the 1945 Act are examined in **Chapter 2**.

8.6.9.2 *Volenti non fit injuria*

We have seen, in **Chapter 2**, that *volenti* is an extremely difficult defence to establish in employer's liability cases. In principle, however, the defence ought to be available. The objection that it would be contrary to public policy to allow it, as in the case of actions for breach of statutory duty, would not apply here. In order to succeed, the defendant would have to establish:

(a) a genuine full **agreement**;

(b) given in the absence of **any** pressure;

(c) a clear assumption of the risk which was the subject of the agreement.

As *Winfield* (p. 220) puts it: '. . . the courts are unwilling to infer an agreement by the worker to run the risk of his employer's negligence merely because he remains in unsafe employment.'. It is suggested, however, by the learned author that the defence might be available where, as the result of a clear agreement to that effect, an employee accepted special remuneration ('danger money') for taking on some specific dangerous task.

As a final question for this chapter, consider whether the *employee* might have any obligations to his employer. After all, the relationship is a consensual one. Can you draw up a list of likely obligations?

Your list of likely obligations might look like this:

(a) an employee owes an implied **contractual** duty to exercise reasonable care in the performance of his or her duties generally;

(b) as a corollary of this duty, where the employee is **solely** to blame for damage caused by his or her tort committed in the course of his or her employment and the employer is found vicariously liable for that tort, the employer may seek an indemnity from the employee. The amount of indemnity payable would depend on what the court considered just in the circumstances;

(c) an employee owes an implied **contractual** duty to take reasonable care of his employer's property which has been entrusted to him;

(d) the Civil Liability (Contribution) Act 1978 provides that where an employer is vicariously liable for an employee's tort, but the employer is also partly responsible for the damage, i.e. he committed a tort himself against the injured person, the employer may seek a contribution from the employee for such amount as the court regards just. The 1978 Act is dealt with in **Chapter 1**.

The leading case is *Lister* v *Romford Ice Co.* [1957] AC 555, in which the appellant and his father were employed by the respondent as lorry-driver and mate. The appellant injured his father through negligent driving. The respondent employer was found vicariously liable for this tort. In contribution proceedings, the House of Lords held that the employer could claim an indemnity from the son, for breach of his contractual duty to his employer.

Vicarious liability is the subject of **Chapter 1**.

8.7 Summary

8.7.1 INTRODUCTION

In this chapter we have dealt with two, **separate**, causes of action:

(a) the action for breach of statutory duty; and
(b) the employer's common law duty of care, in negligence, to his or her employee.

The reason for not having two, discrete chapters dealing with these torts is that they commonly occur together, i.e. in suits brought by employees against their employers. Indeed, it has been pointed out that **vicarious liability** is also of great importance in this context. Vicarious liability is a topic dealt with in **Chapter 1**, but its relationship to employer's liability cannot be ignored; for that reason considerable reference to it is found in the present chapter.

Each of these causes of action involves its own **standards**: liability under statute is **often** strict (in all cases, the relevant standard is contained within the statute in question) and liability in vicarious liability is **strict**. At common law, the employer's duty requires proof of **negligence**.

The word 'absolute' is often used, in the context of statutory standards. 'Absolute' liability carries the implication that there are no defences available and, in the sense that the word is often used as a synonym for 'strict', confusion may often arise. In truth, it is probably better to talk of **degrees** of **strictness**, at least as far as the **law of tort** is concerned.

If a statute which creates a criminal offence, as many of them do, and imposes an 'absolute' or 'strict' standard of care, falls to be considered in the present context, i.e. an action for breach of statutory duty in **tort** is in question, then, whatever the position might be concerning defences to criminal liability, it is likely that the influence of **fault** will manifest itself in the context of **tort** via arguments on **causation:** *Ginty* provides an example of this line of reasoning (see **8.4.2.1**).

8.7.2 BREACH OF STATUTORY DUTY

Whilst the action for breach of statutory duty is of great **practical** importance in the context of industrial injuries, it is of course not confined to such cases; it is of **general** application, as many of the authorities make abundantly clear. In non-employment cases, an action for common law negligence is often combined with an action for breach of statutory duty.

Examples of all types of case appear in this book, and in *Cases and Materials*.

The action for breach of statutory duty, in the sense that we understand it in the **present** context, must be distinguished from those causes of action in tort which have been **specifically created** by statute. An obvious example of this latter type of action can be found in the legislation on occupiers' liability, which is dealt with in **Chapter 7**.

In this chapter we are concerned with statutes which say **nothing** about any remedy in tort. Many of **these** statutes are, in fact, concerned with the imposition of criminal penalties. The action for breach of statutory duty in **this** sense is **implied** at common law, and its basis and rationale is the subject of much confusion. Ultimately, the issue, as in the tort of negligence, is one of policy. As Jones (p. 290) puts it:

> In the vast majority of legislation, however, there is no express provision to indicate whether contravention will be actionable or not. Where the statute is silent the courts purport to 'discover' the intention of Parliament, but the truth is that, Parliament having pointedly omitted to express an intention, the construction of the statute, aided by certain 'presumptions', amounts to little more than judicial legislation, This in itself would not necessarily be a major ground of criticism, if it were possible to discern any coherent guiding principles employed by the courts to determine this question. However, there are so many conflicting 'presumptions' and contradictory statements as to the value of particular presumptions, that it is virtually impossible to predict how the courts will respond to a particular statute.

Again, as *Street* (p. 399) says:

> the existence of a cause of action for violations of a statute thus becomes primarily a matter of construction of the relevant statute. But in the vast majority of statutes to which the tort has been held to extend Parliament has imposed a duty on the defendant, expressly made breach of that duty a crime, and given no indication of whether a cause of action in tort is intended. On occasion, judges will readily imply such an intention. Yet in other circumstances, they equally adamantly deny the existence of any such parliamentary intent. Many of the decided cases can for the most part be regarded as decisions of policy whether breach of particular statutory provisions should be compensated for by way of damages awarded to the victim.

In view of the fact that some of the more modern legislation is explicit on the issue of the availability of an action in tort, for example the Health and Safety at Work Act 1974, it is to be hoped that this practice becomes more widespread.

You may care to consider the extracts from *The Interpretation of Statutes* (The Law Commission, Law Com. No. 21 of 1969) in *Cases and Materials* (8.5.1).

Few examinations in **tort** require **detailed** knowledge of particular legislation **outside those statutes which regulate tortious activity itself**. It is the general principles, such as they are, which are important in respect of any question on the action for breach of statutory duty. **Fictitious** statutes are often given in such contexts, the idea here being to work out a solution based on first principles.

If reference **is** made to a real legislation, it is common practice to set out the actual provision(s) which require attention. Again, unless the particular context dictates otherwise, it is a matter of applying **principle** to the given situation.

8.7.3   THE EMPLOYER'S COMMON LAW DUTY

We have seen that employers, apart from being prone to actions for breach of statutory duty, **also** owe their employees a special, **personal, non-delegable** duty of care at common law. This duty, traditionally known as the **master's** duty to his **servant** ('employment law' was originally labelled 'law of master and servant') is a corollary of the **contractual** relationship between the parties.

This duty requires proof of negligence for its breach and illustrates well how issues of **fact** are paramount outside the rarefied world of 'duty' in 'hard' cases, an issue dealt with in **Chapter 3**.

The **standard** of care, predominantly **the** issue in the present context, is a matter for the common law. It is likely, however, that the standards underpinning the general framework of the health and safety regime set up by the Health and Safety at Work Act 1974, will influence standards of care at common law.

We have seen that the **general** provisions of this Act are **not** amenable to actions in **tort** (**individual regulations** may be actionable, depending on what each set of regulations says) but that does not mean they will be without any effect in the law of tort. The **general** duty imposed on employers, by s. 2 of the 1974 Act, '. . . to ensure, so far as is reasonably practicable, the health, safety and welfare at work of all his employees', is a prime example of potential statutory influence on the common law. In fact, it complements and could be said to strengthen the common law duty; it reads remarkably like the common law duty itself.

Individual regulations will, *a fortiori*, ('with stronger reason') inevitably, also influence the common law obligation. Thus, for example, the Manual Handling Operations Regulations 1992, and the Provision and Use of Work Equipment Regulations 1992, require that where handling cannot be eliminated a detailed assessment must be made regarding the task in question, and employers must make 'suitable and sufficient' assessment of all risks to the health and safety of employees.

The common law duty of care is remarkably vital, as cases like *Walker* v *Northumberland CC* (see **8.6.7**) show. In spite of the fact that it depends on proof of negligence, it is also a stringent duty in the sense that whoever actually **performs** the obligation (it could, for example, be an independent contractor engaged by the employer), the legal responsibility remains with the employer. In *Winfield's* words (p. 221) '. . . the employer's duty is not so much a duty to take care but a duty that care be taken . . .'.

8.8 Further Reading

Specific
Atiyah, P.S., *Accidents, Compensation and the Law*, 5th edn (Peter Cane), London: Butterworths, 1993.
Stanton, K.M., *Breach of Statutory Duty in Tort*, London: Sweet & Maxwell, 1986.

General
Buckley, R.A., 'Liability in Tort for Breach of Statutory Duty' (1984) 100 LQR 204.
Hepple, B.A., and Matthews, M.H., *Tort: Cases and Materials*, 5th edn, London: Butterworths, 1996, chapter 12.
Jones, M., *Textbook on Torts*, 5th edn, London: Blackstone Press, 1996, chapters 5, 9.
Markesinis, B.S., and Deakin, S.F., *Tort Law*, 3rd edn, Oxford: Oxford University Press, 1994, pp. 307–325 and 485–496.
Salmond and Heuston, *Law of Torts*, 21st edn, London: Sweet & Maxwell, 1996, chapter 10 and pp. 464–474.
Street on Torts, 9th edn, London: Butterworths, 1993, Chapters 17, 22.
Weir, T., *Casebook on Tort*, 8th edn, London: Sweet & Maxwell, 1996, pp. 117–122, chapter 3.
Winfield and Jolowicz on Tort, 14th edn, London: Sweet & Maxwell, 1994, chapters 7, 8.

8.9   End of Chapter Assessment Question

Chill Hall is a hall of residence at the University of Radical Thinking. Under the Halls of Residence Act 1995, a fictitious statute, it is provided that all premises coming within the terms of the Act shall be heated from 1st October to 30th April to a temperature of at least 68°F, except between 11.00 p.m. and 6.00 a.m.

During icy winter weather the hall's boiler stops working. The temperature falls gradually during the evening until it is below freezing point. Paul, a student, suffers from frostbite and pneumonia as a result of exposure to the cold. Wally, the University handyman, is called in by the Warden of Chill Hall to attempt to repair the boiler. He is unable to do so and, in an attempt to heat the building, he drags a heavy oil heater out of a storeroom, injuring his back in the process.

Advise Paul and Wally on any rights of action they may have in the law of tort.

See *Cases and Materials* (8.7) for a specimen answer.

CHAPTER NINE

TRESPASS TORTS

9.1 Objectives

By the end of this chapter you should be able to:

■ explain the historical development of the trespass torts;

■ explain how the trespass torts are commonly used to resolve apparently unrelated issues such as disputes over the ownership of goods and the protection of civil liberties;

■ explain the characteristics of the different trespass torts;

■ apply the rules relating to trespass torts in practice.

9.2 Introduction

Make a list of the behaviour which you consider to be trespass on a separate piece of paper. Put this to one side.

9.3 General Historical Background to the Trespass Torts

The protection of the person from deliberately inflicted physical harm and restriction on freedom of movement, and the protection of interests in tangible property, especially the right to non-interference with land and goods, were historically the most important concerns of the law of torts. (*Street on Torts* at p. 5.)

These are very old established torts. They are based on the Writ of Trespass which is one of the original writs developed in medieval times. Strictly speaking this writ only covered direct and intentional harm to the interests referred to above. The action of trespass on the case covered indirect harm, and as the law developed it evolved into the separate action for negligence. Although we say the harm is 'intentional', that word is used in a rather specialised sense, as we will see later in relation to the individual torts.

9.3.1 THE MEANING OF INTENTION

For the moment keep in mind that 'intentional' is not the same as 'deliberate'. It is, in general, more a question of the act being voluntary. In areas covered by trespass you act at your peril, in the sense that if the result of your act is a direct interference with the defendant's interests, you will be liable for the consequences whether you meant to interfere or not.

9.3.2 HOW THE TRESPASS TORTS ARE HANDLED

As these are old torts, it is often the case that their rules are well defined, and can be set out very concisely. There is surprisingly little to say about them in a strictly legal sense. As we go through you will see that the ingredients of each separate tort have been briefly set out. The definitions are usually from *Street on Torts*, 9th edn, edited by Margaret Brazier, but this is my personal preference and does not suggest that *Street* is more definitive than other books. Indeed, I sometimes use another writer's definition if I regard it as more complete, or accurate, or better expressed.

9.3.3 LEGAL INVENTIVENESS

The trespass torts are in fact more interesting from the point of view of legal inventiveness, actions devised for one purpose being adapted to serve others. It is also notable that the various trespass actions are often utilised as the legal mechanism for litigating disputes which are essentially concerned with other areas of the law, such as civil liberties, contract and personal property.

9.3.4 A LIST OF TRESPASSES

There are a number of separate torts comprised within the general heading of trespass. These include:

(a) trespass to the person (assault and battery);

(b) false imprisonment (including wrongful arrest);

(c) trespass to land. This is technically known as trespass *quare clausum fregit* (i.e. in the narrow modern popular sense, by going onto someone's land, literally 'by breaking a boundary');

(d) trespass to goods;

(e) interference with goods (conversion).

How does this compare with the list you made for **Activity 47**?

Although related, each of these torts derived from a different form of writ and represented a different form of action, each with its own detailed procedural rules. There are therefore distinctions between them which can be explained only on an historical basis. You will, however, be relieved to learn that we do not need to carry out any substantial historical investigation. It is enough to know the present scope of each tort.

9.3.5 ALLEGATIONS OF FORCE: FICTIONS AND THE ROYAL COURTS

When instituting an action for trespass there was always an allegation that the defendant had acted *vi et armis, et contra pacem domini regis* (with force of arms and contrary to the

King's Peace). This allegation (which might be, and often was, wholly fictitious) was originally inserted in medieval times to give a royal interest in the subject matter of the action (represented by the breach of the King's Peace) so as to confer jurisdiction on the Royal Court, rather than the competing local courts. It also harks back to the original reasons for giving a civil remedy for such matters at all, which were: first a desire to avoid remedies by way of self-help, which in violent mediaeval times could readily lead to an unacceptable level of feuding; and secondly a wish to reinforce the enforcement of the criminal law.

9.3.6   TRESPASS: TORT AND CRIME

Most trespasses are also crimes; various forms of assault, rape, theft and robbery. The recent cases in which women have sued in trespass to the person in respect of rape, adult victims have sued in respect of child abuse, and the civil action against Michael and Fitzroy Brookes for killing Lynn Siddons: *Halford* v *Brookes* [1991] 1 WLR 428, were very obvious examples of trespass, since it is hard to imagine more obvious examples of the deliberate and direct infliction of physical force.

They sometimes raise interesting issues as to procedure and evidence (e.g. the adoption of the criminal standard of proof in the 'murder' case, which has been adopted in the most recent abuse cases).

They were also unusual as the first modern examples of such actions which were not preceded by a criminal conviction. If such cases are rare, it is because the defendant is not worth powder and shot. In *Stubbings* v *Webb* [1993] 1 All ER 322, where a woman was complaining of physical and sexual abuse by two relatives, the judges pointed out that neither defendant appeared to be in a position to satisfy an award of damages. This is probably an implied criticism of the use of civil proceedings for cathartic purposes (to 'see justice done' and 'work out' the grief and anxiety).

It will sometimes be possible to pursue a claim and recover large damages. In *W* v *Meah* [1986] 1 All ER 935, a minicab driver underwent a personality change as a result of head injuries sustained in a road traffic accident. He then sexually assaulted two women. In these cases it was worthwhile to sue him because he had received damages for his personal injuries. Indeed the issues of liability of the original tortfeasor to pay additional damages by reason of this further damage flowing ultimately from his negligence have also engaged the court: *Meah* v *McCreamer* [1985] 1 All ER 367 and *Meah* v *McCreamer (No. 2)* [1986] 1 All ER 943. (See also **4.4.1.1**.)

In earlier days, the availability of damages was an incentive for the plaintiff to bring the defendant to justice, thus doing the job of the police and justices. The criminal law and civil law of trespass remain closely allied in relation to offences against the person, and cases in one field are generally regarded as authorities in the other, but the criminal law of offences against property has developed along very different lines.

The main difference in relation to offences and trespasses against the person is that the criminal law is more concerned with the degree of moral responsibility of the defendant, in order to ensure that punishment is justified by that moral responsibility. In civil proceedings, the level of compensation is based on the plaintiff's loss. The defendant, as we have seen, 'acts at his peril' and this may result in heavy damages arising from a trivial interference with the plaintiff.

9.3.7   THE PLACE OF TRESPASS

The interests protected by the trespass torts are also the most important recognised by society, although there is perhaps an excess of conservatism in the continuing primacy accorded to tangible belongings over intangible wealth. The state of the law reflects the condition of society at the time it developed, a period when wealth was largely tangible. It is, however, difficult to criticise the survival of this anomaly in trespass when a similar distinction is jealously guarded in negligence and other 'modern' torts in relation to economic loss as opposed to physical injury or damage.

Compare the trespass torts with negligence.

The trespass torts are closely based on a notion of rights, and the action relates to the infringement of the right, rather than the harm caused. On the other hand, only specific areas of activity are within the specific kinds of trespass. In negligence, on the other hand, the emphasis is on compensation and so actual, tangible harm must be shown. Against this, there is considerable room for development; 'the categories of negligence are never closed'. It is thus not necessary to fall within a strictly defined category; provided the claim is analogous to an existing category it can be entertained.

9.4   Trespass to the Person and False Imprisonment

9.4.1   OBJECTIVES

Within the general objectives of this chapter, by the end of this section you should be able to:

■   define both assault and battery in tort;

■   distinguish between criminal and civil assaults and batteries;

■   state what is meant by imprisonment;

■   describe and apply the justifications for imprisonment;

■   explain the relationship between trespass to the person and civil liberties.

9.4.2   TRESPASS TO THE PERSON

There are two forms of trespass to the person, assault and battery, and there is the related *Wilkinson* v *Downton* tort. There is some doubt as to the exact classification of this tort. In this text it is discussed in conjunction with harassment in the chapter on nuisance (i.e. **Chapter 10**). In this area criminal and civil rules as to the substance of the offence/tort (i.e. in criminal terms the *actus reus*) are largely the same, so your study in criminal law of offences under the Offences Against the Person Act 1861 is directly relevant. The crucial distinction is that in tort there is not the same detailed consideration of the mental element, i.e. *mens rea*, and there is no subdivision of the various categories of assault for purposes of sentencing. Since assault is defined by reference to battery, it is logical to consider the latter first.

9.4.3 BATTERY

Battery: Any act of the defendant which directly and either intentionally or negligently causes some physical contact with the person of the plaintiff without the plaintiff's consent. (*Street on Torts* at p. 24.)

We need to consider all the components of the definition.

9.4.3.1 Directly

There must be force, and the contact with the defendant must be the immediate result of the force. This will be a question of fact. If the harm is delayed there may be an action in negligence. The distinction is often illustrated by the example of a log being thrown from a window. If it hits a passer by as it falls to the ground, that is battery. If it falls harmlessly, but a pedestrian later trips over it, that is, at most, negligence. This is one of the distinctions between negligence and trespass.

9.4.3.2 Intentionally or negligently

It is now clear that a mere and innocent accident will not do. In *Fowler* v *Lanning* [1959] 1 All ER 290 (*Cases and Materials* (9.1.1.1)), the defendant discharged a shotgun while out shooting birds. The plaintiff was in the vicinity and sustained pellet wounds. In consequence the plaintiff started proceedings and served a statement of claim alleging that at a stated time and place 'the defendant shot the plaintiff'. There was no suggestion of a deliberate act, and the plaintiff did not allege negligence. Diplock J ruled that in the absence of an allegation of negligence the pleading was inadequate. In other words, even if the plaintiff proved what was in the statement of claim, this did not amount to a battery. It might have been otherwise if the defendant ought to have appreciated the presence of and risk to the plaintiff. The plaintiff was then allowed to amend the statement of claim to allege negligence and the action proceeded to trial. Unfortunately for the plaintiff there were several people in the shooting party and it was impossible to prove from which gun the pellets which had wounded the plaintiff came. She could thus not prove that, on balance, the defendant was responsible.

It is now probably the case that negligence will not be enough. In the USA battery is now restricted to intentional acts, in the sense that contact with the plaintiff was intended, and not merely a negligent side effect. This would mean that, in the example given earlier of the log, it would now be necessary to show that the log was being thrown at someone. English law is still somewhat unclear on the point. It does not matter if it hits someone other than the intended victim: *Livingston* v *Ministry of Defence* [1984] NI 356.

It has been suggested that battery is now confined to intentional acts. In *Letang* v *Cooper* [1964] 2 All ER 929, (*Cases and Materials* (9.1.1.1) the defendant directly harmed the plaintiff by running over her legs in his car while she was sunbathing. It was not intentional, although it was at least arguably negligent. The plaintiff had three years to bring an action in negligence, but omitted to do so. She then brought an action in battery for which the time limit was arguably six years. Since the plaintiff was too late to bring a claim in negligence, she was trying to argue she had longer to bring a claim in trespass. The Court of Appeal held that the absence of intention was fatal to a claim in battery. However the issue before the court was really one of limitation of actions, and the decision could be justified on other grounds. The court concentrated on whether the limitation period differed for trespass and negligence and found that it did not. The plaintiff was therefore too late anyway. While in their comments about the case (*obiter*) the judges were clearly encouraging plaintiffs to bring allegations based on negligence under the tort of negligence, it is not clear that they meant to reach a final and binding decision on the scope of battery.

In *Stubbings* v *Webb* [1993] 1 All ER 322, the House of Lords considered the limitation period applicable to intentional trespass, and concluded, following an analysis of the parliamentary history of the relevant provisions of the Limitation Act, that the intention had been to separate out 'accident' cases from trespass cases generally. The usual limitation for tort, including trespass, is six years, while for accident cases it is three years, with a discretion to extend it. As a result, although *Letang*, which was clearly an accident case, was rightly decided, it was wrong to apply the shorter limitation period to other trespass cases. In *Stubbings* v *Webb* itself this worked against the plaintiff, who was outside the six year period (she was claiming in relation to childhood sexual abuse which she had allegedly 'suppressed' for a number of years since reaching adulthood, and was therefore seeking unsuccessfully to rely on the various extensions permitted in accident cases where the claim cannot be brought within the three year period).

The House did not feel it necessary to consider the passages in *Letang* v *Cooper* as to whether there could be a negligent trespass. It would seem, however, in view of the way in which the procedural rules have been assimilated, that there is no meaningful difference between the two causes of action in an accident type case.

What, after all, is to be gained from suing in trespass rather than negligence if the object of the exercise is to obtain compensation for harm suffered? Virtually any harm amounting to trespass to the person will amount to negligence, and the procedural rules are similar.

Should trespass to the person exclude negligent acts?

It is clear that criminal batteries can be committed recklessly (albeit the recklessness must be of the *Cunningham* type: *R* v *Savage; DPP* v *Parmenter* [1991] 4 All ER 698. See also the Law Commission Paper 122 *Legislating the Criminal Code: Offences against the Person and General Principles* (1992), where the same definition (i.e. intentional or reckless) is used. It may therefore be the case that something short of direct intention will suffice for a civil claim.

It may be however that the wording of *Street's* definition will need to be reviewed sooner rather than later.

9.4.3.3   Physical contact

Injury is not required. As a trespass, battery is actionable *per se*. It is not necessary to prove substantial harm, merely that the plaintiff's rights have been infringed. An action can thus be brought to establish a principle, e.g. in relation to unlawful fingerprinting. It can also be brought where there is indignity but no physical injury. Negligence is of less assistance here since it will provide compensation only for actual tangible loss. It is worth noting, however, that where a technical touching is intended, but what actually transpires is something substantial (as in *Savage*), there is criminal and, by analogy, civil, liability for what actually occurs.

9.4.3.4   Without consent

This raises a number of quite complex issues, which have ramifications beyond the trespass torts.

Express consent
For instance, if you have ever undergone elective surgery you will know that you are required to sign a consent form. This consent must be genuine, but where the plaintiff is really complaining that, although they signed the form, they only did so because they were not properly informed about the implications of treatment, they are regarded as consenting. Any claim must be brought in negligence on the basis that advice on these matters is part of the doctor's professional responsibility: *Chatterton* v *Gerson* [1981] 1 All ER 257 (*Cases and Materials* (**9.1.1.2**)).

Is it reasonable for doctors to operate on you without your full, free and informed consent? If so, why? If not, why not?

There is a very serious issue here; should the *Bolam* test which you have already met as the standard test for medical negligence cases (see **3.7.1**), apply to advice given as to the risks and benefits of proposed treatment, or is some other test applicable? In the USA there must be informed consent. The doctor must tell the patient everything that a prudent patient would want to know about the risks and benefits of the treatment being offered. If not, the patient can sue in battery. In Canada and Australia a similar result is reached in a different way. Such cases are treated as being part of the doctor's professional responsibility, but in deciding whether the doctor has fulfilled that duty, a similar prudent patient test is applied.

Chatterton v *Gerson* concerned the application of intrathecal phenol (acid into the spinal cord!) as a pain relieving measure of last resort. At the time this was still experimental in the UK. Indeed the doctor in the case had learned the technique while working in the USA and there was little evidence of what was the general practice in terms of warnings and advice to patients. The plaintiff framed a claim in battery on the footing that she had not given true or informed consent to the treatment in the absence of proper explanation of the possible complications. This argument was rejected. Bristow J ruled:

> [W]hat the court has to do in each case is to look at all the circumstances and say: 'Was there a real consent?' I think justice requires that in order to vitiate the reality of consent there must be a greater failure of communication between doctor and patient than that involved in a breach of duty if the claim is based on negligence. When the claim is based on negligence the plaintiff must prove not only the breach of duty to inform, but that had the duty not been broken she would not have chosen to have the operation. When the claim is based on trespass to the person, then what the plaintiff would have decided if she had been given the information . . . is irrelevant.

> [O]nce the plaintiff is informed in broad terms of the nature of the procedure which is intended, and gives her consent, that consent is real, and the cause of action on which to base a claim for failure to go into risks and implications is negligence not trespass.

This case was followed in *Hills* v *Potter* [1983] 3 All ER 716 where the trial judge, Hirst J, considered the American case of *Canterbury* v *Spence* (1972) 464 F 2nd 772 (which established the doctrine of informed consent) and the Canadian cases of *Hopp* v *Lepp* (1980) 112 DLR (3rd) 67 and *Reibl* v *Hughes* (1980) 114 DLR (3rd) 1 (which established that the test for negligence was the prudent patient). He used these to support his conclusion that negligence rather than trespass was the appropriate action. Although both English cases were at first instance only, they have been accepted as representing the law.

Although it was now clear that the claim lay in negligence, it could still be argued that the prudent patient test should apply, rather than the *Bolam* test. The position was finally resolved by the House of Lords in the case of *Sidaway* v *Bethlem Royal & Maudsley Hospital Governors* [1985] 1 All ER 643. The case concerned an alleged failure to warn of the risks associated with a particular operation. The risk that eventuated was one which was significantly less than a 1% chance! There were difficulties because the plaintiff's evidence that no warning had been given was not accepted, but the surgeon had died before the trial so could not give evidence as to the scope of the warning. Unfortunately, the House was divided as to the proper test to be applied. The minority view was that one or other version of informed consent should apply, but the majority considered that the *Bolam* test was of universal application. Lord Diplock said:

> In English jurisprudence the doctor's relationship with his patient which gives rise to the normal duty of care to exercise his skill and judgment to improve the patient's health in any particular respect in which the patient has sought his aid has hitherto been treated as a single comprehensive duty covering all the ways in which a doctor is called upon to exercise his skill or judgment in the improvement of the physical or mental condition of the patient . . . This general duty is not subject to dissection into a number of component parts to which different criteria of what satisfy the duty of care apply, such as diagnosis, treatment and advice (including warning of any risks of something going wrong however skilfully the treatment itself is carried out).

His Lordship pointed out that *Bolam* itself concerned an allegation of failure to warn, which had been dealt with in the same terms as the allegation about inappropriate treatment. The US version of informed consent, which created an action based on trespass was again expressly rejected. Reliance was placed on the old case of *Slater* v *Baker* (1767) 95 ER 860, where the patient's action was said to lie in case (in modern terms negligence), not trespass. The Canadian attempt to incorporate 'informed consent' into a negligence context was disapproved.

You may think that applying the *Bolam* test is an abdication of responsibility by the law, thus allowing expert medical evidence to determine the outcome. Two of their Lordships (Lord Bridge and Lord Keith) asserted that medical evidence was not conclusive:

> [E]ven in a case where . . . no expert witness in the relevant medical field condemns the non-disclosure as being in conflict with accepted and responsible medical practice, I am of opinion that the judge might in certain circumstances come to the conclusion that disclosure of a particular risk was so necessary to an informed choice on the part of the patient that no reasonably prudent medical man would fail to make it.

Hirst J said much the same in *Hills* v *Potter*:

> I do not accept that, by adopting the *Bolam* principle, the court in effect abandons its power of decision to the doctors. In every case the court must be satisfied that the standard contended for on [the defendant's] behalf accords with that upheld by a substantial body of medical opinion, and that this body of medical opinion is both respectable and responsible, and experienced in this particular field of medicine.

These fine words have not generally been backed up by action, and it remains the case that medical negligence is one of the hardest things to prove, unless there has been an obvious foul-up, such as the removal of the wrong leg.

ACTIVITY 48

List the advantages and disadvantages of the three approaches to consent to treatment discussed above.

Consent and duress

Consent extorted by fear is void; there is no modern authority, but the proposition is self evident. There are old cases to the contrary, but no one considers they will be followed today. These include *Latter v Braddell* (1881) 50 LJQB 448, where a maid servant's claim that a medical examination which her mistress insisted on, and which she had submitted to in an obviously tearful and distressed condition, amounted to battery was dismissed.

Consent and fraud

Consent given by reason of fraud or abuse of power may be void: *Hegarty v Shine* (1878) 14 Cox CC 145. It will, however, depend on the nature of the fraudulent representation. English law takes a narrow view. If the deception goes to the essence of the transaction it will negative consent, but if it goes only to the surrounding circumstances it will not. Many of the cases are of seduction. If a man seduces a naïve girl by pretending that what he is doing is a surgical operation there is no consent. Seducing a woman by a promise of marriage, or an assurance of infertility is a different matter; the woman does consent to intercourse, although fraud has been used. However, in Canada it has been held that the consent of the 'wife' of a bigamist is no defence to an action for deceit: *Graham v Saville* [1945] 2 DLR 489, and the same logic applies to a participant in a 'sex for drugs' deal with a doctor: *Norberg v Wynrib* (1992) 92 DLR (4th) 449.

ACTIVITY 49

Which approach to consent by deception do you prefer?

Burden of Proof

It is for the plaintiff to negative consent, as in the case where a prisoner objected to medical treatment which he had been given: *Freeman v Home Office* (No. 2) [1984] 1 All ER 1036 CA. See also *L v Bournewood NHS Trust, The Times*, 30 June 1998.

In the context of bona fide medical treatment it may be reasonable to put this onus on the plaintiff; is it always? We are really only considering contexts in which consent can normally be inferred. Given the scope of the defendant's liability, it may be only fair to place this onus on the plaintiff.

9.4.3.5   Implied consent: general social contact

In a crowded society, some unpermitted contact is inevitable. Apart from casual contact in the street or public transport, friends and acquaintances may accept more intrusive behaviour. However, there are limits, especially if the person causing the contact is part of the machinery of government.

In *Wilson* v *Pringle* [1986] 2 All ER 440 (*Cases and Materials* (**9.1.1.3**)), the defendant and the plaintiff were both schoolboys. The defendant, from behind, pulled at a bag on the plaintiff's shoulder. The plaintiff fell and hurt himself. The plaintiff sought summary judgment, on the basis that this was a clear battery. It was held, having regard to the age of the parties, the general habits of schoolboys and the absence of malice (in the sense of actual malevolence), this was not so clearly a battery that summary judgment should be given. This case can be contrasted with *Williams* v *Humphreys, The Times*, 20 February 1975, where the defendant, a 15-year-old, pushed the plaintiff into a swimming pool by way of a prank. The court held this amounted to battery. It went beyond any activity which could be described as permitted child's play.

In *Collins* v *Wilcock* [1984] 3 All ER 374, which is a criminal case, the prosecutrix, a WPC, tried to question the defendant. The defendant walked off; the prosecutrix tried (without arresting her) to restrain her. The defendant tried to break free, and in doing so, scratched the prosecutrix. She was prosecuted for assaulting a police officer in the execution of her duty. The crucial question was whether the prosecutrix had stepped outside the line of duty. The court held that the prosecutrix's action in restraining the defendant amounted to a battery, and as such the prosecutrix ceased to be acting in the execution of her duty. A distinction was drawn between a touch to attract attention and a restraint. A police officer is not on duty to break the law, and doing so cannot be an exercise of duty. It is clear that no physical harm was either intended or caused.

In *Mepstead* v *DPP* [1996] Crim LR 111 the defendant parked illegally. He was asked to move but declined. An officer started to write out a parking ticket and the defendant became seriously annoyed and abusive. Another PC took hold of the defendant's arm to attract his attention to explain what was going on. The defendant hit him and was charged with assault on a police officer in the execution of his duty. He was convicted and appealed. The conviction was upheld. Taking hold of someone to attract or hold their attention, or to give an explanation would be lawful (and therefore within the lawful duties of a constable) if it was 'acceptable by the ordinary standards of everyday life'. This was a question of fact for the justices and there was no suggestion that their decision was perverse.

While this decision certainly suggests greater leeway than *Collins* v *Wilcock*, it is possible to distinguish them, if only on the basis that the defendant in *Collins* had turned away and did not want to talk, while the defendant in *Mepstead* was agitated and not, apparently, addressing his mind to the actions of the police. It may however be better to see the later case as an indication of a less restrictive approach.

Where the police are exercising statutory powers, they are protected from actions for trespass to the person, but it may be necessary to explain what those powers are: *O'Loughlin* v *Chief Constable of Essex, The Times*, 11 December 1997, where the plaintiff succeeded in a claim against the police when he was assaulted and battered during an incident where the police acted without explaining the statutory basis for their actions. (The case is almost a mirror image of *Collins* v *Wilcock*.) See also the wrongful arrest cases discussed under false imprisonment (**9.4.5.4**), where the same issue arises.

SAQ 115

Why were these cases decided as they were?

The distinction is sometimes put on the basis of a hostile touching or touching in anger, as distinct from incidental contact. This is based on a comment by Hale CJ in *Cole* v *Turner* (1704) 6 Mod 149. While this may be a useful test it is not universal. Does it explain why the acts of a surgeon who operates on an unconscious accident victim will not amount to battery, but the lightest restraint by a PC who is not exercising a power of arrest will do so?

9.4.3.6   Sports

What do you think the law says about harm caused by participating in sports and games? There will often be contact which is authorised by the rules of the game, and also contact which results from a clumsy or ineffective failure to abide by the rules. Generally this sort of contact is with the consent of the victim. It is part of the risk accepted when agreeing to play. Deliberate foul play is outside that consent: *Condon* v *Basi* [1985] 2 All ER 453. This case involves soccer, but there have also been cases involving cynical foul play in both codes of rugby, e.g. *R* v *Billinghurst* [1978] Crim LR 553. These appear to have been exclusively criminal in nature. *Condon* is in fact a case in negligence, but it was not suggested that this made any difference so far as this point is concerned. (See also **2.3.**)

9.4.3.7   Other deliberate acts

The limits of consent in areas other than 'manly sports' are now set by *R* v *Brown* [1993] 2 All ER 75. A number of men were prosecuted and convicted for causing actual or grievous bodily harm to adult sado-masochists. The victims had in fact consented. The trial judge ruled that this consent was not legally valid. The House of Lords, dismissing appeals against conviction, held that while consent might be an effective defence in relation to 'manly sports' and other harm of a trivial and transient nature, it could not in law be a defence where there was more serious harm, as there was in this case. The House considered that violence had always to be justified: sport could be justified positively in a way that prizefighting (*R* v *Coney* (1882) 8 QBD 534) and general scuffling and fighting (*A-G's Reference (No. 6 of 1980)* [1981] 2 All ER 1057) could not be. In each case it was the element of disorder or breach of the peace which made the difference. It has always been accepted that consent is not ordinarily a defence in relation to serious and permanent harm, *a fortiori* death. Do you think that this decision cuts down the area for consent too far? You should bear in mind that many, although not all, of the injuries in this case were quite serious, and it is a matter of some surprise that none of the 'victims' required medical treatment or suffered complications or permanent damage. If a 'victim' were to bring civil proceedings claiming damages, defences would be available that are irrelevant in the criminal context, namely *volenti non fit injuria, ex turpi causa non oritur actio* and contributory negligence (which, despite its name, is available whatever the cause of action). There was a very forceful dissent from Lords Mustill and Slynn, who took the view that these were really sexual offences and should be dealt with under the relevant rubric. The Court of Appeal has held that where a husband branded his initials on his wife's buttocks 'at her express request', this was within the scope of legitimate consent: *Wilson* [1996] Crim LR 573, [1996] 3 WLR 125. This appears to be rather different in tone from *Brown*. See also **Chapter 2** on defences generally. The Law Commission, in the criminal context, propose that it should only be an offence to inflict minor harm (love bites, minor bumps etc.) if this is without consent. Consent would only be a defence to the infliction of more serious harm where it is consent to a risk of reckless infliction (e.g. contact sports) or there is specific justification (e.g. medical treatment). This principled approach should avoid the inconsistencies of a case law approach. This specific proposal is however, likely to drive a wedge between civil and criminal trespass to the person as the Theft Act has done in relation to trespass to goods. Consultation Paper 139, November 1995. Cf the draft Offences Against the Person Bill, clause 4.)

On St Valentine's Day Liz approaches John from behind and kisses him passionately on the neck, leaving a love bite which is visible for several days.

Consider Liz's potential liability on the basis that John:

(a) objected from the start to Liz's attentions;

(b) initially welcomed those attentions, but is now upset because of ribald remarks about the lovebite from his friends.

9.4.4 ASSAULT

Assault: Any act of the defendant which directly and intentionally or negligently causes the plaintiff immediately to apprehend a contact with his person. (*Street on Torts* at p. 28.)

You should note that in tort the expression 'assault' is reserved for this threat of contact (or battery). In common parlance, and in the criminal law (assault occasioning actual bodily harm, indecent assault) the word has absorbed the significance of battery as well: see *R v Savage*; *DPP v Parmenter* [1991] 4 All ER 698. The Law Commission (Paper 122 *Legislating the Criminal Code: Offences against the Person and General Principles* (1992)) recognises the way the two expressions are now being used interchangeably.

The law is substantially the same as the law of battery.

9.4.4.1 Act

This used to be regarded as indicating something more than mere words, and indeed it was said that words are no assault (per Holroyd J in *Meade & Belt's Case* (1823) 1 Lewin

184). If the words are clear and threatening enough, very little more by way of gesture was required, however: per Goddard LCJ in *Wilson* [1955] 1 All ER 744. The context of the cases was different. The earlier one was that of an unruly crowd, singing and chanting. This was no doubt intimidatory, but could be said to lack specific and direct threat. The latter concerned a gang of men confronting a single gamekeeper in a isolated place at night. In the criminal law the Public Order Act distinguishes between serious offences involving the use or show of force (ss. 1–3), and lesser offences involving insult and abuse alone (ss. 4, 5). The position has now changed. Lord Steyn (in a speech with which the rest of the House of Lords agreed) said in *Burstow & Ireland* (**Cases and Materials** (**9.1.2.1**)): 'The proposition that a gesture may amount to an assault, but that words can never suffice, is unrealistic and indefensible. A thing said is also a thing done. There is no reason why something said should be incapable of causing an apprehension of unlawful physical violence, e.g. a man accosting a woman in a dark alley saying "come with me or I will stab you". I would, therefore, reject the proposition that an assault can never be committed by words.'

A silent telephone call (or at least a campaign of such calls) had been held capable of amounting to an assault in the same case in the Court of Appeal: *Ireland* [1997] QB 114. The court (Swinton Thomas LJ) indicated that it was immaterial whether words or silence followed the making of the connection, and approved of the ruling in the Australian case *Barton* v *Armstrong* [1969] 2 NSWR 451 that a threat made over the telephone was capable of amounting to an assault. The key issue is said to be whether the victim acquired an apprehension of harm, usually physical, but possibly purely psychological, as a result of the behaviour of the defendant. The House of Lords endorsed this, although accepting that there would need to be proof of a sufficient degree of immediacy of harm, which would not always be present. (Per Lord Steyn and Lord Hope, with both Lord Slynn and Lord Hutton expressing specific caveats on the issue of immediacy.) This behaviour could include, or even be limited to words. It would therefore seem that the original dictum is too narrow, as although the context in which words are deployed will be crucial, if that context is sufficiently menacing, no other overt act will be required. Some commentators (e.g. Allen, 'Look Who'stalking (sic): Seeking a Solution to the Problem of Stalking' [1996] 4 *Web JCLI*; Herring, 'Assault by Telephone' [1997] *CLJ* 11, both discussing the CA decision in *Ireland*) argue that this is an illegitimate extension of the tort/crime of assault to meet the social need for a device to restrain and punish stalkers. However they are mainly concerned with the issues of immediacy and the question whether the defendant has caused harm rather than fear. These issues are discussed further in the context of harassment in **Chapter 10**.

Consider why words alone may not constitute an assault. Do you agree that they should not?

9.4.4.2 Immediately

Words used may negative the threat of a gesture. In *Tuberville* v *Savage* (1669) 1 Mod Rep 3, the plaintiff during an argument with the defendant put his hand on his sword-hilt and said 'An 'twere not assize time, I would not take such language from you'. The defendant drew his own sword and stabbed the plaintiff in the eye. The plaintiff claimed battery and the defendant pleaded self-defence. The court held that this was a battery by the defendant and no self-defence. The plaintiff's conduct did not constitute an assault, because the words counteracted the gesture.

What about a future threat, or a present threat which the defendant manifestly cannot carry out? Generally this will not be an assault. In the first case there is no threat to the peace, the plaintiff can take precautions; in the second, there can be no apprehension. The example usually given is of the threat shouted from one river bank to the other, there being no bridge, boat, ford etc. available. This is illustrated in *Thomas v NUM* [1985] 2 All ER 1. The action was brought on behalf of working miners during the 1984 strike. They were seeking an injunction to restrain aggressive mass picketing by strikers. They claimed, among other things, that the various threats shouted by the strikers as the workers were driven into the pit in buses at some speed and with a substantial police guard, were assaults. There were gestures as well as words. It was held that these threats did not amount to assaults, because there was no basis to fear that they could be carried out then and there. See *Cases and Materials* (9.1.2.2).

So we can conclude that the test is whether the defendant was clearly in a position to carry out the threat. If there was a serious risk, it will be an assault even though the attack is frustrated. In *Stephens v Myers* (1830) 4 C & P 349, the defendant was at a public meeting. He became annoyed at the conduct of the chairman and started to threaten him and move towards him shouting that he would drag him out of the chair. His progress was halted by other members of the audience.

Do you think that this was an assault, bearing in mind all that you have read so far? It was held to be one. It was not a case where the defendant manifestly could **not** carry out his intention.

9.4.4.3 Apprehend

You must consider this aspect from the plaintiff's viewpoint. What construction should he reasonably place on the defendant's conduct? An apparent threat which the defendant knows to be an empty one can thus be an assault, because the plaintiff reasonably perceives it as one. The obvious example is a threat with an unloaded gun. In the USA and in Australia there is no doubt that such a threat is an assault. The same probably applies in England: *R v St George* (1840) 9 C & P 483. Unfortunately there are comments in another case in the same year to the contrary: *Blake v Barnard* (1840) 9 C & P 626. The problem is that the precise effect of these early cases remains disputed. Oddly the issue never seems to have arisen for decision since.

SAQ 117

What torts, if any, have been committed in the following situations:

(a) Just as Alice is sitting down in a chair, but before she has touched it, Beryl, who has crept up from behind, whips the chair from under her. Alice falls to the ground and sustains a fractured coccyx.

(b) Charles is asleep in his seat in a cinema. His feet are stretched out, blocking the passage along the row of seats. Duncan, who wishes to pass, shakes Charles vigorously by the shoulder.

Charles awakes with a start and falls from the seat, sustaining serious injury to his clavicle.

(c) While driving his car Edgar is carved up by Freda, who is driving a large lorry. Edgar shakes his fist at Freda, and leans out of the window of his car to shout that he will swing for her. Freda laughs and drives away.

(d) Grace is having an affair with Horace. Horace has falsely told Grace that he has had a vasectomy. Grace becomes pregnant and Horace arranges for Igor, a surgeon, to carry out a surgical abortion. The formalities prescribed by the Abortion Act have not been complied with. Although Igor was careful, the operation leaves Grace sterile. This is a recognised but accepted side effect in a small minority of cases where the method selected by Igor is employed. Grace is particularly distressed because it was her dearest wish to have children in due course.

(e) Jeremy points a toy gun at Kate as a practical joke. Kate, who is shortsighted, thinks that the gun is real, and faints, hitting her head on the edge of a table.

9.4.5 INTERFERENCE WITH LIBERTY

Here we are concerned with two torts which overlap, namely false imprisonment and wrongful arrest. In many cases the latter is followed by malicious prosecution, but that is outside the scope of this book.

9.4.5.1 False imprisonment

An act of the defendant which directly and intentionally or negligently causes the confinement of the plaintiff within an area delimited by the defendant. (*Street on Torts* at p. 31.)

9.4.5.2 False

The word is not used in the sense of 'not true'. The imprisonment is real enough! It is used in the sense of 'false witness'; something which is improper or unjustified.

9.4.5.3 Imprisonment

This means any confinement or total restriction of freedom of movement. Incarceration in the narrow sense (i.e. locking up in a cell) is a form of imprisonment, but is not necessary. There may, but need not, be an assault or battery associated with a false imprisonment. It depends on whether force or threats were used to restrain the plaintiff. What is the position if the plaintiff voluntarily enters a room and the defendant then locks him in? There is imprisonment but no assault or battery.

What is being protected? It is the plaintiff's freedom of movement; because you 'act at your peril' in relation to trespass, a deliberate act leading inadvertently to imprisonment will be covered. If the defendant locks the plaintiff in a room, the plaintiff's freedom of movement is just as effectively curtailed if the defendant acts deliberately with regard to the plaintiff as where he fails to realise that the plaintiff is in the room. The locking of the door is the direct cause of the restraint in each case. The concept of trespass is that of a class of acts which may not be done unless they are positively justified; this is the concept of acting at one's peril, and certainly mere inadvertence is not a positive justification. However, if the person 'accidentally' imprisoned is acting wrongfully, e.g. by trespassing, or carelessly, e.g. by getting drunk and falling asleep in a corner, there may well be a defence available. In the USA there is no liability in false imprisonment for negligently imprisoning, although there will be for negligently failing to release, e.g. at the end of a period of lawful custody. What is clear is that mistake as to the circumstances is no answer. How far do you think the law should go in protecting plaintiffs and penalising defendants?

How complete must the confinement be? It is not false imprisonment to block off one route but not others, provided these are not unduly hazardous. The plaintiff may not be able to go where he wants, but he still is free to go elsewhere. In *Bird* v *Jones* (1845) 7 QB 742 (*Cases and Materials* (**9.1.3.1**), the defendant improperly erected a temporary grandstand in the highway. The plaintiff entered it. The defendant's servants refused to allow him to go forward as he wished, but did not prevent him from returning, or going in other directions. The court held that such a partial restraint was not an imprisonment. It might amount to a public nuisance. (See **10.5**.)

Being locked in a third floor room would, however, be imprisonment, albeit that the window is open.

The area of confinement may be a defined space, but it will equally be an imprisonment if the plaintiff is constrained to go where the defendant directs. Wrongful arrest often produces an imprisonment of this kind.

Read *Robinson* v *Balmain New Ferry* and *Herd* v *Weardale* in *Cases and Materials* (**9.1.3.2**). Who do you think was in the right?

9.4.5.4   Justification

Consent is a defence to any tort unless excluded by public policy. It is therefore no imprisonment to rely on the terms of an agreement regulating the plaintiff's access to the defendant's premises. In *Robinson* v *Balmain New Ferry Co. Ltd* [1910] AC 295, as you know, the defendant operated a ferry. The plaintiff entered the terminal, paying one penny before travelling, and then changed his mind. The defendant would only allow him to leave on payment of a further penny. The plaintiff tried to climb over the turnstile but was restrained. It was held that there was no false imprisonment.

(a)   First, the plaintiff entered the defendant's premises on the understanding that one penny was payable for passing the turnstile in either direction.

(b)   Secondly, there was nothing to stop the plaintiff leaving on the ferry.

(c)   Thirdly, it was suggested that the defendant was entitled to impose such conditions as he saw fit, whether the plaintiff was told of these or not. An analogy was drawn with a railway passenger, who was only entitled to be set down at a station. Was this a condition in this sense, or was the defendant really detaining the plaintiff in order to compel payment of a civil debt, namely the penny payable on leaving?

Similar issues arose in *Herd* v *Weardale Steel Coal and Coke Co.* [1915] AC 67 HL. The plaintiff was, as you have read, a miner in the defendant's mine. While working underground during a shift, the plaintiff stopped work. He demanded to be taken up to the surface. The defendant refused until the end of the shift. It was held that there was no false imprisonment. The plaintiff had agreed to go down the mine for a particular length of shift. The defendant's obligation was therefore to wind the plaintiff up at the end of the shift, and not before.

Richman attended a match at Fulchester Rovers FC as a guest of Dives plc in their hospitality suite. The local Chief Constable had entered into an agreement with Fulchester Rovers FC to police matches; the agreement provided that the senior police officer present was to control egress from the ground after matches.

Notices were posted around the ground in the following terms: 'Admission to and exit from the ground are subject to police control. Departure from the ground after matches may be delayed in the interests of public safety.' A similar term appeared in the lease of the hospitality suite.

When Richman set out to leave the ground after the match, his way was blocked at the exit from the hospitality suite by Inspector Strangelove, who told him that he could not leave for twenty minutes while an adjoining area was cleared of visiting fans. When Richman made to move past, the Inspector placed his arm across the door.

Was the Inspector's action tortious?

Custody
Imprisonment pursuant to a lawful order of a court is justified.

There has been no successful modern attempt to demonstrate that imprisonment of this kind has become false as a result of the conditions in which the plaintiff is being detained. There have been several unsuccessful attempts, culminating in *R* v *Deputy Governor of Parkhurst Prison, ex parte Hague, Weldon* v *Home Office* [1992] 1 AC 58. These cases raise a number of issues but we concentrate on false imprisonment. (See *Cases and Materials* (9.1.3.2).)

Each case concerned a serving prisoner who alleged that his detention in prison was improper, in that the circumstances and conditions of detention were in breach of the

Prison Act and Prison Rules. In each case it was alleged that a serving prisoner retained a residual liberty, in that the order of the court which sentenced him allowed detention only according to law, and that detention in other circumstances amounted to a deprivation of that liberty which amounted to false imprisonment. This contention had met with some success in the lower courts in *Weldon* but not in *Hague*. The House of Lords unanimously held the following.

(a)   The relevant statutory provisions authorise detention and that *ipso facto* involves a complete loss of liberty. There is thus no concept of residual liberty, and false imprisonment is therefore not available to challenge the circumstances of detention. (It may of course be available to challenge a detention which is itself wrongful, e.g. a failure to release a prisoner on the due date on completion of a sentence.)

(b)   The appropriate remedy for a prisoner who alleges that the Prison Rules have not been applied properly to him, e.g. that he has been placed in solitary confinement without justification, is a public law remedy, i.e. an action for judicial review or for a declaration.

(c)   The prison authorities owe a duty of care to detainees. An action for negligence can be maintained on the usual principles if a breach of this duty results in physical harm. This will certainly cover illness or disease resulting from detention in dangerous or insalubrious conditions. Suggestions in *Middleweek* v *Chief Constable of Merseyside* [1990] 3 All ER 662 that such detention could amount to false imprisonment were firmly disapproved of. In theory this would also include psychiatric illness attributable to the improper detention, but it will be interesting to see how a court approaches any such case which is brought. There have been several cases brought in negligence, some with success, where the prison authorities or police as gaolers have not taken proper care of prisoners who were suicide risks, or at risk from other prisoners, or known to be ill.

In *H* v *Home Office, The Independent*, 6 May 1992, *Weldon* was applied. The plaintiff prisoner alleged that the prison authorities had negligently revealed his background of sexual offences (although his current sentence was for burglary). As a result he had to go on rule 43 (self chosen segregation) for his own protection. The plaintiff's claim was rejected by the Court of Appeal. *Weldon* had decided that there was no cause of action in trespass in respect of unlawful conditions of detention, and this covered the claim here. H was not, so far as can be seen from the brief report, alleging any physical injury.

Arrest and detention
Statute, in the form of the general powers in s. 24 of the Police and Criminal Evidence Act 1984 (and many specific powers in other statutes) and the common law, give powers of arrest to constables and to ordinary citizens. How far will the claim of arrest by a constable (or a citizen) acting within a statutory or common law power of arrest be a sufficient answer to an allegation of false imprisonment? In principle it is such an answer, but the defendant must be able to satisfy all the conditions of the power, and, where he cannot, absence of malice is irrelevant.

This is a significant area in practice. Actions are relatively common, frequently successful and attract substantial damages. Damages for humiliation and distress may themselves exceed £400 per hour of detention, and exemplary damages may be awarded. The Metropolitan Police alone pay out around £1,000,000 each year. The use of the law of trespass to control the function of the police force is a prime example of the revision of the scope of an action already mentioned. The key aspect of these cases is that, for an arrest to be lawful, all the requirements of the provisions giving the power of arrest must be met. So far as police powers are concerned, these are best considered in relation to other aspects of civil rights and liberties.

We do need to consider here how the rules apply to citizen's arrests. The citizen has a limited power of arrest under s. 24 of the Police and Criminal Evidence Act 1984 (*Cases and Materials* (9.1.3.2)). This largely restates the earlier common law position. In *Walters* v *W H Smith* [1911–13] All ER Rep 170 (*Cases and Materials* (9.1.3.2)) W H Smith suspected that the plaintiff, who was the manager of a station bookstall, was stealing money. They therefore arranged for goods to be bought with marked money. The plaintiff was then arrested by a company official and searched. Some of the marked money was found in his possession. He was tried but was subsequently acquitted. It is a condition precedent of the right to make a citizen's arrest that an offence has been committed, and as the acquittal of the only possible defendant demonstrated that there was no offence, it followed that the arrest was unlawful. A similar result followed in *R* v *Self* [1992] 3 All ER 476 (*Cases and Materials* (9.1.3.2)). The defendant was apprehended in a citizen's arrest at the instance of a shopkeeper who believed he had been shoplifting. The defendant resisted the arrest but was finally subdued. He was ultimately acquitted of the theft. His conviction for assault while resisting arrest was quashed; the conditions for a lawful citizen's arrest were not met and the defendant was therefore entitled to use reasonable force in self-defence to prevent a false imprisonment. The same rules would apply to any civil claim.

In *Davidson* v *Chief Constable of North Wales* [1994] 2 All ER 597 the plaintiff and her friend were arrested by the police after a store detective wrongly suspected they had stolen a cassette. The action against the police failed because of their reasonable suspicion based on the initial statement of the store detective. Could the detective, however, be said to have 'instigated, promoted and actively incited' the arrest, thus rendering herself and her employer liable for false imprisonment. No, according to the Court of Appeal. The police had exercised their own judgment, even though the detective said in evidence that she was accustomed to the police acting on her information, and clearly expected them to.

In *L* v *Bournewood Community and Mental Health NHS Trust, The Times*, 30 June 1998 the House of Lords determined that detention of an incompetent person in a mental hospital was not false imprisonment, even though Mental Health Act powers were not used and the patient did not positively consent. The justification was that it was in the best interests of the patient. This patient was too disturbed to indicate an objection. The Court of Appeal had held that this was false imprisonment on the ground that the Mental Health Act machinery replaced the common law of necessity. The House appeared more impressed with arguments that using the formal machinery would be very costly than with the civil liberties arguments.

ACTIVITY 52

Read s. 24 of the Police and Criminal Evidence Act 1984.

Do you consider that the activities of the person arresting in *Walters* and *Self* are or are not legitimate citizen's arrests?

In *Walters* the 'offence' was clearly complete — but in *Self*, should the court have applied s. 24(4)(b) on the basis that, in practical terms, the offence was still in process?

9.4.5.5   Knowledge

Can you be imprisoned without realising it? There are conflicting authorities as to whether there can be a false imprisonment where the plaintiff is in fact under restraint but he does not know this. In *Herring* v *Boyle* (1834) 1 Cr M & R 377 the defendant, a schoolmaster, in effect exercised a lien over a pupil for unpaid fees; in other words he refused to allow him to go home until the fees were paid. The plaintiff (the pupil) was unaware of this, and was not in any obvious way restrained. The plaintiff's mother knew the full story, and brought an action for the plaintiff. This action failed, with the court holding that there could be no false imprisonment in the absence of overt restraint and knowledge. In *Meering* v *Graham-White Aviation* (1919) 122 LT 44 the defendant suspected the plaintiff of theft. The plaintiff was not told of the suspicion. He was asked to wait in an office, and did so voluntarily. In fact, but unbeknown to him, guards were posted who would have prevented him leaving the room if he had tried to, which he did not. The question of whether there had been an imprisonment was left to the jury. What would you have decided? Their verdict was that this was imprisonment. This was upheld on appeal as a proper verdict. The plaintiff's freedom of movement had in fact been curtailed; the state of his knowledge went only to the amount of damages. This view has been supported by comments made obiter in *Murray* v *Ministry of Defence* [1988] 2 All ER 521. (See *Cases and Materials* (**9.1.3.3**).) In this case too Lord Griffiths pointed out that damages should be minimal. The position is again clearer in the USA, where it is laid down that the plaintiff must either be conscious of his confinement or actually harmed by it.

9.5   Interference with Goods

9.5.1   OBJECTIVES

On completion of this section you should be able to:

■   describe what is meant by conversion;

■   explain the mental element for conversion;

■   describe the basic title conflicts rules;

■   apply these rules to actual cases.

9.5.2   CONVERSION AND TRESPASS TO GOODS

This general heading includes two separate torts, namely conversion and trespass to goods. The whole law relating to interference with goods is complex and difficult. It was described by a judge as long ago as 1903 as being particularly technical, and although there has been intervention by Parliament, in the form of the Torts (Interference with Goods) Act 1977, this has affected the rules relating to remedies and procedures, but not the main substantive rules. (See *Cases and Materials* (**9.2.1**) for this Act and the relevant provisions of the Limitation Act 1980.)

9.5.3   LEGAL INVENTIVENESS

You have already seen that the torts of trespass to the person may be relied on where there is an underlying dispute that is, in substance, a matter of civil liberty. The torts relating to interference with goods may, similarly, be the legal format for a dispute which really raises issues in the law of contract or personal property: *Ingram* v *Little* [1961] QB 31 and *Lewis* v *Averay* [1973] 2 All ER 229 are both cases you may recall from contract where this was the case. You should bear in mind that in many cases conversion and trespass to goods cover the same ground (in rather the same way as common law negligence and breach of statutory duty). In practice the plaintiff will normally claim in conversion where he can.

9.5.4 CONVERSION

Conversion is an intentional dealing with goods which is seriously inconsistent with the possession or right to immediate possession of another. (*Street on Torts* at p. 39.)

ACTIVITY 53

List the sort of behaviour you consider might fall within this definition of conversion.

9.5.4.1 Intentional

The act constituting the dealing must be deliberate, as opposed to negligent or accidental. However the consequence of the act is irrelevant. As Cleasby B said in *Fowler* v *Hollins* (1878) LR 7 QB 616:

> The liability . . . is founded upon what has been regarded as a salutary rule for the protection of property, namely, that persons deal with the property in chattels or exercise rights of ownership over them at their peril.

There are any number of instances where the defendant has dealt with goods in entire good faith, with no suggestion of any want of care in all the circumstances, e.g. an auctioneer who sold goods which did not in fact belong to his client. The contract mistake cases also provide any number of instances of morally innocent converters. To this extent the rules in conversion are even more restrictive than in relation to trespass to the person, where innocent accidents are now excluded and negligence is progressively being excluded from the trespass rules. The only real protection against the true owner's claim in most cases is the passage of time. The limitation period for claims in conversion is normally six years from the date of losing possession. However the rules are fairly complex.

There is one statutory exception to the general rule that conversion requires a positive act. This is constituted by s. 2(2) of the Torts (Interference with Goods) Act 1977. This provides that where a bailee of goods (i.e. someone to whom goods have been entrusted by the true owner for safe-keeping, delivery or repair, or for some other limited purpose) who is under a duty of care in relation to the goods fails to prevent their loss or destruction, this will be treated as conversion. Before the Act, such failure did not amount to conversion, although it did amount to the separate tort of detinue. When detinue was abolished by the Act, it was necessary to provide for this situation, and this was done by a statutory extension of the definition of conversion. This form of conversion can occur without any act, intentional or otherwise.

9.5.4.2 Forms of conversion

Dealing with goods covers a number of types of behaviour. The following list aims to cover and explain the main cases, but is not intended to be exhaustive.

Taking goods or dispossessing the plaintiff

Theft, or an unjustified seizure under legal process, will amount to conversion, but merely moving goods (e.g. in order to get at other goods stored behind) is not necessarily conversion, although it might become conversion if the goods were exposed to risk as a result of the removal. You should also note that the limitation rules are different for theft cases than for other forms of conversion. Time under the Limitation Act can never run against a thief. It will only start to run once the thief has sold to a buyer in good faith.

Destroying or altering goods

Damaging goods is not *per se* conversion (although it may amount to trespass to those goods). There is no assertion of ownership in such cases. If the damage is the unintended result of an action, then the appropriate cause of action will be negligence. Destruction of goods will be conversion where this was advertent, and the distinction between damage and destruction is one of fact. Alteration which alters the nature of the goods, e.g. making wine from grapes, or reformatting and using a floppy disk, will amount to conversion. Only the owner has the right to make such irrevocable decisions about the way in which his property is to be exploited. Such dealings are normally advertent in the sense that the defendant means to subject this item to this process, and doing so is clearly asserting the rights of the owner.

Using goods

This assumes that the user has come by the goods legitimately. A bailee who misuses goods does not necessarily convert them. It depends whether his misuse is inconsistent with the bailment. Thus a hirer of a car who crashes it is not converting it, but if he transforms it into a stock car he is doing so. In other circumstances (e.g. finding) use of the goods represents an assumption of the rights of the owner, and thus conversion. There will of course be an action only if the owner finds out where the goods have got to!

Receiving or taking delivery of goods

If the reception of the goods is intentional and represents the completion of a transaction, e.g. a purchase, which is designed to give the defendant rights over the goods, then this will amount to conversion. However, what about someone who receives goods merely as agent for another (e.g. a warehouseman or carrier)? He will not be liable to the original owner merely by taking delivery, since the purpose of the transaction is not to give him rights over the goods. It may be otherwise if he refuses to hand them over to the person entitled to them.

There are a number of exceptions to the rule that receipt of goods is conversion:

(a) market overt (abolished as from 3 January 1995, but still relevant for earlier transactions);

(b) estoppel including the Factors Act 1889;

(c) seller or buyer in possession;

(d) voidable title.

Although a mixed bag, these exceptions reflect the collision at this point of two fundamental principles, namely the primacy of rights of ownership and the need to foster trade by promoting free disposability of goods.

Disposal of goods

The mere agreement to dispose of goods is not a conversion, but a delivery in pursuance of the disposal will be, at all events where the defendant is instrumental in the disposition. In *Fowler* v *Hollins* (see **9.5.4.1**) the defendant was a cotton broker who held cotton actually belonging to the plaintiff, in the belief that it belonged to X. He disposed of it for the benefit of X and was held liable in conversion despite the fact that he was acting in entire good faith and had no ready means of knowing that the goods did not belong to X. Likewise in *Hiort* v *Bott* (1874) LR 9 Exch 86 the plaintiff's agent G fraudulently represented to the plaintiff that the defendant had bought a quantity of oats to the value of £180. The plaintiff sent the goods to a warehouse and an invoice and delivery order to the defendant. G visited the defendant and said that a mistake had been made. He induced the defendant to endorse the delivery order to him by saying that this was the easiest way of returning the goods and cancelling the invoice. G then produced the order to the warehouseman, obtained the goods, sold them and absconded with the proceeds. The defendant was held liable to the plaintiff on the basis that he had, albeit as a result of G's fraud, interfered with the title to the goods by endorsing the delivery order, thus enabling G to obtain them.

Just in case you thought that this sort of case only belongs in the pages of a Dickens novel, here is a rather more up to date example. In *R H Willis and Son* v *British Car Auctions* [1978] 3 All ER 392 X obtained a car on hire purchase from the plaintiff. In breach of the hire purchase agreement he sold the car to Y, using the defendant as auctioneer. X went bankrupt and Y disappeared with the car. The plaintiff sued the defendant for their net loss. Do you think they would win? The Court of Appeal held that the defendant had been instrumental in the sale. Lord Denning departed from tradition in explicitly taking note of the fact that the defendant actually insured itself against the possibility of having to meet conversion claims arising from defective titles by taking a £2 premium from each buyer. The benefit of the insurance went to the defendant and the net result was that the original owner got damages, the defendant was indemnified and the buyer got to keep the car. To refuse a remedy to the plaintiff would have given the defendant's insurers a windfall. See *Cases and Materials* (9.2.2.1 and 9.2.2.2) for *Fowler* and *Willis*.

Refusal to surrender on demand
The motive for the refusal is irrelevant. In *Howard E Perry & Co. Ltd* v *British Rail* [1979] 2 All ER 579 (see *Cases and Materials* (9.2.2.2)) the defendant held steel belonging to the plaintiff but refused to hand it over because this might inflame their own workers at a time of industrial unrest. This was not a valid excuse. Nothing was allowed to interfere with the plaintiff's property rights. It may be reasonable for someone who is storing or otherwise holding goods to seek advice in the face of a demand for them where there is doubt as to the true entitlement, and a delayed response of this kind will not amount to a conversion. After all, the warehouseman is caught between the devil and the deep blue sea, since he often cannot be sure which of two or more claimants is truly entitled. In such cases there is a legal procedure called interpleader, whereby the person in actual possession notifies the court that he has no claim of his own (other than a possible lien for his charges) and asks the court to resolve the issue between the competing parties.

9.5.4.3 Goods

This will include all types of chattels, including crops once severed from the land, with the single exception of cash (although coins as collectors' items or bullion are included). In the case of valuable paper (cheques etc.) the subject matter of the conversion is the paper, but the value for purposes of damages is the commercial value.

9.5.4.4 Possession or the immediate right to possession

The primary concern of conversion is not with ultimate ownership where this is not coincident with possession. *Roberts* v *Wyatt* (1810) 2 Taunt 268 arose out of a conveyancing transaction. The defendant as vendor delivered an abstract of his title to land to the plaintiff. The plaintiff returned it with requisitions endorsed. The defendant could or would not answer these, and retained the abstract (which in strictness he owned since it was written on his paper). The plaintiff successfully sued in conversion, as he was entitled to possession for the purposes of the conveyancing transaction.

List the arguments for and against the imposition of liability without reference to fault and moral blame in conversion.

9.5.4.5   Separation of possession and ownership

In most cases possession and ownership will in fact coincide. The following are the commoner special cases.

Bailment
A bailment arises whenever the owner of goods parts with possession, otherwise than by way of security for a loan or debt. This sounds highly technical, but is in fact an everyday occurrence. Can you think of situations where you get involved in bailments? Amongst other examples are borrowing, lending or hiring out (including hire purchase), or consigning goods for carriage, storage or repair.

While most bailments are contractual in nature there are legal consequences which flow from the bailment as such, and vary with the precise nature of the transaction. The bailee, being in actual possession, will always be able to maintain an action for conversion against someone who has dispossessed him. The bailor will be able to do so only where he has an immediate right to possession. He will have this where the bailment is at will, i.e. terminable forthwith, or if it has already been terminated. The bailor may sue the bailee if the bailee departs from the terms of the bailment, e.g. a repairer who sells the goods.

Lien and pledge
These are security interests (i.e. goods are handed over to secure payment of a debt or loan (pledge), or are retained pending payment of outstanding charges (lien)), but otherwise similar to bailment.

Sale
A party to the sale in actual possession of the goods, whether the seller or the buyer, can maintain conversion against a third party. Whether the other party to the sale has an immediate right to possession will ordinarily depend on whether he has the property in the goods. The situation must be viewed in the light of the general law of personal property.

Finders
The finder's possessory title is good against anyone other than the true owner. This is demonstrated in *Armory* v *Delamirie* [1558–1774] All ER Rep 121 (*Cases and Materials* (**9.2.2.3**)). The plaintiff, a chimney sweep's boy, found a jewel. He took it to the defendant, a goldsmith, for valuation. The plaintiff refused the defendant's offer to buy the jewel; the defendant's servant refused to return the jewel. Did the plaintiff's action succeed? Although he was only a finder, his title dated back to the time of finding. He thus had

a better title than the goldsmith, who also had a possessory title, but a newer one. So the plaintiff won. There are, however, exceptions to this rule:

(a)   an employee who finds in the course of employment has no title as against his employer (but the employer has finder's rights);

(b)   where goods are physically within or attached to land or the structure of a building the property owner has a better right than the finder: *South Staffs Water Co.* v *Sharman* [1896] 2 QB 44 (rings in the mud at the bottom of a pond); *Elwes* v *Brigg Gas Co.* (1886) 33 Ch D 562 (prehistoric canoe six feet underground);

(c)   goods found on or in premises will belong to the owner of the premises rather than the finder if (but only if) the owner has, previously to the finding, manifested an intention to exercise control over the premises and anything found therein or thereon. How does this work in practice?

A passenger at an airport found a valuable gold bracelet in a lounge. He handed it to the airport operator's employee, with a note of his own name and address. He intended to claim it if the owner did not come forward. The airport operator sold the bracelet when the owner did not come forward after several months. The plaintiff claimed its value. Did he succeed?

In *Parker* v *British Airways Board* [1982] 1 All ER 834 on these facts it was held that there was insufficient intention to control. It was a public place and therefore the finder's rights prevailed. There is of course no precedent of fact and other cases must be considered on their merits.

In any case the finder must take reasonable steps to trace the true owner.

9.5.4.6   Complex disputes

It is easy to see that complex situations may arise, with several claimants. In some cases several of them will have rights. Take for instance a car owned by A, leased to B Motor Hire, hired by them to C, stolen from C by D, sold by D to E, an innocent buyer, who has resprayed it and replaced the engine and gear box, which were worn out. Such cases are not uncommon. Can you work out who has rights against whom and why? It is fairly obvious that D has converted the car, but did you spot that E's acts amount to conversion as against C, and possibly A and B depending on the terms of the bailments.

The Torts (Interference with Goods) Act 1977 seeks to deal efficiently and justly with *jus tertii* (or third party rights) which arise in these cases. Section 8 of the Act makes provision for the defendant to bring into the action anyone who has, or may have, a better title than the plaintiff. This is designed to achieve three objectives in relation to which the common law was defective:

(a)   to avoid double liability, i.e. to the plaintiff and the third party;

(b)   to avoid multiplicity of actions;

(b)   to limit the plaintiff's claim to his actual loss.

9.5.4.7   Remedies

The rules relating to remedies for conversion are a detailed subject of study in themselves. What follows is a brief overview.

Damages
The plaintiff can recover the value of his interest in the goods. If the interest is a limited one then the plaintiff will recover only that. Where there are several interested parties, the damages may be apportioned. Prima facie the value will be market value, ascertained as may be appropriate. Consequential loss (e.g. hire of a replacement) is recoverable. The calculation will be done on the basis most favourable to the plaintiff. This may involve an element of restitutionary damages based on the advantage secured by the defendant rather than the loss suffered by the plaintiff. In *Strand Electric* v *Brisford* [1952] 1 All ER 796 the plaintiff hired electrical equipment to the defendant, who failed to return it. The plaintiff's loss would have been nominal if he had had items of that kind still in stock to hire out to others. His loss would have been substantial only if he had had to turn other hirers away. Otherwise all he lost was wear and tear on the items detained. The defendant, on the other hand, got a substantial advantage. He didn't have to pay the market rate for hiring the items from elsewhere. As a result the full hire fee for electrical equipment was recoverable, whether or not the plaintiff could prove he had lost an alternative hiring. Similarly in *Hillesdon Securities* v *Ryjack Ltd* [1983] 2 All ER 184 the contractual hiring charge for a car was due for the period of detention, even though it far exceeded the market value. Is this a fair way of approaching the problem?

Delivery up
See s. 3 of the Torts (Interference with Goods) Act 1977. This is a remedy peculiar to interference with goods, primarily conversion. It is a specific remedy, in the sense that the plaintiff gets back the thing itself rather than compensation for losing it. Such an order may be made whenever the defendant retains the subject matter of the claim. The defendant may be given the option of delivering up the goods or paying their value by way of damages, and the order will in any event carry any consequential damages.

Improvement
Quite frequently someone who acquires goods will repair or upgrade them, thus enhancing their value. How should he be dealt with if the goods have been converted? Equity demands that he be reimbursed for this work, provided he acted in good faith. If he is ordered to pay damages, this will be on the basis of the value at the time of the conversion. If an order for delivery up is made, compensation for the improvement can be ordered: s. 6 Torts (Interference with Goods) Act 1977.

9.5.5   TRESPASS TO GOODS

> Trespass to goods is an intentional or negligent direct interference with goods in the possession of the plaintiff. (*Street on Torts*, slightly amended.)

9.5.5.1   Intentional or negligent

The same observations apply here as in the case of trespass to the person. Accidental damage is no trespass, and if goods are negligently damaged the claim will probably be brought in negligence.

9.5.5.2   Direct

This means immediate in the sense of occasioned by the operation of a physical force set in motion by the defendant.

9.5.5.3   Interference

The tort protects three separate interests of the plaintiff:

(a) retention of possession. In this aspect there is a substantial overlap with conversion and in practice it is the latter which is more usually employed;

(b) physical damage. Appreciable damage to goods is clearly a trespass. It is a moot point whether any alteration of goods is actionable. There are three possible positions, none of which is excluded by the authorities:

   (i) the tort is actionable *per se* on the analogy of the other trespass torts;

   (ii) there must be some element of hostility present to render a nominal interference actionable;

   (iii) substantial harm is a requisite.

Which do you think is correct? Why?

(c) Inviolability. This prevents intermeddling by moving goods and carrying them away even though there may be no damage. The plaintiff is entitled to have his goods where he wants them. The same argument arises in relation to a nominal moving and there is some authority that this is actionable as in *Kirk* v *Gregory* (1876) 1 Ex D 55 where moving rings from room to room in a house was held to be a trespass.

9.5.5.4 Possession

As in conversion the emphasis is on actual possession and not ownership. An immediate legal right to possess (e.g. that of a bailor at will or a trustee) will suffice. An owner who is out of possession cannot maintain an action in trespass, but can maintain an analogous action in relation to the destruction or damage of the goods to his prejudice: *Mears* v *LSWR* (1862) 11 CBNS 850. There will be no claim if the goods are repaired before they were due for return.

9.6 Title Conflicts

[A] person who has neither title nor authority to sell may sometimes confer a good title on a third party. He lacks the right to dispose, for his action is unauthorised, yet has the power of disposal in that in given conditions the law will treat his disposition as effective, binding the true owner even though he did not consent to it. (Goode, *Commercial Law* at p. 392.)

9.6.1 THE GENERAL POSITION

As you will no doubt already have grasped, there are two aspects to a sale of goods transaction, the aspect of obligation (i.e. that there is a contract, performance of which can be enforced, and breaches of which can be compensated) and the aspect of property, or conveyance (i.e. that the end result is intended to be that the goods pass from the ownership of S to that of B). Most of the cases concern outright disposals, usually sales in the strict sense, but some concern disposals for limited purposes, pledges (i.e. deposit of goods or documents as security for a debt or other obligation), hirings-out etc. Although not strictly sales they are dealt with here as the legal analysis is similar, and cases of one kind are often regarded as authority in relation to the other. You should bear in mind that any reference to buyer (B) and seller (S) will also refer to pledges, hirings etc. in most cases. However, the position of the original true owner will be slightly different. In the case of a sale, where the power of the non-owner to give a good title to the goods is recognised, the true owner's rights in the goods are extinguished, although he may have rights against the seller or proceeds of sale. Where the unauthorised disposal is of a limited interest only, the rights of the true owner in the goods are not extinguished, but are postponed to the rights of the owner of the limited interest created by the disposal. So in the case of a pledge the true owner can recover the goods by redeeming the pledge, e.g. by paying the pledgee what is due.

9.6.2   THE BASIC PRINCIPLE: *NEMO DAT QUOD NON HABET* (NO ONE CAN TRANSFER A BETTER RIGHT THAN HE HAS)

What do you suppose this principle means? Rights of ownership are sacred and paramount; in principle an owner can be divested of his rights only by his own voluntary (in the sense of deliberate rather than gratuitous) act in a private law context (the state may possess rights of expropriation or compulsory purchase). Anyone (e.g. a thief) who wrongfully purports to exercise those rights acts without effect; the original rights remain in full vigour and can be enforced at any time and against any person in wrongful possession, even when that person is personally morally blameless and unaware of the earlier depredation (subject only to the Limitation Act 1980 which is quite complex in this area!). This is an example of the general predilection of the common law for the preservation of rights of property. The owner can therefore maintain an action in conversion in respect of his property, in so far as another has interfered with it, except to the extent that the other is protected under the rules set out below, or by the Limitation Act. Any defence to the claim in conversion will be by asserting the rights the defendant believes he has under these rules. See ss. 21 and 23 to 26 of the Sale of Goods Act 1979 in *Cases and Materials* (9.3.1).

9.6.3   THE COUNTER PRINCIPLE: *PACTA SUNT SERVANDA* (EFFECT SHOULD BE GIVEN TO AGREEMENTS)

This is another fundamental consideration. It is a commercial rather than a legal principle. It is connected with the equitable concept of the bona fide purchaser for value without notice. Put in another way, there are contexts in which it is expedient that the rights of the original true owner be postponed to those of one who has acquired goods, or an interest in goods, bona fide and in the ordinary course of commerce. Otherwise the risks of buying goods without good title would be too great.

9.6.4   PROOF OF TITLE

In practical terms much of the difficulty stems from the fact that there is no way of establishing in a convenient way title to tangible personal property (goods or chattels). It is by no means easy to establish and deduce title to real property (land), and the system of conveyancing, registered or unregistered, although developed over centuries with an immense application of intellect and ingenuity, is by no means foolproof (it suffers from boundary disputes, overriding interests and documentary fraud, to name but three bugbears). No such system could by any stretch of the imagination be extended to the vastly greater number of inherently mobile, mutable and largely perishable items of tangible personal property which are the subject of commercial and consumer transactions in a modern economy. This in part explains why the law accepts liability without fault in this area. However, since the buyer must in effect take the seller's title on trust, commerce depends on that trust being protected by the law. This will not of course apply where the buyer has acted in an unbusinesslike manner, or carelessly, let alone where he is party to any species of fraud.

9.6.5   PRIORITY OF CLAIMS

At their simplest these cases involve three parties. The true owner (TO), the 'seller' (S) and the buyer (B). In practice things are often not that simple, as we will see. A common case is theft. If the thief steals goods from TO and in the character of S, purports to sell them to B, and then disappears with the price that B has paid, the net result is that TO and B are competing for the goods. Whoever is awarded the goods is satisfied. The other is left to an action against S either for the value of the goods (TO) or for the return of the price (B). Will this be an acceptable remedy? If not, why not? S will probably be untraceable, and even if he is traceable, he will probably be penniless. The question is which of the claimants should be given the better remedy and which the worse. Other common cases are those where 'S' is a bailee who sells without authority, e.g. the hirer under a hire purchase agreement who sells the goods to a third party, or a wholesaler who sells goods which he has not yet paid for. While problems here are infrequent, since S can usually satisfy the money claim, there is a precisely similar problem whenever S absconds or becomes insolvent before doing so. In each such case can you see that to award the goods to TO is to prefer rights of property, and to award them to B is to accord primacy to the free movement of goods.

9.6.6 APPORTIONMENT

It would in theory be possible to apportion the value of the goods (and the net value of any damages claims) among the *bona fide* claimants, thus spreading the loss. It would also be possible to incorporate in this system differentials to reflect the degree of responsibility of each party for the débâcle that has occurred, by analogy with contributory negligence in the law of tort. Would this be a good idea? This proposal was in fact put forward by Devlin LJ in *Ingram* v *Little* (1960), but was rejected by the Law Reform Committee in their *Twelfth Report on the Transfer of Title to Chattels* (Cmnd 2958: 1966).

9.6.7 AN ALTERNATIVE VIEW

'*En fait de meubles la possession vaut titre*': Code Civil (France), Art. 2279. This has nothing to do with furniture, but is a statement that, under French law, the person in possession of tangible moveables can transfer a good title, i.e. a full recognition of the primacy of commercial considerations over property. In England, however, the main principle is still *nemo dat*, although there are exceptions.

> In the development of our law, two principles have striven for mastery. The first is for the protection of property: no one can give a better title than he himself possesses. The second is the protection of commercial transactions: the person who takes in good faith and for value without notice could get a good title. The first principle has held sway for a long time, but it has been modified by the common law itself and by statute so as to meet the needs of our own times. (*Bishopsgate Motor Finance* v *Transport Brakes Ltd* [1949] 1 KB 322 per Denning LJ.)

SAQ 120

What are the arguments for and against the *nemo dat* principle? What priority would you give to owners' rights and buyers' rights?

9.6.8   PROBLEM AREAS

9.6.8.1   Sale under a voidable title

Where a contract is entered into in circumstances such that it can be avoided by one
party, e.g. where there has been a misrepresentation, but TO has delivered goods in
pursuance of his prima facie obligations, the rule is that, if the contract is avoided, the
rights so created determine and TO resumes his status as such. Until then his buyer has
title and can pass this to any third party. Is this really an exception to the *nemo dat* rule?
It is often described as one. Although in economic, or practical terms, the dispute will
still usually be whether TO or B is entitled to the goods, and therefore which is left to
his action against 'S', the legal analysis is different. The essence of a voidable title is that
it is good unless and until avoided. If B acquires in good faith before TO avoids, he gets
good title, and will not be liable to TO in conversion.

Car and Universal Finance v *Caldwell* [1964] 1 All ER 290, is a standard case of a contract
procured by (fraudulent) misrepresentation, and therefore voidable. TO could not trace
S to give orthodox notice of rescission, but took all practical steps open to him before the
sale to B. This was held to be an effective rescission; the contract was avoided and S's
title annulled before B acquired it. Ordinarily the position will be governed by s. 23 of
the Sale of Goods Act 1979 (see *Cases and Materials* (**9.3.1**)). Can you see why these rules
give rise to an argument as to whether or not certain categories of fraud constitute a
mistake as to identity or a misrepresentation? If the contract is void s. 23 does not apply
and the *nemo dat* rule does.

9.6.8.2   Sale in market overt: s. 22, Sale of Goods Act 1979

This was a very old established (at least 1291) exception to the *nemo dat* rule. It gave
absolute protection to buyers in certain limited circumstances, i.e. to those who made
purchases in lawful markets between sunrise and sundown, and from shops in the City
of London. Other shops were not covered, nor were informal markets (even if on the
boundary of a proper market). It has now been abolished by the Sale of Goods
(Amendment) Act 1994. You do not need to learn it, but it will remain of significance for
at least six years as a defence to claims arising before 1995. It was suggested by the Law
Reform Committee (in Cmnd 2958; see **9.6.6**), that the original purpose of protecting
buyers acting in public would be better served by conferring protection on all sales by
retail from trade premises (shops and markets) and sales by public auction. However, in
the event Parliament opted for simple abolition rather than reform. There had been
complaints that some of the London street markets which were market overt were being
abused and it was a lot simpler to abolish the rule. After all, the vast majority of goods
on sale in shops belong to the shopkeeper, or at least he has the right to sell them.

List and evaluate the arguments for and against retaining, abolishing and reforming
the market overt rule.

9.6.8.3   Estoppel: apparent authority and apparent ownership

In an estoppel, the court is effectively penalising TO by declining to allow him to rely on his usual legal rights because he has in some way, by word or deed, induced B to act to his prejudice, and it is equitable to grant B the better remedy, and therefore deprive TO of his action in conversion. Let us look at the two expressions more closely.

Apparent authority
This is an aspect of agency. An authorised agent can of course sell goods, and his act is regarded in law as the act of the principal. The same result should, in equity, follow where the authority is illusory, but the principal is responsible for creating the illusion.

Apparent ownership
While this may arise in an agency context, it need not. Neither doctrine will operate where TO has merely failed to take care of his property. There is no duty of care to prevent a third party acting to his prejudice. In *Moorgate Mercantile* v *Twitchings* [1976] 2 All ER 641 TO let a car on hire purchase to S. Usually TO registered all hire purchase agreements with a central registry, HPI, who would be consulted by any trade buyer, and would disclose to them any registered transaction. The intention was not to prevent further dealings but to ensure that existing commitments were cleared. In practice, if an agreement were revealed the dealer would obtain a settlement figure and pay this amount to TO. He would pay the balance to the hirer or credit it against another transaction. This agreement was one which slipped through the net; TO simply forgot to register it. When B bought the car he did an HPI search, which came back blank. The House of Lords held:

(a) the blank search did not create an estoppel; it simply stated that there was no registration, and could not be construed as a representation that the car was free of hire purchase altogether;

(b) TO was not negligent; they owed B no duty of care.

TO's claim in conversion against B succeeded.

The crucial question is therefore, what steps will suffice for the court to hold that TO had constituted S the apparent owner, given that mere carelessness will not do?

In *Central Newbury Car Auctions* v *Unity Finance* [1956] 3 All ER 905 TO parted with possession of a car and its log book to S. S sold to B. Held, this was carelessness on the part of TO, but they owed no duty of care and there was no holding out or estoppel. It might have been different if the log book were a document of title, but the vehicle licensing system does not provide a guarantee of ownership. It is the keeper who is registered, and keeping and owning are not at all the same thing. Not many people know that!

In *Eastern Distributors* v *Goldring* [1957] 2 All ER 525 TO gave S certain documents to use as part of a scheme to evade hire purchase controls. The details of the scheme are too complex to set out here. The documents, which included a receipt, showed S to be the owner of TO's vehicle. S used them, not to carry out the proposed fraud, but to sell the vehicle to B. Held: TO was estopped from asserting a claim against B because the effect of the documents was to hold S out as owner. The result was in theory reached without relying on TO's own involvement in the original fraud, but this could quite properly be a consideration when deciding equitable priorities.

SAQ 121

Let us see how well you have grasped how these rules operate. How should the following case be decided?

TO, who knew S reasonably well, and believed him to be honest and respectable (despite the fact that she knew him to be a second-hand car dealer!), enlisted his help to raise a loan on the security of her car. At S's request she signed, without reading in full, what she thought was a loan application, but which in fact was a document which enabled S to represent himself to B as the owner of the car and sell it to B.

These were the facts of *Mercantile Credit* v *Hamblin* [1964] 3 All ER 592 (*Cases and Materials* (**9.3.2.1**)). TO did owe a duty of care to B in respect of the document (*not* in respect of the car itself!) and if she had been negligent would have been estopped, but on the facts was not negligent since there was no reason to be suspicious of S. Most people would say TO was a rather lucky lady.

9.6.8.4 Section 2(1) of the Factors Act 1889

This section is to be found in *Cases and Materials* (**9.3.2.2**) and deals with the position of 'mercantile agents' (defined in s. 1(1) of the Act) who may give good title to buyers of goods in their possession, even though they neither own them nor have actual authority from the owner to sell.

This does not only mean a person habitually carrying on such a business. It can include a one-off transaction, and also such arrangements as 'sale or return'.

Ordinary course of business
This could be construed in two ways:

(a) in the way in which a mercantile agent could in general be expected to act;

(b) in the precise manner in which someone in the trade in question can be expected to act.

Which interpretation is the correct one? In *Oppenheimer* v *Attenborough and Sons* [1908] 1 KB 221 a mercantile agent who was a diamond broker pledged some diamonds belonging to his principal. Diamond brokers do not customarily do so. However s. 2(1) applied because the pledge was not suspiciously carried out, and was the sort of thing which a mercantile agent in general might be expected to do, even though it was not usual for this particular sub-species of agent.

General considerations
Although providing a considerable measure of protection, the Factors Act 1889 is not without technicalities and complexities, which are capable of working injustice. It is also fair to say that the majority of the judges who have applied it have done so from a standpoint that, as an exception to the principle of *nemo dat*, it should be construed narrowly.

What is the position of the buyer from a non-mercantile agent? In *Jerome* v *Bentley & Co.* [1952] 2 All ER 114, TO entrusted a ring to S with a view to S selling it on TO's behalf. S was simply an acquaintance, not in business at all, and thus not a mercantile agent. TO's instructions were to sell at not less than £550, and to return the ring to him after seven days if it was still unsold. S actually sold the ring 11 days later to B at £175, representing himself as the owner. There was no holding out of S as an agent by TO (i.e. TO had not assisted S to masquerade as the owner by anything other than actually giving him possession of the ring, e.g. by giving him documents relating to the ring), and the Factors Act did not apply. The transaction was of course outside S's actual authority, which had in any event come to an end. B had to return the ring to TO in pursuance of a judgment in conversion.

9.6.8.5 Sellers and buyers in possession

The position here is governed by ss. 8 and 9 of the Factors Act 1889 and parallel, but slightly narrower and thus essentially redundant, provisions in the Sale of Goods Act 1979.

Section 24 of the Sale of Goods Act 1979
This section may be found in *Cases and Materials* (**9.3.1**). There is a link with apparent ownership. The seller retaining possession, and probably able to document his original title to the goods as well as anyone, may appear to be the owner, but where s. 8 applies there is no necessity for the first buyer (B1) to have done anything to create this state of affairs. Indeed in the typical case he will at most have given S the opportunity by not taking delivery himself. This may be remiss of him, but would not, under the principles already explained, create a duty of care to possible later buyers. It should be noted that by definition B1 has property (i.e. he already has ownership) but not possession, while the second buyer (B2) must have possession; a sale to B2 will not invoke the section, only delivery of the goods or documents or title in pursuance of that sale. The primacy of possession, i.e. of a conveyance (albeit flawed) over a merely contractual right, reflects a number of equitable principles.

Continues or is in possession
A good example is *Pacific Motor Auctions* v *Motor Credits (Hire Finance)* [1965] 2 All ER 105. S sold a car to B1, but remained in possession as the hirer under a hire purchase agreement with B1. The section was applied to a sale to B2; the character of the continued possession was immaterial. In this case the continued possession (in the character of hirer) was with the consent of B1, but this is not a requirement.

Certain goods may be represented by documents of title, such as bills of lading, warehouse receipts etc. In such cases by usage the documents represent the goods, and transfer of the documents is equivalent to delivery of the goods.

Section 25 of the Sale of Goods Act 1979
This section may be found in *Cases and Materials* (**9.3.1**).

Bought or agreed to buy This does not include the hirer under a hire purchase agreement. Although there is an option to buy at the end of the hire period, and the normal expectation is that that option will be exercised, the hirer is not obliged to do so. This is indeed the vital attribute of hire purchase. It was finally established in the House of Lords decision in *Helby* v *Matthews* [1895] AC 471. It is from this decision that the attractiveness of hire purchase to the finance houses derives. Whatever the legal categorisation of hire purchase in economic terms it is the provision of finance to enable the hirer (H) to have the beneficial use of goods, paying by instalments and with the TO/lender retaining rights over the goods by way of security. This last consideration is an essential part of the deal, and if the rights of TO could routinely be overridden by H selling to B and giving a good title under s. 9 it would become worthless. Today statutory protection under the Consumer Credit Act 1974 and the low resale value of many second hand items make hire purchase less important. It is still significant in commercial financing of plant and machinery. The protective rules do not apply, and the products in question hold their value better than household items.

Other forms of deferred purchase Section 9 does in principle cover such forms of deferred purchase as conditional or credit sale. In practice most such transactions are excluded because any consumer transaction within the Consumer Credit Act 1974 is expressly removed from the scope of s. 9 as the buyer is deemed not to be a person who has bought or agreed to buy goods. Commercial agreements, e.g. where the buyer is a company, will be covered by s. 9.

Consent of the seller   This may have been obtained by fraud. It may have been revoked, e.g. where S under a conditional sale agreement rescinds the agreement because of B's default. This does not matter.

9.6.9   SUMMARY

When two major principles are brought into opposition the result is often unsatisfactory. This is particularly so when the conflict resolution has to be achieved within the common law case-by-case procedure, with a series of narrow precedents established *ad hoc* by judges of differing opinion at times of varying social and economic priorities. Should the rules for bearing loss in the event of merchants' insolvency and dishonesty be the same as those for priority in secured consumer credit? That is what, in essence, we still have. The latter problem could indeed be addressed by the creation of a system of protection of security interests, by registration or otherwise. The former problem may require one solution for consumer cases and others for purely commercial ones.

9.7   Trespass to Land

9.7.1   OBJECTIVES

This is a brief section, but at the end you should be able to:

■   define the behaviour which constitutes trespass to land;

■   indicate what remedies are appropriate.

9.7.2   A DEFINITION

Intentionally or negligently entering or remaining on, or directly causing any physical matter to come into contact with, land in the possession of another. (*Street on Torts* at p. 69.)

9.7.2.1   Intentionally or negligently

It is clear that intentional movement of oneself or one's goods which does put you or them on someone else's land is trespass whether or not you are aware that you have crossed the boundary. There is the same debate as in the other trespass torts over liability for 'pure' negligence. If I park my car, but fail to set the handbrake with the result that it rolls down a hill and into someone's garden, is that trespass?

9.7.2.2   Entering on

This will cover undermining, or entry into that part of the airspace actually in use. So an advertising sign fixed to the side wall of a tall building and projecting into the airspace above the lower neighbouring building is a trespass. That airspace is at least potentially in use, as the building could be extended: *Kelsen* v *Imperial Tobacco* [1957] 2 All ER 343 (*Cases and Materials* (9.4.1.1)). Similarly a site crane swinging over the plaintiff's land will be trespass: *Anchor Brewhouse Developments* v *Berkeley House* (1987) 2 EGLR 187. Where redevelopment is only possible if airspace is encroached on, this can provide a lucrative windfall for adjoining owners, who can demand substantial sums in return for their consent. Is this fair and reasonable?

There is a line to be drawn. Overflying and photographing a house from a safe height is not trespass: *Bernstein* v *Skyview and General* [1977] 2 All ER 902 (*Cases and Materials* (**9.4.1.1**)). Why is this? The area entered is not actually or potentially being utilised. There is statutory provision for civil aviation to be conducted in a normal and proper way. There is no liability for overflying at a reasonable height, and strict liability for actual harm done to person or property on the ground by an aircraft or anything falling from one: s. 76 of the Civil Aviation Act 1982 (see *Cases and Materials* (**9.4.1.1**)).

9.7.2.3 Remaining on

This simply makes it clear that there is a continuing liability .

9.7.2.4 Land

This will include an incorporeal hereditament (e.g. a right of way). It is also a trespass against the owner of the subsoil to commit an abuse of a highway (i.e. use other than for passing and repassing).

9.7.2.5 Possession

A legal estate or equitable interest and exclusive possession (as understood by land law) are required, i.e. the appropriate plaintiff is the freeholder, tenant for years in possession or the equitable owner. There is some argument that a licensee with exclusive possession or a spouse with rights of occupation under the Matrimonial Homes Act 1983 can maintain an action. A squatter acquires no right as against the true owner (although, like the finder of a chattel, he has a right against others), but a tenant in possession has an action against a landlord who wrongfully dispossesses him. A reversioner may have a remedy in an action on the case, provided that the defendant's activities have injured his interest by permanent or long-term damage to the land. Merely walking over the land does not harm the reversion, but extracting minerals, or making tracks with large vehicles may well do.

9.7.3 BASIS OF ACTIONABILITY

It is clear that trespass to land is actionable *per se*.

9.7.4 REMEDIES

9.7.4.1 Damages

If an action is brought for damages, nominal damages at least will be awarded to a successful plaintiff. Substantial damages are available where recompensable damage has occurred.

9.7.4.2 Injunctions

The remedy of choice is often the injunction, which prevents a continuance or repetition of the trespass.

9.7.4.3 Possession orders

These are in practice used against squatters, whose presence is continuous and threatens to be permanent, rather than against the casual user of a short cut or private path. In these cases an injunction is more appropriate. An expedited procedure is available in the case of pure trespassers (i.e. those who have simply entered without any arrangement with the landowner, as opposed to those who have outstayed their welcome in legal terms).

The police have new powers under s. 61 of the Criminal Justice and Public Order Act 1994 to remove squatters on land who have refused to leave on request and who have caused damage, been aggressive, or are present in numbers. The Act also strengthens the powers under the Criminal Law Act 1977 which provide enforcement mechanisms for the civil procedures against squatters in houses.

9.7.4.4 Self-help

Self-help is available in the sense that the landowner or those he authorises may use reasonable force to repel or expel trespassers. This remedy is not available when the trespasser has effectively obtained possession of the property. Why is the use of self-help not encouraged? It may lead to breaches of the peace. Prevention of these was one of the original reasons for developing tort remedies for trespass through the courts as we have seen. The landowner acts at his peril in relation to the degree of force: *R v Chief Constable of Devon & Cornwall, ex parte CEGB* [1982] QB 458.

It is possible to use self-help in cases of a minor, continuing trespass (e.g. by branches or tree roots) or where there is urgency. The law also leans against this form of self-help, for much the same reasons. It will cease to be available (at the latest) once an application for a mandatory injunction has been refused: *Burton v Winters* [1993] 3 All ER 847.

9.7.4.5 Distress damage feasant

A chattel which has 'trespassed' and caused damage may be detained under the ancient remedy of distress damage feasant as security for compensation. This has been applied to a railway engine trespassing on the wrong tracks: *Ambergate Rly v Midland Rly* (1853) 2 E & B 793. Most of the case law relates to cattle trespass, which is now regulated by statute (ss. 7 and 9 of the Animals Act 1971).

9.7.5 A CASE STUDY: WHEEL CLAMPING

There has for some time been concern over the activities of vehicle clampers. It is very much a question of two wrongs not making one right. Both the wrongs are, as it happens, within the trespass categories. The vehicle owner (VO) commits a trespass to land by parking his car on private land without consent. Sometimes it is clear that parking will seriously inconvenience the landowner or his visitors. Sometimes the land is generally vacant or derelict. In many cases there are clear warning signs. In some cases these are inadequate or absent. It has been suggested that decoy cars are sometimes parked to encourage others to believe that parking is tolerated. None of these complaints affects the illegality of the VO's action. The land owner (LO) or his agent immobilises the vehicle. If this were done by a blockade there would be no trespass. If a clamp is physically attached to the vehicle there is apparently a trespass to it. It is probably not a conversion. It is argued that VO is *volens* or consents to the clamping by parking in defiance of the warnings. Large sums are sometimes demanded for release of the vehicle, sometimes where there has been unconscionable behaviour (clamping a VO who is succouring an accident victim, clamping a car with the engine running which has not actually parked). In Scotland this has been held to amount to the criminal offences of theft and extortion: *Black v Carmichael, The Times*, 25 June 1992. If VO uses self help to release the vehicle, this will amount to criminal damage to the clamp: *Lloyd v DPP* [1992] 1 All ER 982. The Queen's Bench Division in that case declined to investigate the civil rights and wrongs. It is understood that VOs who have paid release fees under protest and pursued actions for trespass and money had and received under duress of goods have found LOs settling out of court to avoid a possibly adverse precedent. The Court of Appeal in *Arthur v Anker, The Times*, 1 December 1995, expressly ruled that clamping was in principle lawful, subject to certain conditions:

(a) that there is notice of the operation of the clampers;

(b)   that the release fee is reasonable;

(c)   that the vehicle is released promptly;

(d)   that there is an available means of contacting the clamper.

The police clamp cars parked illegally on the street under statutory powers. While unpopular, this activity is tolerated as lawful. There is no doubt that unauthorised parking can be a nuisance or worse, and that some form of self-help is appropriate. There have been tentative legislative proposals. It may be that a restricted right to clamp is appropriate, but, as in *Arthur* v *Anker*, subject to conditions. There should also be criminal sanctions for improper clamping.

On a separate sheet of paper, draft a short Bill to regulate wheel clamping.

9.8   Summary

There are clearly common threads running through this chapter:

■   The notion of acting at one's peril in relation to the infringement of rights.

■   The emphasis on vindication of the right infringed rather than recompense for harm. If compensation is the desired remedy most trespasses will also be actionable as negligent breach of duty. This has of course led to assertions that merely negligent behaviour is not trespassory.

■   The use of a tortious cause of action as a vehicle for resolving disputes arising out of a wide range of legal areas, such as civil liberties, and ownership of both personal and real property.

9.9   Further Reading

Brazier, M., *Street on Torts*, 10th edn, London: Butterworths, 1997, Part II, Chapters 2 to 6.
Cooke, P.J., and Oughton, D.W., *The Common Law of Obligations*, 2nd edn, London: Butterworths, 1993, Chapter 1.
Herring, J., 'Assault by Telephone' [1997] *CLJ* 11.
Howarth, D., *Textbook on Tort*, London: Butterworths, 1995, Chapters 9 and 10.
Jones, M.A., *Textbook on Torts*, 5th edn, London: Blackstone Press, 1996, Chapters 11 and 12.
Markesinis, B.S., and Deakin, S.F., *Tort Law*, 3rd edn, Oxford: Oxford University Press, 1994, Chapters 4 and 5 (sections 1 and 2 only).
Winfield and Jolowicz on Tort, 14th edn, London: Sweet and Maxwell, 1994, Chapters 4, 13 and 17.

9.10   End of Chapter Assessment Question

Yuri, an official of the St Petersburg Heritage Museum, is in a transit lounge at Heathrow airport when he observes in a corner, behind a counter, an icon which he believes to be one missing from his museum. Although there is a notice on the counter stating 'Authorised Personnel Only Beyond This Point' Yuri goes behind the counter to inspect the icon. Close inspection reinforces his belief that the icon is the missing one. He takes possession of it. He is observed by Susan, a security officer, who suspects him of theft and apprehends him. While she is doing so there is a scuffle, Susan suffers a dislocated finger and the icon is seriously damaged. Yuri is prosecuted for theft and acquitted.

The Airport Authority retains possession of the icon. The icon is claimed by Carlos, who left it in the lounge. Carlos can prove that he bought the icon at a respectable auction two years ago.

The icon is also claimed by Yuri on behalf of the museum. Yuri can prove that the icon was in the museum collection in 1939, and that it has never been officially disposed of by the museum authorities.

Advise Yuri as to his rights and liabilities in tort arising out of this incident.

See *Cases and Materials* (9.6) for a specimen answer.

CHAPTER TEN

NUISANCE AND HARASSMENT

10.1 Objectives

By the end of this chapter you should be able to:

■ describe the elements of the nuisance torts;

■ analyse the factors which lead to particular fact situations being defined as nuisances in law;

■ explain the relationship between nuisance and the law relating to hazardous activities;

■ explain the law relating to harassment and its relationship to nuisance;

■ analyse the relationship between the nuisance torts and other environmental and planning legislation;

■ explain the remedies available and the principles on which they are awarded.

10.2 Introduction

Few words in the legal vocabulary are bedevilled with so much obscurity and confusion as 'nuisance' . . . Much of the difficulty and complexity surrounding the subject stems from the fact that the term 'nuisance' is today applied as a label for an exceedingly wide range of legal situations, many of which have little in common with each other.

Fleming *Law of Torts* 8th edn, at p. 409.

This chapter deals with a number of torts which regulate the way land can be used, and in some cases protect landowners against interference with their occupation by others who are not landowners. Although the emphasis is firmly on the protection of the rights of the individual plaintiff, the nature of the interference in some cases such as air, land, water pollution, does lead to a tie in with environmental and planning law. This is why nuisance has been damned with faint praise by the authors of a critical study of the effectiveness of tort law, *The Wrongs of Tort*, by being nicknamed 'The Pale Green Tort'.

ACTIVITY 57

Find the dictionary definition of the word 'nuisance'. Which parts of this meaning appear to be legally significant?

10.3   Definitions

The first thing to get firmly in mind is that there are two distinct torts with names incorporating the word nuisance, i.e. private nuisance and public nuisance. Some commentators deny that there is anything other than the name in common, and that this similarity of names produces only confusion and an illegitimate tendency to apply rules relating to the one in the context of the other. The two torts certainly do not share a common history, although both deal with activities which are unacceptable as between neighbours.

The word 'nuisance' is, of course, well established in everyday English as being an activity, state of affairs, or person which or who is upsetting, annoying or discommoding, in virtually any context from vexatious litigation (a 'nuisance value offer' is a small sum paid to avoid the hassle, even when you are confident of winning) to sexual harassment ('making a nuisance of himself' is often used as a mild euphemism).

In law the word is restricted to:

(a)   a harmful or noxious activity or state of affairs;

(b)   the harm resulting from (a).

The nuisance must be 'actionable' which means the sub-class of (a) which is within the scope of legal liability.

10.4   Private Nuisance

This occurs where the defendant culpably creates or permits a state of affairs which (a) causes or permits physical damage to the plaintiff's property or (b) appreciably interferes with the plaintiff's enjoyment of his property. This is not taken from the textbooks, but has been drafted specially for this text. This is because recent House of Lords' decisions have significantly affected this area of the law.

The judges tend to reduce the principle of private nuisance to a Latin tag: *sic utere tuo ut alienum non laedas* (you must use your own property so as not to damage the property of others). This does not bring into the equation the balancing of interests. Some word such as 'culpably' is required to qualify 'damage'. This word is used as it is more precise than 'improperly' in suggesting the notion of legal liability.

'Culpably' needs to be handled with care. It is used as a synonym for 'actionably', in the sense that it is bringing into the equation the fact that not all nuisances are recognised and reprehended by the law, and can be analysed into three quite separate elements. The first relates to the mental element of intention or negligence, the second to the foreseeability of the damage complained of and the third to the extent or quality of the interference, which goes to reasonableness.

10.4.1   WHO CAN SUE?

Before we address these issues, it is important to grasp firmly a significant limitation to the scope of private nuisance. It is an action only available to an owner or occupier with a recognised legal or equitable interest (which excludes family of the occupier, visitors etc.), and is in respect of damage to his interest in the land. Although in some cases this damage takes the form of interference through noise or smells, which are actually perceived by the occupier, the claim in nuisance is for the diminution in value or utility of the land which this produces.

In *Malone* v *Laskey* [1907] 2 KB 141 the wife of the occupier was injured when a defective cistern fell on her while she was using the lavatory. Her claim fell between two alternatives. At that time a claim in 'pure' negligence did not lie for defective premises in these circumstances. The position here has now changed (see *AC Billings & Sons Ltd* v *Riden* [1958] AC 240). Although it was found as a fact that the reason for the fall of the cistern was that the supporting bracket had been loosened by vibrations from the working of machinery on the defendants' adjoining property, which is an entirely typical form of nuisance, the plaintiff could not recover in nuisance for her personal injuries as she was regarded as a mere licensee (i.e. having no interest of her own in the land). This case was disapproved of in the Canadian case of *Motherwell* v *Motherwell* (1977) 73 DLR (3rd) 62, where no distinction was made, in granting a remedy for harassment by nuisance phone calls etc., between those family members who owned or leased property and those who occupied by virtue of marital status. The majority of the Court of Appeal took the same view in a similar case in *Khorasandjian* v *Bush* [1993] 3 All ER 669, where the occupation in question was by an adult child of the family. It should, however, be noted that the activity complained of was not really related to the land, but was a species of personal harassment. It can be argued that this is not really private nuisance. The inconvenience complained of is essentially personal, and it is coincidental that the phone calls are received at home rather than at work, or on a mobile phone or car phone. It is now clear that private nuisance is not available in this class of case. The majority of the House of Lords in *Hunter* v *Canary Wharf* [1997] 2 All ER 426 (***Cases and Materials*** (**10.1.1**)) expressly approved *Malone* v *Laskey*. Lord Goff cited with approval passages from an article by Professor Newark asserting a very traditional view of the scope and purpose of nuisance ('The Boundaries of Nuisance' (1949) 65 LQR 480):

> *Disseisina, transgressio* and *nocumentum* [nuisance] covered the three ways in which a man might be interfered with in his rights over land. Wholly to deprive a man of the opportunity of exercising his rights over land was to disseise him, for which he might have recourse to the assize of novel disseisin. But to trouble a man in the exercise of his rights over land without going so far as to dispossess him was a trespass or a nuisance according to whether the act was done on or off the plaintiff's land . . . In true cases of nuisance the interest of the plaintiff which is invaded is not the interest of bodily security but the interest of liberty to exercise rights over land in the amplest manner. A sulphurous chimney in a residential area is not a nuisance because it makes householders cough and splutter but because it prevents them taking their ease in their gardens. It is for this reason that the plaintiff in an action for nuisance must show some title to realty . . . The term 'nuisance' is properly applied only to such actionable user of land as interferes with the enjoyment by the plaintiff of rights in land.

SAQ 122

To what extent do you regard the conservative restatement of the law of private nuisance in *Hunter* as being justified by strict regard for authority and to what extent does it contribute to the development of the law to assist individuals threatened with unacceptable invasions of their 'personal space'?

In the last decade there were many actions similar to *Khorasandjian* v *Bush*. Antisocial behaviour of this kind, often referred to as stalking, was either becoming commoner or attracting more forceful legal action. Assimilating it to private nuisance was clearly an extension of the existing law, but one which could, in principle, be justified by the application of the incremental approach advocated in *Caparo* v *Dickman* [1990] 1 All ER 568. Indeed Lord Cooke endorsed this approach in his very forceful dissent in *Hunter*. However the majority overruled *Khorasandjian* and made it clear that harassment was not a sub-species of private nuisance. The reasoning of Lord Goff is formidable, and certainly draws on and develops in a coherent way the old case law. The existence of the new statutory tort of harassment (see *Cases and Materials* (**10.3.2**)) does remove some of the necessity for the common law to fill this gap. It can, however, be seen as a victory for historical analysis over a developmental one. We will look at this area in more detail when we consider harassment generally (**10.6**).

10.4.2   CULPABILITY I: THE MENTAL ELEMENT

10.4.2.1   Liability for acts

Nuisance is essentially a tort of strict liability, in the sense that it will be no defence to show that the nuisance was not created intentionally, or even that the defendant used all reasonable care. The leading case is *Cambridge Water* v *Eastern Counties Leather* [1994] 1 All ER 53 in *Cases and Materials* (**10.1.2.1**). This case contains a comprehensive restatement of the scope of liability in nuisance and of the relationship between orthodox private nuisance and the rule in *Rylands* v *Fletcher* [1861–73] All ER Rep 1; see *Cases and Materials* (**11.1.1**).

Read the facts of *Cambridge Water* in *Cases and Materials* (**10.1.2.1**)

The first relevant legal finding was that, in a case of this kind, where the nuisance complained of is by way of a positive act of the defendant there is no need to prove intention or want of reasonable care. Thus the mere fact that ECL had acted prudently, in accordance with accepted practice and certainly with no desire or intention to pollute their neighbour's water was not sufficient to exonerate them.

Of course in many cases the behaviour complained of is either deliberate or careless. This is however largely irrelevant to liability **in private nuisance**.

Fred drops a tin of paint stripper as he is trying to open it while standing on his front porch. The stripper splashes. Some goes on Bert's car, which is parked in the street. Some goes onto a planter in the next door garden. The pansies and petunias in the planter are poisoned. They belong to Fred's neighbour, Gladys.

What cause of action do Bert and Gladys have against Fred?

This could easily be seen as negligence – Fred should be careful handling this product. The harm is foreseeable. It is unlikely to be nuisance. Although Bert is a road user whose use of the highway is affected (which could be public nuisance) and Gladys is a neighbour whose property is harmed, this does not arise from a state of affairs but from a single action. It is thus not likely to be nuisance even though it is one neighbour harming another neighbour's property.

Most nuisances do arise from a positive act of the defendant, and are therefore covered by this rule. There are, however, three exceptional cases.

10.4.2.2 Positive duty to act and liability for omissions.

There are a limited number of circumstances where the defendant is under a positive duty, either by a specific assumption of responsibility or by a general rule of law, such as the liability of the owner of premises fronting the highway to keep them in repair: *Tarry* v *Ashton* (1876) 1 QBD 314. This is of course not actually *private* nuisance, but it is treated as equivalent by the courts. The defendant bought a property with a gas lamp suspended from a wall bracket overhanging the pavement. As a prudent man he had this inspected by a competent gas fitter, who negligently reported that it was in good condition. In fact it was old and decayed, and a few months later after it had been weakened when a workman rested a ladder against it, climbed up the ladder, slipped and fell, the lamp itself fell on a passer-by.

HELD Although the defendant was not negligent, he owed a non-delegable duty in relation to the lamp, and remained liable for the non-performance of that duty, notwithstanding the employment of an apparently competent contractor.

A similar duty can arise in a private nuisance context, where for example one property owner has assumed a liability to repair, as in *Wringe* v *Cohen* [1939] 4 All ER 241 (see *Cases and Materials* (**10.1.2.2**), where the Court of Appeal relied on *Tarry* v *Ashton* to hold an owner liable when a wall for which he was responsible collapsed onto his neighbour's shop. Where premises were a nuisance as a result of want of repair, rather than the act of a trespasser or concealed natural forces, liability was strict. The defendant had the right and responsibility to inspect and repair, and would be liable for default. The rule is expressed as relating to harm on the highway or to neighbours where the property fronts the highway. It is thus not universally applicable in nuisance. The defendant was not actually aware of any defects, but he had been fairly lackadaisical in inspecting the property, and could therefore be said to be at fault, but the court considered that immaterial. A similar conclusion was reached in *Spicer* v *Smee* [1946] 1 All ER 489 (defective electrical system causing a fire).

Professor Fleming (*The Law of Torts*, 8th edn, p. 430) suggests that the relevant dicta in *Wringe* v *Cohen* are too wide. There was no evidence of recent inspection and this might amount to culpability in the sense of omission to act. The House of Lords has subsequently regarded liability for trees as dependent on the usual standard of good estate management, not as a strict rule. However the standard required will be high where the tree overhangs a highway because of the high degree of risk of harm: *Caminer* v *Northern and London Investment Trust* [1951] AC 88. A tree on the defendants' premises was internally diseased; a branch fell on a car parked on the adjacent street. The defendants argued that they had employed expert and competent technical experts to advise. It was held that they were not under an absolute liability, but an obligation to act reasonably, albeit up to a very high standard of performance, given the impact of any default on the public. However this may be regarded as an example of the natural causes category, rather than a true *Tarry* v *Ashton* type case.

ACTIVITY 59

List the reasons you can see for and against imposing strict liability.

There is a possible further category of extended strict liability. In *Cambridge Water* the Court of Appeal treated a claim in respect of harm to groundwater percolating under the plaintiff's land as being an interference with the plaintiff's 'natural rights'. This was held to be a nuisance on the authority of *Ballard* v *Tomlinson* (1885) 29 Ch D 115. In this case the defendant had used a well on his land as a cess pit, thus polluting the plaintiff's nearby well and preventing the plaintiff using the water for brewing. This meant that the plaintiff was deprived of his natural right to abstract unpolluted water. The Court of Appeal in the current case was faced with an unchallenged decision at first instance that the defendant had not been negligent in causing the pollution, which was an unintended side effect of the perfectly proper, and as the judge below held, natural user of their land for industrial purposes. The Court was therefore imposing strict liability in nuisance in natural rights cases.

SAQ 124

Was the Court of Appeal right to treat the two cases as being equivalent?

In *Ballard* there was a quite deliberate course of anti-social conduct, and the issue was one of the definition of the right and proof of causation; it is certainly far from clear that a Victorian judge would impose liability for an inadvertent side effect of a proper use. Indeed in three earlier cases of diversion of water referred to by the court in *Ballard* the defendant was exonerated in two cases where his proper activities caused damage to the plaintiff: *Smith* v *Kenrick* (1849) 7 CB 515 and *Wilson* v *Waddell* (1876) 2 App Cas 95, but held liable in a third where he imported water which then escaped and caused harm: *Baird* v *Williamson* (1863) 15 CB (NS) 376. In view of these criticisms, and the fact that the House of Lords certainly did not endorse the approach of the Court of Appeal, the status of this category must be regarded as extremely dubious.

10.4.2.3   Nuisance arising from natural causes

In this situation, the defendant has not brought the nuisance about himself, he is simply the unwilling host to a natural phenomenon. In such cases liability is dependent on fault in a sense equivalent to the position in negligence. The defendant must act reasonably in the position in which he finds himself placed.

Goldman v *Hargrave* [1967] 1 AC 645   A tree on the defendant's land was struck by lightning. The defendant felled the tree and took steps to extinguish the fire which were inadequate; as a result the fire spread. The defendant was liable in nuisance.

Leakey v *National Trust* [1980] 1 All ER 17 (***Cases and Materials*** (**10.1.2.3**)   The plaintiff's property was damaged as a result of natural subsidence of land forming part of the defendant's property. The defendant knew of the situation and was liable in nuisance.

SAQ 125

How do you account for defendants being held responsible for the consequences of the operation of natural forces?

In the above cases it was recognised that the duty owed by the defendant was not absolute; it was conditioned by reference to the defendant's resources. It is also a duty of care, in the sense that, where what is relied on is non-feasance following an extraneous incident, there must be an appreciation (assessed objectively) of the foreseeability of harm. This obviously introduces concepts and terminology familiar from the law of negligence. It has been suggested as a result that nuisance, rather like occupiers' liability, is merely a special case of negligence. This goes too far. It is pointless to deny similarities which do exist, but in nuisance liability for malfeasance depends on the result produced, not on the mental attitude thereto of the producer. In relation to physical harm one acts at one's peril, and in discomfort cases it is not carelessness but the character of the locality and the degree of disturbance which will decide. Consider, however, the observations of Lord Goff in the *Cambridge Water* case which adopt the above analysis of *Leakey* and *Goldman*. Since lack of foreseeability is, in practice, very much a long-stop to deny liability where proper activities, carried out without consciousness of risk creating potential, turn out to have adverse effects, and since those consciously doing things which have a potential to disrupt are well aware of this, foreseeability is not generally a live issue. Markesinis argues that cases like *Leakey* are really cases of negligence arising between neighbours, rather than nuisance, but he does tend to see much of what is generally regarded as nuisance as being something else. The recent claim against Scarborough council over the collapse of the Holbeck Hall Hotel because of lack of support from the council's adjoining land was framed in nuisance by analogy with *Leakey*. although the judge regarded negligence as being a necessary ingredient of the cause of action: *Holbeck Hall Hotel Ltd and Another* v *Scarborough Borough Council, The Times*, 15 October 1997.

10.4.2.4   Acts of third parties

In *Sedleigh-Denfield* v *O'Callaghan* [1940] 3 All ER 349 the local authority put a culvert into a stream on the defendant's land. The culvert was inefficient, and flooded the plaintiff's land when it became clogged with leaves. The defendant knew of the problem (although he had not granted permission for the construction of the culvert), but did nothing either to get those responsible to improve the position or to clear the blockage. This was sufficient to found liability. It was, however, essential to the decision that the defendant was aware of the position and had not acted reasonably in the light of the position in which he was placed, i.e. that there was negligence. It was also the case that the defendant had adopted the nuisance in the sense that he took advantage of the improved drainage of his land which the culvert normally provided.

10.4.3   CULPABILITY II: FORESEEABILITY

Again, the leading case is *Cambridge Water*. Lord Goff, who gave the only speech, considered the case to be within the rule in *Rylands* v *Fletcher*. He did, however, express certain views on liability in nuisance because he regarded *Rylands* v *Fletcher* as essentially a special case of nuisance. In his Lordship's view, there was no strict (in the sense of absolute: note the apparent verbal inconsistency) liability in nuisance. It was an essential prerequisite that there should be foreseeability of the relevant kind of harm. In this respect he relied on the decision in *The Wagon Mound (No. 2)* [1967] 1 AC 617. This does not need further discussion here, as it is the same principle which applies in relation to negligence; see **4.5.1.1** and *Cases and Materials* (**4.3.1.1**). *Ballard* v *Tomlinson* is dealt with rather obliquely. Lord Goff clearly considers that the case is not authority for any proposition that the defendant is liable for unforeseeable harm. It is either an orthodox *Rylands* v *Fletcher* case, or it is a case of private nuisance, subject to the ordinary rules. The harm in *Ballard* was certainly foreseeable, at least in the modern sense. A layman might not appreciate the potential for the spread of pollution, but a reasonable operator of the business would. In *Cambridge Water*, on the other hand, this was not the case, and so the plaintiff's claim failed. The case is discussed in more detail later (**11.3.2.5**).

Does Lord Goff's approach mean that we can forget about the first meaning of 'culpable'?

It is clear that there is now much more emphasis on the effects of the defendant's behaviour. Where action is deliberate you will not need to enquire what the reasonable man ought to have foreseen. The requirement of foresight where the behaviour is not designed to produce the results the plaintiff complains of, does retain some element of fault. A defendant who sees a risk, and runs it, believing that he has the situation under control, is 'culpable' even if only to a very limited extent. At the least he has put his interests ahead of others. The defendant who acts with the best intentions, but who has not weighed up the risks properly, is more clearly 'culpable'. He has not had proper regard for the interests of others.

SAQ 127

Why does the law impose liability for omissions and treat acts as culpable by reference to the results and not to the culpability of the defendant in nuisance, but not in negligence?

Negligence is not a relationship. The only necessary link between the plaintiff and the defendant is the incident. The key is that the defendant must have been at fault in handling the circumstances surrounding the incident. In nuisance the two occupiers each have rights, and it is the infringement of the rights, not the fault involved, which is crucial.

10.4.4 CULPABILITY III: UNREASONABLENESS

What would be a nuisance in Belgrave Square would not necessarily be so in Bermondsey.

Sturges v *Bridgman* (1879) 11 Ch D 852 at p. 865 *per* Thesiger LJ.

10.4.4.1 Striking the balance

Most of our activities impinge on our neighbours. Theirs in turn impinge on us. To a great extent we accept this on a basis of live and let live, or even tit for tat. However, when there is a claim that someone has gone outside this region of civilised co-existence, a balance must be struck. The law generally seeks to hold a fair balance between the gravity, persistence and motive of the defendant's conduct and the nature and quality (but not duration) of the plaintiff's occupation of his land, in the light of the character of the locality. Judges have tried down the years to sum up this process in a single sentence:

Those acts necessary for the common and ordinary use and occupation of land and houses may be done, if conveniently done, without subjecting those who do them to an action.

Bamford v *Turnley* (1862) 3 B & S 62 at p. 83 *per* Bramwell B.

A balance has to be maintained between the right of the occupier to do what he likes with his own and the right of his neighbour not to be interfered with.

Sedleigh-Denfield v *O'Callaghan* [1940] AC 880 at p. 903 *per* Lord Wright.

[A] useful test is perhaps what is reasonable according to the ordinary usages of mankind living in society, or, more correctly, in a particular society.

Ibid.

There is here no dispute that there has been and is likely to be in the future an interference with the plaintiff's enjoyment of [his property]. The only question is whether this is unreasonable. It is a truism to say that this is a matter of degree.

Miller v *Jackson* [1977] 3 All ER 338 *per* Geoffrey Lane LJ.

The judge in concluding that the noise did not constitute an actionable nuisance had applied the correct test, namely whether according to the standards of the average person and taking into account the character of the neighbourhood, the noise was sufficiently serious to constitute a nuisance.

Murdoch v *Glacier Metal Ltd, The Times*, 21 January 1998 *per* Pill LJ.

It is equally a truism that the resolution of this question is going to involve a balancing exercise which will in the end be categorised as a question of fact. This is to be assessed pragmatically, and not by reference to abstract criteria. In the *Glacier Metal* case the judge was held to have rightly refused to accept that noise marginally above a World Health Organisation approved level for disturbance of sleep was itself conclusive that there was an actionable nuisance. On the other hand there are certain recurrent factors which the courts have recognised as having weight where they are relevant. There will inevitably be a degree of overlap, in the sense that certain facts will fit into two or more categories.

ACTIVITY 60

What factors do you consider relevant for the balancing exercise described above? See
Sedleigh-Denfield **and** ***Miller*** **in** ***Cases and Materials*** **(10.1.3.1).**

10.4.4.2 Material considerations

The defendant's unworthy motive
Some activities are either lacking in social utility (e.g. storing unsightly refuse) or are motivated by spite or malice. This will be taken into account when deciding whether they are unreasonable.

In *Christie* v *Davey* [1893] 1 Ch 316 the plaintiff was a music teacher. The defendant took exception to what he perceived as a noise nuisance arising from lessons and other musical activities, and retaliated by creating a cacophony of his own to distract the plaintiff. How should these conflicting interests be reconciled? The judge accepted that the plaintiff's actions were *bona fide*, but the defendant's were not, and appears to have assumed that the plaintiff's actions were not sufficiently disruptive to be unreasonable. The defendant was enjoined from creating a further nuisance because he was not acting *bona fide*. It was not legitimate to use his property for the purpose of annoying his neighbours.

In *Hollywood Silver Fox Farm* v *Emmett* [1936] 1 All ER 825 (*Cases and Materials* (10.1.3.2)) following a difference of opinion over a right of way, the defendant arranged for his son to go shooting near the boundary of the plaintiff's property. There were rooks and other vermin there to be shot, but the defendant also knew that loud noise deterred mating, impeded whelping and provoked infanticide among silver vixens. How do you think the balancing act came out this time? Again the malicious intent was enough to constitute a nuisance. There is no absolute right to make a noise, and motive is relevant.

Utility of the defendant's activity
It is easy to condemn those who are acting out of spite or malice. Should particularly beneficial activities be given special privileges? This is not what happens in practice, although they are not treated with undue rigour. There is also a need to distinguish between the activity as such and an unreasonable approach to carrying it out.

In *Andreæ* v *Selfridge* [1937] 3 All ER 255 the defendant was rebuilding his shop which adjoined the plaintiff's hotel. In order to reduce the period of closure to a minimum, work went on unabated round the clock, rendering sleep impossible. To what extent was this a nuisance? The court acknowledged that a certain amount of disruption during normal working hours was inevitable, and would not be a nuisance, on a basis of mutuality or 'live and let live'. The defendant conceded that he had not in fact had proper regard to the effect of his operations on the plaintiff, with the result that there was an actionable component to the disruption which the plaintiff had suffered.

In *Bellew* v *Irish Cement* [1948] IR 61 an injunction was granted in respect of nuisance from a cement factory, which had the effect of closing the factory down although it was the only domestic source of supply at a time of shortages. What message do we get from this decision? Powerful interests must be at stake if one of the main engines of the economy is being turned off to protect them. On a smaller scale, in *Adams* v *Ursell* [1913] Ch 269 the local fish and chip shop was closed down because it caused unreasonable interference, although it too was, in its way, a valuable local resource.

ACTIVITY 61

Read *Miller* v *Jackson* in *Cases and Materials* (10.1.3.1). What was the basis of the complaint, and what was the reaction of the judges?

In *Miller* v *Jackson* [1977] 3 All ER 338 the defendant was a cricket club, the plaintiff the owner of a house recently built on land adjoining the club, and in easy range of the wicket. It was generally agreed that cricket was a good thing on health and cultural grounds. A majority of the Court of Appeal (Lord Denning dissenting!) held that the regular hitting of balls into the plaintiff's property, with an appreciable risk of damage, constituted a nuisance. The decision was reached reluctantly, but the reluctance was largely on the basis of the plaintiff coming to the nuisance (and taking the benefit of a quiet open area beyond their boundary on all but 20 or 30 days in the year). The utility of cricket as a healthy pastime or essential part of English culture cut little ice with the majority.

Coming to the nuisance
Is it fair for a newcomer to complain? He can see what the defendant is up to, and if he doesn't like it, he should settle down elsewhere. Indeed, if the law had not been laid

down in the last century, when there was much greater stress on rights of property and less respect for activities, this point might have been accepted. However, the position is otherwise.

In *Sturges* v *Bridgman* (1879) 11 Ch D 852 the defendant was a manufacturing confectioner, whose operations were long established, and provoked no complaint until the plaintiff, a physician, erected a consulting room on his property immediately adjacent to the workroom. Noise and vibration in the consulting room were intolerable. The plaintiff's action succeeded. His property right to use his premises as he wished had been interfered with. It was an area where the preponderance of activity was professional rather than industrial. The plaintiff was thus appropriate to the area, the defendant was not. The fact that the plaintiff had 'come to the nuisance' was regarded as subsidiary.

There was some reluctance to accept this argument in *Miller* v *Jackson*, but the matter was regarded as being concluded by authority. If you had the chance to do so, would you change the law to protect established occupiers from complaints by newcomers?

Character of the locality
How is this relevant? Is everyone not entitled to the same level of amenity? It has sometimes been argued that the law of private nuisance operated as a primitive form of town and country planning control. How effective do you think it was to allow the pattern of development to be controlled by those who complained about their neighbours? There may have been some impetus given to the concentration of noxious trades in particular places, on the ground that they would not complain of each other, but this seems to be largely accidental. The factories were certainly well away from the owners' houses, but the owners could afford to move away from the nuisance!

There has, however, traditionally been a distinction drawn between nuisances involving 'material injury to [the plaintiff's] property' and those 'productive of sensible personal discomfort', and we need to consider what this is.

This distinction was made in those terms in *St Helen's Smelting Co.* v *Tipping* (1865) 11 HL Cas 642. In the former category of case, the plaintiff's rights are absolute while in the latter there is an element of relativity. Try working through this example.

Karl operates a chemical plant in Coketown, one of the last centres of heavy industry in England. Fumes from the plant create nasty smells and smuts which make life very messy for Vladimir and Joe. Vladimir is Karl's immediate neighbour, and the operator of a smelting plant. Joe lives half a mile away, across the river on the edge of Squire's Chase, an exclusive residential area. In addition, chemicals in the fumes are eroding the stone mullions of Nikita's boardroom windows. Nikita is Karl's neighbour on the other side, and runs an oil refinery.

Nikita appears to have an action: he has suffered physical damage. Joe also appears to have an action: he is relying on discomfort, but is entitled to the environmental quality appropriate to an exclusive residential area. Only Vladimir is likely to miss out: his claim is based on discomfort, but he is only entitled to the environmental quality appropriate to a heavy industrial zone.

This must of course all be read subject to the question of 'natural rights', which according to *Ballard* v *Tomlinson* are of an unconditional nature. This rediscovery appears to be unaffected by the House of Lords decision in the *Cambridge Water* case, provided that the harm is of a foreseeable kind.

Sensitive users
The concept of reasonableness cuts both ways. If the defendant can cause only a reasonable amount of disturbance, the plaintiff is entitled only to a reasonable quality of amenity. As I hope you can see, this category is confined to the interference type of nuisance.

In *Bridlington Relay* v *Yorkshire Electricity* [1965] 1 All ER 264 the plaintiff claimed that the defendant's main power cable would interfere with TV reception by its relay station. Is such interference a nuisance? The judge was 'prepared to take judicial notice of the fact that the reception of television has become a very common feature of domestic life', but as it was recreational rather than occupational, and there was no (perceived) element of noxious or dangerous interference, it was held no nuisance to interfere with TV reception as such. The plaintiff required a greater freedom from interference than a domestic viewer to justify charging for a relay service. Bridlington at the time had poor reception from domestic aerials because the transmitters were hidden behind hills. The Bridlingtonians, being Yorkshiremen, would only pay for the relay if it gave a much better picture. This need for an ultra-high quality of reception was an undue sensitivity which itself disentitled the plaintiff from a remedy.

Is TV really so unimportant? Couch potatoes will be relieved to learn that the low value placed on TV as such has been rejected in the later Canadian case *Nor-Video* v *Ontario Hydro* (1978) 84 DLR (3rd) 221.

The more serious point is that it is settled law that the plaintiff is not entitled to protection for an ultra-sensitive use of his property, and that what is ultra-sensitive will be a question of fact.

10.4.5 WHO IS LIABLE?

The definition refers to 'cause or permit'. The person actually physically responsible will be liable, as will anyone who actually employed or requested him to do so.

10.4.5.1 The actual perpetrator

The actual perpetrator can be liable whether or not he is in control of premises: *Hubbard* v *Pitt* [1975] 3 All ER 1.

10.4.5.2 Landlords

The test of liability is whether the letting (and the same rule applies to a licensee) necessarily involves the commission of a nuisance: *Tetley* v *Chitty* [1986] 1 All ER 663 (*Cases and Materials* (10.1.5.1)).

Jeremy lets a shop to Ken. Ken undertakes to operate the shop as a fried fish shop and for no other purpose. Jeremy's object is to provide a service to the 5,000 residents of a nearby housing estate with no other fast food outlets. Jeremy lets the house next door to Lout. Lout, as Jeremy knows full well, is a 'neighbour from Hell'. He plays loud music at all hours, his 12 children are totally out of control, and he always has three or four cars semi-dismantled in the garden. This fits in well with Jeremy's plans to upset Minnie, who lives next door, and who once rebuked Jeremy for smoking when he was 11. Minnie also complains that the smell and fumes from the fish shop are adversely affecting her bedroom.

Advise Jeremy as to his potential liability in nuisance.

The landlord will be liable where premises are let solely as a fast food outlet where this is bound to create a nuisance (see *Adams* v *Ursell* [1913] Ch 269 and **10.4.3.2**). The position is different where the nuisance is collateral. In *Smith* v *Scott* [1973] Ch 314 a local authority which put a problem family into a house as tenants was not liable to the next door neighbour in nuisance for their depredations. This was so even though it seemed fairly clear that the local authority wanted to get the plaintiff to move, as he was holding up their development plans, and the tenants had been carefully chosen to cause mayhem. Having answered the question, and considered my response, do you think the law is fair?

There seems to be a separate rule for nuisances arising from want of repair. The landlord remains liable for those parts of the building over which he retains control, but will also be liable for the part which is let, provided that the tenant cannot be shown to be exclusively responsible: *Wringe* v *Cohen* [1940] 1 KB 229, *Mint* v *Good* [1951] 1 KB 517.

10.4.6   PHYSICAL DAMAGE OR APPRECIABLE INTERFERENCE

The interference must be to an interest recognised in law. One of the claims in *Hunter* v *Canary Wharf* [1997] 2 All ER 426 (*Cases and Materials* (**10.1.1**)) was for interference with TV reception because of the 'shadow' cast by the Canary Wharf tower. This was considered to be analogous to interference with a view. This has been consistently held in a series of cases from the sixteenth century onwards not to be actionable as a nuisance or otherwise. TV reception is an important amenity of life, but it cannot outweigh the right to develop one's land in an otherwise reasonable manner. There is no reason why interference caused by the operation of machinery which is not 'suppressed' should not be a nuisance, by way of analogy with vibrations etc. perceived by the occupier directly.

Are these the only categories of harm, or will others do? What if the defendant damages the plaintiff's economic interests by broadcasting racing commentaries from a convenient vantage point? It has been held in Australia that this does not constitute nuisance: *Victoria Park Racing* v *Taylor* (1938) 58 CLR 479.

Interference may be moral. In *Thompson-Schwab* v *Costaki* [1956] 1 All ER 652 the plaintiff's complaint was of the activities of the staff and clients of a brothel operated in a disorderly fashion by the defendant across the road from the plaintiff's property. This was held to be a sufficient potential threat both to current convenience and to property values to be a nuisance. See also *Hubbard* v *Pitt* [1975] 3 All ER 1, where the plaintiff was an estate agent whose activities in relation to tenanted property attracted adverse attention, taking the form of a picket of its premises. Although this was business disturbance it related to preventing the use of premises.

Where do you draw the boundary between those activities which are, and those which are not nuisances, where what is complained of is not the result of physical processes?

The distinction between the cases above is that in the successful claims, occupation of premises became less beneficial in a direct sense. In the unsuccessful case, the real problem was loss of money, not loss of amenity.

10.4.7   DEFENCES

10.4.7.1   Prescription

Do you know what this expression means? If not, look it up in a dictionary (preferably a law dictionary!).

You will now know that it relates to the process whereby a right is acquired by long user. Where the subject matter of the alleged nuisance is capable of being an easement (e.g. a right of eavesdrop) it can be acquired prescriptively (i.e. by 20 years user without action). Many of the nineteenth century cases leave a rather larger ambit for prescription than would be the case today; there is less emphasis on rights of property now.

10.4.7.2   General defences

Most of the general defences will apply, where the facts admit. It is thought that contributory negligence will apply only when the behaviour complained of is other than deliberate, but there is no direct authority.

10.4.7.3   Statutory authority

This defence is available to an individual or authority exercising functions or doing works in pursuance of statute. There is a presumption that Parliament intended the defendant to carry out functions without causing a nuisance so far as practicable: *Metropolitan Asylum District Managers* v *Hill* (1881) 6 App Cas 193.

In *Allen* v *Gulf Oil Refining* [1981] 1 All ER 353 (*Cases and Materials* (**10.1.5.1**)) the defendant was authorised by statute to construct an oil refinery. The plaintiff complained that the refinery as built and operated constituted a nuisance. The defendant pleaded statutory authority. It was held that the defence succeeded in relation to those matters of complaint which related to 'the nuisance which inevitably resulted from any refinery on the site' but not to other matters which might arise because of the economic and operational choices of the defendant as to the actual construction and operation of the refinery. It is sometimes said that the statutory powers must be exercised without negligence, but the word is being used in a special sense; the statutory immunity carries with it an obligation to use all care and skill to avoid harm. In *Gulf Oil* it was also said that the approval of development by statutory authority might alter the prevailing environment, thus 'shifting the goalposts' in relation to nuisances affecting enjoyment of the property.

In *Gillingham BC* v *Medway (Chatham) Dock Co.* [1992] 3 All ER 923 there was a nuisance in fact (it was treated as a public nuisance but this is immaterial for the present discussion) arising out of the use 24 hours a day by commercial traffic of residential streets in the vicinity of the old Chatham dockyard. The local authority sought an injunction (using powers under s. 221 of the Local Government Act 1972 which allow it to act as the custodian of the local public interest). The claim failed because the council had itself granted planning permission for the use of the dock for this purpose, and this had moved the goalposts in the same way. Note that the grant of permission necessarily involved the use of this access to this extent (pending the creation of a new access at some unspecified future date). This was therefore a foreseeable side effect. If the dock company had a choice of access routes and had selected this one for their own convenience the result might have been different. This basis of the decision would, it is submitted, have bound other potential plaintiffs.

SAQ 130

Is it right that the goalposts can be moved in this way? Are the rights of neighbours adequately protected?

While planning authorities are normally careful to research the environmental and disturbance implications of planning decisions, a grant is not normally a binding assurance that the activities can be lawfully carried on (cf. restrictive covenants which may be enforceable by individual neighbours) and it cannot be assumed that the goalposts will be deemed to have moved.

10.4.8   REMEDIES

The remedies of choice will be damages or, more usually, an injunction. The injunction may be *quia timet* (i.e. to restrain a threatened harm) as long as the potential nuisance is established. Harm will be foreseeable if the potential victim can demonstrate that it is liable to occur. An injunction may be granted on terms (i.e. with its full operation suspended) to give the defendant the opportunity to put his house in order. An injunction can only restrain the actionable element of a nuisance, e.g. excessive noise. Damages may be awarded in lieu of an injunction under s. 50 of the Supreme Court Act 1981, but this will not allow the defendant to effect a compulsory purchase of the right to make a nuisance of himself, see *Allen* v *Gulf Oil*; however, an injunction is a discretionary remedy. This may explain the actual decision in *Miller* v *Jackson*.

SAQ 131

Raisa is the proprietress of the 'Tap'n'Tutu Academy of Dance', which is established on the top floor of a three-storey building. The middle floor is used as a lace warehouse until the tenant moves out, and is then let to Shady, the proprietor of the 'Intimate Bliss Massage Parlour'. After three months Shady complains that the noise and vibration of Raisa's tap-dancing classes is disturbing his customers and affecting his trade. A number of parents of Raisa's pupils complain that Shady's customers regularly ogle and occasionally proposition their teenage daughters on the stairs while they are on their way to and from dancing classes.

Advise Raisa as to her rights and liabilities in tort.

The first question is whether the tap dancing is a nuisance; it may be intrusive enough to disturb a normal neighbour, as opposed to a very undemanding one. If so, Raisa will be liable. It is not relevant that she is performing a socially useful function. The harassment of her pupils may be a nuisance. It does directly affect the property. However, it is not clear whether Shady is responsible for the activities of his visitors. This scenario shows up some of the weaknesses of nuisance.

10.5 Public Nuisance

In origin and essence public nuisance was (and is) a crime, although many of the anti-social activities formerly charged as a common law public nuisance are now the subject of specific statutory offences, e.g. offences under the food and drugs legislation, and matters covered by the Environmental Protection Act 1990.

> An act not warranted by law or an omission to discharge a legal duty, which act or omission causes damage or inconvenience to the public in the exercise of rights common to all of Her Majesty's subjects. (Stephen, *Digest of the Criminal Law*, 1883.)

An act or omission which 'materially affects the reasonable comfort and convenience of life of a class of Her Majesty's subjects' (Romer LJ in *AG* v *PYA Quarries Ltd* [1957] 2 QB 169 (*Cases and Materials* (**10.2**)). A nuisance which 'is so widespread in its range or indiscriminate in its effect that it would not be reasonable to expect one person to take proceedings as his own responsibility to stop it' (Lord Denning *ibid*).

10.5.1 SCOPE

As with private nuisance, the judges have consistently avoided general pronouncements seeking to define the scope of public nuisance. Why is this? There are two principal reasons. In the first place, a definition which will comprise disturbance from quarrying, failure to repair highways, permitting an offensive encampment of transients and the incompetent operation of public transport services, all of which have been held to be public nuisances, will be so wide as to be valueless. In the second place, the existence of a definition would fetter the discretion of the courts to declare a novel factual situation to be a nuisance, thus rendering the law less flexible.

This was done, in a rare instance of a criminal prosecution in *Johnson (AT)*, *The Times*, 22 May 1996, where the making of hundreds of obscene phone calls to at least 13 women throughout South Cumbria was held to be not only (self-evidently) a private nuisance in respect of each victim, but also a public nuisance under the above tests (especially Lord Denning's). The decision on private nuisance probably cannot stand after *Hunter* v *Canary Wharf*, but as there is no requirement for an interest in land in public nuisance, this aspect of the decision would seem to be valid. It therefore follows that some matters which are really harassment may qualify as public nuisance, although they would not be private nuisances.

10.5.2 REMEDIES

The primary remedy in public nuisance is by way of prosecution, or by an action for an injunction on the part of the Attorney General, or by a local council under s. 221 of the Local Government Act 1972.

In theory the Attorney General represents the public interest. In practice he is simply invited to lend his name to an action carried on by and at the expense of a private objector (known because of the original legal terminology as a relator). The Attorney General may refuse his consent to the institution of a relator action, but this is very much a reserve power.

10.5.3 PRIVATE ACTIONS

There is a derivative action in tort giving a private remedy in damages where there is special damage, e.g. *Halsey* v *Esso* [1961] 2 All ER 145 (*Cases and Materials* (**10.2.1**)). This is a case where public and private nuisance were both occasioned by the same acts. It is also a rare modern environment/pollution case not brought under specific legislation. Note that the claim for damages is a by-product, not the main reason for an action.

10.5.4 EXAMPLES OF PUBLIC NUISANCES

10.5.4.1 Highway obstruction

Many of the cases relate to highway obstruction. The right to free passage and free access to one's premises is an essentially public one. The only issues for decision are the following.

Reasonableness
A minor obstruction such as a hosepipe across a country lane may not be a nuisance: *Trevett* v *Lee* [1955] 1 All ER 406, but the position will be very different for a busy street: *Farrell* v *John Mowlem & Co.* [1954] 1 Lloyd's Rep 437. Temporary scaffolding for a reasonable purpose may not be a nuisance: *Harper* v *Haden & Sons* [1933] Ch 298. Again it is a question of degree. In many areas there are specific bye-laws which regulate building operations. Scaffolding and other disruptions require a licence. The special damage which the plaintiff must prove will usually be business disruption.

Danger on the highway
There is an overlap with obstruction. Many of these cases are older ones and appear to be nuisance/negligence hybrids. Today there would be a duty of care apparent, and the action would be in negligence, based on this. *Dollman* v *Hillman* [1941] 1 All ER 355 is a good example. A piece of fat was thrown or swept from a butcher's shop onto the pavement, where it was left lying. The plaintiff slipped and injured himself. This was held to be a nuisance. Today the natural cause of action would be negligence. The special damage is fairly obvious; the injuries resulting from exposure to the danger.

Abuse of right of passage
Although there is normally a public right to pass and repass on the highway, a grossly excessive and disruptive use of this right is capable of amounting to a public nuisance: *Gillingham BC* v *Medway (Chatham] Dock Co.* [1992] 3 All ER 923 (see **10.4.7.3**).

10.5.5 STATUS OF THE TORT

A loose parallel can perhaps be drawn with the tort action for breach of statutory duty, although the action derived from public nuisance is of greater antiquity. It may perhaps have influenced the development of the younger tort, but any temptation to draw close parallels should be resisted, as the specific ingredients of the two torts are very disparate.

10.5.6 PARTICULAR DAMAGE

The plaintiff must suffer 'particular damage' over and above the general inconvenience which the defendant's activities cause to the public at large. What does this mean, and why is it necessary? This is generally accepted as a control measure to prevent the opening of the floodgates.

10.5.6.1 Physical harm

As we have seen in relation to *Dollman* v *Hillman* such harm will count. This is as you should expect. This is the form of harm most likely to be compensated. There appears to be a requirement of something akin to negligence in such cases. The situation is confused by the fact that a cause of action in negligence may well co-exist.

10.5.6.2 Economic loss

Economic loss is recognised as constituting particular damage. In *Rose* v *Miles* (1815) 4 M & S 101 the defendant obstructed a waterway, as a result whereof the plaintiff, who was a regular user, was put to the expense of offloading his barges and transporting the cargoes by land round the obstruction. This was held to be particular damage, although no property belonging to the plaintiff had actually been physically harmed in any way.

Why is this recognition of pure economic loss surprising? (You should cross refer to the chapters on negligence).

In negligence pure economic loss is only recoverable in special situations, e.g. where there is a special *Hedley Byrne* relationship, or where it can be shown to be consequential on physical harm.

10.5.6.3 Loss of trade

This may be seen as economic loss, as in *Tate & Lyle* v *GLC* [1983] 1 All ER 1159 (*Cases and Materials* (10.2.2.1)). The defendant's construction of a ferry terminal under statutory powers caused unnecessary silting of the approaches to the plaintiff's jetties. The plaintiff incurred substantial costs in extra dredging. A claim in negligence was dismissed, but a claim in public nuisance for interference with the public right of navigation on the Thames succeeded.

10.5.6.4 Inconvenience

Mere inconvenience will not suffice, but extreme and egregious inconvenience may. There are a number of cases dealing with disruption to the trade of shops by crowds, queues or parked vehicles attracted by neighbouring activities. If the disruption is, on the facts, extreme, a remedy will be given. Is this just the floodgates argument at work?

It could be said that some inconvenience is part of give and take. I have a builder's lorry parked outside my house this week, you have your brother's minibus parked there next week. We each inconvenience the other, but not to such an extent that the law should intervene.

10.5.6.5   Exemplary damages

There is no right to claim exemplary damages: *AB* v *South West Water Services Ltd* [1993] QB 507.

10.6   Harassment

10.6.1   WHAT IS HARASSMENT?

Write down a definition of what you understand by harassment, in the legal sense.

There are many examples of unacceptable behaviour by one person to another. The motive may be personal, when a relationship breaks down, or when one person does not reciprocate the feelings of another, or as a consequence of some other dispute. The modern name for this form of harassment is 'stalking'. Harassment may also be ideological or political, where picketing or protests go too far. The position is complicated by the fact that, especially in 'personal' cases, the defendant may be obsessive or actually mentally ill. In the ideological/political cases, there is a need to balance the civil rights of the protesters with those of the subjects of the protests.

Some activities comprised within harassment amount to existing recognised torts. Physical attacks will amount to assault and/or battery. Entry onto land will be trespass. Verbal attacks may amount to defamation if they are published to others. We have seen how the House of Lords in *Burstow & Ireland* (**Cases and Materials** (9.1.2)) were prepared, against the consensus of academic opinion, to extend the ambit of assault to some verbal threats: 'psychological warfare'. Other activities either do not amount to such torts or only arguably do so. Sending unwanted messages or presents or loitering in public places to observe or speak to the victim are two common examples.

There has thus been a need for an apparent lacuna in the law, which is effectively a gap between trespass and nuisance in the legal sense, to be filled. The key question is whether the common law is still flexible and lively enough to do so, or whether statute is the appropriate method.

10.6.2 REMEDIES FOR HARASSMENT

10.6.2.1 Matrimonial and family harassment

In the area of marital breakdown, statutory provision has long been in place to restrain harassment and molestation. This protection has been gradually extended to cover co-habitees. The current statute is the Family Law Act 1996, which we will look at shortly. This was, however, an exception, although in the last year or two there has been an explosion of statutory protection. Some of this is tortious in nature, but in some cases the matter is treated as being either criminal in nature or a matter of public law, so that a public authority, rather than the victim, takes action.

10.6.2.2 *Wilkinson* v *Downton*

There is one established relevant common law head of liability, the tort in *Wilkinson* v *Downton* (1897) 66 LJQB 493 (*Cases and Materials* (10.3.1.1)):

A wilful act (or statement) calculated to cause physical harm to the plaintiff and in fact causing physical harm to him. (*Street on Torts* slightly modified.)

This is a tort which is in many respects unique; it is not strictly a trespass, since the vector of harm is not direct. It is arguable whether it is actionable *per se*. There is very little authority in England, although the tort has been taken up in the USA, and today the effective overlap with negligence is almost total, although the conceptual basis is very different.

In *Wilkinson* itself the defendant told the plaintiff by way of practical joke that the plaintiff's husband had been seriously injured in an accident. The plaintiff suffered nervous shock amounting to illness. The case was treated as one of first impression. (There were some old cases imposing liability for injuries caused by spring-guns (a kind of man-trap) which are now regarded as representing the same principle.) Wright J was clearly impressed by the fact that this was conduct which was wholly deliberate, unjustified and mischievous. As the law then stood, damages were not readily recoverable for negligently inflicted nervous shock, but a remedy was granted on the basis that this went beyond negligence.

One of the few English cases to apply *Wilkinson* is *Janvier* v *Sweeney* [1919] 2 KB 316 CA (*Cases and Materials* (10.3.1)). The defendant, a private detective, in order to induce the plaintiff to hand over some private letters, threatened to inform the authorities falsely that the plaintiff's fiancé was a traitor. The plaintiff suffered nervous shock amounting to illness.

The modern law would probably allow recovery in negligence on these facts on the usual basis. The special tort is perhaps redundant, but:

■ it is odd to sue in negligence in respect of intentional conduct; there are dicta in *Letang* v *Cooper* which segregate intentional harm (trespass) and negligence, and the limitation period is different;

■ it may be that imputed intention and direct harm cover a different field than foreseeability;

■ in *Khorasandjian* v *Bush* [1993] 3 All ER 669 the defendant was quite deliberately harassing the plaintiff by unwanted telephone calls and in other ways. The plaintiff said in an affidavit that she was under great stress. The court did not regard that as being self-evidently nervous shock amounting to illness, but considered that *Janvier* would apply to such a case if there were the relevant evidence. It was noted that injunctions had been granted in several unreported cases where acute harassment appeared to be causing actual illness. The court granted an injunction in private nuisance. Lord Hoffman in *Hunter* v *Canary Wharf* suggested that the decision in *Khorasandjian* was too restrictive, and that distress was sufficient damage. He would therefore have been prepared to support the decision, but not the reasoning, as Ms Khorasandjian was not an appropriate nuisance plaintiff.

'Harassment' was recognised as a cause of action in *Burris* v *Azadani*, *The Times*, 8 August 1995. It is, however, questionable whether it was seen as an independent tort or a sub-species of trespass to the person or nuisance. The actual use of the phrase appears to have been almost as a piece of shorthand. In the criminal sphere the Court of Appeal held in two decisions by the same court on the same day that harassment by nuisance telephone calls could amount to an assault (and if the victims sustained appropriate psychological trauma, an assault occasioning actual bodily harm): *Ireland*, or alternatively a nuisance, and if widespread a public nuisance: *Johnson (AT)*, *The Times*, 22 May 1996. As we have seen, the former decision has been upheld by the House of Lords, thus extending some protection to victims of harassment. So far as private nuisance is concerned, the decision in *Hunter* has effectively denied the applicability of this tort to personal harassment. Lord Cooke delivered a very powerful dissent, deprecating the wish of the majority to return to the roots of nuisance rather than adapt it to the social circumstances of today.

The net position is that the common law has shown flexibility in relation to expansion of assault to cover harassment and public nuisance may be available (but in practice most stalkers target a single victim) as may *Wilkinson* v *Downton*. Only private nuisance can be excluded.

Return to SAQ 117 and consider whether *Wilkinson* v *Downton* is relevant to any of these scenarios.

If (a) is not a battery (although it seems to be directly inflicted harm) it will clearly fall within *Wilkinson* v *Downton*. Scenario (e) is fairly clearly *Wilkinson* v *Downton*; it is a classic practical joke gone wrong, but with sufficient serious intent to qualify as malice, at least if Jeremy realised Kate was vulnerable.

10.6.3   STATUTORY HARASSMENT

10.6.3.1   Protection from Harassment Act 1997

One reason why the House of Lords excluded private nuisance as a remedy for harassment was that, by the time they decided *Hunter*, the Protection from Harassment Act 1997 (see *Cases and Materials* (**10.3.2.1**)) was on the statute book. This gives both civil and criminal remedies, and the civil remedy is by a specific statutory tort.

Read the extracts from the Protection from Harassment Act 1997, Family Law Act 1996, Housing Act 1996 and Crime and Disorder Act 1998 in *Cases and Materials* (10.3.2.1).

Harassment is not fully defined in the Protection from Harassment Act 1997, although there was considerable debate about this. Indeed a previous private member's Bill introduced by Janet Anderson MP failed to attract government support largely over this issue of definition. There is obviously concern that unwanted but justifiable attention, e.g. of investigative journalists pursuing allegations of financial misconduct, might be the subject of action, although this would probably qualify as reasonable. The Act must also be seen in the context of the European Convention on Human Rights, especially Arts. 8 and 10 which concern the right to privacy and the right to freedom of expression respectively. One particular concern was over the extent that the actions of demonstrators could be classed as harassment. There is now a decision on the point: *Huntingdon Life Sciences Ltd* v *Curtin and Others, The Times*, 11 December 1997, in which Eadie J at an *inter partes* hearing revoked an injunction granted *ex parte* by Schiemann LJ.

The plaintiffs, a company which undertook research on animals, had been granted an *ex parte* injunction against the defendants, among others, restraining them from any course of conduct amounting to harassment. The plaintiffs had complained of a sustained and menacing anti-vivisection campaign directed at itself and its employees, which included many breaches of section 1 of the 1997 Act. In the light of evidence adduced by the defendants for the first time at the *inter partes* hearing, the plaintiffs' allegations could not be sustained and the defendants' application was granted.

Eadie J added that the legislators of the Act would no doubt be surprised to see how widely its terms were perceived to extend by some people. The 1997 Act was clearly not intended by Parliament to be used to clamp down on the discussion of matters of public interest or upon the rights of political protest and public demonstration which was so much a part of our democratic tradition. He had little doubt that the courts would resist any wide interpretation of the Act as and when the occasion arose.

10.6.3.2 Family Law Act 1996

The current provision in family disputes is s. 42 of the 1996 Act. Although this covers many categories, it does not cover boy/girlfriends (other than fiancés) or someone who stalks a stranger or who has fantasised a relationship. There is no jurisdiction to award damages (although if the molestation does amount to assault etc. a separate action could be brought). Very often the defendant is of modest means, so damages are not a practical remedy. Orders may be made by any court with domestic jurisdiction (magistrates and county courts and High Court), although there are some limitations in particular on the powers of magistrates.

Molestation is a word which judges consider has an established and common meaning. It has no legal definition. There must be some element of interference with physical or psychological well-being, although this need not be conduct amounting to a recognised tort. These limits were recently restated in *C* v *C* (*Non-molestation Order: Jurisdiction*), *The Times*, 16 December 1997.

The parties had been married but had obtained a divorce in September 1997. In October two articles detailing the former wife's complaints about her husband appeared in the press and the husband attempted to restrain the wife from providing further information to the newspapers by applying for a non-molestation order under section 42. While there had been no direct threat or molestation in the physical sense, nor any indirect interference by telephone or letter, he contended that her conduct in supplying newspaper reporters with revelations which resulted in the publication of the offending articles justified the making of a non-molestation order. The claim failed. Although there was no legal definition of molestation, the word implied some quite deliberate conduct aimed at a high degree of harassment of the other party sufficient to call for the intervention of the court. Section 42 is in a part of the Act concerned with domestic violence, not breaches of privacy. The behaviour complained of could not be construed as harassment and therefore was not molestation within the Act.

10.6.3.3 Housing Act 1996

A new, specific power to control harassment by injunction is contained in the Housing Act 1996. There has for some time been a power to evict a tenant for anti-social behaviour (Housing Act 1985 for public sector tenants and Housing Act 1988 for private sector tenants) and these powers are strengthened by the 1996 Act.

10.6.3.4 Crime and Disorder Act 1998

More far-reaching powers are contained in the Crime and Disorder Act 1998.

Section 1 provides for 'Antisocial Behaviour Orders'. The protections afforded to the potential subject of the order are significantly less stringent than those afforded at common law or under the statutes considered above. The application is to the magistrates, not to the county or High Court. There is no need to prove violence and, as several speakers in the Second Reading debate in the House of Lords observed, no requirement that those suffering alarm or distress should be of 'reasonable firmness'. There is also provision (in s. 11) for 'Child Safety Orders' which apply to children under 10. One of the conditions for the making of such an order is causing the kind of alarm and distress referred to in s. 1(1). Parenting orders may be made against the parents of children and young persons made the subject of either of the above two orders. However, in all these cases the initiative must come from the public authorities. The victims will no doubt seek to persuade them to act, but these are public law remedies. They are, however, seen as an essential addition to the armoury of the law, particularly to aid those who are too inarticulate, too intimidated or too impecunious to take action themselves:

> Many, many people are afraid to be complainants in court when they have to make public allegations against their neighbours and against people who have made their lives an absolute misery. We are saying that prosecutions under the public order legislation and the Protection from Harassment Act have their place. But this is prior to that. I repeat that it is to endeavour to safeguard the vulnerable in our society, those who have their lives made a daily misery. I regret to say that at the moment our law does not protect them. Therefore, this is a much more considered remedy for a real social evil. (Lord Williams of Mostyn, HL, 3 February 1998, Committee Stage.)

10.6.4 THE OVERALL POSITION ON HARASSMENT

In summary then, the remedies available are:

- common law: action for damages/injunction in trespass to the person or to land; *Wilkinson* v *Downton* or public nuisance;

- statutory private action: damages/injunction, Protection from Harassment Act 1997; non-molestation order, Family Law Act 1996;

- public law: injunction, Housing Act 1996 (Antisocial Behaviour/Child Safety Orders, Crime and Disorder Act 1998).

10.7 Relationship of Public and Private Nuisance

The same factual situation may constitute both public and private nuisance. The plaintiff in public nuisance does not need to be an occupier of property. Although the same facts may give rise to an action in both public and private nuisance, the theoretical basis is different; see *Halsey* v *Esso Petroleum* [1961] 2 All ER 145.

10.7.1 EXAMPLES OF THE OVERLAP

(a) A tumble-down house may fall into the street or onto a neighbouring property.

(b) Pollution from a factory may poison passers by or neighbours.

10.7.2 RELATIONSHIP BETWEEN PUBLIC NUISANCE, PRIVATE NUISANCE AND NEGLIGENCE

10.7.2.1 Test of remoteness of damage

All three share a common test of remoteness of damage: *The Wagon Mound (No. 2)* [1967] 1 AC 617; *Cambridge Water Co.* v *Eastern Counties Leather* [1994] 1 All ER 53.

10.7.2.2 The place of fault

Is fault always required in private nuisance, and if so what degree of fault? What, in any case, is meant by fault? Many commentators suggest that this is one of the instances where there has been an unjustified transfer of rules from negligence to private nuisance via public nuisance, by means of an equation of the two senses of the word nuisance.

Fault is generally required in public nuisance and the category of fault is generally to be equated with the negligence standard.

There are cases in public nuisance where fault has been held not necessary: *Farrell* v *Mowlem* (see **10.5.4.1**). In *Dymond* v *Pearce* [1972] 1 QB 496 it was held that parking a lorry on the road overnight, albeit under a street light and with its own lights lit, was a nuisance. It is hard to see that the defendant was at fault. The plaintiff failed because, on the facts, the nuisance did not cause his loss, but it was said that if there had been fog etc., then as between the creator of the nuisance and the innocent victim, the former would be liable, even though the harm was not foreseeable.

In these residual cases you can see a distinction between negligence and nuisance, at all events public nuisance.

10.7.2.3 Economic loss

Certainly in public nuisance pure economic loss is recoverable. It is not normally recoverable in negligence or private nuisance, but see *Hubbard* v *Pitt* at **10.4.6**.

10.7.3 STATUS OF PRIVATE NUISANCE

On this view private nuisance would simply become a special case of negligence, rather like occupiers' liability. Now that there is a renewed stress on the proper categorisation of torts, and a retreat from the high-water mark of Lord Wilberforce's doctrine of proximity and foreseeability, there appears to be a greater emphasis on the nature of the relationship of the parties, the nature of the interest invaded and the description of harm sustained.

There is also sometimes apparent a confusion between the question: 'did the defendant unreasonably interfere with the plaintiff's enjoyment' and the question: 'did the defendant cause unreasonable interference with the plaintiff's enjoyment?'.

10.8   Summary

We have now seen how the law of tort can protect one's entitlement to enjoyment of land without disturbance or pollution. This is of course only part of the story and much of the protection comes through the powers of local authorities and other statutory bodies (such as the National Rivers Authority) to restrain and punish unacceptable behaviour under statutory powers. The key areas are (always assuming that the defendant is creating a risk of foreseeable harm):

(a)   Private nuisance:

   (i)   Absolute protection against damage arising from a continuing source of harm.

   (ii)   Conditional protection from interference with enjoyment. The level of amenity depends on the nature of the area, and it is far from clear how far the law will deal with injury affecting the emotions rather than the senses.

(b)   Public nuisance:

   (i)   Absolute protection against interference with public rights.

   (ii)   Protection in respect of special harm arising from conduct affecting a large number of people.

(c)   Harassment:

   (i)   Limited common law remedy (although facts may support other torts).

   (ii)   Active development of statutory remedies, both generic and specific. Almost a crusade against antisocial behaviour.

   (iii) Need to balance rights of the parties, and not produce excessive interference with the right to free expression in particular.

Always remember that public nuisance is primarily a crime, and that civil liability is secondary, rather like civil liability for breach of statutory duty.

10.9   Further Reading

Brazier, M., *Street on Torts*, 10th edn, London: Butterworths, 1997, Chapter 19.

Conaghan, J., and Mansell, W., *The Wrongs of Tort*, London: Pluto Press, 1993, Chapter 6.

Cooke, P.J., and Oughton, D.W., *The Common Law of Obligations*, 2nd edn, London: Butterworths, 1993, Chapter 29.

Gearty, C., 'The Place of Private Nuisance in a Modern Law of Torts' [1989] CLJ 214.

Howarth, D., *Textbook on Tort*, London: Butterworths, 1995, Chapter 7 (pp. 360–365) and Chapter 11.

Jones, M.A., *Textbook on Torts*, 5th edn, London: Blackstone Press, 1996, Chapter 7.

Markesinis, B.S., and Deakin, S.F., *Tort Law*, 3rd edn, Oxford: Oxford University Press, 1994, Chapter 5 (section 3 only).

Newark, 'The Boundaries of Nuisance' (1949) 65 LQR 480.

Winfield and Jolowicz on Tort, 14th edn, London: Sweet and Maxwell, 1994, Chapter 14.

10.10   End of Chapter Assessment Question

Harvey is the owner of a small-holding on which he has established a riding school. He has two immediate neighbours, Oenone, an elocution teacher and Sonya, a taxi-driver.

Harvey has a contract to provide weekly riding lessons to the 400 pupils of St Trinian's, a local girls' school. Oenone complains that on the days when the junior girls are receiving lessons, there is so much disturbance and disruption from their chattering, screaming and shouting that she and her own pupils cannot hear themselves think.

Every summer Harvey holds two or three large charity gymkhanas. Sonya complains that on these occasions the approach roads to her house are so congested by parked cars, horseboxes and other vehicles attracted by the gymkhana that she cannot get her taxi out, and she has lost business as a result.

Advise Harvey as to his liability to Oenone and Sonya.

See *Cases and Materials* (10.5) for a specimen answer.

CHAPTER ELEVEN

HAZARDOUS ACTIVITIES

11.1 Objectives

By the end of this chapter you should be able to:

■ identify activities within the special rule for hazardous activities;

■ explain how the law has developed in this area;

■ explain and criticise the present state of the law;

■ explain and discuss the relationship between these rules and the rules of nuisance and negligence;

■ discuss the relative merits of the common law rules and other legal solutions: statutory liability, regulation, and the American rules on 'abnormally dangerous' activities.

11.2 Introduction

You have seen in **Chapter 10** on nuisance that the law of tort has a role, if a limited one, to play in regulating land use. A balance has to be struck between the rights of the owner to carry out his desired activities and those of the neighbours to undisturbed enjoyment of their own property.

There are, however, some activities that appear to demand special treatment because thay have a greater capacity to cause harm than most.

In general these are activities which have been made possible only by the scientific and technical advances of the nineteenth and twentieth centuries: rock blasting, chemical plants, oil refineries, nuclear power stations, aircraft etc. In some cases, such as reservoirs, it is not so much new technology as the increased scale of operation required by modern society which creates the extra risk.

There is one exception, namely 'playing with fire'. Fire has always been a hazard. Although in principle it is on a par with the other risky activities, it is regarded differently in law because it was recognised much earlier. You will look at these differences at **11.4**.

ACTIVITY 65

On a separate piece of paper, make a list of activities you consider would merit special treatment on the grounds set out above. Put it to one side for the present and read on.

It is impossible to prohibit these hazardous activities. Some are essential to modern life, such as oil refineries and chemical plants. Others are at least arguably beneficial, such as nuclear power stations. A balance has to be struck, as in cases of 'ordinary' nuisance, between the rights and responsibilities of those concerned.

11.3   How the 'Hazardous Activities' Rule Developed

The starting point in examining how the law strikes this balance is the leading nineteenth century case, *Rylands* v *Fletcher* (1866) LR 1 Ex 265, Court of Exchequer Chamber; (1868) LR 3 HL 330, House of Lords.

This case has usually been regarded as stating the elements of a discrete tort.

In the latest case in the field, *Cambridge Water Co.* v *Eastern Counties Leather* [1994] 2 All ER 53, Lord Goff prefers to regard it as a species of nuisance. Do you remember this case? If not read it again in *Cases and Materials* (**10.1.2.1**).

It has been adopted in the US, in this instance as the starting point for a new tort imposing strict liability for 'abnormally dangerous activities'.

11.3.1   THE CASE OF *RYLANDS* v *FLETCHER* ITSELF

ACTIVITY 66

Read *Rylands* v *Fletcher* in *Cases and Materials* (11.1.1). What is the basis of liability?

It is clear that the building and operation of the reservoir caused the defendant's loss. It also seems clear that no-one was blaming the defendant. He had done his best. Could he nevertheless be liable?

There seems to be a difference between the reasoning of Blackburn J and that of Lord Cairns. Blackburn J stresses that the defendant brought the water onto his land:

> The person who, for his own purposes, brings on his land and collects and keeps there anything likely to do mischief if it escapes, must keep it in at his peril.

According to Lord Cairns, had the flooding been by the operation of natural forces, albeit altered by works done by the defendant on his land, it was for the plaintiff to take precautions, but if the defendant:

> not stopping at the natural use of their close, had desired to use it for any purpose which I may term a non-natural use . . . and if in consequence of their doing so, or in consequence of any imperfection in the mode of their doing so, the water came to escape . . . [t]hat which the defendants were doing they were doing at their own peril.

SAQ 134

Lord Cairns, after the passage cited above, went on to cite with approval the above passage of Blackburn J's judgment, the principles of which he said led to the same result. Are the two judges indeed saying the same thing, and if not, what is the difference?

Blackburn J gives a number of examples of analogous situations. These fall into two groups:

(a) cattle trespass, which is an old common law tort of strict liability (see today s. 4 of the Animals Act 1971, which gives statutory form to the tort, but retains the strict liability);

(b) situations which appear to be orthodox nuisance, e.g. sewage from a privy flooding a cellar, fumes from an alkali works. There is clearly a state of affairs brought about by the accumulation.

On a narrow view, all that Blackburn J is deciding is that in those circumstances a single escape will create liability. There does not have to be a persistent infliction of damage or inconvenience.

There is no doubt that dangerous escapes arising from the non-natural user of land are a distinct category: it is not entirely clear what sort. It is unlikely that Blackburn J was conscious of creating a new tort, as opposed to developing the law of private nuisance by declaring that it applied to isolated escapes rather than a state of affairs. Lord Goff in *Cambridge Water* confirms this view, as you will see at **11.3.2.3**. Until 1946 there was often a confusion of the specific tort and 'ordinary' nuisance, to such an extent that these earlier cases must often be treated as being of doubtful authority. The confusion was resolved by the decision of the House of Lords in *Read* v *J Lyons* [1946] 2 All ER 471.

Our next task is to establish the rules governing this tort.

11.3.2   THE CURRENT RULES

For the tort to be made out, a number of ingredients must be present:

■ a deliberate accumulation;

■ of things which are hazardous in the event of an escape;

■ in the course of a non-natural user of the land;

■ an actual escape;

■ causing harm which is reasonably foreseeable.

We now need to examine each of these points.

11.3.2.1   Accumulation

The rule does not apply to things which arrive or occur naturally, e.g. rainfall or groundwater: *Wilson* v *Waddell* (1876) 2 App Cas 95, wild vegetation: *Giles* v *Walker* (1890) 24 QBD 656, soil and rock: *Pontardawe RDC* v *Moore-Gwyn* [1929] 1 Ch 656, but will apply to, e.g. planted vegetation, reservoirs, chemicals etc. Where rocks were scattered by blasting the rule can apply, on the basis that the blasting powder had been accumulated: see *AG* v *Cory Bros* [1921] AC 521, and the US case, *Caporale* v *C W Blakeslee Inc* (1961) 149 Conn. 79, 175 A 2d 561.

11.3.2.2   Hazardous things

The cases give a long catalogue of hazardous things: water, electricity, gas, petrol, fumes etc., chair-o-planes and explosives. They do not need to be dangerous *per se* (although many of them will be), merely liable to cause harm if they do escape.

Where the plaintiff's user of his land is abnormally sensitive, it cannot be said that any escape is dangerous if it adversely affects only the sensitive use. There have been decisions which suggest that a defendant may be liable for the actions of people he brings together on his land. In *AG* v *Corke* [1933] Ch 89 the defendant allowed caravan-dwellers on his land; they caused annoyance and damage in the neighbourhood. It was held that the rule could extend to people. However, this has been doubted in New Zealand: *Matheson* v *Northcote College* [1975] 2 NZLR 106 (on the footing that people operate under free will) and an extension to the case of undesirable tenants or licensees (even where put in by way of harassment of the neighbours) has been refused on the ground that the landlord had no sufficient control of the tenants: *Smith* v *Scott* [1973] Ch 314 (see **10.4.5.2**). It is unlikely that people will in future fall within the rule. Is this a good thing?

It is suggested that there is no need to go beyond the questions 'did the defendant bring this onto the scene?' and 'is it likely to cause harm if it escapes from his control?'.

11.3.2.3   Non-natural user

Read *Rickards* v *Lothian* [1913] AC 263 PC and *Cambridge Water* (if you are not entirely familiar with it without re-reading it) in *Cases and Materials* (**11.1.2.1** and **10.1.2.1**).

This requirement is of course based on Lord Cairns' speech in *Rylands* v *Fletcher*. The formulation by Lord Moulton in *Rickards* v *Lothian* has always been considered to be the best:

> It must be some special use, bringing with it increased danger to others, and must not merely be the ordinary use of the land or such a use as is proper for the general benefit of the community.

The question of whether or not a user is non-natural is one of fact and degree, which, being interpreted, means, a question of discretion for the court. In 1919 garaging a car with a full petrol tank was non-natural: *Musgrove* v *Pandelis* [1919] 2 KB 43. In 1964 storage of strips of metal foil was natural: *British Celanese Ltd* v *A H Hunt (Capacitors) Ltd* [1969] 1 WLR 959. During the First World War a munitions factory was non-natural: *Rainham Chemical Works* v *Belvedere Fish Guano* [1921] 2 AC 465; during the Second World War probably natural: *Read* v *J Lyons* [1947] AC 15.

The recent tendency has favoured a narrow approach in order not to stifle proper economic activity. Indeed, the reluctance of courts to declare that user was non-natural was the main limiting factor on the rule, and there were suggestions that the rule was being marginalised by the strict requirements for a user to be non-natural. The high-water mark was probably the decision of Ian Kennedy J at first instance in *Cambridge Water Co.* v *Eastern Counties Leather* (unreported, 31 July 1991).

He decided that, as a matter of policy and balance, industrial activities of the kind carried on by Eastern Counties Leather were not non-natural, at least in this geographical context.

> In reaching this decision I reflect on the innumerable small works that one sees up and down the country with drums stored in their yards. I cannot imagine that all those drums contain milk and water or some other like innocuous substance. Inevitably that storage presents some hazard, but in a manufacturing and outside a primitive and pastoral society such hazards are a part of the life of every citizen.

ACTIVITY 68

Consider the following observations and make a note of your conclusions.

Is there a valid distinction between the metal foil, which was harmful only to immediate neighbours, and was a disruption rather than a toxin, and the TCE, which poisoned a whole aquifer? Can we establish a criterion of the state of the neighbourhood? Is it relevant that at the time when the TCE was being handled without restraint (up to 1976), the hazards which occurred (i.e. pollution of groundwater) were not foreseeable?

Lord Goff rejected the narrow view and preferred a wider concept of what is non-natural:

> I cannot think that it would be right [if the risk of harm were foreseeable] to exempt ECL from liability under the rule in *Rylands* v *Fletcher* on the ground that the use was natural or ordinary. The mere fact that the use is common in the tanning industry cannot, in my opinion, be enough to bring the use within the exception, nor the fact that Sawston contains a small industrial community which is worthy of encouragement or support. Indeed I feel bound to say that the storage of substantial quantities of chemicals on industrial premises should be regarded as an almost classic case of non-natural use.

SAQ 135

Can you reconcile Lord Moulton's concept of non-natural user with Lord Goff's? If not, which seems best adapted to ensuring just results?

11.3.2.4   Escape

ACTIVITY 69

Read *Read* v *J Lyons* [1947] AC 156 in *Cases and Materials* (11.1.2.2). Why did the plaintiff's claim fail?

You should have seen that this case clearly spells out that there must be an escape from the defendant's land or hereditament. As Viscount Simon said:

> Escape from a place where the defendant has occupation of or control over land to a place which is outside his occupation or control.

This was fatal to the plaintiff's claim under the rule, as she was employed on the premises.

What is the 'place' from or to which there is an escape? In either case it need not be premises in the ordinary sense, but may be a conduit under the highway, or a part of a building: *Midwood* v *Manchester* [1905] 2 KB 597. Indeed Taylor J accepted in *Rigby* v *Chief Constable of Northants* [1985] 1 WLR 1242 that the rule might apply in the case of things brought onto the highway and allowed to escape onto other property.

There is no requirement that the defendant have any interest in the property from which the thing escapes, merely that he be in control of the thing: *Benning* v *Wong* (1969) 122 CLR 249.

11.3.2.5   Reasonable foreseeability

The position is now regulated by *Cambridge Water*. The test is whether harm of the kind which transpired was foreseeable. This is the same test, derived from the *Wagon Mound (No. 1)* [1961] 1 All ER 404, which you have already met in relation to nuisance and to negligence generally. Lord Goff's speech is clear support for those who have regarded *Rylands* v *Fletcher* as a species of nuisance rather than an independent entity largely because the *Wagon Mound* test of foreseeability is applied. In the *Cambridge Water* case, his Lordship accepted that, at the time of the escapes, it was not foreseeable that the relevant type of harm would occur because the solvent in question was thought to be so volatile that it presented no risk of contamination of the soil and groundwater.

How has the operation of the rule in *Rylands* v *Fletcher* been affected by the decision in *Cambridge Water*?

You should note that the decision in *Cambridge Water* has been criticised on the basis that the judges wrongly treated the standard of knowledge against which foreseeability was judged as being that of a reasonable foreman, rather than the higher standard to be attributed to a qualified technical director, but the principle is not objectionable, unless the tort is expected to operate as a general purpose absolute environmental protection rule. Lord Goff declined to adopt the general purpose absolute rule approach, and pointed out that the Law Commission had expressed reservations about a strict liability rule for hazardous activities: *Civil Liability for Dangerous Things and Activities* (1970, Law Com No. 32).

He did stress that environmental protection was now regarded as important and was the subject of much legislation, national and international (without referring to the previous UK government's attempts to dismantle significant elements of the EC legislation in this field) and clearly considered that legislation was preferable to an extension of the common law. You will consider these wider issues at **11.3.5**.

11.3.3   SPECIFIC ASPECTS OF THE RULE

11.3.3.1   Who can sue?

An occupier of land can sue. There are *dicta* suggesting that occupation is an essential condition: *Weller* v *Foot & Mouth Disease Research Institute* [1966] 1 QB 569, and *dicta* to the contrary: *Shiffman* v *Order of St John* [1936] 1 All ER 557. If the rule is regarded as being a sub-species of nuisance, then the former are correct; see *Hunter* v *Canary Wharf* (*Cases and Materials* (**10.1.1**)). We have already discussed this. If the rule has become an independent tort, then the restriction is not necessary.

11.3.3.2 Personal injuries

In *Hale* v *Jennings Bros* [1938] 1 All ER 579, the plaintiff was the occupier of a stall at a fair who sustained injury when a chair-o-plane became detached from a neighbouring pitch. Damages for these injuries were recoverable under the rule, although it should be noted that he was an occupier.

There are *dicta* in the Court of Appeal which extend this approach to non-occupiers, although in their case there is the further problem of their title to sue: *Perry* v *Kendricks Transport* [1956] 1 WLR 85.

Against this are *dicta* in the House of Lords in *Read* v *J Lyons* that as the rule 'derives from a conception of mutual duties of neighbouring landowners' there is no liability for personal injuries.

ACTIVITY 70

List the arguments for and against liability under the rule being extended to non-occupiers and/or to personal injuries.

11.3.4 DEFENCES

Although liability is 'strict' there are defences available.

11.3.4.1 Act of war/malicious third parties

An example of this is *Rickards* v *Lothian*. The claim failed not only because the user was natural, but because the harm was caused by a third party for whom the defendant was not liable. But if vandalism was foreseeable, failure to take precautions may result in liability; see *Environment Agency (formerly National Rivers Authority)* v *Empress Car Co.* [1998] 2 WLR 350 (HL).

11.3.4.2 Consent

This may either be to the presence of the source of danger: *Gill* v *Edouin* (1894) 71 LT 762, 72 LT 579 or on the basis that there is a common benefit: e.g. from the mutual use of a gas or electricity supply: *Carstairs* v *Taylor* (1871) LR 6 Ex 217. The consent is to the inherent risks and will not cover negligence: *Prosser* v *Levy* [1955] 1 WLR 1224. Consent is not to be inferred merely because the plaintiff has come to the danger.

11.3.4.3   The plaintiff's default

Contributory negligence will apply: *Lomax* v *Stott* (1870) 39 LJ Ch 834.

11.3.4.4   Statutory authority

This will apply exactly as in nuisance. In *Green* v *Chelsea Waterworks Co.* (1894) 70 LT 547 the defence applied to a water undertaker whose pipes burst, but it was material that the undertaker was under a duty to maintain a supply of water under pressure. In the case of reservoirs and water pipes there is now statutory strict liability which overrides the defence (s. 28 of the Reservoirs Act 1975 and s. 209 of the Water Industry Act 1991 respectively).

11.3.4.5   Sensitive user

You have seen (at **10.4.4.2**) that this is a defence in nuisance. There is little authority under the rule, but in *Eastern SA Telegraph Co.* v *Cape Town Tramways* [1902] AC 381, the defendant was not liable for interference to telegraph instruments by leakage of electric current where the evidence showed that there was a problem only because of the idiosyncratic design of the equipment.

11.3.5   THE STATUS OF THE TORT

There is clearly an anomaly, in that liability for dangerous escapes is subject to a 'strict liability' rule, while in other cases there is a fault principle. The Pearson Commission in 1978 recommended a new statutory tort of strict liability in relation to activities which were either ultra-hazardous (e.g. use or storage of explosive, corrosive or poisonous chemicals) or created a risk of extensive harm (e.g. large buildings such as Ronan Point, or civil engineering works such as the Channel Tunnel or the Dartford bridge). There would be a statutory mechanism for including types of hazard. The scheme appears to reflect in some ways the existing statutory regulation of ionising radiation and civil aviation risks (see Civil Aviation Act 1982 and Nuclear Installations Act 1965 in *Cases and Materials* (**11.1.3**)). It reflects a move from fault to loss-sharing as the rationale of tort, and as such appears to have little legislative priority, except in the environmental area.

The *Cambridge Water* decision has affirmed that there is a role for the tort, limited by the requirement of foreseeability of harm. It remains to be seen how often it will be used.

List the advantages and disadvantages of the various solutions to the problem of dangerous activities or escapes.

11.4 Fire

11.4.1 EARLY HISTORY

There was an early common law remedy by way of trespass on the case in respect of the escape of fire. Although the authorities are obscure the liability was probably regarded as strict in that a man kept a fire at his peril. The tort is seen as analogous with *Rylands v Fletcher*, although it is not so much the escape of something accumulated as the spread of something hazardous. There is also a separate action which now does require proof of negligence.

11.4.2 THE GENERAL NEGLIGENCE BASED ACTION

11.4.2.1 Prohibition of actions where fire accidental

No action . . . shall be prosecuted . . . against any person in whose house . . . or other building or on whose estate any fire shall . . . accidentally begin . . .

Section 86 of the Fires Prevention (Metropolis) Act 1774 (despite its name, this Act applies throughout the country).

11.4.2.2 Meaning of 'accidental'

The word 'accidentally' does not mean non-deliberately. It means by pure accident or where the cause is not established. The defence given by the Act accordingly does not apply to a fire that is started or continued negligently: *Filliter* v *Phippard* (1847) 11 QB 347.

Read *Musgrove* v *Pandelis* **[1919] 2 KB 43** and *Sochacki* v *Sas* **[1947] 1 All ER 344** in *Cases and Materials* **(11.2.1.1). What is the basis of the decisions?**

In each case the court distinguished between two fires. The initial one was 'accidental' in *Musgrove* and deliberate in *Sochacki*. However, this was not the relevant fire. In *Musgrove* the relevant fire was the major one which was due to the chauffeur's negligence. In *Sochacki* the relevant fire was accidental.

11.4.3 QUASI *RYLANDS* V *FLETCHER*

This form of the liability antedates the decision itself, although it was not relied on to support it.

In *Tubervil* v *Stamp* (1698) 1 Salk 13 which was 'an action on the case upon the custom of the realm' [whereby if the defendant so kept a fire in his close that it escaped and burned the plaintiff's property on the plaintiff's own land the defendant was liable], for the fire in his field was his fire as well as that in his house; he made it, and must see that it did no harm, and must answer the damage if he did. Every man must use his own so as not to hurt another.

Vaughan v *Menlove* (1837) 3 Bing NC 468, *per* Park J.

The language used here is archaic, and the reference to using his own so as not to hurt another should remind you of nuisance. It is, however, clear that there is strict liability, in the sense that fault does not need to be proved.

In *Musgrove* v *Pandelis* it was held that this was the same principle as that in *Rylands* v *Fletcher*, and it was also held, as something almost self-evident, that s. 86 of the Fires Prevention (Metropolis) Act would not apply. Why was this? It would not apply to the facts of *Tubervil* v *Stamp* (1698) 1 Salk 13 because the relevant fire was deliberate, or to those of *Musgrove* v *Pandelis*, because the relevant fire was negligent. The latter case was, however, expressly decided on the second ground of *Rylands* v *Fletcher*, it having been decided that the keeping of a motor-car was a non-natural user. How does this help plaintiffs?

11.4.4 THE LATEST WORD ON FIRE

In *Mason* v *Levy Autoparts of England* [1967] 2 All ER 62 (**Cases and Materials (11.2.2)**), the defendant stored large quantities of autoparts, petrol, acetylene and paint in rather cramped conditions in a predominantly residential area. A fire started (the cause was never discovered) and spread to the plaintiff's property. The defendant pleaded the Act.

The plaintiff failed to prove negligence, which meant that for the first time in modern experience, the *Rylands* v *Fletcher* liability was crucial. MacKenna J was not happy with the decision in *Musgrove* v *Pandelis*. Why do you think this was? In the event he decided that he was bound by the earlier decision. He did, however, restate the ingredients of this tort in a rather clearer way.

The defendant is liable if:

(a)   he brought onto the land things which were likely to catch fire . . . and the fire to spread;

(b)   he did so in the course of some non-natural use; and

(c)   the things ignited and the fire spread.

Although fires are common, lawsuits are not. This is because most fire damage is compensated under first party insurance. There will be a need to sue only if the plaintiff is uninsured or under insured, or the plaintiff's insurer exercises his right of subrogation and pursues the defendant for his own benefit

11.5   Summary

It may be the case that this separate chapter will, in future editions, be reabsorbed into the chapter on nuisance as a result of the decision in *Cambridge Water*. It is however too early to say whether this will occur.

It is certainly clear that there is strict liability for dangerous escapes, either of things which are inherently hazardous, things which are hazardous in the context in which they are being used or of a conflagration.

It is immaterial that all due care was used. There must be some degree of enhanced risk from the use of the property, as against ordinary everyday activities (although this is a grey area at present) and the harm must have been foreseeable.

11.6   Further Reading

Brazier, M., *Street on Torts*, 10th edn, London: Butterworths, 1997, Chapter 20.

Cooke, P.J., and Oughton, D.W., *The Common Law of Obligations*, 2nd edn, London: Butterworths, 1993, Chapter 29.

Howarth, D., *Textbook on Tort*, London: Butterworths, 1995, Chapter 11.

Jones, M.A., *Textbook on Torts*, 5th edn, London: Blackstone Press, 1996, Chapter 8.

Markesinis B.S., and Deakin, S.F., *Tort Law*, 3rd edn, Oxford: Oxford University Press, 1994, Chapter 6.

Winfield and Jolowicz on Tort, 14th edn, London: Sweet and Maxwell, 1994, Chapter 15.

11.7   End of Chapter Assessment Questions

What torts, if any, have been committed in the following cases:

(a)   Damian has bought an old rubbish tip to use as a lorry park. Methane from the tip builds up in the basement of Enid's bungalow, which explodes, injuring Enid and her mother, Gertrude, who is visiting her.

(b)   Hamlet establishes a hostel for wayward children. In November the children scour the neighbourhood for timber and remove gates and fences belonging to various neighbours. On Guy Fawkes Night the resultant bonfire causes such dense smoke that the nearby motorway is closed for an hour. On 7 November the fire, which has been left to burn itself out, is revived by a strong wind and burns down the neighbouring bus shelter.

See *Cases and Materials* (11.4) for a specimen answer.

CHAPTER TWELVE

DEFAMATION

12.1 Objectives

At the end of this chapter you should be able to:

- distinguish between the forms of defamation;

- explain the elements of libel and slander;

- account for the respective roles of judge and jury in cases of defamation;

- explain the terms 'defamatory meaning', 'reference to the plaintiff' and 'publication';

- explain the function and scope of the defences to defamation;

- analyse the role of the law of defamation and critically account for its present form.

12.2 Introduction

The law of defamation seeks to protect individual reputation. Its central problem is how to reconcile this purpose with the conflicting demands of free speech. Both are highly valued in our society, the one as perhaps the most dearly prized attribute of civilised man, the other the very foundation of a democratic community.

Fleming, *Law of Torts*, p. 500.

Good name in man and woman, dear my lord
Is the immediate jewel of their souls:
Who steals my purse steals trash; 'tis something, nothing;
'Twas mine, 'tis his, and has been slave to thousands.
But he that filches from me my good name
Robs me of that which not enriches him
And makes me poor indeed.

Shakespeare, *Othello*, Act III, Scene 3.

SAQ 138

How important do you consider reputation to be, weighed against money, physical health and freedom of speech?

12.3   General Considerations

12.3.1   FREEDOM OF SPEECH *VERSUS* THE PROTECTION OF REPUTATION

Some legal systems, such as those of the USA, give primacy to freedom of expression, either by constitutional provision or by general law. Distinctions are often drawn between those who put their characters in issue by seeking public office or status, who are protected only against malicious defamation, and private citizens, who enjoy wider protection. Other systems, such as West Germany and Italy, lay greater emphasis on the right to reply, i.e. to publish a prominent and prompt refutation of the defamatory material than they do on the action for damages.

12.3.2   PROTECTION OF PRIVACY AND PROTECTION OF REPUTATION

Can you see a link between these two 'moral rights'. There is certainly a link in practice between the right to privacy and the right to reputation, although this link is not recognised by the English law in any formal sense. This may be because the two have developed separately so we do not see that each protects an aspect of personal integrity and dignity. French law, for example, has general categories of *préjudice matérielle* and *préjudice morale* to cover those harms which respectively can and cannot be reduced to mere financial loss. Defamation is controversial at the present in view of a number of substantial awards and settlements, which are so obviously disproportionate to damages for serious personal injury as to amount, some argue, to a scandal: Jeffrey Archer (£500,000), Koo Stark (£300,000), Elton John (£1M, including costs and a lot of 'free' publicity and a further £350,000) and Lord Aldington £1.5M (later held, by the European Court of Human Rights, to be excessive and thus an abuse of the defendant's human rights). Perhaps the last part of Iago's observation in *Othello* needs rewriting.

ACTIVITY 72

List the arguments for and against a strong law of defamation.

12.4 Defamation in General

12.4.1 DEFAMATION DEFINED

Defamation is where the defendant publishes a statement about the plaintiff which reflects on the plaintiff's reputation so as to lower him in the estimation of right-thinking members of society or which tends to cause the plaintiff to be shunned and avoided.

Jones, *Textbook on Torts*, slightly altered.

12.4.2 FORMS OF DEFAMATION

12.4.2.1 Historical introduction

As you are probably aware, there are two major subdivisions of defamation, namely libel and slander. What exactly is the difference? The distinction is purely historical in origin. Libel was in medieval times the preserve of the ecclesiastical courts. These were concerned with the moral or spiritual aspect of the tort. The defamer was committing a sin, and recognising and punishing that was the main objective. It was a fortunate side effect that the victim would see his reputation vindicated. A common law action on the case for defamatory words which caused temporal loss (i.e. monetary loss recompensable in damages) then developed independently, becoming known as slander. The ecclesiastical jurisdiction then passed at the Reformation to the Court of Star Chamber and then at the end of the Civil War to the Common Law courts. The two forms of action were never assimilated.

12.4.2.2 Libel

Definition
Libel was originally defamation in written form. The word derives etymologically from the Latin *liber,* a book. It refers now primarily to matter which is both permanent and visible to the eye. What does this cover beyond actual writing? It naturally covers pictures and statues. What about the broadcast media, films, recordings etc.? Although gestures and sign language 'appeal to the eye,' they are transient, and are regarded as slander. It seems to be the case that defamation by e-mail is libel. Although the e-mail is apparently transient, in that it can be deleted, in fact it stays in the system and is of course potentially accessible to others: *Multigroup Bulgaria Holdings Ltd* v *Oxford Analytica Ltd* (1997) (unreported).

Statutory extension

(a) Defamatory material in a stage play is libel by statute: s. 4 of the Theatres Act 1968.

(b) Defamatory material broadcast by means of wireless telegraphy (radio and television) is also libel by statute: s. 166 of the Broadcasting Act 1990. The definition in the Act covers words (including Morse code) and visual methods of conveying meaning (including gestures). It extends only to broadcasts intended for general reception. This will exclude e.g. police frequencies. Cable and satellite TV services are included.

Doubtful cases
Audio tapes and records still constitute a grey area. There is no direct authority. Which side of the line should they fall? Some academic authorities suggest that as there is a permanent medium, the defamation is libel, others that as the actual publication of the material is transient and purely aural, that it will be slander.

In relation to films the authority is *Youssoupoff* v *MGM* (1934) 50 TLR 581. A film about the last years of the Romanovs contained a scene suggesting that Princess Youssoupoff had been raped by Rasputin. The information was primarily conveyed by visual means, although comprehension was aided by the sound-track. The strict *ratio* of the case is that cinematographic images, being perceived by the eye, and being permanent in the sense that the film stock is retained, will be libel and not slander. The case is normally treated as authority that a defamation in the form of an anecdote in the sound track, unaccompanied by any image, will be libel, but the point is technically still open.

Effect of libel
Libel is regarded as being a sufficiently serious invasion of the plaintiff's rights to be actionable *per se*, that is, the plaintiff need not prove actual harm expressible in money terms.

Libel and crime
Libel is a crime as well as a tort although prosecutions are rare. In criminal libel, justification, i.e. the truth of what is said, is not a defence. You may have heard the adage 'the greater the truth, the greater the libel'. What does this mean? It is only in this context that the adage is strictly correct. It is something of a paradox. The essence of the crime is that public order is threatened or public decency outraged. A true allegation is more likely to achieve this than an obvious fabrication.

12.4.2.3 Slander

Now you know what libel is, try working out your own definition of slander.

Definition
Slander is defamation in a form that does not amount to libel, primarily word of mouth. In principle the key factor is transience and the necessarily limited scope of publication, which render slander less damaging, but the case law is not quite as neat and tidy as that.

Effect of slander
Slander is normally actionable only on proof of special damage, e.g. the loss of a job, a tenancy, business etc.

Exceptional cases
Let us look at the four exceptional cases where slander is actionable *per se*.

(a) Imputation of crime   The crime must be a serious one, i.e. it must carry a possible custodial sentence. Why is this sort of allegation an exception? Some say it is because belief in criminality will lead to ostracism, others that it puts the plaintiff in jeopardy. Allegations of conduct that is disreputable, but not technically criminal have been held to fall outside the rule, but an allegation that the plaintiff is a convict to fall within it: *Gray* v *Jones* [1939] 1 All ER 798. Does this help to choose one explanation or the other?

(b)   Imputation of venereal disease   It has been suggested that the rule is wider than venereal disease in the strict sense. It seems to be the case that the disease should not simply be contagious, but should carry some moral opprobrium. AIDS would probably qualify.

(c)   Office, profession, trade, calling or business

In an action for slander in respect of words calculated to disparage the plaintiff in any office [etc], it shall not be necessary to allege or prove special damage, whether or not the words are spoken of the plaintiff in the way of his office [etc]. (Section 2 of the Defamation Act 1952.)

The rule looks to the effect of the words on the plaintiff's employment, not to the context in which they were said; so an allegation of immorality against someone who should be moral, such as a headmaster, or of dishonesty in any case, will count, even though they do not directly relate to the performance of the duties. A voluntary office (office of honour) is within the rule, but the rule is modified so that incompetence will only count if it is of such a degree as to warrant the plaintiff's removal from the office.

(d)   Unchastity of a woman

Words spoken and published . . . which impute unchastity or adultery to any woman or girl, shall not require special damage to render them actionable. (Slander of Women Act 1891.)

Lesbianism is unchastity for this purpose. A male partner cannot rely on the rule. Slang expressions will suffice. Why did women need special protection in 1891? Do they still need it today?

What qualifies as special damage
It must be tangible, pecuniary loss, such as loss of employment or business contracts. Loss of the hospitality of friends will count, but only insofar as this is expressed in tangible form, e.g. food, drink and accommodation.

Nervous shock, or physical illness and financial loss arising therefrom are not special damage (and will not make a slander actionable); if the defamation is otherwise actionable, any such effects may be reflected in the size of the award of general damages. The primary concern of the tort is to protect reputation, not physical integrity.

12.4.2.4   Procedural oddities

(a)   An action is extinguished by the death of either party.

(b)   There is a right to trial by jury (unless a judge considers the case is too complex). This right may be waived by both parties jointly.

(c)   Legal aid is not available.

(d)   The limitation period is 12 months: s. 4A, Limitation Act 1980 (inserted by the Defamation Act 1996).

(e)   Public bodies, such as local authorities: (*Derbyshire CC* v *Times Newspapers Ltd* [1993] AC 534) and political parties (*Goldsmith* v *Bhoyrul* [1997] 4 All ER 268) cannot themselves sue in defamation. Commercial entities may, and of course members and officers may sue in their personal capacity.

SAQ 139

Othello suspects his wife, Desdemona, is having an affair with Cassio. He writes the words 'Cassio is a wife stealer' on the beach between low-and high-water mark. He pays Iago to produce an ice sculpture clearly showing Desdemona and Cassio in a compromising position and puts the sculpture on display in the market place.

What type of defamation do we have here? Will Desdemona or Cassio be able to sue Othello if they cannot prove special damage?

12.5   What is Defamatory?

ACTIVITY 74

What does the plaintiff have to demonstrate in order to show that he has been defamed?

12.5.1   DEFINITION

He must show that a statement has been made about him which reflects on his reputation so as to lower him in the estimation of right-thinking members of society or which tends to cause the plaintiff to be shunned and avoided. At one time the expression 'Brings the plaintiff into hatred, ridicule or contempt' was used, but this is a little wide. To win the case he must also prove the defendant published the statement.

12.5.2   DAMAGE TO REPUTATION

How far does this go? Will a statement which makes the plaintiff a figure of fun suffice, or must there be a 'moral element'? In *Blennerhasset* v *Novelty Sales Services Ltd* (1933) 175 LT Jo 393 the defendant placed a full page advertisement headed 'Beware of Yo Yo' which referred to a Mr Blennerhasset who ate lobster at Pim's and had to be taken to a quiet place in the country after becoming hooked on Yo Yo. The plaintiff was a Mr Blennerhasset who lunched at Pim's and was a stockbroker. He was subjected to ribaldry in the Stock Exchange as a result of the advertisement. This was clearly annoying, but was it actionable? It was held that the words were not capable of being defamatory, as they did not reflect on his moral or social character. In this case the ridicule was transient and transparently unconnected with any moral failing but a satire or lampoon may be defamatory, although it uses the medium of humour.

12.5.3 'RIGHT THINKING MEMBERS OF SOCIETY'

The expression comes from a *dictum* of Lord Atkin in *Sim v Stretch* [1936] 2 All ER 1237. The aim is to exclude the two extremes: those who will tolerate anything, and those who are excessively censorious. This is best illustrated by a rather tongue in cheek decision: *Byrne v Dean* [1937] 2 All ER 204. A golf club had an illegal gaming machine. Someone sneaked to the police, and the machine was suppressed. The defendant composed a squib expressing the hope that the sneak might 'byrne in Hell, whoever he is'. The plaintiff became very unpopular at the club. Was it defamatory to suggest he had advised the police of a breach of the law? It was held that those who would believe the plaintiff to be the sneak and as a result think less of him for doing his duty as a citizen were not 'right-thinking members of society' and so the words were incapable of being defamatory.

12.5.4 HARMFUL, BUT NOT IMPROPER

Why does the second limb of the definition exist? What about an allegation that a woman has been raped? This is clearly not *prima facie* denigratory of her character: *Youssoupoff v MGM* (see **12.4.2.2**). The particular allegation may not be defamatory even in this sense in today's moral climate, where a rape victim is more likely to be pitied and counselled than shunned and victimised. Or is she?

12.5.5 MIXED VIEWS

Problems clearly arise when the allegation is one which, while not absolutely reprehensible, is nevertheless likely to excite strong feelings in a section of the public who are not self evidently wrong thinking, e.g. to call a man a strike breaker, or a Communist. It is probably necessary for such an allegation to carry overtones of hypocrisy. Is it defamatory to say that X is a connoisseur of wine? Would you change your mind if X were a leading temperance campaigner?

12.5.6 A FLAVOUR OF EXAMPLES

Accusations of incompetence or dishonesty in the plaintiff's trade, profession or calling are defamatory (although in an Australian case it was held not defamatory to call a leading rugby player 'fat and cumbersome'). So are allegations of insolvency in the case of a businessman, although it is not defamatory merely to say that the plaintiff has ceased to trade.

Mere words of abuse will not be defamatory, but if, properly understood, they indicate specific wrongdoing or immorality, then they are defamatory.

12.5.7 RESPECTIVE FUNCTIONS OF THE JUDGE AND JURY

12.5.7.1 The judge

The judge is the sole judge of law. It is a question of law whether words (or other communications of meaning) are capable of bearing a particular meaning and whether that meaning is capable of being defamatory.

12.5.7.2   The jury

If the words are so capable it is a question of fact for the jury, who are the sole judges of fact, whether those words do bear that meaning and do defame the plaintiff.

Some cases are heard without a jury. Is it still important to make these distinctions?

12.6   Reference to the Plaintiff

12.6.1   EXPLICIT REFERENCE

There is no problem if the reference is fully explicit: '[the plaintiff] is a damn rogue who has been swindling his customers and sleeping with their wives for years.'. A degree of obliqueness in the reference is not fatal: 'there is a red-headed milkman in this town who . . .' will do just as well.

12.6.2   INDIRECT REFERENCE

There is a division of function (similar to that for defamatory meaning) where the words do not directly refer to the plaintiff. The judge has to rule on whether the words are capable of applying to the plaintiff. This may be so even where there are witnesses who allegedly understood them in this sense. In *Knupffer* v *London Express Newspapers* [1944] 1 All ER 495 (*Cases and Materials* (**12.2.1**)) the defendant published an article suggesting that the Mlado Russ or Young Russia party were a gang of pro-Nazi quislings to be numbered among the 'despised dregs of society'. The plaintiff was the leader of the English branch of Mlado Russ, which had some 40 members. He was not referred to by name in the article, but witnesses testified that they understood the article as referring to the plaintiff. How should the case be decided? The judge held that the words were an unfounded generalisation, applying to a class and not to each and every member and were therefore not capable as a matter of law of referring to the plaintiff, even though as a matter of fact they were clearly so understood. Why do you think the judge flew in the face of apparent common sense here?

12.6.3   MISTAKEN IDENTITY

12.6.3.1   Accidental confusion

It is not necessary that the defendant meant to refer to the plaintiff, or even knew of his existence.

Read *Hulton & Co.* v *Jones* and *Newstead* v *London Express Newspapers* in *Cases and Materials* (**12.2.2.1**). **Does the later case fulfil the fears of those involved in the earlier case?**

Was the defendant in *Hulton & Co.* v *Jones* [1910] AC 20 careless? He could have made it clear that this was a piece of fiction. The denigration of the imaginary character was quite gratuitous, done only to boost sales of the magazine.

Two of the judges in the Court of Appeal were concerned lest allowing the plaintiff's action would expose the defendant to liability where he published a story, true of X, but defamatory of a namesake. They thought such a result would be absurd, and one said it was impossible.

12.6.3.2   Namesakes

Exactly this situation arose in *Newstead* v *London Express Newspapers* [1940] 1 KB 377. The Court of Appeal took the view that the risk should fall on the defendant, and so upheld the decision in favour of the plaintiff, but indicated that such cases would be rare, because the circumstantial detail of the story would usually prevent it being reasonably possible to consider the story to relate to the namesake. Damages were assessed at one farthing, which indicates that the jury had not entirely taken leave of its senses.

Again, it might be said that there was carelessnesss in not giving adequate circumstantial detail.

12.6.3.3   Statutory intervention

ACTIVITY 76

Look up ss. 2–4 of the Defamation Act 1996 in *Cases and Materials* (12.1). What are they designed to achieve?

These sections apply, among other things, to unintentional defamation of the *Newstead* type. The concept of the offer of amends derives from the Defamation Act 1952, but the procedure under that Act was so complex that it was little used, although many newspapers would publish a correction or disclaimer on request anyway. Although the offer of amends under the 1996 Act includes an offer of compensation as well as a correction/apology, it is likely that in a *Newstead* case this compensation will be nil or nominal.

12.6.3.4   The current position

You should now be clear that the question of whether the defendant has defamed the plaintiff is to be answered objectively in the light of the effect of the publication, rather than subjectively in the light of the defendant's intentions and knowledge.

SAQ 140

Is the present law on unintentional defamation unfair? How could it be further reformed?

As we have just seen, cases do arise where a plaintiff can show that an article can be read as applying to him, or at least confusing him with someone else. In practice an informal disclaimer or correction is all that is required, but there is no efficient means of compelling the publisher to make one, or of insisting that the aggrieved party accept one if it is offered. As it is rare for real harm to arise from accidental defamation, it seems unreasonable to involve the publisher in the cost and trouble of a full scale defamation action. The offer of amends is designed to protect the unintentional defamer. If the offer is accepted there will be no trial, and the matter is resolved relatively quickly and cheaply. Even if the offer is rejected it may be pleaded as a defence, and the onus is on the plaintiff to defeat that defence by showing that the defendant believed that the statement referred to the plaintiff. Even if the defence fails it may be relied on in mitigation of damages. It will be a bold, or perhaps foolhardy, plaintiff who launches an action in *Newstead* circumstances in future where there is an offer of amends.

12.6.4 NATURAL MEANING AND INNUENDO

12.6.4.1 Inferences

In many cases it is not just the natural meaning of the words which is claimed to be defamatory, but some subsidiary meaning or inference. There are limits to how far this process can be allowed to go. In *Lewis* v *Daily Telegraph Ltd* [1963] 2 All ER 151 (*Cases and Materials* (**12.2.3.1**)) the defendant published articles headlined 'Fraud Squad Probe Firm' and 'Inquiry on firm by City Police'. The reference was clearly to the plaintiff and his company. Are the words defamatory? The plaintiff alleged that these words meant not only that there was an investigation but, by implication or inference, that there was ground for suspicion, or even a presumption of guilt. (No smoke without fire.) Was this a legitimate meaning? Not according to the judges. This was a case of an attempt to extend the natural and ordinary meaning which failed. It was to draw an inference, not from the facts, but from a further inference which had itself been drawn from the facts. It worked like this:

■ Fact: there was an investigation.

■ First (legitimate) inference: the police considered there were good reasons to investigate.

■ Second (illegitimate) inference: these reasons were valid and the plaintiff was guilty of some offence or other.

12.6.4.2 Innuendo

Do you know what the word means? If not, look it up in the dictionary. Unfortunately this only helps you to a limited extent. The expression 'innuendo' is doubly confusing in the context of defamation. The ordinary meaning of a 'sly' or 'malicious' attack on character is of no help in appreciating the legal meanings, and there are two of these!

12.6.4.3 True (or legal) innuendo

This occurs where the words are harmless in themselves, but become defamatory when considered in the light of other material. Only those with access to the additional evidence will grasp the defamation, but this is immaterial to success in an action.

Read *Morgan* v *Odhams Press* in *Cases and Materials* (12.2.3.2). Can you connect the plaintiff to the story? Can you see how his witnesses did?

In *Morgan* v *Odhams Press* [1971] 1 WLR 1239 the defendant seems to have fallen foul of judges' beliefs that people are all too ready to believe the worst and will do so even if a detailed perusal of the document would show such inconsistencies as to render the conclusion unreasonable. This was stressed by several members of the House of Lords in *Lewis* v *Daily Telegraph*. In the present case, the times did not add up, but the witnesses had not sat down and worked it out. The Court held that the article should be judged in the light of the standards of accuracy and reader sophistication associated with the newspaper in question, *The Sun*.

Similarly, in *Cassidy* v *Daily Mirror* [1929] 2 KB 331 the defendant published a picture of Mr Cassidy and Miss X, 'celebrating their engagement'. How could this be defamatory? The plaintiff was Mrs Cassidy, who was legally married to Mr Cassidy. Although they were effectively separated, Mr Cassidy did spend occasional nights with her. What exactly was she alleging? That the effect of the picture was to lead her friends and neighbours to the conclusion that she was not married to Mr Cassidy but was his kept mistress. The extrinsic facts which made the photo defamatory were a true innuendo, and she succeeded. Nowadays the more obvious inference to draw is that she was now divorced, but divorces were harder to come by in the 1920s.

In *Tolley* v *Fry* [1931] AC 333 the defendant published a caricature of the plaintiff, a well known amateur golfer, as part of its advertising. Can you identify the innuendo? The plaintiff successfully argued that publication of the caricature implied that he had received reward for the use of the picture. This was strictly taboo for an amateur.

A true innuendo must, by Rules of Court, be so pleaded.

12.6.4.4 False innuendo

This is really only the use of an extended meaning. It will usually be pleaded to avoid any suggestion that it is not part of the natural meaning, but there are no extrinsic facts to be specifically put in issue. In *Allsop* v *Church of England Newspaper* [1972] 2 All ER 26 (*Cases and Materials* (12.2.3.3)) the defendant described the plaintiff as 'preoccupied with the bent'. As Lord Denning said, this clearly did not relate to the dictionary meanings (look them up!). It was clearly a slang meaning, and there were several to choose from, involving sexual and financial impropriety as well as merely eccentricity. The plaintiff had, by way of false innuendo, to specify which of the derogatory meanings of the word he was relying on. This was both to help the defendant formulate his line of defence, and to enable the judge to decide whether the meanings actually relied on were capable of being defamatory.

12.6.4.5   The sting

This is a technical expression; what do you think it means? It has nothing to do with complicated frauds and ragtime melodies. It is used to connote the precise defamatory meaning on which the plaintiff relies. If you were the defendant you would want to know this, and the Rules of Court ensure that the defendant is entitled to know what meanings the plaintiff alleges, and what innuendo facts are to be proved. He is entitled to defend each sting independently by the use of any tactic of pleading or defence. Where the plaintiff complains of a lengthy article or passage the defendant may defend by reference to the whole of it, i.e. the plaintiff may not convert an innocent message to a defamation by malicious editing.

A good indication of the correct approach to the last issue is the fairly recent decision in *Charleston* v *News Group Newspapers* [1995] 2 All ER 904. The plaintiffs complained of an item in the *Sun* comprising a photomontage of their heads on bodies forming part of a pornographic photo and accompanying an article. The burden of the text was that the plaintiffs, who were soap actors, were the unwitting victims of entrepreneurs who had manipulated their pictures into images for a pornographic computer game. The impression given by the photos and headlines alone might be that the plaintiffs were willing participants. The court ruled that the defendant was able to have the whole item considered as a whole, even though some readers might have done no more than glance at the picture and caption.

'Some people may think that the law has gone too far in holding that the publisher of a defamatory statement which identifies no one is liable if knowledge of special facts which the publisher could not know causes sensible people to think that the statement applies to someone the publisher had never heard of. That may be arguable . . .' (*Morgan* v *Odhams Press* per Lord Reid).

Should defamation be restricted to those cases where the statement on its face refers to the plaintiff?

Some of the cases appear to go a long way. However, there will be cases where an artful author will 'hide' the identity of his victim, although clues will allow some people to make the connection. There is also the problem of the victim referred to by necessary implication, such as in *Cassidy*. There is a danger of overreacting to extreme cases like *Morgan* v *Odhams Press*.

12.7   Publication

12.7.1   WHAT IS PUBLICATION?

It is an essential element of defamation that the defamatory material should have been published, i.e. have come to the attention of at least one person other than the plaintiff (or the defendant's spouse). Why does this requirement exist?

12.7.2 HARM TO REPUTATION

It is of the essence of defamation that the plaintiff's reputation should be damaged (or at least the possibility of damage exist). Insulting the plaintiff to his face has no effect on his public reputation. The exclusion of spouses can be justified on a variety of grounds; it may be the *de minimis* rule at work (although this would be an anomaly), or it may be a distaste for prying into the realms of matrimonial pillow talk.

12.7.3 EXTENT OF PUBLICATION

12.7.3.1 Number of readers/hearers

A publication to a single person will be enough, although the extent of publication will affect the likely *quantum* of damage to P's reputation and will therefore influence the damages to be awarded.

12.7.3.2 Incidental publication

If the defendant dictates a letter to his secretary, prior to sending it to the plaintiff, there is a publication to the secretary. Other incidental publications, e.g. to a filing or copying clerk will count. There may be a defence of qualified privilege in these circumstances (see **12.9.2.2**): *Bryanston Finance* v *De Vries* [1975] QB 703. This does not affect the principle that this is publication.

12.7.3.3 Untoward events

A publication which is foreseeable, even though unintended, will count. In *Pullman* v *Hill* [1891] 1 QB 524 the defendant wrote a letter addressed to the plaintiff, accusing the plaintiff of obtaining money by false pretences. The letter was not marked as being private and was opened by a clerk employed by the plaintiff, and read by other clerks. This was publication to all the clerks.

But what if the unintended publication was also unforeseeable? In *Huth* v *Huth* [1915] 3 KB 32 the plaintiff's butler opened a letter addressed to the plaintiff in which the defendant (the plaintiff's estranged husband) suggested that the plaintiff and the defendant were not lawfully married, and that their children were illegitimate. The defendant was not responsible for the butler opening and reading the letter in breach of his obligations as a servant. The view of the court may have been coloured by strong suspicions that the butler had been put up to it by his mistress.

It is foreseeable, and will be assumed, that a postcard or telegram will be read by employees of the post office: *Sadgrove* v *Hole* [1901] 2 KB 1. In this case the plaintiff was employed as a quantity surveyor on a building project by the defendant. When the drawings and bills of quantities went out to the builders, the defendant thought they were wrong and sent postcards to some of the builders, saying that the quantities were wrong. There was no overt reference to the plaintiff. As against the builders, the publication was privileged (see **12.9.2.2**). Although it was assumed that the cards would have been read there was no publication *of a libel* to the postal officials etc. who would have seen the cards, because there was no possibility of their connecting the material with the plaintiff.

12.7.4 SERIAL PUBLICATION

Normally each publisher is liable for his own part in the publication process. Who will be the defendants in the case of a book? A newspaper? In the typical case of a book the author, publisher and printer will all be liable, and in the case of a newspaper the author, editor, publisher and printer. The plaintiff has a free choice of whom to sue. A printer will normally have a contractual indemnity from the publisher, but this is only as effective as the publisher's assets. The plaintiff can ignore it.

12.7.5 INNOCENT DISSEMINATORS

At common law many people other than the author of the piece and the editor and publisher responsible for the publication could be liable in defamation. They included the printer and the wholesale and retail distributors, who were often entirely ignorant of the contents of the material which they were handling. A newsagent cannot read every magazine for libel, and even the printer may be working on material in a foreign language or where he is ignorant of the context of the material.

Such people are now protected by s. 1 of the Defamation Act 1996 (see *Cases and Materials* (**12.1**). This section creates a statutory defence for anyone who '[is] not the author, editor or publisher of the statement'. The editor is the person responsible for the decision to publish and the publisher is the person responsible in the commercial sense for the publication in question (not the wider meaning usual in defamation). The printer and distributors are expressly declared not to be the author, editor or publisher: s. 1(3)(a). The defence only applies where the defendant 'took reasonable care in relation to [the] publication' and 'did not know, and had no reason to believe, that what he did caused or contributed to the publication of a defamatory statement'.

The defence is intended to clarify the earlier law. There is, however, a requirement for diligence, and a potentially exempt innocent disseminator may be deemed to have actual knowledge. The limits of the earlier law, and of the scope of the defence can be seen in *Vizetelly* v *Mudie's Select Library* [1900] 2 QB 170. The defendant operated a circulating library. The plaintiff complained of a libel in a book the defendant stocked. The publisher had circulated a notice asking for the book to be returned for the libel to be expunged. The defendant did not employ a reader for libel. The court held that the defendant must prove:

(a)   that he did not know of the libel;

(b)   that he was not put on notice of any libel;

(c)   there was no negligence in not knowing of the libel.

It was not negligent not to employ a reader for libel but the circular meant that the defendant was on notice as to this particular libel. This is some indication of the approach that will be taken to the defence in s. 1. The new defence expressly requires that 'regard shall be had to . . . the previous conduct or character of the author editor or publisher': s. 1(5)(c). It therefore follows that certain periodicals may be suspect and require a higher degree of caution. In *Goldsmith* v *Sperrings Ltd* [1977] 2 All ER 55 (*Cases and Materials* (**12.3.1**)) the plaintiff claimed to have been libelled in *Private Eye*; he was allowed to pursue an action against 37 distributors of the *Eye*, as well as the author, editor and printer. However, all the distributors had been advised of the alleged libel by a circular from the defendant. The defendant suggested that the general reputation of *Private Eye* was such that the distributors were on notice even without the warning.

12.7.6 MERE CARELESSNESS

Intention to defame is unnecessary: *Cassidy* v *Daily Mirror* (see **12.6.4.3**). That case could have been decided on the basis that the information was not adequately checked. It is still not clear whether it will be a defence to prove that the material was published in good faith and that all possible measures were taken to establish that the facts were true. This goes beyond mere innocence, as there is a positive duty to use all due diligence. Look at s. 1 of the Defamation Act 1996 (in *Cases and Materials* (**12.1**)).

SAQ 142

Should there be a defence of due diligence? In other words no one will be liable in defamation unless they ought to have realised that the material was defamatory if they had taken reasonable care to check it.

Which situations which are now actionable will cease to be so? It will not cover those who publish material which is clearly defamatory because they think it is true. It will only cover cases where there is no obvious defamatory meaning and proper care has been taken to check for non-obvious but foreseeable meanings. If s. 4 of the Defamation Act is reformed, this will cover the accidental reference case. Due diligence may help printers, and also cases where the defamatory context arises from circumstances unconnected with the statement which is defamatory. This seems to strike a reasonable balance.

12.8   What Must the Plaintiff Prove?

ACTIVITY 78

List the matters which the plaintiff must prove. What mental element is involved?

You should have written down something along the following lines. The words (etc.) must be proved to be capable of bearing a defamatory meaning, to refer to the plaintiff and to have been published by the defendant; the jury must then find 'libel or no libel'. The truth or otherwise of the words is irrelevant at this stage. The plaintiff is entitled to a verdict in the absence of a relevant defence. Intention and carelessness are not normally relevant.

12.9   Defences

12.9.1   IN GENERAL

How easy is it to establish these elements of defamation which the plaintiff must prove? It seems as though it is fairly simple, at least in principle. As a result defences are of considerably greater significance than in other areas of the law.

It should be remembered that, in accordance with normal practice in civil proceedings, the burden of proof lies upon him who asserts affirmative issues, so in this instance the burden is on the defendant to establish his defence.

12.9.2 PRIVILEGE

The doctrine of privilege is the expression in English law of the primacy of free speech as against the protection of private interests in reputation. A privileged statement, that is one made on a privileged occasion and within the limits of the relevant privilege, is not actionable. There are two species of privilege, absolute and qualified.

12.9.2.1 Absolute privilege

Absolute privilege, as its name implies, is indefeasible. There are three broad categories.

Parliamentary proceedings
No action may be brought on anything said in either House. To do so would be a contempt of Parliament which is itself a High Court. Hence the invitation often extended to MPs who have said something apparently defamatory under the cloak of parliamentary privilege to repeat the remark outside the House.

Judicial proceedings
This covers statements made in the ordinary course of such proceedings by a party, counsel, witness or judge. It extends to quasi-judicial proceedings (e.g. solicitors' or doctors' disciplinary proceedings), but not administrative hearings, such as planning enquiries: *Richards* v *Cresswell, The Times*, 24 April 1987. Anything not said in the course of the case (such as an interjection from the public gallery, or a gratuitous remark by the judge about something unconnected with the trial) is unprotected. The privilege is extended by statute to fair and accurate contemporaneous newspaper reports of such proceedings. There has recently been a clutch of cases on the scope of this head of privilege. In *Daniels* v *Griffiths* (1997) 147 NLJ 1809 it was held that communications to the Parole Board did not attract absolute privilege as the Board was not analogous to a court. In *Waple* v *Surrey CC* [1998] 1 All ER 624 it was held that a solicitor's letter relating to an application for a contribution to child maintenance was too far removed from legal proceedings and in *S* v *Newham LBC, The Times*, 5 March 1998 it was held that statements on the official register of those considered a risk when working with children did not attract absolute privilege.

In all these cases it is accepted that qualified privilege (see below) will apply. There are, however, significant consequences flowing from the denial of absolute privilege. Absolute privilege is a complete defence and all these cases were on the preliminary issue of its existence, since if the defendant won the plaintiff had no case. Although there may be a heavy burden on the plaintiff to negate qualified privilege, the case still has to be fought.

Official communications
The scope of this head is much narrower than the title implies. It relates only to communications between ministers and similarly senior officers of state on official business.

The status of absolute privilege
Is there a common thread between the three types of absolute privilege? Are they all justified? The first two heads are legitimate; while it is not inevitable that the legislature has an absolute right to free speech, any attempt to fetter it would be tendentious. In the case of court proceedings it would similarly be intolerable for the proceedings to be second-guessed by a libel jury. There is a technical link as Parliament is also a court. The third category is perhaps misplaced. A qualified privilege may be all that can be justified, but we do have an excessive veneration for official secrecy. It could be said that it is

equivalent to the others in the sense that they cover between them the three arms of the State, namely Legislature, Judiciary and Executive.

12.9.2.2   Qualified privilege

The qualification is that this category may be defeated by proof of malice, i.e. that the defendant disseminated the material for an improper ulterior motive of, e.g., mischief towards the plaintiff.

Common law qualified privilege

Read *Adam* **v** *Ward* **[1917] AC 309 in** *Cases and Materials* **(12.4.1.1). What is the common law meaning of qualified privilege?**

The key concept seems to be reciprocity and proportionality. While here the use of Hansard to make changes 'made the world the audience', usually the dissemination of the libel must be strictly controlled.

Extent of common law qualified privilege
The privilege attaches to the relationship of the parties to the communication and not to the message itself, if it gets into the 'wrong' hands. In *Watt* v *Longsdon* [1930] 1 KB 130 the defendant was director of a company of which the plaintiff was an overseas director. The defendant received evidence of the plaintiff's misconduct, financial and sexual, and communicated it to colleagues and to the plaintiff's wife, who was an old friend. Was this covered by qualified privilege? The communication to the colleagues was privileged. The misconduct affected the plaintiff's position with the company and there was a clear reciprocity of interest, if not duty. The publication to the wife was, however, excessive and unprivileged. She undoubtedly had an interest in the information, which related in part to the plaintiff's morals, but the defendant had no sufficient duty to her to pass the information on.

A common interest may suffice, as in *Bryanston Finance* v *De Vries* [1975] QB 703 where the defendant dictated a business letter defamatory of the plaintiff to his secretary. There was no other publication. It was held that the defendant and the secretary had a sufficient common interest in the business of the company to confer qualified privilege.

The interest may take various forms, including a complaint about a public official addressed to the proper authorities, or a tenant's complaint to his landlord about work done by the landlord's contractor.

Remember that the rule relates only to bona fide communications. If the defendant is being malicious, the plaintiff will still have an action. While qualified privilege is not concerned with the truth or otherwise of the allegations, it does mitigate for the defendant the harshness of the rule that liability rests on the fact of defamation rather than motive or fault.

Qualified privilege and reports
Fair and accurate reports of parliamentary and judicial proceedings have long attracted qualified privilege, although in the case of Parliament the privilege was hard won. Qualified privilege for court reports is wider than the statutory absolute privilege.

Section 15 of the Defamation Act 1996 extends qualified privilege to a substantial range of reports of proceedings of administrative tribunals, local authorities, foreign legislatures, public enquiries, official registers, trade, professional or sporting regulatory bodies, public meetings and official public notices.

12.9.2.3 Malice

Express malice will defeat qualified privilege (and also the defence of fair comment; see **12.9.4**).

Absence of belief in truth

> By far the most important way of rebutting the privilege is to show that the defendant did not believe in the truth of his statement or was recklessly careless whether the statement be true or false. (*Street on Torts* at p. 451.)

The proposition is clear in principle, although it may be difficult to apply in practice. May there be cases where the nature of the matter and the position of the defendant are such as to sanction the transmission of a message which the defendant believes to be false? Take the case of a manager at a nuclear plant who is advised that a colleague is in the pay of a hostile State. The circumstances would appear to justify transmission of the information to a superior for investigation, even if the defendant firmly disbelieved it.

Abuse of purpose
This is commonly referred to as personal spite or ill will. The wrong motive must be dominant.

Read *Horrocks* v *Lowe* in *Cases and Materials* (12.4.1.2). **Was the defendant telling the truth and making honest comments as he saw the matter? Where is the boundary where the privilege is lost?**

In *Horrocks* v *Lowe* [1975] AC 135 the trial judge found that the plaintiff's conduct was in fact above reproach, and that the defendant had lost the qualified privilege because, although honestly believing what he had said, he was so blinded by gross prejudice that he had abused the occasion, and thus lost the privilege. The Court of Appeal and House of Lords disagreed. It was the honesty of the view which was paramount. It thus follows that honestly expressed opinions enjoy very wide protection.

Excessive publication
The privilege is lost if dissemination goes beyond those covered by the rationale of the privilege: see *Watt* v *Longsdon* (at **12.9.2.2**). This may be used as evidence of malice, or, under a separate though analogous rule, it may negate the privilege. The relevant distinction is that malice is ultimately a question of fact for the jury, but excess of privilege is a question of law for the judge. Excess of privilege may relate to publishing additional, unnecessary matter, as well as to the people to whom publication is made.

12.9.3 JUSTIFICATION

Normally, the plaintiff does not have to prove that the defamatory material is false. It is assumed to be so. A defence of justification is where the defendant tries to prove that the matter is substantially true.

12.9.3.1 Justification and meaning

Whether words can be justified does depend very much on the meaning that is to be attached to them, so the cases on justification are intimately associated with the rules which govern the attachment of meaning to words, as we saw in the section on the rules as to true and false innuendo. In *Lewis* v *Daily Telegraph* (see **12.6.4.1**) the defendant was ready and able to justify the primary meaning of the words used, namely that the plaintiff was under investigation. The case turned on whether the plaintiff was allowed to allege that the words bore a further meaning, namely that the plaintiff was guilty, a meaning that the defendant was unable to justify. When it was ruled that he was not, the defendant was home and dry. Most cases of justification will therefore in the end be seen as turning on interpretation: does the justificatory material cover the whole sting of the defamation?

In *Wakley* v *Cooke* (1849) 4 Exch 511 the defendant called the plaintiff 'a libellous journalist'. He proved that the plaintiff had once had a verdict for libel against him. Did this cover the whole of the sting of the libel? It was held that it did not. The sting was the implication that the plaintiff was an habitual libellist. This case is cited not just for its own significance (although the plaintiff was the founder of *The Lancet* and a celebrated Radical MP), merely as a representative of many others.

Sometimes the boot is on the other foot. In *Clarke* v *Taylor* (1836) 2 Bing NC 654 the defendant accused the plaintiff of being 'involved in a grand swindling concern' at Manchester, adding that the plaintiff had been at Leeds also, and was supposed to have made purchases there, but that it was hoped that his detection had prevented further losses. The defendant justified the Manchester allegation, but could not specifically justify the Leeds allegation. Did this matter? It was held that the Leeds allegation did not of itself add any further allegation of criminality, and so the defendant had met the whole sting.

12.9.3.2 Taking a fair view

The plaintiff cannot select parts of what, on a fair view, is to be seen as a single passage. In other words the defendant is allowed to seek to justify the sting of the passage as a whole, or common sting.

12.9.3.3 Part justification

Look up s. 5 of the Defamation Act 1952 in *Cases and Materials* (12.1). Take a case where the defendant describes the plaintiff as 'a corrupt politician and depraved fornicator who always drives too fast', and justifies the first two counts only. Will he succeed under the section?

On the face of it, there is little left of the plaintiff's reputation, so s. 5 should apply. On the other hand, it might be suggested that there is a separate reputation in relation to driving habits. In such a case, the relative level of harm would be reflected in the level of damages (or at least should be).

12.9.3.4   Failed justification

On the other hand, persistence in an attempt to justify, which fails, and which will have resulted in a redissemination of the defamatory material, is likely to cause the damages to be increased (see *Aldington* v *Watts and Tolstoy* (unreported)). It is for this reason that justification is regarded as tactically risky, to the extent that there is a dictum, attributed to the late Viscount Hailsham, current among the libel bar: 'never justify'. Where the persistence is particularly contumacious (gross, obvious and offensive), a jury may properly award aggravated damages.

12.9.3.5   Effect of justification

With certain limitations in relation to the publication of spent convictions, justification is a complete defence. Malice is irrelevant and, in principle, although there is no case on the point, if the defendant spreads a story which he believes to be false, but which turns out co-incidentally to be true, he may justify.

12.9.4   FAIR COMMENT

What do you understand by fair comment?

Criticism of matters of public interest, in the form of comment upon true or privileged statements of fact, such comment being made honestly by a person who did not believe the statements to be untrue and who was not otherwise actuated by malice. (*Street on Torts* at p. 462.)

12.9.4.1   The public interest

The public interest does not embrace everything in which the public is interested. What does it cover? It will cover the activities of central and local government (including the policies of the opposition parties), and other institutions of a religious or public character. It also covers anything put into the public domain, such as a work of literature, play or film, the work of an architect, or the qualities of goods which are advertised. It does not in theory cover the private morality of public figures except to the extent that this reflects on their fitness to fulfil their public duties.

SAQ 143

Quixote, a Cabinet Minister, is reputed to be a homosexual. He nevertheless always votes against any measure designed to improve the legal position of homosexuals. Snipe, a homosexual rights campaigner, publishes a pamphlet in which he compares Quixote's voting record with that of Oscar, an avowedly homosexual MP and strong supporter of homosexual law reform. Snipe goes on to say 'Honesty is always the best policy. If Quixote won't stand up to be counted on his own sexuality, can he be trusted ever to tell the truth?'.

Advise Snipe how he should defend Quixote's libel action against him.

The main problem is establishing a factual basis. If this can be done, then a defence of fair comment should succeed. The voting record is a matter of fact, and although sexual orientation itself is not a matter of legitimate (as opposed to prurient) public interest, it becomes so where, as here, it impinges on the integrity of a public figure. There is a possibility of malice, but if the facts are correct, strong, even unreasonable, views are protected in the interest of free speech.

12.9.4.2 Comment on true facts

This can cause complications in practice, where there is a single passage of mixed fact and comment: this leads to a defence which is 'rolled-up' so that those statements which are found to be of fact are justified, while those which are comment are alleged to be fair. *Horrocks* v *Lowe* (see **12.9.2.3**) will be relevant here, as will *Kemsley* v *Foot* [1952] AC 345 (*Cases and Materials* (**12.4.2.1**)), where the plaintiff was a newspaper proprietor. The defendant (Michael Foot) attacked another newspaper by referring to it as 'lower than Kemsley'. The defence was fair comment, but can you see how it was argued? It was held in the House of Lords that what Michael Foot said amounted to fair comment on facts which were implied (and true), namely that the Kemsley Press had a bad reputation.

12.9.4.3 Partially true facts

Section 6 of the Defamation Act 1952 makes similar provision to s. 5 in the context of fair comment.

12.9.4.4 Honesty

The law gives considerable latitude to the expression of opinion. Strong feelings, strongly expressed are protected. Some of the cases use words rather loosely, since the extremist is unlikely to appeal in his views to the ordinary reasonable man of moderate habits, although the judges seem to think that the test is one of reasonableness. In effect the result is that only the grossest of calumnies will be seen as dishonest, in the absence of express malice.

12.9.5 AMENDS

This is a new statutory defence under the Defamation Act 1996. Anyone alleged to be guilty of defamation may make an offer of amends, either generally or in respect of a specific defamatory meaning (a 'qualified offer'): s. 2(2). This offer must be in writing, expressed to be an offer of amends under the Act (s. 2(3)), and is an offer:

■ to make a suitable correction and apology;

■ to publish the correction and apology in a reasonable manner;

■ to pay such compensation (if any) and costs as may be agreed or ordered: s. 2(4).

The offer of amends may not be made after a defence has been served in any proceedings which have been brought: s. 2(5).

12.9.5.1 How the procedure operates

If the offer is accepted it is a bar to proceedings for defamation. The only proceedings which may be taken are proceedings to ensure that the offer is carried into effect: s. 3(2) to (6). This may involve the court determining how the apology is to be published and/or fixing compensation.

If the offer is not accepted it will be a defence to proceedings. A qualified offer is a defence only in relation to the defamatory meaning specified: s. 4(2). The defence is disallowed if:

the person by whom the offer was made knew or had reason to believe that the statement complained of:

(a) referred to the aggrieved party or was likely to be understood as referring to him, and

(b) was both false and defamatory of that party;

but it shall be presumed until the contrary is shown that he did not know and had no reason to believe that was the case (s. 4(3)).

It is in this context that amends are a defence for unintentional defamation. It is likely that it would have applied in *Cassidy*, *Newstead* and *Morgan*. It might also have applied in *Hulton* v *Jones*.

The offer of amends thus has a double operation.

■ It protects the inadvertent defamer. In these cases compensation is likely to be very modest (*cf.* the farthing damages in *Newstead*) and the plaintiff is at risk if he does not accept. The plaintiff also bears the burden of proof that the defendant had the requisite knowledge.

■ Even where there is a non-accidental defamation, although the plaintiff has the option of proceedings, he may accept amends if he considers this adequate. He thus avoids the cost, hassle, uncertainty and delay of proceedings. In these cases the compensation is likely to be substantial rather than nominal, although often the retraction and apology is the crucial element.

12.10   Remedies

12.10.1   DAMAGES

The prime remedy is damages. Where the case is tried with a jury, the assessment of damages is purely a question for them, and the judge cannot give anything other than the vaguest of indications of what will be an appropriate level. This does produce some odd results. In the late 1980s there were a number of scandalous awards. As a result the judges have been a little more robust with juries. The Court of Appeal now has power to review an excessive award, rather than remitting the case for retrial.

There is a new summary procedure under ss. 8 and 9, Defamation Act 1996. This allows the court to dismiss a hopeless claim at a preliminary hearing or to give judgment where there is no arguable defence and award summary relief. The plaintiff may elect for summary relief. If he does not the court may impose it but only if the court is satisfied this will provide an adequate remedy. Summary relief may comprise:

■ a declaration that the statement was false and defamatory;

■ an order for the publication of a correction and apology;

■ damages not exceeding £10,000;

■ an order restraining further publication.

The Court of Appeal has also ruled that the judge should give the jury directions on the likely impact of particular awards of damages, so that they understand what any sum they fix on means in terms of purchasing power: *Sutcliffe* v *Pressdram* [1991] 1 QB 153. Where an award is excessive the Court of Appeal may now assess damages itself, rather than order a new trial: s. 8, Courts and Legal Services Act 1990 and will do so if the award appears unreasonable, particularly if it appears to be an unreasonable infringement of freedom of expression: *Rantzen* v *Mirror Group Newspapers* [1993] 4 All ER 975. Count Tolstoy successfully argued before the European Court of Human Rights that the award in his case was excessive and an unlawful restriction on his rights of freedom of expression: *Tolstoy Miloslavsky* v *UK* Case 1995/520, [1995] 20 EHRR 442.

SAQ 144

What appears to be the rationale of the reforms made by the Defamation Act 1996?

It has been long considered that defamation, even more than other litigation, is a form of casino. The worst excesses of this have been addressed by the reform of the level of awards of damages, but this work is continued by the 1996 Act. The changes are all restrictions on the plaintiff: reducing the limitation period, excluding innocent disseminators more effectively from the scope of liability, more effective protection in cases of accidental defamation, and the amends and summary relief procedures. There is also a tilting of the balance towards correction and apology and away from damages.

12.10.2 INJUNCTIONS

Injunctions are available, but there is a well established rule that an injunction will not issue where the defendant proposes to rely on a defence which the plaintiff cannot prove to be wholly spurious.

12.11   Summary

As we have seen the world of defamation is a world apart. The jury still prevails and as a result the old arts of pleading to an issue still largely survive. The art of any text on defamation is to get over a coherent narrative without drowning in procedural complexities relevant only to specialist practitioners. The key issues, as you should now be aware are:

(a) The procedural oddities, including the division of labour between the judge and the jury and the attitude of the appellate courts to jury verdicts.

(b) The often unequal struggle between the protection of free speech (at its strongest in the political context) and the protection of reputation.

(c) The relatively light task faced by the plaintiff, who need only prove publication of defamatory matter referring to him. This must be contrasted with the burden on the defendant who must normally assert a positive defence.

(d) The mismatch of damages for bruised haloes and bruised heads. Not every judge actually gives full guidance about damages as recommended by the Court of Appeal. This criticism was levelled following a £600,000 award in February 1996 to a doctor libelled by allegations of inadequate endeavours to save a patient, and who alleged in turn that he had been scapegoated by the Secretary of State for Health to deflect attention from inadequacies in NHS provision.

12.12   Further Reading

Brazier, M., *Street on Torts*, 10th edn, London: Butterworths, 1997, Part VI.
Howarth, D., *Textbook on Tort*, London: Butterworths, 1995, Chapters 12.
Jones, M.A., *Textbook on Torts*, 4th edn, London: Blackstone Press, 1993, Chapter 13.
Markesinis, B.S., and Deakin, S.F., *Tort Law*, 3rd edn, Oxford: Oxford University Press, 1994, Chapter 7.
Winfield and Jolowicz on Tort, 14th edn, London: Sweet and Maxwell, 1994, Chapter 12.

12.13 End of Chapter Assessment Questions

(1) *The News of the People* recently carried the following story headlined, 'Wife of Acrobat Sues Other Women':

Mrs Rita Kyte, ex-trapeze artist wife of world-famous acrobat Jasper Kyte is suing her husband for divorce citing two women as co-respondents. The first is well known; she is a historian of circuses who has been researching into the history of Big Tops, and was to be seen with Mr Kyte both during and outside working hours in the last two months.

The other is Eleanor Rigby, a 38-year-old spinster from Neasden with a passion for fairs and circuses.

Annabelle Lee, famed for studies of popular entertainment in the 19th and 20th centuries, issues a writ alleging libel. She says that she did do research into Big Tops and that she was to be seen in the company of many circus employees, including Kyte, but that there was never any affair between them.

Eleanor Rigby (the 'real' one) issues a libel writ, as does another lady of the same name.

Advise the paper.

NB: when the Family Law Act 1996 is in force, adultery will no longer be a component of a divorce petition.

(2) During a debate in the House of Commons on the subject of education, questions were raised, by way of example, about the running of a comprehensive school at Eatanswill by the headmaster, Mr Micawber. The speeches of several members showed considerable bias, and some of the charges against Mr Micawber were clearly defamatory and also (no doubt unintentionally) untrue. Next day the *Eatanswill Chronicle*, a local newspaper, published a detailed précis of this part of the debate and also a 'Parliamentary sketch' giving a reporter's impressions of these speeches and referring to the fuller précis. The reporter honestly believed in the truth of what he wrote, but his personal acquaintance with Mr Micawber led him to show unreasonable prejudice against those speakers who had supported the headmaster.

Advise Mr Micawber as to his prospects of a successful action for damages against Wardle & Co. Ltd, the proprietors of the newspaper.

See *Cases and Materials* (**12.6**) for a specimen answer.

CHAPTER THIRTEEN

PRODUCT LIABILITY

13.1 Objectives

By the end of this chapter you should be able to:

■ explain what is meant by product liability;

■ describe the scope of common law manufacturer's liability;

■ explain the development of strict tortious liability;

■ compare the Consumer Protection Act and the Consumer Protection Directive;

■ explain the operation of the Act and the principal difficulties of interpretation which it presents.

13.2 Introduction

Write down what you understand by 'product' and 'product liability'.

In a developed economy such as the United Kingdom, an enormously diverse range of products is manufactured, either directly from raw materials (e.g. smokeless fuel), from partly processed materials (e.g. cutlery, typically produced by the cutler from block or strip steel), or from previously manufactured components which are assembled to form a larger whole (e.g. a motor vehicle).

These processes may be carried out by a single manufacturer, but more typically part processed materials and components are purchased from other manufacturers and further processed or assembled.

The finished product may be intended for consumption (e.g. food, cleaning products), for long term use by consumers (e.g. washing machines), for consumption or long term use in commerce and industry (e.g. copier toner, machine tools respectively) or may be used equally readily by consumers as by commercial organisations (e.g. electricity and gas supplies, products such as stand-by generators and many types of motor vehicle).

In any case the product may be made available to the end user directly by the producer or via one or more middlemen.

The end user may have bought, hired or otherwise acquired the product contractually. However, he may be a family member or employee of the acquirer, or the recipient of a gift. The contractual relationship may only relate indirectly to the product, e.g. the hotel guest scalded by a defective shower unit.

A product which is unsatisfactory may cause damage to person or property, or simply be inadequate or unsuitable. For instance a washing machine might cause injury if the drum continues to revolve with the door open, trapping the user. It may cause property damage if it catches fire following an electrical fault, or it may simply fail to wash very well, or break down altogether. The problem may lie with the instructions rather than the product. If the manual does not explain that the filter must be cleaned regularly, a blockage may occur, leading to flooding.

In the case of a durable product, the harm may only occur well into the product's design life. In the mean time it may or may not have been well looked after; it may even have been modified, or used for purposes other than those it was designed for. It may have passed through the hands of several users.

Some forms of harm may not have been anticipated (e.g. teratogenic or toxic effects of new drugs not revealed by testing).

The law of product liability is, in principle, concerned with all the legal ramifications arising from the above, although emphasis is placed on the position with regard to consumers, and on physical damage to person or property. The primary liability is seen as that of the producer, but there are other potential defendants.

In civil terms all these claims will involve a breach of an obligation, although it may be largely accidental whether that breach is of a duty arising under, or affected by, a contract, or a tortious one amounting to common law negligence or breach of statutory duty. It must, however, be noted that some liabilities are strict, while others depend on the proof of fault.

There may be criminal liability, and as with other areas of statute, there may or may not in such cases be a parallel liability for breach of statutory duty.

For example, it is an offence under s. 75 of the Road Traffic Act 1988 to supply a motor vehicle in an unroadworthy condition. There is no liability in civil proceedings for breach of this statutory duty.

It is an offence to supply goods which contravene the general safety requirement contained in s. 10 of the Consumer Protection Act 1987. It is also an offence to supply goods which contravene safety regulations made under the Act: s. 12. However the latter is also normally actionable civilly while the former is not: s. 41.

At various times this almost random association of the factual harms arising from products and their legal categorisation has led to fairly bizarre results. What was the decision in the following cases? (They are all real ones!)

P purchased a hot water bottle from D. It was used to warm the bed where P and his wife slept. It burst, owing to a manufacturing defect. P and his wife were scalded. Both sued, relying on a breach of implied terms as to fitness.

A mouse crawled into an opaque lemonade bottle to die. The consumer of the lemonade became ill, and sued the manufacturer, alleging negligence.

A purchaser of long johns contracted dermatitis. This was due to an excess of sulphites left over from the manufacturing process. It was the only case known to the manufacturers, who produced millions of items.

D purchased a bottle of W's lemonade from T, asking for it by name. He received a properly sealed bottle. He took it home and drank some, as did his wife. Both became ill, and analysis showed that the lemonade was heavily contaminated with carbolic acid. The manufacturers operated a very up-to-date and 'foolproof' system.

In the first case P could recover both for his own injuries and for the loss of his wife's services. The wife could not recover as there was no contract: *Preist* v *Last* [1903] 2 KB 148.

In the second case it was held that the producer of a product does not, in general owe a duty of care to his ultimate customer: *Mullen* v *Barr & Co.* (1929) 45 SC 245. This may seem like a trick question, since it goes the other way to *Donoghue* v *Stevenson* (but look at the date!).

In the third case it was held that the presence of the sulphites amounted to negligence. The product was within the rule in *Donoghue* v *Stevenson*: *Grant* v *Australian Knitting Mills* [1936] AC 85. The rarity of the occurrence was not fatal to a finding of negligence.

In the final case Lewis J accepted that these facts raised a prima facie case of negligence (i.e. P could rely on *res ipsa loquitur* as lemonade should not emerge from the defendant's plant contaminated). W gave evidence of their washing and bottling process, which the judge accepted was 'fool proof'. The judge therefore held that W had satisfied him that there was in fact no negligence. The obligation was not an absolute one. D, but not his wife, could however recover against T on the basis of the implied terms in his contract with her. The judge noted, acidly, that she was certainly not at fault: *Daniels* v *R White and Sons* [1938] 4 All ER 258.

This is an unscientific, and indeed unfair, sample of cases, but you should now have a rather better idea of the difficulties involved.

13.3   Contractual Remedies

This section is mainly intended for those who haven't studied contract law. If you have studied, or are studying it, all you need to do is skim read this section.

13.3.1   BASIC EXPECTATIONS

When you buy goods, you expect them to be of good quality and safe. This expectation is reflected in the law. Supply of defective goods under a contract of sale, hire, hire purchase etc. is prima facie a breach of the obligations of the seller.

The law merchant recognised this as an incident of merchants' and industrialists' contracts from a relatively early date. Terms as to compliance with description, fitness for purpose and adequate quality were implied unless the contrary was expressed. These implied terms were incorporated into the Sale of Goods Act 1893 when this codification of the law merchant and common law took effect.

This was a powerful weapon for the plaintiff: liability was strict, not fault related, and the measure of damages was the expectation one, which included consequential loss arising from damage to person or property, loss of profit and diminution of value of the goods affected or the cost of repairs.

13.3.2   LIMITATIONS ON CONTRACTUAL REMEDIES

Only the buyer of the goods could sue. Other users/victims were not in privity of contract with the seller.

The implied terms did not cover all aspects of the goods, e.g. durability. The term as to merchantability was particularly complex, and unhelpful to the consumer in that goods were merchantable if suitable for one of the purposes for which they were commonly traded, which might not be the purpose of the consumer.

The implied terms were excludable without any restriction and only applied to sales and not to other transfers of possession.

Sales otherwise than in the course of trade were excluded.

How far do you consider this set of rules protected consumer rights?

Generally speaking the law worked effectively in business transactions. The parties dealt on a basis of equality. If implied terms were excluded, this was on a basis of genuine negotiation. Losses were typically financial. Where appropriate they could be passed down a chain of transactions until they fell either on the person to blame or on someone who had specifically contracted to take the risk.

The position in consumer transactions was very different. Problems arose from the abuse of power by the business party to the transaction, in terms of selecting transaction types where there were no implied terms, excluding implied terms and otherwise imposing unfair terms and conditions.

There was, however, a further problem. Goods in consumer use, if defective, were as likely to harm a third party as they were the buyer. Traded goods were less likely to cause physical harm, otherwise than to the employees of the buyer. These often in turn had a remedy against their employer (although there were many anomalies).

Some of these problems were addressed either by development of the common law or by statutory intervention.

Review the statutes in *Cases and Materials*. **Which of them appear to be part of this process?**

The following developments were amongst those which helped, to some degree, to alleviate the problems:

(a) restrictive construction of exclusion and limitation clauses by the courts;

(b) extension of implied terms to all forms of transfer of possession: Supply of Goods (Implied Terms) Act 1973, Supply of Goods and Services Act 1982;

(c) non-excludability of implied terms: Unfair Contract Terms Act 1977;

(d) non-excludability of certain liabilities: Unfair Contract Terms Act/Unfair Contract Terms Directive 93/13;

(e) extension of employers' common law duty in relation to equipment: Employers' Liability (Defective Equipment) Act 1969;

(f) replacement of 'merchantable quality' by 'satisfactory quality': Sale and Supply of Goods Act 1994.

The rules on privity of contract restricted these developments to the party to the contract only. Such a restriction is not essential. It had largely been abandoned in the USA by

1916 (*MacPherson* v *Buick Motor Co.* (1916) 217 NY 382). The process of allowing third parties to rely on the terms of a warranty had started much earlier: *Thomas* v *Winchester* (1852) 6 NY 397. As a result, consumer claims have been brought against manufacturers and by non-buyers with considerable success.

The Law Revision Committee proposed in 1937 that there should be a general recognition of the rights of third party beneficiaries, but this was not acted upon. The Law Commission is at present considering further proposals for reform. These are aimed at the broad target of privity, but will inevitably affect the product liability aspect.

The net position is that the rights of the consumer purchaser are in principle fully protected. His only risk is the insufficient means of his seller to meet his claim. Subject to this he can claim on a strict liability, non-excludable, basis in relation to shoddy goods and for damage caused by dangerous goods. The only surviving grey area is the interpretation of the term as to 'satisfactory' quality.

The non-purchaser is left in limbo by the rules of privity, and must seek a remedy in tort. He is joined by the purchaser when the latter seeks a remedy against the manufacturer.

A contractual claim, where available, will in principle cover consequential and pure economic loss, but not injury to feelings or loss of enjoyment. It thus follows the usual contract rules.

13.4   Tortious Remedies: Common Law

13.4.1   INTRODUCTION

Initially the common law did not recognise a general duty of a manufacturer or repairer to anyone other than his customer. In a series of cases a range of victims went without remedy: victims of road accidents caused by defective vehicles, workmen damaged by defective plant accquired by their employer, users of defective consumer goods. In all these cases the defect was latent, in the sense that the manufacturer had failed to use proper care, but had not appreciated that the product was defective as a result. The position was different if:

(a)   there was 'fraud' in the sense that the manufacturer was aware of the defect and covered it up, either by lying about it or otherwise;

(b)   the product was inherently dangerous.

In such cases a remedy could be granted. The cases are not set out here, because they are all now obsolete, but they are discussed in full in *Donoghue* v *Stevenson*, if you are interested in them.

When, and why, did this rule change? You will need to read *Donoghue* v *Stevenson* in *Cases and Materials* (13.1.1).

You are well aware of the broader significance of *Donoghue* v *Stevenson* [1932] AC 562 as the home of the neighbour principle. It is also more specifically the leading case on the common law of manufacturer's liability. Lord Atkin said (at p. 599):

> [A] manufacturer of products, which he sells in such a form as to show that he intends them to reach the ultimate consumer in the form in which they left him with no reasonable possibility of intermediate examination and with the knowledge that the absence of reasonable care in preparation or putting up of the products will result in an injury to the consumer's life or property, owes a duty to the consumer to take that reasonable care.

The slightly antiquated expression 'putting up' covers packaging, instructions etc. It is perhaps wrong to read too much into the references to knowledge that absence of care will lead to harm. This suggests *Wagon Mound* foreseeability, but is probably more directed to the issue of want of care, in the sense that there can be no liability without fault.

The scope of liability has been extended by case law and it is necessary to consider the various aspects one by one.

13.4.2 MANUFACTURERS

This includes those who assemble items. In *Malfroot* v *Noxall* (1935) 51 TLR 551, the defendant had fitted a sidecar to a motorcycle. It was successfully argued that the process was akin to manufacturing. Similarly in cases where water undertakers have been held liable for supplying unwholesome water, while they did not 'make' the water, they were in a position analogous to the manufacturer: *Read* v *Croydon Corp* [1938] 4 All ER 631. A further extension by analogy is to the intermediate distributor who ought to be alert to the potential risks of the product, or is specifically instructed to carry out some test or examination, but fails to do so. In *Kubach* v *Hollands* (1937) 53 TLR 1024, the distributor was liable on the latter basis, but the original manufacturer was not. In *Watson* v *Buckley, Osborne Garrett & Co. Ltd* [1940] 1 All ER 174 it was the former aspect. The defendants were wholesalers of a hair dye of 'dubious provenance' and were held negligent in not carrying out their own tests to establish its safety and efficacy.

The liability of repairers and suppliers is perhaps more difficult to classify, if classification be needed. Works of repair are analogous to original manufacture. In *Stennett* v *Hancock & Peters* [1939] 2 All ER 578 the plaintiff was injured when a wheel flange came off a lorry which the defendant had just repaired and mounted the pavement, striking him. This was held to be within *Donoghue* v *Stevenson*.

Generally dealers are not responsible in tort, but there are exceptions. In *Andrews* v *Hopkinson* [1957] 1 QB 229 a second hand car dealer was held liable for supplying a car with dangerously defective steering, about which there was not even a warning. Note however that there was a problem in that the car had been sold to a finance company who let it on hire purchase to the plaintiff. At that time it was easy for the finance company to exclude liability, and the only possibilities of redress were a collateral contract with the garage and tortious liability.

In the more recent case of *Hurley* v *Dyke* [1979] RTR 265 a disclaimer by the seller of a car at auction that it was sold 'As seen and with all its faults' was sufficient to avoid liability to a passenger injured in a crash caused some days later by the defective state of the vehicle. Such a disclaimer would today need to be considered in the light of the Unfair Contract Terms Act 1977 if the seller were acting in the course of a business. Does it amount to an exclusion of liability for negligence, or does it fulfil the duty of care by giving an adequate warning, such that it is unforeseeable that the vehicle will be used until it has at least been checked?

In *Stennett* liability was for misfeasance, and in the other two cases it was for non-feasance. The statutory duty under s. 75 of the Road Traffic Act does not carry a civil action.

Is the dealer's liability the point at which the incremental progression should stop?

A cursory inspection of the cases just referred to shows that most were decided in the 25 years immediately after *Donoghue* v *Stevenson*, i.e. at a time before the neighbour principle had reached general acceptance, and when the categories of negligence exercised a decisive influence. They are perhaps an indication of how life will be after *Caparo* v *Dickman*, if the law of negligence again becomes a series of separate duties.

13.4.3 GOODS

The rules on manufacturers' liability only apply to dangerous goods, i.e. things which go beyond being shoddy and needing repair or replacement. It has never applied to buildings. All the cases on buildings concern economic loss, and are outside this rule for that reason.

How far can disputes over building work be seen as equivalent to product liability? What should the boundary of the law of tort be in this area?

Such protection as there is, is under statute: s. 1 of the Defective Premises Act 1972. *Junior Books* v *Veitchi* may provide an exception where there is a special relationship, despite the rather dismissive treatment by Lord Goff in *Henderson* v *Merrett* [1994] 3 All ER 506.

It is certainly true that in general terms there is no tortious liability of a manufacturer for pure economic loss. As Margaret Brazier puts it in *Street*:

> Economic loss occasioned by defective goods, whether it takes the form of wasted expenditure on the useless product itself, or loss of profits caused by the defective product not doing the job for which it was acquired, is irrecoverable in the tort of negligence save in the most exceptional circumstances.

This certainly seems to follow from *Simaan* v *Pilkington* [1988] QB 758. This sort of harm is covered by a warranty of quality which can only arise in a principal or collateral contract (and in some cases the only function of the collateral contract appears to be a peg to hang this warranty on, as in *Shanklin Pier* v *Detel Products* [1951] 2 KB 854 and *Wells (Merstham) Ltd* v *Buckland Sand & Silica* [1965] 2 QB 170). In these cases the manufacturer actually made efforts to get the user to use the product, but the user actually bought from a middleman. The same conclusion was reached in *Muirhead* v *Industrial Tank Specialities* [1986] QB 507. Even if the item is potentially dangerous, provided this is recognised in time the costs of scrapping or repair are pure economic loss: *Murphy* v *Brentwood District Council* [1991] 1 AC 398.

While it is no doubt the case that the average commercial utiliser of products has only a distant relationship with the manufacturer, there will be exceptions. In most of these there will of course be privity of contract, as the goods will be being produced to an agreed specification. Cases like *Junior Books* are not that rare, although the normal situation may be that typified by *Simaan* v *Pilkington*. This is the situation addressed by Lord Goff in *Henderson* where he denies liability on the ground that there is no assumption of responsibility. He does accept that *Junior Books* has caused 'some difficulty' in this area. It will probably continue to do so, since the general thrust of the latest decision in *Henderson* is to promote the *Hedley Byrne* special relationship even where there is a co-existing contract.

Some difficulty has been caused where the item supplied is itself two separate components, one of which damages the other. This happened in *Aswan Engineering* v *Lupdine* [1987] 1 All ER 135. Waterproofing compound was sent to Kuwait in plastic buckets which could not stand the heat. As a result the compound leaked away and was lost. One view is that this is a single entity and therefore it is economic loss, namely money wasted on the compound. An alternative view is that the buckets were separate, and their failure led to physical damage to the compound. The actual decision was that the harm which had occurred was too remote. The buckets were reasonably fit for their purpose and it was not reasonably foreseeable that they would be left out in the desert sun for long periods. The defendants were therefore not in breach of their duty of care. Nicholls LJ acknowledged that there was force in the argument that the buckets were a separate item, but he thought the argument unattractive as it would lead to any number of disputes as to who was responsible for ensuring that packaging was suitable for intended use, especially when the packaging and contents were separately sourced by a middleman.

The rationale of the rule is that the defect is latent, i.e. one against which a victim cannot protect himself. If the defect is not only patent, but has been noticed, if the plaintiff then chooses to carry on and run the risk, this is a break in the chain of causation, as in *Farr* v *Butters Bros* [1932] 2 KB 606, where the plaintiff's late husband was responsible for erecting a crane manufactured by the defendants. The crane was defective, and the deceased realised this. He nevertheless decided to carry on with the erection and was killed when the defective part failed. This victim fully appreciated the precise defect. A mere general feeling of hazard may not be enough, particularly if there is no safe alternative: *Denny* v *Supplies & Transport* [1950] 2 KB 374. On the other hand this case may be an example of the general rule in negligence, which is broader than the product liability rule and requires a consideration of the total responsibilities of all concerned, as in *Clay* v *A J Crump & Sons* [1964] 1 QB 533, where an architect remained (at least partly) liable for negligently advising the retention of a wall during demolition and rebuilding operations. The wall fell on one of the builders and the fact that the demolition contractors and the builders were on site and in a position to inspect did not absolve the architect.

13.4.4 PROVING NEGLIGENCE

Very often the plaintiff will rely on *res ipsa loquitur*. In effect the burden will then be on the defendant to negative negligence. In the case of a construction defect it is common ground that something has gone wrong. The plaintiff is often in no position to say exactly what, but the inference is that there was some casual or other negligence somewhere in the defendant's operation.

Is it reasonable to expect the plaintiff to prove negligence positively before he can recover damages for a dangerously defective product?

In some cases reliance on this procedure is entirely justified, as in *Mason* v *Williams & Williams and Thomas Turton* [1955] 1 All ER 808 (*Cases and Materials* (**13.1.2**)). The plaintiff lost an eye when a chisel supplied to his employers by the manufacturers shattered because it was too hard (and therefore brittle). This was a case where the source of supply could be traced, and where the manufacturer had, prima facie, produced a dangerously defective chisel as a result of some misapplication of the manufacturing process or casual negligence.

In other cases the burden appears to be a heavy one, as in *Grant* v *Australian Knitting Mills* [1935] All ER Rep 209. It can be rebutted as in *Daniels* v *White and Sons* [1938] 4 All ER 258, although there has been criticism of the judge for failing to address the possibility of casual negligence as opposed to a deficient system. The plaintiff's task is harder if the product has been incorporated into a larger whole as in *Evans* v *Triplex Safety Glass* [1936] 1 All ER 283. This was a rather optimistic claim against the manufacturers of a windscreen which shattered after about 12 months use. As the judge pointed out, a lot of time had passed and there was every possibility of impact damage, the screen had been fitted into an aperture and screwed in place, which might have created stress, the car manufacturer had the opportunity of a visual inspection at least. There was in short no finger of suspicion pointing straight at the manufacturer.

The plaintiff thus gets some help from the maxim *res ipsa loquitur* in respect of manufacturing defects, but is on his own in relation to design defects. These are notoriously problematic. It is very difficult to infer negligence in relation to a design defect. The plaintiff has to prove that the manufacturer ought to have been aware of the problem and ought to have taken action to avoid the defect. The classic example is Thalidomide. The defence was that the tests which were done at the time the drug was developed were the necessary and proper ones in the light of scientific knowledge at the time. This is a powerful argument in relation to 'state of the art' products. A similar process of reasoning was at work in *Roe* v *Minister of Health* [1954] 2 QB 66. This is not strictly a case of product liability, since the complaint was not against the manufacturer of the anaesthetic, but it does show the difficulties in proving a system error as opposed to an operational one.

The duty is, however, a continuing one. If a manufacturer becomes aware of defects affecting a product already in use, it may be necessary to issue a recall or a warning. The principle was accepted in relation to cars in *Walton* v *British Leyland* (1978) (unreported). The discussion was on the question of how many reports of problems are needed to constitute a cluster rather than a coincidence. The defect may be a manufacturing defect affecting a specific batch or a design defect affecting the whole production. The proof of the pudding is in the eating, and if the experience of the product is that there is a problem, action will be required. The most celebrated such case is the Ford Pinto, immortalised in Ralph Nader's book, *Unsafe at any Speed*. In this case the problem was compounded by the apparent callousness of management in refusing to issue the alert in order not to damage the company's reputation.

13.4.5 CURRENT RELEVANCE OF THE COMMON LAW

Common law claims are still the only redress where the Consumer Protection Act (CPA) 1987 does not apply. There are still potential pre-CPA cases in the pipeline. The CPA does not protect businesses, so a common law claim will still be necessary in respect of the allowable heads in cases like *Muirhead*. The same will be true if and to the extent that *Junior Books* makes a comeback.

In particular it may be necessary to rely on this tort action when contribution or indemnity is being sought in respect of complex multi-party actions. These are regulated by the Civil Liability (Contribution) Act 1978, which makes it plain that it is immaterial whether the liability to pay the original victim or to contribute arose in contract or tort (or otherwise). This resolved some earlier complexities.

The limitation period may be more favourable, although this will require quite abnormal circumstances. The CPA has a blanket limit of 10 years from the date of supply: s. 11A, Limitation Act 1980. In tort the limit is six years from the date of harm, with an overriding limit of 15 years: ss. 2 and 14A-B, Limitation Act 1980, unless there are personal injuries, when it is prima facie three years subject to discretionary and theoretically open ended extension: ss. 11 and 33, Limitation Act 1980.

13.5 Statutory Liability

13.5.1 PRESSURE FOR REFORM

The US strict product liability, albeit founded on contract rather than tort was a magnet for consumer groups anxious to secure a similarly broad and transparent basis without the uncertainties and inconsistencies of the narrow rule. This was reinforced by news of legislative implementation of strict product liability by statute in various parts of the common law and civil law world. The Pearson Committee and a joint report of the English and Scottish Law Commissions all recommended a form of strict liability at the end of the 1970s. By this time a product liability directive was also on the agenda of the EC, although it fell victim to the Euro-sclerosis of the 1970s. The UK authorities took no action on the domestic recommendations pending a revival of the EC initiative, This was probably sensible, as it is unlikely that a domestic scheme would have been wholly compatible with the EC one, leading either to early amendment or to the sort of complex interrelationship which has occurred in relation to the Unfair Contract Terms Directive.

The EC proposal, which became Directive 85/374, had two aims, namely levelling the competitive playing field and consumer protection.

The first is clearly an EC objective, as recognised by the first recital to the directive:

> Whereas approximation of the laws of the Member States concerning the liability of the producer for damage caused by the defectiveness of his products is necessary because the existing divergences may distort competition and affect the movement of goods within the common market . . .

This obviously involves both Art 85 (competition) and Art 30 (free movement) of the EC Treaty and gives an EC legitimate interest in creating a level playing field. It is apparently a bit forced, since the benefit of fault based rather than strict liability for faulty products is not a massive advantage competitively or a massive barrier to trade.

The second is more social than economic at first glance. There are clear arguments for imposing strict liability on the basis that employers can in effect insure the risk. As the second recital puts it:

> . . . liability without fault on the part of the producer is the sole means of adequately solving the problem, peculiar to our age of increasing technicality, of a fair apportionment of the risks inherent in modern technological production.

Here one finds the converse difficulty, that this obvious area of utility is not obviously within an area of EC responsibility. At the time consumer protection was not an explicitly defined EC activity, except so far as it came within the general category of 'approximation of the laws of the Member States to the extent required for the proper functioning of the common market'. The directive is expressly made under Art 100 of the EC Treaty which is the provision governing approximation. Following Maastricht there is a specific reference to consumer protection as an activity of the EC. This may seem to be a mere quibble, but objection has successfully been taken to EC legislation on the grounds of want of legal foundation. No such objection was taken to this directive, perhaps because the combination of the firm legal basis and marginal factual one and the firm factual basis and marginal legal one was enough to dissuade potential dissentients.

The recitals are particularly useful in this case as guidance to the policy of the directive.

The UK government enacted the directive into domestic law as it was obliged to do, combining it with other related measures in the Consumer Protection Act 1987. This Act was somewhat rushed through its final stages so as not to fall at the Dissolution preceding the 1987 general election. It may have suffered in the process. It certainly contains a number of departures from the wording, and possibly the sense of the directive. These are still the subject of Art 169 proceedings against the UK government although they do not yet seem to have caused serious problems in practice. There have been few reported cases on the Act as yet, although this is perhaps understandable, given the time it takes litigation to reach the appellate courts.

Leaving aside technical arguments on the scope of EC competence in the field, there has been little complaint as there was a consensus that such a measure was necessary.

The Law Commission had suggested that the main reasons for imposing strict liability were:

(a) that it is economically sound to promote loss sharing, where the producer can insure;

(b) that the producer is in the best position to influence design and safety and provides an incentive to strive proactively for the best standards (this can be challenged on the basis that it is only the highest cost effective level of safety that is so promoted, rather than the best available);

(c) distributors are not usually responsible for quality, although they may be in the sense of inspecting or modifying the product;

(d) there should be a minimum of technical bars to litigation, and multiplicity of actions should be discouraged.

These are all reflected in the directive and are supplemented by a more detailed rationale for the precise scheme created under the directive. The CPA was introduced to give effect to the directive (see s. 1), and although they do not use the same language or follow the same structure, it is possible to place the provisions in parallel.

ACTIVITY 87

List the provisions of the directive and, beside them, the equivalent provisions of the CPA. There is no need to set out the words in full, merely the article/paragraph and section/sub-section numbers at this stage.

13.5.2 THE GENERAL SCHEME OF THE CONSUMER PROTECTION ACT 1987/DIRECTIVE 85/374

When considering the Act and the directive it is important to have the texts to hand. These notes are written on that assumption and will not make proper sense otherwise. You should turn to the sections and articles being discussed and read them carefully as you consider the text below.

The producer of dangerously defective products will be liable to a consumer/user of those goods for death, personal injury and damage to other property (excluding the defective property itself) on proof of the identity of the producer and causation only. Fault is not required, although there are limited defences which must be proved by the defendant. A supplier may be liable if he cannot or will not identify the source of the product.

13.5.2.1 Products

The directive defines these (art. 2) as all movables, even if incorporated into another movable or an immovable. In English terms this means all chattels, even though incorporated into land as fixtures (e.g. a central heating system) and also crops. Electricity is specifically included.

The only exclusion is primary agricultural products and game. These are the produce of the soil, stock farming and fisheries until they have undergone 'initial processing'. It can be argued that these are particularly susceptible to natural defects which are more 'Act of God' than manufacturer's liability. There was a divergence of approach to this class of products and this is reflected in a derogation in art. 15 which allows the member state to include them in the strict liability regime.

The Act defines product as any goods or electricity, including items incorporated into other items (s. 1(2)). By s. 45(1) goods includes substances, growing crops and things comprised in land by virtue of being attached to it, together with ships, vehicles and aircraft. This appears to be the same in substance if not in language.

There is, however, a potential discrepancy, in that agricultural produce and game, although defined in the same way, are excluded until they have undergone 'industrial processing'. So, the UK has not only not taken advantage of the derogation (although the Law Commission recommended the inclusion of strict liability, while the Scottish Law Commission was opposed, and there was a lively debate during the enactment of the Act), but has played around with the wording.

In most cases this will amount to the same thing, but it may not. Is artisanal processing on a farm, or by a wild fowler or a small abattoir actually industrial? The intention of the government was both to exclude activities like harvesting, washing and simple packaging which do not alter the characteristics of the product, and to include such things as freezing, chipping potatoes etc., provided they were done on an industrial scale. (See *Hansard* HL Vol. 483, no. 24, col. 737.) There appears to be no good reason for the discrepancy. One problem is that, if *Hansard* is consulted in any litigation under the rules in *Pepper* v *Hart* [1993] AC 593, the minister appears to be asserting the divergent meaning. This may make it less easy to construe the Act as consistent with the directive.

The exclusion of agricultural products will not affect potential liability in contract or at common law in tort.

13.5.2.2   Defective

The directive defines this concept in art. 6 as follows:

> A product is defective when it does not provide the safety which a person is entitled to expect, taking all circumstances into account, including:
> (a)   the presentation of the product;
> (b)   the use to which it could reasonably be expected that the product would be put;
> (c)   the time when the product was put into circulation.

There is a proviso to the effect that a product is not defective merely because a better one is later put into circulation. The main definition does of course make some allowance for developments in knowledge and techniques.

The Act is somewhat more specific (s. 3):

> There is a defect in a product . . . if the safety of the product is not such as persons generally are entitled to expect; and . . . 'safety', in relation to a product, shall include safety with respect to products comprised within that product and safety in the context of risks of damage to property as well as in the context of risks of death or personal injury.

> In determining . . . what persons generally are entitled to expect in relation to a product all the circumstances shall be taken into account, including:
> (a)   the manner in which, and purposes for which, the product has been marketed, its get-up, the use of any mark in relation to the product and any instructions for, or warnings with respect to, doing or refraining from doing anything with or in relation to the product;
> (b)   what might reasonably be expected to be done with or in relation to the product; and
> (c)   the time when the product was supplied by its producer to another.

There is a similar proviso as to subsequent improvements. The effect of the Act and directive appears to be the same.

Consider the wording of art. 6 and s. 3. How far must a manufacturer go with packaging and labelling to comply with his obligations?

The burden is a heavy one, especially in relation to warnings and instructions. Perhaps some of the American horror stories will not be repeated here, but if hot air paint strippers carry, as they do, a warning that 'This is not a hair dryer', then warnings about not microwaving pets, or mooning out of windows, or swallowing open safety pins, let alone health warnings on beer, may become *de rigueur*. In a case before the Act, *Heil* v *Hedges* [1951] 1 TLR 512, a butcher was held not liable for selling a pork chop which contained parasites. These parasites were common in pork, but were killed by proper cooking. The butcher was entitled to assume that the meat would be properly cooked. This may give some indication of the approach under the Act.

13.5.3 PRODUCERS AND SUPPLIERS

The Act and directive are agreed on defining as the producer the person who manufactures it, and the winner or abstracter or alternatively producer of any raw material. The directive refers specifically to the manufacturer of a component part. The Act by contrast has a negative definition (s. 1(3)):

A person who supplies any product in which products are comprised, whether by virtue of being component parts or raw materials or otherwise, shall not be treated by virtue only of his supply of that product as supplying any of the products so comprised.

The directive appears to impose cumulative liability in relation to a complex product such as a car. Even if the defect can be traced to a specific component supplied by a third party, the car manufacturer remains liable. The Act appears to have the opposite effect, transferring liability onto the component manufacturer. The *intention* appears to have been otherwise. 'Product' is defined in the Act as including a product comprised in another product. This is a remarkably convoluted way of achieving the objective.

The first importer into the European Union (EU) and anyone who holds himself out as producer by applying his own name or trademark to the product (an 'own brander') are assimilated to the producer.

The Act also defines the producer of agricultural produce separately as the person who applies an industrial process to it. The directive does not contain a separate definition of this kind.

Primary liability is on the producer. Suppliers are liable only when they are requested by the potential plaintiff to supply details of the producer within a reasonable time, and where the proposed plaintiff cannot already identify them by other means, and fails either to identify the producer or their own supplier. It is really in this context that s. 1(3) should operate. It is unreasonable for the seller of a TV to identify the source of every transistor etc. in it.

Liability is joint and several.

13.5.4 SCOPE OF LIABILITY

The directive provides:

The producer shall be liable for damage caused by a defect in his product. (art. 1)

The injured person shall be required to prove the damage, the defect and the causal relationship between damage and defect. (art. 4)

The Act provides:

Where any damage is caused wholly or partly by a defect in a product [the producer] shall be liable for the damage. (s. 2(1))

Damage is death, personal injury and property damage (art. 9, s. 5(1)). Contributory negligence will apply (art. 8.2, s. 6(4)). In relation to property damage there are three qualifications:

(a) a threshold of 500ECU (£275);

(b) exclusion of property not ordinarily intended for private use or consumption and used by the injured party for his private use or consumption;

(c) the defective product itself. The Act specifies that this includes any product in which the defective product is comprised. This appears to go beyond the directive, and thus to be invalid. It reflects the traditional distinction between liability in contract for reducing the value of the thing and liability in tort where the thing damages something else, and the inclusion of the whole commodity appears to reflect the decision in *Aswan* v *Lupdine* [1987] 1 All ER 135 that items supplied together are within the economic loss category. The result appears to be that if a car crashes as a result of a defective tyre, the Act applies to the car if the tyre is a replacement, but not if it was original equipment.

13.5.5 DEFENCES

There are strict limitation periods. A claim must be brought within three years of becoming manifest, and within ten years of the supply of the product: s. 11A of the Limitation Act 1980 inserted by the Consumer Protection Act 1987. Contrast the periods at common law discussed at **13.4.5**.

There is no liability if the defect arises from compliance with mandatory public requirements as to the product, e.g. recipe laws. This does not apply simply to licensing procedures if these do not prescribe the composition and processes.

The directive and the Act apply only to business liability, so production and supply otherwise than in the course of business is excluded.

There will be no liability if a product is distributed without the producer's consent, e.g. where something is stolen.

There is no liability if the defect did not exist at the time the product was supplied by the defendant, e.g. if it has been modified by a later supplier, sabotaged or allowed to deteriorate in an unforeseeable way.

There is no liability if the product is not itself defective but when incorporated as a component in a larger product produces a defect attributable to the design of the larger product or the specifications given for the component.

These are all relatively uncontroversial, representing acceptable areas of non-liability.

The final defence is far more controversial. It is the so-called 'development risks defence'. The Act and the directive exclude retrospective liability on the basis of hindsight and improvements in practice, but this defence concerns issues related to the state of the art. In essence the question is whether the developer of an innovative product bears the costs of design or testing defects (in practice spreading them by insurance) or whether these fall on the victim as part of the price of progress. It is somewhat surprising that the directive allows member states to opt in or out of this defence. Some have done so, some have not, while some have applied it to high risk products like pharmaceuticals. There is a serious risk of distortion because drugs will always be tested in areas where the defence applies, and the competitive position of a manufacturer operating in a 'state of the art protected' market is different from that of one in an unprotected market.

The directive provides for a defence as follows:

That the state of scientific and technical knowledge at the time when he put the product into circulation was not such as to enable the existence of the defect to be discovered.

The wording in the Act is distinctly different:

That the state of scientific and technical knowledge at the [time when he supplied the relevant product to another] was not such that a producer of products of the same description as the product in question might be expected to have discovered the defect if it had existed in his products while they were under his control.

The directive test is both clearly objective and absolute. The test under the Act is certainly not absolute, since it appears to envisage different standards for different industries. It was meant to be objective. Lord Lucas of Chilworth said at *Hansard* HL Vol. 483, no. 25 col. 841:

Only if the producer can prove to the court that he took all the steps that a producer of products of that kind might reasonably have been expected to take, and that the state of scientific and technical knowledge would have allowed him to take, will this defence be of any value.

It is not entirely clear that the wording achieves this. In any event the understanding of scientific and technical issues in a given industry may fall short of the knowledge actually extant. The directive catches this situation, but the Act clearly does not.

The Commission took the view that this was defective implementation. Originally it had other complaints but these were resolved during the discussions prior to the commencement of Art 169 proceedings. The ECJ in *Commission* v *UK* (Case C-300/95) [1997] All ER (EC) 481 stated:

The Commission takes the view that inasmuch as section 4(1)(e) of the Act refers to what may be expected of a producer of products of the same description as the product in question, its wording clearly conflicts with Article 7(e) of the Directive in that it permits account to be taken of the subjective knowledge of a producer taking reasonable care, having regard to the standard precautions taken in the industrial sector in question.

That argument must be rejected in so far as it selectively stresses particular terms used in section 4(1)(e) without demonstrating that the general legal context of the provision at issue fails effectively to secure full application of the Directive. Taking that context into account, the Commission has failed to make out its claim that the result intended by Article 7(e) of the Directive would clearly not be achieved in the domestic legal order.

The Court has consistently held that the scope of national laws, regulations or administrative provisions must be assessed in the light of the interpretation given to them by national courts. Yet in this case the Commission has not referred in support of its application to any national judicial decision which, in its view, interprets the domestic provision at issue inconsistently with the Directive.

There is nothing in the material produced to the Court to suggest that the courts in the United Kingdom, if called upon to interpret section 4(1)(e), would not do so in the light of the wording and the purpose of the Directive so as to achieve the result which it has in view and thereby comply with the third paragraph of Article 189 of the Treaty.

Moreover, section 1(1) of the Act expressly imposes such an obligation on the national courts.

In essence, the ECJ did not accept that, as a matter of pure textual analysis, the directive necessarily meant what the Commission said it meant, or that the national court was bound to interpret s. 4(1)(e) contrary to the directive. Although a submission that the proceedings were premature was rejected, the ECJ appears to be saying that it cannot rule on the issue unless and until there is a disputed interpretation of s. 4(1)(e) by the English courts. It is, all in all, a rather unsatisfactory and inconclusive decision.

13.5.6 CONTINUING PROBLEM AREAS

There are three significant areas of possible discrepancy between the Act and the directive, namely processing of agricultural produce, damage to a complex product and the scope of development risks. There are three possible approaches:

(a) benevolent or purposive construction of the Act as implementing legislation following *Pickstone* v *Freemans* [1988] 2 All ER 803 and *Litster* v *Forth Dry Dock Engineering Co. Ltd* [1989] 1 All ER 1134. It is not clear how far ministerial statements asserting a non-congruent intention will be considered;

(b) overriding construction under *Marleasing* Case (106/89) [1992] 1 CMLR 305;

(c) a claim against the government under *Francovich* v *Italian State* (Cases C-6 and 9/90) [1992] IRLR 84).

Causation may be an issue, especially if the consumer has used the product over a period and two or more producers are involved. This has usually saved alcohol and tobacco companies, although in the USA pharmaceutical companies have been held jointly liable in such cases.

It is still much more difficult to prove that a design fault amounts to a defect than a construction or operational fault. This is partly the state of the art and hindsight rule, but it also has a cost benefit aspect. How far is a producer to go to seek out a potential design problem?

The scope of responsibility for products which are used unconventionally is also a grey area. Is unconventional use to absolve the producer on the grounds that the product was safe for its intended and expected uses? Will it be contributory negligence etc.?

13.6 Summary

Product liability is one key area (professional liability is another which you have already met) where causes of action in tort and in contract, and the various rules regulating them can be used in conjunction to provide remedies for a range of claims. You should now understand:

■ The nature and extent of contractual liability for goods which are either defective or dangerous, and the limitations imposed by the doctrine of privity of contract.

■ The development of the common law of negligence in cases where goods are actually dangerous.

■ The theoretical basis of the UK and EC statutory protection, including the difficulties of reconciling the texts.

It is now for the first time probably true to say that there is a comprehensive and effective network of causes of action which should ensure that anyone injured, or suffering property damage, as a result of dangerously defective goods will receive adequate compensation.

13.7　Further Reading

Brazier, M., *Street on Torts*, 10th edn, London: Butterworths, 1997, Chapter 18.
Cooke, P.J., and Oughton, D.W., *The Common Law of Obligations*, 2nd edn, London: Butterworths, 1993, Chapter 24 (especially recommended because it brings the various causes of action and rules together and compares them).
Howarth, D., *Textbook on Tort*, London: Butterworths, 1995, Chapter 8 (pp. 392–433) 1995. (Caution! There is a lot of theoretical and advanced discussion of economics and policy. It is good stuff, but quite difficult.)
Jones, M.A., *Textbook on Torts*, 4th edn, London: Blackstone Press, 1995, Chapter 10.
Markesinis, B.S., and Deakin, S.F., *Tort Law*, 3rd edn, Oxford: Oxford University Press, 1994, Chapter 6.
Winfield and Jolowicz on Tort, 14th edn, London: Sweet & Maxwell, 1994, Chapter 10.

13.8   End of Chapter Assessment Questions

(1)   Latifa buys a fish tank from Allpets Pet Stores. It is fitted with a heater, which came separately packed and labelled as the Allpets Allstar Tankkosy. In fact it was manufactured in China and imported to Finland (in January 1995) by Finchin Impex A/S. Latifa is impressed with the heater and buys a second one for another tank which she has owned for some time. The English instructions simply refer to the need to use a 3 amp fused plug. There are additional instructions, in Finnish and Chinese only, which state that the heater has a dual level transformer which should be set to H for connection to a 230v supply as in the UK and to L for connection to a 110v supply.

After the heaters have been in use for a month there is an explosion because they have been set at L. The two tanks, the valuable fish in them and an antique oriental carpet are destroyed and Latifa's cleaner sustains serious personal injury.

Advise on liability.

Would it affect your advice if Latifa's main source of income was selling fish she had bred?

(2)   Norman recently bought a 'Flamegrill' barbecue set from his local branch of Wyoming Homecare. It incorporated an accessory described as 'The latest miracle of Japanese electronic wizardry: a fully automated, foolproof infrared temperature sensor'. The instructions state that if the sensor is touched against any item of food, a light will flash if the food is fully cooked through. The sensor is preprogrammed to recognise most common barbecued foods, including beef, chicken and pork.

Norman organises a barbecue to raise funds for the village church steeple appeal. The ticket price includes refreshments. Many of the guests, and Norman himself, suffer food poisoning which is diagnosed as resulting from the consumption of marinaded pork spare ribs, which Norman purchased from Bob, the local butcher. These were affected by trichinella. This is commonly present in raw pork, but is killed by adequate heating. The sensor was used on all the ribs and indicated that they were fully cooked.

Most of the guests bought their own tickets. The exceptions were Cynthia, the vicar, who was admitted free, and Ann and Ben who turned up without tickets. Just before leaving, Ann wrote out a cheque for the cost of two tickets.

Considerable development work has been done on this form of sensor. This indicates that it does perform as indicated above. Some three months before this particular barbecue was manufactured, a research paper was delivered to a seminar at Hamburger University, in which it was demonstrated that inaccurate readings could be obtained in respect of 'bone-in' meat, especially pork.

Consider the liability of:

(a)   Norman;

(b)   Any other potential defendant.

See *Cases and Materials* (13.4) for a specimen answer.

CHAPTER FOURTEEN

ANIMALS

14.1 Objectives

By the end of this chapter you should be able to:

■ distinguish the various bases of liability relating to animals;

■ explain the law relating to animals of a dangerous species;

■ explain the circumstances in which there will be liability for harm caused by animals not of dangerous species;

■ explain the modern law of livestock trespass;

■ explain how the general rules of tortious liability apply to harm caused through the agency of animals.

14.2 Introduction

14.2.1 STRICT LIABILITY

At common law there could be strict liability in relation to harm done by animals in three separate situations:

(a) keeping a wild animal, i.e. an animal of a species defined as *ferae naturae* (i.e. 'of a savage disposition');

(b) keeping a domesticated animal which, to your knowledge, had dangerous habits or characteristics. This was referred to as the *scienter* action; *scienter* means 'knowingly' and refers to the requirement of awareness of the particular vice of the animal in question;

(c) trespass of animals onto land of a third party (but not the highway). This action was known as 'cattle trespass' although cattle is used in the old, broad sense of livestock, rather than the modern sense of bulls, cows and bullocks.

An additional statutory strict liability was created in respect of dogs worrying livestock by the Dogs Act 1906.

Read the Animals Act 1971, ss. 1–6 in *Cases and Materials* (14.1.1). How does the Act, in general terms, relate to the common law strict liabilities set out above?

In addition to these strict liabilities, animals may be the agency through which other torts may be committed.

Consider how the following torts might be committed through the agency of animals: trespass to the person, negligence, private nuisance, public nuisance, *Rylands* v *Fletcher* and defamation.

There is no question of special rules for animals in these cases, merely an application of the ordinary rules. The only allowance that has to be made is that animals are sentient beings and may act of their own volition. The keeper may not be liable for such behaviour if it is so unpredictable as to be unforeseeable.

(a) Deliberately setting a dog or other animal on someone would be trespass to the person. Liability would not depend on proving that the animal had unusual characteristics.

(b) Allowing a dog to stray so that it causes a road accident could be negligent, as could creating a hazard with a dog or dogs on leads but not under full control, thus tripping pedestrians. In an actual case (*Clarkson* v *Bransford* (1987) Huddersfield County Court (unreported) but cited in *Winfield & Jolowicz on Tort*) the keeper of some non-poisonous snakes which escaped into a neighbour's house was held liable in negligence for the neighbour's nervous shock.

(c) Smells (e.g. from large quantities of manure) and noise are the obvious forms of animal nuisance (cases about noisy cockerels, and even budgerigars, in quantity, appear in the press with some regularity). The defendant in *Clarkson* v *Bransford* was also held liable in nuisance.

(d) There is no liability in respect of animals straying on the highway unless there is negligence. This represents a change to the common law brought about by s. 8 of the Animals Act 1971. Highway obstruction by quantities of animals may amount to public nuisance as might the pasturing of a bull in a field through which a public right of way runs.

(e) Whimsically, but feasibly, defamatory words uttered by a trained parrot or mynah bird will amount to slander (unless the bird has merely and unforeseeably picked up a remark which it was not intended to repeat!).

14.3   Dangerous Animals

The definition of dangerous species in the Animals Act 1971, s. 6(2), is generally based on the common law definition of *ferae naturae*, although there are new elements. It includes all species not commonly domesticated in the British Islands.

Since 'species' includes sub-species and variety, a dingo would be classed as dangerous. Although of the dog species, and although dogs are commonly domesticated in the British Islands, the sub-species or variety in question is not domesticated here or in Australia.

The wording is slightly ambiguous. Does it mean 'rare in the British Islands whether or not domesticated when found here' or 'not usually domesticated when found here'? In *Tutin* v *Mary Chipperfield Promotions* (1980) 130 NLJ 807 a camel was treated as of a dangerous species. Camels are commonly domesticated (although they are also found in the wild) in various parts of the world. This is irrelevant to the decision. In the British Islands camels are found essentially only in zoos and circuses, many if not most are domesticated to the extent of being broken for riding. It would seem that it was the rarity of the camel, not the status of those camels that there are, which was relied on by the court.

As well as being non-domesticated, the animal must be either likely to cause severe damage (e.g. the large cats) or capable of causing severe damage (e.g. gorillas, which are not usually violent, but can do serious mischief if roused or provoked).

Once a species is regarded as being dangerous, liability extends to all harm which a member causes, whether or not it arises out of its ferocity. In the *Tutin* case the plaintiff fell off a reasonably well mannered camel, but was able to recover on this basis.

Wild animals are an indulgence for any private owner, and zoos ought to be aware of the risks they pose. It is easy to understand the policy of the law, that such animals are kept at the owner's peril. If you choose to acquire beasts which are liable to do harm if they get out of control, you are in much the same position as the person who accumulates potentially dangerous things which escape. This links this aspect of liability fairly closely to *Rylands* v *Fletcher*.

Strict liability for animals from non-dangerous species depends upon the individual animal having particularly dangerous propensities known to the keeper. The Act appears to assume that there are no domesticated species which are normally dangerous. This may be problematical. Clearly dogs, as a species, are not dangerous. The definition includes sub-species and varieties. Four varieties are named in, or in Orders under, the Dangerous Dogs Act 1991 as being so dangerous that they may not be imported and must be kept under strict conditions. Three, the Japanese Tosa, the Dogo Argentino and the Fila Braziliero, are so rare in the UK that they probably qualify as 'not commonly domesticated', but this does not apply to the Pit Bull Terrier. Surely the risk of harm is due to characteristics which are normally found in animals of this variety. This creates a category of dangerous domestic animals caught by neither s. 2(1) nor s. 2(2) of the Act. The courts will be reluctant to create a gap of this kind. In *Curtis* v *Betts* [1990] 1 WLR 459 the Court of Appeal asserted that the relevant group in such a case is 'dogs', but the point was not fully argued.

The propensity must be either an abnormal one for the species, or one which is normal, but only under specific conditions: s. 2(2)(b). These definitions have caused difficulty.

The obvious example of the first sub-type is an animal with a particular vice, such as a horse which rears and panics at the sight of cattle, or a dog which chases cyclists, or bites people carrying bags: *Kite* v *Napp, The Times*, 1 June 1982. It extends to behaviour which is unusual but not vicious: *Wallace* v *Newton* [1982] 2 All ER 106, where a horse which was excitable rather than vicious was held to fall within s. 2(2) (*Cases and Materials* (**14.2**)).

The second sub-type can cover a range of characteristics, such as the tendency of a mother animal to be aggressive only in defence of her young or, more controversially, the tendency of a particular dog to be aggressive in defence of his territory. This was held to fall within the category of 'particular circumstances' although there are authorities on dogs who would argue that this is a normal trait, at least for some breeds: *Curtis* v *Betts* [1990] 1 WLR 459 (*Cases and Materials* (**14.2**)).

When considering whether a characteristic of a dog is abnormal, the comparison is with the breed, not dogs in general: *Hunt* v *Wallis, The Times*, 10 May 1991.

There is strict liability for dogs worrying livestock: s. 3, unless the livestock has strayed onto land where the dog was authorised to be: s. 5(4).

The keeper of the animal must be aware of the characteristic in question. This must be actual knowledge for strict liability to apply. It may be negligent not to know of a harmful characteristic. The knowledge of an employee, or of a child in the family who is the actual keeper of the animal, may be imputed to the employer, or head of the household respectively: s. 2(2)(c).

14.4 Livestock Trespass

The Act provides for strict liability for damage caused by straying livestock to land or property of others and for the expenses of keeping the livestock until it can be restored to its owner: s. 4. However this does not apply where the livestock has strayed from the highway while using it for a lawful purpose, e.g. being moved from one field to another: s. 5(5). There is, however, potentially liability in negligence in relation to animals straying on to the highway: s. 8(1), although it is not negligent to place animals on unfenced common land or where 'fencing is not customary': s. 8(2).

14.5 Defences

Although liability is strict it is not absolute, and a number of defences are provided for in the Act.

There is no liability if the victim is wholly to blame: s. 5(1). A victim is not to blame where livestock trespass just because he could have fenced his own land better, but he is to blame if he was in breach of an obligation to fence: s. 5(6). In rural areas the responsibilities for fencing each field are normally spelled out in the title deeds.

The defence of *volenti non fit injuria* will apply: *s. 5(2)*.

There is no liability to trespassers for harm done by animals not kept for the protection of persons or property (e.g. a guard dog) or by animals kept for those purposes if it was not unreasonable to do so: s. 5(3). There appears to be no good reason for the double negative in this sub-section!

A dog may, under certain circumstances be killed to protect livestock if it is worrying livestock, or has done so: s. 9.

14.6   Summary

This is a very short, self contained chapter. You should however appreciate that liability for animals does connect with other aspects of tort law. The most obvious connection is between cattle trespass and *Rylands* v *Fletcher* which both involve liability for escapes irrespective of fault. There is also a connection between liability for injury by animals and product liability. In each case there is the concept of strict liability (at least so far as dangerous animals are concerned).

In effect there is a distinct group of torts where the emphasis is on the potentially harmful results of the defendant's activity, rather than on his culpability in the sense of objective wrongdoing.

14.7   Further Reading

Howarth, D., *Textbook on Tort*, London: Butterworths, 1995, Chapter 8 (pp. 387–392).
Jones, M.A., *Textbook on Torts*, 5th edn, London: Blackstone Press, 1996, Chapter 8.
Markesinis, B.S., and Deakin, S.F., *Tort Law*, 3rd edn, Oxford: Oxford University Press, 1994, Chapter 6.
Street on Torts, 10th edn, London: Butterworths, 1997, Chapter 21.
Winfield and Jolowicz on Tort, 14th edn, London: Sweet and Maxwell, 1994, Chapter 16.

14.8   End of Chapter Assessment Question

Sheba is a cat. She is normally placid, but dislikes being injected. She then struggles, scratches and bites with surprising ferocity. Her owner, Mary, knows about this. She asks her new boyfriend, John to take Sheba to the vet for her annual injections. Sheba lets fly at the vet and manages to scratch his eye, causing serious injuries.

Advise Mary.

See *Cases and Materials* (14.4) for a specimen answer.

CHAPTER FIFTEEN

REMEDIES

15.1 Objectives

By the end of this chapter you should be able to:

■ identify and describe the various types of remedy available in tort;

■ indicate where each will be relevant;

■ distinguish between the different bases of award of damages;

■ describe in outline the procedure for calculating damages in various categories of case, including personal injury and death;

■ distinguish between the various types of injunctive relief and indicate where each is likely to be relevant.

15.2 Introduction

Remedies are often neglected in the academic study of law. Why this should be so is not clear. It is of course vital to the litigant to know what remedy he may expect to receive if he is successful as plaintiff, and conversely what his liability may be if he is an unsuccessful defendant. One difficulty is that torts are so disparate that it is often easier to discuss remedies in the context of the individual torts, and this has been done sometimes in this book, as you will have noticed. There are, however, a range of more general issues, and it is these that you are about to consider.

There are two distinctions that you must clearly understand at the outset.

15.2.1 LEGAL REMEDIES AND EQUITABLE REMEDIES

Some remedies are described as 'legal' (e.g. damages) and others as 'equitable' (e.g. injunctions). Originally the distinction arose from the division of the courts into those which were courts of common law and those which were courts of equity. A court could only grant remedies from its own side of the divide. This is no longer the case and all courts have for many years administered both law and equity, including the relevant remedies.

The distinction is still important because, while legal remedies are available 'as of right', which means that if the plaintiff proves his case he must obtain the remedy, equitable remedies are discretionary. The court may decline to award them if it would be unreasonable to do so. There are nevertheless well established areas (such as the grant of injunctions to restrain trespass and nuisances) where there are clear guidelines indicating how the discretion is likely to be exercised.

In theory, equity only intervenes to remedy the deficiencies of the common law, and this means that an equitable remedy will only be granted if damages, or some other legal remedy are inadequate. In practice, as stated above, there are areas where the equitable remedy has become the norm.

15.2.2   REMEDIES IN TORT AND REMEDIES IN CONTRACT

Remedies in tort are intended to compensate for harm done or, in some cases, threatened. In contrast, remedies in contract are designed to compensate for failure of the other party to fulfil his promise. The distinction has been discussed many times in the courts. Two succinct expressions of the purpose of damages, which point up the contrast between the two approaches are:

> [The measure of damages is] that sum of money whlch will put the party who has been injured, or who has suffered, in the same position as he would have been in if he had not sustained the wrong for which he is now getting his compensation or reparation.

Lord Blackburn, *Livingstone* v *Rawyards Coal Co.* (1880) 5 App Cas 25.

> The rule of common law is that where a party sustains a loss by reason of a breach of contract he is, so far as money can do it, to be placed in the same situation with respect to damages as if the contract had been performed.

Parke B, *Robinson* v *Harman* (1848) 1 Exch 850.

There is a large area of potential overlap, where a claim can arise in both contract and tort. This is the area of professional responsibility, arising both out of the specific contract and out of the general tortious obligation resulting from the professional undertaking to engage his professional responsibility. This does not, however, cause much difficulty in relation to the remedy. The nature of the contractual obligation is to take reasonable care in carrying out the contract, so, in broad terms, the tortious measure will apply.

ACTIVITY 90

What do you consider to be appropriate and adequate remedies to deal with the following tortious activities? Do not confine yourself to remedies you know or believe the courts can in fact award. If you consider money damages to be appropriate, think what they are designed to cover and how they should be calculated.

■ A prosperous doctor with a young family is rendered quadriplegic in a road accident.

■ A police officer wrongly, but without violence or any public humiliation, arrests and detains (a) a fine upstanding pillar of the community, (b) an habitual criminal, against whom the evidence is not quite strong enough this time.

■ Your next door neighbour proposes to hold a four day rock and reggae festival in his (relatively small) garden.

■ Your next door neighbour deliberately tips a load of hedge trimmings onto your patio.

■ A newspaper is held to have libelled an actress by stating that (a) she engaged in a sexual act with her boyfriend in public, (b) she is a talentless and boring person who cannot convey a character convincingly to save her life, (c) she is a hypocrite because, while publicly espousing animal rights she has a large collection of fur coats. (These are meant to be considered separately.)

15.3   Self-help

In some situations the law allows the victim of a tort to take action without recourse to the courts to put matters right. There is some overlap with the defence of self-defence here. If you consider the case of *Tuberville* v *Savage* (1669) 1 Mod Rep 3, where the plaintiff apparently threatened the defendant by putting his hand on his sword as though to draw it, but negated the threat by saying that he would have done something about the insults the defendant had uttered to him if it had not been assize time, the defendant argued that he was exercising his right to self-help by self-defence in drawing his own sword and getting his retaliation in first. This was a perfectly good argument, but failed on the facts as the defendant was not actually under threat.

There is also an overlap with the defence of necessity. A man may trespass on his neighbour's land to prevent major harm, e.g. to extinguish a fire before it spreads: *Cope* v *Sharpe (No. 2)* [1912] 1 KB 496.

The law does not favour self-help, but tolerates it. There is obviously a danger (as happened in *Tuberville*) that matters will get out of hand. The self-help remedies tend to arise in the context of trespass torts:

(a)   a landowner may use reasonable force to deter or remove a trespasser. The owner of a chattel may likewise use reasonable force to recover it if he is entitled to immediate possession (but not if it has been hired out for a period which has not expired, or he owes money for repairs, storage etc.);

(b)   material which is trespassing may be removed and returned. This may apply to overhanging branches, or to a wall built in the wrong place;

(c)   material which is trespassing may be detained as security for compensation for damage it has caused. There is no right to sell things, but in the case of animals, while the assumption is that the owner will wish to recover them on payment of compensation, there is power under s. 7 of the Animals Act 1971 to sell them if they are not claimed within a specified time.

15.4   Damages

15.4.1   GENERALLY

While damages are normally seen as representing substantial compensation to the victim for harm suffered by him, this is by no means their only function.

Even where damages are compensatory, a distinction must be drawn between those cases where the loss is a money one (loss of earnings following an accident, the cost of repairs to or replacement of a damaged motor car, or loss of profits etc. where allowable) and those where the harm is either physical (death or personal injury) or 'moral' (loss of reputation or infringement of privacy). In the former case there may be complexities of calculation, but the damages do represent direct and actual compensation. In the latter, the award of a cash sum is not direct amends, but an attempt to provide a money equivalent. This is inevitably an imprecise exercise. One of the most notorious examples is the disparity between awards for pain and suffering (where the maximum is around £100,000 for a young adult reduced to quadriplegia, in physical pain and fully aware of his/her plight) and those for defamation (where Lord Aldington was awarded £1,500,000 for allegations that he was implicated in war crimes).

Historically the award of damages was a matter for the jury. Now juries only hear defamation cases, some cases of false imprisonment and some cases of fraud. There is no provision for other types of case to be heard by jury. An attempt was made in the early 1990s to have damages assessed by a jury where the main injury was a traumatic amputation of the penis. It was argued that only a jury could come to a balanced view of the value to be placed on this claim. It was held that there was no jurisdiction to empanel a jury even in an extreme case such as this.

Juries are normally expected to assess damages without specific guidance as to comparables. The foreman of a jury which awarded the late Telly (Kojak) Savalas £30,000 for an allegation that, in effect, he was not a very good actor, wrote to the press to complain of the lack of guidance, saying that the jury felt they could have collectively made a fair stab at the proper award for damage to a car, but they 'were not experts in haloes'. Judges do now give some guidance by reminding them what particular awards mean in practice, so £1,500 will buy a reasonable holiday, £10,000 a new car and £1,000,000 provides an income of £1,000 or more a week for life.

Judges on the other hand can and do have regard to the awards made in comparable cases. There are textbooks such as Kemp & Kemp, *Quantum of Damages*, which simply collate and compare awards, using multipliers to account for inflation. This material is used both in argument in court and when settlements take place out of court. There is in effect a tariff for various types of injury, e.g. £2,000 for a simple fracture of the leg, £10,000–£15,000 for the loss of an eye. This is adjusted in the case of multiple injuries, but there is a fair measure of certainty.

In the USA it is still normal for civil cases to be tried by jury and some of the awards they give appear very high by English standards. There are, however, several factors which in part account for this:

(a) juries know that the plaintiff's attorney will receive a substantial proportion of the award as a contingency fee, and may inflate the award accordingly;

(b) US awards include a higher element for medical expenses;

(c) only the highest awards are reported. This gives a distorted picture. Most jury awards are at or about the level of an English award. Often the higher awards are reduced on appeal, or a settlement is negotiated to avoid an appeal;

(d) some of these awards are made demonstratively, rather than with any expectation of them being satisfied. In one case a jury in New York awarded a woman many millions of dollars for deliberately inflicted facial injuries, although they knew that the defendants were penniless and uninsured. The foreman explained that they were expressing sympathy and indicating what they thought disfigurement was worth in moral terms;

(e) some awards include specified or unspecified sums by way of punitive damages, especially in categories such as product liability, where the producer is, in effect, being fined as well as ordered to make compensation. This punitive element is not distinguished from the compensatory one in ordinary press reports.

ACTIVITY 91

Which procedure, trial by jury or by judge alone, is more likely to produce (a) fair and (b) consistent awards of damages?

15.4.2   ECONOMIC THEORIES

There is a divergence of views on why victims of torts should be compensated. It is highly probable that there is no one basis, since torts are so disparate. There are, however, several bases which have been and are influential in the development and operation of the law.

Fault is the traditional basis for imposing liability for negligent breach of duty. The defendant has culpably failed to live up to the expected standard, and 'ought' to compensate his victim. This leads on to the argument that it is not 'fair' to extend this liability to certain forms of harm which are unforeseeable or otherwise problematic. They fall outwith the defendant's moral responsibility.

Another basis is enterprise liability, or loss distribution. Any enterprise carries a risk of harming others. That risk is run in order to allow the enterprise to operate and accrue benefits for its owners and for those who utilise the goods or services which it produces. If the risks come to pass, compensating the victims is one of the costs of the enterprise, to be absorbed or passed on to the customers. It is immaterial whether the risk arises because of poor organisation and management, which is the 'fault' of the enterprise or the casual negligence of a worker, for which the enterprise is vicariously but not morally liable.

The essential link with moral fault is broken in favour of loss distribution. Similar considerations apply to strict liability. Indeed the major cases of this, product liability and hazardous escapes, are typically cases of enterprise liability.

It can of course be argued that this is merely a half-way house. If loss distribution is the prime concern it can be better achieved by comprehensive insurance schemes, coupled with no fault compensation. In New Zealand most accident claims are covered by such a scheme, largely funded by 'insurance' premiums. In Sweden medical accidents are covered by a government funded, no fault scheme. In the UK, until recently, there was National Insurance no fault compensation for industrial injuries in parallel with the fault based tort scheme. Recent changes have modified National Insurance cover significantly. One interesting comparison is the transaction costs of the two schemes. There are no recent figures, but the Pearson Commission established that in the early 1970s annual tort damages amounted to £202 million, while the legal and other costs of the system amounted to £175 million. Industrial injuries benefits at the same period amounted to £259 million, while the cost of administration was £28 million.

The fault principle is often defended on the basis of deterrence. A rational entrepreneur, aware that if he harms others through fault he will be penalised in damages, will take steps to eliminate fault. What if, however, the cost of the precautions to eliminate the risk exceeds the likely cost of a claim. Market economists will argue that this is inefficient. Resources are being squandered in precautions; it is better to bite the bullet and pay the compensation. This is a largely American approach. Judge Posner gave the example of a railroad company considering whether to install crossing gates, on the assumption that they would be liable to compensate those injured in accidents at ungated crossings. If installing and operating the gates costs $10,000 a year, and the average cost of an accident in compensation and costs is $60,000, it is rational to install the gates if there is likely to be an accident once every five years, but not if it is once every seven years.

This approach can be extended to other torts. In its pure form, the Coase Theorem (named after the American jurist who developed it), the doctrine states that rational parties will maximise resources. He gives the example of a polluter causing a smoke nuisance. If it is worth $100,000 to him to carry on polluting, but the detriment to his neighbour is only $70,000, it is efficient to let him carry on and pay compensation. If the figures are reversed it is not. The actual price paid to continue or stop is of course negotiable in the $70,000–100,000 range. In practice the picture is complicated by the transaction costs, e.g. of litigation or installing alternative technology. There is a close analogy with the principle that the polluter pays for the costs of pollution. He will only meet these costs so long as there is no cheaper alternative.

Economic theories carry little weight in English law. In the first place, they assume that people act only in the manner dictated by economic rationality. This is not true in the real world. Non-economic criteria are interposed, and it is also far from clear in practice where the line of economically rational behaviour is. Secondly, they are based on a particular ideology, of extreme market oriented, *laissez-faire* capitalism. This ideology is not necessarily compatible with established common law doctrine. Thirdly, at best, the economic argument only applies to business liability. It is absurd to suggest that a driver decides to drive carefully to avoid the cost of an accident. There is no clear correlation between good driving and cost, and the individual has only occasional episodes of liability. Businesses, on the other hand, can plausibly be said to plan for liability, and their costs, whether in meeting claims or in insuring, are a material consideration.

SAQ 150

What principles should underlie the imposition of liability in tort?

There is no simple, obvious answer. Fault and loss distribution have some merit, but loss distribution only really works where the liability arises from a prolonged activity. It can also be argued that some interests are so important that they should be protected in all cases, even where there is no fault. See the trespass torts in particular.

15.4.3 COMPENSATORY DAMAGES

15.4.3.1 Land and buildings

Where land or (more likely) buildings are damaged by the defendant, the plaintiff is entitled at least to the diminution in value of this holding, although if it is land being held by way of speculative investment and the destruction of buildings reduces the cost of site clearance, this must be set against the claim: *C R Taylor (Wholesale) Ltd* v *Hepworths Ltd* [1977] 1 WLR 659. This is not mitigation as such but simply an accurate calculation of the net loss. Where the plaintiff is occupying the premises he is entitled to the cost of reinstatement: *Ward* v *Cannock Chase DC* [1986] Ch 546, but may have to settle for a reasonably workmanlike repair rather than meticulous restoration if the latter is dispro-portionately expensive, as the excess amounts to over-compensation: *Dodd Properties (Kent) Ltd* v *Canterbury City Council* [1980] 1 WLR 433 (*Cases and Materials* (**15.1.1.1**)).

This is one area where the English courts have taken some account of efficient use of resources. In *Lodge Holes Colliery Co.* v *Wednesbury Corporation* [1908] AC 323, the council insisted on restoring a road damaged by subsidence exactly, including building it up to its original level, when it could have been left at a lower level just as well and far cheaper. Allowing the plaintiff to insist on exact replacement whatever the cost and whether it benefited him or not 'might lead to a ruinous and wholly unnecessary outlay' (an early instance of 'Wednesbury unreasonableness'?) This was a case where there was no reason to insist on exact replacement, but if the property is of historical, architectural or merely sentimental value, this must be weighed in the equation.

Generally damages are assessed at the time of the tort, but if the cost of repairs is awarded, these will be assessed at the time they were incurred if it was reasonable to defer them until then. In considering what is reasonable, the plaintiff's financial position will be considered, particularly if liability is being denied: *Dodd Properties; London Congregational Union* v *Harriss & Harriss* [1985] 1 All ER 335.

15.4.3.2 Chattels

The basic measure of damage where a chattel is damaged or destroyed is diminution in value. This is usually taken as the cost of repair or replacement, which in turn will normally be market value. Where a unique item is destroyed the compensation, although reflecting the market value will, of course, not allow replacement.

The cost of repair will not be allowed where it is excessive in relation to the pre-accident value. In *Darbishire* v *Warran* [1963] 1 WLR 1067 a vehicle was repaired at a cost of £192, but could have been replaced for under £100. This was held to be a case where the repair cost was disproportionate and the lower figure was awarded. Cf. *O'Grady* v *Westminster Scaffolding* [1962] 2 Lloyd's Rep 238 where repairs costing £450 to a car valued at £150 were allowed because it was a cherished vehicle.

Compensation for loss of use is also recoverable. It is possible to use accountancy and actuarial techniques to calculate this accurately, but the courts have tended not to do this, but to adopt common sense methods. Where the chattel is not being used to make a profit, damages for loss of use are typically calculated by reference to the notional cost of the capital tied up in the chattel. This approach has been taken in respect of publicly owned ships, such as warships and lightships: *Admiralty Commissioners* v *SS Chekiang* [1926] AC 637. An alternative approach is to consider the actual operating cost; this approach was taken in a case involving a Birmingham Corporation bus, although the court was concerned that this might reward inefficiency if the operating cost were unreasonably high: *Birmingham Corporation* v *Sowsbery* [1970] RTR 84.

Where the chattel is a profit earning one, it will normally be appropriate to hire a substitute if it is damaged. This should avoid most claims for loss of profits, although any which arise in the period which elapses before the replacement is in place will be recoverable, as will the hire costs. There will of course be cases where no replacement is available and the measure of damages is then the actual or reasonably anticipated loss of profit.

A similar rule applies where a profit earning chattel is destroyed, but the appropriate response is to replace the chattel as soon as possible. The measure of damages will therefore be the cost of the replacement, including any necessary adaptation and transport to the location of the destroyed item, together with any additional expenses incurred in the intervening period, such as wages for operatives who are kept idle, and compensation payable to third parties for delay: *Liesbosch Dredger* v *SS Edison* [1933] AC 449 (*Cases and Materials* (**15.1.1.2**)). This case is also celebrated for the ruling that the financial position of the plaintiff must be ignored. In this case the owner of a dredger which was sunk did not have the capital available to buy a replacement, although one was available. Instead he hired a replacement. This was more expensive overall, but could be financed out of income earned while completing the dredging contract. The additional cost was not recoverable.

This rule has been forcefully criticised. It is not followed in contractual cases, was held inappropriate in the *Dodd Properties* case (see **15.4.3.1**), and was specifically rejected in a 'consumer' case where the victim of a car accident was held justified in not paying to replace the car until after the litigation was settled, thus incurring higher hire costs and paying more in money terms for the replacement due to inflation: *Mattocks* v *Mann* [1993] RTR 13 (*Cases and Materials* (**15.1.1.2**)). However the *Liesbosch* rule has been upheld against a haulage company who could not afford to replace an uninsured lorry, but were refused hire costs: *Ramwade Ltd* v *W J Emson & Co. Ltd* [1987] RTR 72.

ACTIVITY 92

What is the reason for disallowing claims based on the plaintiff's impecuniosity? Should the rule be specifically abolished or restricted to particular categories of case?

15.4.4 PERSONAL INJURIES

Awards must be broken down into non-pecuniary loss (general damages for pain, suffering and loss of amenities), pecuniary loss (loss of earnings, medical expenses and other outlays) to date, and future pecuniary loss. The main reason is that interest is paid at different rates on these heads. Non-pecuniary loss is assessed at the date of trial and carries a fairly nominal rate of interest from the date the action was commenced. This reflects the fact that the plaintiff gets the benefit of an award at the higher figure appropriate to the date of trial. Interest on pecuniary loss to date runs from the date of the accident at half the normal rate. This is a rough and ready way of reflecting that the loss occurred over the period to trial. No interest is payable on future pecuniary loss; this is in fact a payment in advance: *Jefford* v *Gee* [1970] 2 QB 130.

15.4.4.1 General damages

Loss of amenity and pain and suffering normally attract a single award, but cover different ground. Loss of amenity is in essence the reduction in the capacity to enjoy life. It will depend in part on the nature of the injury, so that it will be greater where there is permanent loss of mobility, or of an organ or limb. Tetraplegia is regarded as the most serious loss of amenity, and attracted an award of £75,000 in 1986 (equivalent to some £100,000 in 1995): *Housecroft* v *Burnett* [1986] 1 All ER 332 (*Cases and Materials* (**15.1.2.1**)). It will also depend in part on the characteristics of the plaintiff, so that there will be a higher award if the injury prevents or curtails continued enjoyment of sport or hobbies: *Moeliker* v *Reyrolle & Co. Ltd* [1977] 1 All ER 9 (*Cases and Materials* (**15.1.2.1**)).

One vexed area has been the level of award appropriate to a plaintiff so seriously injured as to be largely or wholly unaware of the reduction in quality of life. Logically it can be argued that the unconscious patient has not lost any amenity, in the sense of subjective enjoyment of the quality of life, but the practice is to award a reduced figure (it seems to be about 25% of the 'full' figure) on the basis that there is an objective diminution in the quality of life actually enjoyed: *West & Son Ltd* v *Shephard* [1964] AC 326; *Lim Poh Choo* v *Camden & Islington AHA* [1980] AC 174 (*Cases and Materials* (**15.1.2.1**)).

Pain and suffering is essentially subjective, and so no award will be made to a plaintiff who is wholly unconscious. It may include distress due to a consciousness of reduced life expectancy: s. 1(1)(b) of the Administration of Justice Act 1982.

15.4.4.2 Pecuniary loss

Loss of earnings is recoverable, and usually causes little conceptual difficulty. There may be problems establishing exactly what the net loss was, particularly where the employment pattern was irregular, or overall earnings depended on overtime or piecework.

The cost of care is also recoverable. This includes the cost of private medical treatment, and the defendant cannot argue that NHS facilities were available free of charge: s. 2(4) of the Law Reform (Personal Injuries) Act 1948. Problems have arisen in relation to nursing care. If this is provided by a professional, it is clearly recoverable. Where it is provided by a relative out of a sense of moral obligation, it is strictly the case that the plaintiff has not suffered a loss, in the sense of paying for the care. The law takes the common sense view that there is a need which is being met and the plaintiff should be in a position to reward the provider, even though it may, in these family cases, actually amount to compensation to a third party rather than to the accident victim: *Cunningham* v *Harrison* [1973] QB 942. This is the logic behind the refusal to allow the claim where the tortfeasor himself provided the care: *Hunt* v *Severs* [1994] 2 All ER 385 (*Cases and Materials* (**15.1.2.2**)).

It is clearly relatively easy to assess pecuniary loss to date, although in practice, especially in case of average or below average complexity, a settlement figure is reached which can take a broad approach rather than analysing each item of the claim in fine detail.

It is on the other hand extremely difficult to assess future loss. There are three key variables:

(a) the future progress of the injury;

(b) the impact of all the other vagaries of life, such as unrelated illness, on the plaintiff;

(c) the plaintiff's future employment prospects.

Until recently it was necessary to assess all these in every case, as the court was obliged to award a final lump sum to cover all heads of claim.

In all cases assumptions were made. In the case of the development of the injury, the main problem in practice is the uncertainty surrounding such complications as late onset post traumatic epilepsy following head injuries or osteo-arthritis following limb and joint injuries. In these cases the impact of the complication if it occurred is assessed and then discounted by the likelihood of it occurring. Thus if osteo-arthritis has a 'value' in the particular case of £30,000, and there is a 10% chance of it occurring, the damages are increased by £3,000. This of course has the result that the plaintiff is in effect gambling. He is hoping that he is getting £3,000 for 'nothing' against the risk of suffering a substantial uncompensated additional harm. What is clear is that the figure for damages must always be the wrong one.

The other factors, together with the necessary allowances for inflation and for the fact that the plaintiff receives a lump sum now rather than a stream of income over a period, and can invest that lump sum to produce further income, are dealt with by a complex process of discounting. The total loss per annum is calculated, and a multiplier is then used to get the final figure. Calculating such returns, for annuities, life assurance etc. is a highly skilled task, and there is a profession, that of actuary, devoted to it. Judges have traditionally had little time for actuaries. As recently as 1984 Oliver LJ said in *Auty* v *NCB* [1985] 1 All ER 930: 'The predictions of an actuary can be only a little more likely to be accurate (and will almost certainly be less entertaining) than those of an astrologer'. There has been considerable pressure from the Law Commission and elsewhere for a more scientific approach. Shortly after the decision in *Auty* a set of actuarial tables for use in this situation was published by HMSO. In recent cases there have been suggestions that the judges are prepared to use them, at least as the basis for the decision; e.g. Bingham MR in *Hunt* v *Severs* [1993] 4 All ER 180.

The traditional method has been rough and ready at best. In particular it has led to undercompensation because inflation has not been fully allowed for. Further, the courts have been very ready to accept arguments for reducing the multiplier. A young man on the threshold of his working life is unlikely to receive an award based on a multiplier of more than 18, although his potential working life is more than double that.

In *Wells* v *Wells*, *The Times*, 20 July 1998, the House of Lords redressed the balance slightly. Traditionally, it was assumed that damages would be invested in a mixture of shares and government securities as a prudent investor would do with his earnings. This provided a better rate of return, so a smaller capital sum was needed to secure a given annual multiplier. There was however a risk of loss, particularly with the shares. The House accepted that a recipient of very high damages was wholly reliant on them, and could take no risks. A more cautious investment strategy was indicated, and so the capital sum was to be increased accordingly.

Does the tort system achieve full compensation in personal injury cases? If not, how could it be improved?

It is impossible to say what the 'right' level is for pain and suffering. Our awards are low compared to the USA, but this may not mean they are wrong. Compensation to the date of trial is fairly accurately assessed. Thereafter, the use of multipliers and the refusal to give proper weight to actuarial evidence tends to depress the value of awards.

15.4.4.3 Social security and other benefits

Awards of damages are tax free, so the calculations, e.g. of loss of earnings, must all be net of tax: *BTC* v *Gourley* [1956] AC 185.

Where the plaintiff has himself taken out insurance, or is entitled to a pension or other allowance as part of his terms of employment (whether the scheme is contributory or not), benefits received are regarded as independent of the defendant, and will thus not be set against damages. The principle was first established in relation to insurance, being justified on the basis that the plaintiff had paid for and earned those benefits: *Bradburn* v *GWR* (1874) LR 10 Exch 1. It was extended by analogy to the pension situation by *Parry* v *Cleaver* [1970] AC 1, and applies even where the pension provider is also the tortfeasor: *Smoker* v *London Fire & Civil Defence Authority* [1991] 2 AC 502. The defendant is taken to be wearing two separate hats in this situation.

Parry v *Cleaver* is also authority for stating that voluntary payments from charitable or other benevolent sources will be treated as independent and thus not set off.

Until about five years ago a similar rule applied to contributory state benefits. One half of these only could be set off against damages for loss of earnings, on the basis that the plaintiff had in effect insured himself with his own national insurance contribution, so the *Bradburn* principle applied. This rule still applies to small claims up to £2,500, but it is due to be abolished..

The basic rule for state benefits, currently applying to all claims exceeding £2,500, is that all benefits arising during the first five years of the incapacity period may be recouped from damages. The onus is on the defendant to obtain the recoupment figure and account to the Department of Social Security for it. However, recoupment applies only to the amounts awarded for loss of earnings and other specified heads, and applies to benefits which are directly relevant to this head of claim: Social Security (Recovery of Benefits) Act 1997. There is a detailed schedule indicating which benefits are recoupable against loss of earnings, cost of care and loss of mobility respectively.

This has the effect that damages awarded for pain and suffering cannot be recouped. This was the position earlier, and had led to hardship where the whole of the award was being recouped. In such cases plaintiffs were accepting a small payment (i.e. £2,500) to get something, which benefited the defendant, and also left the state out of pocket.

Sick pay received from an employer, or under a scheme administered by the employer will be deducted from the claim. The principle was established in *Hussain* v *New Taplow Paper Mills* [1988] AC 514, where the employer was also the tortfeasor, and the sick pay could be seen as in effect a payment on account of damages. The rule also applies to sick pay where the employer is not the tortfeasor unless the contract of employment contains, as it normally will, an obligation to refund sick pay if it is paid in consequence of a tortiously inflicted injury. In essence the law treats the employee as an agent for the purposes of reimbursing his employer who has shouldered a burden which properly falls on the tortfeasor.

ACTIVITY 93

Consider the various types of payment. What, if any, is the basic rule which determines whether they are or are not deductible from damages? See *Parry, Smoker* and *Hussain* in *Cases and Materials* (15.1.2.3).

15.4.4.4 Provisional damages

There is now a limited exception to the rule that damages must be awarded as a single lump sum. Where there is a recognised potential complication, there is now provision for an award of damages based on the plaintiff's condition on the assumption that this complication or deterioration will not arise. This award is of course itself a lump sum, with the imperfections discussed above.

The court records the nature of the anticipated problem, and the plaintiff is then allowed to apply to the court for a further award if, within the time-scale set by the court, the problem does occur.

This provision (s. 32A of the Supreme Court Act 1981) is useful in some cases, where there is a specific and serious potential complication. It can only be used where there is a clearly identifiable problem; it thus will not assist where the plaintiff's prognosis cannot be firmly established. The provision has been further restricted by the decision in *Willson* v *Ministry of Defence* [1991] 1 All ER 638 (*Cases and Materials* (15.1.2.4)) that the section applies only to a specific 'clear and severable' event rather than the general risk of deterioration posed by conditions such as osteo-arthritis. A further restriction on the use of the provision is the reluctance of insurers to agree to provisional awards. They have to keep their file open and cannot finalise their financial situation. They therefore put pressure on plaintiffs to accept a conventional lump sum settlement.

15.4.4.5 Other exceptions to the lump sum rule

There is power to obtain interim payments of damages on account of the final award. Although there are restrictions these do not apply to the majority of personal injury cases where the defendant will be insured. This power is particularly useful in cases where the plaintiff is suffering financial hardship, but a final resolution cannot be reached because his medical condition has not stabilised.

A recent development is the so-called 'structured settlement'. In these quite elaborate schemes, which are only suitable for the most serious cases, a lump sum award is made for general damages and pecuniary loss to date in the usual way, but all or part of the award for future pecuniary loss is made in the form of the purchase of annuities for the plaintiff by the defendant, rather than in a lump sum. This is cheaper than giving the plaintiff a lump sum to buy his own annuity, as the whole of the receipts under a structured settlement is treated as being capital and is thus not liable to tax, while part of the proceeds of any annuity which the plaintiff bought for himself, and any dividends or interest on investments he made would be taxable. While the plaintiff is thus guaranteed a certain level of income, this must be properly calculated and inflation protected in exactly the same way as a conventional lump sum award.

15.4.5   DEATH

Where the victim dies, the case cannot be treated just as a serious instance of personal injury. The main difference is the treatment of dependants. An award to an injured plaintiff is intended to replace his total income, out of which he is expected to maintain his dependants as he would have done out of his earnings. This is not how fatal cases are treated.

Funeral expenses are payable.

The deceased person's personal representatives may have a claim for personal injuries on behalf of the estate if there was a significant gap between the infliction of injury and death, and this is assessed on the usual principles as set out above. Where death is essentially immediate there will be no claim under this head, as was established in the case brought on behalf of two victims of the Hillsborough disaster: *Hicks* v *Chief Constable of South Yorkshire* [1992] 2 All ER 65.

Statutory damages for bereavement are recoverable by the parents of a deceased minor, and by a bereaved spouse. This is a fixed, conventional sum under s. 1A of the Fatal Accidents Act 1976, which is currently £7,500. It is designed as recognition of, rather than in any real sense compensation for, the grief and distress of close relatives.

At common law no action lay for the death of another, but there is now provision for dependants to make a claim for loss of dependence under the Fatal Accidents Acts 1846–1976.

In law, dependants include all ascendant and descendant relatives, close collateral relatives, established cohabitees and children treated by the deceased as a child of the family. In fact they must prove that they were receiving some support from the deceased.

The usual situation is where the deceased was a breadwinner and supporting the claimant. Such claimants will typically be spouse or children, but if it can be shown that a child is supporting, or would in the future have supported elderly parents etc, then they may claim: *Kandalla* v *BEA* [1981] QB 158. An alternative situation is where the deceased was providing benefits to the dependants by work as a homemaker. The value of the benefit must be established: *Berry* v *Humm & Co.* [1915] 1 KB 627. It may not be the full commercial cost of the services: *Spittle* v *Bunney* [1988] 3 All ER 1031.

In the typical case of a breadwinner with little surplus savable income, the dependence can virtually be calculated as the net income less the amount actually spent by the deceased on himself. When calculating the period of the dependence, allowance must be made for the vagaries of life as they affect the deceased, e.g. the possibility of unemployment, ill health etc., and also as they affect the dependant, including the possibility of premature death, the point at which children are likely to achieve independence, and the possibility of divorce between a widow and the deceased (but not the widow's prospects of re-marriage: s. 3(3) of the Fatal Accidents Act 1976).

15.4.6   AGGRAVATED AND EXEMPLARY DAMAGES

The normal principle for the award of damages in tort is a compensatory one. You have seen this at work in relation to common law negligence, occupiers' liability, breach of statutory duty and product liability. Although this is the dominant principle, it is not the sole one. It is clearly recognised that in certain circumstances exemplary damages may be awarded. These are 'awarded by reference to the defendant's conduct and are intended to deter similar conduct in the future . . . and to signify condemnation or disapproval'. (Law Commission Consultation Paper No. 132, *Aggravated, Exemplary and Restitutionary Damages*, 1993.) Aggravated damages occupy a debatable middle ground between the exemplary and the compensatory principles. They are intended to cover intangible loss arising from injury to feelings, reputation and personality as a result of the nature of the defendant's actions. The Law Commission has now issued its final report (No. 247, December 1997).

15.4.6.1 The present law

At present entitlement to exemplary damages is based on a schematic rather than a principled approach. This derives from Lord Devlin's speech in *Rookes* v *Barnard* [1964] AC 1129 as reinterpreted by the House of Lords in *Broome* v *Cassell* [1972] AC 1027 (***Cases and Materials* (15.1.3.1)**). The schematic approach is reinforced by the decision in *AB* v *South West Water Services Ltd* [1993] QB 507 that exemplary damages are only available in relation to causes of action where they had been established as available before the *Rookes* case.

Until recent cases and statutory reforms which gave the judges some control over the level of awards, there was also concern that jury awards could be capricious. In *Thompson* v *MPC* [1997] 3 WLR 403, the Court of Appeal laid down guidelines for the calculation of damages in police assault/malicious prosecution cases, which are an important category. Other guidance has been given in respect of defamation cases. In *Thompson* it was stressed that exemplary damages are only relevant if a significant amount (say £5,000) would be the minimum figure, but that they are demonstrative, and therefore should be moderate. £25,000 is a high figure, and £50,000 the absolute ceiling for cases involving serious personal misconduct by senior officers.

There are three categories of case where exemplary damages may be awarded.

Oppressive, arbitrary or unconstitutional action by the servants of the government
These terms are *disjunctive*, so unconstitutional action which is not oppressive or arbitrary may qualify.

This derives from the eighteenth century civil liberty cases: *Wilkes* v *Wood* (1763) 98 ER 489, *Huckle* v *Money* (1763) 95 ER 768. The test is now a broad one. It includes policemen, solicitors executing *Anton Piller* orders and EC officials.

Many trespasses to the person fall squarely into this category. The Law Commission points out that it plays 'an important role in the protection of civil liberties' and 'it has been the basis for significant development in the law concerning police misconduct'.

Wrongdoing which is calculated to make a profit
It is not necessary that there be a precise calculation. The concept is a broad one and covers those cases, such as defamation in a tabloid newspaper, where the conduct is designed to be commercially profitable, and also cases of winkling out of tenants to use premises more lucratively. These are of course not typically cases of trespass to the person.

Statutory cases
The main instances are provisions of the Copyright, Designs and Patents Act 1988 which allow additional damages for breach of copyright and design right depending on the flagrancy of the breach and any benefit accruing to the defendant from the breach.

The latter two categories of cases could in fact be said to be restitutionary in nature. Albeit in a rough and ready way the defendant is being deprived of the fruits of his unjust enrichment, obtained by disregarding the plaintiff's legitimate interests.

15.4.6.2   Proposals for reform

The Law Commission has proposed in its Report (No. 247, December 1997) the following reforms:

(a) That exemplary damages be renamed 'punitive damages' and that 'punitive damages would be available for a legal wrong (other than breach of contract) if the defendant has deliberately and outrageously disregarded the plaintiff's rights'. This will replace the current arbitrary and schematic approach: para 1.19–1.23.

(b) That aggravated damages be renamed 'damages for mental distress' and be clearly understood to be compensatory in nature: para 1.9.

(c) That the courts have power to award restitutionary damages in lieu of punitive damages where the justice of the case is best served by depriving the defendant of his improper gains rather than penalising him, but that the detailed development of restitutionary damages be left to the judiciary: para 1.10–1.12.

The central proposals for the reform of exemplary/punitive damages (which are incorporated into a draft Bill) are:

■ the judge will decide on the availability and level of punitive damages;

■ punitive damages will only be available if the defendant has 'deliberately and outrageously disregarded the plaintiff's rights';

■ punitive damages may be awarded for any tort (common law or statutory) or equitable wrong. The cause of action test is to be abolished. No punitive damages are to be awarded for breach of contract;

■ punitive damages are to be additional to other remedies, but only given if the other remedies do not adequately punish the defendant for his conduct. They will not normally be given where the defendant has been convicted of an offence arising out of the same conduct;

■ the amount must be sufficient to punish, but proportional to the gravity of the conduct, and take account of the defendant's culpability, the benefit he sought to achieve and other relevant matters.

ACTIVITY 94

Consider whether there is room in the law of tort for damages which are not compensatory. Is it still part of the function of this branch of the law to punish rather than compensate?

15.4.7 NOMINAL DAMAGES

These are awarded when the plaintiff has established his case, particularly in relation to torts actionable *per se*, such as trespass, but has not shown that there is any actual loss. The award marks his success. It does not reflect badly on the plaintiff, who may have been making an important, if not expensive point about, for instance, the existence of a right of way. There is a conventional figure (currently £5) which is awarded. In a jury trial particularly, if less than this (the traditional figure was a farthing, but it cannot now be less than a penny, being the smallest current coin of the realm) was awarded, this usually indicated that the plaintiff, though legally in the right, had acted harshly or unreasonably, and such an award is known as contemptuous damages. Such an award does of course reflect on the plaintiff.

15.5 Injunctions

Damages are all very well when harm has occurred and can be calculated, but in many cases prevention is better than cure. Also in many cases it will be difficult to work out what loss has been sustained. It is to deal with these cases that the equitable remedy of the injunction was developed. You saw in the introduction at **15.2** how injunctions are designed to supplement the common law remedy of damages and it is now time to explore this remedy in more depth.

The word injunction simply means 'order'. In this context it is an order of a court addressed to a party to litigation and requiring him to do, or refrain from doing, something on pain of punishment for contempt of court by way of fine, imprisonment or sequestration of goods.

It is important to recognise that there are different types of injunctions. The main sub-divisions are between interlocutory and final injunctions and between negative and mandatory injunctions.

The first distinction is as to the stage in the proceedings that the injunction operates. An interlocutory injunction takes effect during the case, usually in order to maintain the *status quo* until the rights and wrongs can be sorted out. A final injunction is normally permanent and represents part of the final disposal of the case. A mandatory injunction positively requires the addressee of the injunction to do something, while a negative injunction requires him not to act. Negative injunctions are much commoner overall, and particularly at the interlocutory stage.

15.5.1 PRINCIPLES OF THE INJUNCTION

The High Court may grant an injunction in any case where it is 'just and convenient' to do so: s. 37(1) of the Supreme Court Act 1981. This may be the only relief sought. In the county court an injunction may only be granted as ancillary to some other relief, but a purely nominal claim for damages will suffice: s. 38 of the County Courts Act 1984.

Although law and equity remain separate, they are administered together and the rules of equity prevail where there is a conflict. This had been recognised in the case of remedies since the *Earl of Oxford's Case* (1615) 21 ER 485, 576.

Equity operates on the conscience, so the judge must consider it to be the right and conscionable thing to do before he will grant an injunction. Injunctions are therefore, in common with all equitable remedies, discretionary. However, this discretion is in the hands of judges, who behave consistently. There are therefore clear guidelines as to when an injunction is likely to be granted, and on what terms.

15.5.2 WHERE INJUNCTIONS ARE LIKELY TO BE USEFUL

There are many areas not involving tort where an injunction will be sought, but in relation to tort the commonest areas of application will be those where there is a course of conduct, rather than a single incident. Unless that incident has been foreshadowed, it will not be practicable to seek an injunction, and damages will have to suffice.

If harm to the plaintiff is being clearly threatened, as where a neighbour is planning a rock festival, then an injunction may well be appropriate on a *quia timet* ('because he fears' (i.e. that there will be a nuisance)) basis.

The victim of a nuisance or repeated trespass, or indeed of harassment falling into the area in between and recognised as a tort by *Khorasandjian v Bush* [1993] 3 WLR 476, is usually more concerned to prevent or halt the defendant than to claim damages. It is now accepted that where proprietary rights are being interfered with by a defendant who intends to carry on doing so, the plaintiff is 'entitled' to an injunction unless there is strong evidence that damages are an appropriate remedy: *Pride of Derby & Derbyshire Angling Association v British Celanese* [1953] Ch 149 (*Cases and Materials* (**15.2.1**)), a case concerning pollution of the River Derwent, over which the plaintiffs had rights, which was likely to damage fish in an unpredictable manner.

An injunction can only be granted in respect of a legal wrong. So when a defendant called his house by the same name as the plaintiff next door, no injunction could be granted. The similarity of names was no doubt annoying, but there is no exclusive right to a house name: *Day v Brownrigg* (1878) 10 Ch D 294. The position might have been different if they were both traders or professionals and the similarity amounted to passing off the defendant as the plaintiff. Similarly, if a plaintiff complains of a range of activities, but not all are held to be tortious, the injunction can apply only to the tortious activities: *Kennaway v Thompson* [1981] 3 All ER 329 (*Cases and Materials* (**15.2.1**)).

15.5.3 INTERLOCUTORY INJUNCTIONS

The court has to be careful in granting these. On the one hand, if the *status quo* is not preserved or restored, one party may be so damaged by what happens in the period before a full trial that he will not enjoy the benefit even if he wins. If, for example, a noise nuisance so affects a music teacher that all his pupils desert him, he may never be able to rebuild his practice. On the other, care must be taken that action is not taken on inadequate evidence, bearing in mind that the full trial is not taking place.

The normal approach is that in *American Cyanamid v Ethicon* [1975] AC 396 (*Cases and Materials* (**15.2.2**)):

(a) the plaintiff must first establish that there is a serious issue to be tried. This is not a major hurdle; it is really designed to weed out the frivolous and hopeless cases;

(b) the court will then investigate whether damages are an adequate remedy. If they will be then, unless there are special circumstances (e.g. that it is quite clear that the defendant will not be able to pay any damages) no injunction will issue;

(c) the court next considers the effect on the defendant of the grant of an injunction. In other words, assuming he wins at trial, whether damages will be an adequate remedy to him for the restrictions on his freedom of action imposed by the injunction.

If the issue remains balanced the court considers whether the plaintiff has acted expeditiously, whether the injunction is designed to restore the *status quo* or to maintain it, and finally, the relative strength of the parties' cases.

15.5.4 NEGATIVE INJUNCTIONS

Although these are the commonest sort they require little further discussion. The defendant is ordered not to behave in a particular way. If he does he is in breach. This is easy for the court to control. Provided the prohibited activity is properly defined it will be easy to recognise when there has been a breach.

It is, however, important to note that the injunction must be framed so as to cover only those activities which are actionable. Thus an injunction against noise from a factory may be expressed to apply only at night and at weekends.

15.5.5 MANDATORY INJUNCTIONS

These can be problematic for the court, in that they require the defendant to do things. The court is not in a position to police this, and there is considerable reluctance to grant a long term mandatory injunction. In *AG* v *Staffordshire CC* [1905] 1 Ch 336 this was given as a reason for not granting an injunction to keep a right of way in a specified state of repair. Injunctions requiring one-off actions, such as demolishing a wall or other structure, will be granted more readily, at least where the application has been made before the work was too far advanced. In *Truckell* v *Stock* [1957] 1 WLR 161 an injunction was granted to remove a completed outbuilding which was built in part over the boundary, and was thus trespassing. It was significant that it was built almost up to an existing wall and this would therefore be very difficult to maintain if the new structure were allowed to remain.

15.5.6 DAMAGES IN LIEU OF AN INJUNCTION

Since, as we have seen, an injunction will not normally be granted where damages is an adequate remedy, it may seem surprising that there is power to award damages on a claim for an injunction. The power originated in Lord Cairns' Act 1858, which reduced the procedural difficulties then existing by allowing the equity courts to award damages, so avoiding the need for a second action if an injunction was refused. It is now contained in s. 50 of the Supreme Court Act 1981. It is sparingly exercised, since the effect of substituting an award of damages where the proper remedy is an injunction is to allow a wealthy defendant compulsorily to purchase the right to infringe the plaintiff's rights. You have already met *Miller* v *Jackson* [1977] 3 All ER 338 in relation to nuisance (see **Activity 61**). The court declined to grant an injunction to restrain a continuing nuisance from cricket balls being hit into a garden. One argument was the relative utility of the activities of the parties, but this was rejected in *Kennaway* v *Thompson* [1981] 3 All ER 329 which is a similar case of nuisance by sporting activities. It is possible to support the decision in *Miller* on the grounds that the plaintiffs moved to the nuisance. This line has been adopted in several US cases.

Where the wrong complained of is one which is commonly resolved by money payments, the judges are more willing to decline to grant an injunction or use this power. See for instance *Wrotham Park Estate* v *Parkside Homes* [1974] 1 WLR 798, where the complaint was that houses were built in breach of a restrictive covenant. It is well known that such covenants are released for cash. The judge indicated that the demolition of these houses would be a criminal waste of resources in the circumstances, which indicates some element of economic utility in his thinking.

15.5.7 UNDERTAKINGS AS TO DAMAGES

These are important in relation to interlocutory injunctions. The plaintiff must normally undertake to pay damages in respect of harm suffered by the defendant if the injunction is granted. Some plaintiffs seek to get round this by applying for a final injunction, without also applying for an interlocutory one. If the defendant carries on in the meantime, and then loses at trial, he may well have to undo all his work. This will be a substantial deterrent if this is, for instance, building work. Normally the plaintiff will be allowed to act like this, as in *Oxy Electric Ltd* v *Zainuddin* [1990] 2 All ER 902 (*Cases and Materials* (**15.2.3**)), where the plaintiffs objected to the defendants' plan to erect a mosque on a particular site. The defendants argued that they could not proceed until after the trial, and that if they won, they would have to build the mosque later and at greater cost. This would have been covered by a cross-undertaking in damages. Nonetheless no order was made preventing the plaintiffs from acting as they did. It might have been otherwise if they had misled the defendants by initially indicating that they had no objection, or were ready to negotiate: *Blue Town Investments* v *Higgs & Hill* [1990] 1 WLR 696.

15.6   Summary

You should by now have some idea of this large but often little explored aspect of the subject. Some of what you have read will no doubt be familiar from other subjects which you may have studied such as contract, land law, trusts and equity. Indeed some of the other chapters of this text have touched on particular aspects of remedies. You can't separate the claim and the remedy, either in real life or in the study of law.

The assessment of damages is a particular issue in tort. In the extracts from the cases in *Cases and Materials*, you will have seen comments from the judges about the imprecision of calculations, the difficulty of accurately predicting the future and the absence of proper guidance (although the House of Lords has had much more to do with remedies in recent years, not always for the better). Many similar comments ended up on the cutting room floor.

You should however have grasped the basic rule, that the plaintiff is to be put back as near as possible into the position he was in before the tort occurred, or that the tortfeasor should compensate for the harm he has done, and also recognised the main problems or anomalies:

■   That as damages for pain, suffering and loss of amenity are consolation not compensation, the level of awards will always depend on judicial interpretation of the level of consolation society deems proper, which may well be too low.

■   That where a plaintiff is too poor to take the cheapest option to restore his position he may not be able to land the defendant with the excess costs.

■   How far the defendant can bring collateral benefits into account.

In recognition of the nature of the topic there is rather more additional reading than usual. This is of particular relevance if you are thinking of becoming a professional lawyer.

Injunctive relief, which we have only touched on, is a rather better ordered branch of the law. Indeed one could almost say, tongue in cheek, that in the case of damages there is a right to a remedy but a fairly capricious allocation of awards, while with injunctions the grant is discretionary, but the discretion is applied on time honoured and consistent principles.

15.7   Further Reading

Burrows, A., *Remedies for Torts and Breach of Contract** 2nd edn, London: Butterworths, 1994.

Cooke, P.J., and Oughton, D.W., *The Common Law of Obligations*, 2nd edn, London: Butterworths, 1993. Section C (Especially recommended because it brings the various causes of action and rules together and compares them; it is a long section of nearly 100 pages).

Harris, D., *Remedies in Contract and Tort* (now a bit dated)*, London: Butterworths, 1988.

Howarth, D., *Textbook on Tort*, London: Butterworths, 1995, Chapter 11 (pp. 522–5 only) and Chapter 13.

Jones, M.A., *Textbook on Torts*, 5th edn, London: Blackstone Press, 1996, Chapter 15.

Law Commission, Consultation Papers and Law Com Papers forming part of the review of damages, especially Nos. 125 and 224 *Structured Settlements and Interim and Provisional Damages*; Nos. 132 and 247 *Aggravated, Exemplary and Restitutionary Damages*; No. 225 *Personal Injury Compensation: How much is enough* and No. 140 *Damages for Personal Injury: Non-pecuniary loss.* (These papers provide a clear account of the present state of the law, the problems identified and proposals for reform. They usually also contain an instructive comparison with the position in other common law jurisdictions.)

Markesinis, B.S., and Deakin, S.F., *Tort Law*, 3rd edn, Oxford: Oxford University Press, 1994, Chapter 8.

Street on Torts, 10th edn, London: Butterworths, 1997, Chapters 28–9.

Winfield and Jolowicz on Tort, 14th edn, London: Sweet and Maxwell, 1994, Chapter 23.

*These are full treatments, at book length.

15.8   End of Chapter Assessment Questions

(1)   Penny, a sole practitioner solicitor and Alf, her husband, who does not work but looks after their two small children are injured in a car crash. This is entirely the fault of the other driver, Dan.

Penny is unable to work for twelve months. Her net profits after tax for the last three years averaged £50,000. She has received state benefits totalling £10,000 in that period. She suffered multiple injuries including a fractured pelvis. She will not be able to have any more children, although she and Alf were hoping to have a family of six. One of her arms has suffered very serious soft tissue damage and may have to be amputated at some time in the future.

Alf is in a coma for two weeks. He then recovers consciousness. He is totally paralysed and helpless. After a further six weeks he dies.

Penny's mother looks after Penny and the children until Penny is able to return to work. Penny then employs a nanny and housekeeper at a total cost of £20,000 per annum.

Advise Dan of the basis on which he will be liable in damages.

You have been given some figures to assist you in working out the likely award under some of the heads of damage, but you will only be able to indicate others in outline.

(2)   Charon operates a number of speedboats on the River Styx. Pluto, who has lived near the river for 30 years and Persephone, who has just moved to the area, both complain about noise. This is mainly when the boats are starting out and when engines are being tested. There is a large fence on Charon's land to deaden the sound, but this has fallen into disrepair. Charon offers to provide double glazing for both the complainants. Pluto rejects the offer out of hand, Persephone provisionally agrees, but later changes her mind. Both Pluto and Persephone apply for a final injunction preventing Charon operating speedboats at all, or in the alternative requiring him to repair and keep in repair the fence. Charon is in the process of erecting a large boathouse.

Advise Charon.

See *Cases and Materials* (15.4) for a specimen answer.

INDEX

Accident, inevitable 34
Act of God 33
Act of war 359
Advocates 82
Aftermath 160, 165, 167, 170, 177, 178
Aircraft surveys, negligent 151
Airspace 320–1
Amends offer 374, 386
Animals 410–15
  accidents caused by 411
  cattle trespass 354, 410, 413
  dangerous animals 412–13
    particular circumstances 413
  dangerous dogs 412–13
  defamatory words (parrots) 412
  defences 413–14
  domestic animals with dangerous habits
    410, 412–13
  guard dogs 414
  livestock trespass 354, 410, 413
  livestock worrying 413
  noise 412
  smells 412
  straying onto highway 412
  strict liability 410–12
  trespass onto land 354, 410, 413
  trespass to person 411
  wild animals 410, 412
Anti-social behaviour orders 348
Apportionment
  between claimants 315
  contributory negligence 60–1
Architects 188, 189–93
Arrest
  false imprisonment 304–5
  wrongful 301
Assault
  act of assault 298–9
  apprehension 300
  negativing threats 299–300
  silence 299
  stalking 299
  threats 298–9
  words only 298–9
  see also Battery
Audio tapes and records 367

Bailment 310
  claims priority 315
Battery 291–8
  attracting attention 296–7
  consent 293–7

Battery – continued
  Bolam test 293, 294
  burden of proof 295–6
  express 293–5
  fraud and 295
  informed 293–4
  direct harm 291
  general social contact 296–7
  hostile touching 296–7
  intention 291–2
  medical treatment 293–4
  negligence 291–2
  physical contact 292
  police actions 296
  sado-masochists 297
  sport 297
Bereavement damages 180, 428
Bills of lading 319
Bolam test 83, 293, 294
Borrowed employees 10–11
Breach of statutory duty 237–66, 283–4
  adequacy of pre-existing common law
    253–4
  alternative remedies 252–5
  background to action 238–9
  breach of statute 255–8
  class protection 240–6
  codes of practice compliance 257
  common law duty 261
  consumer safety regulations 265–6
  damage suffered
    caused by breach 258–60
    within class of risks 260–1
  defences
    contributory negligence 262–4
    general 264–6
    volenti non fit injuria 262
  elements of cause of action 255–61
  employed persons 241
  employer as cause 264
  industrial cases 242–3
  intention of parliament 249
  interpretation 238
  negligence
    common law duty 261
    statutory 256–8
  no remedy provided by statute 237–8, 239,
    249–50, 283
  person duty imposed on 258–60
    plaintiff and defendant 259
  pre-existing common law 253–4
  presumptions 239

Breach of statutory duty – *continued*
  protection of class 240–6
  public authorities 241–2
  public duties 246–7, 250–2
    local authorities 249, 251–2
    public and private law proceedings
      251–2
  remedy not criminal sanction 247–9
  remedy provided in statute 237, 239–49,
      283
    actions against employers 242–3
    benefit of class 240–6
    employed persons 241
    industrial cases 242–3
    presumption that sole remedy 239–40
    public authorities 241–2
    qualified approach 240
    road traffic provisions 243–4
      road users 244
  social service measures 248
  special remedy *see* remedy provided in
      statute
Broadcasts, libel and 367
Builders 188, 189–93
Bullying at work 270
'But for' test 96–7, 99, 117
Bystanders 90, 167, 171, 175, 176–7, 181

Capacity 1–3, 23
  corporations 3
  mentally disordered persons 2, 60, 305
  minors 2–3
  negligence and 82–3
Caparo test 74–5, 91, 92, 136–7
Cattle trespass 354, 410, 413
Causation 96–108
  breaking chain *see* intervening acts
  'but for' test 96–7, 99, 117
  concurrent causes 97
  'egg-shell skull' rule *see* sensitive plaintiffs
  intention 116
  intervening acts 101–8, 117
    by plaintiff 102, 104–5
      to minimise loss 108
    by third parties 103–4
      duty approach 105–6
      reflex actions 108
    contributory negligence 102
    duty approach 105–6
    medical negligence 106–7
    natural and probable consequence 101
    reflex actions 108
  loss of chance 99–100
  material increase in risks 99
  nova causa interveniens 101, 117
  novus actus interveniens see intervening acts
  'probably for' test 99
  proof 98–108, 117
    balance of probabilities 98
    burden 98
  remoteness compared 95–6
  risk, material increase 99
  sensitive plaintiffs 114–16, 117
    allergies 114
    assessing damages 115
    hazardous escapes defence 359
    impecuniosity 115–16
    nervous shock 173–4
    private nuisance and 336–7
  successive acts 97–8

Causation – *continued*
  supervening events 97–8
    see also intervening acts
  taking victim as found *see* sensitive plaintiffs
  see also Remoteness
Children
  capacity 2–3
  child safety orders 348
  Herrington duty 225
  trespassing 208–10
    accompanying adults 209–10
    allurement 208–9
    Herrington duty 222–3, 225
    traps 208–9
Citizen's arrest 304–5
Classification Societies 150
Club premises 233
Coase Theorem 421
Complex structures 191, 192
Consent
  battery 293–7
    attracting attention 296–7
    general social contact 296–7
    hostile touching 296–7
    police actions 296
  Bolam test 293, 294
  burden of proof 295–6
  duress and 35
  express 40, 293–5
  false imprisonment 302
  fraud and 295
  hazardous escapes 359
  implied 40
  informed 293–4
  intentional torts and 39–40
  medical treatment 39, 40, 293–4
  minors 39
  negligence and 83
  sado-masochists 297
  of seller 320
  sport 39, 40, 297
  volenti non fit injuria 39–40
    danger money 51–2
    employment cases 51–3
    must be real 51–6
    rescue *see* rescue cases
Consumer protection
  breach of statutory duty 265–6
  see also Product liability
Contra proferentem construction 40
Contracts
  negligence 152–3
  remedies 417–18
  terms excluding liability 40–1
Contribution 18
  amount 22–3
  apportionment 23
  between tortfeasors 19–23
  eligibility to make claim 21
  general rule 21
  independent tortfeasors 19
  joint tortfeasors 19, 20
  liability to action 21–2
  several concurrent tortfeasors 19, 20
  vicarious liability 18
Contributory negligence 43–4, 45, 47, 48,
    60–4, 65, 67–8
  apportionment 60–1
  breach of statutory duty 262–4
  causation 102

Contributory negligence – *continued*
  dangerous premises and land 220
  emergencies 63
  employer's liability 281
  failure to wear seat belt 62, 63
  headgear for motorcyclists 61, 62
  lifts from drunken motorists 63
  nature of damage 64
  negligence of another 63
  plaintiff's contribution 61–4
  separation of time, space or circumstances
    62
Control test 8–9
Conversion 306–12
  altering goods 308
  damages 312
  destroying goods 308
  disposal of goods 308–9
  dispossessing the plaintiff 308
  forms 307–9
  'goods' meaning 309
  intention 307
  meaning 306
  mistake defence 33
  ownership 310–11
    see also possession
  possession
    bailment 310
    finders 310–11
    immediate right 309
    lien 310
    ownership compared 310–11
    pledge 310
    sale 310
  receiving goods 308
  refusal to surrender on demand 309
  remedies
    damages 312
    delivery up 312
    improvement 312
  several claimants 311
  taking delivery of goods 308
  taking goods 308
  using goods 308
Corporations
  capacity 3
  defamation of 3
Crime and Disorder Act (1998) 348

Damage suffered
  breach of statutory duty
    caused by breach 258–60
    within class of risks 260–1
  dangerous premises and land 220–1
  nuisance *see* private nuisance; public
    nuisance
  private nuisance 338–9, 349
  product liability 391, 405
  psychiatric *see* Nervous shock
  public nuisance 349
    economic loss 343, 349
    inconvenience 343–4
    loss of trade 343
    physical harm 343
  remoteness *see* Remoteness
  repetitive strain injury 279
  sleep deprivation 278
  stress 278–9
  trespass to goods 312–13
Damages 418–31

Damages – *continued*
  aggravated 428–9
  benefits and 426–7
  bereavement 180, 428
  chattels 422–3
  compensatory 419, 422–3
  conversion remedy 312
  death 428
  defamation 387–8
  economic theories 420–2
  enterprise liability 420
  exemplary 428–9
  function 418–19
  funeral expenses 428
  future loss 423, 424–6
    inflation 425
    lump sums 425
  insurance and 420, 426
  interim payments 427
  juries 372, 419
  land and buildings 422
  in lieu of injunction 433
  loss of amenity 424
  loss of chance 99–100
  loss of dependence 428
  loss distribution 420
  loss of earnings 423, 424
  loss of life expectancy 424
  loss of profits 423
  loss of use 422
  lump sums 427–8
  medical expenses 423, 424
  multipliers 425–6
  no fault compensation 420
  nominal 431
  non-pecuniary loss 423
    see also loss of amenity; pain and suffering
  pain and suffering 423, 424
  pecuniary loss 423, 424–6
    future 423, 424–6
    see also loss of earnings; medical expenses
  personal injuries 423–8
  private nuisance remedy 340
  profit earning chattel 423
  provisional 427
  reform proposals 430
  repairs 422
  sensitive plaintiffs 115
  sick pay 426
  social security benefits and 426–7
  trespass to land 321
  undertakings in 433–4
  USA 419–20
Danger money 51–2
Dangerous animals *see* Animals; Dangerous
  dogs
Dangerous dogs 412–13
  guard dogs 414
  livestock worrying 413
Dangerous premises and land 187–234
  architects 188, 189–93
  builders 188, 189–93
  children 208–10
    accompanying adults 209–10
    allurement 208–9
    Herrington duty 222–3, 225
    traps 208–9
  common duty of care 206–15
    see also duty of care
  common humanity duty 222–3

Dangerous premises and land – *continued*
 complex structures 191, 193
 contributory negligence 220
 damage 220–1
  Occupier's Liability Act (1984) 231–2,
   233–4
  personal injury only 231–2, 234
 Defective Premises Act (1972) 196–7, 233
 deterrent measures 221–2
 duty of care 233
  children 208–10
  common 206–15
  exclusion of liability 231
  general nature 207–8
  humanity duty 222–3
  independent contractors 210, 212–15
  minimum standard requirement 219
  OLA (1984) *see* Occupier's Liability Act
   (1984)
  personal injury 231–2, 234
  persons to whom duty owed 223
  res ipsa loquitur 208
  statutory obligation 206
  trespassers 221–32
  warnings 210–12, 216, 229–31
 economic loss 191
 entry by contract 215–16
 exclusion of liability 212
  'business liability' 217
  minimum standard of care required 219
  negligence 217–18
  notices 218–19
  Occupier's Liability Act (1984) 231
  under 1957 Act 216–19
 firefighter injuries 194–5
 health and safety of occupier 191, 192
 Herrington duty 222–3, 225
 independent contractors 193–4, 200–1, 210,
  212–15
 landlords 195–6
 latent defects 188, 192
 lawful visitors 202–6, 233
  abuse of permission 204–5
  canvassers 203–4
  children 208–10
  duty of care *see* common duty of care
  implied permission 202–6
  invitees 203
  licensees 201, 202–3
  rights of way 205–6
 licensees 201, 202–3
 local authorities 190, 191–2
 National House Builders' Protection
  Scheme 197
 negligence liabilities
  architects 188, 189–93
  builders 188, 189–93
  latent defects 188
  lessors 188–9
  local authorities 190, 191–2
  vendors 188–9
 notices 210–12
 occupiers 193–4, 233
  activity duty 198–9
  business 233
  control of premises 200, 201
  licensees 201
  meaning of 199–202
  more than one 200
  occupancy duty 198–9

Dangerous premises and land – *continued*
  Occupier's Liability Act (1984) liability
   223–32
  premises meaning 199
  visitors *see* lawful visitors
  see also duty of care
 Occupier's Liability Act (1984)
  club premises 233
  damage 231–2
  exclusion of liability 231
  liability to trespassers 223–32
  personal injury 231–2, 234
  persons to whom duty owed 223
  volenti non fit injuria 226–9
  warnings 229–31
  see also duty of care
 patent defects 192
 premises meaning 199
 repair costs 191
 rescuers 194–5
 rights of way 205–6
 trespassers 194, 221–32, 234
  common humanity duty 222–3
  deterrent measures 221–2
  Herrington duty 222–3, 225
  intention 221–2, 320
  occupier's duty 221–32
  Occupier's Liability Act (1984) 223–32
  original duty to 221–2
  reckless disregard for safety 222–3
  retributive measures 222
 volenti non fit injuria 219–20, 226–9
 voluntary assumption of risk 212, 219–20
 warning notices 210–12, 216, 229–31
Data protection 127
Defamation 365–89
 apology 373
 by trained birds 412
 carelessness 378–9
 corporations 3
 corrections 373
 death of party 369
 defences 379–86
  amends 374, 386
  fair comment 384–5
  honesty 385
  public interest 384–5
  true facts
   comment on 385
   partially true 385
  see also justification; privilege
 definition 367
 distributors 378
 freedom of speech and 366
 harmful but not improper 371
 history 367
 inferences 374
 innocent disseminators 378
 innuendo 374–6
  false 375–6
  true or legal 375
 intention 378–9
 judge's function 371
 jury's function 372
 justification 383–5
  effect 384
  failed justification 384
  fair view 383
  meaning and 383
  part justification 383–4

Defamation – *continued*
  legal aid 369
  libel
    actionable *per se* 368
    audio tapes and records 367
    broadcasts 367
    criminal liability 368
    definition 367
    films 368
    permanence 367
    sound tracks 368
    statutory extension 367
  limitation period 369
  mistaken identity
    accidental confusion 372–3
    correction and apology 373
    namesakes 373
    statutory intervention 373
  mixed views 371
  offer of amends 374, 386
  photomontages 376
  privacy protection 366
  privilege
    absolute 380–1
    judicial proceedings 380
    official communications 380
    parliamentary 380
    qualified 381–2
      absence of belief in proof 382
      abuse of purpose 382
      common law 381
      excessive publication 382
      malice and 382
      reports 381–2
  proof required 370–2, 379
  public bodies 369
  publication
    extent 377
    foreseeable though unintended 377
    harm to reputation 377
    incidental 377
    innocent disseminators 378
    meaning 376
    number of readers/hearers 377
    serial 377–8
    untoward event 377
  references to plaintiff
    explicit 372
    indirect 372
  remedies
    damages 387–8
    injunctions 388
  reputation
    damage to 370–1
    harm in publication 377
    protection 366
    statement reflects upon 370
  'right thinking members of society' 371
  slander
    definition 368
    disparagement in office 369
    effect 368
    imputation of crime 368–9
    imputation of venereal disease 369
    special damage 369
    unchastity of woman 369
  sting 376
  trial by jury right 369
Defective Premises Act (1972) 196–7, 233
Defences 32–69

Defences – *continued*
  Act of God 33
  animals 413–14
  breach of statutory duty
    contributory negligence 262–4
    general 264–6
    volenti non fit injuria 262
  causation *see* Causation
  consent *see* Consent
  contributory negligence 43–4, 45, 47, 48,
    60–4, 65, 67–8, 339
    accepting lifts from drunken
      motorists 63
    apportionment 60–1
    breach of statutory duty 262–4
    causation 102
    dangerous premises and land
      220
    emergencies 63
    employer's liability 281
    failure to wear seat belt 62, 63
    headgear for motorcyclists 61, 62
    nature of damage 64
    negligence of another 63
    plaintiff's contribution 61–4
    private nuisance 339
    separation of time, space or circumstances
      62
  defamation 379–86
    amends 374, 386
    fair comment 384–5
    honesty 385
    public interest 384–5
    true facts
      comment on 385
      partially true 385
    see also justification; privilege
  duress 34–5
  employer's liability
    contributory negligence 281
    volenti non fit injuria 281
  hazardous activities
    act of war 359
    consent 359
    default of plaintiff 360
    malicious third parties 359
    sensitive user 360
    statutory authority 360
  illegality 65–6
    high speed chases 58–9
    rationale 56
    volenti compared 56–7
  inevitable accident 34
  justification 383–5
    effect 384
    failed justification 384
    fair view 383
    meaning and 383
    part justification 383–4
  mistake 33–4
  necessity 59–60
    protection of the person 59
    protection of property 59–60
    protection of the realm 59
  novus actus interveniens 48
  prescription 339
  private nuisance
    contributory negligence 339
    prescription 339
    statutory authority 339–40

Defences – *continued*
  privilege
    absolute 380–1
    judicial proceedings 380
    official communications 380
    parliamentary 380
    qualified 381–2
      absence of belief in proof 382
      abuse of purpose 382
      common law 381
      excessive publication 382
      malice and 382
      reports 381–2
  product liability
    compliance with public requirements
      405
    developmental risks 405–6
    distribution without consent 405
    later modification 405
    statutory liability 405–7
  of property 38
    another person's property 38
    proportionate response 38
    reasonableness 38
  self-defence 35–7
    characteristics 35
    proportionate response 36–7
    provocation 37
    reasonableness standards 36, 37
  statutory authority 339–40
  volenti non fit injuria 38–56, 65, 66–7
    agreement not to sue 40–1
      danger money 51–2
      employment cases 51–3
      must be real 51–6
      rescue *see* rescue cases
    breach of statutory duty 262
    consent 39–40
      danger money 51–2
      employment cases 51–3
      must be real 51–6
      rescue *see* rescue cases
    dangerous premises and land 219–20
      Occupier's Liability Act (1984) 226–9
    employer's liability 281
    exclusion of liability 40–1
    express 40, 41
    illegality compared 56–7
    implied 67
    implied assumption of risk 41–51
    rescue cases 53–6
      duty to foreseeable rescuer 54
      negligence towards rescuer 56
      nervous shock 55
      no obligation to rescue 53
      professional rescuers 55
      rescuer who makes matters worse
        54–5
      rescuers are volunteers 55
    sports 48–50
    standard of care 48–51
    suicide attempts 45–8
  voluntary assumption of risk 41–51, 67,
    212, 219–20
    agreement 42–8
    alcohol and 43–4
    negligence 42–3
    risk 42
Delegable duties 6–7
Delivery up remedy 312

Dermatitis 277
Developmental risks 399, 405–6
'Diplock qualification' 252–3
Distress damage feasant 322
Documents of title 319
Dogs *see* Dangerous dogs
Donoghue v *Stevenson* 395–6
  see also Neighbour principle
Duress 34–5
  consent and 295
  negativing consent 35
Duties
  dangerous premises 233
  dangerous premises *see* Dangerous
    premises and land, duty of care
  employer to employee *see* Employer's
    liability
  statutory *see* Breach of statutory duty

Economic loss 120–1
  consequential 120
  contractual relationships 125–6
  dangerous premises and land 191
  exceptions to principle 123–6
  Hedley Byrne liability 128–31, 146–7, 152
    advice in usual course of business 130,
      132
    special relationships 129–31
    subsequent developments 129–31
    'without responsibility' disclaimer 128
  Junior Books v *Veitchi* decision 124–5
  manufacturer's liability 121–2, 397–8
  misstatements and 122
  nuisance cause 343, 349
  principle 122–6
  relationships between parties 124, 125–6
  reliance on skill of defendants 124–5
  warranty of care 124
  see also Negligent misstatements
Economic reality test 9
'Egg-shell skull' rule 114–16, 117
  allergies 114
  assessing damages 115
  hazardous escapes defence 359
  impecuniosity 115–16
  nervous shock 173–4, 178
  private nuisance and 336–7
Employees (servants) 5, 7–8
  borrowed 10–11
  control test 8–9
  economic reality test 9
  'frolic of own' 12–13
  integration test 9
  organisation test 9
  regular casual workers 8
Employer's liability
  breach of statutory duty 264
  bullying 270
  common law 266–82
    general nature 267–9
  common law duty 284–5
  competence of supervisors and colleagues
    269–70
  compulsory insurance 281
  contract and tort 278
  damage suffered
    psychiatric damage 278–9
    repetitive strain injury 279
    sleep deprivation 278
    stress 278–9

Employer's liability – *continued*
  defences
    contributory negligence 281
    volenti non fit injuria 281
  dermatitis 277
  disregard for own safety 275–6
  equipment
    maintenance 270
    provision 270–2
  multinational companies 281
  negligent staffing 269–70
  non-delegable duty 267, 284
  passive smoking 280
  personal duty of care 267, 284
  plant and premises 272–4
  practical jokes and pranks 269
  premises 272–4
  safe system of working 274–7
    third party premises 277–8
  supervision
    competence of supervisors 269–70
    safe system of working 276, 277–8
  third party premises 273–4, 277–8
  vicarious liability *see* Employer's vicarious
    liability
Employer's vicarious liability 4–17, 24, 29,
    270
  commission of tort by employee 4
  conditions 4–5
  contract for service 7
  contract of service 7
  employees *see* Employees (servants)
  'in course of business' 4, 11–17, 27
    authorised acts 11–12
    authorised limits of time and space
        12–13, 28
    connection with employer's business
        14–17
    deviation from official route 12–13
    expressly forbidden acts 13–14
    frolic of own 12–13
    meal breaks 28–9
    necessarily incidental acts 14–15
    protection of employer's property 16
    spatial factors 12–13, 28
    trespasser approach 13–14
    unauthorised journeys 13, 28
    unauthorised manner of performance 12
  independent contractors 5, 6–7, 26
  misfeasance in public office 27
  regular casual workers 8
  relationship of employer and employee 4
Employment, consent defence 51–3
Estoppel
  apparent authority 317
  apparent ownership 317–18, 319
Ex turpi causa non oritur actio 56, 58
  dangerous premises and land 226–9
Experts
  negligence and 83–4
  usual practice 85

False imprisonment
  arrest and detention 304–5
  completeness of confinement 302
  conditions turning lawful to false 303–4
  consent 302
  damages 304
  detention in hospital 60, 305
  'false' meaning 301

False imprisonment – *continued*
  'imprisonment' meaning 301–2
  justification 302–5
  knowledge of imprisonment 303–6
Family Law Act (1996) 347
Fiduciary relationships 127
Films, libel and 368
Financial services 127
Finders 310–11
Fire hazard 352
  early history 361
  ingredients of tort 362
  insurance 362
  negligence based action 361
  Rylands v *Fletcher* use 361–2
Firefighter injuries 194–5
Foreseeability
  amount of risk 109, 111
  extent of harm 112
  hazardous escapes 358
  manner of causing damages 111
  nervous shock 163–4, 166
  reasonable 109–11, 117
  relative nature of 112–13
  as test of remoteness 113
Fraud
  consent and battery 295
  consent of seller obtained by 320
Fraudulent misrepresentation 316
'Frolic of own' 12–13

Grief 158
  pathological 158
Guard dogs 414
Guardian *ad litem* 23
Guardians, liability 2

Harassment 327, 350
  anti-social behaviour orders 348
  at work 270
  child safety orders 348
  Crime and Disorder Act (1998) 348
  existing torts and 344
  Family Law Act (1996) 347
  Housing Act (1996) 348
  meaning 344
  Protection from Harassment Act (1997)
      346–7
  remedies
    family harassment 345
    matrimonial harassment 345
  silent phone calls 341, 345
  statutory 346–8
  Willkinnson v *Downton* 345–6
Harm *see* Damage suffered
Hazardous activities 352–64
  accumulation
    meaning 355
    state of affairs brought about by 34353–4
  cattle trespass 354
  control by defendant 358
  defences
    act of war 359
    consent 359
    default of plaintiff 360
    malicious third parties 359
    sensitive user 360
    statutory authority 360
  development of rule 353–60
  escapes 353–4, 355, 357–8

Hazardous activities – *continued*
  fire 353
    early history 361
    ingredients of tort 362
    insurance 362
    negligence based action 361
    Rylands v *Fletcher* use 361–2
  hazardous things 355
  non-natural user 355–7
  personal injuries 359
  persons able to sue 358–9
  reasonable foreseeability 358
  Rylands v *Fletcher* 353–4
    fire hazards and 361–2
  status of tort 360
  strict liability 360
Hedley Byrne liability 128–31, 146–7, 152
  advice in usual course of business 130, 132
  special relationships 129–31
  subsequent developments 129–31
  'without responsibility' disclaimer 128
Herrington duty 222–3, 225
Hillsborough tragedy 168–71, 174, 179–80
  post traumatic stress disorder 174–5
  safe system of work 280
Housing Act (1996) 348

Illegality defence 65–6
  high speed chases 58–9
  rationale 56
  volenti compared 56–7
Improvement remedy 312
Indemnity 18
Independent contractors
  contract for service 7
  control test 8–9
  dangerous premises and land 193–4,
      200–1, 210, 212–15
  demolitions 213–14
  non-delegable duty 6–7, 19, 26
  organisation or integration test 9
  vicarious liability and 5, 6–7, 26
Inevitable accident 34
Inferences, defamation and 374
Injunctions 431–4
  damages in lieu 433
  defamation 388
  final 431
  interlocutory 431, 432
    undertakings in damages 433–4
  mandatory 431, 433
  negative 431, 433
  principles 431
  private nuisance remedy 340
  public nuisance remedy 342
  quia timet 340
  trespass to land 321
  undertakings in damages 433–4
  usefulness 432
Innuendo 374–6
  false 375–6
  true or legal 375
Insurance
  damages remedies and 420, 426
  employer's 281
  fire 362
Integration test 9
Intention
  battery 291–2
  causation and 116

Intention – *continued*
  conversion 307
  defamation 378–9
  trespass 288
  trespass to goods 312
  trespass to land 221–2, 320
Interference with goods 306–13
  conversion 306–12
    altering goods 308
    destroying goods 308
    disposal of goods 308–9
    dispossessing the plaintiff 308
    forms 307–9
    'goods' meaning 309
    intention 307
    meaning 306
    ownership 310–11
      see also Ownership
    possession
      bailment 310
      finders 310–11
      immediate right 309
      lien 310
      ownership compared 310–11
      pledge 310
      sale 310
    receiving goods 308
    refusal to surrender on demand 309
    remedies
      damages 312
      delivery up 312
      improvement 312
    several claimants 311
    taking delivery of goods 308
    taking goods 308
    using goods 308
  sale and purchase *see* Ownership
  title conflicts *see* Ownership
  trespass to goods 306
    direct 312
    intention 312
    interference 312–13
    inviolability 313
    negligence 312
    physical damage 313
    possession 313
    retention of possession 313
    see also Ownership
Interpretation of statute 238
Intervening acts 101–8, 117
  by plaintiff 102, 104–5
    to minimise loss 108
  by third parties 103–4
    duty approach 105–6
    reflex actions 108
  contributory negligence 102
  duty approach 105–6
  medical negligence 106–7
  natural and probable consequence 101
  reflex actions 108

Junior Books v *Veitchi* decision 124–5
Juries, damages awards 372, 419
Justification defence 383–5
  effect 384
  failed justification 384
  fair view 383
  meaning and 383
  part justification 383–4

'Kennedy proviso' 159–60

Land
    dangerous *see* Dangerous premises and land
    trespass *see* Trespass to land
Landlords
    dangerous premises 195–6
    private nuisance 337–8
    repairs 195
Latent defects
    dangerous premises 188, 192
    product liability 398
Legal aid, defamation and 369
Liability
    employer's *see* Employer's liability;
        Employer's vicarious liability
    guardians 2
    parental 2, 108
    personal 3, 4
    vicarious *see* Vicarious liability
Libel
    actionable *per se* 368
    audio tapes and records 367
    broadcasts 367
    criminal liability 368
    definition 367
    films 368
    permanence 367
    sound tracks 368
    statutory extension 367
Licensees 201
Liebosch rule 423
Lien 310
Local authorities
    breach of statutory duties 249, 251–2
    dangerous premises and land 190, 191–2
    defamation 369
    private nuisance 339–40
Loss of chance 99–100
Loss of expectation 100

Manufacture's liability 121–2, 397–8
Market overt sale 316
Mealbreaks 28–9
Medical treatment
    consent 39, 40, 293–4
        lacking capacity 60
    intervening acts 106–7
Mentally disordered persons, capacity 2, 60, 305
Mercantile agents 318
    nemo dat exception 318
    ordinary course of business 318
Minors
    capacity 2–3
    consent 39
'Mischief Rule' 238
Misfeasance in public office 27
Misstatement *see* Negligent misstatements
Mistake 33–4
Mitigation
    financially unable to minimise loss 116
    supervening act of plaintiff 108
Motor Insurers' Bureau 244

National House Builders' Protection Scheme 197
National Insurance 420
Necessity defence 59–60
    protection of the person 59
    protection of property 59–60
    protection of the realm 59

Negligence 70–94
    architects 188, 189–93
    Atkinian test *see* neighbour principle
    balance of probabilities standard 87–9
    Bolam standard 83, 293, 294
    breach of duty 70, 82–9
        burden of proof 87–9
        factors to be considered 82–6
        reasonable man standard 82–5
        resulting damage *see* damage suffered
    builders 188, 189–93
    burden of proof 87–9
    capacity 82–3
    Caparo test 74–5, 91, 92, 136–7
    consent 83
    contract liability 75–6, 152–3
    contributory *see* Contributory negligence
    damage suffered 70, 89
    dangerous premises and land 188–93
        exclusion of liability 217–18
    duty *see* legal duty
    economic loss *see* Economic loss
    experts 83–4
    fire hazards 361
    foreseeability 71, 72, 74, 75, 90
    importance of objective 85
    'just and reasonable' test 74, 75, 78, 91, 92
    latent defects 188, 192
    legal duty 70, 71–5
        advocacy 82
        breach *see* breach of duty
        fairness 72, 74, 78, 91
        omissions 81
        unborn child 81
    lessors 188–9
    local authorities 190, 191–2
    loss of expectation 100
    magnitude of risk 85
    misstatements *see* Negligent misstatement
    neighbour principle 26, 54, 71–2, 73–5, 90–1, 148, 396
        dangerous premises and land liabilities 189
        firefighter injuries 194–5
    nervous shock *see* Nervous shock
    nuisance and 333, 349
    omissions 81
    private nuisance 333
    product liability 398–400
    proximity 72, 74, 75, 90–1, 137–8
    public bodies 77–80
        judicial review 77, 78, 79
        operational and policy decisions 77–8, 79–80
        police under investigation 78–9, 80
        statutory remedies 77
        ultra vires 77
    reasonable man standard 82–5
    'Reid approach' 73, 89
    relationships 71, 72
        assumption of responsibility 132–6, 152–3
        Hedley Byrne liability 129–31
        Henderson 152–3
        proximity requirement 137–8
        three party relationships 141–6, 148–9
    res ipsa loquitur 88–9, 92
    rescuers 56
safety measures 86
seriousness of likely injury 85

Negligence – *continued*
  shock *see* Nervous shock
  standard of care 48–51, 82–5, 92
  state of knowledge 85–6
  statutory 256–8
  tort liability 75–6
  trespass to goods 312
  trespass to land 320
  unborn child 81
  usual practice 85
  vendors 188–9
  voluntary assumption of risk and 42–3
  'Wilberforce approach' 73–4, 167–8
  see also Causation; Remoteness
Negligent misstatements 126–51
  aircraft surveys 151
  assumption of responsibility 132–6, 152–3
  in course of business 130, 132
  data protection 127
  economic loss 122
  fiduciary relationships 127
  financial services 127
  gratuitous advice 132
  Hedley Byrne liability 128–31, 146–7, 152
    advice in usual course of business 130, 132
    special relationships 129–31
    subsequent developments 129–31
    'without responsibility' disclaimer 128
  inducement to enter into contract 128
  nervous shock 179
  omissions 146–7
  physical damage 148–9, 154
  references 142–3
    see also Hedley Byrne liability
  reliance 122, 131–2
  ship surveys 150
  social or casual advice 130, 133
  special relationships
    assumption of responsibility 132–6, 152–3
    fiduciary 127
    Hedley Byrne liability 129–31
    Henderson 152–3
    proximity requirement 137–8
    three party relationships 141–6, 148–9
  three party relationships 141–6
    contract 141–2
    personal injury 148–9
    statute 141
  wills 143–6
Neighbour principle 26, 54, 71–2, 73–5, 148, 396
  dangerous premises and land liabilities 189
  firefighter injuries 194–5
  product liability 397
Nemo dat quot non habet 314
  mercantile agent exception 318
Nervous shock 157–86
  aftermath approach 160, 165, 167, 170, 177, 178
  anxiety 158
  breach of statutory duty 183
  bystanders 90, 167, 171, 175, 176–7, 181
  cause of action 159–80
  class of persons 167
  communication by third party 167
  defendant is own victim 183–4
  duty of care 162–5

Nervous shock – *continued*
  'egg-shell skull' rule 173–4, 178
  elements of claim 160–2, 166–7
  fear for safety of relatives 160
  foreseeability 163–4, 166, 168
  grief 158
    pathological 158
  Hillsborough tragedy 168–71, 174, 179–80
  history 159–60
  immediate aftermath 160, 165, 167, 170, 177, 178
  impact theory 165
  intentionally causing *see* Trespass to the person
  Kennedy proviso 159–60
  live television broadcasts 168, 169–70, 178
  nature of accident 167–8
  negligent misstatements 179
  non-relatives 161–2
  'phlegm and fortitude' 163, 172–4, 176, 178, 181
  plaintiff's reaction 172–4
  police duties 175
  post traumatic stress disorder 159, 161, 174–5
  pre-death suffering 170, 179–80
  presence in area 162–3, 167
  primary victim 178, 181–2
  property damage 162, 172
  proximity, time and space 162, 163, 165, 167, 170
  psychiatric damage 158–9, 278–9
  reform 181–4
  relatives 166, 169, 170
  rescuers 55, 90, 161, 168, 170, 174–5, 178
  secondary victim 181–2
  sorrow 158
  spouses 169
  statutory duty 183
  workmates 161, 178
'Next friend' 3
Non-delegable duties 6–7
Non-molestation orders 347
Nova causa interveniens 101, 117
Novus actus interveniens 48, 101–8, 117
  see also Intervening acts
Nuisance 325–51
  acts and activities 328–30
  animals and 412
  character of locality 336
  coming to the nuisance 335–6
  culpable 326, 328–37
  damage suffered 338–9
    economic loss 343
    inconvenience 343–4
    loss of trade 343
    physical harm 343
  defences
    contributory negligence 339
    prescription 339
    statutory authority 339–40
  definitions 326
  derivative actions 342
  examples 342
  exemplary damages 344
  fault and 349
  foreseeability of harm 331, 332–3
  groundwater harm 330
  highway obstruction 342
  interference with television reception 338

Nuisance – *continued*
  landlords 337–8
  material considerations 334–7
  material injury to property 336
  moral interference 338
  natural causes 331
  negligence and 333, 349
  non-feasance 331
  omissions 329–30
  ordinary usages 333–4
  perpetrator 337
  personal discomfort 336
  persons able to sue 326–8
  persons liable 337–8
  private actions 342
  private nuisance 326–41, 349
  public nuisance 341–4
  remedies 340–1, 342
    damages 340
    injunctions 340, 342
    prosecution 342
  remoteness of damage 349
  Rylands v *Fletcher* case 332
  scope 341
  sensitive users 336–7
  state of affairs creation 329–30
  status of tort 342, 349
  strict liability 330
  third party acts 331–2
  unreasonableness 333–7
  unworthy motive 334–5
  utility of activity 335
  want of repair 329, 338

Occupiers 193–4, 233
  activity duty 198–9
  business 233
  control of premises 200, 201
  liability to lawful visitors 197–221
  licensees 201
  meaning of 199–202
  more than one 200
  occupancy duty 198–9
  premises meaning 199
  vicarious liability 28
  visitors *see* Visitors
  see also Dangerous premises and land;
    Occupier's Liability Act (1984)
Occupier's Liability Act (1984)
  club premises 233
  damage 231–2
  exclusion of liability 231
  liability to trespassers 223–32
  personal injury 231–2, 234
  persons to whom duty owed 223
  volenti non fit injuria 226–9
  warnings 229–31
Offer of amends, defamation 374, 386
Omissions
  negligence 81
  negligent misstatements 146–7
  private nuisance 329–30
Organisation test 9
Overflying 320–1
Ownership
  apparent 317–18, 319
  apportionment 315
  bought or agreed to buy 319
  claims priority 314–15
  consent of seller 320

Ownership – *continued*
  continues or is in possession 319
  conversion 310–11
  deferred purchase 319–20
  documents of title 319
  estoppel
    apparent authority 317
    apparent ownership 317–18, 319
  market overt sale 316
  mercantile agents 318
  nemo dat quot non habet 314
  ordinary course of business 318
  pacta sunt servanda 314
  possession compared 310–11
  proof of title 314
  seller retaining possession 319
  sellers and buyers in possession 319–20
  tangible moveables 315
  title conflicts 313–20
  voidable title sale 316

Pacta sunt servanda 314
Parenting orders 348
Parents, liability 2, 108
Parties 1
Passive smoking 280
Pathological grief 158
Pearson Commission 360, 400, 420
Personal injuries
  damages 423–8
  hazardous activities and 359
  negligent misstatements 148–9
  occupiers liability 231–2, 234
  public service vehicles 40
Personal liability 3–4
Photomontages 376
Physical damage, negligent misstatement and
  148–9, 154
Plant, employer's liability for 272–4
Pledge 310
Possession
  bailment 310
  continues or is in possession 319
  finders 310–11
  immediate right 309
  lien 310
  ownership compared 310–11
  pledge 310
  sale 310
  seller retaining possession 319
  sellers and buyers in possession 319–20
  trespass to goods 313
    retention of possession 313
  trespass to land and 321–2
  see also Conversion; Interference with goods
Possession orders 321–2
Post traumatic stress disorder 159, 161, 174–5
Pre-death suffering 170, 179–80
Premises
  dangerous *see* Dangerous premises and land
  employer's liability for 272–4
    third party premises 273–4, 277–8
Prescription defence 339
Private nuisance
  acts and activities 328–30
  character of locality 336
  coming to the nuisance 335–6
  culpability 328–41
  culpable 326
  damage suffered 338–9

Private nuisance – *continued*
  defences
    contributory negligence 339
    prescription 339
    statutory authority 339–40
  foreseeability of harm 331, 332–3
  groundwater harm 330
  landlords 337–8
  material considerations 334–7
  material injury to property 336
  moral interference 338
  natural causes 331
  negligence and 333, 349
  non-feasance 331
  omissions 329–30
  ordinary usages 333–4
  perpetrator 337
  personal discomfort 336
  persons liable 337–8
  physical damage 338–9
  public nuisance compared 349
  remedies 340–1
    damages 340
    injunctions 340
  Rylands v *Fletcher* case 332
  sensitive users 336–7
  state of affairs creation 329
  status 349, 350
  strict liability 330
  third party acts 331–2
  unreasonableness 333–7
  unworthy motive 334–5
  utility of activity 335
  want of repair 329, 338
Private rights of way 206
Privilege defence
  absolute 380–1
  judicial proceedings 380
  official communications 380
  parliamentary 380
  qualified 381–2
    absence of belief in proof 382
    abuse of purpose 382
    common law 381
    excessive publication 382
    malice and 382
    reports 381–2
Product liability 399–408
  abuse of power by business party 394
  agricultural products and game 402–3, 407
  common law liability
    current relevance 400
    limitation period 400
  common law remedies 395–400
  Consumer Protection Act (1987) 402–7
    see also statutory liability
  continuing duty 399–400
  contractual remedies 393–5
    expectations 393
    implied terms 392, 393–4
    limitations 393–5
    quality 393
  damage suffered 391
    statutory liability 405
  dangerous goods 397–8
  dealers 396
  'defective' definition 403–4
  defences
    compliance with public requirements
      405

Product liability – *continued*
    developmental risks 405–6
    distribution without consent 405
    later modification 405
    statutory liability 405–7
  design defects 399, 406
  developmental risks 399, 405–6
  disclaimers 396
  Donoghue v *Stevenson* 395–6
  durability 393
  fitness 392, 393
  implied terms
    fitness 392, 393
    merchantability 393
    quality 394
  latent defects 398
  liability *see* common law remedies;
      contractual remedies; statutory liability
  limitation periods 405
  manufacturers 396–7
    dangerous goods 397–8
    economic loss 121–2, 397–8
  manufacturing defects 399
  merchantability 393
  modifications 405
  negligence proof 398–400
  neighbour principle 396, 397
  Pearson Committee 400
  privity of contract 394–5, 398
  producers 404
  'product liability' meaning 391–3
  'product' meaning 390–1, 402
  quality 393, 394, 395
  recalls 399–400
  remoteness 392
  repairers 396
  res ipsa loquitur 398–9
  safety requirements 391
  satisfactory quality 394, 395
  state of the art 399, 405–6
  statutory liability
    damage suffered 405
    'defective' definition 403–4
    defences 405–6
    limitation periods 405
    'producer' definition 404
    'product' definition 402
    reform 400–2
    scope 404–5
    suppliers 404
  suppliers 396, 404
  third parties 394–5
  tortious remedies 395–400
  transfers of possession 393–4
  unconventional use 407
  Unfair Contract Terms Directive 400–7
    see also statutory liability
  warnings 399–400
Prosecution remedy 342
Protection from Harassment Act (1997)
    346–7
Provocation 37
Proximity 26, 90–1
  negligence 72, 74, 75, 90–1, 137–8
  nervous shock 162, 163, 165, 167, 170
Psychiatric damage *see* Nervous shock;
    nervous shock
Public bodies
  defamation 369
  negligence 77–80

Public bodies – *continued*
  judicial review 77, 78, 79
  operational and policy decisions 77–8,
    79–80
  police under investigation 78–9, 80
  statutory remedies 77
  ultra vires 77
Public nuisance 341–4, 349, 350
  damage suffered
    economic loss 343
    inconvenience 343–4
    loss of trade 343
    physical harm 343
  derivative actions 342
  examples 342
  exemplary damages 344
  highway obstruction 342
  negligence and 349
  private actions 342
  private nuisance compared 349
  remedies 342
    injunctions 342
    prosecution 342
  scope 341
  status of tort 342
Public rights of way 205–6
Publication
  extent 377
  foreseeable though unintended 377
  harm to reputation 377
  incidental 377
  innocent disseminators 378
  meaning 376
  number of readers/hearers 377
  serial 377–8
  untoward event 377

Reasonable man standard, negligence 82–5
Recoupment 426
References 142–3
  see also Hedley Byrne liability
Reliance, on negligent misstatements 131–2
Remedies
  Coase Theorem 421
  in contract 417–18
  conversion
    delivery up 312
    improvement 312
  damages 418–31
    aggravated 428–9
    benefits and 426–7
    bereavement 180, 428
    chattels 422–3
    compensatory 419, 422–3
    conversion 312
    conversion remedy 312
    death 427–8
    defamation 387–8
    economic theories 420–2
    enterprise liability 420
    exemplary 428–9
    function 418–19
    funeral expenses 428
    future loss 423, 424–6
      inflation 425
      lump sums 425
    insurance 420, 426
    interim payments 427
    juries 372, 419
    land and buildings 422

Remedies – *continued*
  in lieu of injunction 433
  loss of amenity 424
  loss of chance 99–100
  loss of dependence 428
  loss distribution 420
  loss of earnings 423, 424
  loss of life expectancy 424
  loss of profits 423
  loss of use 422
  lump sums 427–8
  medical expenses 423, 424
  multipliers 425–6
  no fault compensation 420
  nominal 431
  non-pecuniary loss 423
    see also loss of amenity; pain and
      suffering
  pain and suffering 423, 424
  pecuniary loss 423, 424–6
    future 423, 424–6
    see also loss of earnings; medical
      expenses
  personal injuries 423–8
  private nuisance remedy 340
  profit earning chattel 423
  provisional 427
  reformn proposals 430
  repairs 422
  sensitive plaintiffs 115
  sick pay 426
  social security benefits and
    426–7
  trespass to land 321
  undertakings in 433–4
  USA 419–20
death of victim 428
defamation
  damages 388
  injunctions 387–8
  offer of amends 374, 386
delivery up 312
distress damage feasant, trespass to land
  322
equitable 416–17
fault principle 420–1
harassment
  family 345
  matrimonial 345
improvement 312
industrial injuries 420–1
injunctions 431–4
  damages in lieu 433
  defamation 388
  final 431
  interlocutory 431, 432
    undertakings in damages 433–4
  mandatory 431, 433
  negative 431, 433
  principles 431
  private nuisance 340
  public nuisance 342
  trespass to land 321
  undertakings in damages 433–4
  usefulness 432
legal 416
Liebosch rule 423
Pearson Commission 420
possession orders 321–2
private nuisance 340–1

Remedies – *continued*
   damages 340
   injunctions 340
  product contractual remedies 393–5
   expectations 393
   implied terms 392, 393–4
   limitations 393–5
   quality 393
  prosecution 342
  public nuisance 342
   injunctions 342
   prosecution 342
  self-help 322, 418
  in tort 417–18
  trespass to land
   damages 321
   distress damage feasant 322
   injunctions 321
   possession orders 321–2
   self-help 322
Remoteness 109–13, 349
  causation compared 95–6
  direct consequences 109–13
  foreseeability
   amount of risk 109, 111
   extent of harm 112
   manner of causing damages 111
   reasonable 109–11, 117
   relative nature of 112–13
   as test of remoteness 113
  see also Causation
Repairs
  compensatory remedy 422
  landlords 195
  nuisance resulting from lack of 329, 338
Repetitive strain injury 279
Reputation
  damage to 370–1
  harm in publication 377
  protection 366
  statement reflects upon 370
Res ipsa loquitur
  inevitable accident and 34
  negligence 88–9, 92
  product liability 398–9
  visitors to dangerous premises and land 208
Rescuers
  dangerous premises and land 194–5
  firefighter injuries 194–5
  nervous shock 90, 161, 168, 170, 174–5, 178
  professional 174–5
  volenti non fit injuria 53–6
   duty to foreseeable rescuer 54
   negligence towards rescuer 56
   nervous shock 55
   no obligation to rescue 53
   professional rescuers 55
   rescuer who makes matters worse 54–5
   rescuers are volunteers 55
Rights of way 205–6
Risk
  causation and 99
  developmental risk defence 405–6
  magnitude and negligence 85
  material increase in 99
Road users, breach of statutory duties 243–4
Rylands v *Fletcher* 332, 353–4
  fire hazards and 361–2

Sado-masochists 297

Scientific knowledge
  developmental risks 399, 405–6
  negligence and 85–6
Self-defence
  characteristics 35
  proportionate response 36–7
  provocation 37
  reasonableness standards 36, 37
Self-help remedy 322, 418
Sensitive plaintiffs 114–16, 117
  allergies 114
  assessing damages 115
  hazardous escapes defence 359
  impecuniosity 115–16
  nervous shock 173–4
  private nuisance and 336–7
Ship surveys, negligent 150
Shock *see* Nervous shock
Silence, assault by 299, 341, 345
Slander
  definition 368
  disparagement in office 369
  effect 368
  imputation of crime 368–9
  imputation of venereal disease 369
  special damage 369
  unchastity of woman 369
Smoking, passive 280
Social security benefits 426–7
  recoupment 426
Sound tracks, libel and 368
Sport
  consent 39, 40, 297
  standard of care 48–51
  volenti non fit injuria 48–50
Squatters 321
Stalking 299, 341, 345
Statutory authority defence
  hazardous escapes 359
  private nuisance 339–40
Statutory duty breach *see* Breach of statutory
   duty
Sting 376
Suicides
  intervening acts and causation 104–5
  volenti non fit injuria 45–8
Supervening events 97–8
  see also Intervening acts

Technical knowledge
  developmental risks 399, 405–6
  negligence and 85–6
Television reception, interference 338
Third parties
  communications causing nervous shock
   167
  dangerous premises and land 215–16
  employer's liability for premises of 273–4
  harmed by defective products 394
  intervening acts by 103–4
  malicious, defence 359
  private nuisance acts 331–2
Trespass
  cattle trespass 354, 410, 413
  crime and 289
  expressly forbidden acts 13–14
  force 288–9
  historical background 287–90
  importance of 289–90
  intention meaning 288

Trespass – *continued*
  interests protected 289–90
  King's Peace breach 288–9
  tort and 289
  Writ of Trespass 287
  see also Conversion; False imprisonment;
    Interference with goods; Trespass to
    goods; Trespass to land; Trespass to the
    person
Trespass to goods 306
  direct 312
  intention 312
  interference 312–13
  inviolability 313
  negligence 312
  physical damage 313
  possession 313
  retention of possession 313
  see also Interference with goods
Trespass to land 320–3
  actionable *per se* 321
  airspace 320–1
  cattle trespass 354, 410, 413
  dangerous premises and land 194
  entering on 320–1
  intention 221–2, 320
  land meaning 321
  mistake defence 33
  negligence 320
  overflying 320–1
  possession 321
  remaining on 321
  remedies
    damages 321
    distress damage feasant 322
    injunctions 321
    possession orders 321–2
    self-help 322
  squatters 321
  wheel clamping 322–3
Trespass to the person 290–301
  arrest 304–5
  assault
    act of assault 298–9
    apprehension 300
    negativing threats 299–300
    silence 299
    stalking 299
    threats 298–9
    words only 298–9
    see also battery
  battery 291–8
    attracting attention 296–7
    consent 293–7
      Bolam test 293, 294
      burden of proof 295–6
      duress and 295
      express 293–5
      fraud and 295
      informed 293–4
    direct harm 291
    general social contact 296–7
    hostile touching 296–7
    intention 291–2
    medical treatment 293–4
    negligence 291–2
    physical contact 292
    police actions 296
    sado-masochists 297
    sport 297

Trespass to the person – *continued*
  by animals 411
  citizen's arrest 304–5
  detention 304–5
  false imprisonment
    arrest and detention 304–5
    completeness of confinement 302
    conditions turning lawful to false 303–4
    consent 302
    damages 304
    'false' meaning 301
    'imprisonment' meaning 301–2
    justification 302–5
    knowledge of imprisonment 305–6
  interference with liberty *see* arrest; false
    imprisonment
  shock 158
  Wilkinson v *Downton* (1897) tort 345–6
  wrongful arrest 301
  see also Trespass
Trespassers 194, 234
  common humanity duty 222–3
  deterrent measures 221–2
  Herrington duty 222–3, 225
  intentional harm 221–2
  occupier's duty 221–32
  Occupier's Liability Act (1984) 223–32
  original duty to 221–2
  reckless disregard for safety 222–3
  retributive measures 222

Unborn children 81
Unchastity imputation 369
Unfair Contract Terms Directive 400–7
  see also Product liability, statutory liability

Vehicles
  exclusion of liability for injury 40–1
  failure to wear seat belt 62, 63
  lifts from drunken motorists 63
  vicarious liability of owners 17–18, 24, 28
Venereal disease imputation 369
Vicarious liability 23–4
  agency 16, 17–18, 19, 24
  contribution 18
    amount 22–3
    apportionment 23
    between tortfeasors 19–23
    eligibility to make claim 21
    general rule 21
    independent tortfeasors 19
    joint tortfeasors 19, 20
    liability to action 21–2
    several concurrent tortfeasors 19, 20
  employer's 4–17, 24, 29, 270
    commission of tort by employee 4
    conditions 4–5
    contract for service 7
    contract of service 7
    employees (servants) 5, 7–8
      borrowed 10–11
      control test 8–9
      economic reality test 9
      integration test 9
      organisation test 9
      regular casual workers 8
    'in course of business' 4, 11–17, 27
      authorised acts 11–12
      authorised limits of time and space
        12–13, 28

Vicarious liability – *continued*
    connection with employer's business
      14–17
    deviation from official route   12–13
    expressly forbidden acts   13–14
    frolic of own   12–13
    meal breaks   28–9
    necessarily incidental acts   14–15
    protection of employer's property
      16
    spatial factors   12–13, 28
    trespasser approach   13–14
    unauthorised journeys   13, 28
    unauthorised manner of performance
      12
    independent contractors   5, 6–7
    misfeasance in public office   27
    regular casual workers   8
    relationship of employer and employee
      4
  indemnity   18
  independent contractors   26
  meaning   3
  occupier's liability and   28
  primary liability and   29
  vehicle owners   17–18, 24, 28
Visitors   202–6, 233
  abuse of permission   204–5
  canvassers   203–4
  children   208–10
  duty of care *see* common duty of care
  implied permission   202–6
  invitees   203
  licensees   202–3
  rights of way   205–6
Voidable title sale   316
Volenti non fit injuria   38–56, 65, 66–7
  agreement not to sue   40–1
    danger money   51–2
    employment cases   51–3
    must be real   51–6
    rescue *see* rescue cases
  breach of statutory duty   262
  consent   39–40
    danger money   51–2

Volenti non fit injuria – *continued*
    employment cases   51–3
    must be real   51–6
    rescue *see* rescue cases
  dangerous premises and land   219–20
    Occupier's Liability Act (1984)   226–9
  employer's liability   281
  exclusion of liability   40–1
  express   40, 41
  illegality compared   56–7
  implied   67
  implied assumption of risk   41–51
  rescue cases   53–6
    duty to foreseeable rescuer   54
    negligence towards rescuer   56
    nervous shock   55
    no obligation to rescue   53
    professional rescuers   55
    rescuer who makes matters worse   54–5
    rescuers are volunteers   55
  sports   48–50
  standard of care   48–51
  suicide attempts   45–8
  voluntary assumption of risk *see* Voluntary
    assumption of risk
Voluntary assumption of risk   41–51, 67, 212,
  219–20
  agreement   42–8
  alcohol and   43–4
  negligence   42–3
  risk   42

Warehouse receipts   319
Warnings
  dangerous premises and land   210–12, 216,
    229–31
  product defects   399–400
Wheel clamping   322–3
'Wilberforce approach'   73–4, 167–8
Wilkinson v *Downton* (1897) tort   345–6
Wills, negligently drawn up   143–6
Workmates   161, 178
Writ of Trespass   287
Wrongful arrest   301
Wrongful birth   81